THE PAPERS OF

WOODROW WILSON

VOLUME 4

1885

SPONSORED BY THE WOODROW WILSON
FOUNDATION
AND PRINCETON UNIVERSITY

THE PAPERS OF

WOODROW WILSON

ARTHUR S. LINK, *EDITOR*

JOHN WELLS DAVIDSON AND DAVID W. HIRST
ASSOCIATE EDITORS

T. H. VAIL MOTTER, *CONSULTING EDITOR*

JOIIN E. LITTLE AND WILLIAM M. LEARY, JR.
ASSISTANT EDITORS

JEAN MACLACHLAN, *CONTRIBUTING EDITOR*

Volume 4 · 1885

PRINCETON, NEW JERSEY
PRINCETON UNIVERSITY PRESS
1968

INTRODUCTION

THIS fourth volume of *The Papers of Woodrow Wilson* records the climax and culmination of events in Volumes 2 and 3. The present book opens with Wilson's receipt of the first copies of *Congressional Government* on January 24, 1885, and the text of the work that catapulted its author into national prominence. Then follow, in chronological order, letters relating to Wilson's first academic appointment, at the new Bryn Mawr College, reviews of *Congressional Government*, Wilson's personal and rapidly growing professional correspondence, his occasional writings, and his section for the projected but never published "History of Political Economy in the United States."

However, a large portion of the pages following the text of *Congressional Government* is filled with the letters between Woodrow Wilson and his fiancée, Ellen Louise Axson. These letters, like their predecessors in Volumes 2 and 3, shed brilliant light on the daily lives of their authors and the world in which they moved. But they are even more noteworthy for their revelation of a mutual love that grew in intensity and found increasingly eloquent expression as the long courtship reached its climax. We can only be grateful that Woodrow and his "matchless sweetheart" were separated during this period and, as Wilson put it, under bondage to the pen, for theirs will surely rank among the great love letters in the English language. This portion of their correspondence goes down to the eve of their wedding, and the book ends, appropriately, with a notice of the ceremony in Savannah on June 24, 1885.

Printed as addenda at the end of the volume are two letters written in 1884 by Wilson to Albert Shaw. They were discovered by their owner, Virginia Shaw English, too late to be included in their chronological sequence in Volume 3.

The single editorial innovation in this fourth volume has been the expansion of the Index to include all names and all authorities and books mentioned in the documents. It might be well to remind readers that the Editors reproduce documents in their repairing or correcting in square brackets misspelled words or other mistakes except where absolutely necessary for clarity. original form insofar as it is typographically possible, without Exceptions to this rule in the printing of Ellen Axson's letters have been noted in the Introduction to Volume 2. An additional exception, which the Editors have adopted for this and future volumes, is the silent correction of obvious typographical errors in *copies* of letters—for example, the copies of Wilson's letters to Albert Shaw.

Reference librarians, scholars, and other individuals have unstintingly contributed documents and information for notes. The Editors are particularly indebted to Dr. Thomas H. Spence, Jr., and Mrs. Michael N. Lane of the Historical Foundation, Montreat, N. C., for materials relating to the southern Presbyterian Church; to Professor Arthur Dudden of Bryn Mawr College, for materials relating to Wilson's appointment to the faculty of that college; to President Katharine McBride of the same institution, for permission to print portions of the minutes of the Executive Committee of the Bryn Mawr Board of Trustees; to Misses Margaret Godley of the Savannah Public Library, Katharine Howell of the Wilmington, N. C., Public Library, and Elizabeth C. Litsinger and Martha Ann Peters of the Enoch Pratt Free Library of Baltimore, for an endless stream of answers to queries. The Editors are also grateful to Margaret Hale Ely for supplying the original text of Wilson's section for a "History of Political Economy in the United States," and to Virginia Shaw English for making available her copies of Wilson's letters to Albert Shaw. Finally, the Editors are grateful to Mrs. Bryant Putney of Princeton University Press for copyediting and other assistance.

T. H. Vail Motter, Consulting Editor since 1964, retired during the completion of this volume. His colleagues take this occasion to record their gratitude to Dr. Motter for his invaluable contributions during the formative years of this series, and to wish for him a happy and productive retirement. The Editors also take this opportunity to welcome Jean MacLachlan to the staff as Contributing Editor.

THE EDITORS

Princeton, New Jersey

October 11, 1967

CONTENTS

ILLUSTRATIONS

Following page 360

TEXT ILLUSTRATION

ABBREVIATIONS

ALI	autograph letter initialed
ALS	autograph letter signed
API	autograph postal initialed
att(s).	attached, attachment(s)
ELA	Ellen Louise Axson
ELAhw	Ellen Louise Axson handwriting
enc(s).	enclosed, enclosure(s)
env.	envelope
hw	handwritten
hwL	handwritten letter
JRW	Joseph Ruggles Wilson
JWW	Janet Woodrow Wilson
TCL	typed copy of letter
TLS	typed letter signed
WW	Woodrow Wilson
WWhw	Woodrow Wilson handwriting or handwritten
WWsh	Woodrow Wilson shorthand
WWT	Woodrow Wilson typed

ABBREVIATIONS FOR COLLECTIONS AND LIBRARIES

Following the National Union Catalogue of the
Library of Congress

DLC	Library of Congress
MdBJ	Library of The Johns Hopkins University
Meyer Coll., DLC	Meyer Collection, Library of Congress
MH	Harvard University Library
MHi	Massachusetts Historical Society
NjP	Princeton University Library
PBm	Bryn Mawr College Library
RSB Coll., DLC	Ray Stannard Baker Collection of Wilsoniana, Library of Congress
ViU	University of Virginia Library
WC, NjP	Woodrow Wilson Collection, Princeton University Library
WP, DLC	Woodrow Wilson Papers, Library of Congress

SYMBOLS

[blank]	blanks in the text
[----]	undecipherable words in text, each dash representing one word
[* *]	undecipherable shorthand, each asterisk representing one shorthand outline
[ ]	word or words in original text which Wilson omitted in copying
⟨ ⟩	matter deleted from manuscript by Wilson and restored by the editors
[Sept. 8, 1884]	publication date of a published writing; also date of document when date is not part of text
[*Sept. 8, 1884*]	latest composition date of a published writing
[[Sept. 8, 1884]]	delivery date of a speech if publication date differs

THE PAPERS OF

WOODROW WILSON

VOLUME 4

1885

THE PAPERS OF
WOODROW WILSON

To Ellen Louise Axson

My own darling,　　　Balto., Saturday morning, Jany 24th, 1885

I received two copies of "Congressional Government" last evening and immediately reversed the wrappers about one of them
and sent it off to you—in hopes that you would get it before Sunday. I took time only to write your name upon the fly-leaf: but
that cost some ten minutes, because it was so hard to decide what
to write! Of course, however, I had to refrain from putting anything more than I did put. I had to say everything or nothing—
and what I wanted to put would have been out of place on the
public face of a book. I *wanted* to say that everything in the book
was yours already, having been written in the light and under
the inspiration of your love; that every word of it was written as
if to you, with thoughts of what you would think of it, and speculations as to your delight should it receive favour from the publishers and the public; that, as your love runs through this my
first book, so it must be the enabling power in all that I may write
hereafter, for without your entire love and faith and sympathy
it must be also the *last* book into which I could put any of my
self; that, in presenting it to you, I was presenting it to one whose
praise and approval are a thousand times sweeter and more essential to me than the praise and approval of the whole world of
critics and readers. In sending you my first book, darling, I renew
the gift of my self. My *mind* is yours, Eileen,—yours to strengthen
and freshen with a woman's whole-hearted sympathy, yours to
rule with a woman's love. If my book is precious to you for my
sake, if it has beauty and value in your eyes because I wrote it,
if it has delights for you because it represents my first adventure
as an author, then I will try to forget its so numerous defects and
to be satisfied with it because my Eileen esteems it precious. My
darling, if the book fails, I have your love to enable me to forget
the failure, and to strive to retrieve it; if it succeeds, I shall have
the delight of knowing that the success is sweet to you, of knowing that I have so far achieved the absorbing desire of my heart
—the desire of making my precious little sweetheart happy. You
see, therefore, little lady, that this gift of my book though trifling

in itself, is made great by the fact that it includes the gift of my heart, of my life. With such contents, I hope that the little volume will acquire a dignity and a sacredness in your eyes which otherwise it must lack. With it I give all that a man can give to a woman!

The longer of the two newspaper clippings I enclose is taken from the Charlotte [Raleigh] (N.C.) *Chronicle* of Jany. 20—a paper edited by [Walter H. Page] a one-time Fellow of the Hopkins, a great chum of Renick's, whom I met once in Atlanta. I suppose Renick gave him the "points" of the editorial.[1] The other extract is from the Wilmington *Star* of the 22nd.—and is certainly very cordial for Mr. Kingsbury.[2]

A young North Carolinian here gave me Page's editorial, and father sent me the other piece. Father's letter, however, which came after I had mailed my letter to you yesterday, contained news which drove everything else from my head. Mother and Josie[3] are away, in Columbia, where sister Annie's[4] precious little Jessie is at the point of death with brain fever. Possibly the dear little girl is dead by this time, as the event in such a case must be promptly decided, one way or the other, and brother George was "not at all hopeful as to the result." God grant that it may not be so! Her little life has been one of singular beauty and promise; and if she is taken away, it will come near to break my heart. She seemed to belong to me—sister Annie can hardly love her more than I do. What would I not give to be able to do something for the little pet! If she does go, there could be no sweeter memory than her sunshiny life and her brave suffering.

This sudden call to Columbia took dear mother away before she and father could come to any final decision as to that part of their plans which must affect ours. Dear father says: "As to *our* plans, on which *yours* may somewhat depend, I can write nothing definitely until I shall have consulted your mother, who will probably arrange for a couple of months' board—April and May and a part of June—*in Columbia*." He evidently takes it as a matter of course that our plan, for a marriage in June, is a *proper* one—the only open question being as to the date and their preparation to receive us in Tennessee.

I had intended, my darling, to say nothing more about Mr. Goodrich,[5] but my surprise at one or two things in your recent notes leads me to say just one word more. To go with him to the theatre on Monday, to prayer-meeting on Wednesday, and to the theatre again the next week is scarcely discouraging his attentions—is it, little lady? I suggest this, my pet, altogether in love—

for your sake;—not because of any chagrin or pique at having my advice neglected, but because I am exceedingly jealous for your dignity and because I know how hard it must be to tell what to do under such delicate circumstances. And it is a mere suggestion. I have no desire to dictate your course in the least particular. I know that you will do what is *right*: my only fear is that your generous lack of all suspicion, and trust in all professions, will lead you to do what may in the event prove to have been inexpedient. Let my love atone for the mistake, if I am mistaken.

It is hard, *so* hard, to write these things, my precious. I cannot but be frank with you—and yet frankness so often seems like harshness on the written page. I could no more be harsh to you, my darling, than I could be untrue. As you have all my heart, in completest homage, so you must take my mind as well—tho' its judgments can never be given to you except in tenderness and as proof of love. I want to be admitted to your counsels as I have been admitted to your heart—my purpose, my longing, my ambition are to serve you through a life-time which shall prove that I am altogether and with all my heart

Your own   Woodrow.

ALS (WC, NjP). Encs.: clippings from Raleigh, N.C., *State Chronicle*, Jan. 20, 1885, and Wilmington, N.C., *Morning Star*, Jan. 22, 1885.

[1] WW's supposition was correct. See E. I. Renick to WW, Jan. 24, 1885.

[2] Theodore Bryant Kingsbury, editor of the Wilmington *Morning Star*, a son-in-law of William H. Bernard, founder and former editor of the paper.

[3] Joseph R. Wilson, Jr.

[4] Mrs. George Howe, Jr.

[5] Arthur Goodrich, who was in warm pursuit of Ellen and was the subject of many letters between Woodrow and Ellen printed in Vol. 3.

CONGRESSIONAL GOVERNMENT

Wilson's failure to find publication for his book-length polemical essay, "Government by Debate,"[1] had revealed that it was not easy for an unknown young author to break into print with a tract for the times. As Wilson wrote to Robert Bridges on May 13, 1883, he could do nothing but accept the failure and try to profit from the experience while striving "to deserve better at the next trial." The disappointed author, at Bridges' suggestion, did salvage a segment of "Government by Debate" in "Committee or Cabinet Government?" published in *The Overland Monthly* in January 1884.[2] But this was not "the next trial."

The catalyst of the conception of a different kind of book seems to have been Wilson's re-reading of Walter Bagehot's *The English Constitution*. He had of course read this classic comparison between the Cabinet and presidential-congressional systems long before 1883—at least by the time that he began writing "Cabinet Government in the United States"[3] in late January or early February of 1879. This article and another, "Congressional Government,"[4] written in the following October, reveal Wilson's heavy reliance upon Bagehot and, to a lesser degree, Gamaliel Bradford and other American commentators. But, as the Editorial Note on "Government by Debate" has pointed out,[5] Wilson's single objective in all his political writings between "Cabinet Government in the United States" and "Government by Debate" was to encourage and lead, if he could, a great national movement for reform of the American governmental system through a modified adoption of the Cabinet system. He purchased a copy of the most recent edition of *The English Constitution* in early August 1883,[6] while in Wilmington, North Carolina, and he re-read the book while on vacation in Arden, North Carolina, completing it, as his reading date at the end of the book reveals, on September 12, 1883.

It was surely during these weeks that the plan for a new book took form in Wilson's mind. He would change course sharply and abandon the objective of attempting, *directly and openly*, to promote specific reforms. Instead, he would do for the American constitutional system what Bagehot had done for the British—describe the American system as it had developed historically and as it actually operated in his own day, not according to what Bagehot had called the "literary theory." Bagehot had vindicated the British system by comparing it with the American. Wilson would show the weaknesses of the presidential-congressional system by comparing them with the strengths of the Cabinet system. He explained his purposes fully and clearly in letters to Ellen Axson, Bridges, and Dabney. The following extracts bear

[1] Printed at Dec. 4, 1882, Vol. 2.
[2] Printed at Jan. 1, 1884, Vol. 2.
[3] Printed at Aug. 1, 1879, Vol. 1.
[4] Printed at Oct. 1, 1879, Vol. 1.
[5] Printed in Vol. 2; see also the Editorial Note on "Cabinet Government in the United States," in Vol. 1.
[6] Receipted bill from J. B. Lippincott & Co., Aug. 2, 1883 (WP, DLC). WW's copy was Walter Bagehot, *The English Constitution and Other Political Essays*, "Latest Revised Edition," published in New York by D. Appleton in 1882.

repetition here even though they have been printed in Volumes 2 and 3, and, in the case of the letter to Dabney, will appear in Volume 5:

I want to contribute to our literature what no American has ever contributed, studies in the philosophy of our institutions, not the abstract and occult, but the practical and suggestive, philosophy which is at the core of our governmental methods; their use, their meaning, "the spirit that makes them workable." I want to divest them of the theory that obscures them and present their weakness and their strength without disguise, and with such skill and such plenitude of proof that it shall be seen that I have succeeded and that I have added something to the resources of knowledge upon which statecraft must depend. [To Ellen Axson, Oct. 30, 1883]

I've planned a set of four or five essays . . . in which it is my purpose to show, as well as I can, our constitutional system as it looks in operation. My desire and ambition are to treat the American constitution as Mr. Bagehot . . . has treated the English Constitution. His book has inspired my whole study of our government. He brings to the work a fresh and original method which has made the British system much more intelligible to ordinary men than it ever was before, and which, if it could be succcessfully applied to the exposition of our federal constitution, would result in something like a revelation to those who are still reading the Federalist as an authoritative constitutional manual. An immense literature has already accumulated upon this subject; but I venture to think that the greater part of it is either irrelevant or already antiquated. [To Ellen Axson, Jan. 1, 1884]

It's the same old thing—Committee government—but it's worked up in very different shape from that of the essays ["Government by Debate"]. . . . I leave out all advocacy of Cabinet government— all advocacy, indeed, of *any* specific reform—and devote myself to a careful analysis of Congressional government. I have abandoned the evangelical for the exegetical—so to speak! [To Robert Bridges, Nov. 19, 1884]

If ever any book was written with fulness and earnestness of conviction, with purpose of imparting conviction, that book was: and, in my view, the extent to which it realizes that purpose is the standard of its success. Of course I should like to be able to believe that it was to stand as a permanent piece of constitutional criticism by reason of some depth of historical and political insight: but its mission was to *stir* thought and to carry irresistible practical suggestion, and it was as such a missionary that it carried my hopes and ambitions with it. I carefully kept all advocacy of particular reforms out of it, because I wanted it to be, so far as I could make it such, a permanent piece of work, not a political pamphlet, which couldn't succeed without destroying its own reason for being; but I hoped at the same time that it might catch hold of its readers' convictions and set reform a-going in a very definite direction. [To Richard H. Dabney, Oct. 28, 1885]

As Wilson would later say in the preface to *Congressional Government,* his purpose in comparing the British and American systems was to clarify the actual conditions of the American federal government. He would offer, "not a commentary, but an outspoken presentation of such cardinal facts as may be sources of practical suggestion."

That Wilson had come to such a complete understanding of his purposes by the late summer of 1883 might well be doubted. But by this time he had resolved to write a book modeled after Bagehot's, for he was so impressed after re-reading Bagehot (and perhaps already so excited about plans for his own book) that he talked at length about his British mentor to Ellen Axson on Friday night, September 14, 1883, as they sat on the verandah of the Eagle Hotel in Asheville.

Wilson went to Baltimore and The Johns Hopkins University a few days later. He spent some time getting into academic harness; and at first he feared that his chief professor, Herbert Baxter Adams, would insist that he do research in the sources and historical writing of a monographic kind for the Seminary of Historical and Political Science. These fears were relieved when Adams, in a conference on October 16, 1883, not only freed his student from the obligation to pursue conventional historical work, but also encouraged him to go on with his comparative constitutional studies.[7] Wilson wrote *Congressional Government* entirely on his own. There is no evidence to suggest that Adams or Wilson's other professors either advised him in his research or edited his manuscript in any way.

However eager Wilson may have been after his conference with Adams to complete research on his favorite topic, the normal demands of graduate school seem to have diverted him temporarily. In addition, he devoted a considerable portion of his time during the first three weeks in November to preparing his lecture on Adam Smith for delivery in Dr. Richard T. Ely's undergraduate course in political economy.[8]

Soon afterward, probably during the last week in November, he began research on *Congressional Government.* Of course he did not begin *de novo.* He had been studying the American, British, and French governments comparatively and with singleness of purpose at least since late 1878 or early 1879. He undoubtedly had at hand his earlier writings as well as the scrapbook in which he had pasted articles, editorials, and letters to the editor, and which he had used in writing "Government by Debate."[9] In this new research for *Congressional Government,* Wilson did not use the topical note-card system but kept a special notebook—almost entirely in shorthand.[10] Into this notebook he copied extracts from various authorities and sources, jotted down bibliographical references, and occasionally interspersed some of his own ideas growing out of his reading. Since he filled the pages (numbered 1-20) consecutively, these notes provide evidence

[7] WW to ELA, Oct. 16, 1883, Vol. 2.

[8] See the Editorial Note "Wilson's Lecture on Adam Smith," and the fragmentary draft of WW's lecture, printed at Nov. 20, 1883, Vol. 2.

[9] Scrapbook inscribed on cover "T. Woodrow Wilson 1881," described at Jan. 1, 1881, Vol. 2.

[10] Described at Nov. 1, 1883, Vol. 2.

A page of *Wilson's* shorthand research notes for
CONGRESSIONAL GOVERNMENT

of when he had substantially completed his research. For instance, on page 18 he included a reference to the *Congressional Record* of January 8, 1884, when the House was considering a revision of its rules. Thus, though his research as represented in this notebook overlapped the writing of his introduction, the evidence indicates that he finished the main body of his research by the middle of January 1884.

Wilson began writing the introductory chapter of *Congressional Government* on January 1, 1884, and completed the final chapter on about September 1 of that same year. He did not follow what later became his usual practice of noting the composition dates at the ends of chapters, but his letters and other documents enable us to reconstruct the chronology almost completely. The following is offered as a guide, the dates referring to documents printed in Volumes 2 and 3:

January 1, 1884: Wilson tells Ellen Axson that he has begun composition of the introductory essay.

January 16, 1884: Wilson intimates to Ellen that the writing of the first essay is going very well.

February 12, 1884: Wilson writes to Ellen that he is struggling with the second essay and describes his objectives in fine detail.

March 4, 1884: Wilson informs Ellen that he has finished the second chapter.

March 11, 1884: Wilson, in response to a question from Ellen, says that he has not yet decided upon a title but has tentatively adopted "The Government of the Union."

March 23, 1884: Wilson tells Ellen that the third essay is moving quite prosperously.

March 30, 1884: Wilson writes Ellen that he finished the third chapter on March 26; and that he had spent March 27, 28, 29, and 30 copying all but forty pages of the first three chapters on his Caligraph.

April 4, 1884: Wilson submits the first three chapters to Houghton Mifflin for publication and says that he will complete the book if they like the first part. Indicates that he has changed the title to "Congressional Government."

April 28, 1884: Houghton Mifflin reply that they are favorably impressed and encourage Wilson to continue.

May 2, 1884: Wilson asks Houghton Mifflin to keep the second and third chapters and to return the first, or introductory, essay, as he may want to add some references to the recent legal tender decision and the Blair bill for federal aid to education if it passes.

May 5, 1884: Houghton Mifflin comply, referring to the book as "Congressional Government."

May 8, 1884: Wilson reads the introduction to the Seminary of Historical and Political Science.

May 15, 1884: Wilson reads the second chapter to the Seminary.

June 3, 1884: Wilson tells Ellen that he has earlier submitted the first three chapters with his application for a fellowship at the university. (He had been notified on May 26 that he had won the fellowship.)

June 26, 1884: Wilson writes Ellen that he has had little time since his arrival in Wilmington to work on the fourth chapter because he has been preoccupied with the Minutes of the General Assembly of the southern Presbyterian Church; and that he wrote a few pages on the preceding night to get started.

July 3, 13, and 15, 1884: Wilson reports to Ellen on his progress on the fourth chapter.

July 22, 1884: Wilson writes Ellen that he has completed the fourth chapter and is copying it on his Caligraph.

August 2, 1884: Wilson intimates to Ellen that he has begun the fifth chapter.

August 10, 1884: Wilson reports that Chapter V is a little more than half completed.

August 23, 1884: Wilson tells Ellen that he finished the fifth chapter the "other evening" and will begin the sixth and final essay on August 25.

September 6, 1884: Wilson writes Ellen that he finished the last chapter "some days ago" and now has to make two Caligraph copies of Chapters V and VI as he did of the other chapters.

October 7, 1884: Wilson tells Ellen that he has just prepared his manuscript to be sent to Houghton Mifflin and is about to start for the express office.

October 17, 1884: Wilson reads the third chapter before the Historical Seminary.

November 18, 1884: Wilson writes Ellen that it has been six weeks since he sent the manuscript to Houghton Mifflin. He wonders what they have done with it.

November 26, 1884: Houghton Mifflin offer to publish *Congressional Government*.

December 10, 1884: Wilson writes Ellen that he received first proofs of his book on the preceding day.

December 15, 1884: Wilson tells Ellen that he has proofs to read.

January 11, 1885: Wilson tells Ellen that the last proofs came this morning.

January 24, 1885: Wilson writes Ellen that he received two copies of *Congressional Government* last evening and mailed one to her.

Wilson seems to have done little additional research while writing *Congressional Government*, so intense was his concentration upon organization and composition. But he did obtain information about the preparation of budget estimates by the various federal departments from his former law partner, Edward I. Renick, before starting and while he was writing the third chapter, in which he used this information.[11] He also, in the last stages of composition in Wilmington, kept returning to Bagehot as his principal source and authority.[12] In addition, he began, almost certainly in the autumn of 1884, to take the research notes which he entitled "*Congressional Government. Notes.* 1884 to [blank]."[13] But he took most of these after the book

[11] E. I. Renick to WW, Feb. 28, March 2, and March 29, 1884, Vol. 3.
[12] As the pocket notebook described at May 16, 1884, Vol. 3, reveals.
[13] He recorded these in the "private notebook" described at Jan. 1, 1881, Vol. 2.

had gone to press; and he used only one of them—a quotation from Lord Roseberry on the Senate—in his text. It is also worth noting that at no time during the research for and writing of *Congressional Government* did Wilson go to Washington to observe Congress at first hand.[14]

A glance at the drafts of *Congressional Government* reveals Wilson's method of working toward a final text. He wrote his first draft in longhand, editing it heavily for stylistic improvement and copying some of the pages on his Caligraph. Then he made a first Caligraphscript for his own reference, putting footnotes in brackets in the body of the text. He next edited this copy lightly and copied it on his Caligraph in final form for the printer, with footnotes at the bottom of the pages.

Congressional Government was the crystallization and apogee of Wilson's thinking at least since 1876 about the American and British political systems. His thought during these years of maturing was a continuous and developing stream, and nothing was lost as he progressed from one literary formulation to the next. So complete is the documentation that it would be possible by close textual analysis and study of Wilson's research notebooks, scrapbooks, and marginal notes to show what in *Congressional Government* was derivative and what original and, moreover, the extent to which Wilson used authorities without following customary practice in acknowledging his indebtedness. Since such a task is beyond the scope of this essay, the following is offered only to indicate a possible method and probable results.

The analyst might begin by comparing the text of *Congressional Government* with that of its immediate predecessor, "Government by Debate." Such comparison would isolate the new portions of the former, and our analyst could then locate the sources of the new text by studying Wilson's footnotes and research notes. He would also recognize the continuing predominant influence of Bagehot and the lesser contribution of Gamaliel Bradford. The comparison would also reveal the extensive portions of "Government by Debate" that Wilson incorporated in more or less revised form into *Congressional Government*. The analyst, by following the same methods, could also separate the new portions of "Government by Debate" from portions drawn from earlier essays, all the way back to "Cabinet Government in the United States" of 1879. The result would be to show how Wilson built systematically upon the foundation of this essay over the years, adding and expanding in his accretions but still adhering to his controlling purpose of exposing the defects of the presidential-congressional system in the light of the merits of the Cabinet system.

Wilson's largely handwritten first draft, entitled "The Government of the Union," is in the Wilson Papers in the Library of Congress. This collection also contains Wilson's first Caligraphscript, minus the sixth chapter. His second Caligraphscript, which he sent to Houghton Mifflin, is now in the Library of The Johns Hopkins University because Wilson later submitted it as his doctoral dissertation. It contains a few emendations and insertions by Wilson but no signs of copyediting by Houghton Mifflin except a few markings for the printer,

[14] As WW said in his letter to ELA of Jan. 22, 1885, Vol. 3.

which Horace E. Scudder may have made. The text printed below is that of the first edition, including its few typographical errors, altered only by two kinds of silent editorial changes. Quotation marks, which Wilson usually printed outside semicolons, have been moved inside semicolons; and footnotes have been numbered consecutively by chapter.

Congressional Government subsequently went through many printings or "editions," and Wilson never changed the text. He added an index to the third printing in 1885 and wrote a new preface to the fifteenth "edition" in 1900.

Wilson's First Published Book

[c. Jan. 24, 1885]

Congressional Government: A Study
in American Politics

PREFACE.

The object of these essays is not to exhaust criticism of the government of the United States, but only to point out the most characteristic practical features of the federal system. Taking Congress as the central and predominant power of the system, their object is to illustrate everything Congressional. Everybody has seen, and critics without number have said, that our form of national government is singular, possessing a character altogether its own; but there is abundant evidence that very few have seen just wherein it differs most essentially from the other governments of the world. There have been and are other federal systems quite similar, and scarcely any legislative or administrative principle of our Constitution was young even when that Constitution was framed. It is our legislative and administrative *machinery* which makes our government essentially different from all other great governmental systems. The most striking contrast in modern politics is not between presidential and monarchical governments, but between Congressional and Parliamentary governments. Congressional government is Committee government; Parliamentary government is government by a responsible Cabinet Ministry. These are the two principal types which present themselves for the instruction of the modern student of the practical in politics: administration by semi-independent executive agents who obey the dictation of a legislature to which they are not responsible, and administration by executive agents who are the accredited leaders and accountable servants of a legislature virtually supreme in all things. My chief aim in these essays has been, therefore, an adequate illustrative contrast of these two types of government, with a view to making as plain as possible the actual conditions of federal administration. In short, I offer, not a commentary, but an outspoken presentation of such cardinal facts as may be sources of practical suggestion.   WOODROW WILSON.

JOHNS HOPKINS UNIVERSITY, *October* 7, 1884.

I.

INTRODUCTORY.

The laws reach but a very little way. Constitute government how you please, infinitely the greater part of it must depend upon the exercise of powers, which are left at large to the prudence and uprightness of ministers of state. Even all the use and potency of the laws depends upon them. Without them your commonwealth is no better than a scheme upon paper; and not a living, active, effective organization.—BURKE.

The great fault of political writers is their too close adherence to the forms of the system of state which they happen to be expounding or examining. They stop short at the anatomy of institutions, and do not penetrate to the secret of their functions.—JOHN MORLEY.

It would seem as if a very wayward fortune had presided over the history of the Constitution of the United States, inasmuch as that great federal charter has been alternately violated by its friends and defended by its enemies. It came hard by its establishment in the first place, prevailing with difficulty over the strenuous forces of dissent which were banded against it. While its adoption was under discussion the voices of criticism were many and authoritative, the voices of opposition loud in tone and ominous in volume, and the Federalists finally triumphed only by dint of hard battle against foes, formidable both in numbers and in skill. But the victory was complete,—astonishingly complete. Once established, the new government had only the zeal of its friends to fear. Indeed, after its organization very little more is heard of the party of opposition; they disappear so entirely from politics that one is inclined to think, in looking back at the party history of that time, that they must have been not only conquered but converted as well. There was well-nigh universal acquiescence in the new order of things. Not everybody, indeed, professed himself a Federalist, but everybody conformed to federalist practice. There were jealousies and bickerings, of course, in the new Congress of the Union, but no party lines, and the differences which caused the constant brewing and breaking of storms in Washington's first cabinet were of personal rather than of political import. Hamilton and Jefferson did not draw apart because the one had been an ardent and the other only a lukewarm friend of the Constitution, so much as because they were so different in natural bent and temper that they would have been like to disagree and come to drawn points wherever or however brought into contact. The one had inherited warm blood and a bold sagacity, while in the other a negative philosophy ran suitably through cool veins. They had not been meant for yoke-fellows.

There was less antagonism in Congress, however, than in the cabinet; and in none of the controversies that did arise was there shown any serious disposition to quarrel with the Constitution itself; the contention was as to the obedience to be rendered to its provisions. No one threatened to withhold his allegiance, though there soon began to be some exhibition of a disposition to confine obedience to the letter of the new commandments, and to discountenance all attempts to do what was not plainly written in the tables of the law. It was recognized as no longer fashionable to say aught against the principles of the Constitution; but all men could not be of one mind, and political parties began to take form in antagonistic schools of constitutional construction. There straightway arose two rival sects of political Pharisees, each professing a more perfect conformity and affecting greater "ceremonial cleanliness" than the other. The very men who had resisted with might and main the adoption of the Constitution became, under the new division of parties, its champions, as sticklers for a strict, a rigid, and literal construction.

They were consistent enough in this, because it was quite natural that their one-time fear of a strong central government should pass into a dread of the still further expansion of the power of that government, by a too loose construction of its charter; but what I would emphasize here is not the motives or the policy of the conduct of parties in our early national politics, but the fact that opposition to the Constitution as a constitution, and even hostile criticism of its provisions, ceased almost immediately upon its adoption; and not only ceased, but gave place to an undiscriminating and almost blind worship of its principles, and of that delicate dual system of sovereignty, and that complicated scheme of double administration which it established. Admiration of that one-time so much traversed body of law became suddenly all the vogue, and criticism was estopped. From the first, even down to the time immediately preceding the war, the general scheme of the Constitution went unchallenged; nullification itself did not always wear its true garb of independent state sovereignty, but often masqueraded as a constitutional right; and the most violent policies took care to make show of at least formal deference to the worshipful fundamental law. The divine right of kings never ran a more prosperous course than did this unquestioned prerogative of the Constitution to receive universal homage. The conviction that our institutions were the best in the world, nay more, the model to which all civilized states must sooner or later conform, could not be laughed out of us by foreign critics, nor shaken out of us by the roughest jars of the system.

Now there is, of course, nothing in all this that is inexplicable, or even remarkable; any one can see the reasons for it and the benefits of it without going far out of his way; but the point which it is interesting to note is that we of the present generation are in the first season of free, outspoken, unrestrained constitutional criticism. We are the first Americans to hear our own countrymen ask whether the Constitution is still adapted to serve the purposes for which it was intended; the first to entertain any serious doubts about the superiority of our own institutions as compared with the systems of Europe; the first to think of remodeling the administrative machinery of the federal government, and of forcing new forms of responsibility upon Congress.

The evident explanation of this change of attitude towards the Constitution is that we have been made conscious by the rude shock of the war and by subsequent developments of policy, that there has been a vast alteration in the conditions of government; that the checks and balances which once obtained are no longer effective; and that we are really living under a constitution essentially different from that which we have been so long worshiping as our own peculiar and incomparable possession. In short, this model government is no longer conformable with its own original pattern. While we have been shielding it from criticism it has slipped away from us. The noble charter of fundamental law given us by the Convention of 1787 is still our Constitution; but it is now our *form of government* rather in name than in reality, the form of the Constitution being one of nicely adjusted, ideal balances, whilst the actual form of our present government is simply a scheme of congressional supremacy. National legislation, of course, takes force now as at first from the authority of the Constitution; but it would be easy to reckon by the score acts of Congress which can by no means be squared with that great instrument's evident theory. We continue to think, indeed, according to long-accepted constitutional formulae, and it is still politically unorthodox to depart from old-time phraseology in grave discussions of affairs; but it is plain to those who look about them that most of the commonly received opinions concerning federal constitutional balances and administrative arrangements are many years behind the actual practices of the government at Washington, and that we are farther than most of us realize from the times and the policy of the framers of the Constitution. It is a commonplace observation of historians that, in the development of constitutions, names are much more persistent than the functions upon which they were originally bestowed; that institutions constantly undergo essential alterations of character, whilst retaining the names conferred upon them in their first estate; and the history of our own Constitution is but another illustration of this universal principle of institutional change. There has been a constant growth of legislative and administrative practice, and a steady accretion of precedent in the management of federal affairs, which have broadened the sphere and altered the functions of the government without perceptibly affecting the vocabulary of our constitutional language. Ours is, scarcely less than the British, a living and fecund system. It does not, indeed, find its rootage so widely in the hidden soil of unwritten law; its tap-root at least is the Constitution; but the Constitution is now, like Magna Carta and the Bill of Rights, only the sap-centre of a system of government vastly larger than the stock from which it has branched,—a system some of whose forms have only very indistinct and rudimental beginnings in the simple substance of the Constitution, and which exercises many functions apparently quite foreign to the primitive properties contained in the fundamental law.

The Constitution itself is not a complete system; it takes none but the first steps in organization. It does little more than lay a foundation of principles. It provides with all possible brevity for the establishment of a government having, in several distinct branches, executive, legislative, and judicial powers. It vests executive power in a single chief magistrate, for whose election and inauguration it makes carefully definite provision, and whose privileges and prerogatives it defines with succinct clearness; it grants specifically enumerated powers of legislation to a representative Congress, outlining the organization of the two houses of that body and definitely providing for the election of its members, whose number it regulates and the conditions of whose choice it names; and it establishes a Supreme Court with ample authority of constitutional interpretation, prescribing the manner in which its judges shall be appointed and the conditions of their official tenure. Here the Constitution's work of organization ends, and the fact that it attempts nothing more is its chief strength. For it to go beyond elementary provisions would be to lose elasticity and adaptability. The growth of the nation and the consequent development of the governmental system would snap asunder a constitution which could not adapt itself to the new conditions of an advancing society. If it could not stretch itself to the measure of the times, it must be thrown off and left behind, as a bygone device; and there can, therefore, be no question that our Constitution has proved lasting because of its simplicity. It is a corner-stone, not a complete building; or, rather, to return to the old figure, it is a root, not a perfect vine.

The chief fact, therefore, of our national history is that from this vigorous tap-root has grown a vast constitutional system,—a system branching and expanding in statutes and judicial decisions, as well as in unwritten precedent; and one of the most striking facts, as it seems to me, in the history of our politics is, that that system has never received complete and competent critical treatment at the hands of any, even the most acute, of our constitutional writers. They view it, as it were, from behind. Their thoughts are dominated, it would seem, by those incomparable papers of the "Federalist," which, though they were written to influence only the voters of 1788, still, with a strange, persistent longevity of power, shape the constitutional criticism of the present day, obscuring much of that development of constitutional practice which has since taken place. The Constitution in operation is manifestly a very different thing from the Constitution of the books. "An observer who looks at the living reality will wonder at the contrast to the paper description. He will see in the life much which is not in the books; and he will not find in the rough practice many refinements of the literary theory."[1] It is, therefore, the difficult task of one who would now write at once practically and critically of our national government to escape from theories and attach himself to facts, not allowing himself to be confused by a knowledge of what that government was intended to be, or led away into conjectures as to what it may one day become, but striving to catch its present phases and to photograph the delicate organism in all its characteristic parts exactly

[1] These are Mr. Bagehot's words with reference to the British constitutional system. See his *English Constitution* (last American edition), p. 69.

as it is today; an undertaking all the more arduous and doubtful of issue because it has to be entered upon without guidance from writers of acknowledged authority.

The leading inquiry in the examination of any system of government must, of course, concern primarily the real depositaries and the essential machinery of power. There is always a centre of power: where in this system is that centre? in whose hands is self-sufficient authority lodged, and through what agencies does that authority speak and act? The answers one gets to these and kindred questions from authoritative manuals of constitutional exposition are not satisfactory, chiefly because they are contradicted by self-evident facts. It is said that there is no single or central force in our federal scheme; and so there is not in the federal *scheme*, but only a balance of powers and a nice adjustment of interactive checks, as all the books say. How is it, however, in the practical conduct of the federal government? In that, unquestionably, the predominant and controlling force, the centre and source of all motive and of all regulative power, is Congress. All niceties of constitutional restriction and even many broad principles of constitutional limitation have been overridden, and a thoroughly organized system of congressional control set up which gives a very rude negative to some theories of balance and some schemes for distributed powers, but which suits well with convenience, and does violence to none of the principles of self-government contained in the Constitution.

This fact, however, though evident enough, is not on the surface. It does not obtrude itself upon the observation of the world. It runs through the undercurrents of government, and takes shape only in the inner channels of legislation and administration which are not open to the common view. It can be discerned most readily by comparing the "literary theory" of the Constitution with the actual machinery of legislation, especially at those points where that machinery regulates the relations of Congress with the executive departments, and with the attitude of the houses towards the Supreme Court on those occasions, happily not numerous, when legislature and judiciary have come face to face in direct antagonism. The "literary theory" is distinct enough; every American is familiar with the paper pictures of the Constitution. Most prominent in such pictures are the ideal checks and balances of the federal system, which may be found described, even in the most recent books, in terms substantially the same as those used in 1814 by John Adams in his letter to John Taylor. "Is there," says Mr. Adams, "a constitution upon record more complicated with balances than ours? In the first place, eighteen states and some territories are balanced against the national government. . . . In the second place, the House of Representatives is balanced against the Senate, the Senate against the House. In the third place, the executive authority is, in some degree, balanced against the legislative. In the fourth place, the judicial power is balanced against the House, the Senate, the executive power, and the state governments. In the fifth place, the Senate is balanced against the President in all appointments to office, and in all treaties. . . . In the sixth place, the people hold in their hands the balance against their own representatives, by biennial . . . elections. In the seventh place, the legislatures of the several states are balanced against the Senate by sextennial elections. In the eighth place, the electors are balanced against the people in the choice of the President. Here is a complicated refinement of balances, which, for anything I recollect, is an invention of our own and peculiar to us."[2]

All of these balances are reckoned essential in the theory of the Constitution; but none is so quintessential as that between the national and the state governments; it is the pivotal quality of the system, indicating its principal, which is its federal characteristic. The object of this balance of thirty-eight States "and some territories" against the powers of the federal government, as also of several of the other balances enumerated, is not, it should be observed, to prevent the invasion by the national authorities of those provinces of legislation by plain expression or implication reserved to the States,—such as the regulation of municipal institutions, the punishment of ordinary crimes, the enactment of laws of inheritance and of contract, the erection and maintenance of the common machinery of education, and the control of other such like matters of social economy and everyday administration,—but to check and trim national policy on national questions, to turn Congress back from paths of dangerous encroachment on middle or doubtful grounds of jurisdiction, to keep sharp, when it was like to become dim, the line of demarcation between state and federal privilege, to readjust the weights of jurisdiction whenever either state or federal scale threatened to kick the beam. There never was any great likelihood that the national government would care to take from the States their plainer prerogatives, but there was always a violent

---

[2] *Works*, vol. vi., p. 467: "Letter to Jno. Taylor." The words and sentences omitted in the quotation contain Mr. Adams's opinions as to the value of the several balances, some of which he thinks of doubtful utility, and others of which he, without hesitation, pronounces altogether pernicious.

probability that it would here and there steal a march over the borders where territory like its own invited it to appropriation; and it was for a mutual defense of such border-land that the two governments were given the right to call a halt upon one another. It was purposed to guard not against revolution, but against unrestrained exercise of questionable powers.

The extent to which the restraining power of the States was relied upon in the days of the Convention, and of the adoption of the Constitution, is strikingly illustrated in several of the best known papers of the "Federalist"; and there is no better means of realizing the difference between the actual and the ideal constitutions than this of placing one's self at the point of view of the public men of 1787–89. They were disgusted with the impotent and pitiable Confederation, which could do nothing but beg and deliberate; they longed to get away from the selfish feuds of "States dissevered, discordant, belligerent," and their hopes were centred in the establishment of a strong and lasting union, such as could secure that concert and facility of common action in which alone there could be security and amity. They were, however, by no means sure of being able to realize their hopes, contrive how they might to bring the States together into a more perfect confederation. The late colonies had but recently become compactly organized, self-governing States, and were standing somewhat stiffly apart, a group of consequential sovereignties, jealous to maintain their blood-bought prerogatives, and quick to distrust any power set above them, or arrogating to itself the control of their restive wills. It was not to be expected that the sturdy, self-reliant, masterful men who had won independence for their native colonies, by passing through the flames of battle, and through the equally fierce fires of bereavement and financial ruin, would readily transfer their affection and allegiance from the new-made States, which were their homes, to the federal government, which was to be a mere artificial creation, and which could be to no man as his home government. As things looked then, it seemed idle to apprehend a too great diminution of state rights: there was every reason, on the contrary, to fear that any union that could be agreed upon would lack both vitality and the ability to hold its ground against the jealous self-assertion of the sovereign commonwealths of its membership. Hamilton but spoke the common belief of all thinking men of the time when he said: "It will always be far more easy for the state governments to encroach upon the national authorities than for the national government to encroach upon the state authorities"; and he seemed to furnish abundant support for the opinion, when he added, that "the proof of this proposition turns upon the greater degree of influence which the state governments, if they administer their affairs uprightly and prudently, will generally possess over the people; a circumstance which, at the same time, teaches us that there is an inherent and intrinsic weakness in all federal constitutions, and that too much pains cannot be taken in their organization to give them all the force that is compatible with the principles of liberty."[3]

Read in the light of the present day, such views constitute the most striking of all commentaries upon our constitutional history. Manifestly the powers reserved to the States were expected to serve as a very real and potent check upon the federal government; and yet we can see plainly enough now that this balance of state against national authorities has proved, of all constitutional checks, the least effectual. The proof of the pudding is the eating thereof, and we can nowadays detect in it none of that strong flavor of state sovereignty which its cooks thought they were giving it. It smacks, rather, of federal omnipotence, which they thought to mix in only in very small and judicious quantities. "From the nature of the case," as Judge Cooley says, "it was impossible that the powers reserved to the States should constitute a restraint upon the increase of federal power, to the extent that was at first expected. The federal government was necessarily made the final judge of its own authority, and the executor of its own will, and any effectual check to the gradual amplification of its jurisdiction must therefore be found in the construction put by those administering it upon the grants of the Constitution, and in their own sense of constitutional obligation. And as the true line of division between federal and state powers has, from the very beginning, been the subject of contention and of honest differences of opinion, it must often happen that to advance and occupy some disputed ground will seem to the party having the power to do so a mere matter of constitutional duty."[4]

During the early years of the new national government there was, doubtless, much potency in state will; and had federal and state powers then come face to face, before Congress and the President had had time to overcome their first awkwardness and timidity, and to discover the safest walks of their authority and the most effectual means of exercising their power, it is probable that state prerogatives would have prevailed. The central govern-

[3] *Federalist*, No. 17.
[4] Cooley's *Principles of Const. Law*, p. 143.

ment, as every one remembers, did not at first give promise of a very great career. It had inherited some of the contempt which had attached to the weak Congress of the Confederation. Two of the thirteen States held aloof from the Union until they could be assured of its stability and success; many of the other States had come into it reluctantly, all with a keen sense of sacrifice, and there could not be said to be any very widespread or undoubting belief in its ultimate survival. The members of the first Congress, too, came together very tardily, and in no very cordial or confident spirit of coöperation; and after they had assembled they were for many months painfully embarrassed, how and upon what subjects to exercise their new and untried functions. The President was denied formal precedence in dignity by the Governor of New York, and must himself have felt inclined to question the consequence of his official station, when he found that amongst the principal questions with which he had to deal were some which concerned no greater things than petty points of etiquette and ceremonial; as, for example, whether one day in the week would be sufficient to receive visits of compliment, "and what would be said if he were sometimes to be seen at quiet tea-parties."[5] But this first weakness of the new government was only a transient phase in its history, and the federal authorities did not invite a direct issue with the States until they had had time to reckon their resources and to learn facility of action. Before Washington left the presidential chair the federal government had been thoroughly organized, and it fast gathered strength and confidence as it addressed itself year after year to the adjustment of foreign relations, to the defense of the western frontiers, and to the maintenance of domestic peace. For twenty-five years it had no chance to think of those questions of internal policy which, in later days, were to tempt it to stretch its constitutional jurisdiction. The establishment of the public credit, the revival of commerce, and the encouragement of industry; the conduct, first, of a heated controversy, and finally of an unequal war with England; the avoidance, first, of too much love, and afterwards of too violent hatred of France; these and other like questions of great pith and moment gave it too much to do to leave it time to think of nice points of constitutional theory affecting its relations with the States.

But still, even in those busy times of international controversy, when the lurid light of the French Revolution outshone all others, and when men's minds were full of those ghosts of '76, which took

[5] McMaster, *Hist. of the People of the U.S.*, vol. i., p. 564.

the shape of British aggressions, and could not be laid by any charm known to diplomacy,—even in those times, busy about other things, there had been premonitions of the unequal contest between state and federal authorities. The purchase of Louisiana had given new form and startling significance to the assertion of national sovereignty, the Alien and Sedition Laws had provoked the plain-spoken and emphatic protests of Kentucky and Virginia, and the Embargo had exasperated New England to threats of secession.

Nor were these open assumptions of questionable prerogatives on the part of the national government the most significant or unequivocal indications of an assured increase of federal power. Hamilton, as Secretary of the Treasury, had taken care at the very beginning to set the national policy in ways which would unavoidably lead to an almost indefinite expansion of the sphere of federal legislation. Sensible of its need of guidance in those matters of financial administration which evidently demanded its immediate attention, the first Congress of the Union promptly put itself under the direction of Hamilton. "It is not a little amusing," says Mr. Lodge, "to note how eagerly Congress, which had been ably and honestly struggling with the revenue, with commerce, and with a thousand details, fettered in all things by the awkwardness inherent in a legislative body, turned for relief to the new secretary."[6] His advice was asked and taken in almost everything, and his skill as a party leader made easy many of the more difficult paths of the new government. But no sooner had the powers of that government begun to be exercised under his guidance than they began to grow. In his famous Report on Manufactures were laid the foundations of that system of protective duties which was destined to hang all the industries of the country upon the skirts of the federal power, and to make every trade and craft in the land sensitive to every wind of party that might blow at Washington; and in his equally celebrated Report in favor of the establishment of a National Bank, there was called into requisition, for the first time, that puissant doctrine of the "implied powers" of the Constitution which has ever since been the chief dynamic principle in our constitutional history. "This great doctrine, embodying the principle of liberal construction, was," in the language of Mr. Lodge, "the most formidable weapon in the armory of the Constitution; and when Hamilton grasped it he knew, and his opponents felt, that here was something capable of conferring on the federal government powers of almost any ex-

[6] Lodge's *Alexander Hamilton* (Am. Statesmen Series), p. 85.

tent."[7] It served first as a sanction for the charter of the United States Bank,—an institution which was the central pillar of Hamilton's wonderful financial administration, and around which afterwards, as then, played so many of the lightnings of party strife. But the Bank of the United States, though great, was not the greatest of the creations of that lusty and seductive doctrine. Given out, at length, with the sanction of the federal Supreme Court,[8] and containing, as it did, in its manifest character as a doctrine of legislative prerogative, a very vigorous principle of constitutional growth, it quickly constituted Congress the dominant, nay, the irresistible, power of the federal system, relegating some of the chief balances of the Constitution to an insignificant rôle in the "literary theory" of our institutions.

Its effect upon the status of the States in the federal system was several-fold. In the first place, it clearly put the constitutions of the States at a great disadvantage, inasmuch as there was in them no like principle of growth. Their stationary sovereignty could by no means keep pace with the nimble progress of federal influence in the new spheres thus opened up to it. The doctrine of implied powers was evidently both facile and irresistible. It concerned the political discretion of the national legislative power, and could, therefore, elude all obstacles of judicial interference; for the Supreme Court very early declared itself without authority to question the legislature's privilege of determining the nature and extent of its own powers in the choice of means for giving effect to its constitutional prerogatives, and it has long stood as an accepted canon of judicial action, that judges should be very slow to oppose their opinions to the legislative will in cases in which it is not made demonstrably clear that there has been a plain violation of some unquestionable constitutional principle, or some explicit constitutional provision. Of encroachments upon state as well as of encroachments upon federal powers, the federal authorities are, however, in most cases the only, and in all cases the final, judges. The States are absolutely debarred even from any effective defense of their plain prerogatives, because not they, but the national authorities, are commissioned to determine with decisive and unchallenged authoritativeness what state powers shall be recognized in each case of contest or of conflict. In short, one of the privileges which the States have resigned into the hands of the federal government is the all-inclusive privilege of deter-

[7] Lodge's *Alexander Hamilton*, p. 105.
[8] Its final and most masterly exposition, by C. J. Marshall, may be seen in McCulloch *v.* Maryland, 4 Wheaton, 316.

mining what they themselves can do. Federal courts can annul state action, but state courts cannot arrest the growth of congressional power.[9]

But this is only the doctrinal side of the case, simply its statement with an "if" and a "but." Its practical issue illustrates still more forcibly the altered and declining status of the States in the constitutional system. One very practical issue has been to bring the power of the federal government home to every man's door, as, no less than his own state government, his immediate overlord. Of course every new province into which Congress has been allured by the principle of implied powers has required for its administration a greater or less enlargement of the national civil service, which now, through its hundred thousand officers, carries into every community of the land a sense of federal power, as the power of powers, and fixes the federal authority, as it were, in the very habits of society. That is not a foreign but a familiar and domestic government whose officer is your next-door neighbor, whose representatives you deal with every day at the post-office and the custom-house, whose courts sit in your own State, and send their own marshals into your own county to arrest your own fellow-townsman, or to call you yourself by writ to their witness-stands. And who can help respecting officials whom he knows to be backed by the authority and even by the power of the whole nation, in the performance of the duties in which he sees them every day engaged? Who does not feel that the marshal represents a greater power than the sheriff does, and that it is more dangerous to molest a mail-carrier than to knock down a policeman? This personal contact of every citizen with the federal government,—a contact which makes him feel himself a citizen of a greater state than that which controls his everyday contracts and probates his father's will,—more than offsets his sense of dependent loyalty to local authorities by creating a sensible bond of

[9] The following passage from William Maclay's *Sketches of Debate in the First Senate of the United States* (pp. 292-3) illustrates how clearly the results of this were forecast by sagacious men from the first: "The system laid down by these gentlemen (the Federalists) was as follows, or rather the development of the designs of a certain party: The general power to carry the Constitution into effect by a constructive interpretation would extend to every case that Congress may deem necessary or expedient. . . . The laws of the United States will be held paramount to all" state "laws, claims, and even constitutions. The supreme power is with the general government to decide in this, as in everything else, for the States have neglected to secure any umpire or mode of decision in case of difference between them. Nor is there any point in the Constitution for them to rally under. They may give an opinion, but the opinions of the general government must prevail. . . . Any direct and open act would be termed usurpation. But whether the gradual influence and encroachments of the general government may not gradually swallow up the state governments, is another matter."

allegiance to what presents itself unmistakably as the greater and more sovereign power.

In most things this bond of allegiance does not bind him oppressively nor chafe him distressingly; but in some things it is drawn rather painfully tight. Whilst federal postmasters are valued and federal judges unhesitatingly obeyed, and whilst very few people realize the weight of customs-duties, and as few, perhaps, begrudge license taxes on whiskey and tobacco, everybody eyes rather uneasily the federal supervisors at the polls. This is preëminently a country of frequent elections, and few States care to increase the frequency by separating elections of state from elections of national functionaries. The federal supervisor, consequently, who oversees the balloting for congressmen, practically superintends the election of state officers also; for state officers and congressmen are usually voted for at one and the same time and place, by ballots bearing in common an entire "party ticket"; and any authoritative scrutiny of these ballots after they have been cast, or any peremptory power of challenging those who offer to cast them, must operate as an interference with state no less than with federal elections. The authority of Congress to regulate the manner of choosing federal representatives pinches when it is made thus to include also the supervision of those state elections which are, by no implied power even, within the sphere of federal prerogative. The supervisor represents the very ugliest side of federal supremacy; he belongs to the least liked branch of the civil service; but his existence speaks very clearly as to the present balance of powers, and his rather hateful privileges must, under the present system of mixed elections, result in impairing the self-respect of state officers of election by bringing home to them a vivid sense of subordination to the powers at Washington.

A very different and much larger side of federal predominance is to be seen in the history of the policy of internal improvements. I need not expound that policy here. It has been often enough mooted and long enough understood to need no explanation. Its practice is plain and its persistence unquestionable. But its bearings upon the status and the policies of the States are not always clearly seen or often distinctly pointed out. Its chief results, of course, have been that expansion of national functions which was necessarily involved in the application of national funds by national employees to the clearing of inland water-courses and the improvement of harbors, and the establishment of the very questionable precedent of expending in favored localities moneys raised by taxation which bears with equal incidence upon the people of all sections of the country; but these chief results by no means constitute the sum of its influence. Hardly less significant and real, for instance, are its moral effects in rendering state administrations less self-reliant and efficient, less prudent and thrifty, by accustoming them to accepting subsidies for internal improvements from the federal coffers; to depending upon the national revenues, rather than upon their own energy and enterprise, for means of developing those resources which it should be the special province of state administration to make available and profitable. There can, I suppose, be little doubt that it is due to the moral influences of this policy that the States are now turning to the common government for aid in such things as education. Expecting to be helped, they will not help themselves. Certain it is that there is more than one State which, though abundantly able to pay for an educational system of the greatest efficiency, fails to do so, and contents itself with imperfect temporary makeshifts because there are immense surpluses every year in the national treasury which, rumor and unauthorized promises say, may be distributed amongst the States in aid of education. If the federal government were more careful to keep apart from every strictly local scheme of improvement, this culpable and demoralizing state policy could scarcely live. States would cease to wish, because they would cease to hope, to be stipendiaries of the government of the Union, and would address themselves with diligence to their proper duties, with much benefit both to themselves and to the federal system. This is not saying that the policy of internal improvements was either avoidable, unconstitutional, or unwise, but only that it has been carried too far; and that, whether carried too far or not, it must in any case have been what it is now seen to be, a big weight in the federal scale of the balance.

Still other powers of the federal government, which have so grown beyond their first proportions as to have marred very seriously the symmetry of the "literary theory" of our federal system, have strengthened under the shadow of the jurisdiction of Congress over commerce and the maintenance of the postal service. For instance, the Supreme Court of the United States has declared that the powers granted to Congress by the Constitution to regulate commerce and to establish post-offices and post-roads "keep pace with the progress of the country and adapt themselves to new developments of times and circumstances. They extend from the horse with its rider to the stage-coach, from the sailing vessel to the steamer, from the coach and the steamer to the railroad, and from the railroad to the telegraph, as these new agencies are successively brought into use to meet the demands of increasing population and wealth. They are intended for the government of the business to which they relate, at all times and under all circumstances. As they were intrusted to the general government for the good of the nation, it is not only the right but the duty of Congress to see to it that the intercourse between the States and the transmission of intelligence are not obstructed or unnecessarily encumbered by state legislation."[10] This emphatic decision was intended to sustain the right of a telegraph company chartered by one State to run its line along all post-roads in other States, without the consent of those States, and even against their will; but it is manifest that many other corporate companies might, under the sanction of this broad opinion, claim similar privileges in despite of state resistance, and that such decisions go far towards making state powers of incorporation of little worth as compared with federal powers of control.

Keeping pace, too, with this growth of federal activity, there has been from the first a steady and unmistakable growth of nationality of sentiment. It was, of course, the weight of war which finally and decisively disarranged the balance between state and federal powers; and it is obvious that many of the most striking manifestations of the tendency towards centralization have made themselves seen since the war. But the history of the war is only a record of the triumph of the principle of national sovereignty. The war was inevitable, because that principle grew apace; and the war ended as it did, because that principle had become predominant. Accepted at first simply because it was imperatively necessary, the union of form and of law had become a union of sentiment, and was destined to be a union of institutions. That sense of national unity and community of destiny which Hamilton had sought to foster, but which was feeble in his day of long distances and tardy inter-communication, when the nation's pulse was as slow as the stage-coach and the postman, had become strong enough to rule the continent when Webster died. The war between the States was the supreme and final struggle between those forces of disintegration which still remained in the blood of the body politic and those other forces of health, of union and amalgamation, which had been gradually building up that body in vigor and strength as the system passed from youth to

---

[10] Pensacola Tel. Co. *v.* West. Union, 96 U.S. 1, 9. (Quoted by Judge Cooley in his *Principles of Constitutional Law.*)

maturity, and as its constitution hardened and ripened with advancing age.

The history of that trenchant policy of "reconstruction," which
followed close upon the termination of the war, as at once its
logical result and significant commentary, contains a vivid picture of the altered balances of the constitutional system which is
a sort of exaggerated miniature, falling very little short of being
a caricature, of previous constitutional tendencies and federal
policies. The tide of federal aggression probably reached its highest shore in the legislation which put it into the power of the
federal courts to punish a state judge for refusing, in the exercise of his official discretion, to impanel negroes in the juries of
his court,[11] and in those statutes which gave the federal courts
jurisdiction over offenses against state laws by state officers.[12]
But that tide has often run very high, and, however fluctuating
at times, has long been well-nigh irresistible by any dykes of constitutional state privilege; so that Judge Cooley can say without
fear of contradiction that "The effectual checks upon the encroachments of federal upon state power must be looked for, not
in state power of resistance, but in the choice of representatives,
senators, and presidents holding just constitutional views, and
in a federal supreme court with competent power to restrain all
departments and all officers within the limits of their just authority, so far as their acts may become the subject of judicial cognizance."[13]

Indeed it is quite evident that if federal power be not altogether
irresponsible, it is the federal judiciary which is the only effectual balance-wheel of the whole system. The federal judges hold
in their hands the fate of state powers, and theirs is the only authority that can draw effective rein on the career of Congress.
If their power, then, be not efficient, the time must seem sadly
out of joint to those who hold to the "literary theory" of our Constitution. By the word of the Supreme Court must all legislation
stand or fall, so long as law is respected. But, as I have already
pointed out, there is at least one large province of jurisdiction
upon which, though invited, and possibly privileged to appropri-

---

[11] 18 Stat., part 3, 336. See Ex parte Virginia, 100 U.S. 339.

[12] Sect. 5515 Rev. Stats. See Ex parte Siebold, 100 U.S. 371. Equally extensive
of federal powers is that "legal tender" decision (Juilliard v. Greenman) of
March, 1884, which argues the existence of a right to issue an irredeemable paper currency from the Constitution's grant of other rights characteristic of sovereignty, and from the possession of a similar right by other governments. But
this involves no restriction of state powers; and perhaps there ought to be offset
against it that other decision (several cases, October, 1883), which denies constitutional sanction to the Civil Rights Act.

[13] *Principles of Constitutional Law*, pp. 143, 144.

ate it, the Supreme Court has, nevertheless, refused to enter, and by refusing to enter which it has given over all attempt to guard one of the principal, easiest, and most obvious roads to federal supremacy. It, has declared itself without authority to interfere with the *political discretion* of either Congress or the President, and has declined all effort to constrain these its coordinate departments to the performance of any, even the most constitutionally imperative act.[14] "When, indeed, the President exceeds his authority, or usurps that which belongs to one of the other departments, his orders, commands, or warrants protect no one, and his agents become personally responsible for their acts. The check of the courts, therefore, consists in their ability to keep the executive within the sphere of his authority by refusing to give the sanction of law to whatever he may do beyond it, and by holding the agents or instruments of his unlawful action to strict accountability."[15] But such punishment, inflicted not directly upon the chief offender but vicariously upon his agents, can come only after all the harm has been done. The courts cannot forestall the President and prevent the doing of mischief. They have no power of initiative; they must wait until the law has been broken and voluntary litigants have made up their pleadings; must wait nowadays many months, often many years, until those pleadings are reached in the regular course of clearing a crowded docket.

Besides, in ordinary times it is not from the executive that the most dangerous encroachments are to be apprehended. The legislature is the aggressive spirit. It is the motive power of the government, and unless the judiciary can check it, the courts are of comparatively little worth as balance-wheels in the system. It is the subtile, stealthy, almost imperceptible encroachments of policy, of political action, which constitute the precedents upon which additional prerogatives are generally reared; and yet these are the very encroachments with which it is hardest for the courts to deal, and concerning which, accordingly, the federal courts have declared themselves unauthorized to hold any opinions. They have naught to say upon questions of policy. Congress must itself judge what measures may legitimately be used to supplement or make effectual its acknowledged jurisdiction, what are the laws "necessary and proper for carrying into execution" its own peculiar powers, "and all other powers vested by" the "Constitution in the government of the United States, or in any de-

---

[14] Marbury *v.* Madison, 1 Cranch, 137.
[15] Cooley's *Principles*, p. 157.

partment or officer thereof." The courts are very quick and keen-eyed, too, to discern prerogatives of political discretion in legis-lative acts, and exceedingly slow to undertake to discriminate between what is and what is not a violation of the spirit of the Constitution. Congress must wantonly go very far outside of the plain and unquestionable meaning of the Constitution, must bump its head directly against all right and precedent, must kick against the very pricks of all well-established rulings and inter-pretations, before the Supreme Court will offer it any distinct rebuke.

Then, too, the Supreme Court itself, however upright and ir-reproachable its members, has generally had and will undoubt-edly continue to have a distinct political complexion, taken from the color of the times during which its majority was chosen. The bench over which John Marshall presided was, as everybody knows, staunchly and avowedly federalist in its views; but during the ten years which followed 1835 federalist justices were rapidly displaced by Democrats, and the views of the Court changed ac-cordingly. Indeed it may truthfully be said that, taking our politi-cal history "by and large," the constitutional interpretations of the Supreme Court have changed, slowly but none the less surely, with the altered relations of power between the national parties. The Federalists were backed by a federalist judiciary; the period of democratic supremacy witnessed the triumph of democratic principles in the courts; and republican predominance has driven from the highest tribunal of the land all but one representative of democratic doctrines. It has been only during comparatively short periods of transition, when public opinion was passing over from one political creed to another, that the decisions of the fed-eral judiciary have been distinctly opposed to the principles of the ruling political party.

But, besides and above all this, the national courts are for the most part in the power of Congress. Even the Supreme Court is not beyond its control; for it is the legislative privilege to increase, whenever the legislative will so pleases, the number of the judges upon the supreme bench,—to "dilute the Constitution," as Web-ster once put it, "by creating a court which shall construe away its provisions"; and this on one memorable occasion it did choose to do. In December, 1869, the Supreme Court decided against the constitutionality of Congress's pet Legal Tender Acts; and in the following March a vacancy on the bench opportunely occur-ring, and a new justiceship having been created to meet the emergency, the Senate gave the President to understand that no nominee unfavorable to the debated acts would be confirmed, two justices of the predominant party's way of thinking were appointed, the hostile majority of the court was outvoted, and the obnoxious decision reversed.[16]

The creation of additional justiceships is not, however, the only means by which Congress can coerce and control the Supreme Court. It may forestall an adverse decision by summarily depriving the court of jurisdiction over the case in which such a decision was threatened,[17] and that even while the case is pending; for only a very small part of the jurisdiction of even the Supreme Court is derived directly from the Constitution. Most of it is founded upon the Judiciary Act of 1789, which, being a mere act of Congress, may be repealed at any time that Congress chooses to repeal it. Upon this Judiciary Act, too, depend not only the powers but also the very existence of the inferior courts of the United States, the Circuit and District Courts; and their possible fate, in case of a conflict with Congress, is significantly foreshadowed in that Act of 1802 by which a democratic Congress swept away, root and branch, the system of circuit courts which had been created in the previous year, but which was hateful to the newly-successful Democrats because it had been officered with Federalists in the last hours of John Adams's administration.

This balance of judiciary against legislature and executive would seem, therefore, to be another of those ideal balances which are to be found in the books rather than in the rough realities of actual practice; for manifestly the power of the courts is safe only during seasons of political peace, when parties are not aroused to passion or tempted by the command of irresistible majorities.

As for some of the other constitutional balances enumerated in that passage of the letter to John Taylor which I have taken as a text, their present inefficacy is quite too plain to need proof. The constituencies may have been balanced against their representatives in Mr. Adams's day, for that was not a day of primaries and of strict caucus discipline. The legislatures of the States, too, may have been able to exercise some appreciable influence upon the action of the Senate, if those were days when policy was the predominant consideration which determined elections to the Senate, and the legislative choice was not always a matter of astute management, of mere personal weight, or party ex-

16 For an incisive account of the whole affair, see an article entitled "The Session," *No. Am. Review*, vol. cxi., pp. 48, 49.

17 7 Wall. 506.

pediency; and the presidential electors undoubtedly did have at one time some freedom of choice in naming the chief magistrate, but before the third presidential election some of them were pledged, before Adams wrote this letter the majority of them were wont to obey the dictates of a congressional caucus, and for the last fifty years they have simply registered the will of party conventions.

It is noteworthy that Mr. Adams, possibly because he had himself been President, describes the executive as constituting only *"in some degree"* a check upon Congress, though he puts no such limitation upon the other balances of the system. Independently of experience, however, it might reasonably have been expected that the prerogatives of the President would have been one of the most effectual restraints upon the power of Congress. He was constituted one of the three great coördinate branches of the government; his functions were made of the highest dignity; his privileges many and substantial—so great, indeed, that it has pleased the fancy of some writers to parade them as exceeding those of the British crown; and there can be little doubt that, had the presidential chair always been filled by men of commanding character, of acknowledged ability, and of thorough political training, it would have continued to be a seat of the highest authority and consideration, the true centre of the federal structure, the real throne of administration, and the frequent source of policies. Washington and his Cabinet commanded the ear of Congress, and gave shape to its deliberations; Adams, though often crossed and thwarted, gave character to the government; and Jefferson, as President no less than as Secretary of State, was the real leader of his party. But the prestige of the presidential office has declined with the character of the Presidents. And the character of the Presidents has declined as the perfection of selfish party tactics has advanced.

It was inevitable that it should be so. After independence of choice on the part of the presidential electors had given place to the choice of presidential candidates by party conventions, it became absolutely necessary, in the eyes of politicians, and more and more necessary as time went on, to make expediency and availability the only rules of selection. As each party, when in convention assembled, spoke only those opinions which seemed to have received the sanction of the general voice, carefully suppressing in its "platform" all unpopular political tenets, and scrupulously omitting mention of every doctrine that might be looked upon as characteristic and as part of a peculiar and original programme, so, when the presidential candidate came to be chosen, it was recognized as imperatively necessary that he should have as short a political record as possible, and that he should wear a clean and irreproachable insignificance. "Gentlemen," said a distinguished American public man, "I would make an excellent President, but a very poor candidate." A decisive career which gives a man a well-understood place in public estimation constitutes a positive disability for the presidency; because candidacy must precede election, and the shoals of candidacy can be passed only by a light boat which carries little freight and can be turned readily about to suit the intricacies of the passage.

I am disposed to think, however, that the decline in the character of the Presidents is not the cause, but only the accompanying manifestation, of the declining prestige of the presidential office. That high office has fallen from its first estate of dignity because its power has waned; and its power has waned because the power of Congress has become predominant. The early Presidents were, as I have said, men of such a stamp that they would under any circumstances have made their influence felt; but their opportunities were exceptional. What with quarreling and fighting with England, buying Louisiana and Florida, building dykes to keep out the flood of the French Revolution, and extricating the country from ceaseless broils with the South American Republics, the government was, as has been pointed out, constantly busy, during the first quarter century of its existence, with the adjustment of foreign relations; and with foreign relations, of course, the Presidents had everything to do, since theirs was the office of negotiation.

Moreover, as regards home policy also those times were not like ours. Congress was somewhat awkward in exercising its untried powers, and its machinery was new, and without that fine adjustment which has since made it perfect of its kind. Not having as yet learned the art of governing itself to the best advantage, and being without that facility of legislation which it afterwards acquired, the Legislature was glad to get guidance and suggestions of policy from the Executive.

But this state of things did not last long. Congress was very quick and apt in learning what it could do and in getting into thoroughly good trim to do it. It very early divided itself into standing committees which it equipped with very comprehensive and thorough-going privileges of legislative initiative and control, and set itself through these to administer the government.

Congress is (to adopt Mr. Bagehot's description of Parliament) "nothing less than a big meeting of more or less idle people. In proportion as you give it power it will inquire into everything, settle everything, meddle in everything. In an ordinary despotism the powers of the despot are limited by his bodily capacity, and by the calls of pleasure; he is but one man; there are but twelve hours in his day, and he is not disposed to employ more than a small part in dull business: he keeps the rest for the court, or the harem, or for society." But Congress "is a despot who has un-limited time,—who has unlimited vanity,—who has, or believes he has, unlimited comprehension,—whose pleasure is in action, whose life is work." Accordingly it has entered more and more into the details of administration, until it has virtually taken into its own hands all the substantial powers of government. It does not domineer over the President himself, but it makes the Secretaries its humble servants. Not that it would hesitate, upon occasion, to deal directly with the chief magistrate himself; but it has few calls to do so, because our latter-day Presidents live by proxy; they are the executive in theory, but the Secretaries are the executive in fact. At the very first session of Congress steps were taken towards parceling out executive work amongst sev-eral departments, according to a then sufficiently thorough divi-sion of labor; and if the President of that day was not able to direct administrative details, of course the President of to-day is infinitely less able to do so, and must content himself with such general supervision as he may find time to exercise. He is in all every-day concerns shielded by the responsibility of his subor-dinates.

It cannot be said that this change has raised the cabinet in dignity or power; it has only altered their relations to the scheme of government. The members of the President's cabinet have al-ways been prominent in administration; and certainly the early cabinets were no less strong in political influence than are the cabinets of our own day; but they were then only the President's advisers, whereas they are now rather the President's colleagues. The President is now scarcely the executive; he is the head of the administration; he appoints the executive. Of course this is not a legal principle; it is only a fact. In legal theory the President can control every operation of every department of the executive branch of the government; but in fact it is not practicable for him to do so, and a limitation of fact is as potent as a prohibition of law.

But, though the heads of the executive departments are thus

no longer simply the counselors of the President, having become in a very real sense members of the executive, their guiding power in the conduct of affairs, instead of advancing, has steadily diminished; because while they were being made integral parts of the machinery of administration, Congress was extending its own sphere of activity, was getting into the habit of investigating and managing everything. The executive was losing and Congress gaining weight; and the station to which cabinets finally attained was a station of diminished and diminishing power. There is no distincter tendency in congressional history than the tendency to subject even the details of administration to the constant supervision, and all policy to the watchful intervention, of the Standing Committees.

I am inclined to think, therefore, that the enlarged powers of Congress are the fruits rather of an immensely increased efficiency of organization, and of the redoubled activity consequent upon the facility of action secured by such organization, than of any definite and persistent scheme of conscious usurpation. It is safe to say that Congress always had the desire to have a hand in every affair of federal government; but it was only by degrees that it found means and opportunity to gratify that desire, and its activity, extending its bounds wherever perfected processes of congressional work offered favoring prospects, has been enlarged so naturally and so silently that it has almost always seemed of normal extent, and has never, except perhaps during one or two brief periods of extraordinary political disturbance, appeared to reach much beyond its acknowledged constitutional sphere.

It is only in the exercise of those functions of public and formal consultation and coöperation with the President which are the peculiar offices of the Senate, that the power of Congress has made itself offensive to popular conceptions of constitutional propriety, because it is only in the exercise of such functions that Congress is compelled to be overt and demonstrative in its claims of over-lordship. The House of Representatives has made very few noisy demonstrations of its usurped right of ascendency; not because it was diffident or unambitious, but because it could maintain and extend its prerogatives quite as satisfactorily without noise; whereas the aggressive policy of the Senate has, in the acts of its "executive sessions," necessarily been overt, in spite of the closing of the doors, because when acting as the President's council in the ratification of treaties and in appointments to office its competition for power has been more formally and directly a contest with the executive than were those really more significant legislative acts by which, in conjunction with the House, it has habitually forced the heads of the executive departments to observe the will of Congress at every important turn of policy. Hence it is that to the superficial view it appears that only the Senate has been outrageous in its encroachments upon executive privilege. It is not often easy to see the true constitutional bearing of strictly legislative action; but it is patent even to the least observant that in the matter of appointments to office, for instance, senators have often outrun their legal right to give or withhold their assent to appointments, by insisting upon being first consulted concerning nominations as well, and have thus made their constitutional assent to appointments dependent upon an unconstitutional control of nominations.

This particular usurpation has been put upon a very solid basis of law by that Tenure-of-Office Act, which took away from President Johnson, in an hour of party heat and passion, that independent power of removal from office with which the Constitution had invested him, but which he had used in a way that exasperated a Senate not of his own way of thinking. But though this teasing power of the Senate's in the matter of the federal patronage is repugnant enough to the original theory of the Constitution, it is likely to be quite nullified by that policy of civil-service reform which has gained so firm, and mayhap so lasting, a footing in our national legislation; and in no event would the control of the patronage by the Senate have unbalanced the federal system more seriously than it may some day be unbalanced by an irresponsible exertion of that body's semi-executive powers in regard to the foreign policy of the government. More than one passage in the history of our foreign relations illustrates the danger. During the single congressional session of 1868–9, for example, the treaty-*marring* power of the Senate was exerted in a way that made the comparative weakness of the executive very conspicuous, and was ominous of very serious results. It showed the executive in the right, but feeble and irresolute; the Senate masterful, though in the wrong. Denmark had been asked to part with the island of St. Thomas to the United States, and had at first refused all terms, not only because she cared little for the price, but also and principally because such a sale as that proposed was opposed to the established policy of the powers of Western Europe, in whose favor Denmark wished to stand; but finally, by stress of persistent and importunate negotiation, she had been induced to yield; a treaty had been signed and sent to the Senate; the people of St. Thomas had signified their consent to the cession by a formal vote; and the island had been actually transferred to an authorized agent of our government, upon the faith, on the part of the Danish ministers, that our representatives would not have trifled with them by entering upon an important business transaction which they were not assured of their ability to conclude. But the Senate let the treaty lie neglected in its committee-room; the limit of time agreed upon for confirmation passed; the Danish government, at last bent upon escaping the ridiculous humiliation that would follow a failure of the business at that stage, extended the time and even sent over one of its most eminent ministers of state to urge the negotiation by all dignified means; but the Senate cared nothing for Danish feelings and could afford, it thought, to despise President Grant and Mr. Fish, and at the next session rejected the treaty, and left the Danes to repossess themselves of the island, which we had concluded not to buy after all.

It was during this same session of 1868–9 that the Senate teased the executive by throwing every possible obstacle in the way of the confirmation of the much more important treaty with Great Britain relative to the Alabama claims, nearly marring for good and all one of the most satisfactory successes of our recent foreign policy;[18] but it is not necessary to dwell at length upon these well-known incidents of our later history, inasmuch as these are only two of innumerable instances which make it safe to say that from whatever point we view the relations of the executive and the legislature, it is evident that the power of the latter has steadily increased at the expense of the prerogatives of the former, and that the degree in which the one of these great branches of government is balanced against the other is a very insignificant degree indeed. For in the exercise of his power of veto, which is of course, beyond all comparison, his most formidable prerogative, the President acts not as the executive but as a third branch of the legislature. As Oliver Ellsworth said, at the first session of the Senate, the President is, as regards the passage of bills, but a part of Congress; and he can be an efficient, imperative member of the legislative system only in quiet times, when parties are pretty evenly balanced, and there are no indomitable majorities to tread obnoxious vetoes under foot.

Even this rapid outline sketch of the two pictures, of the theory and of the actual practices of the Constitution, has been suffi-

18 For a brilliant account of the senatorial history of these two treaties, see the article entitled "The Session," *No. Am. Rev.*, vol. cviii. (1869), p. 626 *et seq.*

cient, therefore, to show the most marked points of difference between the two, and to justify that careful study of congressional government, as the real government of the Union, which I am about to undertake. The balances of the Constitution are for the most part only ideal. For all practical purposes the national government is supreme over the state governments, and Congress predominant over its so-called coördinate branches. Whereas Congress at first overshadowed neither President nor federal judiciary, it now on occasion rules both with easy mastery and with a high hand; and whereas each State once guarded its sovereign prerogatives with jealous pride, and able men not a few preferred political advancement under the governments of the great commonwealths to office under the new federal Constitution, seats in state legislatures are now no longer coveted except as possible approaches to seats in Congress; and even governors of States seek election to the national Senate as a promotion, a reward for the humbler services they have rendered their local governments.

What makes it the more important to understand the present mechanism of national government, and to study the methods of congressional rule in a light unclouded by theory, is that there is plain evidence that the expansion of federal power is to continue, and that there exists, consequently, an evident necessity that it should be known just what to do and how to do it, when the time comes for public opinion to take control of the forces which are changing the character of our Constitution. There are voices in the air which cannot be misunderstood. The times seem to favor a centralization of governmental functions such as could not have suggested itself as a possibility to the framers of the Constitution. Since they gave their work to the world the whole face of that world has changed. The Constitution was adopted when it was six days' hard traveling from New York to Boston; when to cross East River was to venture a perilous voyage; when men were thankful for weekly mails; when the extent of the country's commerce was reckoned not in millions but in thousands of dollars; when the country knew few cities, and had but begun manufactures; when Indians were pressing upon near frontiers; when there were no telegraph lines, and no monster corporations. Unquestionably, the pressing problems of the present moment regard the regulation of our vast systems of commerce and manufacture, the control of giant corporations, the restraint of monopolies, the perfection of fiscal arrangements, the facilitating of economic exchanges, and many other like national concerns, amongst which may possibly be numbered the question of marriage and divorce; and the greatest of these problems do not fall within even the enlarged sphere of the federal government; some of them can be embraced within its jurisdiction by no possible stretch of construction, and the majority of them only by wresting the Constitution to strange and as yet unimagined uses. Still there is a distinct movement in favor of national control of all questions of policy which manifestly demand uniformity of treatment and power of administration such as cannot be realized by the separate, unconcerted action of the States; and it seems probable to many that, whether by constitutional amendment, or by still further flights of construction, yet broader territory will at no very distant day be assigned to the federal government. It becomes a matter of the utmost importance, therefore, both for those who would arrest this tendency, and for those who, because they look upon it with allowance if not with positive favor, would let it run its course, to examine critically the government upon which this new weight of responsibility and power seems likely to be cast, in order that its capacity both for the work it now does and for that which it may be called upon to do may be definitely estimated.

Judge Cooley, in his admirable work on "The Principles of American Constitutional Law," after quoting Mr. Adams's enumeration of the checks and balances of the federal system, adds this comment upon Mr. Adams's concluding statement that that system is an invention of our own. "The invention, nevertheless, was suggested by the British Constitution, in which a system almost equally elaborate was then in force. In its outward forms that system still remains; but there has been for more than a century a gradual change in the direction of a concentration of legislative and executive power in the popular house of Parliament, so that the government now is sometimes said, with no great departure from the fact, to be a government by the House of Commons." But Judge Cooley does not seem to see, or, if he sees, does not emphasize the fact, that our own system has been hardly less subject to "a gradual change in the direction of a concentration" of all the substantial powers of government in the hands of Congress; so that it is now, though a wide departure from the form of things, "no great departure from the fact" to describe ours as a government by the Standing Committees of Congress. This fact is, however, deducible from very many passages of Judge Cooley's own writings; for he is by no means insensible of that expansion of the powers of the federal government and that crystallization of its methods which have practically made obsolete the early constitutional theories, and even the modified theory which he himself seems to hold.

He has tested the nice adjustment of the theoretical balances by the actual facts, and has carefully set forth the results; but he has nowhere brought those results together into a single comprehensive view which might serve as a clear and satisfactory delineation of the Constitution of to-day; nor has he, or any other writer of capacity, examined minutely and at length that internal organization of Congress which determines its methods of legislation, which shapes its means of governing the executive departments, which contains in it the whole mechanism whereby the policy of the country is in all points directed, and which is therefore an essential branch of constitutional study. As the House of Commons is the central object of examination in every study of the English Constitution, so should Congress be in every study of our own. Any one who is unfamiliar with what Congress actually does and how it does it, with all its duties and all its occupations, with all its devices of management and resources of power, is very far from a knowledge of the constitutional system under which we live; and to every one who knows these things that knowledge is very near.

II.

THE HOUSE OF REPRESENTATIVES.

No more vital truth was ever uttered than that freedom and free institutions cannot long be maintained by any people who do not understand the nature of their own government.

Like a vast picture thronged with figures of equal prominence and crowded with elaborate and obtrusive details, Congress is hard to see satisfactorily and appreciatively at a single view and from a single stand-point. Its complicated forms and diversified structure confuse the vision, and conceal the system which underlies its composition. It is too complex to be understood without an effort, without a careful and systematic process of analysis. Consequently, very few people do understand it, and its doors are practically shut against the comprehension of the public at large. If Congress had a few authoritative leaders whose figures were very distinct and very conspicuous to the eye of the world, and who could represent and stand for the national legislature in the thoughts of that very numerous, and withal very respectable, class of persons who must think specifically and in concrete forms when they think at all, those persons who can make something out of men but very little out of intangible generalizations, it would be quite within the region of possibilities for the majority of the nation to follow the course of legislation without any very serious confusion of thought. I suppose that almost everybody who just now gives any heed to the policy of Great Britain, with regard even to the reform of the franchise and other like strictly legislative questions, thinks of Mr. Gladstone and his colleagues rather than of the House of Commons, whose servants they are. The question is not, What will Parliament do? but, What will Mr. Gladstone do? And there is even less doubt that it is easier and more natural to look upon the legislative designs of Germany as locked up behind Bismarck's heavy brows than to think of them as dependent upon the determinations of the Reichstag, although as a matter of fact its consent is indispensable even to the plans of the imperious and domineering Chancellor.

But there is no great minister or ministry to represent the will and being of Congress in the common thought. The Speaker of the House of Representatives stands as near to leadership as any one; but his will does not run as a formative and imperative power in legislation much beyond the appointment of the committees who are to lead the House and do its work for it, and it is, therefore, not entirely satisfactory to the public mind to trace all legislation to him. He may have a controlling hand in starting it; but he sits too still in his chair, and is too evidently not on the floor of the body over which he presides, to make it seem probable to the ordinary judgment that he has much immediate concern in legislation after it is once set afoot. Everybody knows that he is a staunch and avowed partisan, and that he likes to make smooth, whenever he can, the legislative paths of his party; but it does not seem likely that all important measures originate with him, or that he is the author of every distinct policy. And in fact he is not. He is a great party chief, but the hedging circumstances of his official position as presiding officer prevent his performing the part of active leadership. He appoints the leaders of the House, but he is not himself its leader.

The leaders of the House are the chairmen of the principal Standing Committees. Indeed, to be exactly accurate, the House has as many leaders as there are subjects of legislation; for there are as many Standing Committees as there are leading classes of legislation, and in the consideration of every topic of business the House is guided by a special leader in the person of the chairman of the Standing Committee, charged with the superintendence of measures of the particular class to which that topic belongs. It is this multiplicity of leaders, this many-headed leadership, which makes the organization of the House too complex to afford uninformed people and unskilled observers any easy clue to its methods of rule. For the chairmen of the Standing Committees do not constitute a coöperative body like a ministry. They do not consult and concur in the adoption of homogeneous and mutually helpful measures; there is no thought of acting in concert. Each Committee goes its own way at its own pace. It is impossible to discover any unity or method in the disconnected and therefore unsystematic, confused, and desultory action of the House, or any common purpose in the measures which its Committees from time to time recommend.

And it is not only to the unanalytic thought of the common observer who looks at the House from the outside that its doings seem helter-skelter, and without comprehensible rule; it is not at once easy to understand them when they are scrutinized in their daily headway through open session by one who is inside the House. The newly-elected member, entering its doors for the first time, and with no more knowledge of its rules and customs than the more intelligent of his constituents possess, always experiences great difficulty in adjusting his preconceived ideas of congressional life to the strange and unlooked-for conditions by which he finds himself surrounded after he has been sworn in and has become a part of the great legislative machine. Indeed there are generally many things connected with his career in Washington to disgust and dispirit, if not to aggrieve, the new member. In the first place, his local reputation does not follow him to the federal capital. Possibly the members from his own State know him, and receive him into full fellowship; but no one else knows him, except as an adherent of this or that party, or as a new-comer from this or that State. He finds his station insignificant, and his identity indistinct. But this social humiliation which he experiences in circles in which to be a congressman does not of itself confer distinction, because it is only to be one among many, is probably not to be compared with the chagrin and disappointment which come in company with the inevitable discovery that he is equally without weight or title to consideration in the House itself. No man, when chosen to the membership of a body possessing great powers and exalted prerogatives, likes to find his activity repressed, and himself suppressed, by imperative rules and precedents which seem to have been framed for the deliberate purpose of making usefulness unattainable by individual members. Yet such the new member finds the rules and precedents of the House to be. It matters not to him, because it is not apparent on the face of things, that those rules and precedents have grown, not out of set purpose to curtail the privileges of new members as such, but out of the plain necessities of business; it remains the fact that he suffers under their curb, and it is not until "custom hath made it in him a property of easiness" that he submits to them with anything like good grace.

Not all new members suffer alike, of course, under this trying discipline; because it is not every new member that comes to his seat with serious purposes of honest, earnest, and duteous work. There are numerous tricks and subterfuges, soon learned and easily used, by means of which the most idle and self-indulgent members may readily make such show of exemplary diligence as will quite satisfy, if it does not positively delight, constituents in Buncombe. But the number of congressmen who deliberately court uselessness and counterfeit well-doing is probably small. The great majority doubtless have a keen enough sense of their duty, and a sufficiently unhesitating desire to do it; and it may safely be taken for granted that the zeal of new members is generally hot and insistent. If it be not hot to begin with, it is like to become so by reason of friction with the rules, because such men must inevitably be chafed by the bonds of restraint drawn about them by the inexorable observances of the House.

Often the new member goes to Washington as the representative of a particular line of policy, having been elected, it may be, as an advocate of free trade, or as a champion of protection; and it is naturally his first care upon entering on his duties to seek immediate opportunity for the expression of his views and immediate means of giving them definite shape and thrusting them upon the attention of Congress. His disappointment is, therefore, very keen when he finds both opportunity and means denied him. He can introduce his bill; but that is all he can do, and he must do that at a particular time and in a particular manner. This he is likely to learn through rude experience, if he be not cautious to inquire beforehand the details of practice. He is likely to make a rash start, upon the supposition that Congress observes the ordinary rules of parliamentary practice to which he has become accustomed in the debating clubs familiar to his youth, and in the mass-meetings known to his later experience. His bill is doubtless ready for presentation early in the session, and some day, taking advantage of a pause in the proceedings, when there seems to be no business before the House, he rises to read it and move its adoption. But he finds getting the floor an arduous and precarious undertaking. There are certain to be others who want it as well as he; and his indignation is stirred by the fact that the Speaker does not so much as turn towards him, though he must have heard his call, but recognizes some one else readily and as a matter of course. If he be obstreperous and persistent in his cries of "Mr. Speaker," he may get that great functionary's attention for a moment,—only to be told, however, that he is out of order, and that his bill can be introduced at that stage only by unanimous consent: immediately there are mechanically-uttered but emphatic exclamations of objection, and he is forced to sit down confused and disgusted. He has, without knowing it, obtruded himself in the way of the "regular order of business," and been run over in consequence, without being quite clear as to how the accident occurred.

Moved by the pain and discomfiture of this first experience to respect, if not to fear, the rules, the new member casts about, by study or inquiry, to find out, if possible, the nature and occasion of his privileges. He learns that his only safe day is Monday. On that day the roll of the States is called, and members may introduce bills as their States are reached in the call. So on Monday he essays another bout with the rules, confident this time of being on their safe side,—but mayhap indiscreetly and unluckily overconfident. For if he supposes, as he naturally will, that after his bill has been sent up to be read by the clerk he may say a few words in its behalf, and in that belief sets out upon his long-considered remarks, he will be knocked down by the rules as surely as he was on the first occasion when he gained the floor for a brief moment. The rap of Mr. Speaker's gavel is sharp, immediate, and peremptory. He is curtly informed that no debate is in order; the bill can only be referred to the appropriate Committee.

This is, indeed, disheartening; it is his first lesson in committee government, and the master's rod smarts; but the sooner he learns the prerogatives and powers of the Standing Committees the sooner will he penetrate the mysteries of the rules and avoid the pain of further contact with their thorny side. The privileges of the Standing Committees are the beginning and the end of the rules. Both the House of Representatives and the Senate conduct their business by what may figuratively, but not inaccurately, be called an odd device of *disintegration*. The House virtually both deliberates and legislates in small sections. Time would fail it to discuss all the bills brought in, for they every session number thousands; and it is to be doubted whether, even if time allowed, the ordinary processes of debate and amendment would suffice to sift the chaff from the wheat in the bushels of bills every week piled upon the clerk's desk. Accordingly, no futile attempt is made to do anything of the kind. The work is parceled out, most of it to the forty-seven Standing Committees which constitute the regular organization of the House, some of it to select committees appointed for special and temporary purposes. Each of the almost numberless bills that come pouring in on Mondays is "read a first and second time,"—simply perfunctorily read, that is, by its title, by the clerk, and passed by silent assent through its first formal courses, for the purpose of bringing it to the proper stage for commitment,—and referred without debate to the appropriate Standing Committee. Practically, no bill escapes commitment—save, of course, bills introduced by committees, and a few which may now and then be crowded through under a suspension of the rules, granted by a two-thirds vote—though the exact disposition to be made of a bill is not always determined easily and as a matter of course. Besides the great Committee of Ways and Means and the equally great Committee on Appropriations, there are Standing Committees on Banking and Currency, on Claims, on Commerce, on the Public Lands, on Post-Offices and Post-Roads, on the Judiciary, on Public Expenditures, on Manufactures, on Agriculture, on Military Affairs, on Naval Affairs, on Mines and Mining, on Education and Labor, on Patents, and on a score of other branches of legislative concern; but careful and differential as is the topical division of the subjects of legislation which is represented in the titles of these Committees, it is not always evident to which Committee each particular bill should go. Many bills affect subjects which may be regarded as lying as properly within the jurisdiction of one as of another of the Committees; for no hard and fast lines separate the various classes of business which the Committees are commissioned to take in charge. Their jurisdictions overlap at many points, and it must frequently happen that bills are read which cover just this common ground. Over the commitment of such bills sharp and interesting skirmishes often take place. There is active competition for them, the ordinary, quiet routine of matter-of-course reference being interrupted by rival motions seeking to give very different directions to the disposition to be made of them. To which Committee should a bill "to fix and establish the maximum rates of fares of the Union Pacific and Central Pacific Railroads" be sent,—to the Committee on Commerce or to the Committee on the Pacific Railroads? Should a bill which prohibits the mailing of certain classes of letters and circulars go to the Committee on Post-Offices and Post-Roads, because it relates to the mails, or to the Committee on the Judiciary, because it proposes to make any transgression of its prohibition a crime? What is the proper disposition of any bill which thus seems to lie within two distinct committee jurisdictions?

The fate of bills committed is generally not uncertain. As a rule, a bill committed is a bill doomed. When it goes from the clerk's desk to a committee-room it crosses a parliamentary bridge of sighs to dim dungeons of silence whence it will never return. The means and time of its death are unknown, but its friends never see it again. Of course no Standing Committee is privileged to take upon itself the full powers of the House it represents, and formally and decisively reject a bill referred to it; its disapproval, if it disapproves, must be reported to the House in the form of a recommendation that the bill "do not pass." But it is easy, and therefore common, to let the session pass without making any report at all upon bills deemed objectionable or unimportant, and to substitute for reports upon them a few bills of the Committee's own drafting; so that thousands of bills expire with the expiration of each Congress, not having been rejected, but having been simply neglected. There was not time to report upon them.

Of course it goes without saying that the practical effect of this Committee organization of the House is to consign to each of the Standing Committees the entire direction of legislation upon those subjects which properly come to its consideration. As to those subjects it is entitled to the initiative, and all legislative action with regard to them is under its overruling guidance. It gives shape and course to the determinations of the House. In one respect, however, its initiative is limited. Even a Standing Committee cannot report a bill whose subject-matter has not been referred to it by the House, "by the rules or otherwise"; it cannot volunteer advice on questions upon which its advice has not been asked. But this is not a serious, not even an operative, limitation upon its functions of suggestion and leadership; for it is a very simple matter to get referred to it any subject it wishes to introduce to the attention of the House. Its chairman, or one of its leading members, frames a bill covering the point upon which the Committee wishes to suggest legislation; brings it in, in his capacity as a private member, on Monday, when the call of States is made; has it referred to his Committee; and thus secures an opportunity for the making of the desired report.

It is by this imperious authority of the Standing Committees that the new member is stayed and thwarted whenever he seeks to take an active part in the business of the House. Turn which way he may, some privilege of the Committees stands in his path. The rules are so framed as to put all business under their management; and one of the discoveries which the new member is sure to make, albeit after many trying experiences and sobering adventures and as his first session draws towards its close, is, that under their sway freedom of debate finds no place of allowance, and that his long-delayed speech must remain unspoken. For even a long congressional session is too short to afford time for a full consideration of all the reports of the forty-seven Committees, and debate upon them must be rigidly cut short, if not altogether excluded, if any considerable part of the necessary business is to be gotten through with before adjournment. There are some subjects to which the House must always give prompt attention; therefore reports from the Committees on Printing and on Elections are always in order; and there are some subjects to which careful consideration must always be accorded; therefore the Committee of Ways and Means and the Committee on Appropriations are clothed with extraordinary privileges; and revenue and supply bills may be reported, and will ordinarily be considered, at any time. But these four are the only specially licensed Committees. The rest must take their turns in fixed order as they are called on by the Speaker, contenting themselves with such crumbs of time as fall from the tables of the four Committees of highest prerogative.

Senator Hoar, of Massachusetts, whose long congressional experience entitles him to speak with authority, calculates[1] that, "supposing the two sessions which make up the life of the House to last ten months," most of the Committees have at their disposal during each Congress but two hours apiece in which "to report upon, debate, and dispose of all the subjects of general legislation committed to their charge." For of course much time is wasted. No Congress gets immediately to work upon its first assembling. It has its officers to elect, and after their election some time must elapse before its organization is finally completed by the appointment of the Committees. It adjourns for holidays, too, and generally spares itself long sittings. Besides, there are many

[1] In an article entitled "The Conduct of Business in Congress" (*No. Am. Rev.*, p. 121), to which I am indebted for many details of the sketch in the text.

things to interrupt the call of the Committees upon which most of the business waits. That call can proceed only during the morning hours,—the hours just after the reading of the "Journal," —on Tuesdays, Wednesdays, and Thursdays; and even then it may suffer postponement because of the unfinished business of the previous day which is entitled to first consideration. The call cannot proceed on Mondays because the morning hour of Mondays is devoted invariably to the call of the States for the introduction of bills and resolutions; nor on Fridays, for Friday is "private bill day," and is always engrossed by the Committee on Claims, or by other fathers of bills which have gone upon the "private calendar." On Saturdays the House seldom sits.

The reports made during these scant morning hours are ordered to be printed, for future consideration in their turn, and the bills introduced by the Committees are assigned to the proper calendars, to be taken up in order at the proper time. When a morning hour has run out, the House hastens to proceed with the business on the Speaker's table.

These are some of the plainer points of the rules. They are full of complexity, and of confusion to the uninitiated, and the confusions of practice are greater than the confusions of the rules. For the regular order of business is constantly being interrupted by the introduction of resolutions offered "by unanimous consent," and of bills let in under a "suspension of the rules." Still, it is evident that there is one principle which runs through every stage of procedure, and which is never disallowed or abrogated,— the principle that the Committees shall rule without let or hindrance. And this is a principle of extraordinary formative power. It is the mould of all legislation. In the first place, the speeding of business under the direction of the Committees determines the character and the amount of the discussion to which legislation shall be subjected. The House is conscious that time presses. It knows that, hurry as it may, it will hardly get through with one eighth of the business laid out for the session, and that to pause for lengthy debate is to allow the arrears to accumulate. Besides, most of the members are individually anxious to expedite action on every pending measure, because each member of the House is a member of one or more of the Standing Committees, and is quite naturally desirous that the bills prepared by his Committees, and in which he is, of course, specially interested by reason of the particular attention which he has been compelled to give them, should reach a hearing and a vote as soon as possible. It must, therefore, invariably happen that the Committee holding the floor at any particular time is the Committee whose proposals the majority wish to dispose of as summarily as circumstances will allow, in order that the rest of the forty-two unprivileged Committees to which the majority belong may gain the earlier and the fairer chance of a hearing. A reporting Committee, besides, is generally as glad to be pushed as the majority are to push it. It probably has several bills matured, and wishes to see them disposed of before its brief hours of opportunity[2] are passed and gone.

Consequently, it is the established custom of the House to accord the floor for one hour to the member of the reporting Committee who has charge of the business under consideration; and that hour is made the chief hour of debate. The reporting committee-man seldom, if ever, uses the whole of the hour himself for his opening remarks; he uses part of it, and retains control of the rest of it; for by undisputed privilege it is his to dispose of, whether he himself be upon the floor or not. No amendment is in order during that hour, unless he consent to its presentation; and he does not, of course, yield his time indiscriminately to any one who wishes to speak. He gives way, indeed, as in fairness he should, to opponents as well as to friends of the measure under his charge; but generally no one is accorded a share of his time who has not obtained his previous promise of the floor; and those who do speak must not run beyond the number of minutes he has agreed to allow them. He keeps the course both of debate and of amendment thus carefully under his own supervision, as a good tactician, and before he finally yields the floor, at the expiration of his hour, he is sure to move the previous question. To neglect to do so would be to lose all control of the business in hand; for unless the previous question is ordered the debate may run on at will, and his Committee's chance for getting its measures through slip quite away; and that would be nothing less than his disgrace. He would be all the more blameworthy because he had but to ask for the previous question to get it. As I have said, the House is as eager to hurry business as he can be, and will consent to almost any limitation of discussion that he may demand; though, probably, if he were to throw the reins upon its neck, it would run at large from very wantonness, in scorn of such a driver. The previous question once ordered, all amendments are

[2] No Committee is entitled, when called, to occupy more than the morning hours of two successive days with the measures which it has prepared; though if its second morning hour expire while the House is actually considering one of its bills, that single measure may hold over from morning hour to morning hour until it is disposed of.

precluded, and one hour remains for the summing-up of this same privileged committee-man before the final vote is taken and the bill disposed of.

These are the customs which baffle and perplex and astound the new member. In these precedents and usages, when at length he comes to understand them, the novice spies out the explanation of the fact, once so confounding and seemingly inexplicable, that when he leaped to his feet to claim the floor other members who rose after him were coolly and unfeelingly preferred before him by the Speaker. Of course it is plain enough now that Mr. Speaker knew beforehand to whom the representative of the reporting Committee had agreed to yield the floor; and it was no use for any one else to cry out for recognition. Whoever wished to speak should, if possible, have made some arrangement with the Committee before the business came to a hearing, and should have taken care to notify Mr. Speaker that he was to be granted the floor for a few moments.

Unquestionably this, besides being a very interesting, is a very novel and significant method of restricting debate and expediting legislative action,—a method of very serious import, and obviously fraught with far-reaching constitutional effects. The practices of debate which prevail in its legislative assembly are manifestly of the utmost importance to a self-governing people; for that legislation which is not thoroughly discussed by the legislating body is practically done in a corner. It is impossible for Congress itself to do wisely what it does so hurriedly; and the constituencies cannot understand what Congress does not itself stop to consider. The prerogatives of the Committees represent something more than a mere convenient division of labor. There is only one part of its business to which Congress, as a whole, attends,—that part, namely, which is embraced under the privileged subjects of revenue and supply. The House never accepts the proposals of the Committee of Ways and Means, or of the Committee on Appropriations, without due deliberation; but it allows almost all of its other Standing Committees virtually to legislate for it. In form, the Committees only digest the various matter introduced by individual members, and prepare it, with care, and after thorough investigation, for the final consideration and action of the House; but, in reality, they dictate the course to be taken, prescribing the decisions of the House not only, but measuring out, according to their own wills, its opportunities for debate and deliberation as well. The House sits, not for serious discussion, but to sanction the conclusions of its Committees as rapidly as possible. It legislates in its committee-rooms; not by the determinations of majorities, but by the resolutions of specially-commissioned minorities; so that it is not far from the truth to say that Congress in session is Congress on public exhibition, whilst Congress in its committee-rooms is Congress at work.

Habit grows fast, even upon the unconventional American, and the nature of the House of Representatives has, by long custom, been shaped to the spirit of its rules. Representatives have attained, by rigorous self-discipline, to the perfect stature of the law under which they live, having purged their hearts as completely as may be of all desire to do that which it is the chief object of that law to forbid by giving over a vain lust after public discussion. The entire absence of the instinct of debate amongst them, and their apparent unfamiliarity with the idea of combating a proposition by argument, was recently illustrated by an incident which was quite painfully amusing. The democratic majority of the House of the Forty-eighth Congress desired the immediate passage of a pension bill of rather portentous proportions; but the republican minority disapproved of the bill with great fervor, and, when it was moved by the Pension Committee, late one afternoon, in a thin House, that the rules be suspended, and an early day set for a consideration of the bill, the Republicans addressed themselves to determined and persistent "filibustering" to prevent action. First they refused to vote, leaving the Democrats without an acting quorum; then, all night long, they kept the House at roll-calling on dilatory and obstructive motions, the dreary dragging of the time being relieved occasionally by the amusement of hearing the excuses of members who had tried to slip off to bed, or by the excitement of an angry dispute between the leaders of the two parties as to the responsibility for the dead-lock. Not till the return of morning brought in the delinquents to recruit the democratic ranks did business advance a single step. Now, the noteworthy fact about this remarkable scene is, that the minority were not manœuvring to gain opportunity or time for debate, in order that the country might be informed of the true nature of the obnoxious bill, but were simply fighting a preliminary motion with silent, dogged obstruction. After the whole night had been spent in standing out against action, the House is said to have been "in no mood for the thirty-minutes' debate allowed by the rules," and a final vote was taken, with only a word or two said. It was easier and more natural, as everybody saw, to direct attention to the questionable character of what was being attempted by the majority by creating a somewhat scandalous "scene," of which every one would talk, than by making speeches which nobody would read. It was a notable commentary on the characteristic methods of our system of congressional government.

One very noteworthy result of this system is to shift the theatre of debate upon legislation from the floor of Congress to the privacy of the committee-rooms. Provincial gentlemen who read the Associated Press dispatches in their morning papers as they sit over their coffee at breakfast are doubtless often very sorely puzzled by certain of the items which sometimes appear in the brief telegraphic notes from Washington. What can they make of this for instance: "The House Committee on Commerce to-day heard arguments from the congressional delegation from" such and such States "in advocacy of appropriations for river and harbor improvements which the members desire incorporated in the River and Harbor Appropriations Bill"? They probably do not understand that it would have been useless for members not of the Committee on Commerce to wait for any opportunity to make their suggestions on the floor of Congress, where the measure to which they wish to make additions would be under the authoritative control of the Committee, and where, consequently, they could gain a hearing only by the courteous sufferance of the committee-man in charge of the report. Whatever is to be done must be done by or through the Committee.

It would seem, therefore, that practically Congress, or at any rate the House of Representatives, delegates not only its legislative but also its deliberative functions to its Standing Committees. The little public debate that arises under the stringent and urgent rules of the House is formal rather than effective, and it is the discussions which take place in the Committees that give form to legislation. Undoubtedly these siftings of legislative questions by the Committees are of great value in enabling the House to obtain "undarkened counsel" and intelligent suggestions from authoritative sources. All sober, purposeful, business-like talk upon questions of public policy, whether it take place in Congress or only before the Committees of Congress, is of great value; and the controversies which spring up in the committee-rooms, both amongst the committee-men themselves and between those who appear before the Committees as advocates of special measures, cannot but contribute to add clearness and definite consistency to the reports submitted to the House.

There are, however, several very obvious reasons why the most thorough canvass of business by the Committees, and the most exhaustive and discriminating discussion of all its details in their rooms, cannot take the place or fulfill the uses of amendment and debate by Congress in open session. In the first place, the proceedings of the Committees are private and their discussions unpublished. The chief, and unquestionably the most essential, object of all discussion of public business is the enlightenment of public opinion; and of course, since it cannot hear the debates of the Committees, the nation is not apt to be much instructed by them. Only the Committees are enlightened. There is a conclusive objection to the publication of the proceedings of the Committees, which is recognized as of course by all parliamentary lawyers, namely, that those proceedings are of no force till confirmed by the House. A Committee is commissioned, not to instruct the public, but to instruct and guide the House.

Indeed it is not usual for the Committees to open their sittings often to those who desire to be heard with regard to pending questions; and no one can demand a hearing as of right. On the contrary, they are privileged and accustomed to hold their sessions in absolute secrecy. It is made a breach of order for any member to allude on the floor of the House to anything that has taken place in committee, "unless by a written report sanctioned by a majority of the Committee"; and there is no place in the regular order of business for a motion instructing a Committee to conduct its investigations with open doors. Accordingly, it is only by the concession of the Committees that arguments are made before them.

When they do suffer themselves to be approached, moreover, they generally extend the leave to others besides their fellow-congressmen. The Committee on Commerce consents to listen to prominent railroad officials upon the subject of the regulation of freight charges and fares; and scores of interested persons telegraph inquiries to the chairman of the Committee of Ways and Means as to the time at which they are to be permitted to present to the Committee their views upon the revision of the tariff. The speeches made before the Committees at their open sessions are, therefore, scarcely of such a kind as would be instructive to the public, and on that account worth publishing. They are as a rule the pleas of special pleaders, the arguments of advocates. They have about them none of the searching, critical, illuminating character of the higher order of parliamentary debate, in which men are pitted against each other as equals, and urged to sharp contest and masterful strife by the inspiration of political principle and personal ambition, through the rivalry of parties and the competition of policies. They represent a joust between antagonistic interests, not a contest of principles. They could scarcely either inform or elevate public opinion, even if they were to obtain its heed.

For the instruction and elevation of public opinion, in regard to national affairs, there is needed something more than special pleas for special privileges. There is needed public discussion of a peculiar sort: a discussion by the sovereign legislative body itself, a discussion in which every feature of each mooted point of policy shall be distinctly brought out, and every argument of significance pushed to the farthest point of insistence, by recognized leaders in that body; and, above all, a discussion upon which something—something of interest or importance, some pressing question of administration or of law, the fate of a party or the success of a conspicuous politician—evidently depends. It is only a discussion of this sort that the public will heed; no other sort will impress it.

There could, therefore, be no more unwelcome revelation to one who has anything approaching a statesman-like appreciation of the essential conditions of intelligent self-government than just that which must inevitably be made to every one who candidly examines our congressional system; namely, that, under that system, such discussion is impossible. There are, to begin with, physical and *architectural* reasons why business-like debate of public affairs by the House of Representatives is out of the question. To those who visit the galleries of the representative chamber during a session of the House these reasons are as obvious as they are astonishing. It would be natural to expect that a body which meets ostensibly for consultation and deliberation should hold its sittings in a room small enough to admit of an easy interchange of views and a ready concert of action, where its members would be brought into close, sympathetic contact; and it is nothing less than astonishing to find it spread at large through the vast spaces of such a chamber as the hall of the House of Representatives, where there are no close ranks of coöperating parties, but each member has a roomy desk and an easy revolving chair; where broad aisles spread and stretch themselves; where ample, soft-carpeted areas lie about the spacious desks of the Speaker and clerks; where deep galleries reach back from the outer limits of the wide passages which lie beyond "the bar": an immense, capacious chamber, disposing its giant dimensions freely beneath the great level lacunar ceiling through whose glass panels the full light of day pours in. The most vivid impression the visitor gets in looking over that vast hall is the impression of space. A speaker must needs have a voice like O'Connell's, the practical visitor is apt to think, as he sits in the gallery, to fill even the silent spaces of that room; how much more to overcome the disorderly noises that buzz and rattle through it when the representatives are assembled,—a voice clear, sonorous, dominant, like the voice of a clarion. One who speaks there with the voice and lungs of the ordinary mortal must content himself with the audience of those members in his own immediate neighborhood, whose ears he rudely assails in vehement efforts to command the attention of those beyond them, and who, therefore, cannot choose but hear him.

It is of this magnitude of the hall of the representatives that those news telegrams are significant which speak of an interesting or witty speech in Congress as having drawn about the speaker listeners from all parts of the House. As one of our most noted wits would say, a member must needs take a Sabbath day's journey to get within easy hearing distance of a speaker who is addressing the House from the opposite side of the hall; for besides the space there are the noises intervening, the noises of loud talking and of the clapping of hands for the pages, making the task of the member who is speaking "very like trying to address the people in the omnibuses from the curbstone in front of the Astor House."[3]

But these physical limitations to debate, though serious and real, are amongst the least important, because they are amongst the least insuperable. If effective and business-like public discussions were considered indispensable by Congress, or even desirable, the present chamber could readily be divided into two halls: the one a commodious reading-room where the members might chat and write at ease as they now do in the House itself; and the other a smaller room suitable for debate and earnest business. This, in fact, has been several times proposed, but the House does not feel that there is any urgency about providing facilities for debate, because it sees no reason to desire an increase of speech-making, in view of the fact that, notwithstanding all the limitations now put upon discussion, its business moves much too slowly. The early Congresses had time to talk; Congresses of to-day have not. Before that wing of the Capitol was built in which the representative chamber now is, the House used to sit in the much smaller room, now empty save for the statuary to whose exhibition it is

[3] Quoted from an exceedingly life-like and picturesque description of the House which appeared in the New York *Nation* for April 4, 1878.

devoted; and there much speech-making went on from day to day; there Calhoun and Randolph and Webster and Clay won their reputations as statesmen and orators. So earnest and interesting were the debates of those days, indeed, that the principal speeches delivered in Congress seemed to have been usually printed at length in the metropolitan journals.[4] But the number and length of the speeches was even then very much deplored; and so early as 1828 a writer in the "North American Review" condemns what he calls "the habit of congressional debating," with the air of one who speaks against some abuse which every one acknowledges to be a nuisance.[5] Eleven years later a contributor to the "Democratic Review"[6] declared that it had "been gravely charged upon" Mr. Samuel Cushman, then a member of the Twenty-fifth Congress from New Hampshire, "that he moves the previous question. Truly," continues the essayist, "he does, and for that very service, if he had never done anything else, he deserves a monument as a public benefactor. One man who can arrest a tedious, long-winded, factious, time-killing debate, is worth forty who can provoke or keep one up. It requires some moral courage, some spirit, and some tact also, to move the previous question, and to move it, too, at precisely the right point of time."

This ardent and generous defense of Mr. Cushman against the odious accusation of moving the previous question would doubtless be exquisitely amusing to the chairman of one of the Standing Committees of the Forty-eighth Congress, to whom the previous question seems one of the commonest necessities of life. But, after all, he ought not to laugh at the ingenuous essayist, for that was not the heyday of the rules; they then simply served and did not tyrannize over the House. They did not then have the opportunity of empire afforded them by the scantiness of time which hurries the House, and the weight of business which oppresses it; and they were at a greater disadvantage in a room where oratory was possible than they are in a vast chamber where the orator's voice is drowned amidst the noises of disorderly inattention. Nowadays would-be debaters are easily thrust out of Congress and forced to resort to the printing-office; are compelled to content themselves with speaking from the pages of the "Record" instead of from their places in the House. Some people who live very far from Washington may imagine that the speeches which are spread at large in the columns of the "Congressional

---

[4] *No. Am. Rev.*, vol. xxvi., p. 162.
[5] *Id.*, the same article.
[6] "Glances at Congress," *Dem. Rev.*, March, 1839.

Record," or which their representative sends them in pamphlet form, were actually delivered in Congress; but every one else knows that they were not; that Congress is constantly granting leave to its members to insert in the official reports of the proceedings speeches which it never heard and does not care to hear, but which it is not averse from printing at the public expense, if it is desirable that constituents and the country at large should read them. It will not stand between a member and his constituents so long as it can indulge the one and satisfy the others without any inconvenience to itself or any serious drain upon the resources of the Treasury. The public printer does not object.

But there are other reasons still more organic than these why the debates of Congress cannot, under our present system, have that serious purpose of search into the merits of policies and that definite and determinate party—or, if you will, partisan—aim without which they can never be effective for the instruction of public opinion, or the cleansing of political action. The chief of these reasons, because the parent of all the rest, is that there are in Congress no authoritative leaders who are the recognized spokesmen of their parties. Power is nowhere concentrated; it is rather deliberately and of set policy scattered amongst many small chiefs. It is divided up, as it were, into forty-seven seigniories, in each of which a Standing Committee is the court-baron and its chairman lord-proprietor. These petty barons, some of them not a little powerful, but none of them within reach of the full powers of rule, may at will exercise an almost despotic sway within their own shires, and may sometimes threaten to convulse even the realm itself; but both their mutual jealousies and their brief and restricted opportunities forbid their combining, and each is very far from the office of common leader.

I know that to some this scheme of distributed power and disintegrated rule seems a very excellent device whereby we are enabled to escape a dangerous "one-man power" and an untoward concentration of functions; and it is very easy to see and appreciate the considerations which make this view of committee government so popular. It is based upon a very proper and salutary fear of *irresponsible* power; and those who most resolutely maintain it always fight from the position that all leadership in legislation is hard to restrain in proportion to its size and to the strength of its prerogatives, and that to divide it is to make it manageable. They aver, besides, that the less a man has to do—that is to say, the more he is confined to single departments and to definite details—the more intelligent and thorough will his work be. They like the Committees, therefore, just because they are many and weak, being quite willing to abide their being despotic within their narrow spheres.

It seems evident, however, when the question is looked at from another stand-point, that, as a matter of fact and experience, the more power is divided the more irresponsible it becomes. A mighty baron who can call half the country to arms is watched with greater jealousy, and, therefore, restrained with more vigilant care than is ever vouchsafed the feeble master of a single and solitary castle. The one cannot stir abroad upon an innocent pleasure jaunt without attracting the suspicious attention of the whole country-side; the other may vex and harry his entire neighborhood without fear of let or hindrance. It is ever the little foxes that spoil the grapes. At any rate, to turn back from illustration to the facts of the argument, it is plain enough that the petty character of the leadership of each Committee contributes towards making its despotism sure by making its duties uninteresting. The Senate almost always discusses its business with considerable thoroughness; and even the House, whether by common consent or by reason of such persistent "filibustering" on the part of the minority as compels the reporting Committee and the majority to grant time for talk, sometimes stops to debate committee reports at length; but nobody, except, perhaps, newspaper editors, finds these debates interesting reading.

Why is it that many intelligent and patriotic people throughout this country, from Virginia to California,—people who, beyond all question, love their State and the Union more than they love our cousin state over sea,—subscribe for the London papers in order to devour the parliamentary debates, and yet would never think of troubling themselves to make tedious progress through a single copy of the "Congressional Record"? Is it because they are captivated by the old-world dignity of royal England with its nobility and its court pageantry, or because of a vulgar desire to appear better versed than their neighbors in foreign affairs, and to affect familiarity with British statesmen? No; of course not. It is because the parliamentary debates are interesting and ours are not. In the British House of Commons the functions and privileges of our Standing Committees are all concentrated in the hands of the Ministry, who have, besides, some prerogatives of leadership which even our Committees do not possess, so that they carry all responsibility as well as great power, and all debate wears an intense personal and party interest. Every important discussion is an arraignment of the Ministry by the Opposition,—an arraignment of the majority by the minority; and every important vote is a party defeat and a party triumph. The whole conduct of the government turns upon what is said in the Commons, because the revelations of debate often change votes, and a Ministry loses hold upon power as it loses hold upon the confidence of the Commons. This great Standing Committee goes out whenever it crosses the will of the majority. It is, therefore, for these very simple and obvious reasons that the parliamentary debates are read on this side of the water in preference to the congressional debates. They affect the ministers, who are very conspicuous persons, and in whom, therefore, all the intelligent world is interested; and they determine the course of politics in a great empire. The season of a parliamentary debate is a great field day on which Liberals and Conservatives pit their full forces against each other, and people like to watch the issues of the contest.

Our congressional debates, on the contrary, have no tithe of this interest, because they have no tithe of such significance and importance. The committee reports, upon which the debates take place, are backed by neither party; they represent merely the recommendations of a small body of members belonging to both parties, and are quite as likely to divide the vote of the party to which the majority of the Committee belong as they are to meet with opposition from the other side of the chamber. If they are carried, it is no party triumph; if they are lost, it is no party discomfiture. They are no more than the proposals of a mixed Committee, and may be rejected without political inconvenience to either party or reproof to the Committee; just as they may be passed without compliment to the Committee or political advantage to either side of the House. Neither party has any great stake in the controversy. The only importance that can attach to the vote must hang upon its relation to the next general election. If the report concern a question which is at the time so much in the public eye that all action upon it is likely to be marked and remembered against the day of popular action, parties are careful to vote as solidly as possible on what they conceive to be the safe side; but all other reports are disposed of without much thought of their influence upon the fortunes of distant elections, because that influence is remote and problematical.

In a word, the national parties do not act in Congress under the restraint of a sense of immediate responsibility. Responsibility is spread thin; and no vote or debate can gather it. It rests not so much upon parties as upon individuals; and it rests upon individuals in no such way as would make it either just or efficacious to visit upon them the iniquity of any legislative act. Looking at government from a practical and business-like, rather than from a theoretical and abstractly-ethical point of view,—treating the business of government as a business,—it seems to be unquestionably and in a high degree desirable that all legislation should distinctly represent the action of parties as parties. I know that it has been proposed by enthusiastic, but not too practical, reformers to do away with parties by some legerdemain of governmental reconstruction, accompanied and supplemented by some rehabilitation, devoutly to be wished, of the virtues least commonly controlling in fallen human nature; but it seems to me that it would be more difficult and less desirable than these amiable persons suppose to conduct a government of the many by means of any other device than party organization, and that the great need is, not to get rid of parties, but to find and use some expedient by which they can be managed and made amenable from day to day to public opinion. Plainly this cannot be effected by punishing here and there a member of Congress who has voted for a flagrantly dishonest appropriation bill, or an obnoxious measure relating to the tariff. Unless the punishment can be extended to the party—if any such be recognizable—with which these members have voted, no advantage has been won for self-government, and no triumph has been gained by public opinion. It should be desired that parties should act in distinct organizations, in accordance with avowed principles, under easily recognized leaders, in order that the voters might be able to declare by their ballots, not only their condemnation of any past policy, by withdrawing all support from the party responsible for it; but also and particularly their will as to the future administration of the government, by bringing into power a party pledged to the adoption of an acceptable policy.

It is, therefore, a fact of the most serious consequence that by our system of congressional rule no such means of controlling legislation is afforded. Outside of Congress the organization of the national parties is exceedingly well-defined and tangible; no one could wish it, and few could imagine it, more so; but within Congress it is obscure and intangible. Our parties marshal their adherents with the strictest possible discipline for the purpose of carrying elections, but their discipline is very slack and indefinite in dealing with legislation. At least there is within Congress no *visible*, and therefore no *controllable* party organization. The only bond of cohesion is the caucus, which occasionally whips a party together for coöperative action against the time for casting its vote upon some critical question. There is always a majority and a minority, indeed, but the legislation of a session does not represent the policy of either; it is simply an aggregate of the bills recommended by Committees composed of members from both sides of the House, and it is known to be usually, not the work of the majority men upon the Committees, but compromise conclusions bearing some shade or tinge of each of the variously-colored opinions and wishes of the committee-men of both parties.

It is plainly the representation of both parties on the Committees that makes party responsibility indistinct and organized party action almost impossible. If the Committees were composed entirely of members of the majority, and were thus constituted representatives of the party in power, the whole course of congressional proceedings would unquestionably take on a very different aspect. There would then certainly be a compact opposition to face the organized majority. Committee reports would be taken to represent the views of the party in power, and, instead of the scattered, unconcerted opposition, without plan or leaders, which now sometimes subjects the propositions of the Committees to vexatious hindrances and delays, there would spring up debate under skillful masters of opposition, who could drill their partisans for effective warfare and give shape and meaning to the purposes of the minority. But of course there can be no such definite division of forces so long as the efficient machinery of legislation is in the hands of both parties at once; so long as the parties are mingled and harnessed together in a common organization.

It may be said, therefore, that very few of the measures which come before Congress are party measures. They are, at any rate, not brought in as party measures. They are indorsed by select bodies of members chosen with a view to constituting an impartial board of examination for the judicial and thorough consideration of each subject of legislation; no member of one of these Committees is warranted in revealing any of the disagreements of the committee-room or the proportions of the votes there taken; and no color is meant to be given to the supposition that the reports made are intended to advance any party interest. Indeed, only a very slight examination of the measures which originate with the Committees is necessary to show that most of them are framed with a view to securing their easy passage by giving them as neutral and inoffensive a character as possible. The manifest object is to dress them to the liking of all factions.

Under such circumstances, neither the failure nor the success of any policy inaugurated by one of the Committees can fairly be charged to the account of either party. The Committee acted honestly, no doubt, and as they thought best; and there can, of course, be no assurance that, by taking away its congressional majority from the party to which the greater number of the committee-men belong, a Committee could be secured which would act better or differently.

The conclusion of the whole matter is, then, that public opinion cannot be instructed or elevated by the debates of Congress, not only because there are few debates seriously undertaken by Congress, but principally because no one not professionally interested in the daily course of legislation cares to read what is said by the debaters when Congress does stop to talk, inasmuch as nothing depends upon the issue of the discussion. The ordinary citizen cannot be induced to pay much heed to the details, or even to the main principles, of law-making, unless something else more interesting than the law itself be involved in the pending decision of the law-makers. If the fortunes of a party or the power of a great political leader are staked upon the final vote, he will listen with the keenest interest to all that the principal actors may have to say, and absorb much instruction in so doing; but if no such things hang in the balance, he will not turn from his business to listen; and if the true issues are not brought out in eager public contests which catch his ear because of their immediate personal interest, but must be sought amidst the information which can be made complete only by reading scores of newspapers, he will certainly never find them or care for them, and there is small use in printing a "Record" which he will not read.

I know not how better to describe our form of government in a single phrase than by calling it a government by the chairmen of the Standing Committees of Congress. This disintegrate ministry, as it figures on the floor of the House of Representatives, has many peculiarities. In the first place, it is made up of the elders of the assembly; for, by custom, seniority in congressional service determines the bestowal of the principal chairmanships; in the second place, it is constituted of selfish and warring elements; for chairman fights against chairman for use of the time of the assembly, though the most part of them are inferior to the chairman of Ways and Means, and all are subordinate to the chairman of the Committee on Appropriations; in the third place, instead of being composed of the associated leaders of Congress, it consists of the dissociated heads of forty-eight "little legislatures" (to borrow Senator Hoar's apt name for the Committees); and, in the fourth place, it is instituted by appointment from Mr. Speaker, who is, by intention, the chief judicial, rather than the chief political, officer of the House.

It is highly interesting to note the extraordinary power accruing to Mr. Speaker through this pregnant prerogative of appointing the Standing Committees of the House. That power is, as it were, the central and characteristic inconvenience and anomaly of our constitutional system, and on that account excites both the curiosity and the wonder of the student of institutions. The most esteemed writers upon our Constitution have failed to observe, not only that the Standing Committees are the most essential machinery of our governmental system, but also that the Speaker of the House of Representatives is the most powerful functionary of that system. So sovereign is he within the wide sphere of his influence that one could wish for accurate knowledge as to the actual extent of his power. But Mr. Speaker's powers cannot be known accurately, because they vary with the character of Mr. Speaker. All Speakers have, of late years especially, been potent factors in legislation, but some have, by reason of greater energy or less conscience, made more use of their opportunities than have others.

The Speaker's privilege of appointing the Standing Committees is nearly as old as Congress itself. At first the House tried the plan of balloting for its more important Committees, ordering, in April, 1789, that the Speaker should appoint only those Committees which should consist of not more than three members; but less than a year's experience of this method of organizing seems to have furnished satisfactory proof of its impracticability, and in January, 1790, the present rule was adopted: that "All committees shall be appointed by the Speaker, unless otherwise specially directed by the House." The rules of one House of Representatives are not, however, necessarily the rules of the next. No rule lives save by biennial readoption. Each newly-elected House meets without rules for its governance, and amongst the first acts of its first session is usually the adoption of the resolution that the rules of its predecessor shall be its own rules, subject, of course, to such revisions as it may, from time to time, see fit to make. Mr. Speaker's power of appointment, accordingly, always awaits the passage of this resolution; but it never waits in vain, for no House, however foolish in other respects, has yet been foolish enough to make fresh trial of electing its Committees. That mode may do well enough for the cool and leisurely Senate, but it is not for the hasty and turbulent House.

It must always, of course, have seemed eminently desirable to all thoughtful and experienced men that Mr. Speaker should be no more than the judicial guide and moderator of the proceedings of the House, keeping apart from the heated controversies of party warfare, and exercising none but an impartial influence upon the course of legislation; and probably when he was first invested with the power of appointment it was thought possible that he could exercise that great prerogative without allowing his personal views upon questions of public policy to control or even affect his choice. But it must very soon have appeared that it was too much to expect of a man who had it within his power to direct affairs that he should subdue all purpose to do so, and should make all appointments with an eye to regarding every preference but his own; and when that did become evident, the rule was undoubtedly retained only because none better could be devised. Besides, in the early years of the Constitution the Committees were very far from having the power they now possess. Business did not then hurry too fast for discussion, and the House was in the habit of scrutinizing the reports of the Committees much more critically than it now pretends to do. It deliberated in its open sessions as well as in its private committee-rooms, and the functionary who appointed its committees was simply the nominator of its advisers, not, as is the Speaker of to-day, the nominor of its rulers.

It is plain, therefore, that the office of Speaker of the House of Representatives is in its present estate a constitutional phenomenon of the first importance, deserving a very thorough and critical examination. If I have succeeded, in what I have already said, in making clear the extraordinary power of the Committees in directing legislation, it may now go without the saying that he who appoints those Committees is an autocrat of the first magnitude. There could be no clearer proof of the great political weight of the Speaker's high commission in this regard than the keen strife which every two years takes place over the election to the speakership, and the intense interest excited throughout the country as to the choice to be made. Of late years, the newspapers have had almost as much to say about the rival candidates for that office as about the candidates for the presidency itself, having come to look upon the selection made as a sure index of the policy to be expected in legislation.

The Speaker is of course chosen by the party which commands the majority in the House, and it has sometimes been the effort of scheming, self-seeking men of that majority to secure the elevation of some friend or tool of their own to that office, from which he can render them service of the most substantial and acceptable sort. But, although these intrigues have occasionally resulted in the election of a man of insignificant parts and doubtful character, the choice has usually fallen upon some representative party man of well-known antecedents and clearly-avowed opinions; for the House cannot, and will not willingly, put up with the intolerable inconvenience of a weak Speaker, and the majority are urged by self-respect and by all the weightiest considerations of expediency, as well as by a regard for the interests of the public business, to place one of their accredited leaders in the chair. If there be differences of opinion within the party, a choice between leaders becomes a choice between policies and assumes the greatest significance. The Speaker is expected to constitute the Committees in accordance with his own political views, and this or that candidate is preferred by his party, not at all because of any supposed superiority of knowledge of the precedents and laws of parliamentary usage, but because of his more popular opinions concerning the leading questions of the day.

Mr. Speaker, too, generally uses his powers as freely and imperatively as he is expected to use them. He unhesitatingly acts as the legislative chief of his party, organizing the Committees in the interest of this or that policy, not covertly and on the sly, as one who does something of which he is ashamed, but openly and confidently, as one who does his duty. Nor does his official connection with the Committees cease upon their appointment. It is his care to facilitate their control of the business of the House, by recognizing during the consideration of a report only those members with whom the reporting committee-man has agreed to share his time, and by keeping all who address the House within the strictest letter of the rules as to the length of their speeches, as well as by enforcing all those other restrictions which forbid independent action on the part of individual members. He must see to it that the Committees have their own way. In so doing he is not exercising arbitrary powers which circumstances and the habits of the assembly enable him safely to arrogate; he is simply enforcing the plain letter and satisfying the evident spirit of the rules.

A student of Roman law and institutions, looking at the Rules of the House of Representatives through glasses unaccustomed to search out aught but antiquities, might be excused for claiming that he found in the customs of the House a striking reproduction of Roman legislative methods. The Roman assembly, he would remind us, could not vote and debate at the same time; it had no privileges of amendment, but had to adopt every law as a whole or reject it as a whole; and no private member had a right to introduce a bill, that being the exclusive prerogative of the magistrates. But though he might establish a parallel satisfactory to himself between the magistrates of Rome and the Committees at Washington, and between the undebatable, unamendable laws of the ancient, and the undebated, unamended laws of the modern, republic, he could hardly find in the later system that compensating advantage which scholars have noted as giving to Roman legislation a clearness and technical perfection such as is to be found in none of the modern codes. Since Roman laws could not be amended in their passage, and must carry their meaning plainly to the comprehension of the commons, clear and brief drafting was cultivated as of the first necessity in drawing up measures which were first to gain popular approval and then to succeed or fail in accomplishing their ends according as they proved workable or impracticable.

No such comparison of our own with other systems can, however, find any favor in the eyes of a certain class of Americans who pride themselves upon being nothing if not patriotic, and who can consequently find no higher praise for the peculiar devices of committee government than that they are our own invention. "An ill-favored thing, sir, but mine own." No one will readily believe, however, that congressmen—even those of them who belong to this dutiful class—cherish a very loving admiration for the discipline to which they are nowadays subjected. As the accomplished librarian of Congress has declared, "the general conviction may be said to exist, that, under the great control over legislation and current business by the Speaker, and by the powerful Committee on Appropriations, combined with the rigor of the Rules of the House, there is less and less opportunity for individual members to make any influential mark in legislation. Independence and ability are repressed under the tyranny of the rules, and practically the power of the popular branch of Congress is concentrated in the Speaker and a few—very few—expert parliamentarians." And of course members of Congress see this. "We have but three forces in this House," exclaimed a jocose member from the Pacific coast, "the Brahmins of the Committee of Ways and Means—not the brains but the Brahmins of the House; the white-button mandarins of the Appropriations Committee; the dignified oligarchy called the Committee on Rules; the Speaker of the House; and the illustrious gentleman from Indiana." Naturally all men of independent spirit chafe under the arbitrary restraints of such a system, and it would be much more philosophical to conclude that they let it stand because they can devise nothing better, than that they adhere to its inconvenient practices because of their admiration for it as an American invention.

However that may be, the number of those who misuse the rules is greater than the number of those who strive to reform them. One of the most startling of the prevalent abuses is the hasty passage of bills under a suspension of the rules, a device "by means of which," says Senator Hoar, "a large proportion, perhaps the majority, of the bills which pass the House are carried through." This practice may be very clearly understood by following further Mr. Hoar's own words: "Every Monday after the morning hour, and at any time during the last ten days of a session, motions to suspend the rules are in order. At these times any member may move to suspend the rules and pass any proposed bill. It requires two thirds of the members voting to adopt such a motion. Upon it no debate or amendment is in order. In this way, if two thirds of the body agree, a bill is by a single vote, without discussion and without change, passed through all the necessary stages, and made a law, so far as the House of Representatives can accomplish it; and in this mode hundreds of measures of vital importance receive, near the close of an exhausting session, without being debated, amended, printed, or understood, the constitutional assent of the representatives of the American people."

One very obvious comment to be made upon habits of procedure so palpably pernicious is, that nothing could be more natural under rules which repress individual action with so much stringency. Then, too, the mills of the Committees are known to grind slowly, and a very quick and easy way of getting rid of minor items of business is to let particular bills, of apparently innocent meaning or laudable intent, run through without commitment. There must be some outlet, too, through which the waters of delayed and accumulated business may be drained off as the end of a session draws near. Members who know how to take the House at an indulgent moment, and can in a few words make out a *primâ facie* case for the action they urge, can almost always secure a suspension of the rules.

To speak very plainly, it is wonderful that under such a system of government legislation is not oftener at sixes and sevens than it actually is. The infinitely varied and various interests of fifty millions of active people would be hard enough to harmonize and serve, one would think, were parties efficiently organized in the pursuit of definite, steady, consistent policies; and it is therefore simply amazing to find how few outrageously and fatally foolish, how few bad or disastrous, things have been done by means of our disintegrate methods of legislation. The Committees of the House to whom the principal topics of legislation are allotted number more than thirty. We are ruled by a score and a half of "little legislatures." Our legislation is conglomerate, not homogeneous. The doings of one and the same Congress are foolish in pieces and wise in spots. They can never, except by accident, have any common features. Some of the Committees are made up of strong men, the majority of them of weak men; and the weak are as influential as the strong. The country can get the counsel and guidance of its ablest representatives only upon one or two subjects; upon the rest it must be content with the impotent service of the feeble. Only a very small part of its most important business can be done well; the system provides for having the rest of it done miserably, and the whole of it taken together done at haphazard. There could be no more interesting problem in the doctrine of chances than that of reckoning the probabilities of there being any common features of principle in the legislation of an opening session. It might lighten and divert the leisure of some ingenious mathematician to attempt the calculation.

It was probably some such reflections as these which suggested the proposal, made not long since in the House, that there should be appointed, along with the usual Standing Committee, a new committee which should be known as the Executive Committee of the House, and should be empowered to examine and sort all the bills reported favorably by the other Standing Committees, and bring them forward in what might seem to it the order of their importance; a committee which should, in short, digest pending measures and guide the House in arranging its order of business. But it is seriously to be doubted whether such an addition to the present organization would do more than tighten the tyranny of committee rule and still further restrict freedom of debate and action. A committee to superintend committees would add very little to the efficiency of the House, and would certainly contribute nothing towards unifying legislation, unless the new committee were to be given the power, not yet thought of, of revising the work of the present Standing Committees. Such an executive committee is not quite the device needed.

Apparently committee government is but one of many experiments in the direction of the realization of an idea best expressed —so far as my reading shows—by John Stuart Mill; and is too much like other experiments to be quite as original and unique as some people would like to believe. There is, said Mr. Mill, a "distinction between the function of *making* laws, for which a numerous popular assembly is radically unfit, and that of *getting good laws made*, which is its proper duty, and cannot be satisfactorily fulfilled by any other authority"; and there is, consequently, "need of a legislative commission, as a permanent part of the constitution of a free country; consisting of a small number of highly-trained political minds, on whom, when parliament has determined that a law shall be made, the task of making it should be devolved; parliament retaining the power of passing or rejecting the bill when drawn up, but not of altering it otherwise than by sending proposed amendments to be dealt with by the commission."[7] It would seem, as I have said, that committee government is one form of the effort, now making by all self-governing peoples, to set up a satisfactory legislative commission somewhat after this order; and it might appear to some as if the proposed executive committee were a slight approximation to that form of the effort which is typified in the legislative functions of the British cabinet. It cannot, of course, be claimed that the forty-eight legislative commissions of the House of Representatives always answer the purpose when the House wants to get good laws made, or that each of them consists invariably of "a small number of highly-trained political minds"; but everybody sees that to say that they fall short of realizing the ideal would be nothing less than hypercritical.

In saying that our committee government has, germinally, some of the features of the British system, in which the ministers of the crown, the cabinet, are chosen from amongst the leaders of the parliamentary majority, and act not only as advisers of the sovereign but also as the great standing committee or "legislative commission" of the House of Commons, guiding its business and digesting its graver matters of legislation, I mean, of course, only that both systems represent the common necessity of setting apart some small body, or bodies, of legislative guides through whom a "big meeting" may get laws made. The difference between our device and the British is that we have a Standing Committee, drawn from both parties, for the consideration of each topic of legislation, whereas our English cousins have but

[7] *Autobiography*, pp. 264, 265.

a single standing committee that is charged with the origination of legislation,—a committee composed of the men who are recognized as the leaders of the party dominant in the state, and who serve at the same time as the political heads of the executive departments of the government.

The British system is perfected party government. No effort is made in the Commons, such as is made in the House of Representatives in the composition of the Committees, to give the minority a share in law-making. Our minorities are strongly represented on the Standing Committees; the minority in the Commons is not represented at all in the cabinet. It is this feature of closely organized party government, whereby the responsibility for legislation is saddled upon the majority, which, as I have already pointed out, gives to the debates and action of parliament an interest altogether denied to the proceedings of Congress. All legislation is made a contest for party supremacy, and if legislation goes wrong, or the majority becomes discontented with the course of policy, there is nothing for it but that the ministers should resign and give place to the leaders of the Opposition, unless a new election should procure for them a recruited following. Under such a system mere silent voting is out of the question; debate is a primary necessity. It brings the representatives of the people and the ministers of the Crown face to face. The principal measures of each session originate with the ministers, and embody the policy of the administration. Unlike the reports of our Standing Committees, which are intended to be simply the digested substance of the more sensible bills introduced by private members, the bills introduced into the House of Commons by the cabinet embody the definite schemes of the government; and the fact that the Ministry is made up of the leaders of the majority and represents always the principles of its party, makes the minority only the more anxious to have a chance to criticise its proposals. Cabinet government is a device for bringing the executive and legislative branches into harmony and cooperation without uniting or confusing their functions. It is as if the majority in the Commons deputized its leaders to act as the advisers of the Crown and the superintendents of the public business, in order that they might have the advantage of administrative knowledge and training in advising legislation and drafting laws to be submitted to parliament. This arrangement enlisted the majority in behalf of successful administration without giving the ministers any power to coerce or arbitrarily influence legislative action. Each session of the Lords and

Commons becomes a grand inquest into the affairs of the empire. The two estates sit as it were in committee on the management of the public business—sit with open doors, and spare themselves no fatigue in securing for every interest represented a full, fair, and impartial hearing.

It is evident why public debate is the very breath of life to such a system. The Ministry's tenure of office depends upon the success of the legislation they urge. If any of their proposals are negatived by parliament, they are bound to accept their defeat as an intimation that their administration is no longer acceptable to the party they represent, and are expected to resign, or to appeal, if they prefer, to the country for its verdict, by exercising their privilege of advising the sovereign to dissolve parliament and issue writs for a new election. It is, consequently, inevitable that the Ministry should be subjected to the most determined attacks and the keenest criticisms of the Opposition, and should be every day of the session put to the task of vindicating their course and establishing anew their claim to the confidence of their party. To shrink from discussion would be to confess weakness; to suffer themselves to be worsted in discussion would be seriously to imperil their power. They must look to it, therefore, not only that their policy be defensible, but that it be valiantly defended also.

As might be expected, then, the Ministry seldom find the task of leading the House an easy one. Their plans are kept under an unceasing fire of criticism from both sides of the House; for there are independent sharp-shooters behind the ministers as well as heavy batteries in front of them; and there are many amongst their professed followers who give aid and comfort to the enemy. There come ever and again showers of stinging questions, too, from friends and foes alike,—questions great and small, direct and indirect, pertinent and impertinent, concerning every detail of administration and every tendency of policy.

But, although the initiative in legislation and the general direction of the business of parliament are the undisputed prerogatives of "the government," as the Ministry is called, they have not, of course, all the time of the House at their disposal. During the session, certain days of each week are set apart for the introduction and debate of bills brought in by private members, who, at the opening of the session, draw lots to decide the precedence of their bills or motions on the orders of the day. If many draw, those who get last choice of time find the session near its end, and private members' days being absorbed by belated government measures, before their opportunity has come, and must content themselves with hoping for better fortune next year; but time is generally found for a very fair and full consideration of a large number of private members' bills, and no member is denied a chance to air his favorite opinions in the House or to try the patience of his fellow-members by annual repetitions of the same proposition. Private members generally find out by long experience, however, that they can exert a more telling influence upon legislation by pressing amendments to government schemes, and can effect more immediate and satisfactory results by keeping the Ministry constantly in mind of certain phases of public opinion, than they could hope to exert or effect by themselves introducing measures upon which their party might hesitate to unite. Living as he does under a system which makes it the minister's wisest policy to allow the utmost freedom of debate, each member can take as prominent a part in the proceedings of the House as his abilities give him title to take. If he have anything which is not merely frivolous to say, he will have repeated opportunities to say it; for the Commons cough down only the bores and the talkers for the sake of talk.

The House of Commons, as well as our House of Representatives, has its committees, even its standing committees, but they are of the old-fashioned sort which merely investigate and report, not of the new American type which originate and conduct legislation. Nor are they appointed by the Speaker. They are chosen with care by a "Committee of Selection" composed of members of both parties. The Speaker is kept carefully apart from politics in all his functions, acting as the impartial, judicial president of the body. "Dignity of presence, courtliness of manner, great physical endurance, courage and impartiality of judgment, a consummate tact, and familiarity, 'born of life-long experience,' with the written and unwritten laws of the House,"—such are the qualities of the ideal Speaker. When he takes the chair he turns his back on partisan alliances and serves both parties alike with even hand. Such are the traditions of the office that its occupant feels himself as strictly bound to unbiased judgment as is the chiefest judge of the realm; and it has become no uncommon thing for a Speaker of tried ability to preside during several successive Parliaments, whether the party to whose suffrages he originally owed his elevation remains in power or no. His political principles do not affect his fitness for judicial functions.

The Commons in session present an interesting picture. Constrained by their habits of debate to sit in quarters suitable for the purpose, they crowd together in a hall of somewhat cramped proportions. It seems a place fit for hand to hand combats. The cushioned benches on which the members sit rise in close series on either side of a wide central aisle which they face. At one end of this aisle is raised the Speaker's chair, below and in front of which, invading the spaces of the aisle, are the desks of the wigged and gowned clerks. On the front benches nearest the Speaker and to his right sit the cabinet ministers, the leaders of the Government; opposite, on the front benches to the Speaker's left, sit the leaders of the Opposition. Behind and to the right of the ministers gather the majority; behind and to the left of their leaders, the minority. Above the rear benches and over the outer aisles of the House, beyond "the bar," hang deep galleries from which the outside world may look down upon the eager contests of the two parties which thus sit face to face with only the aisle between them. From these galleries the fortunate listen to the words of leaders whose names fill the ear of the world.

The organization of the French Assembly is in the main similar to that of the British Commons. Its leaders are the executive officers of the government, and are chosen from the ranks of the legislative majority by the President of the Republic, much as English cabinets are chosen by English sovereigns. They too are responsible for their policy and the acts of their administration to the Chamber which they lead. They, like their British prototypes, are the executive committee of the legislative body, and upon its will their tenure of office depends.

It cannot be said, however, that the proceedings of the French Assembly very closely resemble those of the British Commons. In the hall of the Deputies there are no close benches which face each other, and no two homogeneous parties to strive for the mastery. There are parties and parties, factions and factions, coteries and coteries. There are Bonapartists and Legitimatists, Republicans and Clericals, stubborn reactionists and headlong radicals, stolid conservatives and vindictive destructionists. One hears of the Centre, the Right Centre and the Left Centre, the Right, the Left, the Extreme Right and the Extreme Left. Some of these are, of course, mere factions, mere groups of irreconcilables; but several of them are, on the other hand, numerous and powerful parties upon whose mutual attractions and repulsions depend the formation, the authority, and the duration of cabinets.

Of course, too, there is in a body so made up a great deal of combustible material which the slightest circumstance suffices to kindle into a sudden blaze. The Assembly would not be French if it were not always excitable and sometimes uproarious. Absolute turbulence is so probable a contingency in its economy that a very simple and quickly applicable device is provided for its remedy. Should the deputies lose their heads altogether and become unmanageable, the President may *put on his hat,* and by that sign, unless calm be immediately restored, the sitting is adjourned for one hour, at the expiration of which time it is to be expected that the members may resume the business of the day in a cooler frame of mind. There are other rules of procedure observed in the Chamber which seem to foreign eyes at first sight very novel; but which upon closer examination may be seen to differ from some of the practices of our own House of Representatives in form rather than in essence. In France greater freedom of speech is allowed individual members than is possible under committee government, but recognition is not given to just any one who first gets the floor and catches the presiding officer's eye, as it is in the House of Commons, where none but the ministers are accorded any right of precedence in gaining a hearing. Those who wish to speak upon any pending question "inscribe" their names beforehand on a list in the keeping of the President, and the discussion is usually confined to those members who have "inscribed." When this list has been exhausted, the President takes the sense of the Chamber as to whether the debate shall be closed. The Chamber need not wait, however, to hear all the gentlemen who have put their names upon the list. If *une portion notable* of it tires sooner of the discussion or thinks itself sufficiently informed before all who wish to inform it have spoken, it may demand that the debate be brought to an end. Of course such a demand will not be heeded if it come from only a few isolated members, and even *une portion notable* may not interrupt a speaker with this peremptory call for what we should denominate the previous question, but which the French parliamentarian knows as the *clôture.* A demand for the *clôture* is not debatable. One speech may be made against it, but none in its favor. Unless it meet with very powerful resistance, it is expected to go through of its own weight. Even the *clôture,* however, must give way if a member of the Ministry claims the right to speak; for a minister must always be heard, and after he has spoken, moreover, there must always be allowed one speech in reply. Neither can the *clôture* be pronounced unless a majority of the deputies are present; and in case of doubt as to the will of the Chamber in the matter, after two votes have been taken without eliciting a full-voiced and indubitable assent, the discussion is tacitly suffered to proceed.

These rules are not quite so compulsive and inexorable as are those which sustain the government of our Standing Committees, nor do they seem quite imperative enough for the effectual governance of rampant deputies in their moments of wildest excitement; but they are somewhat more rigid than one would expect to find under a system of ministerial responsibility, the purity of whose atmosphere depends so directly upon a free circulation of debate. They are meant for a body of peculiar habits and a fiery temperament,—a body which is often brought screaming to its feet by the words of a passionate speaker, which is time and again betrayed into stormy disquiet, and which is ever being blown about by every passing wind of excitement. Even in its minor points of observance, the Chamber is essentially un-English. Members do not speak from their seats, as we are accustomed to see members of our public assemblies do, but from the "tribune," which is a conspicuous structure erected near the desks of the President and secretaries,—a box-like stand, closely resembling those narrow, quaintly-fashioned pulpits which are still to be seen in some of the oldest of our American churches. And since deputies must gain its commanding top before they may speak, there are said to be many exciting races for this place of vantage. Sometimes, indeed, very unseemly scenes take place, when several deputies, all equally eager to mount the coveted stand, reach its narrow steps at the same moment and contest the privilege of precedence,—especially if their friends rally in numbers to their assistance.

The British House of Commons and the French Chamber, though so unlike in the elements which compose them, and so dissimilar in their modes of procedure, are easily seen to be alike in constitutional significance, being made close kin by the principle of cabinet government, which they both recognize and both apply in its fullest efficacy. In both England and France a ministry composed of the chief officers of the executive departments are constituted at once the leaders of legislation and the responsible heads of administration,—a binding link between the legislative and executive branches of the government. In this regard these two systems present a strong contrast to our own. They recognize and support simple, straightforward, inartificial party government, under a standing committee of responsible party leaders, bringing legislature and executive side by side in intimate but open coöperation; whilst we, preferring to keep

Congress and the departments at arm's length, permit only a less direct government by party majorities, checking party action by a complex legislative machinery of two score and eight composite, semi-ministerial Committees. The English take their parties straight,—we take ours mixed.

There is another aspect, however, in which all three of these systems are alike. They are alike in their essential purpose, which is to enable a mass meeting of representatives to superintend administration and get good laws made. Congress does not deal so directly with our executive as do the French and English parliaments with theirs, and cannot, therefore, control it quite so effectually; there is a great deal of friction amongst the many wheels of committee government; but, in the long run, Congress is quite as omnipotent as either the Chamber of Deputies or the House of Commons; and, whether there be two score committees with functions mainly legislative, or only one with functions half legislative, half executive, we have one form or another of something like Mr. Mill's "legislative commission."

III.

THE HOUSE OF REPRESENTATIVES.

REVENUE AND SUPPLY.

The highest works of statesmanship require these three things: Great power in the minister, genius to counsel and support him, enlightenment in parliament to weigh and decide upon his plans.—PROFESSOR SEELEY.

When men are not acquainted with each other's principles, nor experienced in each other's talents, nor at all practiced in their mutual habitudes and dispositions by joint efforts of business; no personal confidence, no friendship, no common interest subsisting among them; it is evidently impossible that they can act a public part with uniformity, perseverance, or efficacy.—BURKE.

"It requires," says Mr. Bagehot, "a great deal of time to have opinions," and if one is to judge from the legislative experience of some very enlightened nations, it requires more time to have opinions about finance than about any other subject. At any rate, very few nations have found time to have correct opinions about it. Governments which never consult the governed are usually content with very shabby, short-sighted methods of taxation,—with any methods, indeed, which can be made to yield the desired revenues without much trouble; and the agents of a self-governing people are quite sure to be too busy with elections and party management to have leisure to improve much upon the practices of autocrats in regard to this important care of administration. And yet this subject of finance seems to be interesting enough in a way. It is one of the commonplaces of our history that, ever since long before we came westward across the ocean, we have been readier to fight about taxation than about any other one thing,—than about a good many other things put together, indeed. There are several sadly bloody spots in the financial history of our race. It could probably be shown, however, if one cared to take time to show it, that it is easy to get vexed about mismanagement of the finances without knowing how they might be better managed. What we do not like is that we are taxed,—not that we are stupidly taxed. We do not need to be political economists to get angry about it; and when we have gotten angry about it in the past our rulers have not troubled themselves to study political economy in order to find out the best means of appeasing us. Generally they have simply shifted the burden from the shoulders of those who complained, and were able to make things unpleasant, to the shoulders of those who might complain, but could not give much trouble.

Of course there are some taxes which are much more hateful than others, and have on that account to be laid more circumspectly. All direct taxes are heartily disliked by every one who has to pay them, and as heartily abused, except by those who have never owned an ounce or an inch of property, and have never seen a tax-bill. The heart of the ordinary citizen regards them with an inborn aversion. They are so straightforward and peremptory in their demands. They soften their exactions with not a grain of consideration. The tax-collector, consequently, is never esteemed a lovable man. His methods are too blunt, and his powers too obnoxious. He comes to us, not with a "please," but with a "must." His requisitions always leave our pockets lighter and our hearts heavier. We cannot, for the life of us, help thinking, as we fold up his receipt and put it away, that government is much too expensive a luxury as nowadays conducted, and that that receipt is incontestable documentary proof of unendurable extortion. What we do not realize is, that life would be robbed of one of its chief satisfactions if this occasion of grumbling were to be taken away.

Indirect taxes, on the other hand, offend scarcely anybody. It is one of the open secrets of finance that in almost every system of taxation the indirect overcrow the direct taxes by many millions, and have a knack for levying on the small resources of insignificant persons which direct taxes have never learned. They know how to coax pennies out of poor people whose names have never been on the tax-collector's books. But they are very sly, and have at command a thousand successful disguises. High or complicated tariffs afford them their most frequent and abundant opportunities. Most people have very short thoughts, which do not extend beyond the immediate phenomena of direct vision, and so do not recognize the hand of the government in the high prices charged them in the shops. Very few of us taste the tariff in our sugar; and I suppose that even very thoughtful topers do not perceive the license-tax in their whiskey. There is little wonder that financiers have always been nervous in dealing with direct, but confident and free of hand in laying indirect, taxes.

It may, therefore, be accounted one of the customary advantages which our federal government possesses over the governments of the States, that it has almost always, in ordinary times, derived its entire revenue from prompt and facile indirect taxes, whilst the States have had to live upon the tardy and begrudged income derivable from a direct levy. Since we have had to support two governments it has been widely resolved to let us, as long as possible, feel the weight of only one of them,—and that the one which can get at us most readily, and, at the same time, be most easily and promptly controlled by our votes. It is a plain, convenient, and, on the whole, satisfactory division of domain, though the responsibility which it throws on state legislatures is more apt to pinch and prove vexatious than is that which it lays upon Congress. Mr. Gladstone, the greatest of English financiers, once playfully described direct and indirect taxes as two sisters, —daughters of Necessity and Invention,—"differing only as sisters may differ, . . . the one being more free and open, the other somewhat more shy, retiring, and insinuating"; and frankly owned that, whether from "a lax sense of moral obligation or not," he, as Chancellor of the Exchequer, "thought it not only allowable, but even an act of duty, to pay his addresses to them both." But our chancellors of the exchequer, the chairmen of the Committee of Ways and Means, are bound by other traditions of courtship, and have, besides, usually shown no susceptibility to the charms of the blunt and forward elder of these two sisters. They have been constant, even if now and again a little wayward, in their devotion to the younger.

I suppose that no one ever found the paths of finance less thorny and arduous than have our national publicists. If their tasks be compared with those of European and English financiers, it is plain to see that their lines have fallen in pleasant places. From almost the very first they have had boundless resources to draw upon, and they have certainly of late days had free leave to spend limitless revenues in what extravagances they pleased. It has come to be infinitely more trouble to spend our enormous national income than to collect it. The chief embarrassments have arisen, not from deficits, but from surpluses. It is very fortunate that such has been the case, because for the best management of the finances of a nation, when revenue is scant and economy imperative, it is absolutely necessary to have financial administration in the hands of a few highly-trained and skillful men acting subject to a very strict responsibility, and this is just what our committee system does not allow. As in other matters of legislation, so in finance, we have many masters acting under a very dim and inoperative accountability. Of course under such ministration our financial policy has always been unstable, and has often strayed very far from the paths of wisdom and providence; for even when revenue is superabundant and extravagance easy, irresponsible, fast and loose methods of taxation and expenditure must work infinite harm. The only difference is that during such times the nation is not so sensitive to the ill effects wrought by careless policy. Mismanagement is not generally blamed until a great many people have discovered it by being hurt by it. Meantime, however, it is none the less interesting and important to study our government, with a view to gauging its qualities and measuring accurately its capabilities for good or bad service; and the study can doubtless be much more dispassionately conducted before we have been seriously hurt by foolish, unsteady administration than afterwards. The forces of the wind can be reckoned with much more readily while they are blowing only a gale than after they have thrown a hurricane upon us.

The national income is controlled by one Committee of the House and one of the Senate; the expenditures of the government are regulated by fifteen Committees of the House and five of the Senate; and the currency is cared for by two Committees of the House and one of the Senate; by all of which it appears that the financial administration of the country is in the hands of twenty-four Committees of Congress,—a mechanism of numerous small and great functions, quite complex enough to be worth careful study, perhaps too complex to be studied directly without an aiding knowledge of some simpler system with which it may be compared. Our own budget may be more readily followed through all the vicissitudes of committee scrutiny, and all the varied fortunes of committee action, after one has traced some other budget through the simpler processes of some other system of government.

The British system is, perhaps, in its main features, the simplest in existence. It is, besides, the pattern after which the financial systems of the chief governments of Europe have been modeled, and which we have ourselves in a measure copied; so that by prefacing the study of other systems by a careful examination of the British, in its present form, one may start with the great advantage of knowing the characteristics of what may fairly be called the parent stock. Parliament, then, in the first place, simply controls, it does not originate, measures of financial administration. It acts through the agency and under the guidance of the ministers of the Crown. Early in each annual session "the estimates" are submitted to the Commons, which, when hearing such statements, sits in Committee of the Whole House, known as Committee of Supply. The estimates come before the House in truly formidable shape. Each department presents its estimates in a huge quarto volume, "crammed with figures and minute entries of moneys wanted for the forthcoming year."[1] But the House itself does not have to digest this various and overwhelming mass of figures. The digesting is done in the first instance by the official leaders of the House. "The ministers in charge of the naval and military services lay before the Committee [of Supply] their respective statements of the sums which will be required for the maintenance of those services; and somewhat later in the session a common estimate for the various civil services is submitted also." Those statements are, as it were, condensed synopses of the details of the quartos, and are made with the object of rendering quite clear to the House, sitting under the informal rules of Committee, the policy of the expenditures proposed and the correctness of the calculations upon which they are based. Any member may ask what pertinent questions he pleases of the minister who is making the statement, so that nothing needing elucidation may be passed by without full explanation. After the statement has been completed to the satisfaction of the Committee, a vote is taken, at the motion of the minister, upon each item of expenditure, and the duties of the Committee of Supply have been performed.

The estimates are always submitted "on the collective responsibility of the whole cabinet." "The army and navy estimates

---

[1] *The National Budget, etc.* (English Citizen Series), p. 146. In what I have to say of the English system, I follow this volume, pp. 146-149, and another volume of the same admirable series, entitled *Central Government*, pp. 36-47, most of my quotations being from the latter.

have, as a rule, been considered and settled in cabinet council before being submitted to the House; and the collective responsibility of the Ministry is in this case, therefore, not technical merely, but substantial." If the estimates are resisted and rejected by the Committee, the ministers, of course, resign. They "cannot acquiesce in a refusal on the part of parliament to sanction the expenditure which" they "have assumed the responsibility of declaring necessary for the support of the civil government, and the maintenance of the public credit at home and abroad." The votes in Committee of Supply are, therefore, vital in the history of every administration, being taken as sure indexes of the amount of confidence placed by the House in the government.

But the votes in Committee of Supply are only the first steps in parliament's annual supervision of the public finances. They are simply the spending votes. In order to consider the means by which money is to be raised to meet the outlays sanctioned by the Committee of Supply, the House resolves itself into Committee of the Whole, under the name of the Committee of Ways and Means. It is to this Committee that the Chancellor of the Exchequer submits his budget every year, on or soon before the fifth of April, the date at which the national accounts are made up, the financial year closing on the thirty-first of March. In order to prepare his budget, the Chancellor must of course have early knowledge of the estimates made for the various services. Several months, therefore, before the estimates are laid before the House in Committee of Supply, the various departments are called upon by the Treasury to send in statements of the sums required to defray the expenses of the current year, and these estimates are carefully examined by the Chancellor, with a view not only to exercising his duty of keeping the expenditures within the limits of economy, but also to ascertaining how much revenue he will have to secure in order to meet the proper expenditure contemplated. He must balance estimated needs over against estimated resources, and advise the House in Committee of Ways and Means as to the measures by which taxation is to be made to afford sufficient revenue. Accordingly he calls in the aid of the permanent heads of the revenue departments who furnish him with "their estimates of the public revenue for the ensuing year, upon the hypothesis that taxation will remain unchanged."

Having with such aids made up his budget, the Chancellor goes before the Committee of Ways and Means prepared to give a clear history of the financial administration of the year just closed, and to submit definite plans for adjusting the taxation and providing for the expected outlays of the year just opening. The precedents of a wise policy of long standing forbid his proposing to raise any greater revenue than is absolutely necessary for the support of the government and the maintenance of the public credit. He therefore never asks the Committee to lay taxes which promise a considerable surplus. He seeks to obtain only such an overplus of income as will secure the government against those slight errors of underestimation of probable expenses or of overestimation of probable revenue as the most prudent of administrations is liable to make. If the estimated revenue considerably exceed the estimated expenses, he proposes such remissions of taxation as will bring the balance as near equality as prudence will permit; if the anticipated expenses run beyond the figure of the hoped-for revenue, he asks that certain new taxes be laid, or that certain existing taxes be increased; if the balance between the two sides of the forecast account shows a pretty near approach to equilibrium, so the scale of revenue be but a little the heavier of the two, he contents himself with suggesting such a readjustment of existing taxes as will be likely to distribute the burden of taxation more equitably amongst the taxpaying classes, or facilitate hampered collections by simplifying the complex methods of assessment and imposition.

Such is the budget statement to which the House of Commons listens in Committee of Ways and Means. This Committee may deal with the proposals of the Chancellor of the Exchequer with somewhat freer hand than the Committee of Supply may use in passing upon the estimates. The Ministry is not so stiffly insistent upon having its budget sanctioned as it is upon having its proposed expenditures approved. It is understood to pledge itself to ask for no more money than it honestly needs; but it simply advises with the House as to the best way of raising that money. It is punctiliously particular about being supplied with the funds it asks for, but not quite so exacting as to the ways and means of supply. Still, no Ministry can stand if the budget be rejected out of hand, or if its demands for the means of meeting a deficiency be met with a flat refusal, no alternative means being suggested by the Opposition. Such votes would be distinct declarations of a want of confidence in the Ministry, and would of course force them to resign.

The Committee of Ways and Means, then, carries out, under the guidance of the Chancellor of the Exchequer, the resolutions of the Committee of Supply. The votes of the latter Committee, authorizing the expenditures mapped out in the estimates, are embodied in "a resolution proposed in Committee of Ways and Means for a general grant out of the Consolidated Fund 'towards making good the supply granted to Her Majesty' "; and that resolution, in order that it may be prepared for the consideration of the House of Lords and the Crown, is afterwards cast by the House into the form of a Bill, which passes through the regular stages and in due course becomes law. The proposals of the Chancellor of the Exchequer with reference to changes in taxation are in like manner embodied in resolutions in Committee of Ways and Means, and subsequently, upon the report of the Committee, passed by the House in the shape of Bills. "Ways and Means Bills" generally pass the Lords without trouble. The absolute control of the Commons over the subjects of revenue and supply has been so long established that the upper House would not now dream of disputing it; and as the power of the Lords is simply a privilege to accept or reject a money bill as a whole, including no right to amend, the peers are wont to let such bills go through without much scrutiny.

But so far I have spoken only of that part of parliament's control of the finances which concerns the future. The "Ways and Means Bills" provide for coming expenses and a prospective revenue. Past expenses are supervised in a different way. There is a double process of audit by means of a special Audit Department of the Civil Service, which is, of course, a part of the permanent organization of the administration, having it in charge "to examine the accounts and vouchers of the entire expenditure," and a special committee nominated each year by the House "to audit the Audit Department." This committee is usually made up of the most experienced business men in the Commons, and before it "all the accounts of the completed financial year are passed in review." "Minute inquiries are occasionally made by it into the reasons why certain items of expenditure have occurred; it discusses claims for compensation, grants, and special disbursements, in addition to the ordinary outgoings of the department, mainly, to be sure, upon the information and advice of the departments themselves, but still with a certain independence of view and judgment which must be valuable."

The strictness and explicitness with which the public accounts are kept of course greatly facilitate the process of audit. The balance which is struck on the thirty-first of every March is of the most definite sort. It deals only with the actual receipts and disbursements of the completed fiscal year. At that date all unexpended credits lapse. If the expenditure of certain sums has been sanctioned by parliamentary vote, but some of the granted moneys remain undrawn when April comes in, they can be used only after a regrant by the Commons. There are, therefore, no unclosed accounts to obscure the view of the auditing authorities. Taxes and credits have the same definite period, and there are no arrears or unexpended balances to confuse the book-keeping. The great advantages of such a system in the way of checking extravagances which would otherwise be possible, may be seen by comparing it with the system in vogue in France, in whose national balance-sheet "arrears of taxes in one year overlap with those of other years," and "credits old jostle credits new," so that it is said to be "always three or four years before the nation can know what the definitive expenditure of a given year is."

For the completion of this sketch of financial administration under the Commons it is of course necessary to add a very distinct statement of what I may call the *accessibility* of the financial officers of the government. They are always present to be questioned. The Treasury department is, as becomes its importance, exceptionally well represented in the House. The Chancellor of the Exchequer, the working chief of the department, is invariably a member of the Commons, "and can be called to account by interrogation or motion with respect to all matters of Treasury concern"—with respect, that is, to well-nigh "the whole sphere of the discipline and economy of the Executive Government"; for the Treasury has wide powers of supervision over the other departments in all matters which may in any way involve an outlay of public money. "And not only does the invariable presence of the Chancellor of the Exchequer in the House of Commons make the representation of that department peculiarly direct, but, through the Secretary of the Treasury, and, with respect to certain departmental matters, through the Junior Lords, the House possesses peculiar facilities for ascertaining and expressing its opinion upon the details of Treasury administration." It has its responsible servants always before it, and can obtain what glimpses it pleases into the inner workings of the departments which it wishes to control.

It is just at this point that our own system of financial administration differs most essentially from the systems of England, of the Continent, and of the British colonial possessions. Congress does not come into direct contact with the financial officers of the government. Executive and legislature are separated by a hard and fast line, which sets them apart in what was meant to be independence, but has come to amount to isolation. Correspondence between them is carried on by means of written communications, which, like all formal writings, are vague, or by means of private examinations of officials in committee-rooms to which the whole House cannot be audience. No one who has read official documents needs to be told how easy it is to conceal the essential truth under the apparently candid and all-disclosing phrases of a voluminous and particularizing report; how different those answers are which are given with the pen from a private office from those which are given with the tongue when the speaker is looking an assembly in the face. It is sufficiently plain, too, that resolutions which call upon officials to give testimony before a committee are a much clumsier and less efficient means of eliciting information than is a running fire of questions addressed to ministers who are always in their places in the House to reply publicly to all interrogations. It is reasonable to conclude, therefore, that the House of Representatives is much less intimately acquainted with the details of federal Treasury affairs than is such a body as the House of Commons, with the particulars of management in the Treasury which it oversees by direct and constant communication with the chief Treasury officials.

This is the greater drawback in our system, because, as a further result of its complete separation from the executive, Congress has to originate and perfect the budget for itself. It does not hear the estimates translated and expounded in condensed statements by skilled officials who have made it their business, because it is to their interest, to know thoroughly what they are talking about; nor does it have the benefit of the guidance of a trained, practical financier when it has to determine questions of revenue. The Treasury is not consulted with reference to problems of taxation, and motions of supply are disposed of with no suggestions from the departments beyond an itemized statement of the amounts needed to meet the regular expenses of an opening fiscal year.

In federal book-keeping the fiscal year closes on the thirtieth of June. Several months before that year expires, however, the estimates for the twelve months which are to succeed are made ready for the use of Congress. In the autumn each department and bureau of the public service reckons its pecuniary needs for the fiscal year which is to begin on the following first of July (making explanatory notes, and here and there an interjected prayer for some unwonted expenditure, amongst the columns of figures), and sends the resulting document to the Secretary of the Treasury. These reports, including of course the estimates of the various bureaux of his own department, the Secretary has printed in a thin quarto volume of some three hundred and twenty-five pages, which for some reason or other, not quite apparent, is called a "Letter from the Secretary of the Treasury transmitting estimates of appropriations required for the fiscal year ending June 30," . . . and which boasts a very distinct arrangement under the heads Civil Establishment, Military Establishment, Naval Establishment, Indian Affairs, Pensions, Public Works, Postal Service, etc., a convenient summary of the chief items, and a complete index.

In December this "Letter" is sent, as a part of the Secretary of the Treasury's annual report to Congress, to the Speaker of the House of Representatives, immediately after the convening of that body, and is referred to the Standing Committee on Appropriations. The House itself does not hear the estimates read; it simply passes the thin quartos over to the Committee; though, of course, copies of it may be procured and studied by any member who chooses to scrutinize the staring pages of columned figures with the dutiful purpose of keeping an eye upon the uses made of the public revenue. Taking these estimates into consideration, the Committee on Appropriations found upon them the "general appropriation bills," which the rules require them to report to the House "within thirty days after their appointment, at every session of Congress, commencing on the first Monday in December," unless they can give satisfactory reasons in writing for not doing so. The "general appropriation bills" provide separately for legislative, executive, and judicial expenses; for sundry civil expenses; for consular and diplomatic expenses; for the Army; for the Navy; for the expenses of the Indian department; for the payment of invalid and other pensions; for the support of the Military Academy; for fortifications; for the service of the Post-Office department, and for mail transportation by ocean steamers.

It was only through the efforts of a later-day spirit of vigilant economy that this practice of making the appropriations for each of the several branches of the public service in a separate bill was established. During the early years of the Constitution very loose methods of appropriation prevailed. All the moneys for the year were granted in a single bill, entitled "An Act making Appropriations for the support of the Government"; and there was no attempt to specify the objects for which they were to be spent. The gross sum given could be applied at the discretion of the heads of the executive departments, and was always large enough to allow much freedom in the undertaking of new schemes of administration, and in the making of such additions to the clerical force of the different offices as might seem convenient to those in control. It was not until 1862 that the present practice of somewhat minutely specifying the uses to be made of the funds appropriated was reached, though Congress had for many years been by slow stages approaching such a policy. The history of appropriations shows that "there has been an increasing tendency to limit the discretion of the executive departments, and bring the details of expenditure more immediately under the annual supervision of Congress"; a tendency which has specially manifested itself since the close of the recent war between the States.[2] In this, as in other things, the appetite for government on the part of Congress has grown with that perfection of organization which has rendered the gratification of its desire for power easily attainable. In this matter of appropriations, however, increased care has unquestionably resulted in a very decided curtailment of extravagance in departmental expenditure, though Congress has often shown a blind ardor for retrenchment which has fallen little short of parsimony, and which could not have found place in its legislation had it had such adequate means of confidential communication with the executive departments as would have enabled it to understand their real needs, and to discriminate between true economy and those scant allowances which only give birth to deficiencies, and which, even under the luckiest conditions, serve only for a very brief season to create the impression which they are usually meant to beget,—that the party in power is the party of thrift and honesty, seeing in former appropriations too much that was corrupt and spendthrift, and desiring to turn to the good ways of wisdom and frugality.

There are some portions of the public expenditure which do not depend upon the annual gifts of Congress, but which are provided for by statutes which run without limit of date. These are what are known as the "permanent appropriations." They cover, on the one hand, such indeterminate charges as the interest on the public debt, the amounts annually paid into the sinking fund, the outlays of refunding, the interest on the bonds

[2] See an article entitled "National Appropriations and Misappropriations," by the late President Garfield, *North American Review*, pp. 578 *et seq.*

issued to the Pacific Railways; and, on the other hand, such specific charges as the maintenance of the militia service, the costs of the collection of the customs revenue, and the interest on the bequest to the Smithsonian Institution. Their aggregate sum constitutes no insignificant part of the entire public expense. In 1880, in a total appropriation of about $307,000,000, the permanent appropriations fell short of the annual grant by only about sixteen and a half millions. In later years, however, the proportion has been smaller, one of the principal items, the interest on the public debt, becoming, of course, continually less as the debt is paid off, and other items reaching less amounts, at the same time that the figures of the annual grants have risen rather than fallen.

With these permanent grants the Committee on Appropriations has, of course, nothing to do, except that estimates of the moneys to be drawn under authority of such grants are submitted to its examination in the Secretary of the Treasury's "Letter," along with the estimates for which special appropriations are asked. Upon these latter estimates the general appropriations are based. The Committee may report its bills at any stage of the House's business, provided only that it does not interrupt a member who is speaking; and these bills when reported may at any time, by a majority vote, be made a special order of the day. Of course their consideration is the most imperative business of the session. They must be passed before the end of June, else the departments will be left altogether without means of support. The chairman of the Committee on Appropriations is, consequently, a very masterful authority in the House. He can force it to a consideration of the business of his Committee at almost any time; and by withholding his reports until the session is well advanced can crowd all other topics from the docket. For much time is spent over each of the "general appropriation bills." The spending of money is one of the two things that Congress invariably stops to talk about; the other being the raising of money. The talk is made always in Committee of the Whole, into which the House at once resolves itself whenever appropriations are to be considered. While members of this, which may be called the House's Committee of Supply, representatives have the freest opportunity of the session for activity, for usefulness, or for meddling, outside the sphere of their own committee work. It is true that the " 'five-minutes' rule" gives each speaker in Committee of the Whole scant time for the expression of his views, and that the House can refuse to accord full freedom of debate to its other self, the

Committee of the Whole, by limiting the time which it is to devote to the discussion of matters referred to it, or by providing for its discharge from the further consideration of any bill committed to it, after it shall have acted without debate on all amendments pending or that may be offered; but as a rule every member has a chance to offer what suggestions he pleases upon questions of appropriation, and many hours are spent in business-like debate and amendment of such bills, clause by clause and item by item. The House learns pretty thoroughly what is in each of its appropriation bills before it sends it to the Senate.

But, unfortunately, the dealings of the Senate with money bills generally render worthless the painstaking action of the House. The Senate has been established by precedent in the very freest possible privileges of amendment as regards these bills no less than as regards all others. The Constitution is silent as to the origination of bills appropriating money. It says simply that "all bills for *raising revenue* shall originate in the House of Representatives," and that in considering these "the Senate may propose or concur with amendments as on other bills" (Art. I., Sec. VII.); but, "by a practice as old as the Government itself, the constitutional prerogative of the House has been held to apply to all the general appropriation bills,"[3] and the Senate's right to amend these has been allowed the widest conceivable scope. The upper house may add to them what it pleases; may go altogether outside of their original provisions and tack to them entirely new features of legislation, altering not only the amounts but even the objects of expenditure, and making out of the materials sent them by the popular chamber measures of an almost totally new character. As passed by the House of Representatives, appropriation bills generally provide for an expenditure considerably less than that called for by the estimates; as returned from the Senate, they usually propose grants of many additional millions, having been brought by that less sensitive body up almost, if not quite, to the figures of the estimates.

After passing their ordeal of scrutiny and amendment in the Senate, the appropriation bills return with their new figures to the House. But when they return it is too late for the House to put them again into the crucible of Committee of the Whole. The session, it may be taken for granted, was well on towards its middle age before they were originally introduced by the House Committee on Appropriations; after they reached the Senate they were referred to its corresponding Committee; and the report of

[3] Senator Hoar's article, already several times quoted.

that Committee upon them was debated at the leisurely length characteristic of the weightier proceedings of the upper chamber; so that the last days of the session are fast approaching when they are sent down to the House with the work of the Senate's hand upon them. The House is naturally disinclined to consent to the radical alterations wrought by the Senate, but there is no time to quarrel with its colleague, unless it can make up its mind to sit through the heat of midsummer, or to throw out the bill and accept the discomforts of an extra session. If the session be the short one, which ends, by constitutional requirement, on the 4th of March, the alternative is the still more distasteful one of leaving the appropriations to be made by the next House.

The usual practice, therefore, is to adjust such differences by means of a conference between the two Houses. The House rejects the Senate's amendments without hearing them read; the Senate stoutly refuses to yield; a conference ensues, conducted by a committee of three members from each chamber; and a compromise is effected, by such a compounding of disagreeing propositions as gives neither party to the quarrel the victory, and commonly leaves the grants not a little below the amounts asked for by the departments. As a rule, the Conference Committee consists, on the part of the House, of the chairman of its Committee on Appropriations, some other well-posted member of that Committee, and a representative of the minority. Its reports are matters of highest prerogative. They may be brought in even while a member is speaking. It is much better to silence a speaker than to delay for a single moment, at this stage of the session, the pressing, imperious question of the supplies for the support of the government. The report is, therefore, acted upon immediately and in a mass, and is generally adopted without debate. So great is the haste that the report is passed upon before being printed, and without giving any one but the members of the Conference Committee time to understand what it really contains. There is no chance of remark or amendment. It receives at once sanction or rejection as a whole; and the chances are, of course, in favor of its being accepted, because to reject it would but force a new conference and bring fresh delays.

It is evident, therefore, that after all the careful and thorough-going debate and amendment of Committee of the Whole in the House, and all the grave deliberation of the Senate to which the general appropriations are subjected, they finally pass in a very chaotic state, full of provisions which neither the House nor the Senate likes, and utterly vague and unintelligible to every one save the members of the Conference Committee; so that it would seem almost as if the generous portions of time conscientiously given to their consideration in their earlier stages had been simply time thrown away.

The result of the under-appropriation to which Congress seems to have become addicted by long habit in dealing with the estimates, is, of course, the addition of another bill to the number of the regular annual grants. As regularly as the annual session opens there is a Deficiency Bill to be considered. Doubtless deficiencies frequently arise because of miscalculations or extravagance on the part of the departments; but the most serious deficiencies are those which result from the close-fistedness of the House Committee on Appropriations, and the compromise reductions which are wrung from the Senate by conference committees. Every December, consequently, along with the estimates for the next fiscal year, or at a later period of the session in special communications, come estimates of deficiencies in the appropriations for the current year, and the apparent economies of the grants of the preceding session have to be offset in the gifts of the inevitable Deficiency Bill. It is as if Congress had designedly established the plan of making semi-annual appropriations. At each session it grants part of the money to be spent after the first of July following, and such sums as are needed to supplement the expenditures previously authorized to be made after the first of July preceding. It doles out their allowances in installments to its wards, the departments.

It is usual for the Appropriations Committees of both Houses, when preparing the annual bills, to take the testimony of the directing officers of the departments as to the actual needs of the public service in regard to all the principal items of expenditure. Having no place upon the floor of the House, and being, in consequence, shut out from making complete public statements concerning the estimates, the heads of the several executive departments are forced to confine themselves to private communications with the House and Senate Committees. Appearing before those Committees in person, or addressing them more formally in writing, they explain and urge the appropriations asked in the "Letter" containing the estimates. Their written communications, though addressed only to the chairman of one of the Committees, frequently reach Congress itself, being read in open session by some member of the Committee in order to justify or interpret the items of appropriation proposed in a pending bill. Not infrequently the head of a department exerts himself to secure desired supplies by dint of negotiation with individual members of the Committee, and by repeated and insistent private appeals to their chairman.

Only a very small part of the relations between the Committees and the departments is a matter of rule. Each time that the estimates come under consideration the Committees must specially seek, or the departments newly volunteer, information and advice. It would seem, however, that it is now less usual for the Committees to ask than for the Secretaries to offer counsel and suggestion. In the early years of the government it was apparently not uncommon for the chairman of spending committees to seek out departmental officials in order to get necessary enlightenment concerning the mysteries of the estimates, though it was often easier to ask for than to get the information wanted. An amusing example of the difficulties which then beset a committee-man in search of such knowledge is to be found in the private correspondence of John Randolph of Roanoke. Until 1865 the House Committee of Ways and Means, which is one of the oldest of the Standing Committees, had charge of the appropriations; it was, therefore, Mr. Randolph's duty, as chairman of that Committee in 1807, to look into the estimates, and he thus recounts, in an interesting and exceedingly characteristic letter to his intimate friend and correspondent, Nicholson, this pitiful experience which he had had in performing that duty: "I called some time since at the navy office to ask an explanation of certain items of the estimate for this year. The Secretary called upon his chief clerk, who knew very little more of the business than his master. I propounded a question to the head of the department; he turned to the clerk like a boy who cannot say his lesson, and with imploring countenance beseeches aid; the clerk with much assurance gabbled out some commonplace jargon, which I could not take for sterling; an explanation was required, and both were dumb. This pantomime was repeated at every item, until, disgusted and ashamed for the degraded situation of the principal, I took leave without pursuing the subject, seeing that my object could not be attained. There was not one single question relating to the department that the Secretary could answer."[4] It is to be hoped that the Secretaries of to-day are somewhat better versed in the affairs of their departments than was respectable Robert Smith, or, at any rate, that they have chief clerks who can furnish inquiring chairmen with something better than commonplace jargon which no shrewd man can take for sterling information; and it is al-

4 Adams's *John Randolph*. American Statesman Series, pp. 210, 211.

together probable that such a scene as the one just described would nowadays be quite impossible. The book-keeping of later years has been very much stricter and more thorough than it was in the infancy of the departments; the estimates are much more thoroughly differentiated and itemized; and a minute division of labor in each department amongst a numerous clerical force makes it comparatively easy for the chief executive officers to acquaint themselves quickly and accurately with the details of administration. They do not wait, therefore, as a general thing, to be sought out and questioned by the Committees, but bestir themselves to get at the ears of the committee-men, and especially to secure, if possible, the influence of the chairmen in the interest of adequate appropriations.

These irregular and generally informal communications between the Appropriations Committees and the heads of the departments, taking the form sometimes of pleas privately addressed by the Secretaries to individual members of the Committees, and again of careful letters which find their way into the reports laid before Congress, stand in our system in the place of the annual financial statements which are in British practice made by the ministers to parliament, under circumstances which constitute very full and satisfactory public explanations and the freest replies to all pertinent questions invariable features of the supervision of the finances by the Commons. Our ministers make their statements to both Houses indirectly and piecemeal, through the medium of the Committees. They are mere witnesses, and are in no definite way responsible for the annual appropriations. Their secure four-year tenure of office is not at all affected by the treatment the estimates receive at the hands of Congress. To see our cabinet officers resign because appropriations had been refused for the full amount asked for in the Secretary of the Treasury's "Letter" would be as novel in our eyes as would be, in the view of our English cousins, the sight of a Ministry of the Crown remaining in office under similar circumstances. Indeed, were our cabinets to stake their positions upon the fortunes of the estimates submitted to Congress, we should probably suffer the tiresome inconvenience of yearly resignations; for even when the heads of the departments tax all their energies and bring into requisition all their arts of persuasion to secure ample grants from the Committees, the House Committee cuts down the sums as usual, the Senate Committee adds to them as before, and the Conference Committee strikes a deficient compromise balance according to time-honored custom.

There is in the House another appropriations committee besides the Committee on Appropriations. This is the Committee on Rivers and Harbors, created in December, 1883, by the Forty-eighth Congress, as a sharer in the too great prerogatives till then enjoyed by the Committee on Commerce. The Committee on Rivers and Harbors represents, of course, the lately-acquired permanency of the policy of internal improvements. Until 1870 that policy had had a very precarious existence. Strenuously denied all tolerance by the severely constitutional Presidents of the earlier days, it could not venture to declare itself openly in separate appropriations which offered an easy prey to the watchful veto, but skulked in the unobtrusive guise of items of the general grants, safe under the cover of respectable neighbor items. The veto has never been allowed to seek out single features in the acts submitted to the executive eye, and even such men as Madison and Monroe, stiff and peremptory as they were in the assertion of their conscientious opinions, and in the performance of what they conceived to be their constitutional duty, and much as they disapproved of stretching the Constitution to such uses as national aid to local and inland improvements, were fain to let an occasional gift of money for such purposes pass unforbidden rather than throw out the general appropriation bill to which it was tacked. Still, Congress did not make very frequent or very flagrant use of this trick, and schemes of internal improvement came altogether to a standstill when faced by President Jackson's imperious disfavor. It was for many years the settled practice of Congress to grant the States upon the seaboard leave to lay duties at their ports for the improvement of the harbors, and itself to undertake the expense of no public works save those upon territory actually owned by the United States. But in later years the relaxation of presidential opposition and the admission of new States lying altogether away from the sea, and, therefore, quite unwilling to pay the tariffs which were building up the harbors of their eastern neighbors without any recompensing advantage to themselves who had no harbors, revived the plans which the vetoes of former times had rebuffed, and appropriations from the national coffers began freely to be made for the opening of the great water highways and the perfecting of the sea-gates of commerce. The inland States were silenced, because satisfied by a share in the benefits of national aid, which, being no longer indirect, was not confined to the sanctioning of state tariffs which none but the sea-board commonwealths could benefit by, but which consumers everywhere had to pay.

The greatest increase in appropriations of this class took place just after 1870. Since that date they have occupied a very prominent place in legislation, running from some twelve millions in the session of 1873–4 up and down through various figures to eighteen millions seven hundred thousand in the session of 1882–3, constituting during that decade the chief business of the Committee on Commerce, and finally having a special Standing Committee erected for their superintendence. They have thus culminated with the culmination of the protective tariff, and the so-called "American system" of protective tariffs and internal improvements has thus at last attained to its perfect work. The same prerogatives are accorded this new appropriations committee which have been secured to the greater Committee which deals with the estimates. Its reports may be made at any time when a member is not speaking, and stand in all respects upon the same footing as the bills proposing the annual grants. It is a special spending committee, with its own key to the Treasury.

But the Appropriation Committees of the two Houses, though, strictly speaking, the only committees of supply, have their work increased and supplemented by the numerous Committees which devote time and energy to creating demands upon the Treasury. There is a pension list in the estimates for whose payment the Committee on Appropriations has to provide every year; but the Committee on Pensions is constantly manufacturing new claims upon the public revenues.[5] There must be money forthcoming to build the new ships called for by the report of the Committee on Naval Affairs, and to meet the charges for the army equipment and reforms recommended by the Committee on Military Affairs. There are innumerable fingers in the budget pie.

It is principally in connection with appropriations that what has come to be known in our political slang as "log-rolling" takes place. Of course the chief scene of this sport is the private room of the Committee on Rivers and Harbors, and the season of its highest excitement, the hours spent in the passage of the River

[5] On one occasion "the House passed thirty-seven pension bills at one sitting. The Senate, on its part, by unanimous consent, took up and passed in about ten minutes seven bills providing for public buildings in different States, appropriating an aggregate of $1,200,000 in this short time. A recent House feat was one in which a bill, allowing 1,300 war claims in a lump, was passed. It contained one hundred and nineteen pages full of little claims, amounting in all to $291,-000; and a member, in deprecating criticism on this disposition of them, said that the Committee had received ten huge bags full of such claims, which had been adjudicated by the Treasury officials, and it was a physical impossibility to examine them."–N. Y. Sun, 1881.

and Harbor Bill. "Log-rolling" is an exchange of favors. Representative A. is very anxious to secure a grant for the clearing of a small water-course in his district, and representative B. is equally solicitous about his plans for bringing money into the hands of the contractors of his own constituency, whilst representative C. comes from a sea-port town whose modest harbor is neglected because of the treacherous bar across its mouth, and representative D. has been blamed for not bestirring himself more in the interest of schemes of improvement afoot amongst the enterprising citizens of his native place; so it is perfectly feasible for these gentlemen to put their heads together and confirm a mutual understanding that each will vote in Committee of the Whole for the grants desired by the others, in consideration of the promise that they will cry "aye" when his item comes on to be considered. It is not out of the question to gain the favoring ear of the reporting Committee, and a great deal of tinkering can be done with the bill after it has come into the hands of the House. Lobbying and log-rolling go hand in hand.

So much for estimates and appropriations. All questions of revenue are in their first stages in the hands of the House Committee of Ways and Means, and in their last, in charge of the Senate Committee on Finance. The name of the House Committee is evidently borrowed from the language of the British Parliament; the English Committee of Ways and Means is, however, the Commons itself sitting in Committee of the Whole to consider the statement and proposals of the Chancellor of the Exchequer, whilst ours is a Standing Committee of the House composed of eleven members, and charged with the preparation of all legislation relating to the raising of the revenue and to providing ways and means for the support of the government. We have, in English parliamentary phrase, put our Chancellorship of the Exchequer into commission. The chairman of the Committee figures as our minister of finance, but he really, of course, only represents the commission of eleven over which he presides.

All reports of the Treasury department are referred to this Committee of Ways and Means, which also, like the Committee on Appropriations, from time to time holds other more direct communications with the officers of revenue bureaux. The annual reports of the Secretary of the Treasury are generally quite full of minute information upon the points most immediately connected with the proper duties of the Committee. They are explicit with regard to the collection and disbursement of the revenues, with regard to the condition of the public debt, and with regard to the operation of all laws governing the financial policy of the departments. They are, in one aspect, the great yearly balance sheets, exhibiting the receipts and expenditures of the government, its liabilities and its credits; and, in another aspect, general views of the state of industry and of the financial machinery of the country, summarizing the information compiled by the bureau of statistics with reference to the condition of the manufactures and of domestic trade, as well as with regard to the plight of the currency and of the national banks. They are, of course, quite distinct from the "Letters" of the Secretary of the Treasury, which contain the estimates, and go, not to the Committee of Ways and Means, but to the Committee on Appropriations.

Though the duties of the Committee of Ways and Means in supervising the management of the revenues of the country are quite closely analogous to those of the British Chancellor of the Exchequer, the lines of policy in which they walk are very widely separated from those which he feels bound to follow. As I have said, the object which he holds constantly in view is to keep the annual balances as nearly as possible at an equilibrium. He plans to raise only just enough revenue to satisfy the grants made in Committee of Supply, and leave a modest surplus to cover possible errors in the estimates and probable fluctuations in the returns from taxation. Our Committee of Ways and Means, on the other hand, follow a very different policy. The revenues which they control are raised for a double object. They represent not only the income of the government, but also a carefully erected commercial policy to which the income of the government has for many years been incidental. They are intended to foster the manufactures of the country as well as to defray the expenses of federal administration. Were the maintenance of the government and the support of the public credit the chief objects of our national policy of taxation, it would undoubtedly be cast in a very different pattern. During a greater part of the lifetime of the present government, the principal feature of that policy has been a complex system of duties on imports, troublesome and expensive of collection, but nevertheless yielding, together with the license taxes of the internal revenue which later years have seen added to it, immense surpluses which no extravagances of the spending committees could exhaust. Duties few, small, and comparatively inexpensive of collection would afford abundant revenues for the efficient conduct of the government, besides comporting much more evidently with economy in financial administration. Of course, if vast revenues pour in over the barriers of an exacting and exorbitant tariff, amply sufficient revenues would flow in through the easy conduits of moderate and simple duties. The object of our financial policy, however, has not been to equalize receipts and expenditures, but to foster the industries of the country. The Committee of Ways and Means, therefore, do not concern themselves directly with regulating the income of the government—they know that that, in every probable event, will be more than sufficient—but with protecting the interests of the manufacturers as affected by the regulation of the tariff. The resources of the government are made incidental to the industrial investments of private citizens.

This evidently constitutes a very capital difference between the functions of the Chancellor of the Exchequer and those of our Committee of Ways and Means. In the policy of the former the support of the government is everything; with the latter the care of the industries of the country is the beginning and the end of duty. In the eyes of parliament enormous balances represent ignorant or improper management on the part of the ministers, and a succession of them is sure to cast a cabinet from office, to the lasting disgrace of the Chancellor of the Exchequer; but to the mind of Congress vast surpluses are indicative of nothing in particular. They indicate of course abundant returns from the duties, but the chief concern is, not whether the duties are fruitful, but whether they render the trades prosperous. Commercial interests are the essential consideration; excess of income is a matter of comparative indifference. The points of view characteristic of the two systems are thus quite opposite: the Committee of Ways and Means subordinates its housekeeping duties to its much wider extra-governmental business; the Chancellor of the Exchequer subordinates everything to economical administration.

This is evidently the meaning of the easy sovereignty, in the practice of the House, of questions of supply over questions of revenue. It is imperative to grant money for the support of the government, but questions of revenue revision may be postponed without inconvenience. The two things do not necessarily go hand in hand, as they do in the Commons. The reports of the Committee of Ways and Means are matters of quite as high privilege as the reports of the Committee on Appropriations, but they by no means stand an equal chance of gaining the consideration of the House and reaching a passage. They have no inseparable connection with the annual grants; the needed supplies will be forthcoming without any readjustments of taxation to meet the anticipated demands, because the taxes are not laid in the first instance with reference to the expenses which are to be paid out of their proceeds. If it were the function of the Committee of Ways and Means, as it is of the Chancellor of the Exchequer, to adjust the revenue to the expenditures, their reports would be as essential a part of the business of each session as are the reports of the Committee on Appropriations; but their proposals, occupying, as they do, a very different place in legislation, may go to the wall just as the proposals of the other Committees do at the demand of the chairman of the great spending Committee. The figures of the annual grants do not run near enough to the sum of the annual receipts to make them at all dependent on bills which concern the latter.

It would seem that the supervision exercised by Congress over expenditures is more thorough than that which is exercised by the Commons in England. In 1814 the House created a Standing Committee on Public Expenditures whose duty it should be "to examine into the state of the several public departments, and particularly into laws making appropriations of money, and to report whether the moneys have been disbursed conformably with such laws; and also to report from time to time such provisions and arrangements as may be necessary to add to the economy of the departments and the accountability of their officers"; but this Committee stood as the only committee of audit for but two years. It was not then abolished, but its jurisdiction was divided amongst six other Committees on Expenditures in the several departments, to which was added in 1860 a seventh, and in 1874 an eighth. There is thus a separate Committee for the audit of the accounts of each of the executive departments, beside which the original single Committee on Public Expenditures stands charged with such duties as may have been left it in the general distribution.[6] The duties of these eight Committees are specified with great minuteness in the rules. They are "to examine into the state of the accounts and expenditures respectively submitted to them, and to inquire and report particularly," whether the expenditures

---

[6] Congress, though constantly erecting new Committees, never gives up old ones, no matter how useless they may have become by subtraction of duties. Thus there is not only the superseded Committee on Public Expenditures but the Committee on Manufactures also, which, when a part of the one-time Committee on Commerce and Manufactures, had plenty to do, but which, since the creation of a distinct Committee on Commerce, has had nothing to do, having now, together with the Committee on Agriculture and Indian Affairs, no duties assigned to it by the rules. It remains to be seen whether the Committee on Commerce will suffer a like eclipse because of the gift of its principal duties to the new Committee on Rivers and Harbors.

of the respective departments are warranted by law; "whether the claims from time to time satisfied and discharged by the respective departments are supported by sufficient vouchers, establishing their justness both as to their character and amount; whether such claims have been discharged out of funds appropriated therefor, and whether all moneys have been disbursed in conformity with appropriation laws; and whether any, or what, provisions are necessary to be adopted, to provide more perfectly for the proper application of the public moneys, and to secure the government from demands unjust in their character or extravagant in their amount." Besides exercising these functions of careful audit, they are, moreover, required to "report from time to time" any plans for retrenchment that may appear advisable in the interests of economy, or any measures that may be necessary to secure greater efficiency or to insure stricter accountability to Congress in the management of the departments; to ferret out all abuses that may make their appearance; and to see to it that no department has useless offices in its bureaux, or over or under-paid officers on its rolls.

But, though these Committees are so many and so completely armed with powers, indications are not wanting that more abuses run at large in the departments than they, with all their eyes, are able to detect. The Senate, though it has no similar permanent committees, has sometimes discovered dishonest dealings that had altogether escaped the vigilance of the eight House Committees; and even these eight occasionally, by a special effort, bring to light transactions which would never have been unearthed in the ordinary routine course of their usual procedure. It was a select committee of the Senate which, during the sessions of the Forty-seventh Congress, discovered that the "contingent fund" of the Treasury department had been spent in repairs on the Secretary's private residence, for expensive suppers spread before the Secretary's political friends, for lemonade for the delectation of the Secretary's private palate, for bouquets for the gratification of the Secretary's busiest allies, for carpets never delivered, "ice" never used, and services never rendered;[7] although these were secrets of which the honest faces of the vouchers submitted with the accounts gave not a hint.

[7] See the report of this Committee, which was under the chairmanship of Senator Windom.

An illustration of what the House Committees find by special effort may be seen in the revelations of the investigation of the expenses of the notorious "Star Route Trials" made by the Forty-eighth Congress's Committee on Expenditures in the department of Justice.

It is hard to see how there could have been anything satisfactory or conclusive in the annual supervision of the public accounts during any but the latest years of this system of committee audit. Before 1870 our national book-keeping was much like that still in vogue in France. Credits once granted ran on without period until they were exhausted. There were always unexpended balances to confuse the accounts; and when the figures of the original grants had been on a too generous scale, as was often the case, these balances accumulated from year to year in immense surpluses, sometimes of many millions, of whose use no account was given, and which consequently afforded means for all sorts of extravagance and peculation. In 1870 this abuse was partially corrected by a law which limited such accumulations to a period of two years, and laid hands, on behalf of the Treasury, on the $174,000,000 of unexpended balances which had by that time been amassed in the several departments; but it was not till 1874 that such a rule of expenditure and accounting was established as would make intelligent audit by the Committees possible, by a proper circumscription of the time during which credits could be drawn upon without a regrant.[8]

Such is a general view, in brief and without technical detail, of the chief features of our financial system, of the dealings of Congress with the questions of revenue, expenditure, and supply. The contrast which this system offers to the old-world systems, of which the British is the most advanced type, is obviously a very striking one. The one is the very opposite of the others. On the one hand is a financial policy regulated by a compact, coöperative ministry under the direction of a representative chamber, and on the other hand a financial policy directed by the representative body itself, with only clerical aid from the executive. In our practice, in other words, the Committees are the ministers, and the titular ministers only confidential clerks. There is no concurrence, not even a nominal alliance, between the several sections of this committee-ministry, though their several duties are clearly very nearly akin and as clearly mutually dependent. This feature of disintegration in leadership runs, as I have already pointed out, through all our legislation; but it is manifestly of much more serious consequence in financial administration than in the direction of other concerns of government. There can be no doubt that, if it were not for the fact that our revenues

[8] See General Garfield's article, already once quoted, *North American Review*, vol. 128, p. 583.

are not regulated with any immediate reference to the expenditures of the government, this method of spending according to the suggestions of one body, and taxing in obedience to the suggestions of another entirely distinct, would very quickly bring us into distress; it would unquestionably break down under any attempt to treat revenue and expenditure as mutually adjustable parts of a single, uniform, self-consistent system. They can be so treated only when they are under the management of a single body; only when all financial arrangements are based upon schemes prepared by a few men of trained minds and accordant principles, who can act with easy agreement and with perfect confidence in each other. When taxation is regarded only as a source of revenue and the chief object of financial management is the graduation of outlays by income, the credit and debit sides of the account must come under a single eye to be properly balanced; or, at the least, those officers who raise the money must see and be guided by the books of those who spend it.

It cannot, therefore, be reasonably regarded as matter of surprise that our financial policy has been without consistency or coherency, without progressive continuity. The only evidences of design to be discovered in it appear in those few elementary features which were impressed upon it in the first days of the government, when Congress depended upon such men as Hamilton and Gallatin for guidance in putting the finances into shape. As far as it has any invariable characteristics, or any traceable heredity, it is the handiwork of the sagacious men who first presided over the Treasury department. Since it has been altogether in the hands of congressional Committees it has so waywardly shifted from one rôle to another, and has with such erratic facility changed its principles of action and its modes of speech, to suit the temper and tastes of the times, that one who studies it hardly becomes acquainted with it in one decade before he finds that that was a season quite apart from and unlike both those which went before and those which succeeded. At almost every session Congress has made some effort, more or less determined, towards changing the revenue system in some essential portion; and that system has never escaped radical alteration for ten years together. Had revenue been graduated by the comparatively steady standard of the expenditures, it must have been kept stable and calculable; but depending, as it has done, on a much-debated and constantly fluctuating industrial policy, it has been regulated in accordance with a scheme which has passed through as many phases as there have been vicissitudes and vagaries in the fortunes of commerce and the tactics of parties.

This is the more remarkable because upon all fiscal questions Congress acts with considerable deliberation and care. Financial legislation usually, if not always, occupies by far the most prominent place in the business of each session. Though other questions are often disposed of at odd moments, in haste and without thought, questions of revenue and supply are always given full measure of debate. The House of Representatives, under authority of the Rule before referred to, which enables it, as it were, to project the previous question into Committee of the Whole, by providing for the discharge of that Committee from the further consideration of any bill that is in its hands, or that may be about to be referred to it, after all amendments "pending and that may be offered" shall have been acted upon without debate, seldom hesitates, when any ordinary business is to be considered, to forbid to the proceedings of Committee of the Whole all freedom of discussion, and, consequently, almost all discussion as to the action to be taken; but this muzzle is seldom put upon the mouth of the Committee when appropriation or tariff bills are to be considered, unless the discussion in Committee wanders off into fields, quite apart from the proper matter of the measure in hand, in which case the House interposes to check the irrelevant talk. Appropriation bills have, however, as I have shown, a much higher privilege than have bills affecting the tariff, and instances are not wanting in which the chairman of the Committee on Appropriations has managed to engross the time of the House in the disposal of measures prepared by his Committee, to the entire exclusion of any action whatever on important bills reported by the Committee of Ways and Means after the most careful and laborious deliberation. His prerogatives are never disputed in such a contest for consideration between a supply and a revenue bill, because these two subjects do not, under our system, necessarily go hand in hand. Ways and Means bills may and should be acted upon, but Supply bills must be.

It should be remarked in this connection, moreover, that much as Congress talks about fiscal questions, whenever permitted to do so by the selfish Appropriations Committee, its talk is very little heeded by the big world outside its halls. The noteworthy fact, to which I have already called attention, that even the most thorough debates in Congress fail to awaken any genuine or active interest in the minds of the people, has had its most striking illustrations in the course of our financial legislation; for, though the discussions which have taken place in Congress upon financial questions have been so frequent, so protracted, and so thorough, engrossing so large a part of the time of the House on their every recurrence, they seem, in almost every instance, to have made scarcely any impression at all upon the public mind. The Coinage Act of 1873, by which silver was demonetized, had been before the country many years, ere it reached adoption, having been time and again considered by Committees of Congress, time and again printed and discussed in one shape or another, and having finally gained acceptance apparently by sheer persistence and importunity. The Resumption Act of 1875, too, had had a like career of repeated considerations by Committees, repeated printings, and a full discussion by Congress; and yet when the "Bland Silver Bill" of 1878 was on its way through the mills of legislation, some of the most prominent newspapers of the country declared with confidence that the Resumption Act had been passed inconsiderately and in haste, almost secretly indeed; and several members of Congress had previously complained that the demonetization scheme of 1873 had been pushed surreptitiously through the courses of its passage, Congress having been tricked into accepting it, doing it scarcely knew what.

This indifference of the country to what is said in Congress, pointing, as it obviously does, to the fact that, though the Committees lead in legislation, they lead without concert or responsibility, and lead nobody in particular, that is, no compact and organized party force which can be made accountable for its policy, has also a further significance with regard to the opportunities and capacities of the constituencies. The doubt and confusion of thought which must necessarily exist in the minds of the vast majority of voters as to the best way of exerting their will in influencing the action of an assembly whose organization is so complex, whose acts are apparently so haphazard, and in which responsibility is spread so thin, throws constituencies into the hands of local politicians who are more visible and tangible than are the leaders of Congress, and generates, the while, a profound distrust of Congress as a body whose actions cannot be reckoned beforehand by any standard of promises made at elections or any programmes announced by conventions. Constituencies can watch and understand a few banded leaders who display plain purposes and act upon them with promptness; but they cannot watch or understand forty odd Standing Committees, each of which goes its own way in doing what it can without any special regard to the pledges of either of the parties from which its membership is drawn. In short, we lack in our political life the conditions most essential for the formation of an active and effective public opinion. "The characteristics of a nation capable of public opinion," says Mr. Bagehot, most sagacious of political critics, "is that . . . parties will be *organized*; in each there will be a leader, in each there will be some looked up to, and many who look up to them; the opinion of the party will be formed and suggested by the few, it will be criticised and accepted by the many."[9] And this is just the sort of party organization which we have not. Our parties have titular leaders at the polls in the persons of candidates, and nominal creeds in the resolutions of conventions, but no select few in whom to trust for guidance in the general policy of legislation, or to whom to look for suggestions of opinion. What man, what group of men, can speak for the Republican party or for the Democratic party? When our most conspicuous and influential politicians say anything about future legislation, no one supposes that they are speaking for their party, as those who have authority; they are known to speak only for themselves and their small immediate following of colleagues and friends.

The present relations between Congress and public opinion remind us of that time, in the reign of George III., when "the bulk of the English people found itself powerless to control the course of English government," when the government was divorced from "that general mass of national sentiment on which a government can alone safely ground itself." Then it was that English public opinion, "robbed as it was of all practical power, and thus stripped of the feeling of responsibility which the consciousness of power carries with it," "became ignorant and indifferent to the general progress of the age, but at the same time . . . hostile to Government because it was Government, disloyal to the Crown, averse from Parliament. For the first and last time . . . Parliament was unpopular, and its opponents secure of popularity."[10] Congress has in our own day become divorced from the "general mass of national sentiment," simply because there is no means by which the movements of that national sentiment can readily be registered in legislation. Going about as it does to please all sorts of Committees composed of all sorts of men,—the dull and the acute, the able and the cunning, the honest and the careless,— Congress evades judgment by avoiding all coherency of plan in

[9] *Essays on Parliamentary Reform.*
[10] Green's *History of the English People*, vol. iv., pp. 202, 203.

its action. The constituencies can hardly tell whether the works of any particular Congress have been good or bad; at the opening of its sessions there was no determinate policy to look forward to, and at their close no accomplished plans to look back upon. During its brief lifetime both parties may have vacillated and gone astray, policies may have shifted and wandered, and untold mischief, together with some good, may have been done; but when all is reviewed, it is next to impossible oftentimes to distribute justly the blame and the praise. A few stubborn committee-men may be at the bottom of much of the harm that has been wrought, but they do not represent their party, and it cannot be clear to the voter how his ballot is to change the habits of Congress for the better. He distrusts Congress because he feels that he cannot control it.

The voter, moreover, feels that his want of confidence in Congress is justified by what he hears of the power of corrupt lobbyists to turn legislation to their own uses. He hears of enormous subsidies begged and obtained; of pensions procured on commission by professional pension solicitors; of appropriations made in the interest of dishonest contractors; and he is not altogether unwarranted in the conclusion that these are evils inherent in the very nature of Congress, for there can be no doubt that the power of the lobbyist consists in great part, if not altogether, in the facility afforded him by the Committee system. He must, in the natural course of things, have many most favorable opportunities for approaching the great money-dispensing Committees. It would be impracticable to work up his schemes in the broad field of the whole House, but in the membership of a Committee he finds manageable numbers. If he can gain the ear of the Committee, or of any influential portion of it, he has practically gained the ear of the House itself; if his plans once get footing in a committee report, they may escape criticism altogether, and it will, in any case, be very difficult to dislodge them. This accessibility of the Committees by outsiders gives to illegitimate influences easy approach at all points of legislation, but no Committees are affected by it so often or so unfortunately as are the Committees which control the public moneys. They are naturally the ones whose favor is oftenest and most importunately, as well as most insidiously, sought; and no description of our system of revenue, appropriation, and supply would be complete without mention of the manufacturers who cultivate the favor of the Committee of Ways and Means, of the interested persons who walk attendance upon the Committee on Rivers and Harbors, and of the mail-contractors and subsidy-seekers who court the Committee on Appropriations.

My last point of critical comment upon our system of financial administration I shall borrow from a perspicacious critic of congressional methods who recently wrote thus to one of the best of American journals: "So long as the debit side of the national account is managed by one set of men, and the credit side by another set, both sets working separately and in secret, without any public responsibility, and without any intervention on the part of the executive official who is nominally responsible; so long as these sets, being composed largely of new men every two years, give no attention to business except when Congress is in session, *and thus spend in preparing plans the whole time which ought to be spent in public discussion of plans already matured*, so that an immense budget is rushed through without discussion in a week or ten days,—just so long the finances will go from bad to worse, no matter by what name you call the party in power. No other nation on earth attempts such a thing, or could attempt it without soon coming to grief, our salvation thus far consisting in an enormous income, with practically no drain for military expenditure."[11] Unquestionably this strikes a very vital point of criticism. Congress spends its time working, in sections, at preparing plans, instead of confining itself to what is for a numerous assembly manifestly the much more useful and proper function of debating and revising plans prepared beforehand for its consideration by a commission of skilled men, old in political practice and in legislative habit, whose official life is apart from its own, though dependent upon its will. Here, in other words, is another finger pointing to Mr. Mill's question as to the best "legislative commission." Our Committees fall short of being the best form of commission, not only in being too numerous but also in being integral parts of the body which they lead, having no life apart from it. Probably the best working commission would be one which should make plans for government independently of the representative body, and in immediate contact with the practical affairs of administration, but which should in all cases look to that body for the sanctioning of those plans, and should be immediately responsible to it for their success when put into operation.

11 'G. B." in N. Y. *Nation*, Nov. 30, 1882.

IV.

THE SENATE.

This is a Senate, a Senate of equals, of men of individual honor and personal character, and of absolute independence. We know no masters, we acknowledge no dictators. This is a hall for mutual consultation and discussion, not an arena for the exhibition of champions.—DANIEL WEBSTER.

The Senate of the United States has been both extravagantly praised and unreasonably disparaged, according to the predisposition and temper of its various critics. In the eyes of some it has a stateliness of character, an eminency of prerogative, and, for the most part, a wisdom of practice such as no other deliberative body possesses; whilst in the estimation of others it is now, whatever it may have been formerly, but a somewhat select company of leisurely "bosses," in whose companionship the few men of character and high purpose who gain admission to its membership find little that is encouraging and nothing that is congenial. Now of course neither of these extreme opinions so much as resembles the uncolored truth, nor can that truth be obtained by a judicious mixture of their milder ingredients. The truth is, in this case as in so many others, something quite commonplace and practical. The Senate is just what the mode of its election and the conditions of public life in this country make it. Its members are chosen from the ranks of active politicians, in accordance with a law of natural selection to which the state legislatures are commonly obedient; and it is probable that it contains, consequently, the best men that our system calls into politics. If these best men are not good, it is because our system of government fails to attract better men by its prizes, not because the country affords or could afford no finer material.

It has been usual to suppose that the Senate was just what the Constitution intended it to be; that because its place in the federal system was exalted the aims and character of its members would naturally be found to be exalted as well; that because its term was long its foresight would be long also; or that because its election was not directly of the people demagogy would find no life possible in its halls. But the Senate is in fact, of course, nothing more than a part, though a considerable part, of the public service, and if the general conditions of that service be such as to starve statesmen and foster demagogues, the Senate itself will be full of the latter kind, simply because there are no others available. There cannot be a separate breed of public men reared specially for the Senate. It must be recruited from the lower branches of the representative system, of which it is only the topmost part. No stream can be purer than its sources. The Senate can have in it no better men than the best men of the House of Representatives; and if the House of Representatives attract to itself only inferior talent, the Senate must put up with the same sort. I think it safe to say, therefore, that, though it may not be as good as could be wished, the Senate is as good as it can be under the circumstances. It contains the most perfect product of our politics, whatever that product may be.

In order to understand and appreciate the Senate, therefore, one must know the conditions of public life in this country. What are those conditions? Well, in the first place, they are not what they were in the early years of the federal government; they are not what they were even twenty years ago; for in this, as in other things, the war between the States ends one distinct period and opens another. Between the great constructive statesmen of the revolutionary days and the reconstructing politicians of the sixties there came into public place and legislative influence a great race of constitutional lawyers. The questions which faced our statesmen while the Constitution was a-making were in the broadest sense questions of politics; but the questions which dominated our public life after the federal government had been successfully set up were questions of legal interpretation such as only lawyers could grapple with. All matters of policy, all doubts of legislation, even all difficulties of diplomacy, were measured by rules of constitutional construction. There was hardly a single affair of public concern which was not hung upon some peg of constitutional dogma in the testing-rooms of one or another of the contending schools of constitutional interpretation. Constitutional issues were ever the tides, questions of administrative policy seldom more than the eddies, of politics.

The Republicans under Jefferson drew their nourishment from constitutional belief no less than did the Federalists; the Whigs and Democrats of a later day lived on what was essentially the same diet, though it was served in slightly different forms; and the parties of to-day are themselves fain to go to these cooks of the olden time whenever they desire strong meat to fortify them against their present debility. The great questions attending the admission of new States to the Union and the annexation of foreign territory, as well as all the controversies which came in the train of the contest over slavery and the reserved powers of the States, were of the Constitution constitutional; and what other questions were then living—save those which found root in the great charter's implied powers, about which there was such constant noise of debate? It will be remembered that very few publicists opposed internal improvements, for instance, on the ground that they were unwise or uncalled for. No one who took a statesmanlike view of the matter could fail to see that the opening up of the great water-ways of the country, the construction of roads, the cutting of canals, or any public work which might facilitate inter-State commerce by making inter-course between the various portions of the Union easy and rapid, was sanctioned by every consideration of wisdom, as being in conformity with a policy at once national in its spirit and universal in its benefits. The doubt was, not as to what it would be best and most provident to do, but as to what it would be law-ful to do; and the chief opponents of schemes of internal improve-ment based their dissent upon a careful meditation of the lan-guage of the Constitution. Without its plain approval they would not move, even if they had to stand still all their days.

It was, too, with many professions of this spirit that the tariff was dealt with. It ran suddenly to the front as a militant party question in 1833, not as if a great free-trade movement had been set afoot which was to anticipate the mission of Cobden and Bright, but as an issue between federal taxation and the consti-tutional privileges of the States. The agricultural States were being, as they thought, very cruelly trodden down under the iron heel of that protectionist policy to whose enthronement they had themselves consented, and they fetched their hope of escape from the Constitution. The federal government unquestionably pos-sessed, they admitted, and that by direct grant of the funda-mental law, the right to impose duties on imports; but did that right carry with it the privilege of laying discriminating duties for other purposes than that of raising legitimate revenue? Could the Constitution have meant that South Carolina might be taxed to maintain the manufactures of New England?

Close upon the heels of the great tariff controversy of that time came the stupendous contest over the right of secession and the abolition of slavery; and again in this contest, as in all that had gone before, the party which was being hard driven sought refuge in the Constitution. This too was, in its first stages at least, a lawyer's question. It eventually slipped out of all lawyerly con-trol, and was given over to be settled by the stern and savage processes of war; but it stayed with the constitutional lawyers as long as it could, and would have stayed with them to the end had it not itself been bigger than the Constitution and mixed with such interests and such passions as were beyond the control of legislatures or of law courts.

Such samples of the character which political questions have hitherto borne in this country are sufficient to remind all readers of our history of what have been the chief features of our politics, and may serve, without further elaboration, to illustrate the point I wish to emphasize. It is manifest how such a course of politics would affect statesmanship and political leadership. While questions affecting the proper construction of the Constitution were the chief and most imperative questions pressing for settlement, great lawyers were in demand; and great lawyers were, accordingly, forthcoming in satisfaction of the demand. In a land like ours, where litigation is facilitated by the establishment of many open and impartial courts, great lawyers are a much more plentiful product than great administrators, unless there be also some extraordinary means for the encouragement of administrative talents. We have, accordingly, always had plenty of excellent lawyers, though we have often had to do without even tolerable administrators, and seem destined to endure the inconvenience of hereafter doing without any constructive statesmen at all. The constitutional issues of former times were so big and so urgent that they brought great advocates into the field, despite all the tendencies there were in our system towards depriving leadership of all place of authority. In the presence of questions affecting the very structure and powers of the federal government, parties had to rally with definite purpose and espouse a distinct creed; and when the maintenance or overthrow of slavery had ceased to be a question of constitutional right, and had become a matter of contention between sentiment and vested rights,—between interested and passionate feeling,—there was of course a hot energy of contest between two compact hosts and a quick elevation of forceful leaders.

The three stages of national growth which preceded the war between the States were each of them creative of a distinct class of political leaders. In the period of erection there were great architects and master-builders; in the period of constitutional interpretation there were, at a distance from the people, great political schoolmen who pondered and expounded the letter of the law, and, nearer the people, great constitutional advocates who cast the doctrines of the schoolmen into policy; and in the period of abolitionist agitation there were great masters of feeling and leaders of public purpose. The publicists of the second period kept charge of the slavery question, as I have said, as long as they could, and gave place with bitter reluctance to the anti-slavery orators and pro-slavery champions who were to talk the war-feeling into a flame. But it was of course inevitable that the new movement should have new leaders. It was essentially revolutionary in its tone and in its designs, and so quite out of the reach of those principles of action which had governed the policy of the older school of politicians. Its aim was to change, not to vindicate, the Constitution. Its leaders spoke, not words of counsel, but words of passion and of command. It was a crusade, not a campaign; the impetuous movement of a cause, not the canvass of a mooted measure. And, like every big, stirring cause, it had its leaders—leaders whose authority rested upon the affections and sympathies of the people rather than upon any attested wisdom or success of statesmanship. The war was the work, mediately, of philanthropists; and the reconstructions which followed the war were the hasty strokes of these same un-balanced knights of the crusade, full of bold feeling, but not of steady or far-sighted judgment.

The anti-slavery movement called forth leaders who, from the very nature of their calling, were more picturesque than any who had figured on the national stage since the notable play of the Revolution had gone off the boards; but it was no better cast in leading parts than had been the drama which immediately pre-ceded it. When the constitution of a self-governing people is be-ing consciously moulded by the rapid formation of precedent dur-ing the earliest periods of its existence, there are sure to be an-tagonistic beliefs, distinct and strong and active enough to take shape in the creeds of energetic parties, each led by the greatest advocates of its cherished principles. The season of our consti-tutional development, consequently, saw as fine a race of states-men at the front of national affairs as have ever directed the civil policy of the country; and they, in turn, gave place to men brave to encounter the struggles of changed times, and fit to solve the doubts of a new set of events.

Since the war, however, we have come into a fourth period of national life, and are perplexed at finding ourselves denied a new order of statesmanship to suit the altered conditions of govern-ment. The period of federal construction is long passed; questions of constitutional interpretation are no longer regarded as of press-ing urgency; the war has been fought, even the embers of its issues being now almost extinguished; and we are left to that un-exciting but none the less capitally important business of everyday peaceful development and judicious administration to whose execution every nation in its middle age has to address itself with what sagacity, energy, and prudence it can command. It cannot be said that these new duties have as yet raised up any men eminently fit for their fulfillment. We have had no great administrators since the opening of this newest stage, and there is as yet no visible sign that any such will soon arise. The forms of government in this country have always been unfavorable to the easy elevation of talent to a station of paramount authority; and those forms in their present crystallization are more unfavorable than ever to the toleration of the leadership of the few, whilst the questions now most prominent in politics are not of such a nature as to compel skilled and trustworthy champions to come into the field, as did the constitutional issues and revolutionary agitations of other days. They are matters of a too quiet, business-like sort to enlist feeling or arouse enthusiasm.

It is, therefore, very unfortunate that only feeling or enthusiasm can create recognized leadership in our politics. There is no office set apart for the great party leader in our government. The powers of the Speakership of the House of Representatives are too cramped and covert; the privileges of the chairmanships of the chief Standing Committees are too limited in scope; the presidency is too silent and inactive, too little like a premiership and too much like a superintendency. If there be any one man to whom a whole party or a great national majority looks for guiding counsel, he must lead without office, as Daniel Webster did, or in spite of his office, as Jefferson and Jackson did. There must be something in the times or in the questions which are abroad to thrust great advocates or great masters of purpose into a non-official leadership, which is theirs because they represent in the greatest actions of their lives some principle at once vital and widely loved or hated, or because they possess in their unrivaled power of eloquent speech the ability to give voice to some such living theme. There must be a cause to be advanced which is greater than the trammels of governmental forms, and which, by authority of its own imperative voice, constitutes its advocates the leaders of the nation, though without giving them official title—without need of official title. No one is authorized to lead by reason of any official station known to our system. We call our real leaders by no names but their own: Mr. Webster was always Mr. Webster and never Prime Minister.

In a country which governs itself by means of a public meeting, a Congress or a Parliament, a country whose political life is representative, the only real leadership in governmental affairs must be legislative leadership—ascendency in the public meeting which decides everything. The leaders, if there be any, must be those who suggest the opinions and rule the actions of the representative body. We have in this country, therefore, no real leadership; because no man is allowed to direct the course of Congress, and there is no way of governing the country save through Congress, which is supreme. The chairman of a great Committee like the Committee of Ways and Means stands, indeed, at the sources of a very large and important stream of policy, and can turn that stream at his pleasure, or mix what he will with its waters; but there are whole provinces of policy in which he can have no authority at all. He neither directs, nor can often influence, those other chairmen who direct all the other important affairs of government. He, though the greatest of chairmen, and as great, it may be, as any other one man in the whole governmental system, is by no means at the head of the government. He is, as he feels every day, only a big wheel where there are many other wheels, some almost as big as he, and all driven, like himself, by fires which he does not kindle or tend.

In a word, we have no supreme executive ministry, like the great "Ministry of the Crown" over sea, in whose hands is the general management of legislation; and we have, consequently, no great prizes of leadership such as are calculated to stimulate men of strong talents to great and conspicuous public services. The Committee system is, as I have already pointed out, the very opposite of this. It makes all the prizes of leadership small, and nowhere gathers power into a few hands. It cannot be denied that this is in ordinary times, and in the absence of stirring themes, a great drawback, inasmuch as it makes legislative service unattractive to minds of the highest order, to whom the offer of really great place and power at the head of the governing assembly, the supreme council of the nation, would be of all things most attractive. If the presidency were competitive,—if it could be won by distinguished congressional service,—who can doubt that there would be a notable influx of talents into Congress and a significant elevation of tone and betterment of method in its proceedings; and yet the presidency is very far from being equal to a first-rate premiership.

There is, I know, one distinctive feature of legislative leadership which makes it seem to some not altogether to be desired; though it scarcely constitutes such an objection as to make no leadership at all seem preferable. It is the leadership of orators;

it is the ascendency of those who have a genius for talking. In the eyes of those who do not like it it, seems a leadership of artful dialecticians, the success of tricks of phrase, the victory of rushing declamation—government, not by the advice of statesmanlike counselors, but by the wagging of ready tongues. Macaulay pointed out with his accustomed force of statement just the fact which haunts those who hold to such objections. The power of speaking, he said, which is so highly prized by politicians in a popular government, "may exist in the highest degree without judgment, without fortitude, without skill in reading the characters of men or the signs of the times, without any knowledge of the principles of legislation or of political economy, and without any skill in diplomacy or in the administration of war. Nay, it may well happen that those very intellectual qualities which give peculiar charm to the speeches of a public man may be incompatible with the qualities which would fit him to meet a pressing emergency with promptitude and firmness. It was thus with Charles Townshend. It was thus with Windham. It was a privilege to listen to those accomplished and ingenious orators. But in a perilous crisis they would be found inferior in all the qualities of rulers to such a man as Oliver Cromwell, who talked nonsense, or as William the Silent, who did not talk at all."

Nevertheless, it is to be observed that neither Windham nor Townshend rose to places of highest confidence in the assembly which they served, and which they charmed by their attractive powers of speech; and that Cromwell would have been as unfit to rule anything but an autocratic commonwealth as would have been William the Silent to be anything but a Dutch governor. The people really had no voice in Cromwell's government. It was absolute. He would have been as much out of place in a representative government as a bull in a china shop. We would not have a Bismarck if we could.

Every species of government has the defects of its own qualities. Representative government is government by advocacy, by discussion, by persuasion, and a great, miscellaneous voting population is often misled by deceitful pleas and swayed by unwise counsels. But if one were to make a somewhat freer choice of examples than Macaulay permitted himself, it would be easy to multiply the instances of ruling orators of our race who have added to their gifts of eloquence conspicuous sagacity in the administration of affairs. At any rate, the men who have led popular assemblies have often been, like Hampden, rarely endowed with judgment, foresight, and steadfastness of purpose; like Walpole, amazingly quick in "reading the characters of men and the signs of the times"; like Chatham, masterful in ordering the conquests and the policies of the world; like Burke, learned in the profoundest principles of statecraft; like Canning, adroit in diplomacy; like Pitt, safe in times of revolution; like Peel, sagacious in finance; or, like Gladstone, skilled in every branch of political knowledge and equal to any strain of emergency.

It is natural that orators should be the leaders of a self-governing people. Men may be clever and engaging speakers, such as are to be found, doubtless, at half the bars of the country, without being equipped even tolerably for any of the high duties of the statesman; but men can scarcely be orators without that force of character, that readiness of resource, that clearness of vision, that grasp of intellect, that courage of conviction, that earnestness of purpose, and that instinct and capacity for leadership which are the eight horses that draw the triumphal chariot of every leader and ruler of free men. We could not object to being ruled again by such men as Henry and Otis and Samuel Adams; but they were products of revolution. They were inspired by the great causes of the time; and the government which they set up has left us without any ordinary, peaceful means of bringing men like them into public life. We should like to have more like them, but the violent exercise of revolution is too big a price to pay for them. Some less pungent diet is to be desired for the purpose of giving health to our legislative service. There ought to be some quiet, effective tonic, some mild stimulant, such as the certain prospect of winning highest and most honorable office, to infuse the best talent of the nation into our public life.

These, then, are the conditions of public life which make the House of Representatives what it is, a disintegrate mass of jarring elements, and the Senate what it is, a small, select, and leisurely House of Representatives. Or perhaps it would be nearer the whole truth to say that these are the circumstances and this the frame of government of which the two Houses form a part. Were the Senate not supplied principally by promotions from the House, —if it had, that is, a membership made up of men specially trained for its peculiar duties,—it would probably be much more effective than it is in fulfilling the great function of instructive and business-like debate of public questions; for its duties are enough unlike those of the House to be called peculiar. Men who have acquired all their habits in the matter of dealing with legislative measures in the House of Representatives, where committee work is everything and public discussion nothing but "talking to the country," find themselves still mere declaimers when they get into the Senate, where no previous question utters its interrupting voice from the tongues of tyrannical committee-men, and where, consequently, talk is free to all.[1] Only superior talents, such as very few men possess, could enable a Representative of goln [long] training to change his spots upon entering the Senate. Most men will not fit more than one sphere in life; and after they have been stretched or compressed to the measure of that one they will rattle about loosely or stick too tight in any other into which they may be thrust. Still, more or less adjustment takes place in every case. If a new Senator knock about too loosely amidst the free spaces of the rules of that august body, he will assuredly have some of his biggest corners knocked off and his angularities thus made smoother; if he stick fast amongst the dignified courtesies and punctilious observances of the upper chamber, he will, if he stick long enough, finally wear down to such a size, by jostling, as to attain some motion more or less satisfactory.

But it must be said, on the other hand, that even if the Senate were made up of something better than selections from the House, it would probably be able to do little more than it does in the way of giving efficiency to our system of legislation. For it has those same radical defects of organization which weaken the House. Its functions also, like those of the House, are segregated in the prerogatives of numerous Standing Committees.[2] In this regard Congress is all of a piece. There is in the Senate no more opportunity than exists in the House for gaining such recognized party leadership as would be likely to enlarge a man by giving him a sense of power, and to steady and sober him by filling him with a grave sense of responsibility. So far as its organization controls it, the Senate, notwithstanding the one or two special excellences which make it more temperate and often more rational than the House, has no virtue which marks it as of a different nature. Its proceedings bear most of the charac-

---

[1] An attempt was once made to bring the previous question into the practices of the Senate, but it failed of success, and so that imperative form of cutting off all further discussion has fortunately never found a place there.

[2] As regards all financial measures indeed committee supervision is specially thorough in the Senate. "All amendments to general appropriation bills reported from the Committees of the Senate, proposing new items of appropriation, shall, one day before they are offered, be referred to the Committee on Appropriations, and all general appropriation bills shall be referred to said Committee; and in like manner amendments to bills making appropriations for rivers and harbors shall be again referred to the Committee to which such bills shall be referred." —Senate Rule 30.

teristic features of committee rule.[3] Its conclusions are suggested now by one set of its members, now by another set, and again by a third; an arrangement which is of course quite effective in its case, as in that of the House, in depriving it of that leadership which is valuable in more ways than in imparting distinct purpose to legislative action, because it concentrates party responsibility, attracts the best talents, and fixes public interest.

Some Senators are, indeed, seen to be of larger mental stature and built of stauncher moral stuff than their fellow-members, and it is not uncommon for individual members to become conspicuous figures in every great event in the Senate's deliberations. The public now and again picks out here and there a Senator who seems to act and to speak with true instinct of statesmanship and who unmistakably merits the confidence of colleagues and of people. But such a man, however eminent, is never more than *a* Senator. No one is *the* Senator. No one may speak for his party as well as for himself; no one exercises the special trust of acknowledged leadership. The Senate is merely a body of individual critics, representing most of the not very diversified types of a society substantially homogeneous; and the weight of every criticism uttered in its chamber depends upon the weight of the critic who utters it, deriving little if any addition to its specific gravity from connection with the designs of a purposeful party organization. I cannot insist too much upon this defect of congressional government, because it is evidently radical. Leadership with authority over a great ruling party is a prize to attract great competitors, and is in a free government the only prize that will attract great competitors. Its attractiveness is abundantly illustrated in the operations of the British system. In England, where members of the Cabinet, which is merely a Committee of the House of Commons, are the rulers of the empire, a career in the Commons is eagerly sought by men of the rarest gifts, because a career there is the best road, is indeed the only road, to membership of the great Committee. A part in the life of Congress, on the contrary, though the best career opened to men of ambition by our system, has no prize at its end greater than membership of some one of numerous Committees, between which there is some choice, to be sure, because some of them have great and others only small jurisdictions, but none of which has the distinction of supremacy in policy or of recognized au-

[3] The twenty-nine Standing Committees of the Senate are, however, chosen by ballot, not appointed by the Vice-President, who is an appendage, not a member, of the Senate.

thority to do more than suggest. And posts upon such Committees are the highest posts in the Senate just as they are in the House of Representatives.

In an address delivered on a recent occasion,[4] in the capacity of President of the Birmingham and Midland Institute, Mr. Froude, having in mind, of course, British forms of government, but looking mediately at all popular systems, said very pointedly that "In party government party life becomes like a court of justice. The people are the judges, the politicians the advocates, who," he adds caustically rather than justly, "only occasionally and by accident speak their real opinions." "The truly great political orators," he exclaims, "are the ornaments of mankind, the most finished examples of noble feeling and perfect expression, but they rarely understand the circumstances of their time. They feel passionately, but for that reason they cannot judge calmly." If we are to accept these judgments from Mr. Froude in the face of his reputation for thinking somewhat too independently of evidence, we should congratulate ourselves that we have in this country hit upon a system which, now that it has reached its perfection, has left little or no place for politicians to make false declarations or for the orator to coin fine expression for views which are only feelings, except outside of the legislative halls of the nation, upon the platform, where talk is all that is expected. It would seem as if the seer had a much more favorable opportunity in the committee-room than the orator can have, and with us it is the committee-room which governs the legislative chamber. The speech-making in the latter neither makes nor often seriously affects the plans framed in the former; because the plans are made before the speeches are uttered. This is self-evident of the debates of the House; but even the speeches made in the Senate, free, full, and earnest as they seem, are made, so to speak, after the fact—not to determine the actions but to air the opinions of the body.

Still, it must be regarded as no inconsiderable addition to the usefulness of the Senate that it enjoys a much greater freedom of discussion than the House can allow itself. It permits itself a good deal of talk in public about what it is doing,[5] and it commonly talks a great deal of sense. It is small enough to make it safe to allow individual freedom to its members, and to have, at the same time, such order and sense of proportion in its pro-

---

[4] In the Birmingham Town Hall, November 3, 1882. I quote from the report of the *London Times*.

[5] "No Senator shall speak more than twice, in any one debate, on the same day, without leave of the Senate."—Senate Rule 4.

ceedings as is characteristic of small bodies, like boards of college trustees or of commercial directors, who feel that their main
object is business, not speech-making, and so say all that is
necessary without being tedious, and do what they are called
upon to do without need of driving themselves with hurrying
rules. Such rules, they seem to feel, are meant only for big assemblies which have no power of self-control. Of course the
Senate talks more than an average board of directors would,
because the corporations which it represents are States, made
up, politically speaking, of numerous popular constituencies to
which Senators, no less than Representatives, must make
speeches of a sort which, considering their fellow-members alone,
would be unnecessary if not impertinent and out of taste, in the
Senate chamber, but which will sound best in the ears of the
people, for whose ears they are intended, if delivered there.
Speeches which, so to say, run in the name of the Senate's business will generally be more effectual for campaign uses at home
than any speech could be which should run in the name of the
proper topics of the stump. There is an air of doing one's duty
by one's party in speaking party platitudes or uttering party de-
fiances on the floor of the Senate or of the House.

Of course, however, there is less temptation to such speech-
making in the Senate than in the House. The House knows the
terrible possibilities of this sort in store for it, were it to give
perfect freedom of debate to its three hundred and twenty-five
members, in these days when frequent mails and tireless tongues
of telegraphy bring every constituency within easy earshot of
Washington; and it therefore seeks to confine what little discussion it indulges in to the few committee-men specially in charge
of the business of each moment. But the Senate is small and of
settled habits, and has no such bugbear to trouble it. It can afford
to do without any *clôture* or previous question. No Senator is
likely to want to speak on all the topics of the session, or to prepare more speeches than can conveniently be spoken before adjournment is imperatively at hand. The House can be counted
upon to waste enough time to leave some leisure to the upper
chamber.

And there can be no question that the debates which take place
every session in the Senate are of a very high order of excellence.
The average of the ability displayed in its discussions not infrequently rises quite to the level of those controversies of the past
which we are wont to call great because they furnished occasion
to men like Webster and Calhoun and Clay, whom we cannot

now quite match in mastery of knowledge and of eloquence. If the debates of the present are smothered amongst the innumerable folios of the "Record," it is not because they do not contain utterances worthy to be heeded and to gain currency, but because they do not deal with questions of passion or of national existence, such as ran through all the earlier debates, or because our system so obscures and complicates party rule in legislation as to leave nothing very interesting to the public eye dependent upon the discussions of either House or Senate. What that is picturesque, or what that is vital in the esteem of the partisan, is there in these wordy contests about contemplated legislation? How does anybody know that either party's prospects will be much affected by what is said when Senators are debating, or, for that matter, by what is voted after their longest flights of controversy?

Still, though not much heeded, the debates of the Senate are of great value in scrutinizing and sifting matters which come up from the House. The Senate's opportunities for open and unrestricted discussion and its simple, comparatively unencumbered forms of procedure, unquestionably enable it to fulfill with very considerable success its high functions as a chamber of revision.

When this has been claimed and admitted, however, it still remains to be considered whether two chambers of equal power strengthen by steadying, or weaken by complicating, a system of representative government like our own. The utility and excellence of a bicameral system has never, I believe, been seriously questioned in this country; but M. Turgot smiles with something like contempt at our affectation in copying the House of Lords without having any lords to use for the purpose; and in our own day Mr. Bagehot, who is much more competent to speak on this head than was M. Turgot, has avowed very grave doubts as to the practical advantage of a two-headed legislature—each head having its own independent will. He finds much to recommend the House of Lords in the fact that it is not, as theory would have it, coordinate and coequal with the House of Commons, but merely "a revising and suspending House," altering what the Commons have done hastily or carelessly, and sometimes rejecting "Bills on which the House of Commons is not yet thoroughly in earnest, —upon which the nation is not yet determined."[6] He points out the fact that the House of Lords has never in modern times been,

[6] These quotations from Bagehot are taken from various parts of the fifth chapter of his *English Constitution*.

as a House, coequal in power with the House of Commons. Before the Reform Bill of 1832 the peers were all-powerful in legislation; not, however, because they were members of the House of Lords, but because they nominated most of the members of the House of Commons. Since that disturbing reform they have been thrown back upon the functions in which they never were strong, the functions of a deliberative assembly. These are the facts which seem to Mr. Bagehot to have made it possible for legislation to make easy and satisfactory progress under a system whose theory provided for fatal dead-locks between the two branches of the supreme legislature.

In his view "the evil of two coequal Houses of distinct natures is obvious." "Most constitutions," he declares, "have committed this blunder. The two most remarkable Republican institutions in the world commit it. In both the American and Swiss Constitutions the Upper House has as much authority as the second; it could produce the maximum of impediment—a dead-lock, if it liked; if it does not do so, it is owing not to the goodness of the legal constitution, but to the discreetness of the members of the Chamber. In both these constitutions this dangerous division is defended by a peculiar doctrine. . . . It is said that there must be in a federal government some institution, some authority, some body possessing a veto in which the separate States comprising the Confederation are all equal. I confess this doctrine has to me no self-evidence, and it is assumed, but not proved. The State of Delaware is not equal in power or influence to the State of New York, and you cannot make it so by giving it an equal veto in an Upper Chamber. The history of such an institution is indeed most natural. A little State will like, and must like, to see some token, some memorial mark, of its old independence preserved in the Constitution by which that independence is extinguished. But it is one thing for an institution to be natural, and another for it to be expedient. If indeed it be that a federal government compels the erection of an Upper Chamber of conclusive and coördinate authority, it is one more in addition to the many other inherent defects of that kind of government. It may be necessary to have the blemish, but it is a blemish just as much."

It would be in the highest degree indiscreet to differ lightly with any conclusion to which Mr. Bagehot may have come in viewing that field of critical exposition in which he was supreme, the philosophical analysis, namely, of the English Constitution; and it must be apparent to any one who reads the passage I have just now quoted that his eye sees very keenly and truly even when he looks across sea at institutions which were repugnant to his own way of thinking. But it is safe to say that he did not see all in this instance, and that he was consequently in error concerning the true nature of our federal legislative system. His error, nevertheless, appears, not when we look only at the facts which he held up to view, but when we look at other facts which he ignored. It is true that the existence of two coequal Houses is an evil when those two Houses are of distinct natures, as was the case under the Victorian Constitution to which Mr. Bagehot refers by way of illustrative example. Under that Constitution all legislative business was sometimes to be seen quite suspended because of irreconcilable differences of opinion between the Upper House, which represented the rich wool-growers of the colony, and the Lower Assembly, which represented the lesser wool-growers, perhaps, and the people who were not wool-growers at all. The Upper House, in other words, was a class chamber, and thus stood quite apart from anything like the principle embodied in our own Senate, which is no more a class chamber than is the House of Representatives.

The prerogatives of the Senate do, indeed, render our legislative system more complex, and for that reason possibly more cumbersome, than the British; for our Senate can do more than the House of Lords. It can not only question and stay the judgment of the Commons, but may always with perfect safety act upon its own judgment and gainsay the more popular chamber to the end of the longest chapter of the bitterest controversy. It is quite as free to act as is any other branch of the government, and quite as sure to have its acts regarded. But there is safety and ease in the fact that the Senate never wishes to carry its resistance to the House to that point at which resistance must stay all progress in legislation; because there is really a "latent unity" between the Senate and the House which makes continued antagonism between them next to impossible—certainly in the highest degree improbable. The Senate and the House are of different origins, but virtually of the same nature. The Senate is less democratic than the House, and consequently less sensible to transient phases of public opinion; but it is no less sensible than the House of its ultimate accountability to the people, and is consequently quite as obedient to the more permanent and imperative judgments of the public mind. It cannot be carried so quickly by every new sentiment, but it can be carried quickly enough. There is a main chance of election time for it as well as for the House to think about.

By the mode of its election and the greater length of the term by which its seats are held, the Senate is almost altogether removed from that temptation to servile obedience to the whims of popular constituencies to which the House is constantly subject, without as much courage as the Senate has to guard its virtue. But the men who compose the Senate are of the same sort as the members of the House of Representatives, and represent quite as various classes. Nowadays many of the Senators are, indeed, very rich men, and there has come to be a great deal of talk about their vast wealth and the supposed aristocratic tendencies which it is imagined to breed. But even the rich Senators cannot be said to be representatives of a class, as if they were all opulent wool-growers or great land-owners. Their wealth is in all sorts of stocks, in all sorts of machinery, in all sorts of buildings, in possessions of all the sorts possible in a land of bustling commerce and money-making industries. They have made their money in a hundred different ways, or have inherited it from fathers who amassed it in enterprises too numerous to imagine; and they have it invested here, there, and everywhere, in this, that, and everything. Their wealth represents no class interests, but all the interests of the commercial world. It represents the majority of the nation, in a word; and so they can probably be trusted not to neglect one set of interests for another; not to despoil the trader for the sake of the farmer, or the farmer for the sake of the wool-grower, or the wool-grower for the behoof of the herder of short-horned cattle. At least the Senate is quite as trustworthy in this regard as is the House of Representatives.

Inasmuch as the Senate is thus separated from class interests and quite as representative of the nation at large as is the House of Representatives, the fact that it is less quickly sensitive to the hasty or impulsive movements of public opinion constitutes its value as a check, a steadying weight, in our very democratic system. Our English cousins have worked out for themselves a wonderfully perfect scheme of government by gradually making their monarchy unmonarchical. They have made of it a republic steadied by a reverenced aristocracy and pivoted upon a stable throne. And just as the English system is a limited monarchy because of Commons and Cabinet, ours may be said to be a limited democracy because of the Senate. This has in the trial of the scheme proved the chief value of that upper chamber which was instituted principally as an earnest of the abiding equality

and sovereignty of the States. At any rate, this is the most conspicuous, and will prove to be the most lasting, use of the Senate
in our system. It is valuable in our democracy in proportion as
it is undemocratic. I think that a philosophical analysis of any
successful and beneficent system of self-government will disclose
the fact that its only effectual checks consist in a mixture of elements, in a combination of seemingly contradictory political principles; that the British government is perfect in proportion as it
is unmonarchical, and ours safe in proportion as it is undemocratic; that the Senate saves us often from headlong popular
tyranny.

"The value, spirit, and essence of the House of Commons," said
Burke, "consists in its being the express image of the feelings of
the nation"; but the image of the nation's feelings should not be
the only thing reflected by the constitution of a free government.
It is indispensable that, besides the House of Representatives
which runs on all fours with popular sentiment, we should have
a body like the Senate which may refuse to run with it at all
when it seems to be wrong—a body which has time and security
enough to keep its head, if only now and then and but for a
little while, till other people have had time to think. The Senate
is fitted to do deliberately and well the revising which is its prop-
erest function, because its position as a representative of state
sovereignty is one of eminent dignity, securing for it ready and
sincere respect, and because popular demands, ere they reach it
with definite and authoritative suggestion, are diluted by passage
through the feelings and conclusions of the state legislatures,
which are the Senate's only immediate constituents. The Senate
commonly feels with the House, but it does not, so to say, feel so
fast. It at least has a chance to be the express image of those
judgments of the nation which are slower and more temperate
than its feelings.

This it is which makes the Senate "the most powerful and
efficient second chamber that exists,"[7] and this it is which constitutes its functions one of the effectual checks, one of the real
balances, of our system; though it is made to seem very insignificant in the literary theory of the Constitution, where the
checks of state upon federal authorities, of executive prerogatives
upon legislative powers, and of Judiciary upon President and
Congress, though some of them in reality inoperative from the
first and all of them weakened by many "ifs" and "buts," are made

[7] These are the words of Lord Rosebery—testimony from the oldest and most
celebrated second chamber that exists.

to figure in the leading rôles, as the characteristic Virtues, triumphing over the characteristic Vices, of our new and original political Morality-play.

It should, however, be accounted a deduction from the Senate's usefulness that it is seldom sure of more than two thirds of itself for more than four years at a time. In order that its life may be perpetual, one third of its membership is renewed or changed every two years, each third taking its turn at change or renewal in regular succession; and this device has, of course, an appreciably weakening effect on the legislative sinews of the Senate. Because the Senate mixes the parties in the composition of its Committees just as the House does, and those Committees must, consequently, be subjected to modification whenever the biennial senatorial elections bring in new men, freshly promoted from the House or from gubernatorial chairs. Places must be found for them at once in the working organization which busies itself in the committee-rooms. Six years is not the term of the Senate, but only of each Senator. Reckoning from any year in which one third of the Senate is elected, the term of the majority,—the two thirds not affected by the election,—is an average of the four and the two years which it has to live. There is never a time at which two thirds of the Senate have more than four years of appointed service before them. And this constant liability to change must, of course, materially affect the policy of the body. The time assured it in which to carry out any enterprise of policy upon which it may embark is seldom more than two years, the term of the House. It may be checked no less effectually than the lower House by the biennial elections, albeit the changes brought about in its membership are effected, not directly by the people, but indirectly and more slowly by the mediate operation of public opinion through the legislatures of the States.

In estimating the value of the Senate, therefore, as a branch of the national legislature, we should offset the committee organization, with its denial of leadership which disintegrates the Senate, and that liability to the biennial infusion of new elements which may at any time interrupt the policy and break the purpose of the Senate, against those habits of free and open debate which clear its mind, and to some extent the mind of the public, with regard to the nation's business, doing much towards making legislation definite and consistent, and against those great additions to its efficiency which spring from its observation of "slow and steady forms" of procedure, from the mediate election which gives it independence, and from its having a rational and august cause for existing.

When we turn to consider the Senate in its relations with the executive, we see it no longer as a legislative chamber, but as a consultative executive council. And just here there is to be noted an interesting difference between the relations of the Senate with the President and its relations with the departments, which are in constitutional theory one with the President. It deals directly with the President in acting upon nominations and upon treaties. It goes into "executive session" to handle without gloves the acts of the chief magistrate. Its dealings with the departments, on the other hand, are, like those of the House, only indirect. Its legislative, not its executive, function is the whip which coerces the Secretaries. Its will is the supreme law in the offices of the government; and yet it orders policy by no direct word to the departments. It does not consult and negotiate with them as it does with the President, their titular head. Its immediate agents, the Committees, are not the recognized constitutional superiors of Secretary A. or Comptroller B.; but these officials cannot move a finger or plan more than a paltry detail without looking to it that they render strict obedience to the wishes of these outside, uncommissioned, and irresponsible, but none the less authoritative and imperative masters.

This feature of the Senate's power over the executive does not, however, call for special emphasis here, because it is not a power peculiar to the Senate, this overlordship of the departments, but one which it possesses in common with the House of Representatives,—simply an innate and inseparable part of the absolutism of a supreme legislature. It is the Senate's position as the President's council in some great and many small matters which call for particular discussion. Its general tyranny over the departments belongs rather with what I am to say presently when looking at congressional government from the stand-point of the executive.

The greatest consultative privilege of the Senate,—the greatest in dignity, at least, if not in effect upon the interests of the country,—is its right to a ruling voice in the ratification of treaties with foreign powers. I have already alluded to this privilege, for the purpose of showing what weight it has had in many instances in disarranging the ideal balance supposed to exist between the powers of Congress and the constitutional prerogatives of the President; but I did not then stop to discuss the organic reasons which have made it impossible that there should be any real consultation between the President and the Senate upon such business, and which have, consequently, made disagreement and even antagonism between them probable outcomes of the system. I do not consult the auditor who scrutinizes my accounts when I submit to him my books, my vouchers, and a written report of the business I have negotiated. I do not take his advice and seek his consent; I simply ask his endorsement or invite his condemnation. I do not sue for his coöperation, but challenge his criticism. And the analogy between my relations with the auditor and the relations of the President with the Senate is by no means remote. The President really has no voice at all in the conclusions of the Senate with reference to his diplomatic transactions, or with reference to any of the matters upon which he consults it; and yet without a voice in the conclusion there is no consultation. Argument and an unobstructed interchange of views upon a ground of absolute equality are essential parts of the substance of genuine consultation. The Senate, when it closes its doors, upon going into "executive session," closes them upon the President as much as upon the rest of the world. He cannot meet their objections to his courses except through the clogged and inadequate channels of a written message or through the friendly but unauthoritative offices of some Senator who may volunteer his active support. Nay, in many cases the President may not even know what the Senate's objections were. He is made to approach that body as a servant conferring with his master, and of course deferring to that master. His only power of compelling compliance on the part of the Senate lies in his initiative in negotiation, which affords him a chance to get the country into such scrapes, so pledged in the view of the world to certain courses of action, that the Senate hesitates to bring about the appearance of dishonor which would follow its refusal to ratify the rash promises or to support the indiscreet threats of the Department of State.

The machinery of consultation between the Senate and the President is of course the committee machinery. The Senate sends treaties to its Standing Committee on Foreign Relations, which ponders the President's messages accompanying the treaties and sets itself to understand the situation in the light of all the information available. If the President wishes some more satisfactory mode of communication with the Senate than formal message-writing, his only door of approach is this Committee on Foreign Relations. The Secretary of State may confer with its chairman or with its more influential members. But such a mode of conference is manifestly much less than a voice in the deliberations of the Senate itself,—much less than meeting that body face to face in free consultation and equal debate. It is almost as distinctly dealing with a foreign power as were the negotiations preceding the proposed treaty. It must predispose the Senate to the temper of an overseer.[8]

Still, treaties are not every-day affairs with us, and exceptional business may create in Senators an exceptional sense of responsibility, and dispose them to an unwonted desire to be dispassionate and fair. The ratification of treaties is a much more serious matter than the consideration of nominations which every session constitutes so constant a diversion from the more ponderous business of legislation. It is in dealing with nominations, however, that there is the most friction in the contact between the President and his overlord, the Senate. One of the most noteworthy instances of the improper tactics which may arise out of these relations was the case of that Mr. Smythe, at the time Collector for the port of New York, whom, in 1869, President Grant nominated Minister to the Court of St. Petersburg. The nomination, as looking towards an appointment to diplomatic service, was referred to the Committee on Foreign Relations, of which Mr. Charles Sumner was then chairman. That Committee rejected the nomination; but Smythe had great influence at his back and was himself skilled beyond most men in the arts of the lobby. He accordingly succeeded in securing such support in the Senate as to become a very formidable dog in the manger, not himself gaining the appointment, but for a time blocking all other appointments and bringing the business of the Senate altogether to a standstill, because he could not.[9] Smythe himself is forgotten; but no observer of the actual conditions of senatorial power can fail to see the grave import of the lesson which his case teaches, because his case was by no means an isolated one. There have been scores of others quite as bad; and we could have no assurance that there might not in the future be hundreds more, had not recent movements in the direction of a radical reform of the civil service begun to make nominations represent, not the personal preference of the President or the intrigues of other people, but honest, demonstrated worth, which the Sen-

[8] There seems to have been at one time a tendency towards a better practice. In 1813 the Senate sought to revive the early custom, in accordance with which the President delivered his messages in person, by requesting the attendance of the President to consult upon foreign affairs; but Mr. Madison declined.

[9] *North American Review*, vol. 108, p. 625.

ate is likely to feel forced to accept without question, when the reform reaches the highest grades of the service.

In discussing the Senate's connection with the civil service and the abuses surrounding that connection, one is, therefore, discussing a phase of congressional government which promises soon to become obsolete. A consummation devoutly to be wished! —and yet sure when it comes to rob our politics of a feature very conspicuous and very characteristic, and in a sense very entertaining. There are not many things in the proceedings of Congress which the people care to observe with any diligence, and it must be confessed that scandalous transactions in the Senate with reference to nominations were among the few things that the country watched and talked about with keen relish and interest. This was the personal element which always had spice in it. When Senator Conkling resigned in a huff because he could not have whom he liked in the collectorship of the port of New York, the country rubbed its hands; and when the same imperious politician sought reëlection as a vindication of that unconstitutional control of nominations which masqueraded as "the courtesy of the Senate," the country discussed his chances with real zest and chuckled over the whole affair in genuine glee. It was a big fight worth seeing. It would have been too bad to miss it.

Before the sentiment of reform had become strong enough to check it, this abuse of the consultative privileges of the Senate in the matter of nominations had assumed such proportions as to seem to some the ugliest deformity in our politics. It looked as if it were becoming at once the weakest and the most tried and strained joint of our federal system. If there was to be a break, would it not be there, where was the severest wear and tear? The evil practices seemed the more ineradicable because they had arisen in the most natural manner. The President was compelled, as in the case of treaties, to obtain the sanction of the Senate without being allowed any chance of consultation with it; and there soon grew up within the privacy of "executive session" an understanding that the wishes and opinions of each Senator who was of the President's own party should have more weight than even the inclinations of the majority in deciding upon the fitness or desirability of persons proposed to be appointed to offices in that Senator's State. There was the requisite privacy to shield from public condemnation the practice arising out of such an understanding; and the President himself was always quite out of earshot, hearing only of results, of final votes.

All through the direct dealings of the Senate with the President there runs this characteristic spirit of irresponsible dictation. The President may tire the Senate by dogged persistence, but he can never deal with it upon a ground of real equality. He has no real presence in the Senate. His power does not extend beyond the most general suggestion. The Senate always has the last word. No one would desire to see the President possessed of authority to overrule the decisions of the Senate, to treat with foreign powers, and appoint thousands of public officers, without any other than that shadowy responsibility which he owes to the people that elected him; but it is certainly an unfortunate feature of our government that Congress governs without being put into confidential relations with the agents through whom it governs. It dictates to another branch of the government which was intended to be coördinate and coequal with it, and over which it has no legalized authority as of a master, but only the authority of a bigger stockholder, of a monopolist indeed, of all the energetic prerogatives of the government. It is as if the Army and Navy Departments were to be made coördinate and coequal, but the absolute possession and control of all ammunition and other stores of war given to the one and denied the other. The executive is taken into partnership with the legislature upon a salary which may be withheld, and is allowed no voice in the management of the business. It is simply charged with the superintendence of the employees.

It was not essentially different in the early days when the President in person read his message to the Senate and the House together as an address, and the Senate in a body carried its reply to the executive mansion. The address was the formal communication of an outsider just as much as the message of to-day is, and the reply of the Senate was no less a formal document which it turned aside from its regular business to prepare. That meeting face to face was not consultation. The English Parliament does not consult with the sovereign when it assembles to hear the address from the throne.

It would, doubtless, be considered quite improper to omit from an essay on the Senate all mention of the Senate's President; and yet there is very little to be said about the Vice-President of the United States. His position is one of anomalous insignificance and curious uncertainty. Apparently he is not, strictly speaking, a part of the legislature,—he is clearly not a member,—yet neither is he an officer of the executive. It is one of the remarkable things about him, that it is hard to find in sketching the government any proper place to discuss him. He comes in most naturally along with the Senate to which he is tacked; but he does not come in there for any great consideration. He is simply a judicial officer set to moderate the proceedings of an assembly whose rules he has had no voice in framing and can have no voice in changing. His official stature is not to be compared with that of the Speaker of the House of Representatives. So long as he is Vice-President, he is inseparable officially from the Senate; his importance consists in the fact that he may cease to be Vice-President. His chief dignity, next to presiding over the Senate, lies in the circumstance that he is awaiting the death or disability of the President. And the chief embarrassment in discussing his office is, that in explaining how little there is to be said about it one has evidently said all there is to say.

V.

THE EXECUTIVE.

Every political constitution in which different bodies share the supreme power is only enabled to exist by the forbearance of those among whom this power is distributed.—LORD JOHN RUSSELL.

Simplicity and logical neatness are not the good to be aimed at in politics, but freedom and order, with props against the pressure of time, and arbitrary will, and sudden crises.—THEO. WOOLSEY.

Nothing, indeed, will appear more certain, on any tolerable consideration of this matter, than that *every sort of government ought to have its administration correspondent to its legislature.*—BURKE.

It is at once curious and instructive to note how we have been forced into practically amending the Constitution without constitutionally amending it. The legal processes of constitutional change are so slow and cumbersome that we have been constrained to adopt a serviceable framework of fictions which enables us easily to preserve the forms without laboriously obeying the spirit of the Constitution, which will stretch as the nation grows. It would seem that no impulse short of the impulse of self-preservation, no force less than the force of revolution, can nowadays be expected to move the cumbrous machinery of formal amendment erected in Article Five. That must be a tremendous movement of opinion which can sway two thirds of each House of Congress and the people of three fourths of the States. Mr. Bagehot has pointed out that one consequence of the existence of this next to immovable machinery "is that the most obvious evils cannot be quickly remedied," and "that a clumsy working and a curious technicality mark the politics of a rough-

and-ready people. The practical arguments and legal disquisitions in America," continues he, "are often like those of trustees carrying out a misdrawn will,—the sense of what they mean is good, but it can never be worked out fully or defended simply, so hampered is it by the old words of an old testament."[1] But much the greater consequence is that we have resorted, almost unconscious of the political significance of what we did, to extra-constitutional means of modifying the federal system where it has proved to be too refined by balances of divided authority to suit practical uses,—to be out of square with the main principle of its foundation, namely, government by the people through their representatives in Congress.

Our method of choosing Presidents is a notable illustration of these remarks. The difference between the actual and the constitutional modes is the difference between an ideal nonpartisan choice and a choice made under party whips; the difference between a choice made by independent, unpledged electors acting apart in the States and a choice made by a national party convention. Our Executive, no less than the English and French Executives, is selected by a representative, deliberative body, though in England and France the election is controlled by a permanent legislative chamber, and here by a transient assembly chosen for the purpose and dying with the execution of that purpose. In England the whole cabinet is practically elective. The French Chambers formally elect the President, the titular head of the government, and the President regards only the will of the Assembly in appointing the Prime Minister, who is the energetic head of the government, and who, in his turn, surrounds himself with colleagues who have the confidence of the legislature. And the French have but copied the English constitution, which makes the executive Ministry the representatives of the party majority in the Commons. With us, on the other hand, the President is elected by one representative body, which has nothing to do with him after his election, and the cabinet must be approved by another representative body, which has nothing directly to do with them after their appointment.

Of course I do not mean that the choice of a national convention is literally election. The convention only nominates a candidate. But that candidate is the only man for whom the electors of his party can vote; and so the expression of the preference of the convention of the dominant party is practically equivalent to election, and might as well be called election by any one who is

[1] *English Constitution*, chap. viii., p. 293.

writing of broad facts, and not of fine distinctions. The sovereign in England picks out the man who is to be Prime Minister, but he must pick where the Commons point; and so it is simpler, as well as perfectly true, to say that the Commons elect the Prime Minister. My agent does not select the particular horse I instruct him to buy. This is just the plain fact,—that the electors are the agents of the national conventions; and this fact constitutes more than an amendment of that original plan which would have had all the electors to be what the first electors actually were, trustworthy men given *carte blanche* to vote for whom they pleased, casting their ballots in thirteen state capitals in the hope that they would happen upon a majority agreement.

It is worth while, too, to notice another peculiarity of this elective system. There is a thorough-going minority representation in the assemblies which govern our elections. Across the ocean a Liberal Prime Minister is selected by the representatives only of those Liberals who live in Liberal constituencies; those who live elsewhere in a helpless minority, in a Conservative district, having of course no voice in the selection. A Conservative Premier, in like manner, owes nothing to those Conservatives who were unable to return a member to Parliament. So far as he is concerned, they count for Liberals, since their representative in the Commons is a Liberal. The parliaments which select our Presidents, on the contrary, are, each of them, all of a kind. No state district can have so few Republicans in it as not to be entitled to a representative in the national Republican convention equal to that of the most unanimously Republican district in the country; and a Republican State is accorded as full a representation in a Democratic convention as is the most Democratic of her sister States.

We had to pass through several stages of development before the present system of election by convention was reached. At the first two presidential elections the electors were left free to vote as their consciences and the Constitution bade them; for the Constitution bade them vote as they deemed best, and it did not require much discretion to vote for General Washington. But when General Washington was out of the race, and new parties began to dispute the field with the Federalists, party managers could not help feeling anxious about the votes of the electors, and some of those named to choose the second President were, accordingly, pledged beforehand to vote thus and so. After the third presidential election there began to be congressional oversight of the matter. From 1800 to 1824 there was an unbroken succession of caucuses of the Republican members of Congress to direct the action of the party electors; and nomination by caucus died only when the Republican party became virtually the only party worth reckoning with,—the only party for whom nomination was worth while,—and then public opinion began to cry out against such secret direction of the monopoly. In 1796 the Federalist congressmen had held an informal caucus to ascertain their minds as to the approaching election; but after that they refrained from further experiment in the same direction, and contented themselves with now and then a sort of convention until they had no party to convene. In 1828 there was a sort of dropping fire of nominations from state legislatures; and in 1832 sat the first of the great national nominating conventions.

There was, therefore, one form of congressional government which did not succeed. It was a very logical mode of party government, that of nominating the chief magistrate by congressional caucus, but it was not an open enough way. The French chamber does not select premiers by shutting up the members of its majority in caucus. Neither does the House of Commons. Their selection is made by long and open trial, in debate and in business management, of the men in whom they discover most tact for leading and most skill for planning, as well as most power for ruling. They do not say, by vote, give us M. Ferry, give us Mr. Gladstone; but Her Majesty knows as well as her subjects know that Mr. Gladstone is the only man whom the Liberal majority will obey; and President Grévy perceives that M. Ferry is the only man whom the Chambers can be made to follow. Each has elected himself by winning the first place in his party. The election has openly progressed for years, and is quite different from the private vote of a caucus about an outsider who is to sit, not in Congress, but in the executive mansion; who is not their man, but the people's.

Nor would nominations by state legislatures answer any rational purpose. Of course every State had, or thought she had,—which is much the same thing,—some citizen worthy to become President; and it would have been confusion worse confounded to have had as many candidates as there might be States. So universal a competition between "favorite sons" would have thrown the election into the House of Representatives so regularly as to replace the nominating caucus by an electing caucus.

The virtual election of the cabinet, the real executive, or at least the Prime Minister, the real head of the executive, by the Commons in England, furnishes us with a contrast rather than with a parallel to the election of our premier, the head of our executive, by a deliberative, representative body, because of the difference of function and of tenure between our Presidents and English Prime Ministers. William Pitt was elected to rule the House of Commons, John Adams to hold a constitutional balance against the Houses of Congress. The one was the leader of the legislature; the other, so to say, the colleague of the legislature. Besides, the Commons can not only make but also unmake Ministries; whilst conventions can do nothing but bind their parties by nomination, and nothing short of a well-nigh impossible impeachment can unmake a President, except four successions of the seasons. As has been very happily said by a shrewd critic, our system is essentially astronomical. A President's usefulness is measured, not by efficiency, but by calendar months. It is reckoned that if he be good at all he will be good for four years. A Prime Minister must keep himself in favor with the majority, a President need only keep alive.

Once the functions of a presidential elector were very august. He was to speak for the people; they were to accept his judgment as theirs. He was to be as eminent in the qualities which win trust as was the greatest of the Imperial Electors in the power which inspires fear. But now he is merely a registering machine, —a sort of bell-punch to the hand of his party convention. It gives the pressure, and he rings. It is, therefore, patent to every one that that portion of the Constitution which prescribes his functions is as though it were not. A very simple and natural process of party organization, taking form first in congressional caucuses and later in nominating conventions, has radically altered a Constitution which declares that it can be amended only by the concurrence of two thirds of Congress and three fourths of the States. The sagacious men of the constitutional convention of 1787 certainly expected their work to be altered, but can hardly have expected it to be changed in so informal a manner.

The conditions which determine the choice of a nominating convention which names a President are radically different from the conditions which facilitate the choice of a representative chamber which selects for itself a Prime Minister. "Among the great purposes of a national parliament are these two," says Mr. Parton:[2] "first, to train men for practical statesmanship; and secondly, to exhibit them to the country, so that, when men of ability are wanted, they can be found without anxious search

[2] *Atlantic Monthly*, vol. xxv., p. 148.

and perilous trial." In those governments which are administered by an executive committee of the legislative body, not only this training but also this exhibition is constant and complete. The career which leads to cabinet office is a career of self-exhibition. The self-revelation is made in debate, and so is made to the nation at large as well as to the Ministry of the day, who are looking out for able recruits, and to the Commons, whose ear is quick to tell a voice which it will consent to hear, a knowledge which it will pause to heed. But in governments like our own, in which legislative and executive services are altogether dissociated, this training is incomplete, and this exhibition almost entirely wanting. A nominating convention does not look over the rolls of Congress to pick a man to suit its purpose; and if it did it could not find him, because Congress is not a school for the preparation of administrators, and the convention is supposed to be searching not for an experienced committeeman, but for a tried statesman. The proper test for its application is not the test by which congressmen are assayed. They make laws, but they do not have to order the execution of the laws they make. They have a great deal of experience in directing, but none at all in being directed. Their care is to pass bills, not to keep them in running order after they have become statutes. They spend their lives without having anything to do directly with administration, though administration is dependent upon the measures which they enact.

A Presidential convention, therefore, when it nominates a man who is, or has been, a member of Congress, does not nominate him because of his congressional experience, but because it is thought that he has other abilities which were not called out in Congress. Andrew Jackson had been a member of Congress, but he was chosen President because he had won the battle of New Orleans and had driven the Indians from Florida. It was thought that his military genius evinced executive genius. The men whose fame rests altogether upon laurels won in Congress have seldom been more successful than Webster and Henry Clay in their candidacy for the chief magistracy. Washington was a soldier; Jefferson cut but a sorry figure in debate; Monroe was a diplomatist; it required diligent inquiry to find out what many of our Presidents had been before they became candidates; and eminency in legislative service has always been at best but an uncertain road to official preferment.

Of late years a tendency is observable which seems to be making the gubernatorial chairs of the greater States the nearest offices to the Presidency; and it cannot but be allowed that there is much that is rational in the tendency. The governorship of a State is very like a smaller Presidency; or, rather, the Presidency is very like a big governorship. Training in the duties of the one fits for the duties of the other. This is the only avenue of subordinate place through which the highest place can be naturally reached. Under the cabinet governments abroad a still more natural line of promotion is arranged. The Ministry is a legislative Ministry, and draws its life from the legislature, where strong talents always secure executive place. A long career in Parliament is at least a long contact with practical statesmanship, and at best a long schooling in the duties of the practical statesman. But with us there is no such intimate relationship between legislative and executive service. From experience in state administration to trial in the larger sphere of federal administration is the only natural order of promotion. We ought, therefore, to hail the recognition of this fact as in keeping with the general plan of the federal Constitution. The business of the President, occasionally great, is usually not much above routine. Most of the time it is *mere* administration, mere obedience of directions from the masters of policy, the Standing Committees. Except in so far as his power of veto constitutes him a part of the legislature, the President might, not inconveniently, be a permanent officer; the first official of a carefully-graded and impartially regulated civil service system, through whose sure series of merit-promotions the youngest clerk might rise even to the chief magistracy.[3] He is part of the official rather than of the political machinery of the government, and his duties call rather for training than for constructive genius. If there can be found in the official systems of the States a lower grade of service in which men may be advantageously drilled for Presidential functions, so much the better. The States will have better governors, the Union better Presidents, and there will have been supplied one of the most serious needs left unsupplied by the Constitution,—the need for a proper school in which to rear federal administrators.

Administration is something that men must learn, not something to skill in which they are born. Americans take to business of all kinds more naturally than any other nation ever did, and the executive duties of government constitute just an exalted kind of business; but even Americans are not Presidents in their cradles. One cannot have too much preparatory training and ex-

[3] Something like this has been actually proposed by Mr. Albert Stickney, in his interesting and incisive essay, *A True Republic*.

perience who is to fill so high a magistracy. It is difficult to perceive, therefore, upon what safe ground of reason are built the opinions of those persons who regard short terms of service as sacredly and peculiarly republican in principle. If republicanism is founded upon good sense, nothing so far removed from good sense can be part and parcel of it. Efficiency is the only just foundation for confidence in a public officer, under republican institutions no less than under monarchs; and short terms which cut off the efficient as surely and inexorably as the inefficient are quite as repugnant to republican as to monarchical rules of wisdom. Unhappily, however, this is not American doctrine. A President is dismissed almost as soon as he has learned the duties of his office, and a man who has served a dozen terms in Congress is a curiosity. We are too apt to think both the work of legislation and the work of administration easy enough to be done readily, with or without preparation, by any man of discretion and character. No one imagines that the drygoods or the hardware trade, or even the cobbler's craft, can be successfully conducted except by those who have worked through a laborious and unremunerative apprenticeship, and who have devoted their lives to perfecting themselves as tradesmen or as menders of shoes. But legislation is esteemed a thing which may be taken up with success by any shrewd man of middle age, which a lawyer may now and again advantageously combine with his practice, or of which any intelligent youth may easily catch the knack; and administration is regarded as something which an old soldier, an ex-diplomatist, or a popular politician may be trusted to take to by instinct. No man of tolerable talents need despair of having been born a Presidential candidate.

These must be pronounced very extraordinary conclusions for an eminently practical people to have accepted; and it must be received as an awakening of good sense that there is nowadays a decided inclination manifested on the part of the nation to supply training-schools for the Presidency in like minor offices, such as the governorships of the greater States. For the sort of Presidents needed under the present arrangement of our federal government, it is best to choose amongst the ablest and most experienced state governors.

So much for nomination and election. But, after election, what then? The President is not all of the Executive. He cannot get along without the men whom he appoints, with and by the consent and advice of the Senate; and they are really integral parts of that branch of the government which he titularly contains in his one single person. The characters and training of the Secretaries are of almost as much importance as his own gifts and antecedents; so that his appointment and the Senate's confirmation must be added to the machinery of nomination by convention and election by automatic electors before the whole process of making up a working executive has been noted. The early Congresses seem to have regarded the Attorney-General and the four Secretaries[4] who constituted the first Cabinets as something more than the President's lieutenants. Before the republican reaction which followed the supremacy of the Federalists, the heads of the departments appeared in person before the Houses to impart desired information, and to make what suggestions they might have to venture, just as the President attended in person to read his "address." They were always recognized units in the system, never mere ciphers to the Presidential figure which led them. Their wills counted as independent wills.

The limits of this independence would seem, however, never to have been very clearly defined. Whether or not the President was to take the advice of his appointees and colleagues appears to have depended always upon the character and temper of the President. Here, for example, is what was reported in 1862. "We pretend to no state secrets," said the New York "Evening Post,"[5] "but we have been told, upon what we deem good authority, that no such thing as a combined, unitary, deliberative administration exists; that the President's brave willingness to take all responsibility has quite neutralized the idea of a joint responsibility; and that orders of the highest importance are issued, and movements commanded, which cabinet officers learn of as other people do, or, what is worse, which the cabinet officers disapprove and protest against. Each cabinet officer, again, controls his own department pretty much as he pleases, without consultation with the President or with his coadjutors, and often in the face of determinations which have been reached by the others." A picture this which forcibly reminds one of a certain imperious Prime Minister, in his last days created Earl of Chatham. These reports may have been true or they may have been mere rumors; but they depict a perfectly possible state of affairs. There is no influence except the ascendency or tact of the President himself to keep a Cabinet in harmony and to dispose it to coöperation; so that it would be very difficult to lay down any rules as to what elements really constitute an Executive. Those elements can be

---

[4] State, Treasury, War, Navy.
[5] As quoted in *Macmillan's Magazine*, vol. vii., p. 67.

determined exactly of only one administration at a time, and of that only after it has closed, and some one who knows its secrets has come forward to tell them. We think of Mr. Lincoln rather than of his Secretaries when we look back to the policy of the war-time; but we think of Mr. Hamilton rather than of President Washington when we look back to the policy of the first administration. Daniel Webster was bigger than President Fillmore, and President Jackson was bigger than Mr. Secretary Van Buren. It depends for the most part upon the character and training, the previous station, of the cabinet officers, whether or not they act as governing factors in administration, just as it depends upon the President's talents and preparatory schooling whether or not he is a mere figure-head. A weak President may prove himself wiser than the convention which nominated him, by overshadowing himself with a Cabinet of notables.

From the necessity of the case, however, the President cannot often be really supreme in matters of administration, except as the Speaker of the House of Representatives is supreme in legislation, as appointer of those who are supreme in its several departments. The President is no greater than his prerogative of veto makes him; he is, in other words, powerful rather as a branch of the legislature than as the titular head of the Executive. Almost all distinctively executive functions are specifically bestowed upon the heads of the departments. No President, however earnest and industrious, can keep the Navy in a state of creditable efficiency if he have a corrupt or incapable Secretary in the Navy Department; he cannot prevent the army from suffering the damage of demoralization if the Secretary of War is without either ability, experience, or conscience; there will be corrupt jobs in the Department of Justice, do what he will to correct the methods of a deceived or deceitful Attorney-General; he cannot secure even-handed equity for the Indian tribes if the Secretary of the Interior chooses to thwart him; and the Secretary of State may do as much mischief behind his back as can the Secretary of the Treasury. He might master the details and so control the administration of some one of the departments, but he can scarcely oversee them all with any degree of strictness. His knowledge of what they have done or are doing comes, of course, from the Secretaries themselves, and his annual messages to Congress are in large part but a recapitulation of the chief contents of the detailed reports which the heads of the departments themselves submit at the same time to the Houses.

It is easy, however, to exaggerate the power of the Cabinet.

After all has been said, it is evident that they differ from the permanent officials only in not being permanent. Their tenure of office is made to depend upon the supposition that their functions are political rather than simply ministerial, independent rather than merely instrumental. They are made party representatives because of the fiction that they direct policy. In reality the First Comptroller of the Treasury has almost, if not quite, as much weight in directing departmental business as has the Secretary of the Treasury himself, and it would practically be quite as useful to have his office, which is in intention permanent, vacated by every change of administration as to have that rule with regard to the office of his official chief. The permanent organization, the clerical forces of the departments, have in the Secretaries a sort of *sliding top*; though it would probably be just as convenient in practice to have this lid permanent as to have it movable. That the Secretaries are not in fact the directors of the executive policy of the government, I have shown in pointing out the thorough-going supervision of even the details of administration which it is the disposition of the Standing Committees of Congress to exercise. In the actual control of affairs no one can do very much without gaining the ears of the Committees. The heads of the departments could, of course, act much more wisely in many matters than the Committees can, because they have an intimacy with the workings and the wants of those departments which no Committee can possibly possess. But Committees prefer to govern in the dark rather than not to govern at all, and the Secretaries, as a matter of fact, find themselves bound in all things larger than routine details by laws which have been made for them and which they have no legitimate means of modifying.

Of course the Secretaries are in the leading-strings of statutes, and all their duties look towards a strict obedience to Congress. Congress made them and can unmake them. It is to Congress that they must render account for the conduct of administration. The head of each department must every year make a detailed report of the expenditures of the department, and a minute account of the facilities of work and the division of functions in the department, naming each clerk of its force. The chief duties of one cabinet officer will serve to illustrate the chief duties of his colleagues. It is the duty of the Secretary of the Treasury[6] "to prepare plans for the improvement and management of the

---

[6] I quote from an excellent handbook, *The United States Government*, by Lamphere.

revenue and for the support of the public credit; to prescribe forms of keeping and rendering all public accounts; to grant all warrants for moneys to be issued from the Treasury in pursuance of appropriations made by Congress; to report to the Senate or House, in person or in writing, information required by them pertaining to his office; and to perform all duties relating to finance that he shall be directed to perform." "He is required to report to Congress annually, on the first Monday in June, the results of the information compiled by the Bureau of Statistics, showing the condition of manufactures, domestic trade, currency, and banks in the several States and Territories." "He prescribes regulations for the killing in Alaska Territory and adjacent waters of minks, martens, sable, and other fur-bearing animals." "And he must lay before Congress each session the reports of the Auditors, showing the applications of the appropriations made for the War and Navy Departments, and also abstracts and tabulated forms showing separate accounts of the moneys received from internal duties."

Of course it is of the utmost importance that a Secretary who has within his choice some of the minor plans for the management of the revenue and for the maintenance of the public credit should be carefully chosen from amongst men skilled in financial administration and experienced in business regulation; but it is no more necessary that the man selected for such responsible duties should be an active politician, called to preside over his department only so long as the President who appointed him continues to hold office and to like him, than it is to have a strictly political officer to fulfill his other duty of prescribing game laws for Alaska and Alaskan waters. Fur-bearing animals can have no connection with political parties,—except, perhaps, as "spoils." Indeed, it is a positive disadvantage that Mr. Secretary should be chosen upon such a principle. He cannot have the knowledge, and must therefore lack the efficiency, of a permanent official separated from the partisan conflicts of politics and advanced to the highest office of his department by a regular series of promotions won by long service. The general policy of the government in matters of finance, everything that affects the greater operations of the Treasury, depends upon legislation, and is altogether in the hands of the Committees of Ways and Means and of Finance; so that it is entirely apart from good sense to make an essentially political office out of the post of that officer who controls only administrative details.

And this remark would seem to apply with still greater force to the offices of the other Secretaries. They have even less energetic scope than the Secretary of the Treasury has. There must under any system be considerable power in the hands of the officer who handles and dispenses vast revenues, even though he handle and dispense them as directed by his employers. Money in its goings to and fro makes various mares go by the way, so to speak. It cannot move in great quantities without moving a large part of the commercial world with it. Management even of financial details may be made instrumental in turning the money-markets upside down. The Secretary of the Treasury is, therefore, less a mere chief clerk than are his coadjutors; and if his duties are not properly political, theirs certainly are not.

In view of this peculiarity of the Secretaries, in being appointed as partisans and endowed as mere officials, it is interesting to inquire what and whom they represent. They are clearly meant to represent the political party to which they belong; but it very often happens that it is impossible for them to do so. They must sometimes obey the opposite party. It is our habit to speak of the party to which the President is known to adhere and which has control of appointments to the offices of the civil service as "the party in power"; but it is very evident that control of the executive machinery is not all or even a very large part of power in a country ruled as ours is. In so far as the President is an executive officer he is the servant of Congress; and the members of the Cabinet, being confined to executive functions, are altogether the servants of Congress. The President, however, besides being titular head of the executive service, is to the extent of his veto a third branch of the legislature, and the party which he represents is in power in the same sense that it would be in power if it had on its side a majority of the members of either of the other two branches of Congress. If the House and Senate are of one party and the President and his ministers of the opposite, the President's party can hardly be said to be in power beyond the hindering and thwarting faculty of the veto. The Democrats were in power during the sessions of the Twenty-fifth Congress because they had a majority in the Senate as well as Andrew Jackson in the White House; but later Presidents have had both House and Senate against them.[7]

[7] "In America the President cannot prevent any law from being passed, nor can he evade the obligation of enforcing it. His sincere and zealous coöperation is no doubt useful, but it is not indispensable, in the carrying on of public affairs. All his important acts are directly or indirectly submitted to the legislature, and of his own free authority he can do but little. It is, therefore, his weakness, and not his power, which enables him to remain in opposition to

It is this constant possibility of party diversity between the Executive and Congress which so much complicates our system of party government. The history of administrations is not necessarily the history of parties. Presidential elections may turn the scale of party ascendency one way, and the intermediate congressional elections may quite reverse the balance. A strong party administration, by which the energy of the State is concentrated in the hands of a single well-recognized political organization, which is by reason of its power saddled with all responsibility, may sometimes be possible, but it must often be impossible. We are thus shut out in part from real party government such as we desire, and such as it is unquestionably desirable to set up in every system like ours. Party government can exist only when the absolute control of administration, the appointment of its officers as well as the direction of its means and policy, is given immediately into the hands of that branch of the government whose power is paramount, the representative body. Roger Sherman, whose perception was amongst the keenest and whose sagacity was amongst the surest in the great Convention of 1787, was very bold and outspoken in declaring this fact and in proposing to give it candid recognition. Perceiving very clearly the omnipotence which must inevitably belong to a national Congress such as the convention was about to create, he avowed that "he considered the executive magistracy as nothing more than an institution for carrying the will of the legislature into effect; that the person or persons [who should constitute the executive] ought to be appointed by, and accountable to, the legislature only, which was the depository of the supreme will of the society." Indeed, the executive was in his view so entirely the servant of the legislative will that he saw good reason to think that the legislature should judge of the number of persons of which the executive should be composed; and there seem to have been others in the convention who went along with him in substantial agreement as to these matters. It would seem to have been only a desire for the creation of as many as possible of those balances of power which now decorate the "literary theory" of the Constitution which they made that prevented a universal acquiescence in these views.

The anomaly which has resulted is seen most clearly in the

Congress. In Europe, harmony must reign between the Crown and the other branches of the legislature, because a collision between them may prove serious; in America, this harmony is not indispensable, because such a collision is impossible."—De Tocqueville, i. p. 124.

party relations of the President and his Cabinet. The President is a partisan,—is elected because he is partisan,—and yet he not infrequently negatives the legislation passed by the party whom he represents; and it may be said to be nowadays a very rare thing to find a Cabinet made up of truly representative party men. They are the men of his party whom the President likes, but not necessarily or always the men whom that party relishes. So low, indeed, has the reputation of some of our later Cabinets fallen, even in the eyes of men of their own political connection, that writers in the best of our public prints feel at full liberty to speak of their members with open contempt. "When Mr. ——— was made Secretary of the Navy," laughs the New York "Nation," "no one doubted that he would treat the Department as 'spoils,' and consequently nobody has been disappointed. He is one of the statesmen who can hardly conceive of a branch of the public Administration having no spoils in it." And that this separation of the Cabinet from real party influence, and from the party leadership which would seem properly to belong to its official station, is a natural result of our constitutional scheme is made patent in the fact that the Cabinet has advanced in party insignificance as the system has grown older. The connection between the early Cabinets and the early Congresses was very like the relations between leaders and their party. Both Hamilton and Gallatin led rather than obeyed the Houses; and it was many years before the suggestions of heads of departments ceased to be sure of respectful and acquiescent consideration from the legislative Committees. But as the Committees gained facility and power the leadership of the Cabinet lost ground. Congress took command of the government so soon as ever it got command of itself, and no Secretary of to-day can claim by virtue of his office recognition as a party authority. Congress looks upon advice offered to it by anybody but its own members as gratuitous impertinence.

At the same time it is quite evident that the means which Congress has of controlling the departments and of exercising the searching oversight at which it aims are limited and defective. Its intercourse with the President is restricted to the executive messages, and its intercourse with the departments has no easier channels than private consultations between executive officials and the Committees, informal interviews of the ministers with individual members of Congress, and the written correspondence which the cabinet officers from time to time address to the presiding officers of the two Houses, at stated intervals, or in response to formal resolutions of inquiry. Congress stands almost helplessly outside of the departments. Even the special, irksome, ungracious investigations which it from time to time institutes in its spasmodic endeavors to dispel or confirm suspicions of malfeasance or of wanton corruption do not afford it more than a glimpse of the inside of a small province of federal administration. Hostile or designing officials can always hold it at arm's length by dexterous evasions and concealments. It can violently disturb, but it cannot often fathom, the waters of the sea in which the bigger fish of the civil service swim and feed. Its dragnet stirs without cleansing the bottom. Unless it have at the head of the departments capable, fearless men, altogether in its confidence and entirely in sympathy with its designs, it is clearly helpless to do more than affright those officials whose consciences are their accusers.

And it is easy to see how the commands as well as the questions of Congress may be evaded, if not directly disobeyed, by the executive agents. Its Committees may command, but they cannot superintend the execution of their commands. The Secretaries, though not free enough to have any independent policy of their own, are free enough to be very poor, because very unmanageable, servants. Once installed, their hold upon their offices does not depend upon the will of Congress. If they please the President, and keep upon living terms with their colleagues, they need not seriously regard the displeasure of the Houses, unless, indeed, by actual crime, they rashly put themselves in the way of its judicial wrath. If their folly be not too overt and extravagant, their authority may continue theirs till the earth has four times made her annual journey round the sun. They may make daily blunders in administration and repeated mistakes in business, may thwart the plans of Congress in a hundred small, vexatious ways, and yet all the while snap their fingers at its dissatisfaction or displeasure. They are denied the gratification of possessing real power, but they have the satisfaction of being secure in a petty independence which gives them a chance to be tricky and scheming. There are ways and ways of obeying; and if Congress be not pleased, why need they care? Congress did not give them their places, and cannot easily take them away.

Still it remains true that all the big affairs of the departments are conducted in obedience to the direction of the Standing Committees. The President nominates, and with legislative approval appoints, to the more important offices of the government, and the members of the Cabinet have the privilege of advising him as to matters in most of which he has no power of final action without the concurrence of the Senate; but the gist of all policy is decided by legislative, not by executive, will. It can be no great satisfaction to any man to possess the barren privilege of suggesting the best means of managing the every-day routine business of the several bureaux so long as the larger plans which that business is meant to advance are made for him by others who are set over him. If one is commanded to go to this place or to that place, and must go, will he, nill he, it can be but small solace to him that he is left free to determine whether he will ride or walk in going the journey. The only serious questions are whether or not this so great and real control exerted by Congress can be exercised efficiently and with sufficient responsibility to those whom Congress represents, and whether good government is promoted by the arrangement.

No one, I take it for granted, is disposed to disallow the principle that the representatives of the people are the proper ultimate authority in all matters of government, and that administration is merely the clerical part of government. Legislation is the originating force. It determines what shall be done; and the President, if he cannot or will not stay legislation by the use of his extraordinary power as a branch of the legislature, is plainly bound in duty to render unquestioning obedience to Congress. And if it be his duty to obey, still more is obedience the bounden duty of his subordinates. The power of making laws is in its very nature and essence the power of directing, and that power is given to Congress. The principle is without drawback, and is inseparably of a piece with all Anglo-Saxon usage; the difficulty, if there be any, must lie in the choice of means whereby to energize the principle. The natural means would seem to be the right on the part of the representative body to have all the executive servants of its will under its close and constant supervision, and to hold them to a strict accountability: in other words, to have the privilege of dismissing them whenever their service became unsatisfactory. This is the matter-of-course privilege of every other master; and if Congress does not possess it, its mastery is hampered without being denied. The executive officials are its servants all the same; the only difference is that if they prove negligent, or incapable, or deceitful servants Congress must rest content with the best that can be got out of them until its chief administrative agent, the President, chooses to appoint better. It cannot make them docile, though it may compel them to be obedient in all greater matters. In authority of rule Congress is made master, but in means of rule it is made mere magistrate.

It commands with absolute lordship, but it can discipline for disobedience only by slow and formal judicial process.

Upon Machiavelli's declaration that "nothing is more important to the stability of the state than that facility should be given by its constitution for the accusation of those who are supposed to have committed any public wrong," a writer in the "Westminster Review" makes this thoughtful comment: "The benefit of such a provision is twofold. First, the salutary fear of the probable coming of a day of account will restrain the evil practices of some bad men and self-seekers; secondly, the legal outlet of accusation gives vent to peccant humors in the body politic, which, if checked and driven inward, would work to the utter ruin of the constitution; . . . the distinction is lost between accusation and calumny."[8] And of course it was these benefits which our federal Constitution was meant to secure by means of its machinery of impeachment. No servant of the state, not even the President himself, was to be beyond the reach of accusation by the House of Representatives and of trial by the Senate. But the processes of impeachment, like those of amendment, are ponderous and difficult to handle. It requires something like passion to set them a-going; and nothing short of the grossest offenses against the plain law of the land will suffice to give them speed and effectiveness. Indignation so great as to overgrow party interest may secure a conviction; nothing less can. Indeed, judging by our past experiences, impeachment may be said to be little more than an empty menace. The House of Representatives is a tardy grand jury, and the Senate an uncertain court.

Besides, great crimes such as might speed even impeachment are not ordinary things in the loosest public service. An open-eyed public opinion can generally give them effective check. That which usually and every day clogs and hampers good government is folly or incapacity on the part of the ministers of state. Even more necessary, therefore, than a power clothed with authority to accuse, try, and punish for public crime is some ultimate authority, whose privilege it shall be to dismiss for inefficiency. Impeachment is aimed altogether above the head of business management. A merchant would not think it fair, even if it were lawful, to shoot a clerk who could not learn the business. Dismissal is quite as effective for his purposes, and more merciful to the clerk. The crying inconvenience of our system is, therefore, that the constitutional authority whose prerogative it is to direct policy and oversee administration has fewer facilities for getting its

8 *Westminster Review*, vol. lxvi., p. 193.

work well done than has the humblest citizen for obtaining satisfactory aid in his own undertakings. The authority most interested in appointments and dismissals in the civil service has little to do with the one and less to do with the other. The President appoints with the sanction of the Senate, and cannot dismiss his advisers without legislative consent;[9] yet the ministers in reality serve, not the President, but Congress, and Congress can neither appoint nor dismiss. In other words, the President must in both acts take the initiative, though he is not the real master; and Congress, which is the real master, has in these vital matters only a consultative voice, which it may utter, through its upper chamber, only when its opinion is asked. I should regard my business as a hopeless undertaking if my chief agent had to be appointed by a third party, and, besides being himself put beyond my power of control, were charged with the choice and discipline of all his subordinates, subject not to my directions, but simply to my acquiescence!

The relations existing between Congress and the departments must be fatally demoralizing to both. There is and can be between them nothing like confidential and thorough coöperation. The departments may be excused for that attitude of hostility which they sometimes assume towards Congress, because it is quite human for the servant to fear and deceive the master whom he does not regard as his friend, but suspects of being a distrustful spy of his movements. Congress cannot control the officers of the executive without disgracing them. Its only whip is investigation, semi-judicial examination into corners suspected to be dirty. It must draw the public eye by openly avowing a suspicion of malfeasance, and must then magnify and intensify the scandal by setting its Committees to cross-examining scared subordinates and sulky ministers. And after all is over and the murder out, probably nothing is done. The offenders, if any one has offended, often remain in office, shamed before the world, and ruined in the estimation of all honest people, but still drawing their salaries and comfortably waiting for the short memory of the public mind to forget them. Why unearth the carcass if you cannot remove it?

Then, too, the departments frequently complain of the incessant exactions made upon them by Congress. They grumble that they are kept busy in satisfying its curiosity and in meeting the demands of its uneasy activity. The clerks have ordinarily as much as they can do in keeping afoot the usual routine business

[9] Tenure of Office Act, already discussed.

of their departments; but Congress is continually calling upon them for information which must be laboriously collected from all sorts of sources, remote and accessible. A great speech in the Senate may cost them hours of anxious toil: for the Senator who makes it is quite likely beforehand to introduce a resolution calling upon one of the Secretaries for full statistics with reference to this, that, or the other topic upon which he desires to speak. If it be finance, he must have comparative tables of taxation; if it be commerce or the tariff, he cannot dispense with any of the minutest figures of the Treasury accounts; whatever be his theme, he cannot lay his foundations more surely than upon official information, and the Senate is usually unhesitatingly ready with an easy assent to the resolution which puts the whole clerical force of the administration at his service. And of course the House too asks innumerable questions, which patient clerks and protesting Secretaries must answer to the last and most minute particular. This is what the departmental officials testily call the tyranny of Congress, and no impartial third person can reasonably forbid them the use of the word.

I know of few things harder to state clearly and within reasonable compass than just how the nation keeps control of policy in spite of these hide-and-seek vagaries of authority. Indeed, it is doubtful if it does keep control through all the roundabout paths which legislative and executive responsibility are permitted to take. It must follow Congress somewhat blindly; Congress is known to obey without altogether understanding its Committees: and the Committees must consign the execution of their plans to officials who have opportunities not a few to hoodwink them. At the end of these blind processes is it probable that the ultimate authority, the people, is quite clear in its mind as to what has been done or what may be done another time? Take, for example, financial policy,—a very fair example, because, as I have shown, the legislative stages of financial policy are more talked about than any other congressional business, though for that reason an extreme example. If, after appropriations and adjustments of taxation have been tardily and in much tribulation of scheming and argument agreed upon by the House, the imperative suggestions and stubborn insistence of the Senate confuse matters till hardly the Conference Committees themselves know clearly what the outcome of the disagreements has been; and if, when these compromise measures are launched as laws, the method of their execution is beyond the view of the Houses, in the semi-privacy of the departments, how is the comprehension—not to speak of the will—of the people to keep any sort of hold upon the course of affairs? There are no screws of responsibility which they can turn upon the consciences or upon the official thumbs of the congressional Committees principally concerned. Congressional Committees are nothing to the nation: they are only pieces of the interior mechanism of Congress. To Congress they stand or fall. And, since Congress itself can scarcely be sure of having its own way with them, the constituencies are manifestly unlikely to be able to govern them. As for the departments, the people can hardly do more in drilling them to unquestioning obedience and docile efficiency than Congress can. Congress is, and must be, in these matters the nation's eyes and voice. If it cannot see what goes wrong and cannot get itself heeded when it commands, the nation likewise is both blind and dumb.

This, plainly put, is the practical result of the piecing of authority, the cutting of it up into small bits, which is contrived in our constitutional system. Each branch of the government is fitted out with a small section of responsibility, whose limited opportunities afford to the conscience of each many easy escapes. Every suspected culprit may shift the responsibility upon his fellows. Is Congress rated for corrupt or imperfect or foolish legislation? It may urge that it has to follow hastily its Committees or do nothing at all but talk; how can it help it if a stupid Committee leads it unawares into unjust or fatuous enterprises? Does administration blunder and run itself into all sorts of straits? The Secretaries hasten to plead the unreasonable or unwise commands of Congress, and Congress falls to blaming the Secretaries. The Secretaries aver that the whole mischief might have been avoided if they had only been allowed to suggest the proper measures; and the men who framed the existing measures in their turn avow their despair of good government so long as they must intrust all their plans to the bungling incompetence of men who are appointed by and responsible to somebody else. How is the schoolmaster, the nation, to know which boy needs the whipping?

Moreover, it is impossible to deny that this division of authority and concealment of responsibility are calculated to subject the government to a very distressing paralysis in moments of emergency. There are few, if any, important steps that can be taken by any one branch of the government without the consent or coöperation of some other branch. Congress must act through the President and his Cabinet; the President and his Cabinet must wait upon the will of Congress. There is no one supreme, ultimate head—whether magistrate or representative body—which can decide at once and with conclusive authority what shall be done at those times when some decision there must be, and that immediately. Of course this lack is of a sort to be felt at all times, in seasons of tranquil rounds of business as well as at moments of sharp crisis; but in times of sudden exigency it might prove fatal,—fatal either in breaking down the system or in failing to meet the emergency.[10] Policy cannot be either prompt or straightforward when it must serve many masters. It must either equivocate, or hesitate, or fail altogether. It may set out with clear purpose from Congress, but get waylaid or maimed by the Executive.

If there be one principle clearer than another, it is this: that in any business, whether of government or of mere merchandising, *somebody must be trusted*, in order that when things go wrong it may be quite plain who should be punished. In order to drive trade at the speed and with the success you desire, you must confide without suspicion in your chief clerk, giving him the power to ruin you, because you thereby furnish him with a motive for serving you. His reputation, his own honor or disgrace, all his own commercial prospects, hang upon your success. And human nature is much the same in government as in the dry-goods trade. *Power and strict accountability for its use* are the essential constituents of good government. A sense of highest responsibility, a dignifying and elevating sense of being trusted, together with a consciousness of being in an official station so conspicuous that no faithful discharge of duty can go unacknowledged and unrewarded, and no breach of trust undiscovered and unpunished,—these are the influences, the only influences, which foster practical, energetic, and trustworthy statesmanship. The best rulers are always those to whom great power is intrusted in such a manner as to make them feel that they will surely be abundantly honored and recompensed for a just and patriotic use of it, and to make them know that nothing can shield them from full retribution for every abuse of it.

It is, therefore, manifestly a radical defect in our federal system that it parcels out power and confuses responsibility as it does. The main purpose of the Convention of 1787 seems to have been to accomplish this grievous mistake. The "literary theory" of checks and balances is simply a consistent account

[10] These "ifs" are abundantly supported by the executive acts of the war-time. The Constitution had then to stand aside that President Lincoln might be as prompt as the seeming necessities of the time.

of what our constitution-makers tried to do; and those checks and balances have proved mischievous just to the extent to which they have succeeded in establishing themselves as realities. It is quite safe to say that were it possible to call together again the members of that wonderful Convention to view the work of their hands in the light of the century that has tested it, they would be the first to admit that the only fruit of dividing power had been to make it irresponsible. It is just this that has made civil service reform tarry in this country and that makes it still almost doubtful of issue. We are in just the case that England was in before she achieved the reform for which we are striving. The date of the reform in England is no less significant than the fact. It was not accomplished until a distinct responsibility of the Ministers of the Crown to one, and to only one, master had been established beyond all uncertainty. This is the most striking and suggestive lesson to be gathered from Mr. Eaton's interesting and valuable history of Civil Service in Great Britain. The Reform was originated in 1853 by the Cabinet of Lord Aberdeen. It sprang from the suggestion of the appointing officers, and was carried through in the face of opposition from the House of Commons, because, paradoxically enough, the Ministry had at last come to feel their responsibility to the Commons, or rather to the nation whom the Commons represented.

Those great improvements which have been made in the public service of the British empire since the days of Walpole and Newcastle have gone hand in hand with the perfecting of the system now known as responsible Cabinet government. That system was slow in coming to perfection. It was not till long after Walpole's day that unity of responsibility on the part of the Cabinet—and that singleness of responsibility which made them look only to the Commons for authority—came to be recognized as an established constitutional principle. "As a consequence of the earlier practice of constructing Cabinets of men of different political views, it followed that the members of such Cabinets did not and could not regard their responsibility to Parliament as one and indivisible. The resignation of an important member, or even of the Prime Minister, was not regarded as necessitating the simultaneous retirement of his colleagues. Even so late as the fall of Sir Robert Walpole, fifty years after the Revolution Settlement (and itself the first instance of resignation in deference to a hostile parliamentary vote) we find the King requesting Walpole's successor, Pulteney, 'not to distress the Government by making too many changes in the midst of a session'; and Pulteney replying that he would be satisfied, provided 'the main forts of the Government,' or, in other words, the principal offices of state, were placed in his hands. It was not till the displacement of Lord North's ministry by that of Lord Rockingham in 1782 that a whole administration, with the exception of the Lord Chancellor, was changed by a vote of want of confidence passed in the House of Commons. Thenceforth, however, the resignation of the head of a Government in deference to an adverse vote of the popular chamber has invariably been accompanied by the resignation of all his colleagues."[11] But, even after the establishment of that precedent, it was still many years before Cabinets were free to please none but the Commons,—free to follow their own policies without authoritative suggestion from the sovereign. Until the death of the fourth George they were made to feel that they owed a double allegiance: to the Commons and to the King. The composition of Ministries still depended largely on the royal whim, and their actions were hampered by the necessity of steering a careful middle course between the displeasure of parliament and the ill-will of His Majesty. The present century had run far on towards the reign of Victoria before they were free to pay undivided obedience to the representatives of the people. When once they had become responsible to the Commons alone, however, and almost as soon as they were assured of their new position as the servants of the nation, they were prompted to even hazardous efforts for the reform of the civil service. They were conscious that the entire weight and responsibility of government rested upon their shoulders, and, as men regardful of the interests of the party which they represented, jealous for the preservation of their own fair names, and anxious, consequently, for the promotion of wise rule, they were naturally and of course the first to advocate a better system of appointment to that service whose chiefs they were recognized to be. They were prompt to declare that it was the "duty of the executive to provide for the efficient and harmonious working of the civil service," and that they could not "transfer that duty to any other body far less competent than themselves without infringing a great and important constitutional principle, already too often infringed, to the great detriment of the public service." They therefore determined themselves to inaugurate the merit-system without waiting for the assent of parliament, by simply surrendering their power of appointment in the various departments to a non-partisan examining board, trusting to the power of public opinion to induce par-

[11] *Central Government* (Eng. Citizen Series), H. D. Traill, p. 20.

liament, after the thing had been done, to vote sufficient money to put the scheme into successful operation. And they did not reckon without their host. Reluctant as the members of the House of Commons were to resign that control of the national patronage which they had from time immemorial been accustomed to exercise by means of various crooked indirections, and which it had been their pleasure and their power to possess, they had not the face to avow their suspicious unwillingness in answer to the honorable call of a trusted Ministry who were supported in their demand by all that was honest in public sentiment, and the world was afforded the gratifying but unwonted spectacle of party leaders sacrificing to the cause of good government, freely and altogether of their own accord, the "spoils" of office so long dear to the party and to the assembly which they represented and served.

In this country the course of the reform was quite the reverse. Neither the Executive nor Congress began it. The call for it came imperatively from the people; it was a formulated demand of public opinion made upon Congress, and it had to be made again and again, each time with more determined emphasis, before Congress heeded. It worked its way up from the convictions of the many to the purposes of the few. Amongst the chief difficulties that have stood in its way, and which still block its perfect realization, is that peculiarity of structure which I have just now pointed out as intrinsic in the scheme of divided power which runs through the Constitution. One of the conditions precedent to any real and lasting reform of the civil service, in a country whose public service is moulded by the conditions of self-government, is the drawing of a sharp line of distinction between those offices which are political and those which are *non*-political. The strictest rules of business discipline, of merit-tenure and earned promotion, must rule every office whose incumbent has naught to do with choosing between policies; but no rules except the choice of parties can or should make and unmake, reward or punish, those officers whose privilege it is to fix upon the political purposes which administration shall be made to serve. These latter are not many under any form of government. There are said to be but fifty such at most in the civil service of Great Britain; but these fifty go in or out as the balance of power shifts from party to party. In the case of our own civil service it would, I take it, be extremely hard to determine where the line should be drawn. In all the higher grades this particular distinction is quite obscured. A doubt exists as to the Cabinet itself. Are the

Secretaries political or non-political officers? It would seem that they are exclusively neither. They are at least semi-political. They are, on the one hand, merely the servants of Congress, and yet, on the other hand, they have enough freedom of discretion to mar and color, if not to choose, political ends. They can wreck plans, if they cannot make them. Should they be made permanent officials because they are mere Secretaries, or should their tenure depend upon the fortunes of parties because they have many chances to render party services? And if the one rule or the other is to be applied to them, to how many, and to which of their chief subordinates, is it to be extended? If they are not properly or necessarily party men, let them pass the examinations and run the gauntlet of the usual tests of efficiency, let errand-boys work up to Secretaryships; but if not, let their responsibility to their party be made strict and determinate. That is the cardinal point of practical civil service reform.

This doubt as to the exact *status* in the system of the chief ministers of state is a most striking commentary on the system itself. Its complete self is logical and simple. But its complete self exists only in theory. Its real self offers a surprise and presents a mystery at every change of view. The practical observer who seeks for facts and actual conditions of organization is often sorely puzzled to come at the real methods of government. Pitfalls await him on every side. If constitutional lawyers of strait-laced consciences filled Congress and officered the departments, every clause of the Constitution would be accorded a formal obedience, and it would be as easy to know beforehand just what the government will be like inside to-morrow as it is now to know what it was like outside yesterday. But neither the knowledge nor the consciences of politicians keep them very close to the Constitution; and it is with politicians that we have to deal nowadays in studying the government. Every government is largely what the men are who constitute it. If the character or opinions of legislators and administrators change from time to time, the nature of the government changes with them; and as both their characters and their opinions do change very often it is very hard to make a picture of the government which can be said to have been perfectly faithful yesterday, and can be confidently expected to be exactly accurate to-morrow. Add to these embarrassments, which may be called the embarrassments of human nature, other embarrassments such as our system affords, the embarrassments of subtle legal distinctions, a fine theoretical plan made in delicate hair-lines, requirements of law which can hardly be met and can easily and naturally be evaded or disregarded, and you have in full the conception of the difficulties which attend a practical exposition of the real facts of federal administration. It is not impossible to point out what the Executive was intended to be, what it has sometimes been, or what it might be; nor is it forbidden the diligent to discover the main conditions which mould it to the forms of congressional supremacy; but more than this is not to be expected.

VI.

CONCLUSION.

Political philosophy must analyze political history; it must distinguish what is due to the excellence of the people, and what to the excellence of the laws; it must carefully calculate the exact effect of each part of the constitution, though thus it may destroy many an idol of the multitude, and detect the secret of utility where but few imagined it to lie.—BAGEHOT.

Congress always makes what haste it can to legislate. It is the prime object of its rules to expedite law-making. Its customs are fruits of its characteristic diligence in enactment. Be the matters small or great, frivolous or grave, which busy it, its aim is to have laws always a-making. Its temper is strenuously legislative. That it cannot regulate all the questions to which its attention is weekly invited is its misfortune, not its fault; is due to the human limitation of its faculties, not to any narrow circumscription of its desires. If its committee machinery is inadequate to the task of bringing to action more than one out of every hundred of the bills introduced, it is not because the quick clearance of the docket is not the motive of its organic life. If legislation, therefore, were the only or the chief object for which it should live, it would not be possible to withhold admiration from those clever hurrying rules and those inexorable customs which seek to facilitate it. Nothing but a doubt as to whether or not Congress should confine itself to law-making can challenge with a question the utility of its organization as a facile statute-devising machine.

The political philosopher of these days of self-government has, however, something more than a doubt with which to gainsay the usefulness of a sovereign representative body which confines itself to legislation to the exclusion of all other functions. Buckle declared, indeed, that the chief use and value of legislation nowadays lay in its opportunity and power to remedy the mistakes of the legislation of the past; that it was beneficent only when it carried healing in its wings; that repeal was more blessed than enactment. And it is certainly true that the greater part of the labor of legislation consists in carrying the loads recklessly or bravely shouldered in times gone by, when the animal which is now a bull was only a calf, and in completing, if they may be completed, the tasks once undertaken in the shape of unambitious schemes which at the outset looked innocent enough. Having got his foot into it, the legislator finds it difficult, if not impossible, to get it out again. "The modern industrial organization, including banks, corporations, joint-stock companies, financial devices, national debts, paper currency, national systems of taxation, is largely the creation of legislation (not in its historical origin, but in the mode of its existence and in its authority), and is largely regulated by legislation. Capital is the breath of life to this organization, and every day, as the organization becomes more complex and delicate, the folly of assailing capital or credit becomes greater. At the same time it is evident that the task of the legislator to embrace in his view the whole system, to adjust his rules so that the play of the civil institutions shall not alter the play of the economic forces, requires more training and more acumen. Furthermore, the greater the complication and delicacy of the industrial system, the greater the chances for cupidity when backed by craft, and the task of the legislator to meet and defeat the attempts of this cupidity is one of constantly increasing difficulty."[1]

Legislation unquestionably generates legislation. Every statute may be said to have a long lineage of statutes behind it; and whether that lineage be honorable or of ill repute is as much a question as to each individual statute as it can be with regard to the ancestry of each individual legislator. Every statute in its turn has a numerous progeny, and only time and opportunity can decide whether its offspring will bring it honor or shame. Once begin the dance of legislation, and you must struggle through its mazes as best you can to its breathless end,—if any end there be.

It is not surprising, therefore, that the enacting, revising, tinkering, repealing of laws should engross the attention and engage the entire energy of such a body as Congress. It is, however, easy to see how it might be better employed; or, at least, how it might add others to this overshadowing function, to the

[1] Professor Sumner's *Andrew Jackson* (American Statesmen Series), p. 226. "Finally," adds Prof. S., "the methods and machinery of democratic republican self-government—caucuses, primaries, committees, and conventions—lend themselves perhaps more easily than any other methods and machinery to the uses of selfish cliques which seek political influence for interested purposes."

infinite advantage of the government. Quite as important as legislation is vigilant oversight of administration; and even more
important than legislation is the instruction and guidance in political affairs which the people might receive from a body which
kept all national concerns suffused in a broad daylight of discussion. There is no similar legislature in existence which is so
shut up to the one business of lawmaking as is our Congress.
As I have said, it in a way superintends administration by the
exercise of semi-judicial powers of investigation, whose limitations and insufficiency are manifest. But other national legislatures command administration and verify their name of "parliaments" by talking official acts into notoriety. Our extra-constitutional party conventions, short-lived and poor in power as they
are, constitute our only machinery for that sort of control of the
executive which consists in the award of personal rewards and
punishments. This is the cardinal fact which differentiates Congress from the Chamber of Deputies and from Parliament, and
which puts it beyond the reach of those eminently useful functions whose exercise would so raise it in usefulness and in dignity.

An effective representative body, gifted with the power to rule,
ought, it would seem, not only to speak the will of the nation,
which Congress does, but also to lead it to its conclusions, to
utter the voice of its opinions, and to serve as its eyes in super-
intending all matters of government,—which Congress does not
do. The discussions which take place in Congress are aimed at
random. They now and again strike rather sharply the tender
spots in this, that, or the other measure; but, as I have said, no
two measures consciously join in purpose or agree in character,
and so debate must wander as widely as the subjects of debate.
Since there is little coherency about the legislation agreed upon,
there can be little coherency about the debates. There is no one
policy to be attacked or defended, but only a score or two of separate bills. To attend to such discussions is uninteresting; to be
instructed by them is impossible. There is some scandal and discomfort, but infinite advantage, in having every affair of administration subjected to the test of constant examination on the
part of the assembly which represents the nation. The chief use
of such inquisition is, not the direction of those affairs in a way
with which the country will be satisfied (though that itself is of
course all-important), but the enlightenment of the people,
which is always its sure consequence. Very few men are unequal
to a danger which they see and understand; all men quail before

a threatening which is dark and unintelligible, and suspect what is done behind a screen. If the people could have, through Congress, daily knowledge of all the more important transactions of the governmental offices, an insight into all that now seems withheld and private, their confidence in the executive, now so often shaken, would, I think, be very soon established. Because dishonesty *can* lurk under the privacies now vouchsafed our administrative agents, much that is upright and pure suffers unjust suspicion. Discoveries of guilt in a bureau cloud with doubts the trustworthiness of a department. As nothing is open enough for the quick and easy detection of peculation or fraud, so nothing is open enough for the due vindication and acknowledgment of honesty. The isolation and privacy which shield the one from discovery cheat the other of reward.

Inquisitiveness is never so forward, enterprising, and irrepressible as in a popular assembly which is given leave to ask questions and is afforded ready and abundant means of getting its questions answered. No cross-examination is more searching than that to which a minister of the Crown is subjected by the all-curious Commons. "Sir Robert Peel once asked to have a number of questions carefully written down which they asked him one day in succession in the House of Commons. They seemed a list of everything that could occur in the British empire or to the brain of a member of parliament."[2] If one considered only the wear and tear upon ministers of state, which the plague of constant interrogation must inflict, he could wish that their lives, if useful, might be spared this blight of unending explanation; but no one can overestimate the immense advantage of a facility so unlimited for knowing all that is going on in the places where authority lives. The conscience of every member of the representative body is at the service of the nation. All that he feels bound to know he can find out; and what he finds out goes to the ears of the country. The question is his, the answer the nation's. And the inquisitiveness of such bodies as Congress is the best conceivable source of information. Congress is the only body which has the proper motive for inquiry, and it is the only body which has the power to act effectively upon the knowledge which its inquiries secure. The Press is merely curious or merely partisan. The people are scattered and unorganized. But Congress is, as it were, the corporate people, the mouthpiece of its will. It is a sovereign delegation which could ask questions with dignity, because with authority and with power to act.

[2] Bagehot: *Essay on Sir Robert Peel*, p. 24.

Congress is fast becoming the governing body of the nation, and yet the only power which it possesses in perfection is the power which is but a part of government, the power of legislation. Legislation is but the oil of government. It is that which lubricates its channels and speeds its wheels; that which lessens the friction and so eases the movement. Or perhaps I shall be admitted to have hit upon a closer and apter analogy if I say that legislation is like a foreman set over the forces of government. It issues the orders which others obey. It directs, it admonishes, but it does not do the actual heavy work of governing. A good foreman does, it is true, himself take a hand in the work which he guides; and so I suppose our legislation must be likened to a poor foreman, because it stands altogether apart from that work which it is set to see well done. Members of Congress ought not to be censured too severely, however, when they fail to check evil courses on the part of the executive. They have been denied the means of doing so promptly and with effect. Whatever intention may have controlled the compromises of constitution-making in 1787, their result was to give us, not government by discussion, which is the only tolerable sort of government for a people which tries to do its own governing, but only *legislation* by discussion, which is no more than a small part of government by discussion. What is quite as indispensable as the debate of problems of legislation is the debate of all matters of administration. It is even more important to know how the house is being built than to know how the plans of the architect were conceived and how his specifications were calculated. It is better to have skillful work—stout walls, reliable arches, unbending rafters, and windows sure to "expel the winter's flaw"—than a drawing on paper which is the admiration of all the practical artists in the country. The discipline of an army depends quite as much upon the temper of the troops as upon the orders of the day.

It is the proper duty of a representative body to look diligently into every affair of government and to talk much about what it sees. It is meant to be the eyes and the voice, and to embody the wisdom and will of its constituents. Unless Congress have and use every means of acquainting itself with the acts and the disposition of the administrative agents of the government, the country must be helpless to learn how it is being served; and unless Congress both scrutinize these things and sift them by every form of discussion, the country must remain in embarrassing, crippling ignorance of the very affairs which it is most important that it should understand and direct. The informing function of Congress should be preferred even to its legislative function. The argument is not only that discussed and interrogated administration is the only pure and efficient administration, but, more than that, that the only really self-governing people is that people which discusses and interrogates its administration. The talk on the part of Congress which we sometimes justly condemn is the profitless squabble of words over frivolous bills or selfish party issues. It would be hard to conceive of there being too much talk about the practical concerns and processes of government. Such talk it is which, when earnestly and purposefully conducted, clears the public mind and shapes the demands of public opinion.

Congress could not be too diligent about such talking; whereas it may easily be too diligent in legislation. It often overdoes that business. It already sends to its Committees bills too many by the thousand to be given even a hasty thought; but its immense committee facilities and the absence of all other duties but that of legislation make it omnivorous in its appetite for new subjects for consideration. It is greedy to have a taste of every possible dish that may be put upon its table, as an "extra" to the constitutional bill of fare. This disposition on its part is the more notable because there is certainly less need for it to hurry and overwork itself at law-making than exists in the case of most other great national legislatures. It is not state and national legislature combined, as are the Commons of England and the Chambers of France. Like the Reichstag of our cousin Germans, it is restricted to subjects of imperial scope. Its thoughts are meant to be kept for national interests. Its time is spared the waste of attention to local affairs. It is even forbidden the vast domain of the laws of property, of commercial dealing, and of ordinary crime. And even in the matter of caring for national interests the way has from the first been made plain and easy for it. There are no clogging feudal institutions to embarrass it. There is no long-continued practice of legal or of royal tyranny for it to cure, —no clearing away of old débris of any sort to delay it in its exercise of a common-sense dominion over a thoroughly modern and progressive nation. It is easy to believe that its legislative purposes might be most fortunately clarified and simplified, were it to square them by a conscientious attention to the paramount and controlling duty of understanding, discussing, and directing administration.

If the people's authorized representatives do not take upon themselves this duty, and by identifying themselves with the actual work of government stand between it and irresponsible, half-informed criticism, to what harassments is the executive not exposed? Led and checked by Congress, the prurient and fear-less, because anonymous, animadversions of the Press, now so often premature and inconsiderate, might be disciplined into serviceable capacity to interpret and judge. Its energy and sagacity might be tempered by discretion, and strengthened by knowledge. One of our chief constitutional difficulties is that, in opportunities for informing and guiding public opinion, the free-dom of the Press is greater than the freedom of Congress. It is as if newspapers, instead of the board of directors, were the sources of information for the stockholders of a corporation. We look into correspondents' letters instead of into the Congressional Record to find out what is a-doing and a-planning in the departments. Congress is altogether excluded from the arrangement by which the Press declares what the executive is, and conventions of the national parties decide what the executive shall be. Editors are self-constituted our guides, and caucus delegates our government directors.

Since all this curious scattering of functions and contrivance of frail, extra-constitutional machinery of government is the re-sult of that entire separation of the legislative and executive branches of the system which is with us so characteristically and essentially constitutional, it is exceedingly interesting to inquire and important to understand how that separation came to be in-sisted upon in the making of the Constitution. Alexander Hamil-ton has in our own times, as well as before, been "severely re-proached with having said that the British government was the 'best model in existence.' In 1787 this was a mere truism. How-ever much the men of that day differed they were all agreed in despising and distrusting *a priori* constitutions and ideally perfect governments, fresh from the brains of visionary enthusiasts, such as sprang up rankly in the soil of the French revolution. The Con-vention of 1787 was composed of very able men of the English-speaking race. They took the system of government with which they had been familiar, improved it, adapted it to the circum-stances with which they had to deal, and put it into successful operation. Hamilton's plan, then, like the others, was on the British model, and it did not differ essentially in details from that finally adopted."[3] It is needful, however, to remember in this con-nection what has already been alluded to, that when that conven-tion was copying the English Constitution, that Constitution was

[3] H. C. Lodge's *Alexander Hamilton* (Am. Statesmen Series), pp. 60, 61.

in a stage of transition, and had by no means fully developed the features which are now recognized as most characteristic of it. Mr. Lodge is quite right in saying that the Convention, in adapting, improved upon the English Constitution with which its members were familiar,—the Constitution of George III. and Lord North, the Constitution which had failed to crush Bute. It could hardly be said with equal confidence, however, that our system as then made was an improvement upon that scheme of responsible cabinet government which challenges the admiration of the world to-day, though it was quite plainly a marked advance upon a parliament of royal nominees and pensionaries and a secret cabinet of "king's friends." The English constitution of that day had a great many features which did not invite republican imitation. It was suspected, if not known, that the ministers who sat in parliament were little more than the tools of a ministry of royal favorites who were kept out of sight behind the strictest confidences of the court. It was notorious that the subservient parliaments of the day represented the estates and the money of the peers and the influence of the King rather than the intelligence and purpose of the nation. The whole "form and pressure" of the time illustrated only too forcibly Lord Bute's sinister suggestion, that "the forms of a free and the ends of an arbitrary government are things not altogether incompatible." It was, therefore, perfectly natural that the warnings to be so easily drawn from the sight of a despotic monarch binding the usages and privileges of self-government to the service of his own intemperate purposes should be given grave heed by Americans, who were the very persons who had suffered most from the existing abuses. It was something more than natural that the Convention of 1787 should desire to erect a Congress which would not be subservient and an executive which could not be despotic. And it was equally to have been expected that they should regard an absolute separation of these two great branches of the system as the only effectual means for the accomplishment of that much desired end. It was impossible that they could believe that executive and legislature could be brought into close relations of coöperation and mutual confidence without being tempted, nay, even bidden, to collude. How could either maintain its independence of action unless each were to have the guaranty of the Constitution that its own domain should be absolutely safe from invasion, its own prerogatives absolutely free from challenge? "They shrank from placing sovereign power anywhere. They feared that it would generate tyranny; George III. had been a tyrant to them, and come what might they would not make a George III."[4] They would conquer, by dividing, the power they so much feared to see in any single hand.

"The English Constitution, in a word," says our most astute English critic, "is framed on the principle of choosing a single sovereign authority, and making it good; the American, upon the principle of having many sovereign authorities, and hoping that their multitude may atone for their inferiority. The Americans now extol their institutions, and so defraud themselves of their due praise. But if they had not a genius for politics, if they had not a moderation in action singularly curious where superficial speech is so violent, if they had not a regard for law, such as no great people have ever evinced, and infinitely surpassing ours, the multiplicity of authorities in the American Constitution would long ago have brought it to a bad end. Sensible shareholders, I have heard a shrewd attorney say, can work *any* deed of settlement; and so the men of Massachusetts could, I believe, work *any* constitution."[5] It is not necessary to assent to Mr. Bagehot's strictures; but it is not possible to deny the clear-sighted justice of this criticism. In order to be fair to the memory of our great constitution-makers, however, it is necessary to remember that when they sat in convention in Philadelphia the English Constitution, which they copied, was not the simple system which was before Mr. Bagehot's eyes when he wrote. Its single sovereign authority was not then a twice-reformed House of Commons truly representative of the nation and readily obeyed by a responsible Ministry. The sovereignty was at see-saw between the throne and the parliament,—and the throne-end of the beam was generally uppermost. Our device of separated, individualized powers was very much better than a nominal sovereignty of the Commons which was suffered to be overridden by force, fraud, or craft, by the real sovereignty of the King. The English Constitution was at that time in reality much worse than our own; and, if it is now superior, it is so because its growth has not been hindered or destroyed by the too tight ligaments of a written fundamental law.

The natural, the inevitable tendency of every system of self-government like our own and the British is to exalt the representative body, the people's parliament, to a position of absolute supremacy. That tendency has, I think, been quite as marked in our own constitutional history as in that of any other country, though its power has been to some extent neutralized, and its

4 Bagehot, *Eng. Const.*, p. 293.
5 Bagehot, *Eng. Const.*, p. 296.

progress in great part stayed, by those denials of that supremacy which we respect because they are written in our law. The political law written in our hearts is here at variance with that which the Constitution sought to establish. A written constitution may and often will be violated in both letter and spirit by a people of energetic political talents and a keen instinct for progressive practical development; but so long as they adhere to the forms of such a constitution, so long as the machinery of government supplied by it is the only machinery which the legal and moral sense of such a people permits it to use, its political development must be in many directions narrowly restricted because of an insuperable lack of open or adequate channels. Our Constitution, like every other constitution which puts the authority to make laws and the duty of controlling the public expenditure into the hands of a popular assembly, practically sets that assembly to rule the affairs of the nation as supreme overlord. But, by separating it entirely from its executive agencies, it deprives it of the opportunity and means for making its authority complete and convenient. The constitutional machinery is left of such a pattern that other forces less than that of Congress may cross and compete with Congress, though they are too small to overcome or long offset it; and the result is simply an unpleasant, wearing friction which, with other adjustments, more felicitous and equally safe, might readily be avoided.

Congress, consequently, is still lingering and chafing under just such embarrassments as made the English Commons a nuisance both to themselves and to everybody else immediately after the Revolution Settlement had given them their first sure promise of supremacy. The parallel is startlingly exact. "In outer seeming the Revolution of 1688 had only transferred the sovereignty over England from James to William and Mary. In actual fact it had given a powerful and decisive impulse to the great constitutional progress which was transferring the sovereignty from the King to the House of Commons. From the moment when its sole right to tax the nation was established by the Bill of Rights, and when its own resolve settled the practice of granting none but annual supplies to the Crown, the House of Commons became the supreme power in the State. . . . But though the constitutional change was complete, the machinery of government was far from having adapted itself to the new conditions of political life which such a change brought about. However powerful the will of the Commons might be, it had no means of bringing its will directly to bear on the control of public affairs. The ministers who had charge of them were not its servants but the servants of the Crown; it was from the King that they looked for direction, and to the King that they held themselves responsible. By impeachment or more indirect means the Commons could force a king to remove a minister who contradicted their will; but they had no constitutional power to replace the fallen statesman by a minister who would carry out their will.

"The result was the growth of a temper in the Lower House which drove William and his ministers to despair. It became as corrupt, as jealous of power, as fickle in its resolves and factious in its spirit as bodies always become whose consciousness of the possession of power is untempered by a corresponding consciousness of the practical difficulties or the moral responsibilities of the power which they possess. It grumbled . . . and it blamed the Crown and its ministers for all at which it grumbled. But it was hard to find out what policy or measures it would have preferred. Its mood changed, as William bitterly complained, with every hour. . . . The Houses were in fact without the guidance of recognized leaders, without adequate information, and destitute of that organization out of which alone a definite policy can come."[6]

The cure for this state of things which Sunderland had the sagacity to suggest, and William the wisdom to apply, was the mediation between King and Commons of a cabinet representative of the majority of the popular chamber,—a first but long and decisive step towards responsible cabinet government. Whether a similar remedy would be possible or desirable in our own case it is altogether aside from my present purpose to inquire. I am pointing out facts,—diagnosing, not prescribing remedies. My only point just now is, that no one can help being struck by the closeness of the likeness between the incipient distempers of the first parliaments of William and Mary and the developed disorders now so plainly discernible in the constitution of Congress. Though honest and diligent, it is meddlesome and inefficient; and it is meddlesome and inefficient for exactly the same reasons that made it natural that the post-Revolutionary parliaments should exhibit like clumsiness and like temper: namely, because it is "without the guidance of recognized leaders, without adequate information, and destitute of that organization out of which alone a definite policy can come."

The dangers of this serious imperfection in our governmental machinery have not been clearly demonstrated in our experience

6 Green: *Hist. of the English People* (Harpers' ed.), iv., pp. 58, 59.

hitherto; but now their delayed fulfillment seems to be close at hand. The plain tendency is towards a centralization of all the greater powers of government in the hands of the federal authorities, and towards the practical confirmation of those prerogatives of supreme overlordship which Congress has been gradually arrogating to itself. The central government is constantly becoming stronger and more active, and Congress is establishing itself as the one sovereign authority in that government. In constitutional theory and in the broader features of past practice, ours has been what Mr. Bagehot has called a "composite" government. Besides state and federal authorities to dispute as to sovereignty, there have been within the federal system itself rival and irreconcilable powers. But gradually the strong are overcoming the weak. If the signs of the times are to be credited, we are fast approaching an adjustment of sovereignty quite as "simple" as need be. Congress is not only to retain the authority it already possesses, but is to be brought again and again face to face with still greater demands upon its energy, its wisdom, and its conscience, is to have ever-widening duties and responsibilities thrust upon it, without being granted a moment's opportunity to look back from the plough to which it has set its hands.

The sphere and influence of national administration and national legislation are widening rapidly. Our populations are growing at such a rate that one's reckoning staggers at counting the possible millions that may have a home and a work on this continent ere fifty more years shall have filled their short span. The East will not always be the centre of national life. The South is fast accumulating wealth, and will faster recover influence. The West has already achieved a greatness which no man can gainsay, and has in store a power of future growth which no man can estimate. Whether these sections are to be harmonious or dissentient depends almost entirely upon the methods and policy of the federal government. If that government be not careful to keep within its own proper sphere and prudent to square its policy by rules of national welfare, sectional lines must and will be known; citizens of one part of the country may look with jealousy and even with hatred upon their fellow-citizens of another part; and faction must tear and dissension distract a country which Providence would bless, but which man may curse. The government of a country so vast and various must be strong, prompt, wieldy, and efficient. Its strength must consist in the certainty and uniformity of its purposes, in its accord with national sentiment, in its unhesitating action, and in its honest aims. It must be steadied and approved by open administration diligently obedient to the more permanent judgments of public opinion; and its only active agency, its representative chambers, must be equipped with something besides abundant powers of legislation.

As at present constituted, the federal government lacks strength because its powers are divided, lacks promptness because its authorities are multiplied, lacks wieldiness because its processes are roundabout, lacks efficiency because its responsibility is indistinct and its action without competent direction. It is a government in which every officer may talk about every other officer's duty without having to render strict account for not doing his own, and in which the masters are held in check and offered contradiction by the servants. Mr. Lowell has called it "government by declamation." Talk is not sobered by any necessity imposed upon those who utter it to suit their actions to their words. There is no day of reckoning for words spoken. The speakers of a congressional majority may, without risk of incurring ridicule or discredit, condemn what their own Committees are doing; and the spokesmen of a minority may urge what contrary courses they please with a well-grounded assurance that what they say will be forgotten before they can be called upon to put it into practice. Nobody stands sponsor for the policy of the government. A dozen men originate it; a dozen compromises twist and alter it; a dozen offices whose names are scarcely known outside of Washington put it into execution.

This is the defect to which, it will be observed, I am constantly recurring; to which I recur again and again because every examination of the system, at whatsoever point begun, leads inevitably to it as to a central secret. It is the defect which interprets all the rest, because it is their common product. It is exemplified in the extraordinary fact that the utterances of the Press have greater weight and are accorded greater credit, though the Press speaks entirely without authority, than the utterances of Congress, though Congress possesses all authority. The gossip of the street is listened to rather than the words of the law-makers. The editor directs public opinion, the congressman obeys it. When a presidential election is at hand, indeed, the words of the political orator gain temporary heed. He is recognized as an authority in the arena, as a professional critic competent to discuss the good and bad points, and to forecast the fortunes of the contestants. There is something definite in hand, and he is known to have studied all its bearings. He is one of the managers, or is thought to be well acquainted with the management. He speaks "from the card." But let him talk, not about candidates, but about measures or about the policy of the government, and his observations sink at once to the level of a mere individual expression of opinion, to which his political occupations seem to add very little weight. It is universally recognized that he speaks without authority, about things which his vote may help to settle, but about which several hundred other men have votes quite as influential as his own. Legislation is not a thing to be known beforehand. It depends upon the conclusions of sundry Standing Committees. It is an aggregate, not a simple, production. It is impossible to tell how many persons' opinions and influences have entered into its composition. It is even impracticable to determine from this year's law-making what next year's will be like.

Speaking, therefore, without authority, the political orator speaks to little purpose when he speaks about legislation. The papers do not report him carefully; and their editorials seldom take any color from his arguments. The Press, being anonymous and representing a large force of inquisitive news-hunters, is much more powerful than he chiefly because it *is* impersonal and seems to represent a wider and more thorough range of information. At the worst, it can easily compete with any ordinary individual. Its individual opinion is quite sure to be esteemed as worthy of attention as any other individual opinion. And, besides, it is almost everywhere strong enough to deny currency to the speeches of individuals whom it does not care to report. It goes to its audience; the orator must depend upon his audience coming to him. It can be heard at every fireside; the orator can be heard only on the platform or the hustings. There is no imperative demand on the part of the reading public in this country that the newspapers should report political speeches in full. On the contrary, most readers would be disgusted at finding their favorite columns so filled up. By giving even a notice of more than an item's length to such a speech, an editor runs the risk of being denounced as dull. And I believe that the position of the American Press is in this regard quite singular. The English newspapers are so far from being thus independent and self-sufficient powers, —a law unto themselves,—in the politics of the empire that they are constrained to do homage to the political orator whether they will or no. Conservative editors must spread before their readers *verbatim* reports not only of the speeches of the leaders of their own party, but also of the principal speeches of the leading Liberal orators; and Liberal journals have no choice but to print every syllable of the more important public utterances of the

Conservative leaders. The nation insists upon knowing what its public men have to say, even when it is not so well said as the newspapers which report them could have said it.

There are only two things which can give any man a right to expect that when he speaks the whole country will listen: namely, genius and authority. Probably no one will ever contend that Sir Stafford Northcote was an orator, or even a good speaker. But by proof of unblemished character, and by assiduous, conscientious, and able public service he rose to be the recognized leader of his party in the House of Commons; and it is simply because he speaks as one having authority,—and not as the scribes of the Press,—that he is as sure of a heedful hearing as is Mr. Gladstone, who adds genius and noble oratory to the authority of established leadership. The leaders of English public life have something besides weight of character, prestige of personal service and experience, and authority of individual opinion to exalt them above the anonymous Press. They have definite authority and power in the actual control of government. They are directly commissioned to control the policy of the administration. They stand before the country, in parliament and out of it, as the responsible chiefs of their parties. It is their business to lead those parties, and it is the matter-of-course custom of the constituencies to visit upon the parties the punishment due for the mistakes made by these chiefs. They are at once the servants and scapegoats of their parties.

It is these well-established privileges and responsibilities of theirs which make their utterances considered worth hearing,— nay, necessary to be heard and pondered. Their public speeches are their parties' platforms. What the leader promises his party stands ready to do, should it be intrusted with office. This certainty of audience and of credit gives spice to what such leaders have to say, and lends elevation to the tone of all their public utterances. They for the most part avoid buncombe, which would be difficult to translate into Acts of Parliament. It is easy to see how great an advantage their station and influence give them over our own public men. We have no such responsible party leadership on this side the sea; we are very shy about conferring much authority on anybody, and the consequence is that it requires something very like genius to secure for any one of our statesmen a universally recognized right to be heard and to create an ever-active desire to hear him whenever he talks, not about candidates, but about measures. An extraordinary gift of eloquence, such as not every generation may hope to see, will always hold, because it will always captivate, the attention of the people. But genius and eloquence are too rare to be depended upon for the instruction and guidance of the masses; and since our politicians lack the credit of authority and responsibility, they must give place, except at election-time, to the Press, which is everywhere, generally well-informed, and always talking. It is necessarily "government by declamation" and editorial-writing.

It is probably also this lack of leadership which gives to our national parties their curious, conglomerate character. It would seem to be scarcely an exaggeration to say that they are homogeneous only in name. Neither of the two principal parties is of one mind with itself. Each tolerates all sorts of difference of creed and variety of aim within its own ranks. Each pretends to the same purposes and permits among its partisans the same contradictions to those purposes. They are grouped around no legislative leaders whose capacity has been tested and to whose opinions they loyally adhere. They are like armies without officers, engaged upon a campaign which has no great cause at its back. Their names and traditions, not their hopes and policy, keep them together.

It is to this fact, as well as to short terms which allow little time for differences to come to a head, that the easy agreement of congressional majorities should be attributed. In other like assemblies the harmony of majorities is constantly liable to disturbance. Ministers lose their following and find their friends falling away in the midst of a session. But not so in Congress. There, although the majority is frequently simply conglomerate, made up of factions not a few, and bearing in its elements every seed of discord, the harmony of party voting seldom, if ever, suffers an interruption. So far as outsiders can see, legislation generally flows placidly on, and the majority easily has its own way, acting with a sort of matter-of-course unanimity, with no suspicion of individual freedom of action. Whatever revolts may be threatened or accomplished in the ranks of the party outside the House at the polls, its power is never broken inside the House. This is doubtless due in part to the fact that there is no freedom of debate in the House; but there can be no question that it is principally due to the fact that debate is without aim, just because legislation is without consistency. Legislation is conglomerate. The absence of any concert of action amongst the Committees leaves legislation with scarcely any trace of determinate party courses. No two schemes pull together. If there is a coincidence of principle between several bills of the same session, it is generally accidental; and the confusion of policy which prevents intelligent coöperation also, of course, prevents intelligent differences and divisions. There is never a transfer of power from one party to the other during a session, because such a transfer would mean almost nothing. The majority remains of one mind so long as a Congress lives, because its mind is very vaguely ascertained, and its power of planning a split consequently very limited. It has no common mind, and if it had, has not the machinery for changing it. It is led by a score or two of Committees whose composition must remain the same to the end; and who are too numerous, as well as too disconnected, to fight against. It stays on one side because it hardly knows where the boundaries of that side are or how to cross them.

Moreover, there is a certain well-known piece of congressional machinery long ago invented and applied for the special purpose of keeping both majority and minority compact. The legislative caucus has almost as important a part in our system as have the Standing Committees, and deserves as close study as they. Its functions are much more easily understood in all their bearings than those of the Committees, however, because they are much simpler. The caucus is meant as an antidote to the Committees. It is designed to supply the cohesive principle which the multiplicity and mutual independence of the Committees so powerfully tend to destroy. Having no Prime Minister to confer with about the policy of the government, as they see members of parliament doing, our congressmen confer with each other in caucus. Rather than imprudently expose to the world the differences of opinion threatened or developed among its members, each party hastens to remove disrupting debate from the floor of Congress, where the speakers might too hastily commit themselves to insubordination, to quiet conferences behind closed doors, where frightened scruples may be reassured and every disagreement healed with a salve of compromise or subdued with the whip of political expediency. The caucus is the drilling-ground of the party. There its discipline is renewed and strengthened, its uniformity of step and gesture regained. The voting and speaking in the House are generally merely the movements of a sort of dress parade, for which the exercises of the caucus are designed to prepare. It is easy to see how difficult it would be for the party to keep its head amidst the confused cross-movements of the Committees without thus now and again pulling itself together in caucus, where it can ask itself its own mind and pledge itself anew to eternal agreement.

The credit of inventing this device is probably due to the Democrats. They appear to have used it so early as the second session of the eighth Congress. Speaking of that session, a reliable authority says: "During this session of Congress there was far less of free and independent discussion on the measures proposed by the friends of the administration than had been previously practiced in both branches of the national legislature. It appeared that on the most important subjects, the course adopted by the majority was the effect of caucus arrangement, or, in other words, had been previously agreed upon at meetings of the Democratic members held in private. Thus the legislation of Congress was constantly swayed by a party following feelings and pledges rather than according to sound reason or personal conviction."[7] The censure implied in this last sentence may have seemed righteous at the time when such caucus pledges were in disfavor as new-fangled shackles, but it would hardly be accepted as just by the intensely practical politicians of to-day. They would probably prefer to put it thus: That the silvern speech spent in caucus secures the golden silence maintained on the floor of Congress, making each party rich in concord and happy in coöperation.

The fact that makes this defense of the caucus not altogether conclusive is that it is shielded from all responsibility by its sneaking privacy. It has great power without any balancing weight of accountability. Probably its debates would constitute interesting and instructive reading for the public, were they published; but they never get out except in rumors often rehearsed and as often amended. They are, one may take it for granted, much more candid and go much nearer the political heart of the questions discussed than anything that is ever said openly in Congress to the reporters' gallery. They approach matters without masks and handle them without gloves. It might hurt, but it would enlighten us to hear them. As it is, however, there is unhappily no ground for denying their power to override sound reason and personal conviction. The caucus cannot always silence or subdue a large and influential minority of dissentients, but its whip seldom fails to reduce individual malcontents and mutineers into submission. There is no place in congressional jousts for the free lance. The man who disobeys his party caucus is understood to disavow his party allegiance altogether, and to assume that dangerous neutrality which is so apt to degenerate into mere caprice, and which is almost sure to destroy his in-

[7] *Statesman's Manual,* i. p. 244.

fluence by bringing him under the suspicion of being unreliable, —a suspicion always conclusively damning in practical life. Any individual, or any minority of weak numbers or small influence, who has the temerity to neglect the decisions of the caucus is sure, if the offense be often repeated, or even once committed upon an important issue, to be read out of the party, almost without chance of reinstatement. And every one knows that nothing can be accomplished in politics by mere disagreement. The only privilege such recalcitrants gain is the privilege of disagreement; they are forever shut out from the privilege of confidential coöperation. They have chosen the helplessness of a faction.

It must be admitted, however, that, unfortunate as the necessity is for the existence of such powers as those of the caucus, that necessity actually exists and cannot be neglected. Against the fatal action of so many elements of disintegration it would seem to be imperatively needful that some energetic element of cohesion should be provided. It is doubtful whether in any other nation, with a shorter inheritance of political instinct, parties could long successfully resist the centrifugal forces of the committee system with only the varying attraction of the caucus to detain them. The wonder is that, despite the forcible and unnatural divorcement of legislation and administration and the consequent distraction of legislation from all attention to anything like an intelligent planning and superintendence of policy, we are not cursed with as many factions as now almost hopelessly confuse French politics. That we have had, and continue to have, only two national parties of national importance or real power is fortunate rather than natural. Their names stand for a fact, but scarcely for a reason.

An intelligent observer of our politics[8] has declared that there is in the United States "a class, including thousands and tens of thousands of the best men in the country, who think it possible to enjoy the fruits of good government without working for them." Every one who has seen beyond the outside of our American life must recognize the truth of this; to explain it is to state the sum of all the most valid criticisms of congressional government. Public opinion has no easy vehicle for its judgments, no quick channels for its action. Nothing about the system is direct and simple. Authority is perplexingly subdivided and distributed, and responsibility has to be hunted down in out-of-the-way corners. So that the sum of the whole matter is that the means of

[8] Mr. Dale, of Birmingham.

working for the fruits of good government are not readily to be found. The average citizen may be excused for esteeming government at best but a haphazard affair, upon which his vote and all of his influence can have but little effect. How is his choice of a representative in Congress to affect the policy of the country as regards the questions in which he is most interested, if the man for whom he votes has no chance of getting on the Standing Committee which has virtual charge of those questions? How is it to make any difference who is chosen President? Has the President any very great authority in matters of vital policy? It seems almost a thing of despair to get any assurance that any vote he may cast will even in an infinitesimal degree affect the essential courses of administration. There are so many cooks mixing their ingredients in the national broth that it seems hopeless, this thing of changing one cook at a time.

The charm of our constitutional ideal has now been long enough wound up to enable sober men who do not believe in political witchcraft to judge what it has accomplished, and is likely still to accomplish, without further winding. The Constitution is not honored by blind worship. The more open-eyed we become, as a nation, to its defects, and the prompter we grow in applying with the unhesitating courage of conviction all thoroughly-tested or well-considered expedients necessary to make self-government among us a straightforward thing of simple method, single, unstinted power, and clear responsibility, the nearer will we approach to the sound sense and practical genius of the great and honorable statesmen of 1787. And the first step towards emancipation from the timidity and false pride which have led us to seek to thrive despite the defects of our national system rather than seem to deny its perfection is a fearless criticism of that system. When we shall have examined all its parts without sentiment, and gauged all its functions by the standards of practical common sense, we shall have established anew our right to the claim of political sagacity; and it will remain only to act intelligently upon what our opened eyes have seen in order to prove again the justice of our claim to political genius.

From Edward Ireland Renick

My dear Wilson: Washington, D. C., Jan'y 24, 1885.

As you will probably be able to believe by aid of the Raleigh Chronicle, which I now send you, I have written & prevailed upon Walter Page (one of the editors) to give editorial prominence to, a few comments upon you & your book,[1] which I trust you will not take amiss. . . .

Of course I could speak in only a general way, & had to be guided almost wholly by your expressed intentions last winter, when engaged on the work—which, probaby were subsequently changed. . . .

If you have time, I would like to have the *result* of your investigation relative to the right residing exclusively in the lower House to take the initiative in appropriation bills as well as in *raising* revenue. Mr. Hurd[2]—as you have seen—holds that it does—& objects to the Blair bill, because raised in the Senate. Hammond,[3] of the judiciary committee—speaking for himself & for the majority of that committee, denies that this privilege of the House extends to appropriation bills.

In great haste, my dear fellow, but with renewed expressions of affection and congratulation,

I am,   Yours most sincerely   E. I. Renick

ALS (WP, DLC) with WWhw notation on env.: "Ans. Jany 28, 1885." Enc.: clipping from the Raleigh, N. C., *State Chronicle*, Jan. 20, 1885.
  [1] *Congressional Government.*
  [2] Rep. Frank H. Hurd of Ohio.
  [3] Rep. Nathaniel J. Hammond of Georgia.

Two Letters from Ellen Louise Axson

My darling Woodrow,   New York, Jan. 24/85

I had an engagement last night with a party of "Leaguers"[1]—(of which more anon) which prevented my writing as I so much wished to do. I rushed home from the League as soon as I could to get my letter, and if possible answer it before dinner; but that would not work. I was busy until dinner-time *reading* and re-reading it, and thinking about [it]. It was a sweet and precious letter my darling. I can't speak of it this morning further than to tell you that it has served it's purpose. It was indeed an *answer* to mine; and my heart is satisfied, ay, and my *head* too. I will and I *do* trust your judgment entirely, dearest, in this as in all things. The question is simply as to what will be best for your happiness, and, as you say, *you* ought to *know* best about that! So it must be as you wish.

As to Eddie [Axson],—I think it will be best to talk with Uncle Henry [Hoyt] before reaching any conclusion on that point. If he is as anxious to have him as ever, it might be well to leave him there next winter. It would certainly be as well or better for him. My desire to have him is in great measure selfish, and if I can do without him this winter when I am alone I surely can then. Indeed I think it would be pleasant to be for a time like other young people!—alone together! But I must write no more this morning, for it is very cold. I am *straining* my promise to write *so* much. I love you, my darling. I love you; you do not know even yet *how* much.

With all my heart,   Your own   Eileen.

[1] Members of the Art Students' League of New York, which Ellen was then attending.

New York, Jan. 24/84 [1885].

Many, many thanks, my darling, for *the book* which reached me safely tonight, and is now lying under my hand. Didn't it "give you a turn"! to see it? It made me "feel queer," as well as happy; though it is'nt the first time, by any means, that I have "seen your name in print"! It is a very nicely gotten up, and attractive looking book, is it not? It's truly delightful to behold it,— almost as delightful as to read it. It seems to me, darling, that it sounds better than ever "in print"! The style is really wonderful; not the most fascinating novel could "hold" one more closely,—it is so strong and racy and so finished. And it seems to be as hard to put down as a novel; the sequence of ideas is so fine, that one is carried along irresistably by the current of thought;—that has been my experience tonight, and I have been absorbed in it most of the evening though I *have* read it before.[1]

Have you sent one to Wil. yet? You must tell me what your father says about the dedication. I think it is simply delightful. I suppose you managed to keep the secret till now? I wish I could see them when they receive the book.

I wonder if you know half how much I admire you, my darling. How perfectly absurd it seems that you should care for *me*! I have had time to grow "used to" that idea now, yet sometimes it strikes me afresh and in an almost ludicrous light! And to think that you should fear that you ask a *sacrifice*! of the woman *you love* when you ask her to marry you! I assure you she *does* not and will not "feel poor"; she is the richest little girl in the world, and she knows it. And she is one of the happiest too, happy in your success, happy in your love, happy in that you are *yourself*. I could find it in my heart to wish ours a less unequal bargain,—that I might be "trebled twenty times myself." But at least I can match you in loving; my *heart* is as great as yours. This is a charming plan, dearest, which you have devised,—for "purveying for each other" I mean.[2] We will certainly put it into practice; it will be *delightful*. Ah if I only can give you some sort—*any* sort of aid"! And now I *must* say goodnight my darling

    With all my heart,   Your own Eileen.

ALS (WP, DLC).
    [1] In Wilmington, N. C., during her visit with the Wilsons in September 1884.
    [2] See WW to ELA, Jan. 23, 1885, Vol. 3.

To Ellen Louise Axson

My own darling,   Balto., Sabbath afternoon, Jany. 25, 1885
    I believe it's my privilege—isn't it?—to repent in my Sunday letter of what I wrote in its companion of Saturday. I don't repent of what I said yesterday about your engagements with Mr. Goodrich,[1] because I said only what I honestly thought—but I repent that I *said* it, because I am quite sure that it was unnecessary. 'You have already cautioned this little lady who is the light of your eyes, Woodrow, you insistent, too urgent fellow, you; why make her think that she needs *re*cautioning?'
    I am trying to be hopeful about dear little Jessie's[2] condition because I haven't heard anything further and that, so far as it means anything, means hope.
    The little note that I fetched from the post-office this morning was, and is, specially precious to me, darling, because it is so essentially and so perfectly a *love*-message all the way through. That makes it serve, too, as an excuse for my doing what I so love to do on Sunday (and never do any other day!), namely, writing a love-letter in reply. Why do I delight so, I wonder, in telling you of my love for you over and over again, my little sweetheart? You *know* that I love you—and, even if you don't know *how much*, there's no use trying to tell you *that*—because I've tried often enough to know that I can't. It must be that I like to try again because I can be sure that what I write will be read with the eyes of a love which will supply from its own riches all that my words lack, that there is a heart that will respond to everything I say. And I can say something very definite in answer to

the crowning, the most precious sentence of this sweet note. "So it must be as you wish." As I wish! *Can* it be true that I am to have, as my heart's own most inestimable treasure, the loving wife for whom my life has so long waited? Is my Eileen to be my *constant* companion, my counsellor in all life's *little* things even? Is she really to be my bride, my life-long sweetheart, the joy and pride of my manhood, and, if God will, the comfort and strength of my old age? Yes, she has promised! And I? What will I give in return? There is very little that I can give—except love. That is much—and she shall be rich in that; but I want to give more, by way of *proving* my love. I want for her sake to drive all these black spirits of despondency and over-anxiety out of my heart— to let the sweet sunlight of her love drive all else thence but tender loyalty, steady courage, undismayed hope, fresh and confident purpose. If my heart—if my love for her—could shape my life, I would be the delight of her bridal days, the unfailing joy and comfort and pride of her womanhood, and the stay of her old age. If love can make a true husband, I will be one to my darling, my matchless little queen, my own Eileen, whom I love more and more as the day for our marriage approaches, and whom then I shall serve as   Her own   Woodrow.

ALS (WC, NjP).
¹ See WW to ELA, Jan. 24, 1885.
² Jessie Howe, daughter of Annie Wilson Howe.

From Ellen Louise Axson

My darling Woodrow,   New York Jan 25/85
     I have just been reading over for the "severelth" time your sweet letters of the last few days; trying to make them take the place of the one which is, alas! in the post-office, instead of being in my possession. I ought not to feel the want of it so much, after all, when these others are still so far from being worn out,—when both my heart and my thoughts are still so filled and satisfied by them. I wonder if it is because you are a man of genius that you are able to write such wonderful love-letters, or can it be that the power comes from love alone? I am trying to decide whether it would be possible for an ordinary man, however well he loved, to say always so exactly the right thing, and to say it so perfectly,— whether he could play with such skill upon that delicate instrument, the heart, as do you upon mine. You do what you will with mine, dear love,—you are complete *master* of the instrument. At your lightest touch it thrills with an unspeakable love and tender-

ness. After all it *cannot* be genius, but love; no other power is so great. To put it exactly, I think it is a genius for loving that you have;—you[r] heart is as great and beyond compare as you[r] mind. I wonder how much such love there is in this world of ours. (Isnt this an original way to write down poetry?)[1] "I will not gainsay *love—called* love forsooth! I have heard love talked in my early youth . . . and tis not much—will turn that thing call[ed] love aside to hate or else to oblivion. But *thou* art not such a lover, my Beloved!"[2] Do you know I did not even dream in Asheville that I had found such a lover! You see it is true that "God's gifts put man's best dreams to shame." Perhaps it was because you had told me that you were "undemonstrative" and because you seemed grave and calm, but certain it is, I did not even hope to be loved so well. I only knew that you *loved* me, and that whether much or little, my time had come and I *must* give *all my* love in return. Perhaps I rather expected the common woman's fate,—to give much and receive little—after perhaps a few weeks or months of blind, unreasonable infatuation! How little I knew you! How little I thought that my own heart must needs grow ever larger to hold the treasures of love that were to be poured into it! This is one reason why your love is still such a wonder to me, as it is also the reason why mine for you grows daily deeper and stronger. As I learn to know you better I *must* love you more even when further increase would seem impossible.

I did not have an opportunity to tell you about my Friday night's frolic. I was tempted to join a small party they were forming at the League to see Booth in "Macbeth." You see I *have*, as I told you, gone wild over him! Oh! it was magnificent!—but I hav'nt time to discuss it now,—and besides I ought not, on Sunday. Our chaperon was Miss Granger of whom I suppose you have heard me speak, as she is one of my special favourites. She is a Cong[regation]al minister's daughter from New England and a delightful old lady,—not exactly *old* either, though he[r] hair is as white as snow,—about forty I suppose. It seemed very queer to go to such a place without a gentleman, but I asked my *mentor*, Miss LeConte, and she said *of course* there was not the slightest impropriety. In fact, so far as I can make out, the people here seem to think it more proper to go alone with a chaperon than alone with a young gentleman!

I joined the Bible class at my church[3] this morning and like it exceedingly.

Monday morning—I have just read your sweet letters, my darling, and *must* write a word of explanation, hurried as I am. No, I admit that in view of those three engagements it doesnt look as if I were discouraging Mr. G.—and yet if you consulted him he would tell you truly that he *was* very much discouraged! The engagements are not all of it, you see. You know we decided that I was not to break positive engagements already formed, and these were all of that character; even the prayer-meeting was a special service which I had promised to attend three weeks ago. I am sorry that I had made these engagements,—they will *certainly be the last.* But I have naturally a very strong desire to avoid any unpleasant termination to this affair & to break a positive engagement would certainly have resulted in an open breach. And indeed I did not think the situation *justified* me in doing so. *Of course* you are right, dear, to tell me just what you think on this subject, as on all,—and I thank you for it.

For what price can you get copies of your book? You must be sure to send the notices of it that you see, or tell me where they are to be found. Goodnight, my darling. I wonder if you have been thinking of me more than usual today!—why is it that my heart has been yearning toward you even more than usual all day. I could almost *cry* to see you! If the spirit of sleep doesn't take pity on me and show you to me in my dreams I *shall cry*(!)

     As ever,   Your own   Eileen

Oh I am *so* sorry about dear little Jessie—and so shocked! I did not know children ever had brain fever. What *could* have caused it? How I hope and pray that she is indeed better.

                            Lovingly   Eileen.

(excuse haste)

ALS (WP, DLC).
  1 Ellen added this comment at the top of the page, referring to the fact that these lines of verse are run on in her letter like prose.
  2 From Elizabeth Barrett Browning, *Sonnets from the Portuguese*, No. XL.
  3 The Scotch Presbyterian Church of New York.

From Joseph R. Wilson, Jr.

My dearest brother: Wilmington N. C. Jan. 25th '85

I enclose a letter which I have written to Miss Ellie, and which I send to you to forward to her as I do not know her address.[1] Please read it, seal it up, and send it to her. Please give me her address also.

Mother and I returned from Columbia Saturday morning. We would have stayed until Jessie was better but we could not do anything as Jessie would not let any one but her mother and Nannie nurse her. The poor little girl was hardly any better I suppose, but she was a little quieter. We got a postal this morning saying that she was about the same, only a little quieter, having screamed none at all that day (Saturday)[.] I will let you know should she get either worse or better. She is a *very very* ill little girl brother George says.

We are all well, although mother almost makes her-self sick by anxiety about Jessie.

We all send *unbounded* love to you. We are *so* glad you have accepted the professorship.[2]   Your aff. brother   Joseph.

ALS (WP, DLC).
  [1] See WW to ELA, Jan. 28, 1885.
  [2] At Bryn Mawr College.

To Ellen Louise Axson

My own darling, •   Balto., Monday afternoon, Jany. 26, 1885
Do you think that you know enough of the strength and tenderness of my love for you to frame a probable guess as to my sensations when I read the praise of my book and the precious declarations of love for myself contained in the note I received this morning? If you do, it is only because you yourself know what it is to love with all your heart, and to value more than aught else the praise that comes from the one you love best in all the world. My precious! Do you really think the little volume so good? I am *so* glad, darling! How many kisses I would like to give my lovely little sweetheart for these words of generous admiration, and above all for the sweet love that is in them! I shall write all my books for you, Eileen.

Yes, I have kept the dedication a secret—I am still keeping it a secret indeed, because the publishers are slow about sending me the extra copies they have promised, and I have had none to send to Wilmington[.] Counting on the prompt arrival of the additional copies, I gave the one I had to 'the Seminary,'[1] and to-day when I went down to *buy* one to send to father, I found that all that had been sent to the book-sellers here were already sold, there being only one firm here that gets the new books. I had a comical experience, by the way, in my attempt to make the purchase. The first clerk I approached did not know of the book and asked me "if I remembered who it was by"! I simulated an air of difficult recollection and told him that it was written by a man named Wilson. He inquired of an elderly gentleman about "Wilson's 'Congressional Government' " and was told that all the copies had been sold but that more had been ordered.

I am so glad, my pet, that your cold is gone—and that you are going to see Booth in Hamlet. It makes me very happy to know that my darling is both well and enjoying herself.

I don't wish, Miss, that you "might be 'trebled twenty times yourself' "—and it is not kind of you to wish it for my sake! Because, if it were so, what would become of me? I already love you to a pitch that absolutely frightens me: and if you were twenty times yourself how could I keep my head at all! Does it seem to you "perfectly absurd that I should care for you"? Well, it oughtn't to seem so. Admitting that you are quite as unworthy a little woman as you suppose—an admission which I find it hard to make, even for the sake of argument—you have yourself supplied reason enough for my loving you with all my heart. Don't *you* love *me* with all your heart: and oughtn't such treasures of love to be reckoned rich enough dower for any man's wife? Ah, my darling, my little queen, *I* see the *other* riches you have promised to give me with yourself: and, since you are so delighted with the principle of my 'purveying' plan, I am more sure than ever—if one *can* be more than *perfectly* sure—that, with the gift of yourself, you will fill the measure of blessing to

Your own   Woodrow.

P.S. Do my letters reach you in the afternoon now, my pet? If so, I shall write at night, as you do—if you would prefer getting them in the morning. Afternoon and evening are the only times from which I can take an hour for my letter nowadays.

No news yet from Columbia, I am glad to say.

In scratching haste,   Lovingly   W.

ALS (WC, NjP).
1 The Seminary of Historical and Political Science of The Johns Hopkins University.

From James E. Rhoads

My dear Friend,   Philadelphia 1 mo. 26. 1885.
Thine of the 24th with its enclosures is at hand and I am truly glad thou hast decided to come to Bryn Mawr. I trust it will prove no less advantageous to thy self than to us.

In arranging the course in History it should be a matter of careful consideration whether the History of France should be the connecting link between ancient & modern History; or whether the History of some part of the German peoples should be the one. However greatly France has influenced the governments of Europe, her history has not been so full of interest to

English speaking peoples as those of Germany and England.

Should thou wish to take one of the cottages at Bryn Mawr please inform me—also whether furnished or not.

Very truly thy friend   James E Rhoads

ALS (WP, DLC) with WWhw notation on env.: "Ans. Jany 28/85."

From Ellen Louise Axson

My darling Woodrow,   New York Jan. 27 1885

Once again I must try to content myself with a brief and hurried note, for "Hamlet," you know, is a very long play, and it was too late for writing when I returned last night. It is hardly necessary to say that I was *delighted*—beyond measure by that great piece of acting; the part exactly suits him and he suits the part. It was really a revelation, "so to speak"!—as Mr. Guerry[1] says.

Many thanks for the notices of your book, they are very good —are they not. I was *wondering* as I glanced over the longer one, by what possible means the N. C. editor had been able to speak of it so intelligibly;—and as for Mr. Kingsberry![2]—why he is not so bad, after all!

Ah yes, my darling, I think I *do* know what comes to me with this gift of your book! It *has* for *many* reasons a dignity and sacredness in my eyes. How can it be other than *sacred* to me when it seems to be a *part of you*. It is indeed *most* precious to me,—my most precious possession, saving only the love of the giver. What can I give you in return, my darling! Very little, alas! but you may be sure it is my little *all*. I give the *whole* of *me*, my "entire love and faith and whole-hearted sympathy." And I would wrong myself to even imply that that part of me called the *heart* is *little*. Such love is as great as you could wish,—in short I can give you quite as much of *that* as you will know what to do with!

As ever   Your own   Eileen.

(excuse haste)

ALS (WP, DLC).
    [1] One of the residents of Ellen's boardinghouse at 120 W. 11th St., New York.
    [2] These enclosures are noted in WW to ELA, Jan. 24, 1885. "Mr. Kingsberry" was Theodore B. Kingsbury, editor of the Wilmington, N. C., *Morning Star*.

To Ellen Louise Axson

My own darling,   Balto., Tuesday afternoon, Jany 27, 1885

The postman on this 'beat' now brings us our mail about 10 o'clock, so that the reading of your letter serves as a delightful recess in my work. I generally sit down resolutely to my book (whatever it may be) about 9 o'clock, and usually I have waded through forty or fifty pages of more or less irksome lore by the time the ring at the door-bell for which I've been listening comes and I go down stairs to fetch my letter from the hall table. The great difficulty about the arrangement is, that, after I have read the letter, it takes a *very* long time and a very big effort to coax my attention back to the contents of my book. The first result is to make me read several times over pages which really—as I at length discover—do not merit more than one perusal. A second result—after my attention is partially under command again—is that you are brought into the most incongruous surroundings of historical recital and constitutional theories. This morning you played a very prominent part, for instance, in the slavery question! Indeed Mr. von Holst had a peculiarly difficult task to perform in winning my thoughts from a certain letter which was written on Sunday evening. I don't believe he was *altogether* successful in the end. That letter filled my heart with a music which his thunderous sentences could by no means drown, and my mind with thoughts much too nimble for his slow sense to catch. Oh, my darling, how am I rewarded for the insistence by which I have coaxed and teased you into putting your love into words! At least, I love to *think* that my persuasion has had a part in winning for me this delight, though I know that love like my little sweetheart's *must* sooner or later make freest confession of itself. My precious! If I have "a genius for loving," you have a genius for making me expend all my love on *you*! In other words, you have a genius for showing yourself irresistibly lovely! This confession of your first estimate (your Asheville estimate) of my powers of loving is extremely instructive, Miss! And did it take you *very* long to discover your mistake? I had a much more adequate conception then of what sort of lover I was capable of being than you had: I knew that I could love with an intensity that would absorb my whole nature. But even I did not know then, little sweetheart, of what my nature was capable—*how* deep my heart was. It is just the proof of proofs that I found in you the only woman I *could* love with all my heart that I found my love for you growing even beyond the great proportions I had thought possible for it. My mistake about *you* in Asheville was of another sort. I suspected—nay, I *knew*—that you *could* love even as now I know you love me; but I couldn't for a long time credit the possibility of your bestowing such love upon *me*—except by an effort of the imagination, adding to me what was lovable. But you have taught me this other lesson, darling, that I did myself injustice by such thoughts—because you have taught me that I can give a love such as *must* be worthy even of your acceptance. My love *entitles* me to be   Your own   Woodrow.

P.S. I have received a postal card, darling, from bro. Geo (Dr. Howe) which takes away all hope![1] He says that Jessie's disease is *meningitis*, and that "there is no hope of her recovery." Oh, it nearly breaks my heart to think that I am not to see that precious little girl again! She seemed almost to belong to me—certainly she belonged to my heart. But God's will be done!
Lovingly yours   Woodrow.

ALS (WC, NjP).
    [1] This postal is missing. On its receipt Wilson wrote a "note of love & sympathy," to which Annie Wilson Howe to WW, c. Jan. 29, 1885, ALS (WP, DLC), is the reply.

From Ellen Louise Axson

My darling Woodrow,   New York Jan 27/85.
    That *was* a queer and comical experience you had in trying to buy your own book! I should like to have seen your face at the time! It must give one a very peculiar sensation to make such a purchase. With what remarkable rapidity your book-seller managed to get "sold out"! All the copies gone almost before they had time to get there! That is quite a triumph,—the success of the book seems insured already. Have they a great poster in the store window, with your name on it in immense letters? Mr. Goodrich brought me up one as a curiosity;[1]—they prepare them here I believe and send them about the country for that purpose.
    And you have heard nothing still from Columbia? Strange, but surely it *must* mean that she is better, for as you say, the disease soon runs it[s] course and there must have been *some* change ere this, of which if for the worse you would have been informed. Oh! I *hope* it is so! It would indeed be heart-breaking to think of that beautiful bright little life so early cut off.
    No,—your letters still reach me as a rule in the morning, to my entire satisfaction; for I do much prefer getting them then, for so I can carry it with me "to keep the long day warm"; I can peep into it occasionally and think of it constantly. Sometimes I carry some special message of love back and forth with me for days; not the copy of them in my heart alone, but also the original written words. I don't know that I can *ever* part from that one of last Sunday. I feel as though I would keep it always close,— ah very close to my heart! Do you know, darling, that it was the

sweetest letter ever written,—and yet hardly more so than the one of the day before. I have no words to tell you how precious *these* words are to me. You *will* be all that to me, dearest, my delight—the joy and comfort and pride of my womanhood. I pray God make me as surely all that you describe to you. "If love can make a true" *wife* "I will be one to my darling," whom I shall *live* to love and serve as   Your own   Eileen.

ALS (WP, DLC).
 [1] He was connected with Houghton Mifflin's New York office.

To Ellen Louise Axson

My own darling   Balto., Wednesday afternoon, Jany. 28, 1885
    The accompanying letter, from "Dode," was sent me by that promising youth to be forwarded to you—he being ignorant of your address. He left it open for my perusal—and you may imagine my amazement at the part of the contents concerning the family plans for the summer! In one of his letters to *me*[1] this same young gentleman had alluded to the fine times we would have during the summer "in the north," and I was sorely puzzled by the reference. I credited my younger brother with too just a geographical sense to speak of Tenn. as "the north," and yet no *other* north had been so much as mentioned in the letters from home! Really the way I've been kept in the dark about those mysterious plans would be ludicrous, if it were not downright provoking! Naturally—and as you will be quite ready to believe—I am intensely interested in the movements of those three people during the summer: and not a single definite detail—beyond what I quoted from father's last letter—have I been able to extract from them.[2] Manifestly *father* sees nothing in their plans to interfere with our wishes as to June:[3] but one would like to know how he reconciles things—and I *will* know, if a letter of prayer and protest can prove of any avail.
    Dode's letter is rather a formal, embarrassed one for a self-confident, free-and-easy fellow, isn't it?
    At last H. M. & Co. sent me the copies of "Cong. Govt." promised me, and yesterday I mailed one to dear father.
    You ask the price of the book, my pet. Do you want to send copies of it to Georgia?—how many? The retail price is $1.25; but I can get it cheaper than that through the "New Book Department" of the Hopkins, so you better let me get and send as you wish. I don't want *you* to be spending money for it.
    "Dode's" letter to me, accompanying the one to you, represents

dear little Jessie's case as *not* altogether hopeless. Indeed he and mother seem to have come away expecting her to get well, and because they could be of no use—the poor little girl not suffering anyone but her mother and her nurse to touch her. But brother George's postal was written the same day as "Dode's" letter, and is, I am afraid, decisive.

There was a brief analysis of my book in Monday afternoon's *Post* my pet. I enclose it.

I am so glad, darling, that you have been able to see Booth so often. I suppose that it is safe to say that there is no greater actor now on the stage—and I can well understand your delight in his acting. That Macbeth party must have been very jolly!

'What can you give me in return for my love?' little lady! Why you can give me—and you have given me—the greatest thing within the gift of any woman, *your love*. And that love is more to me than the love of all the rest of the world put together. If all the rest of the world loved me and you did not, I should be unhappy; though all the rest of the world should frown upon me, if *you* will love me, I can be happy. My darling! *Nothing* can compare in my eyes with the gift of your love! 'The whole of you' is the greatest treasure—the one treasure—that my heart covets. I am nothing if I may not be   Your own   Woodrow.

ALS (WC, NjP). Encs.: J. R. Wilson, Jr., to ELA, Jan. 26, 1885, ALS (WP, DLC), and "Brief Mention of New Books," clipping from the New York *Evening Post*, Jan. 26, 1885.

1 J. R. Wilson, Jr., to WW, Jan. 5, 1885, ALS (WP, DLC).

2 Wilson did learn very soon about his family's plans for the summer. See JWW to WW, Jan. 26, 1885, printed as an enclosure with WW to ELA, Jan. 29, 1885.

3 That is, their plans for a June wedding.

From Ellen Louise Axson

My darling Woodrow,   New York Jan 28/85.

What sad, sad news your morning's letters brings me, dearest. Oh, I am *so* sorry! I can't tell you how my heart aches for you all. The poor mother! Yes! I knew how dearly you loved her, my darling, & I too loved her well, though I had seen so little of her; —but it would be impossible to see her even *once without* loving her. I have been able to think of but little else today but the lovely little creature,—of her sweet ways and her exquisite face as I saw it last on the piazza at Arden Park.[1] I think she was the most beautiful creature I ever saw. It seems almost too strange and sad to be true,—what had she to do with *death*? But "all is of God that is or is to be,—and God is *Love.*" Whatever betide we may always *trust* him.

I received today a lovely little picture of Jessie's baby[2]—taken in Chicago. It was so kind in her to send it. I wish she had managed to drop me a few lines with it;—would like so much to hear something about her life in her new home; do you ever hear? Is it true that Marions[3] health was so poor that she was obliged to leave school and go to her sister? So I heard recently from Annie Lester.

But I must make haste to close for I have been busy all the evening, and now it grows late.

Your letter this morning discovers to me once again the great advantage which I have over you in the fact that thoughts of you and your letters don't interfere *seriously* with my work. I don't know what would become of me if they did. I fear my winter at the League would prove a very unprofitable one; for to keep such thoughts very long in the background is altogether out of my power. But, in truth, those thoughts help rather than hinder my work, for they make me *happier*, and you know "a merry heart goes all the day, but a sad one tires in a mile, sir!" That is a very sweet word in this morning's letter, darling. I must steal it out of your mouth, for you *are* beginning to teach *me* that I "can give a love such as *must* be worthy even of *your* acceptance." And you are indeed entitled by right of love and of *many* other things to my whole heart.   As ever   Your own   Eileen.

By the way, darling, I must do here what I have been intending to do for several days, viz. enter a protest against your allowing your mind to dwell so much on that June arrangement! I really don't see, as I told you at first, how it is possible; and all my "thinking of ways to make it possible" fails to throw much light on the subject. I think it would be better for you to give up the idea now, once for all, for I have often observed that the more we allow ourselves to *think* of what we *want* to do, the harder it is to see clearly what we *ought* to do!   Lovingly   Ellie

ALS (WP, DLC).
  1 She refers to her trip with Woodrow to Arden Park, N. C., on September 15, 1883, when she first met Mrs. Wilson and Annie Wilson Howe and her children.
  2 Marion Brower, daughter of Jessie Bones Brower.
  3 Marion McGraw Bones, daughter of James W. Bones.

To Robert Bridges

Dear Bobby,   Balto., Md., Jany 28/85

You have certainly reduced "brief mention" to a science. The little analysis of "Congressional Government" in Monday's paper was excellent.[1] I am very anxious to hear your candid critical judgment of the little volume: and, if you find both the time and the inclination to read it through, I hope that you will tell me just what you think, without thought of my feelings. Do you think that the *Nation* will speak to posterity at any length about it?

I hope that you had a jolly good time at the wedding in Buffalo. I thought of you often, and wanted very much to wait for your return; but Miss Axson decided to spend New Years and a few days following with her uncle in Philadelphia,[2] and of course I went along as escort. And since then I have been overwhelmed, as usual, with well-nigh unmanageable masses of work.

The "Cow"[3] is basking in the favour of his fair victrix, and seems on the whole to enjoy basking. He will ever be the same old boy.

I have accepted a position in the new Quaker college (the "Miss Johns Hopkins") at Bryn Mawr, near Phila., and shall begin work there at its opening next September. I hope, therefore, to be married some time before the 15th of Sept.—for I wont "go it alone" any longer than that if I can help it!

Love to Pete and any of the rest of our crowd that you may see.

As usual in great haste,

Yours affectionately,   Woodrow Wilson

ALS (Meyer Coll., DLC).
[1] New York *Evening Post*, Jan. 26, 1885.
[2] The Rev. Thomas A. Hoyt.
[3] Hiram Woods, Jr.

To Albert Shaw

My dear Shaw,   Balto., Md., Jany 28/85

I have been waiting to answer your delightful letter of a month ago[1] till I could send my book along with my reply: I sent the modest volume west this afternoon, and now I proceed to dispatch "these presents" after it. I hope that you will tell me just what you think of the essays as completed—should you find time to read them—because I value your judgment, as you know, more

than that of any one here: and tell me without too much consideration for my feelings. I was *very* sorry to hear, from Bemis,[2]
that you had been *sick*. I sincerely hope that you are quite well
again by this time. Was it your old enemy, nervousness? You will
be pleased to know that we are about to be launched once more
into a delightful series of "quizzes" on topics general and particular, according to the newest programme of the amiable head of
the department: and you will doubtless be *amused* to hear that I,
your humble servant, am under agreement to give my services
next year to furthering the higher education of women! Possibly
you have heard of the new Quaker college to be opened at Bryn
Mawr (ten miles from Phila.) in September next? In these parts
it is familiarly known as the "Miss Johns Hopkins"—for it is to be
modelled quite closely after the system prevailing here—even in
the ranking of the teachers, I am sorry to say: for it is at Bryn
Mawr that I am to teach. The institution is richly endowed, is
to be administered upon very liberal principles, and is situate in
just the part of the country in which I want to be—namely, where
one can make friends, can find all needed material, and can command a desirable audience. Such, briefly, are the considerations
that determined my decision. I shall be head of my department,
of course—its organizer, in fact—and so have a large measure of
freedom in my work.

Did you know that [Charles H.] Shinn had gone on a visit to
the Pacific Coast? He went principally to boom the "Overland" for
his sister, and some men in New York who have taken hold of it,
and had free passes for a tour of the continent—going by way of
New Orleans, Texas, &c. and expecting to return by the Northern
Pacific.

I am at present going through the not too exciting round of von
Holst, Bancroft, Curtis, &c, which you possibly remember having
taken yourself when '84 was about as old as '85 is now—and I
call upon you for sympathy. It's a "demnition horrid grind" and,
like grinding, it is wearing me out. I fear that the bloom upon my
cheek has departed. I have shaved off my "siders" until cramming
is no more!

Our Seminary meetings have been peculiarly home-like this
year. We have been cultivating domestic industry almost exclusively—and it must surely need *more* protection, for it is not
exceedingly productive. A crisis (of under-production) is approaching: we must have either free importation of foreign *articles* or enormous bounties! Levermore[3] can't *keep* the market full.

Wright and Miss Ashton[4] send love—and I know that a much bigger stock would be sent if it were generally known that I am writing to "Shaw."

Yours affectionately   W. Wilson

TCL (in possession of Virginia Shaw English).

  [1] Albert Shaw to WW, Dec. 19, 1884, Vol. 3, pp. 556-58.
  [2] Edward Webster Bemis, who was teaching at the University of Chicago and received his Ph.D. from the Johns Hopkins in 1885.
  [3] Identified at Albert Shaw to WW, Feb. 5, 1885, n. 4.
  [4] Charles B. Wright, a graduate student in English at the Johns Hopkins, and Mary Jane Ashton, who ran the boardinghouse at 8 McCulloh Street where Wilson lived.

To Ellen Louise Axson, with Enclosure

My own darling,   Balto., Thursday afternoon, Jany 29, 1885

Dr. Rhoads's reply to my letter of acceptance reached me on Tuesday, and contains this very cordial opening passage: "Thine of the 24th with its enclosure is at hand and I am truly glad thou hast decided to come to Bryn Mawr. I trust it will prove no less advantageous to thyself than to us." He then proceeds with some suggestions about the choice of topics for the history course. He is certainly a most affable gentleman, and much more satisfactory and agreeable to deal with than sleek, plausible, slippery Dan'l C. Gilman.

I received a letter from dear mother yesterday, my pet, which I enclose for your perusal. It certainly tur[ns] *our* plans topsy turvy, though the dear lady herself does not seem to think so, and we must now take very frank counsel together as to what it may be best and most feasible to do. I have begged dear mother's advice; but, in any case, *we* must *decide*. I shall take it for granted, my precious little sweetheart,—f[or] you *have* granted it, and my heart cannot lose the delight of the confession—that you are as anxious as I am that our marriage should take place as soon as possible; that you don't *want* to put me off till September, when we could have not more than one week of free enjoyment before going to B.M., and even that *not* free from the cares of preparation[.] A summer spent with you would be infinitely more to my advantage, as well as to our mutual s[at]isfaction. It would make me ready for work—no o[ther] arrangement would. Now, I expect to have abo[ut] $500 in all to get married on[1]—and, since we shall both of us have to be wanderers during the summer anyhow, why shouldn't we wander together? Would it not be the very *best* of plans to find some quiet, unfashionable place to board, and spend July and August—or part of them—off to ourselves somewhere? At any rate, we might lose ourselves to the rest of the world for five or six weeks, and spend the rest of the time visiting our friends. These are mere suggestions, darling; but I put them down in the confident hope that your woman's wit can construct some definite plan out of them. Having had no experience(!) in getting married, I can't tell very clearly how much of the $500 will remain after the ceremony; but I should think quite enough for any modest, economical plan.

Wont [y]ou meet me *more* than half way in deciding this [ma]t-ter, darling? Somehow I feel, as if *everything* were hanging upon the decision: and you must be my *co-conspirator*—in a conspiracy to hasten the event for which our hearts are so longingly waiting. Tell me *just* what you think, my Eileen, and just what occurs to you by way of suggestion—I do so much want this proof of our already accomplished oneness of heart and purpose: and I *know*, my darling, that the dear folks at home will *altogether* approve any plan we may make.

Little sweetheart, Mr. [William T.] Walters is to open his gallery again as he did last year, on certain days of each week during Feby, March, and April: is there no *possibility* of your being able to come down for just a day or two to take a peep at the great collection?

Oh what shall I say to my darling's precious promise, in this morning's let[ter,] to be 'a true wife to her darling'! If I could tell you h[ow] and what my heart felt as it read those precious wor[ds,] my queen, I could tell you why I am irrevocably, h[ap]pi-ly, and with all my heart   Your own   Woodrow.

ALS (WC, NjP). MS. damaged.
¹ See JRW to WW, Jan. 22, 1885, Vol. 3.

E N C L O S U R E

From Janet Woodrow Wilson

Monday Night [Jan. 26, 1885]
My precious boy—   Wilmington, N.C.
I am not in very good condition for letter-writing tonight—the agitation and anxiety of the past week—and my continued anxiety about our precious little sick girl—having quite unnerved me. But I cannot delay writing with reference to the very important matter with regard to which you write. . . .

Your father expects to resign his pastorate here on the 1st of

April—then he is to have his teeth drawn—and replaced by Dr. Brown of Augusta. By the time this is accomplished, it will be time for him to go to the Assembly. It is possible—though not certain—that he will be expected to deliver his inaugural at Clarkesville on his return from the Assembly (i.e. 3d June)[1]—as you already know. Then he expects to go North—some place in the neighborhood of New York—so that he can have access to the libraries in the city—to aid him in his preparation for his new work. You know we are not due in Clarkesville before Sep 1st. And we are told it will be very doubtful whether we can procure [a] h[ouse] [e]ven then! As to Josie & myself—we are in doubt as to how we can spend the time between April 1st & the date when we can join dear papa again—for we are to be with him, I am glad to say, during the summer. I hope we will be able to go to Columbia—if Annie would only consent to let us board with her! I am not without hope that the matter may be arranged. Of course I will let you know anything as soon as we know ourselves.

I cannot tell you how glad I am that you are to have your dear little wife so soon! (In June, that is—according to my announcement of our plans—W)[2] Write me dear, as soon as possible, and tell me everything about your plans. How I wish you *could* come home to us to spend the summer. But unfortunately we will have no home! I comfort my self with the thought that Clarkesville will [be a pleas]ant place for you to come to us in *future* summers! But that is a long time to wait.

We had a Postal from George yesterday. Jessie was still lying unconscious. We heard nothing today. I am afraid to hope for her recovery—for the desease may leave her a hopeless invalid. How mysterious are God's dealings! But they *are right* we know. Good bye my precious boy. I am so glad for you. Papa & Josie join me in love inexpressible to you & dear Ellie.

Yours as always   Mother

ALS (WP, DLC). MS. damaged.
  [1] JRW's insertion. The General Assembly of the southern Presbyterian Church met in Houston, May 21-28, 1885.
  [2] WW's insertion.

To Ellen Louise Axson

Balto., Thursday evening, Jany 29, 1885
I must write to you to-night, my precious, instead of to-morrow, because I shall have scarcely a half hour to myself then, whereas now my evening's work is done and it still lacks an hour of bedtime. What is to keep me so busy to-morrow? Why, I shall be in

attendance upon lectures till one o'clock; from two to five I am
expected to act as "proctor" at an examination; at 8 o'clock the
Seminary meets; and at half past nine I am to go over to Prof.
Morris's[1] for the rest of the evening. Prof. Morris is "Collegiate
Prof. of Latin and Greek." He is a jolly, whole-souled Englishman
and delights in serving up nice little suppers on Friday evenings
to a few students—with whom his invitations now and then mix
a teacher or two. He does just what all the professors ought to do,
brings the men together in informal fashion for his own and
their enjoyment. He had the Glee Club with him once or twice in
a body last year.

To preside as "proctor" at an examination—to sit the examination through, that is, to see that the fellows behave themselves
—is one of the very few official duties which a Fellow is liable to
be called upon to perform.

It has more than once occurred to me, little lady, that the letter which I despatch on Friday has a peculiar mission to perform;
it is the letter which must last my darling through Sunday: it
must be able to *wear* for two days: it ought to contain *something*
that my little sweetheart will like to think about. Shall I tell you
this time what *I* like to think about on Sundays? I like to look
forward to the time when my precious Eileen will have come to
me to show me day by day what it is to be loved by a wife whose
delight it is to love and to manifest her love; when we shall go
to church together and feel our love for each other sanctified by
our common love for the gracious God who brought us together;
when we shall pause from the week-day work to talk as we please
the sweet confidences of love, to look each other in the eyes and
know that we are the same sweethearts as of old, only with *more*
love and a more precious intimacy added to the old intercourse,
and to commune with the Father in Heaven whose children we
delight to be; when we can forget worry in love, can find happy,
careless moments in which to be like gleeful children in our love-
making, and can cheer each other for work and plans ahead. And
you will please observe, Miss, how firm are the foundations of my
castles in the air. They are not built upon fancy, but upon fact—
upon the great, the delightful fact that *we love each other*—a
fact which seems to me to be worth more than all the other happy
facts of the world put together. Why, that fact is my fortune!
Without love I should die: *with* love—with faith and courage and
love before me in my Eileen's eyes, and in her loving services—I
can live the best, the strongest life of which I am capable. See
what you have given me, my darling! Every time that you de-

clare how much you love me you are simply estimating the treasure which is all in all to   Your own   Woodrow.

ALS (WC, NjP).
1 Dr. George Sylvester Morris.

From Ellen Louise Axson

My darling Woodrow,   New York Jan 29/85.

Many thanks for the nice notice of your book received this morning, also for the envelopes—also for sending me "Dode's" letter. It was a *great* pleasure to me both to receive and to read it. He was a dear boy to think of writing me, and I appreciate it very highly.

I am sure that this plan of your fathers for spending the summer at the north will be a delightful one for you all and just the thing for your mother. The change of scene coupled with the complete freedom from "the cares of bread" as Mrs. Carlyle, or rather Mazzini, calls them, will be sure to do her good. The interval between getting one house off of her mind and another *on* will be just the time for a real good rest, and I am glad they are wise enough to avail themselves of the exceptional opportunity.

Yes, I wanted to send copies of your book to Grandfather[1] and Uncle Will [Hoyt], and I thought you could probably get them cheaper than common folks! But I *will* pay for them, sir. I won't have them on any other terms.

Do you suppose Mr. Bridges wrote this excellent notice of it? I am looking out for the "Nation's" with the greatest impatience.

I thought I had a fair chance to get a hundred dollar prize at the Metropolitan,[2] but my hopes are nipped in the bud. Mr. Stimson has circumvented us.[3] The prize was offered for the best drawing from the head, and it seemed certain that one of the Leaguers would get it—there are five of us working there,—for it is assuredly not boasting to say that we can do better than the students at the "Met.,"—the standard for admission being by no means so high there. But of course Mr. Stimson would have felt it as a reflection upon *himself*, if the honour, such as it is, had been carried off by a Leaguer; so he has made the rule that no one may try for it who has not worked there from the beginning of the season. Quite a neat device for getting ahead of us! eh? Good night, my darling. Believe me, love, yours with all my heart.

Yours forever   Eileen.

ALS (WP, DLC).
1 I. S. K. Axson.
2 The Metropolitan Museum Art School, where Ellen and other Leaguers were attending a class in sketching from live models.
3 John Ward Stimson, director of the Art School.

From Edward Miles Gadsden

My dear Wilson: Washington, D. C. Jan. 29th. 1885

Two weeks ago I saw in the "Nation"[1] that a book would soon come out from the press of Houghton Miflin, & Co, the author of which was Woodrow Wilson, and this afternoon walking down the Ave. my attention was attracted to a large placard, put out by a book seller, announcing the fact that "Congressional Governments" by Woodrow Wilson, was for sale. Permit me my friend to shake your paw, and to say that no one can and does more warmly congratulate you on this you[r] first success than your humble servant. Renick has told me how eagerly the publisher, that holy terror to all authors, seized the opportunity of being the first to give to the world the sage wisdom contained in those covers. Naturally they knew a good thing when they saw it. You should feel justly proud at the compliment they paid you, and your work. . . . Besides being kept very busy at the office, I am preparing to be married on the 12th proximo. As might be expected I am a little preoccupied just now, to put it mildly, and until this painful excitement is over I am unfit for much sober thought. Please as opportunity offers let me hear from you, and know that you have not forgotten me. I hope we shall meet again in the near future, and that I shall also have the pleasure of hearing soon that Mrs. Woodrow Wilson is with you.

Sincerely, your friend,   E. M. Gadsden

ALS (WP, DLC) with WWhw notation on env.: "Ans. Fcby. 8, 1885."
[1] New York *Nation*, XL (Jan. 15, 1885), 55.

From Ellen Louise Axson

My darling Woodrow,   New York, Jan. 30/85.

I have spent so much time this evening in thinking about the contents of your sweet letter of this morning that I have left myself very little in which to return a more tangible answer. But perhaps it is just as well, for I am hardly ready to make answer yet. I must think still a little longer—I must "*sleep* over it"! However I *can* give you an answer upon one point, my darling, and that is that I am ready to give you any proof you want of our oneness of heart and purpose; I *will* tell you just what I think, as soon as I am sure that I have thought anything definite, and I will in the meantime "talk it over bravely" and frankly.

You know, of course, that your parents' change of plan is not the only difficulty in the way;—there are a number of perplexing features in the case on my side,—obstacles, which as yet I can't see any way to surmount. But very probably there *is* a way. I havn't had time to bring my "woman's wit" fully to bear upon the problem. At least I shan't make the humiliating confession that it is unequal to *any* emergency(!). And it is worth making some effort to bring to pass that sweet vision of two long months alone together, buried from the world, not even an imperative duty to call you away and remind us that we still belong to it. Yes, dear, you may take for granted anything you wish as to the answer my heart gives to your questions. I can't tell as yet whether that which you suggest would be "the very best of plans," but I am sure that it would be the most delightful. Will that "do" for the present? I too must ask advice, Aunt Ella's,[1] before I can say more. I have never mentioned this subject yet in writing to Sav. and of course I must hear from there, before saying anything positive.

By-the-way I have just heard from there, and Grandmother[2] has been very ill, but is now better, is "sitting up." This is my first information with regard to it. Give my dearest love to your dear parents and to Josie. With all my heart,

Your own,   Eileen.

ALS (WP, DLC).
  [1] Mrs. Randolph Axson of Savannah.
  [2] Mrs. I. S. K. Axson.

From Robert Bridges

Dear Tommy: New York, Jan 30th '85
    You have my sincerest thanks for the copy of your book which arrived yesterday. I hope that it is only the beginning of a long row by the same author which may some day stand in stately half-calf in all well-regulated libraries.

I have given the book a pretty thorough skimming for ideas and am now reading it leisurely for the style. (I don't mean to insinuate that the cream of ideas is not equal in bulk to the skim-milk of literary finish.) I will send you a paragraph in *Life* which expresses my sincerest judgment—in a very condensed shape.[1] I do not doubt that it will meet with careful and scholarly consideration by the small but growing class of men who are giving thought to political questions. It seems to me that the book is likely to have a steady sale, because it covers a new field—and one in which young men are gradually becoming interested.

Mr. Garrison[2] assured me that the book would be sent to a first-class *Nation* man for review. That will insure it a notice of some length. The *Nation* moves slowly and it probably will not appear for some weeks.

I am glad that you have decided to accept the Bryn Mawr place. It will keep you in range with the Eastern Colleges and the chair at Princeton which I believe awaits you.

The marriage which goes with it will, I doubt not, be a favoring sail to help you onward. You are fairly and prosperously launched.   God speed you.   Bob Bridges.

ALS (WP, DLC).
   [1] Droch [Robert Bridges], "Two Admirable Books," *Life*, v (Feb. 5, 1885), 76.
   [2] Wendell Phillips Garrison, literary editor of the *Nation*.

From John Randolph Tucker

                          House of Representatives U.S.,
Dear Sir   Washington, D.C., Jan 30 1885.
I thank you for your kindness in sending me your book—which I shall read with pleasure, when this Congressional Machine stops running—and shall weigh its suggestions on Congressional Govt with good hope of being greatly benefitted thereby.[1]
              I am very truly yours   J. R. Tucker

ALS (WP, DLC).
   [1] Wilson may have sent his book to Tucker because of the Virginian's sponsorship, in 1880, of reform of the rules of the House of Representatives relating to a quorum.

From James E. Rhoads

Dear Friend   Philadelphia, 1 mo. 30. 1885.
Thine of 28th is recd. The address of the lady who keeps the Boarding House is, "Mrs. Hawkins, Bryn Mawr, Montgomery Co, Penna." I do not know her first name. There is another Bg. House nearer the college—not so good, I fear, but comfortable. I have not the address of the lady—will try to get it.

Thy work on Congressional Government came duly. Please accept my very hearty thanks for it.

I have glanced through it, enough to learn that its analysis and account of the actual modes of organization & action of the Departments of our government, will be a revelation to many intelligent Americans. The comparison of our government in its practical working with those of Great Britain & France, is admirable, bringing out likeness & contrasts well, and very instructively. It shows an author who can discern not the facts alone, but the principles of History. Some modification of this government by irresponsible standing Committees must come. I think this book will hasten it. Sooner or later there must be a responsible Ministry or something to stand for it.

There must be sooner or later, too, at least a few *trained* men in our government. A practical people like ours when it has arranged the civil service system, will see that leaders as well as subordinates should have fitness for office. The style is clear, agreeable—pleasant to read. There are a few phrases, idiomatic, which do not add to the dignity of the volume, but it is a very valuable contribution to the political history of the United States. I most heartily congratulate thee upon being its author and believe it is the precursor of yet more powerful wks, which shall help to mould our national life.

Thine very truly,   James E Rhoads

ALS (WP, DLC).

From Edward Ireland Renick

My dear Wilson,   Washington, D. C., Jan'y 31, 1885.

Your book, for which please take my warmest thanks, has been in part devoured, Mrs Renick being a partner at the feast—& for it we have only praise, unqualified praise. Mrs Renick thinks it as entertaining as Green—she *can* go no higher than that. I, with far better insight into the true workings of our governmental machinery than I ever possessed when you & I were together, am amazed at the book—its practicalness, & correctness of minutiae. I expect to see it well reviewed & favorably—& especially by the Nation.

On page 157, 158[1]—I hoped to find an answer to enquiries which I have lately repeatedly put to persons who ought to be capable of leaving no doubt in my mind—but from whom I have received conflicting statements.

The general functions of Conference Committees I well understand—but can they assume—or as a matter of fact, do they as of course arrogate to themselves the right to tack new features to a bill? By "new features" I mean, of course, not something entirely foreign to the bill upon which they endeavor to secure harmonious views, but something not provideded for at all by either house—as for instance—the providing for compensation for Commissioners to be appointed by the Prest. with advice & consent of Senate to negotiate a treated [treaty] with Mexico, or to ascertain the best modes of securing more intimate Commercial relations between the U. S. and South America—in a bill making appropriations for the fiscal year for the Consular & Diplomatic Service—

said provision not having been suggested to or by either Committe[e] on Appropriation of the House or Senate. Judge [William] Lawrence—1st Comptroller and ex-member of Congress says yes. I can hardly credit it.

Must go to work.

Very sincerely,   As ever yours   E I Renick

ALS (WP, DLC) with WWhw notation on env.: "Ans. Feby. 21/85."
 1 Printed on p. 92 of the present volume.

From Joseph R. Wilson, Jr.

My dearest brother: Wilmington N. C. Jan. 31st '85.

Dear little Jessie died last night, (Friday Jan. 30th) and father expects to leave to-night for Columbia to be in time for the funeral which takes place tomorrow. Mother and I will not go over as father can be of more comfort to poor sister Annie. I think perhaps it is a blessing to the dear little girl that she did die, as she would probably have been a sufferer for the rest of her life. Now we can think of her as being in heaven with God whom she seemed to love very much. They say she would take a bible and sit down and read it just like a grown person, and speak of Jesus and how she loved him.

We have been receiving a postal from sister Annie every day, and Jessie has been in a sort of stupor, so I dont suppose she suffered much, if at all.

I must close now and write a note to sister Marion. We received your letter this morning, and I suppose mother will write just as soon as she can. We are pretty well and send unbounded love to you.   Your loving bro.   Joseph.

ALS (WP, DLC) with WWhw notation on env.: "Ans."

To Ellen Louise Axson, with Enclosure

My own darling,   Balto., Sunday morning, Feby. 1st., 1885

I did not write yesterday simply because I couldn't: I tried, but had to give it up: my pains were 'too many' for me. The fact of the matter is, little sweetheart, that I was miserably unwell yesterday and the day before. My head felt as big as a bushel-basket, and was full of an ache bigger than any bushel-basket could have held, while very merciless pains chased each other actively throughout every part of my frame. I was not particularly alarmed, because I had met those pains before, and had never found the gentlemen capable of inflicting permanent damage;

but I was sufficiently miserable! Miss Ashton and the men here are just as kind and attentive as possible: but, after all, their care is not like the loving attention one gets at home, and it's a desperately desolate business to be sick when one is away off from those who care most for him! But I am *very much* better this morning, and I think that by keeping to my room for twenty-four hours and claiming all the indulgences of an invalid I can effect a perfect cure of my petty malady.

Mr. Wright was kind enough to go to the Post Office for me this morning, so that I have your sweet letter of Friday night before me, with its precious, satisfying reply to my letter about our plans. Yes, darling, I do know that the change of plan on the part of my home-folks is not the only difficulty in the way of our making possible the plan which our hearts are cherishing: though, as you are doubtless aware, Miss, I have so far been left to *guess* what the "perplexing features" and "obstacles" on your side are. If our marriage early in the summer will necessitate your rushing to Savannah immediately after the closing of the League to plunge into a mass of *sewing* and like preparation which will serve only to wear you out, if not to break you down completely, I must of course withdraw my plea for the plan. *Any* length of waiting would be preferable to risking my darling's health in the slightest. Indeed, I must confess that there is only one fact that has kept me from feeling that I was altogether selfish in urging the plan upon which I have so much insisted: and that is, that my darling *wants* to make it possible as much as I do. My *argument* has been altogether selfish: namely, that a summer spent with you would prepare me for my winter's work, a summer spent away from you, harass and fret me, and to that extent render me unfit for that work. (By-the-way, Miss, I opened my eyes very wide at your being "*sure*" that this plan of father's for spending the summer at the north "will be a *delightful* one" for us all! *I* couldn't promise to be very *constantly* delighted with half a dozen States between yourself and me!)

But I don't mean to be—or wish even to *seem*—unreasonable, and you may be *quite* "sure" that, whatever your decision may be, I will accept it with perfect loyalty, because I shall know that you have given the utmost that love can give, have made as great sacrifices as love could demand. My fortunes are in your hands, my precious; and I know of no greater possible good fortune than to have them in such keeping! This little letter here on the table before me would prove—if I had not known it long ago— that my fortunes are, in your heart's view, identical with your own; that you will give me anything within your gift. The only thing I have to beg *now*, therefore, my little queen, is that you will wait to know all the facts that may remain to be known both on your side and on mine before you make any decision final. In the meantime, I will be content—who would *not* be!—with the sweet assurance that your *heart* desires unreservedly all that mine does. Oh, my darling, what a world of hope and delight there is for me in your precious love, so sweetly and so freely given! *I love you*, sweetheart!

You queer, shy little maiden! You actually had not *mentioned the* subject in writing to Savannah? I hope that when you did write you put *my* side of the case as strongly as your own—provided my side is different from yours in your view of the case!

Do you know, young lady, that a very grave suspicion has been growing upon me of late with reference to yourself? Yes; it's even so! The habitual, uniform brevity of your letters, and the evidences they bore of having been written late in the evening, have led me to suspect that you have been continuing your art work into the evenings, that you have taken to drawing or painting *at night*! I most sincerely *hope* that it is *not* so, my darling, for I think that it would be a very, very great mistake on your part to do anything of the sort. But I mustn't scold you on the strength of a *supposition*!

I will send copies of "Cong. Govt." to your Grandfather, my pet, and "uncle Will," as soon as I can get them, and you may 'settle' with me for them when you catch me.

Yes, Bridges wrote the notice I sent you, and will have another one in "Life." He says, in a letter thanking me for a copy of the book which I sent him: "Mr. Garrison ['literary editor' of the *Nation* and *Post*][1] assured me that the book would be sent to a first-class *Nation* man for review. That will insure it a notice of some length. The *Nation* moves slowly and it probably will not appear for some weeks."

The letter which I enclose speaks for itself. You can imagine the feelings with which I read it. What greater pleasure could a man have than to *give* pleasure to such a father!

Oh! my darling, that matchless little girl, our precious little Jessie is dead! She is to be buried to-day. The news of the end did not come upon me as a great blow, however, because I expected it—and because I knew that recovery from meningitis must be attended with the risk of *imbecility*! I had suffered as much as I could when I heard of her desperate sickness and knew what the end must be—and to learn of her death was almost a relief—

a relief from the fear of another result. What a vision of brightness that little life was! I know that I am the better for having
seen it and shared part of it. Oh my poor sister—how my heart
bleeds for her! May God give her strength!

Good-bye, my love—I feel still better after having poured my
heart out to you. With love unspeakable

Your own   Woodrow.

ALS (WC, NjP).
1 WW's brackets.

ENCLOSURE

From Joseph Ruggles Wilson

My precious Son—   Wilmington, Friday, Jan. 30, 85

Your book has been received and gloated over. The "dedication"[1] took me by surprise, and never have I felt such a blow of
love. Shall I confess it?—I wept and sobbed in the stir of the glad
pain. God bless you, my noble child, for such a token of your
affection.

I cannot write you at length touching the contents of the volume which is so dear to my pride. I have read portions of it, more
than once, with an ever-new admiration. You have cause for
thankfulness and for courage.

The love we all feel for you is as large as possible.

Your own affc   Father.

ALS (WP, DLC).
1 It is printed in Vol. 3, p. 503.

Two Letters from Ellen Louise Axson

My darling Woodrow,   New York, Feb. 1/85.

I was unable to write last night "for reasons to[o] numerous
to mention"; and this morning of course it was a rush to get off
to Bible class. So I have been forced to put off until my return
from church, and now I must write a hasty line only, and run to
the corner and mail it before dinner, that it may be in time for
the postman.

Speaking of the Bible class—I am perfectly *charmed* with it and
my teacher. He is a beautiful old man,—tall, rather large, with
a noble, massive head and face;—it is ruddy and smooth-shaven
with gray hair, and the sweetest kindliest smile always lurking
about his mouth and eyes,—just the sort of face you like, except
that, while there is no weakness in it, benevolence—love,—rather
than power, is it's most striking characteristic. You perceive, I

have placed him among *my* old men! I am always in love with,—
raving over!—two or three of that type. I heard this Mr. Carter[1]
pray at the first prayer-meeting that I attended and lost my heart
to him then, so I was delighted when I found that he was my
teacher. By the way, *you* know the Carter Bros.—publishers of
religious books;—this is one of them, Robert Carter's younger
brother.

He told me today that he thought last Sunday that my name
was familiar, and that it was associated in his mind somehow
with the Southern Church, but having a bad memory he couldn't
recall at the time that it was the name of a minister in Sav.
of whom he had often heard and to whom he had sold many
books. Was I related to him? "He had three initials,—let me see—
I. S.—I. S.![''] He really seemed quite triumphant,—he fairly
beamed,—when he learned that he had found me out.

I had a sweet letter from Grandmother yesterday,—was overjoyed to hear from her again. She has been very ill, but is now
slowly recovering strength. But I *must* close or it will be too late.
Surely I might wait until tonight to say the rest. With all my
heart I am forever   Your own Eileen.

[1] Probably Peter Carter, a long-time partner of Robert Carter in publishing
and selling religious books.

My darling Woodrow,   New York Feb. 1, 1885.
I have just finished writing a long letter to Aunt Ella, the answer to which will, I hope, enable me to give *you* a positive answer with regard to certain matters of interest to us. What
wouldn't I give for one little talk with her! It is very tiresome to
be obliged to write such volumes—to anyone but you;—and it has
left me but a fragment of an evening in which to answer that
sweet letter which has indeed lasted me two days. It is sweet to
know, darling, that on these happy Sabbath days you and I are
perchance thinking the same thoughts; for I too, always, but then
most of all, like to look forward to the time when I may show you,
day by day, what it is to be loved by a wife whose delight it is to
love and to manifest her love;—to think how—by what means—I
may *best* manifest that love,—best prove how true and strong
and real a thing it is. And I too like above all then to look forward
to our *Sabbaths* together, to think of how we may take sweet
counsel together and ["] go up to the house of the Lord in company." So absorbing are those thoughts that—would you believe
it?—they have the curious effect of tempting me to stay away

from that house now! It is so much pleasanter to stay at home &
dream of you than go to that second service. But of course now
that I have made it *my* church I feel that I ought.

Do you know I fear I shall be obliged to fill another letter with
Mr. Goodrich! It is a great bore, and I hardly know why I do it,
when I have so many other more interesting things to discuss; but
then if I did not tell you all, I should feel somehow that I had
not been *true*. So remember that whenever Miss Cunningham
makes love to you I shall expect you to tell me all about it, even
thought the result should be an uninteresting letter! We had another tilt last night. It began with my refusing to go and see
"Julius Caesar"; for like Julius himself, I gave him to understand
that "cannot is false; and that I dare not falser; I *will* not go tonight." I scorned to make excuses,—or to be candid, I was *tired*
of making them, I had had enough of that role. But, of course,
he was deeply hurt, and in his excitement said things (about his
regard for me,) that he did not mean to say. So I told him that
self-respect would not permit me to hear such things, and I said
moreover,—remembering your words—that I did not understand
him and I feared he misunderstood me. I had thought when I
told him I was engaged, it was enough; but I was afraid he
thought, because it was not my way to wear my heart upon my
sleeve, that an engagement, after all, was a very small matter,
and to be easily overlooked; so I wished to tell him that I was not
only engaged to you, but I also *loved* you,—loved you more than
my own soul, and would love you forever. Well! he said it was
impossible to misunderstand me either now or at any time before,
I was the truest, purest noblest woman he had even seen! &c. &c.
—(Can't you see why I object to telling even you what other men
have said to me? it makes me feel too silly!) And then he lost his
head and said that he too *must* tell *me* something,—it was that
he loved *me* more than his own soul. Upon that I of course immediately *froze*, and was about to take my departure; but he,
shocked grieved, and mortified at what he had done, pleaded so
piteously for forgiveness that I could not but be moved. So when
he asked me if I would always despise him, I told him,—"no,"—
because I believed that he had not *meant* to say it;—and he said,
—upon his soul, he had not and he would never say it, or anything
approaching it again. He added with a miserable sort of laugh
that something had forced him to be, like me, perfectly straightforward; for that one time. Then he asked what I would have him
do, and I told him the only wise thing for him to do was to see as
little of me as he could,—if possible absolutely nothing (I really

wanted him to leave the house, as he was intending to do when
I came,) and the only *kind* thing for me to do was to co-operate
with him to that end. Then he entreated me not to end it so, and
added in a very manly way that I must allow him to judge what
was kindest—what was *best* for him, trying only, on my part, to
be *just* to him. It was not as though he had been *disappointed*,
in that case he would have left the house at once, never to see me
again; but as I had never allowed him, from the first, a moment's hope, there was no pain—no *new* pain that could result
from what had just passed. His love was altogether unselfish and
he wished now above all else to be my friend,—to render me the
services of friendship; he would be my brother. I said it would
do no good to trifle with the situation—to ignore the facts of the
case—he could not be my brother because he had not the feelings
of a brother! But he insisted he had, (!) that quite apart from his
always hopeless love he felt for me the truest, strongest *friendship*; he would not but for that wish for *my* friendship,—he wished
for it because he respected and revered me (one can't always
choose the right word, you see) more than any human being—
because he felt that it was good for him to be with me. I *must*
know that my influence had done him good, and would do
him still more; even this experience, bitter as it was, had been
good for him. It had not shamed or humiliated him;—he did not
even feel that his love was wasted because to love such a woman
as I, (!) hopelessly or not, was a privilege in itself, and could
never bring one anything but good. He would be a better man
for it all his life though he now put it away out of sight forever.
He asked why I should refuse to him, who so much wished it, the
friendship, which it seemed to be the stereotyped thing for
women to offer men who did *not* wish it, because they had hoped
for something more. He begged me then again to be just to him,
not to cast him aside as though I did not trust him, and would
not even give him an opportunity to *prove* himself *worthy* of my
confidence and friendship—for he *would* prove it! Now what am I
to do? don't you think that this is a manly, noble young fellow?
As for his love, anyone can see the sort of poetical thing it is;—
he says he has been in love with an ideal since he was two years
old and—so forth! Is it necessary for me to be harsh with him?
Would it be right or just in me to drop him? Would it compromise my dignity to accept his friendship? Is'nt it a similar case
to Mr. Baker's and Mr. Thornwell's[1] whose friendship I have never
hesitated to accept, always feeling for them, indeed, a peculiarly
warm regard and admiration because they were able and content

to give me such pure, disinterested friendship. And then is it necessary for me to humiliate him before this household, as would be the case if I dropped him, for every one would know the cause, and even if he does'nt think of that I must think of it for him. I dont ask all these questions by way of argument, you *know*, but simply to get your opinion. I sorely need another view of the case "from a man's stand-point," for unless it is absolutely necessary from that standpoint, I *can't* be unkind to him,—I am too sorry about it all.

By-the-way, he did not mean what you thought, when he said he "knew I was engaged but had made himself half believe otherwise"; he only meant that he had persuaded himself that my *hints* were *not* hints! I had made no direct statement, and while what I did say was enough to convince an outsider it was *not* enough to convince one in his state of mind. I was wrong not to think of that. I said that if I could be had by anyone but *you* I wouldn't be worth having! And he said he quite agreed with me, that was one thing he admired most in me!

But *my*! I didnt mean to write a regular *novel* about Mr. Goodrich. I'll venture to say that you never read such a rig-a-marole as this before! At any rate I have the honour of having invented a perfectly original style of letter, and you have to thank me for a brand new experience; your presence has been allowed at such a scene as you could never have witnessed under any other circumstances!—for your own case don't count. You have been admitted to the *sweet* (!) privileges of girlhood!—have heard things sacred to their ears! You have been as it were transformed into a girl for the time being!—don't you feel like one? If you do you feel very miserable. Oh dear! I wish I had never seen Mr. Goodrich. I never believed much in anybody's love but yours, but this is too good an imitation. What a pity I am not like Miss Arnold!— then I wouldn't get into so much trouble; Mr. G. says the trouble is that I am *not* the least bit of a flirt. If I was I would'nt do half the mischief! for I wouldn't have half the power. The idea of any human being suffering a heart-ache on *my* account! It is *too* preposterous. If I could only in *some* way open their eyes to see me as I am! But I think it is *about* bed time. Goodnight, my darling, I love, love, *love* you! I live for you, my dearest wish is to render you that "loving service."

As ever   Your own Eileen.

ALS (WP, DLC).
¹ Baker and Thornwell were earlier suitors of Ellen's.

To Ellen Louise Axson

My own darling,   Balto., Monday noon, Feby. 2nd, 1885

I am not as much better this morning as I had hoped and expected to be: but the most distressing features of my ailment have disappeared, and I am left with nothing more serious than a wretched cold in my head which makes study next to impossible. I shall go out for a short time this afternoon to pay a duty call of consultation upon Dean Martha;[1] but, with that imperative exception, I intend to keep within doors as much as possible. My darling need not be alarmed about me in the least. The malady in its present form amounts to little more than a serious inconvenience, temporarily interrupting my work and destroying my comfort. My *spirits* are really the only *sufferers*.

I received two letters this morning, my pet, from which, I think, you will like to hear extracts: the one was from Josie, the other from Renick. Speaking of precious little Jessie, Dode says: "I think perhaps it is a blessing to the dear little girl that she did die, as she would probably have been a sufferer for the rest of her life. Now we can think of her as being in heaven with God whom she seemed to love very much. They say she would take a Bible and sit down and read it just like a grown person, and speak of Jesus and how she loved him." Isn't that a beautiful picture, darling! One couldn't wish for a sweeter attitude for that lovely little figure.

I too am "overjoyed" at your receipt of a letter from your dear Grandmother. That she could write it is evidence that she is really *very much* better. I am so glad!—and, since the issue of her illness has been what it has, I am glad that you *didn't* know of it sooner. What does that dear family in Savannah do without Dr. Thomas[2] in case of illness?

But I must not forget the extract from Renick's letter. It concerns my book. He had taken so much trouble to have it favourably announced in various quarters (in Atlanta and at the Univ. of Va.,—as well as in the Charlotte paper[3]—whose editorial he wrote himself, by-the-way—) that I sent him a copy. After according it "only praise, unqualified praise," he says: "I, with far better insight into the true workings of our governmental machinery than I ever possessed when you and I were together, am amazed at the book—its practicalness and correctness of minutiae." Rather gratifying testimony from a governmental official! I am getting rather impatient for the *adverse* criticisms to make themselves heard!

I am delighted, little lady, that you have found so lovable and admirable a teacher for your Bible class. Yes, of course I know of Robert Carter and brothers—and I think that quite a charming little episode of quasi-recognition.

I feel sufficiently lonely and downcast shut up here in my room with nobody but myself and my cold for company; but when the experience threatens to become intolerable, I know of an infallible spell with which to lay all evil spirits and that is the spell that is so full of blessing and of hope—your love for

Your own   Woodrow.

ALS (WC, NjP).
1 Martha Carey Thomas.
2 James G. Thomas, M.D., who had recently died.
3 Actually, it was in the Raleigh, N. C., *State Chronicle*, Jan. 20, 1885.

From Ellen Louise Axson

New York Feb. 3 1885.

I am *so* sorry—*so distressed*, my darling to hear of your sickness, and that it is such a sharp and painful attack. It makes my heart ache to think of you suffering among strangers—or at least away from home,—it *must* be the most desolate business in the world. I think if I were ill here, I should almost die, not of the desease but of the attendant homesickness. But I am *so* glad to hear that you are "very much better"; take good care of yourself darling, and don't call yourself well until you *are*. Don't try to get out and to work again before it is prudent.

Many thanks for sending me the charming little note from your father. I think I can imagine the feelings with which you read it, because my own feeling of delight in both your happiness and his was so strong. Happy—thrice happy son!—to be able to give *such* pleasure to such a father!

You are very good *and* very naughty to take the business of sending the book to *my* friends in your hands after that fashion! I *shall* settle with you when I catch you,—in the meantime—on paper—I suppose I must be resigned to thank you!

Why did you *tell* me of Mr. Walter's exhibition? I can't get it out of my mind!—can't avoid doing that most foolish of things, dwelling on the impossible. One trouble is that I hear so much of it at school now, I *must* think of it. The whole life class has just been down on an excursion to see it. They went by invitation, someone, Mr. Walters I presume, paying their railroad fare. So they are all full of it. Yet you know, that after all, it is'nt the pictures which draw me most strongly in that direction, so that I almost refuse to believe that it *is* impossible. What wouldn't I give for a glimpse of you!—for just one nice long talk with you, at this particular time!

Oh, dearest I can't tell you how my heart bleeds for your sister and all of you in this great trouble. I can't forget it for a moment. But there is nothing to *say*, that would not be almost a mockery. We can only be still and know that He is God. It is indeed a sweet and beautiful memory that she has left us, all—who ever saw her.

Good-bye, darling, for the present. Hoping to hear soon that you are quite well I am *with all my heart*

Your own Eileen.

ALS (WP, DLC).

From Robert Bridges

Dear Tommy: New York, Feb 3 '85

I enclose a number of clippings which I have met with in my reading. Will send more when I get a bunch of them.

Mr. Garrison handed me a note yesterday from the *Nation* critic who will handle your book. He says, "Woodrow Wilson's book is admirable, and I shall go into that *con amore.*" I am permitted to violate a rule of the office and tell you that he is Gaml Bradford of Boston. Yours Bob B.

ALS (WP, DLC) with WWhw notation on env.: "Ans. Feby. 7, 1885." Encs. missing.

Wilson's Courses of Study for Students in History and Political Science[1]

[c. Feb. 3, 1885]
HISTORY

The courses indicated suggest the topical plan of instruction which is to be followed. The histories of Greece and Rome are taken as representative of ancient history, those of France and England as representative of mediæval and modern history; and in following these special lines the work of the classes will consist largely in the preparation by individuals of reports on specific topics and important episodes in the histories studied. These reports will be founded, not only upon the text-books used, but also upon all the standard authorities available.

Constant text-book drill will be combined with instruction by means of frequent lectures, whose object will be to give life to the narrative of the text-book used in recitation by recounting the most important contemporary events in the history of other countries, and by pointing out the chief and most memorable characteristics of the periods studied, as well as the philosophical connection of leading facts and tendencies. The general purpose of the lectures will be to group and explain facts separated in the narrative, and to keep the student mindful of the broad views of history to which the events in the lives of individual nations stand related.

The courses on the Italian Renaissance and the German Reformation will be lecture courses.

Each year's work will be introduced by a brief course of lectures on the philosophy of history and the method of study.

First Year.   Major Course.
(Ancient History.)

History of Greece. *Three times weekly during the first semester.*

History of Rome. *Three times weekly during the second semester.*

It is intended to supplement this course by the reading of several of the principal Greek and Latin historians in the original, under the instructors of the Classical Department.

Second Year.
(Modern History.)

History of France. *Three times weekly, on alternate weeks throughout the year.*

History of England. *Three times weekly, on alternate weeks throughout the year.*

Italian Renaissance and German Reformation. *Twice weekly during the first semester.*

Lectures on special topics in American History. *Twice weekly during the second semester.*

Either year of the major courses in History may be taken separately as a minor course.

Group. History and Political Science. Students who elect this group may take as required studies, instead of one year of science and one year of history, one year of science and one year of French, Italian or Spanish.

POLITICAL SCIENCE

First Year.   Major Course.

Elements of Political Economy. Text-book drill and lectures. *Three times weekly throughout the year.*

History of Political Opinion. Lectures and class reports. *Twice weekly throughout the year.*

Second Year.

English and American Constitutional History. Lectures. *Three times weekly throughout the year.*

History of Political Institutions. Lectures. *Twice weekly throughout the year.*

Group. History and Political Science.

Printed in *Bryn Mawr College Program, 1885-86* (Philadelphia, 1885), pp. 28-30.
  1 For a description of Wilson's actual course work during his first year at Bryn Mawr, see the Editorial Note, "Wilson's Teaching at Bryn Mawr, 1885-86," Vol. 5.

To Ellen Louise Axson

Metropolitan Hotel, N. Y.,
Wednesday morning [Feb. 4, 1885].

If Eileen will stay at home this morning she will see someone she loves. He promises himself a sight of her, and as many kisses as she will give him, at *nine o'clock A. M.* Is she glad? Is she as glad as he is impatient?

ALS (WC, NjP).

From Albert Shaw

My Dear Colonel: Minneapolis, Feb. 5. 1885.

I was delighted to get the book, and equally "proud" (as they say in New England) to have the news of your fortunate appointment in the "Miss Johns Hopkins." It was with much sense of reflected glory that I walked into our principal book-store yesterday, picked up a copy of "Congressional Government" and remarked to the proprietor that the author of that book was an intimate friend of mine. It so happened that [George Edward] Woodberry's "Poe" and [Josiah] Royce's metaphysical volume lay beside it; and the three books set me to thinking of all the great men it had been my privilege to meet. I thought with amusement of my attempt to *cicerone* Woodberry through the Bluntschli, and how we swapped sarcasms and "exchanged profanities," figuratively speaking, for you know I never swear. I thought Woodberry was a dude and an ass; and doubtless he thought I was a donkey and a cow-boy.

Your book has been many times in my hands and much in my sight since it came, but I have been so unwontedly busy that I have not found time to read three consecutive pages, and there-

fore I cannot yet say, intelligently, how I like the new chapters
of the book. I shall very soon have time to peruse the whole book
carefully. I shall make a presentation of it before the Political
Science Club of the Univ. of Minnesota, a small society recently
organized by Prof. Folwell, Prof. Peebles (a Princeton post-graduate under Dr. McCosh), Bemis,[1] and myself. I have written to
Mr. Browne of the Chicago *Dial*[2] bespeaking a good notice for the
book. I hope he will let me write it, but I don't know that he will.
By the way, I have wondered who wrote the flattering review of
"Icaria" in the *Nation*.[3] It was so complimentary that I felt certain it must have been inspired or written by a friend. I believe
you are a correspondent of the *Evening Post*. Just find out for me
who is my benefactor. That notice was worth a great deal to me.
So [Charles H.] Shinn has gone West. I haven't heard from him
for some time. Perhaps I owe him a letter. It is very hard for me
to get any letters written. I am glad to hear he is coming back
by the Northern Pacific. I shall try to have him make me a little
visit here. . . .

Your prospects must seem very attractive. You will be near,
Philadelphia, Baltimore, New York, and Washington, and will be
in a school which is certain to become famous. You will, I suppose, have some leisure—as you will have ample materials—for
study and writing. With the immediate future so well cared for,
you can easily resign yourself to the inevitable grind of cramming
and examinations. Are there other candidates for Ph. D. in the Department besides yourself and Levermore?[4] Does D[avis]. Dewey
come up this year?

I must positively wind this up and cast about for subjects editorial. Give my grip of fellowship to Wright and my salutations
to the other lads, besides giving my love to Miss Ashton and the
ladies of the household.   Sincerely yours   Albert Shaw.

ALS (WP, DLC) with WWhw notation on env.: "Ans. Feby 21/85."
  1 William Watts Folwell, Thomas Peebles, and Edward Webster Bemis.
  2 Francis Fisher Browne, editor.
  3 New York *Nation*, xxxix (Dec. 4, 1884), 488-89, reviewing Shaw's *Icaria:
A Chapter in the History of Communism* (New York, 1884).
  4 Charles Herbert Levermore, born Mansfield, Conn., Oct. 15, 1856. A.B., Yale
University, 1879; Ph.D., The Johns Hopkins University, 1886. Taught history
at the Hopkins Grammar School, New Haven, Conn., 1885-86, and at the Massachusetts Institute of Technology, 1888-93. Principal, Adelphi Academy, Brooklyn, 1893-96. Founded Adelphi College in Brooklyn in 1896 and served as president until 1912. Associated with the World Peace Foundation of Boston, 1913-17.
Became secretary of the New York Peace Society in 1917, of the World Court
and League of Nations Union in 1919, and of the American Association for
International Cooperation in 1922. Helped to organize the League of Nations
Non-Partisan Association in 1923 and served as vice-president until his death.
In 1924 he won the Bok Peace Award for "the best practicable plan by which
the United States may co-operate with other nations to achieve and preserve the
peace of the world." Died Oct. 20, 1927.

To Ellen Louise Axson

My own darling: [Baltimore] Friday [Feb. 6, 1885] 8:15 P.M.

It is just possible that I can get these few lines to you by to-morrow if I rush off to the P. O. with them now. They are to say that I am safe at home with a heart full of the sweetest thoughts about the sweetest of sweet maidens, and full of precious memories of the last two days

In the greatest haste—and with love unspeakable,

Your own   Woodrow.

ALS (WC, NjP).

From Ellen Louise Axson

My darling Woodrow,   New York Feb. 6/85.

I suppose you won't expect anything more than a short message of love so soon as this; and I don't feel disposed to send you more because,—because to tell the truth I have the *blues*, and it is rather against my principles to write much in such a case. My letters might become of the same shade, and that would hardly be fair to the unfortunate recipients, to whom in my character of letter-writer I am already so unmerciful. Am I not the most unreasonable of mortals to be so melancholy when I have had such a sweet visit from the noblest, truest, tenderest lover in the world,—from a lover so lovable and so well-beloved. Such a visit ought to have an exhilerating effect. I ought to be the happiest girl in the world,—and so indeed I *am*! Deep down below all surface changes of mood I am *always* happy, it [is] so great and wonderful a joy to love, and be loved by, you. It seems to me sometimes that I never knew what happiness was until I knew you, that even the happiness of childhood—that *most* blissful period as I have generally agreed with the rest of the world in thinking,—is but a small and shallow stream compared with the deep, full flood of *blessedness* which follows true love given and returned. And so though I do feel a little lonely and sad tonight with my darling so far away, deep down in my heart, from which he is *never* absent, there is always sunshine and good cheer.

One trouble tonight is that I have just had it out with Mr. G. Such a scene! I do think it was rather weak and unmanly in him to plead and protest so much. But he seemed to think he was being treated very unjustly, and he could not help rebelling. However I think he reached a satisfactory conclusion (to me!) and without exciting on his part any very hard feeling toward me. He speaks of leaving, and I hope he will except on Miss Beatty's[1] account.

Good night, my darling, you don't know even yet how very very dear you are to me.

As ever,   Your own Eileen.

The "Thing"[2] has been *out* all the evening. *Isn't* she "aggravating"?

ALS (WP, DLC).
   [1] Elizabeth Beatty, proprietress of ELA's boardinghouse.
   [2] Miss Beatty.

To Robert Bridges

Dear Bobby,   Balto., Md., Feby. 7, 1885

Many thanks for the notices of "Cong. Govt." from your exchanges—but most of all for the paragraph in *Life*. I was just wishing that I might have a chance to see something like a complete collection of the newspaper opinions on my book—and your thoughtful kindness has anticipated the wish. As for the paragraph in *Life*, I am exceedingly gratified by it, especially since I know that it expresses your deliberate opinion. It relieves me of much anxiety, too, to be assured of a favourable review in the *Nation*. It quite delighted me to learn that Mr. Bradford is the man chosen to formulate posterity's judgment. I sent him a copy of my *Overland* article[1] last winter and received, in return, a long and very complimentary letter from him assuring me of his entire sympathy.[2] I knew that he had made a special study of Congress and its methods.

What a terrible thing this Khartoum business is!—but how strange that it did not happen long ago, that Gordon was able to control the situation so long. I wish the Gladstone ministry a happy deliverance from their difficulties, but it is hard to see whence it is to come. I can think of little else since Thursday.

In love and haste, Yours as ever   Woodrow Wilson

ALS (Meyer Coll., DLC).
   [1] "Committee or Cabinet Government?", printed at Jan. 1, 1884, Vol. 2.
   [2] G. Bradford to WW, Feb. 13, 1884, Vol. 3.

Two Letters to Ellen Louise Axson

Balto., Saturday afternoon, Feby. 7, 1885

Oh, my darling, what a blessing it is to have seen you once more!—and what a misfortune to have lost your sweet presence again! With what bright, joyful memories those two days have enriched me, and with what an increase of longing they have filled me for the time of completed joy and hope that is to come! What a little witch you are, my matchless little sweetheart! what wonderful lessons of love you teach me without so much as trying! I love you—*I love you—I love you.*

I had a queer 'run of luck' getting home. After leaving you, I took the same lines of cars we had taken, proceeded quietly to my hotel, where I paid my bill. I got my satchell, and then, without any hurry, mounted 'the elevated' and sought Cordtlandt St, having not the remotest idea of catching any train, but thinking that I would sit in the station and read my paper until one should happen to be going. But it was as exactly in time for a fast Phila. express as if I had calculated my arrival to the minute. I got aboard and was off. Arrived in Phila., I found that there was just time enough for a comfortable lunch before the next accommodation for Bryn Mawr; and, coming back from B. M., still without plan as to hours, I made close connection with my old 4 o'clock train for Balto. Starting out not caring where I might be delayed, I was not in the least delayed anywhere: with no plans to guide me, I proceeded like a machine!

I found a letter from Bob. Bridges awaiting me with the enclosed notices. His business is to read 'exchanges' from all parts of the country—and he promises to send me all the notices he finds of "Cong. Govt." In his note he says: "Mr. Garrison handed me a note yesterday from the *Nation* critic who will handle your book. He says 'Woodrow Wilson's book is admirable, and I shall go into that *con amore.*' I am permitted to violate a rule of the office and tell you that he is Gam'l Bradford, of Boston." Now isn't that jolly! Gamaliel Bradford is the man who is most interested in just the subjects my book discusses—the man I should myself have chosen for critic—and I am assured of appreciative notice in the *Nation.* I sent Mr. Bradford a copy of my *Overland* article last winter, and received, in reply, a long and exceedingly complimentary letter from him. Truly the fates seem propitious to me nowadays! May they retain their present temper until they bring me the prize without which all others are nothing—until they make my sweetheart my bride!

I shall be very anxious to hear, my darling, how Mr. Goodrich receives the decision. His manner of receiving it will be a much finer test of his manliness than any he has been subjected to before. Oh, my pet, how sweetly you fulfilled my wishes in your acceptance *for yourself* of my view of the case! It was *you* who hit upon the true solution of the matter—and I am *so* glad!

My precious, the parting was terribly hard—I came away like one who leaves *behind* all that can give *joy*—and yet no price was too great to pay for those two blessed days! I have seen my darling and felt again what a supreme delight it is to be

Your own   Woodrow.

My own darling,   Balto., Sabbath afternoon, Feby. 8, 1885

How I wish I could give you a score of kisses for this precious little note that came this morning! Nobody but you, little sweetheart, could have written it—because no heart but yours could have conceived the sweet love that prompted its wonderful message of love. Ah, my darling! And *have* I made you so happy?—*have* I taught you a happiness greater even that [than] that of childhood, and which asserts itself even in the midst of the grief of losing me for a little while? Oh! what a delight it is to think that I have! I would cheerfully, gladly make *any* sacrifice to make my Eileen happy—that is what I live for—and I have been able to do it simply by loving her with all my heart, simply by doing what my whole nature bade me do! My precious! And have you not made me the happiest and proudest of men by the inestimable gift of your love? I am quite sure that *I* never knew what it was to be happy until you loved me: and—if you would know a secret of which I have recently become possessed—I never knew *how* happy I could be until this week just past. I had never before had, when with my darling, so certain a prospect of our marriage, so clear an assurance of the early realization of our hopes. Since I had seen you last, my plans had taken definite shape and certainty. I knew that *very soon*, Providence permitting, I would have a home to offer you, and that not even the most untoward circumstances could long delay my winning the sweetest bride in the world. I saw for the first time *how* soon our partings must be over, *how* soon that companionship which is more to me than all the world would be mine for good and aye—and it seemed to me that this knowledge was revealing to me as I never saw it before my darling's nearness and dearness to me. My heart needs for its satisfaction as great love as woman can give: and every glimpse I get of my Eileen's heart shows me that *she can* satisfy it. Her caresses teach me that I have found what I need more than wealth or power or opportunity; and when I realized last week how soon that priceless thing was to become part of my everyday life, my happiness was unspeakably and beyond all imagination sweet. Your *love* is the light of my life, darling; but

only that *communion* of love which your presence alone can secure can make me *perfectly* happy, can satisfy my heart's yearnings. When I hold you in my arms and feel the warmth of your
pretty cheek against mine, the position, so sweet to me, seems to
my mind a figure of the days to come when we shall live as it were
a single life, when every throb of my heart shall find an answering throb in yours, when every impulse of your heart shall find a
mirror in mine, when my arm shall sustain you and your eyes
shall infuse strength into me—when I may forget my*self* because
I have you to live for and to serve. There is a very deep meaning,
my love, in my desire that you should give yourself to me in June.
If that plan can be realized, I shall have nothing but hope and
confidence for the work at Bryn Mawr; if it may not be, I shall
fear that work's beginning. Even you, Eileen, can hardly have an
idea of the sense in which I *need* you. It is no ordinary lover's
impatience that makes me stick to this plan. I stick to it as a man
would to life: I am *afraid* to have it prove impossible! My darling,
your husband will be made strong for any work *because* you are
his wife!

I had a rather amusing visit to Mrs. Hawkins'[1] house at Bryn
Mawr, my pet: she charges enormous prices with *such* assurance. The view of the case that must comfort you, and silence
your unselfish objections, is that it would cost *one* person almost
as much for board there as it would cost *two*. It pleases Mrs. H.
to charge ten dollars apiece for two and "about fifteen" for one!
I have heard of another place, further from the college, where we
can probably do better and pay less. At any rate, I think we can
command lower rates than Mrs. Hawkins', even from that lady
herself in the end. The difficulty is that all the houses up there
take a great many summer boarders and we cannot *secure* particular rooms beforehand—many of the people staying much later
than the 15th of Sept. I am not at all worried about the prospect:
it's just about what I expected: the unsatisfactory part is having
to delay definite arrangements till the very last moment.

So Mr. G. sought his fate at once, did he? My brave, true, noble
little sweetheart! You have acted just as I would have had you
act! But what shall I say for him? If he pleaded and protested,
and thought himself unjustly treated, I don't wonder that you
saw how weak and unmanly the whole thing was on his part!
Why, Eileen, I can't conceive of a *man's* making it *necessary*
that you should have a "scene" with him. I had almost said that
if he don't know that you are the wronged, the cruelly and dis-
gracefully wronged, party to this affair, he is either a fool or a

knave; but I have no inclination to abuse him. I can only pity and despise a man who hasn't the manliness to see that he *owes* it to you to *anticipate* your wish to have nothing more to do with him; and I cannot sufficiently rejoice that you are finally rid of the attentions of a man whose lack of true gentlemanly instinct must have exposed you to repeated mortification and humiliation. I sincerely hope that he *will* leave the house. Otherwise, you can have no assurance that he will not be weak and childish and selfish enough to seek again and again a reinstatement in your favour, which he has already so grossly abused.

Did you think, pet, that I did not notice your sweet change of *pronunciation*? I noticed it with delight; but I did not say anything about it for fear of making you self-conscious in the use of the novel sounds. You don't *know*, darling, how sweet it sounded in my ears—or how prettily you spoke the 'Italian' *a*. It made me fairly love the words that you spoke so for my sake!

Good-bye, precious. Will you take the kisses put here on your name—Eileen—by   Your own   Woodrow.

ALS (WC, NjP).
¹ Lizzie R. Hawkins, referred to in J. E. Rhoads to WW, Jan. 30, 1885, with whom Wilson will have some correspondence.

Two Letters from Ellen Louise Axson

My darling Woodrow,   New York, Feb. 8 1885.

For some reason, or rather for *many* reasons,—it seems impossible for me to get my letter written on Sat. night, so I must again this morning write a short note and make haste to mail it. Your little note reached me last night; many thanks for it, dear. It was well for me that it did come, for I fear that my common sense alone would not have prevented my being most foolishly excited over that accident of yesterday morning. As it was—in spite of the *evidence* of an alibi which I held in my hand—my heart gave a most curious and unreasonable throb when, at the dinner table, I heard the words "accident on the Penn. R. R." I suppose it was at the thought of how easily you *might* have been there.

I am going at two o'clock away down to Spring St. to take a class in the mission school there. They asked me last Sunday to do so; but I told them that I did not think work of that sort amounted to much unless you could follow the children up in their homes, and I was as yet too much of a stranger to the city to attempt that; my family would not consent, it was about as much as they could "stand," to have me finding my way alone about the *avenues*! But they said that while of course it was better if one could visit among them, it was not absolutely necessary in this case because they had a city missionary regularly employed for the purpose. But they needed *teachers* very much. So I have decided to go; am very glad of the opportunity, for I feel that I am leading a very selfish life here, doing only my *own* work all day long;—not even looking for my share of God's work. But I must close at once, my time is so short. More tonight. I love you, darling, with all my heart, and I am forever,

Your own Eileen.

My darling Woodrow,   New York Feb. 8, 1885.

Well, the labours of the day are over at last, and I can afford to take good solid Sunday comfort in the way I like best, that is, to sit cosily by the fire in dressing-gown and slippers toasting my toes and dreaming of you or writing to you;—or doing each by turn as I feel most disposed. I have only been to church four times today,—bible-class, morning and afternoon service and the mission school;—though it is rather a misnomer to call the latter *church*, "seeing as how" it is situated over a *bar-room*. I was rather pleased with my first experience of a city mission. It is a big room-full of noisy bright very clean and respectable looking little darkies,—did I tell you it was a coloured school? It is Mr. Carter's special property,—he has had charge of it for thirty years. Miss Carter teaches the infant school, Miss Carter Jun. is organist, and the old gentleman's two young hopefuls, two of the handsomest, brightest most wide-awake little scamps I ever saw, act as "under-secretaries" and general managers. The youngest Miss Carter I have never met before, she is exceedingly pretty and sweet looking. She is, next year, to marry a young minister, Mr. Dodd[1] and go with him as missionary to Turkey. He is at present taking a course of medicine here as a preparation for his work. All this I was told by Mr. C. himself in her presence almost immediately after our introduction. Arn't northan people *queer* about engagements! I walked home from church this afternoon by way of fifth Ave., and was overtaken by Dr. Hamilton[2] with whom I had a nice little talk,—the longest I have ever had. He is very delightful, I think. He has been wanting to call on me, but—&c. &c.—is coming soon.

Well, I believe I have given you a complete history of the day! —except indeed an account of my mental disquietude concerning

Mr. Goodrich! I don't know whether he is trying to act out a third-rate melodrama or not but it looks like it. Yesterday he was an object ghastly to behold—ate nothing, and when I, meeting him on the stair, said "how do you do," he answered that he was ill—he *couldn't* bear it! &c. &c. Today he failed to make his appearance at breakfast or dinner; I asked Lizzie after dinner if he was sick; she said "yes, but he was getting better, he had been *out of his head* in the morning.["] Think of it! I hope for his own sake that when he is "out of his head" he recites Mother Goose's melodies. But as you may imagine I was "scared!" However it's all right now and I am immensely relieved. He was on hand at the supper table,—said it was a terrible head-ache; he had often had them, as a child, so severe that they affected him in that way. So I hope the drama isn't to have the full five acts at any rate.

What—do you think—are poor Gordon's chances now! Yesterday they said he was living, and today that he has been killed at best and perhaps also subjected to sickening tortures,—but I don't believe that. Oh, I *hope* we may hear soon![3] I don't know whether I am most sorry for him or Gladstone, but I am inclined to think it is Gladstone.

How glad I will be when tomorrow morning comes and I have a letter. It seems so long since I have had one. I am just "wearying" for the sight of the postman. Dear postman! how I love him! In fact I love them *all*. You know how one feels when one sees anything they like very much one [*sic*] the street,—or elsewhere, —a pretty child, for instance, or the mass of flowers in a florist window, or the sunset glow in the sky with the church towers dark against it, as one looks down fifth Ave,—a strange delicious *warmth* goes creeping all up and down and over and through one —as if one were standing over a *register*! Well I have exactly that same feeling whenever I see a postman! Good-night, my darling, with a heart full of love for you, of happy thoughts of you & of longing to render you service in some degree commensurate with my love, I am as ever   Your own Eileen.

ALS (WP, DLC).
    [1] William Schauffler Dodd, who went as a Presbyterian medical missionary to Turkey in 1886.
    [2] Rev. Dr. Samuel M. Hamilton, pastor of the Scotch Presbyterian Church.
    [3] Though General Gordon was killed in late January, the *New York Times* could not confirm the fact until February 10, 1885, and even then did not know the details of his death. See ELA to WW, Feb. 15, 1885, second letter of that date.

To Ellen Louise Axson

My own darling,   Balto., Feby. 9, 1885

It will not add to my peace of mind on Sabbaths to know that you have undertaken missionary labours on Spring St. I have no disposition to interfere in the least with your discretion in such matters: you must of course decide for yourself what your duty may be with reference to work like that; but I cannot see that you were under any moral obligations to take part in the school of which you speak. One who is not a New Yorker must be entirely inexperienced in the ways of approaching the gamins of a city missionary school, and must be exposed to risks in the work to which city-wise and city-hardened persons would not be subject. I trust that my darling may be protected from these and that she may derive satisfaction from her new work as great as her motives are pure in undertaking it: but I have my misgivings. I entirely sympathize with and admire your feelings in the matter; but I cannot help questioning the wisdom of the arrangement. Be sure to tell me all about your experiences in the work.

The notice I enclose is from the N. Y. *Sun* of yesterday, the 8th. Here is one from the *Independent*: "Mr. Woodrow Wilson, a Fellow of Johns Hopkins, publishes *Congressional Government, a Study in American Politics*, which indicates industrious reading and a bright mind, but is not remarkable for any broad, mature grasp on the complexities of the subject."[1] Quite a summary way of damning the book!—and evidently suggested by the author's *title*, amongst other things.

I am beginning to feel the inevitable reaction from that little visit of last week, and am warned that I shall need all my forces to fight off a tremendous army of "blues." The process in my case seems to be the opposite of the process in yours. The *first* effect of such a visit with me is exhilaration. During the few days that immediately succeed it, its spell of joy seems to be still upon me. But the excitement wears off and the dull contrast of separation with its indefinitely long prospect of desolate loneliness fills me with a desperate sort of despondency that it is sometimes next to impossible to throw off. It is then that I feel to the full my *need* of you—that need that fills all the days of my separation from you and makes me long to push time to still greater speed, or, failing that, to plunge myself so deep in work as to forget the tedious slowth of the dragging months. This is after I have realized that the visit is *over*: that my darling is far away: that I am alone, and to be alone for long weeks to come: that I may wish till I have wished my life away without bringing nearer by a single hour thereby the time when she will once more look with her sweet eyes into mine that are so longing for a sight of her lovely face.

Good-bye, my precious. This is too doleful a way of talking love. Don't forget that, in spite of this passing mood, your love is my delight, that I am happy because I am with all my heart

Your own   Woodrow

ALS (WC, NjP). The enc., a clipping from the New York *Sun*, Feb. 8, 1885, is missing. The review was titled "The Functions of Congress."

¹ Wilson quoted this notice verbatim from the *Independent*, xxxvii (Feb. 5, 1885), 12.

From Ellen Louise Axson

New York Feb. 9/85

How can I thank you, my darling, for those sweet letters received this morning? Nobody but you could have written *them*, because nobody else could love me so well or so exactly as I wish to be loved. Ah, what a treasure is that love! it were strange, indeed, if I were not happy,—if I did not feel that my life is full to over-flowing with the sweetest and purest joy. It seems almost impossible that I could be *more* happy, and yet I know right well that some day I *shall* be;—and shall continue to be just as long as my darling continues to be happier,—more at hearts-ease—with me,—just as long as he is sure that he *needs* me. That is the sweetest thought in the world to me, dear. Shall I too tell *you*,—tell you again,—how glad I am that the time draws nearer when I may *live* to satisfy that need,—when I may give daily proof of my love.

How *very* glad I am, that the "Nation" is treating you so well! The whole thing is perfectly delightful,—couldn't be better. I was so anxious for you to get a satisfactory notice from that paper of all others. Now I am *wild* to see it.

Your friend Mrs. Hawkins is simply preposterous. I should let her severely alone. Such extortion amounts to dishonesty! I suppose she thinks she has the matter altogether in her own hands; I should say the crying need at Bryn Mawr is competition in trade, these women seem to have the people at their mercy. If it comes to that—to such absurd prices, I mean, how would it do to stay temporarily in the city, where you would have the power of choice. What sort of hours do you suppose you will have at the college? Must you be there off and on all day, or half the day only, or how? Good-night, my darling. Yes, I will take the kisses you send and return them here on your name—Woodrow—*Woodrow*, see how well I can say it. As ever   Your own Eileen.

ALS (WP, DLC) with WWhw and WWsh notation on env.: "The Procedure of the House of Commons J.E.T. Rogers, Contemp. Rev. [xli] March 1882 [pp. 503-518]."

From Janet Woodrow Wilson

My precious Son,   Wilmington, N. C. Monday Feb. 9th [1885]

I need not apologize for my delay in writing—even under the circumstance, when you so naturally desired an immediate reply to your last letter. I cannot help grieving for the loss of our beautiful little darling—but I am sure it is all for the best. . . .

As to the important matter you wrote about I hardly know how to advise you, darling. First of all—as to the *money*—I would not have *you* write to James B[ones]. about it.[1] Fortunately, I received a letter from him a few weeks ago—not referring to business matters at all—but begging for a renewal of correspondence. This makes it necessary for me to write him—which I will try to do today—when I will ask him to do me the favor of paying the note before it is due. I suppose he *can* do it, as he writes that his present business is a success. Of course I will not tell him what I want with the money—except that I will explain that as your father is not to receive any salary during the next five months, we will *need* all we can get from other sources. Will that do? As to the other matter I am utterly at a loss what to advise. If we only *could* go at once to Clarkesville and have our home there ready to receive you! How delightful it would be! But, in the first place, we are not *expected* there before September. Then we have reason to believe that we will not be able to go to housekeeping at once when we do go. We hear that houses are very scarce there —that Prof. [John W.] Caldwell's house was taken at once.[2] I confess I am very much at a loss as to what it is best for *me* to do. The plan proposed now for April & May is, that Josie & I should go to Columbia—while papa attends to his teeth, & then goes to the Ass[embly]. I am not sure that I would not rather go to some quiet place—where I know nobody, and just *rest*. I scarcely know why it is—but I feel *so tired* these late days!

It seems to me, dear, that you may safely arrange for your marriage in June in any case—Ellie will likely wish to spend part of her time with her relatives—but if you wanted to go off to yourselves it would not involve any great expense. We have been enquiring as to board in *Yonkers*, and are told that very desirable board can be gotten at from *seven to nine dollars per week*. You see that this is not so high as in most of the mountain resorts. I have been making these calculations with reference to our own movements as it will be necessary for us to be exceedingly economical to get on without embarrassment. For although your father's salary has been larger you know the demands upon it have been equally so. Please write further as to what you propose, dear. We will be very anxious to hear. I will be content about you when you have your sweet little wife all to yourself. Love unbounded to her from us each one.

We are exceedingly busy getting ready for our move *indirectly* —for we have not disarranged any of our rooms yet—but are packing up every thing we can do without—and arranging for the rest. Next month we will be compelled to break up. Your father notified the Session last week, formally, of his intention to leave. They behaved very well—are sincerely grieved—*everybody* seems really distressed. A congregational meeting will be held on the 26th of this month—when your father will request them to join in his request to be released from the pastorate[.] Presbytery meets early next month. Ask Prof C[aldwell]. about Clarksville, please—I am anxious to hear *something* of our future home. I hear he is in the same house with you. Good bye my darling boy. *Are you quite well now.* I long for a good long letter telling me all about yourself & dear Ellie. Papa and Josie join me in warmest love.

Yours lovingly   Mother

ALS (WP, DLC) with WWhw notation on env.: "Ans. Feby 18, 1885."
   [1] JRW to WW, Jan. 22, 1885, Vol. 3, had informed Woodrow that Dr. and Mrs. Wilson intended to give him as a wedding gift a note for $500 which James W. Bones owed Mrs. Wilson.
   [2] He had recently taught at the South-Western Presbyterian University in Clarksville and was at this time studying at the Johns Hopkins and living at Wilson's boardinghouse.

From Marion Wilson Kennedy

My dearest brother: Little Rock 2/9/85.

Last week and week before were so full of, first, anxiety about Annie's baby, and then, sympathy for the poor father and mother, that I did not feel as if it were possible to for me to write an ordinary letter, even to you. How sad their loss is! Of course, it is a blessed change for little Jessie, but the realization of that always comes gradually, I imagine. . . .

Woodrow dear, we are delighted with your book, and it seems the critics are too, as far as it has been seen. We have a young lawyer friend, just about your age, who is anxious to read your book, and I will tell you what he thinks of it—though he is only just an ordinary man, I suppose, with rather extraordinary energy and ambition, for this part of the world. . . .

We are all pretty well—but I am not in a writing mood today. Ross[1] & the boys join me in warmest love.

Your sister   Marion.

P.S. Why did dear Mother leave Annie after going over there to her? I wanted dreadfully to go to the poor child, and think I should have done so, whether able or not, if I had not been so confident that Mother was with her, and I knew *she* could console Annie better than I could. Poor Annie must have felt quite *alone* in her great, first heavy trouble. It has puzzled me greatly. Can you explain?

ALS (WP, DLC) with WWhw notation on env.: "Ans. Mar. 7/85."
¹ The Rev. A. Ross Kennedy, Marion's husband.

From George Frisbie Hoar

My dear Sir,   Senate Chamber [Washington] Feb. 9/85
   I thank you for the copy of your book on Congressional Government, which you have been so kind as to send me. The book had already attracted my attention and I had purchased a copy and read a great part of it. It is very interesting, unquestionably the result of much thought and investigation, and likely to stimulate its readers to thought and investigation.
   Although we have a written constitution, yet it is a document of a very few pages, and the form and substance of our government must depend in very large degree upon administrative and legislative usages which in this country almost as much as in England get to have the force of a constitution[.] Your book will teach many persons this truth, who would otherwise get a very imperfect notion of the working of our institutions.
   You have fallen into one or two errors. I suppose by accepting other persons statements without original investigation. There is not the slightest truth in the statements on p. 38¹ in regard to the appointment of Judges with a view of reversing the decision of the Court in regard to the Legal Tender Act. The new Judgeship was created long before the decision of the court declaring the act unconstitutional was pronounced; Mr. Stanton was nominated confirmed and appointed to the place and died. Judge Hoar was nominated to Judge Grier's place and rejected. Judges Strong and Bradley were then nominated to the two vacancies and their names sent to the Senate before the decision of the Court which was afterward overruled. The whole story was in its origin a miserable and foolish campaign slander. Its only refuge was the suggestion that the decision of the Court might have leaked out before it was formally announced and that the administration might have heard of it. This is met by the positive statement of Pres. Grant, Secretary Fish and Attorney General Hoar, each of

whom has given a positive and unqualified denial to the whole charge and must be convicted of falsehood if it is believed. The Attorney General who recommended the judges stated that he had no knowledge of the opinions of Judge Bradley on the question, except that he had heard that he advised a corporation for which he was counsel, that they were bound in honor to pay their bonds in gold. Judge Strong had been offered the place of Atty General in Grants cabinet, when it was expected Mr. Hoar would leave it; he was the person whom Judge Grier desired for his successor; he belonged to Pennsylvania, which had no representative in the cabinet, and as his great judicial career has shown, he was in every way the fittest person suggested for the place from the circuit to which Judge Grier belonged. Both he & Judge Bradley would have been appointed, if there had never been a legal tender act on the statute book.

But this is a single and quite excusable mistake in an otherwise most excellent work.

I am   Yrs very respectfully   Geo F Hoar

ALS (WP, DLC) with WWhw notation on env.: "Ans. Feby 16, 1885."
 1 Printed on pages 32-33 of the present volume.

To Ellen Louise Axson

My own darling,   Balto., Feby. 10, 1885

I ought to begin by telling you that I am in ever so much better spirits this morning—and nothing has helped me to the improvement more than that delightful letter written on Sunday night by a little lady in dressing-gown and slippers toasting her feet at her fire. I would say—what I am constantly thinking—that I ought not to have distressed you with a confession of my low spirits yesterday, were it not that I would not for anything have you draw the inference which might seem naturally to flow from such a declaration on my part: namely, that *you* ought not to allow your moods free reflection in your letters to me. What I wish more than anything else in connection with our correspondence is that your letters *should* reflect your moods, should contain just the thoughts that are uppermost as you write. I love not only these delightful little pictures of my darling's home-life—of her figure before the fire in the sacred privacy of her own room—but quite as much pictures of her spontaneous thoughts, even of her whims and fancies—of those things in the home-life of her mind that *can* be shown to no one but the one whose home is in her heart of hearts. I know of nothing in the world that could compare, in power to control my life, with the fact that that heart is full of love for me: and there is nothing that so fills me with delight and sweet content as the evidence of that fact borne upon the words that tell me freely all your thoughts of me and of those private affairs of the life and of the heart which concern *only* yourself. What man with a heart *could* have the "blues" when such sweet letters are sent him by the woman he loves and admires above all others as this one lying before me? Darling! your love shall be a sacred trust with me! and oh, I shall try *so* hard to prove worthy of it! I would rather satisfy that love than make conquest of the whole world of letters and of eloquence! I would rather *die* than *not* satisfy it!

My darling, if Mr. Goodrich's rather dramatic illness was *not* "a third-rate melodrama," it makes me all the more thankful that you have conclusively broken with him. If your decision was really the cause—or even *a* cause—of his illness, what more startling proof could one have that it was high *time* to break with him? It would have been playing with fire—would have been both compromising yourself and torturing him—to continue to allow him the privilege of seeing you alone, to allow him to continue nominally your friend while really, *confessedly*, your almost desperate lover. More clearly than ever I see your *necessity* of self-defence; and I am profoundly thankful that the affair is ended, so far as you can end it!

I have gotten quite steadily to work again, and could feel that any amount even of reading was attainable if only I could *know* that five months will end for good and aye that separation from my darling which every day grows harder to bear—and which, by Dec. might altogether break me down from sheer *strain* at the heart! So entirely am I   Your own   Woodrow.

ALS (WC, NjP).

From Ellen Louise Axson

My darling Woodrow,   New York, Feb. 10/85.
You must not let my "missionary labours" disturb your peace of mind, for I assure you there is no cause. The way thither lies through streets that are altogether respectable—so say the people who are "city-wise"—and the children are neat and well-behaved so that there is not even anything *disagreeable* about it. And even if there were some little risk or unpleasantness connected with it, it don't seem quite right to think first and altogether of *that*, letting it keep us from even *trying* to do anything. True I can't ac-

complish as *much* as one with more experience, but that would hardly excuse my doing *nothing.* I must do what I can,—especially as they *need* teachers badly, so that I am not taking the place of others who could be more useful.

By-the-way, all this reminds me of our model for the week; who is a little "darkie"—not *very* dark however. She is really pretty and exceedingly picturesque, with the most remarkable Pre-Raphealite hair.

What a singularly stupid, absurd criticism (!) is that you quote! Evidently the man made up his mind before-hand that it was a college-boy performance and therefore *must* be immature; —and quite as evidently he is incapable of judging a book on any other evidence than that afforded by the title-page. Such men really criticise *themselves* alone. What *is* the "Independent," by the way—where published? Nor do I think the long notice *very* much more sensible!

I swore off the other night from any further mention of Mr. Goodrich, but his last caper is *too* rich! I must tell it. He stopped me last night as I was passing through the hall, and showed me a great pile of papers which he held in his hand,—they were all poems, he said, about me! "What should he do with them?" I said *I* didn't care; and he thereupon proceeded to burn them over the gas! that is he *began* to burn them but changed his mind and decided, it seems, to preserve a dozen or two.

The fire is almost entirely out so I must "turn *in.*" Good-night, my darling, I am sorry you are threatened with the blues. I want you to miss me but not so much as that;—yet after all[,] this longing for the one we love is a sweet pain, which I wouldn't be without. It comes nearer to happiness that [than] a low form of un-expectant content. With truest love, As ever,

Your own Eileen.

ALS (WP, DLC).

To Ellen Louise Axson

My own darling,   Balto., Feby. 11, 1885

Granting, for the sake of argument, that the letters I wrote on Saturday and Sunday were as 'sweet' as you thought them, I am quite sure that I should be capable of writing many more like them for the sake of such a reply as I received this morning. When my darling fills two pages of one of her precious notes with such wonderfully perfect declarations of love as these I have just read, it seems to me that the sunlight is made brighter, that my heart receives afresh the full measure of that satisfying joy which can come only with the assurance that one is loved with perfect trust, and with supreme joy in the loving, by the woman to whom he has given all that is best in his heart and life. Here's the reason, my precious little pet, why you are satisfied and made happy by my love: I love you with all my heart, without reserve; I have given you all that a man can give to a woman, absolute fealty, perfect honour, and unbounded love. And oh, Eileen, my matchless sweetheart, what sweet delight there is for me in this renewed confession that you are glad "that the time draws nearer" when we may live for each other in the sacred relation of man and wife! That time not only draws "nearer," precious; it draws *near*! I received a long letter from dear mother yesterday in which she expresses her opinions about our plans as freely as I had asked her to do; and here are the words of her conclusion: "*It seems to me, dear, that you may safely arrange for your marriage in June in any case.*" And you may be sure that this is the *family* judgment in the matter: because one of the chief characteristics of our household is, that its opinions upon such subjects are always *consultative* opinions. Mother discusses again her own plans, and confesses that she cannot yet advise us exactly what plan to pursue after the wedding—whether to go north or stay south: but she is sure that the first, the essential, the delightful part of the programme can "*safely*" be determined upon. Here is another passage from her letter: "Please write further as to what you propose, dear—We will be very anxious to hear. I will be content about you when you have your sweet little wife all to yourself. Love unbounded to her from us each one." And *now*, my queen, that *settles* the matter as far as I am concerned—and I *know* that you will let nothing not *insuperable* prevent on your side. I cannot put too strongly my *need* in the matter. I *cannot* wait unless I *must*; and if I must, I cannot but be hurt by the necessity. How easy work seems when I think that only *four months* stand between me and the highest, dearest, best wish my heart ever had or ever can have—between me and that life of love that shall give me the sympathy and consequently the strength that I need above all things else—between me and that service of love that will enable me to forget my small self in the big fact, the blessed fact, that I am   Your own   Woodrow!

ALS (WC, NjP).

From James E. Rhoads

My dear Friend,   Philadelphia, 2 mo. 11. 1885.

I have examined thy schedule of studies in History & Political Economy and am much pleased with it.[1] It covers the most important parts of Ancient History—the most germinant to us—, the thread of mediaeval and modern history is well lapt by using those of England & France, The Renaissance & Reformation seem essential; the topical method—the combination of lectures, reading, "drill," reports and directed research forms a good method. When the pressure on thy time will permit please send me a list of books which *must* be had for the library attached to the Historical department, and also the periodicals we should take for the same.

Please also indicate what text-books for students in History we ought to purchase and keep on hand to sell to them.

A more careful reading of "Congressional Government" has but raised my first estimate of its value.

With regard truly thy friend,   James E Rhoads

ALS (WP, DLC) with WWhw notation on env.: "Ans. Feby 13/85" and WWhw figures.
    [1] See Wilson's Courses of Study for Students in History and Political Science, printed at Feb. 3, 1885.

Gamaliel Bradford's Review of *Congressional Government*

[Feb. 12, 1885]

We have no hesitation in saying that this is one of the most important books, dealing with political subjects, which have ever issued from the American press. We have often been asked by students of politics and by foreign visitors for some book which would explain the real working of our Government, and have been obliged to confess that there was none in existence. Of those which explain the origin of the Constitution, the intentions of its framers, and the meaning of its provisions, the name is legion; but of what the Government established by it has actually become after a century of history, if there is any expositor it has escaped our search. Of histories of the United States, again, down to the adoption of the Constitution there is no end, including those which follow the political growth and union of the colonies; but those of the period since are mere catalogues of events. Even the 'Constitutional History' of Von Holst, though it begins with some general observations, soon falls into a bald narration. This want Mr. Wilson has come forward to supply. His book is evidently modelled on Mr. Bagehot's 'English Constitution,' and it will, though the praise is so high as to be almost extravagant, bear comparison with that inestimable work.

The introductory chapter shows how steadily the Federal Government has extended its power over the States, the probability that this tendency will still further increase, and the consequent necessity that the machinery of the Government shall be carefully studied and corrected, so that it may be fitted for the momentous duties which, with the growth of population and wealth, await it. The procedure of the House of Representatives is then analyzed in a way which is the more effective from the entire absence of denunciation. Nearly all the critics of Congress inveigh against the inefficiency, stupidity, and prevalent corruption of its members, with the result that the world at large has come to believe what is so persistently asserted at home. Mr. Wilson's analysis shows conclusively that these appearances of evil are mainly owing to the helplessness of anarchy. You may take a regiment of the bravest men that ever lived, and if sent into battle without officers and without training in subordination, they flee in panic at the first attack. Nor will it help the matter to denounce them as cowards. Mr. Wilson says: "I know not how better to describe our form of Government in a single phrase than by calling it a Government by the Chairmen of the Standing Committees of Congress." And this text covers an infinitude of consequences. He shows how Congress has absorbed all the powers of the Government, reducing Executive and Supreme Court to comparative and constantly increasing insignificance. He dwells, we think with hardly sufficient force, on the dangerous and irresponsible power of the Speaker, and very much understates the fearful influence of the lobby in the committee-rooms. The Senate, though he does justice to its valuable qualities, he describes as substantially a second House of Representatives, nearly duplicating the chaos of its forty-eight committees, whereby all consistent and systematic legislation is rendered impossible. His account of the Executive reminds us of the famous one of the snakes in Iceland. He might have pointed his tale by adding that this absorption of all power by the Legislature exists in all the States and nearly all the cities, and constitutes by far the greatest political danger now threatening this country.

In comparison with this, Mr. Wilson gives an account of Cabinet government in England, where all executive power is in the hands of the Ministry, resting upon organized party support, and held in check by an opposition also organized under regular leadership. Mr. Bagehot, in his quiet assumption of superiority, describes ours as Presidential government, having its essential features as above described. We hold this distinction to be entirely fanciful, and unfortunately for it the Presidential government of France since 1870, and since Mr. Bagehot's book was written, has proceeded, if with less perfect development, yet upon exactly the same principles as that of the English Cabinet, which, indeed, is true to a greater or less extent of every government in Europe which has a legislature at all. Debarred from this distinction, Mr. Wilson falls back upon calling ours Congressional government, though we cannot see that the distinction between this and Parliamentary has any better foundation than the other.

It was with extreme surprise that we found on reaching the end of the book that Mr. Wilson was satisfied to draw the distinction and leave the matter there. He has described the danger with perfect clearness, if not in its fullest force, but offers no hint of a remedy. Yet that this is not his last word upon the subject we know from other sources. In an article in the *Overland Monthly* for January, 1884, he said that a gain might be made "by making them [members of Congress][1] also members of the President's Cabinet, and thus at once the executive chiefs of the Department of State and the leaders of their party on the floor of Congress—in a word, by having done with the standing committees, and constituting the Cabinet advisers both of President and Congress." He closes the same article by saying: "Committee government is too clumsy and too clandestine a system to last. Other methods of government must sooner or later be sought, and a different economy established. First or last, Congress must be organized in conformity with what is now the prevailing legislative practice of the world. English precedent and the world's fashion must be followed in the institution of Cabinet government in the United States." In the book under review he has this forcible summary of our constitutional history:

"In the period of erection there were great architects and master builders; in the period of constitutional interpretation there were, at a distance from the people, great political schoolmen, who pondered and expounded the letter of the law, and, nearer the people, great constitutional advocates, who cast the doctrines of the schoolmen into policy; and in the period of abolitionist agitation there were great masters of feeling and leaders of public purpose. The period of Federal construction is long passed; questions of constitutional interpretation are no longer regarded as of pressing urgency; the war has been fought, even the embers of its issues being now almost extinguished; and we are left to that unexciting but none the less capitally important business of every-day peaceful development and judicious administration, to whose execution every nation in its middle age has to address itself with what sagacity, energy, and prudence it can command. It cannot be said that these new duties have as yet raised up any men eminently fit for their fulfilment."

Feeling thus, how is it possible that he should have passed over without an allusion the only arrangement which, according to his own view, offers us a chance of obtaining the men desired? The answer to this question is not far to seek. He thinks that amendments to the Constitution are an essential prerequisite. In the article already referred to, he speaks of two: first, that in the clause "and no person holding any office under the United States shall be a member of either House during his continuance in office," there should be inserted the words "except a Cabinet office"; and, second, that the terms both of Congress and the President should be lengthened. If such a course is necessary, we do not wonder that he has passed over in silence the reform which it is intended to bring about. It would be hard enough to obtain any action from Congress, but to secure the coöperation of three-fourths of the State legislatures—every one of which is steadily striving to extend its own power and to reduce that of the executive—would be a perfectly hopeless task. It may pretty safely be said that the only constitutional amendments which have any chance in the future, as the Government is now carried on, are of two kinds—those which tend to increase the power of Congress as against the Executive, with which the State legislatures would have an instinctive sympathy; and those in favor of which such a national passion may be aroused as to carry them with a rush. Any move toward placing Congress under executive leadership would meet with solid resistance from local politicians, while the people do not understand it enough to lend effective support.

We maintain, however, that no constitutional amendment is necessary—that the practical result may be arrived at by a much easier process. The secretaries, as Mr. Wilson shows, do now on occasion appear in the committee rooms. There needs only a vote of the House of Representatives authorizing and requiring them to do the same thing on the floor of the House, with the right of taking part in debate, but without a vote. The difference in one respect, indeed, would be immense, for as the committees work in secret, independently, and largely at cross purposes, what the officials say is of no consequence. But if the same officials should lift up their voices before the whole House, advocating a policy or criticising procedure, the attention of the country would be at once aroused, and instead of looking on as now in cold contempt, it would manifest a lively interest. All the rest can be left to time. Whether the Cabinet should introduce and explain bills or be mere witnesses and critics; whether they should resign individually or collectively in case of defeat, or maintain themselves as best they could till a new election; whether the short term of Congress would answer for the dissolution which is the *ultima ratio* of a British ministry; what would be the position of the President; whether the Cabinet should be outside of Congress or members of it—and a constitutional amendment to this effect would then have a very different aspect from what it would have now—these and many other points must be settled in the light of experience. The first step is simple and needs only agitation. It is of not much direct use for scholars to argue about it, and of just as little to advocate it in Congress, as we believe the late President Garfield did as far back as 1864, or as Mr. Pendleton did within a few years in the Senate, because Congress is solidly if silently hostile. It must be carried to the people, and we have a strong conviction that its popularity would be great; that the country is charged with a sentiment in this direction, as a black cloud is with electricity, needing only a point to draw it. If Senator Pendleton could make up his mind to stump the country on behalf of his plan, he would arrive at a very different result. If President Cleveland, in his opening message to Congress, would make the suggestion, with a simple statement of the argument in its favor, it could be carried before his term was over.

We believe, with Mr. Wilson, that the present state of things is too intolerable to last; that the change proposed is the only thing which will give any relief, and that it must come; but, with a natural desire to live to see it, we are looking anxiously for some statesman with mind enough and courage enough to see that in a resolute advocacy of such a proposition lies the broadest and most open road to the Presidency.

Printed in the New York *Nation*, xl (Feb. 12, 1885), 142-43; title omitted.
    1 Bradford's brackets.

From Ellen Louise Axson

My darling Woodrow,   New York Feb 12/85.

I was so busy over my perspective last night, that my fire which had been misbehaving all the evening finally went out altogether, before I had an opportunity to write. It is quite as cold this morning, so I must mind my promise and write only a few lines. What bitter weather it is! therm. "8 below" yesterday. The "Met" seems terribly far away today;—but "this too will pass"! as they [say] in Turkey.

I wanted to tell you the various facts I learned yesterday about cheap summer resorts—but that can wait,—decidedly! The girls at the "Met." have been for the last few days engaged in the most unseasonable occupation of making their plans for the *summer*. Three of them have a delightful scheme on foot in which they have invited Annie Lester and myself to join them. They are going to rent for next to nothing the old J. Howard Payne Academy at Hampton Beach which Mr. Stimson had last year, and of which he now has the refusal. Then with the mother of one of them as chaperone they are going to keep house in gypsy fashion. Mr. Stimson will board next door and give them lessons— in landscape, principally. The whole thing will cost them only fifteen or twenty dollars a month each. Is'nt that a lovely plan? I told them I would join them for a month at least,—*perhaps*!

But my fingers are too frozen to write, I must stop. I wonder if the postman is frozen too, this morning; he is late in coming.

I love you, darling, with all my heart, and am now and always,

Your own Eileen.

ALS (WP, DLC).

To Ellen Louise Axson, with Enclosure

My own darling,   Balto., Feby. 12, 1885

I don't know yet whether or not it would be practicable for us to board in Philadelphia in order to escape Mrs. Hawkins and her ilk; but I had thought of that plan, as you had, and it may be worth a trial. If you should have occasion to write to your uncle[1] soon, would you mind inquiring of him the usual rates in Philadelphia for such accommodation as we should want? Give him my love, if you do write—and send my warmest regards to the rest of the family.

I received a letter this morning from sister Annie which I shall enclose with this—not only that you may enjoy the sweet Christian resignation that it breathes and the beautiful pen-picture of dear little Jessie which it contains, but also that you may consider the part that concerns yourself. I wish that you *could* do what sister suggests; but of course I know perfectly all the obstacles in the way, and I mention it only that you may have the request before you just in the shape and the spirit in which dear sister meant it to go to you. You will understand her letter, and will know what to say in reply: will know whether or not you can promise to do it *some*time.

The *Independent*—the paper that contained the brief and curt criticism which I quoted—is the most prominent, and, according to a very common opinion, the ablest religious (or semi-religious) newspaper in the country. It is published in New York. Its judgments carry great weight.

I did not object to the remarks of the *Sun*. Of course the critic has mistaken the character and purpose of my book; but, as he understood its chief object, his criticism was quite legitimate—even evident. An intention such as he ascribes to me *would* make a tour of South American republics and a closer look at France desirable, if not necessary. Such criticisms are helpful, in a way, as indicating what lines of inquiry *might* be taken up with a prospect of exciting favourable attention and imparting desired information. An elaborate comparative study of presidential systems may be well worth while some of these days.

At last I have seen Shinn's book.[2] It has made its appearance on the shelves of our new book department—and a very good appearance it is! I have not had time to read it yet, of course,—nor opportunity—but I dipped into it enough to discover that S. has improved it amazingly since I saw it in *mss.*—I mean as to the *style*: the *matter* always was excellent. I am sure that the book will create a very good and a very great impression, and that he will make a very enviable reputation through it.

I stole a march on you yesterday. I sent copies of "Cong. Govt." to your Grandfather and Dr. [W. D.] Hoyt with my 'regards' written boldly upon the fly-leaves! You couldn't have the hardihood to offer to *pay* for presents I make in my own name!

I don't think that you judged very fairly the character of my objections to your mission-school work. I did not mean to base them upon a selfish disregard for duty. But we wont quarrel about that. I am sure you did what was right and for the best.

That absurd performance of Mr. G's serves to confirm my opinion of him—poor, dangerous baby.

  With unbounded love,   Your own   Woodrow.

ALS (WC, NjP).
[1] Thomas A. Hoyt.
[2] Charles H. Shinn, *Mining-Camps: A Study in American Frontier Government* (New York, 1885).

From Annie Wilson Howe

My darling brother,   Columbia, Feb. 10th 1885
Thank you ever so much for the copy of your book. I prize it
very highly—and am very proud that the author is *my* brother. I
want to thank you, too, for your sweet letters of sympathy to us.
They did me a world of good. I know that you loved our darling
Jessie—and she loved you *very* dearly—loved to talk about "uncle,"
and often wished she could see you. I cannot tell you how lonely
I am without her. She was my constant companion, never seeming to expect to go out with "the children"—especially after she
became lame—and perfectly happy with me. Her ankle was much
better before she was taken sick. She called me to her one day
as she left the room & when I got to her, she put down her
crutches and stepped on her lame foot—saying that it did not
hurt her at all. I kissed her and she said "Now, Mama, I am happy because I have made *you* happy." But, Woodrow, I am so
thankful that I do not feel rebellious in the least. I *know* that it
was best for her to go—hard as it is to give her up. She would
possibly have suffered, more or less, all her life with that ankle.
And then after that long illness I was *afraid* to see her recover—
her brain would probably have been affected—and *that* would
have been worse than death. It is a great comfort to think of her
as safe forever more—but we cannot help weeping—and longing
for her. There is no sin in that if we do not rebel against God's
will.
Woodrow, do you think it would be out of the way for us to ask
your dear Ellie to make a picture of little Jessie, from her photograph, for us? We cannot let her do it except upon condition that
she will let us pay for it just as anyone else would. There is no
one about *here* that I would trust with it—and I would rather have
her do it than anyone else. If you think best, will you mention it
to her?
Write to me when you can, dear. Even a little note now and
then would do me much good. I will write again before long.
George unites with me in unbounded love to our precious brother.
                                                         · Annie.
ALS (WP, DLC).

From Ellen Louise Axson

My darling Woodrow,   New York, Feb. 12, 1885.
I have just finished reading your review in the "Nation." They

have given you their very full and respectful attention. How do you like it? That is certainly very high praise which they accord you in the first paragraph. And I suppose that when they place you side by side with your "master," Bagehot, they give you just the praise you most desire. He doesn't seem quite to understand or appreciate your desire to avoid appearing as an advocate, of any particular method, or especially as an Anglo-maniac. He wants you not only to drive in the nail but also to clinch it on the other side. Yet I should think the method you chose—of allowing people to think for themselves—of calmly stating the facts and leaving them to reach their own conclusions,—would be much more effective, and would have much more weight with many people.

What shall I say, my darling, in answer to your letter of this morning? with regard to our plans I mean. I cannot as yet say or feel that the matter is *settled*; and yet when my darling wishes anything of me, as much as he says he wishes this I cannot *but* feel that it is *settled* "as far as I am concerned." My heart leaps forth to give it's answer far in advance of the tardy judgement. I hardly know what I ought to do. Don't you think we had better leave the matter *unsettled* for the present, and await further developments?

How shall I ever thank your dear mother enough, or love her enough, for her wonderful goodness to me; for it *is* wonderful that she should be "content" to give you to *me*;—or indeed to *anyone*. A love so perfect, so unselfish is rare even in a mother. Please give my *best* love to her—and all. By the way, Grandmother and the rest including Mrs. Duncan *always* send their love to you; and of late many congratulations on the success of your book. I heard from Aunt Ella a day or so ago; she gives me the "consultative opinion" of that household on our case in very nearly your mothers words. She think[s] June will be better than *Sept.* at all events on account of Grandfather's absence. Goodnight my darling. I love you more—ah *how* much more—than life, and I am forever   Your own Eileen.

ALS (WP, DLC).

To Ellen Louise Axson

My own darling,   Balto., Feby. 13, 1885
I wish that I could school myself to some sort of patient content in my work here. I often grow savagely out of humour with my present state of pupilage—and yet, if my analysis of my own

case be correct—the compulsory drill of pupilage is just what I most need. The fault of my mind is that it is creative without being patient and docile in learning *how* to create. I am like one who would play on the piano, not only without any knowledge of the laws and theory of music, but with only a superficial acquaintance with notation and no practice at all in the management of the fingers; like one who would solve the mysteries of astronomy before getting further than the easier processes of arithmetic; like one who would build a house of such odds and ends of material as happen to be at hand, and on the first vacant spot to be found, like one who would write a code of laws out of his inner consciousness, as if no other code had ever existed; like one who would rush to give battle to von Moltke without knowing so much as the drill manual; like a child ready to undertake the care of his father's business; like a mechanic ready to try his hand at watch-making before he has learned to blow a furnace decently well. A few glimpses of a great subject are enough to set me to sketching a treatment of it elaborate enough to fill a volume. I at once buy a blank-book and begin to accumulate matter (principally thoughts without facts) for a treatise. I should make a capital hack-writer! All the equipment that I should need would be a hint or two from somebody who understood the subject, plenty of paper and ink: my enthusiasm for thinking without the necessary material for thought would render superfluous (for the production, that is, of *an* article) any special preparation—any *reading* such as ordinary folks do! Give me a pen. Let me write a volume on the philosophy of history! True I know precious little history; but philosophy isn't narrative. I can do some golden philosophizing with a very few facts to go upon. What the world wants is *thought*—and the smaller the ingredient of dull fact the purer the intellectual product! Be a sort of literary tramp: walk about the world and *observe*—pick up your sustenance of fact by the wayside! Don't earn an intellectual living the stupid orthodox way, in the reputable reading trade; don't serve a grinding apprenticeship to erudition; scholarship is a narrow, too confining trade! Live by your wits!

Excuse this nonsense—I love to ridicule myself now and then just for the sake of a good laugh at myself. I am *such* a droll fool in some respects, and it would be a shame to lose all the fun of seeing it! My *alter ego* must be allowed to enjoy the joke now and then. Besides, it is less lonely to have two selves to quarrel with each other.

With unbounded love,   Your own   Woodrow

ALS (WC, NjP).

From Ellen Louise Axson

My darling Woodrow,   New York, Feb. 13/84. [1885]

Yes, I think you *have* stolen a march on me in sending the books in your own name. But they will appreciate them much more highly as coming from the distinguished author himself—and it was very kind of you, dear, to do it. You don't know how much an attention of that sort—or even the smallest thing that proves one had been thinking of him,—pleases and touches dear Uncle Will.

I read the sweet letter from your sister this morning, with the deepest interest; it does indeed show a most beautiful spirit. I will be delighted, dear, to do the picture, if they have a satisfactory photograph. I am afraid that if the one I have seen is the best, it would be a very doubtful experiment, however, for to me that gave *no idea* of the beautiful little face; I shouldn't have known it. But perhaps they like it better than we do;—or perhaps they have a better photograph. At all events it would be a great pleasure to me to do—or rather to *try* to do—anything they wish;—to do anything that I *can*.

I am delighted to hear such good accounts of Mr. Shinn's book, —hope I may have the opportunity before very long to see the book itself. Strange, that you have heard nothing of it from him. I wonder what *has* become of him!

You ask for information from Uncle Tom as to board in Phil. As it happens I heard them say something on that point while there. They said they thought it a much cheaper place to live than New York, that one could get much better accommodations for the same price; for seven dollars one could do very well indeed.

By the way, I didn't tell you about the cheap summer resorts! One is in the Catskills, and the price is five dollars a week. It is a farm-house but is said to be quite comfortable. The other I am given to understand is *perfectly lovely* in every respect—exquisite scenery, an interesting and delightful old village, and a most charming family who might accommodate *me* on this lady's account for six dollars. They don't take boarders now, you understand, but they would probably receive me into the bosom of their family for the sake of our mutual friend,—who is, by-the-way, a very pleasant lady from Baltimore. The village—over which she really *raves*—is Greenfield Mass. hard by old Deerfield.

No, darling, I don't think I misjudged the character of your objections to to [sic] my mission. I did not for a moment imagine that you based them upon "a selfish *disregard* for duty"; you simply wished to suggest that under the circumstances it was *not* my duty: you thought, very naturally and sensibly, that the fact of my being a stranger here lessened my obligation in such matters; while at the same time it increases the risk;—provided there be any, to begin with. And I quite agree with you on both points. I merely wished to explain that in this case there *was* no risk; and that while I know it is not an imperative duty I might as well do what I can,—for my own satisfaction! I assure you I appreciate, dear, the watchful care you show in such things for my well-being.

With all my heart, believe me, dear love, now and always,

Your own Eileen.

ALS (WP, DLC).

To Richard Heath Dabney

My dear Heath,   Balto., Feby 14th, 1885

Your postal card of Jany. 24th reached me the other day, and I was pricked e'en to the heart thereby. Not that I had really *neglected* you; but I had certainly *seemed* to neglect you. The fact is that your letter of last year (!)[1] came just when I was in the thickest of the fight with my University work—and with other things in addition: for, if the whole truth must be confessed, I was *writing a book*, and the writing thereof absorbed all my time and energy from Jany. to summer vacation, and through summer vacation till my return here in October—that is, all the strength and time that were left over from my other duties—to wit, University reading and *courting*! But I made the writing count for all it was worth. I read the first essays of my series before our Historical Seminary here—and lo! such was the fame of them that they won the appointment of Fellow for me for this year. And on the 24th of Jany just passed Houghton, Mifflin, & Co. of Boston issued a neat duodecimo entitled "Congressional Government: a Study in American Politics," by Woodrow Wilson, Fellow in History, Johns Hopkins University. Yes, I've been saying my final say about my hobby, the comparative merits of congressional and parliamentary government. I wont bore you with an analysis of the book, because I am going to send you a copy of it as soon as I can obtain it from the publishers; but I can tell you what the indications are as to its success. There have been a great many notices of it in the papers and all of them very favourable indeed so far as I have seen or heard. The *Nation* of this week has a three-column review of it which quite takes my breath away by starting out in this fashion: "We have no hesitation in saying that this is one of the most important books, dealing with political subjects, which have ever issued from the American press," with more to the same effect! The publishers accepted my *mss.* in an exceedingly flattering manner, offering me their very best terms. But that's enough for that. To write all this down seems too much like bald self-laudation, even though I *know* that I am writing it only because I know that it will gratify your big, genuine old West Range heart[2] to learn that a fellow you care something for has had a bit of success.

I am reading for my Ph.D.—contrary to my one-time determination, and mayhap with too tardy a change of plan to leave myself time for completing the needful preparation—because it's this year or never. I could keep my Fellowship next year and take the degree then with some little comfort and ease; but I am anxious to get to work—for many reasons which you can surmise without any aid from me—and a position was offered to me for next year which, because of its possibilities rather than because of its immediate returns, was much too good to refuse. A benevolent member of the Society of Friends (alias the Quakers) resident in New Jersey,[3] but having his heart, it would seem, warm towards the city where citizens of his persuasion most do congregate and multiply and wax strong in spirit, made provision for the founding of a college for the young women of the land to be situate at Bryn Mawr, a few miles out from Philadelphia, and then died, leaving the scheme in charge of sundry wise and Friendly men, one or two of whom are also Trustees of "the Hopkins." These gentlemen, after the thrifty manner of their kind—a manner which was also enjoined, be it said, in the aforesaid founder's last will and testament—set about erecting, upon the interest of Mr. Taylor's $800,000, the necessary buildings, meantime concocting a course of instruction which was to warrant the wits of this University in dubbing the new college "the Miss Johns Hopkins" or "the Johanna Hopkins." The buildings are now almost completed; the first session is to open next September; and your humble servant has been invited to be one of the new faculty and spread himself in the organization of a department of History and Political Science. There are to be several women in the faculty—the Dean[4] (a Ph.D. of Zürich) is to be a woman—but there are to be more men—and the President is a man.[5] The great advantages of the plan are its situation in the midst of the most cultivated portion of the country and the freedom of method, the comparatively limited number of topics to teach, and the comparatively small number of hours per week in teaching them, that will be given each instructor. And the salary will be sufficient from the first to support two persons. You don't wonder that I accepted the place—do you—in view of the probable alternative of having to teach this, that, and everything somewhere away off from all the great libraries and from the lively, stimulating centres of thought?

But I am handicapped for my degree because of the extra work with which I was indiscreet enough to saddle myself. Dr. [Richard T.] Ely (our economist) is preparing a history of political economy, and, as an episode in his labours in that field, wishes to publish a volume on the history of the science in this country. But he has impressed me and another "graduate student"[6] into this part of the voyage and I am to wade—am wading, indeed—through innumerable American text writers of the orthodox Ricardian school (Perry, Bowen, Wayland, Vethake, and the rest) for the purpose of writing, with as profound an air of erudite criticism and infallible insight as I can by any means counterfeit, about one-third of the projected treatise.[7] I am to get full credit as joint author of the volume: but the question that is worrying me at present is, will it be creditable?

I am considerably better contented with the University courses this year than I was last: whether because I am enjoying the acceptable emolument of the Fellowship stipend or because the courses—or rather the *coursers*—have taken a brace is too recondite a problem for my present powers of solution. Doubtless the real truth of the matter is that I expected too much at first, neglecting the principle you point out in your letter, that everything of progress comes from one's private reading—not from lectures; that professors can give you always copious bibliographies and sometimes inspiration or suggestion, but never learning. Of course I did not hope to be given the latter through lectures—I looked for too much inspiration and suggestion, and was too little content with mere recreation and book-lists.

I have many times regretted, my dear fellow, that I had absolutely no chance of meeting your aunts and grandfather here. I know that I should find them delightful—and that's just the sort of delight that I need to relieve this "demnition horrid grind": but I just can't make calls and my degree both in the same year. I have to endure daily the scowls and remonstrances of my several Princeton classmates dwelling here because I frequent their company seldom or never. As a 'Varsity friend of mine would say, for a time I positively must "herd alone."

I received the volume of Bagby's writings[8] you were so thoughtful as to have sent to me and got much diversion out of the same. One or two of the pieces were easily recognizable as old friends. When the book came with your name in your own familiar fist on the cover, my first thought was that you were at home—for a moment my wish was father to the thought that you were once more on this side the water. You *will* be back within the twelvemonth, wont you? I hope so, for the sake of my sore eyes. When you do get back make a small pilgrimage to Bryn Mawr and—if the gods permit meanwhile the plan by which I am to be married in June—I will introduce you to Mrs. Wilson, as a sufficient explanation of why I did not remain single.

Give my warmest love to all the old friends to be found in Berlin and keep lots for yourself. What would I not give to see you, thou very ass—oh thou illimitable idiot! I will be in the penitentiary before I cease to be

Your loving friend   Woodrow Wilson

ALS (Wilson-Dabney Correspondence, ViU).
[1] R. H. Dabney to WW, May 6, 1884, Vol. 3.
[2] Dabney had lived near Wilson's room, 31 West Range, at the University of Virginia.
[3] Dr. Joseph W. Taylor of Burlington, N. J.
[4] Martha Carey Thomas.
[5] Dr. James E. Rhoads.
[6] Davis R. Dewey.
[7] See the Editorial Note, "Wilson's Research for a 'History of Political Economy in the United States,' " in Vol. 3.
[8] George William Bagby, *Selections from the Miscellaneous Writings of Dr. George W. Bagby* (2 vols., Richmond, 1884-85).

From Gamaliel Bradford

Dear Sir: Boston, Feb 14 1885

You will probably have seen my notice of your book in the Nation and I trust that you will not be dissatisfied with it. I have a hope that you will be disposed to accept my view that it is best to push for the admission of the cabinet officers to Congress under the constitution as it is rather than attempt the far harder and more uncertain task of getting the constitution amended

To show how long this has been a cherished hobby of mine I take the liberty of sending you a copy of an address which I delivered in 1873   Very truly yours   Gamaliel Bradford

ALS (WP, DLC) with WWhw notation on env.: "Ans. Feby 17, 1885." Enc. missing.

To Ellen Louise Axson

My own darling,   Balto., Feby. 14th, 1885

I find myself sorely puzzled by the contents of the sweet letter I received this morning, and reading it again and again only adds to my perplexity. If the counsel of your counsellors in Savannah is the same as that given by my counsellors concerning our plans, why do you hesitate to promise? *why* does your judgment lag behind your heart's wish? What "further developments" are there to wait for? Of course there is the *possibility* that the note in which my money is locked up may not be paid when it falls due; but that is violently improbable—much too small an 'if' to stand in the way of the making of definite plans even about so all-important a matter. At what does your judgment halt? Be frank with me, darling, and tell me—for the doubt is making me sick. If you could know my intense feeling about the matter, you could not entertain any doubt about your lover's wishing this of you "as much as he says he wishes" it. I cannot express my need any more strongly than I have expressed it—and yet no expression I have given to it has come near the full measure of my heart's desire. Is it possible, then, that my darling shrinks from a promise that would bring our marriage so near? Is it possible that second thought has led her to prefer Hampton Beach and a little longer period of freedom? Of course it is *not* possible: my darling has said that she longs for our wedding day to come! But *something* holds her back from the promise which would ensure the consummation of her wish. She cannot "say or feel that the matter is settled," and yet all that is necessary to settle it is her own consent. I don't *want* it to be settled because *I* wish it: it shall remain unsettled until *you* wish, and will, it!

Pardon me, my darling, for arguing this question (*this* question of all others!) so baldly. Every thought of it, or of anything that affects it, fills my heart with an unspeakable tenderness for my precious little sweetheart. But I know that for me everything depends on our present decision and I know the wound that my heart would receive if your judgment in the matter should be based upon considerations withheld from my knowledge. I *must* argue the question—must even suspect my little sweetheart of preferring a summer sketching class to my company—if by any means I can induce her to reveal the *reasons* that make her plead against an immediate settlement of the most important plan of our lives—be those reasons great or small, of the heart or of the head, little inconveniences or big sentiments. The decision would not be an irrevocable proclamation. We would not say to the world, 'On such and such a day of June next you may expect the marriage of Ellen L. Axson and Woodrow Wilson.' It would be none of the world's business: it would be nobody's business but our own. It would be our own most sacred confidence. It would be but the confirmation of those sacred tacit pledges we made to each other on that doubly hallowed Sabbath in Asheville.[1] It would simply be saying: 'God's providence permitting, we will fulfil those pledges, and our heart's desire, next June.' Do you fear the promise, Eileen? Would you rather say: 'Let some slight drawbacks decide us to wait until December: that's quite soon enough for reasonable people: my ardent, impatient lover wont suffer so much as he thinks'? That seems to be the alternative. I shall not again urge my own interests: I would have you absolutely free to follow your own will. Apparently every real obstacle to our early marriage—every obstacle that cannot with a little exertion be removed—has been taken away. You are *free* to choose, and it will be a genuine kindness to me if you will choose at once. You may be absolutely sure that I shall receive any decision that you may make with loving acquiescence: that no denial of my wishes will raise a single questioning or rebellious thought in my heart. You have my *perfect* trust and allegiance; and the only thing I beg is that you will decide soon (since it is not *necessary*, it would be cruel to keep me longer in suspense), and that, if you decide upon a postponement, you will, if possible, frankly give me your reasons for doing so. I have only to add a fresh declaration of my love for my darling. I love you, my precious! I accord you absolute homage as the queen of my heart. My life waited for you—it still waits for a wife's love, such as only you can ever give. Your love has brought a world of joy and of beauty into my life: it will always be to that life as a crown! It has completed my manhood by opening wide my heart to all that purifies and enobles: and it shall always keep that heart open to its sweet influences, perfecting day by day my power of love and my delight in the reciprocal services of love! My queen shall reign with ever-increasing dominion, and I shall be freed from myself by the perfect freedom of loving and being loved!

What a privilege it is to be allowed to give one's whole heart to the woman one loves! Until the love is accepted—until one is given *leave* to love—pride holds one back and makes love almost a bitter torture; but once love is accepted and a like love given in return, all the secret fountains of chivalric devotion, all the elevating impulses—of which one never so much as dreamed himself possessed—are opened, and the *blessedness* of loving is revealed! What would I have been without you, darling! An incomplete creature, selfish in spite of a keen desire to love somebody, or to serve some noble end, to the elimination of self; anxious and feverish in every undertaking because there was no heart in whose trust and sympathy I could find repose and calm courage; suspicious of the world, because practically alone in it. Under any circumstances, I am inclined to take life too *intensely*, and it is an inestimable advantage to me that I may live, not for myself, but for you. Your love *rests* at the same time that it inspires me. My heart would wear itself away in its own service, but it will only grow younger so long as I am

Your own   Woodrow

ALS (WC, NjP).
1 See the Editorial Note, "The Engagement," Vol. 2.

From Edward Ireland Renick

My dear Wilson,   Washington D. C. Feb. 15, 1885.
As I expected, the *Nation* has accorded your book the highest possible praise.

You may be glad to hear that ever since its publication, Mr. [E. R. A.] Gould, the professor of History & Polit. Econ. in our High School here, & a Johns Hopkins man, has been urging his pupils to an earnest study of it.

Gadsden is here with his bride. He married on Thursday.

I do not like to advise unsolicited, but I cannot help but hold up a warning finger, when you at this time are about to make a contract with a female seminary—I mean at this time when you are just becoming known, and are apt to receive very much better offers, though the one made to you is flattering.

I am sick. But I write to ask you to write & to tell me all, if you please, with old time frankness that has been said & written of your book. Try to see us soon.

As ever,   Sincerely,   Renick

ALS (WP, DLC) with WWhw notation on env.: "Ans. Feby. 21/85."

From Ellen Louise Axson

My darling Woodrow,   New York Feb 15/85.
What a perfect—what a glorious day it! I dont think I ever saw the city so beautiful; the snow looks as pure and white as country snow, and the air is as sweet and delicious. I have just re-

turned from church—came down fifth Avenue that I might have the pleasure of seeing the snow in the church-yard there. It is so lovely to see it in such wide, sunlit, or shadowed masses. The air is full of the sound of sleigh-bells,—very naughty, of course, for people generally go sleigh-riding for pleasure alone, but it sounds very sweetly. It must be delicious on such a day as this, —not too cold to be pleasant.

We had a rousing sermon today—and a very pointed one on personal accountability. And by-the-way he preached *secession*! he actually did, though I don't suppose he meant to. But he used the very word;—if any corporation or party or—&c. &c. of which we are a member pursues a course of action which we consider wrong and our protest is unheeded then secession there-from becomes our duty! But I must not begin on that, for I have hardly a moment to write; am expecting the dinner-bell at any time,— so no more until tonight. How I wish you were with me this beautiful Sabbath day! then it would be perfect indeed. Believe me darling, with all my heart,   Your own   Eileen.

ALS (WP, DLC).

To Ellen Louise Axson

My own darling,   Balto., Feby. 15, 1885
    I was disappointed in the *Nation*'s notice just as you were, and for the same reasons. I knew that responsible cabinet government for this country was Mr. Bradford's hobby; but I did not suppose that he would ride it into this review with such extraordinary demonstration; and of course he misjudges my purpose altogether. If the conclusion to be drawn from the book is so evident and so irresistible, why not let its readers draw it for themselves? They will like it much better if it seems to be their own than if it were thrust in their face. I do not consider constitutional amendments necessary *at first*, to make way for a *beginning*, any more than Mr. Bradford does; but I think that they would be necessary eventually, as he does. A magazine article is a proper enough place to advocate such a change, but such a book as I tried to write is not; and Mr. B. has done it a great disservice by bringing in my *Overland* piece to supplement it.

    I suppose that it is ungracious to take exception to the warm praise of my work with which the notice opens, but I may confide to you the fact that it seems to me almost ridiculous. I should like above all things to be able to write something comparable with Bagehot's "inestimable work"; but of course it will be evident to every one who has read both my essays and his that I am as yet *very* far from having approached the excellencies of my master; and this critic's rhapsody will, I fear, be read with elevated eyebrows and a smile of disbelief. The publishers will find it useful for their advertisements, but it will scarcely advance the fame of the book.

Probably no author is ever satisfied with any review of his writings—because critics are seldom or never of the number of those bosom friends of the author to whom alone the real *spirit* of his work is revealed—and doubtless these three columns in the *Nation* contain infinitely more of appreciation and sympathy than most writers can ever hope to get from contemporary criticism; but I may pour into *your* ear the disappointments which come to my sensitive secret heart when what I have worked so hard to accomplish is partially marred by being placed in a false light by the very persons who ought to have understood it best.

I am conscious of being in all things *too* sensitive. Most men of my age and in the earliest, most critical stages of their careers would be willing to pay any price for such a notice from such a paper as the *Nation*; and would enjoy very keenly such congratulations as it has brought me. But the object that I have placed before myself is so dear, so sacred in my eyes that anything that in the least obstructs it or diminishes the chances of achieving it hurts me like a slap in the face. I want to contribute something substantial to the political knowledge and the political science of the country, to the end that our forms of government and our means of administration may be perfected. Since I am shut out from realizing my first ambition, to become a public servant and actively participate in the direction of affairs, it is my heart's dearest desire that I may become one of the guides of public policy by becoming one of the guides of public thought. To be effective in such a rôle, it is imperative that I should stand apart from advoc[ac]y of radical measures for which the public mind may not be ripe—at least in all that I write which is intended to be of *permanent* value, like this exposition of our present governmental methods. Magazine articles are essentially ephemeral and can quite appropriately be used as spurs to definite action; but the last chapter of a book should not be a propagandist pamphlet. I am too anxious to succeed not to be sorry that Mr. Bradford ever saw my *Overland* essay.

Of course I was deeply interested, darling, in what you report about cheap boarding places in New England. It seems more than possible that we shall fare best in every way by going north rather than staying south. Do you think the family in Greenfield would take you *and me* into their common bosom for the sake of your friend in New York? I am afraid that it would make a great deal of difference that you were going to bring a man along: wouldn't it? The account you give of the place and surroundings is very attractive. Maybe it would be just the place for us. I don't know any place that *would'*nt be delightful under the circumstances, though. I could not by searching find anything but delights in a place where my little sweetheart would be with me as my bride! Still I admit that prudence prompts me to look for a comparatively inexpensive place, and consideration for you prompts me to seek an altogether comfortable and attractive place. And, since my darling has a better opportunity than I just now to hear of some such place, I am delighted that she is on the lookout. It is another illustration of one of the chief things that makes me love her with all my heart: her willingness to work frankly and her power to work sweetly and modestly for the consummation of the common object of our love, of our lives!

And do those dear folks in Savannah always remember me with their love, my pet? Well, you may be sure that I pay them back in fullest measure: and I hope that you have not been forgetting my request to send my love to them all—including Mrs. Duncan *of course*—whenever you write. I love them, darling, almost as much as you do.

By-the-way, Miss, what would Aunt Ella think of the strength of your desire to get married in June if she knew that, after asking her favourable judgment, you hesitated to act upon it? Sweetness, wont you promise that I may come to you in June—may come to claim you as my own? My heart shall stand still until Wednesday morning brings me an answer to my yesterday's letter—and yet I *know* that my darling will not refuse, because she loves me—and *does* want me a little!

Did you receive the "Franklin Square" edition of Geo. Eliot's Life that I sent to you, precious?[1]

Oh, Eileen, dear sister Annie will be *so* much delighted at your glad consent to do little Jessie's picture—and *I* am so glad that you feel as you do about it. Do you mean that you would like to, and can, do it *now*?

It certainly looks as if we *could* board in Philadelphia to greater advantage than at Bryn Mawr—provided the Penn. R.R. sells cheap season tickets. But could you let me go for the whole day several times a week, as would likely be necessary under such an arrangement?

God bless you, my darling, for the joy and strength you bring me: and may he help me to be as worthily as I am devotedly
Your own   Woodrow.

ALS (WC, NjP).
[1] J. W. Cross (ed.), *George Eliot's Life as related in her Letters and Journals* (3 vols., New York, 1885).

From Ellen Louise Axson

My darling Woodrow,   New York Feb. 15/85
I was highly entertained by that fine phlippic of which you are at once the author and the victim. It was a noble burst of eloquence! I hope you will profit by your castigation. I have no doubt you find a great deal to chafe you in the "present state of pupilage"; it isn't exactly the natural state for a mature man with ideas of his own and a very strong mind of his own, and I am glad you find so much of good in the situation, and so much that is laughable. I believe in laughing away our annoyances whenever it is possible. I have been in a great many situations when it would have been equally easy to laugh or to cry, I had only to decide for myself,—one would afford just as much relief and the same sort of relief as the other;—and of course I always decided on the former,—unless it was very late at night. But seriously, however much you may have needed the compulsory drill of pupilage, I think you have had about enough of it, and I am glad it is almost over; a very vast amount of patient docility is hardly to be expected from you in your relations towards Dr. [Herbert B.] Adams, or any of his kind.

So poor Gordon is really dead! Oh how terrible it is!—and what is to come of it all? Did you ever see a paper so entirely without fear or favour as that "Nation"[?] They would not "flatter Neptune for his trident," &c. They surely have the courage of their convictions. The idea of their saying at this juncture, when "all Christendom thrills with passionate sorrow for the lost hero," that he was a half crazy fanatic whose folly was the cause of all the troubles, past, present, and to come.[1]

Poor Mr. Goodrich has lost his father; he has been in very poor health for a long time, but died suddenly, yesterday I suppose, at least he received the telegram and left yesterday afternoon.

But, having wasted the whole evening, I find it is now half past ten and I must close. So you did notice my very spasmodic change in pronunciation! I was wondering if you perceived it, for otherwise I knew you must have been puzzled at my unreasonable merriment on certain occasions,—I hadn't learned to carry it off demurely in your presence. By-the-way, I had intended to ask you for the rule again and that list of sounds,—I think I have forgotten some of them. I seem to have the matter fairly on my mind at last, and I believe I can make some progress. And certainly now is my time to change. You had better write me out some of the other cases in which a departure from the Southern standard would be desirable. All those cases which can be classified,—grouped under some rule,—I might manage; I despair of the isolated words;—unless indeed there is something about it that strikes me comically,—I shall never forget rise—rice! I shall never be stinted, dearest, in that pleasure than which Tenneyson tells us there is no greater,—you remember how he describes it

> "And what delights can equal those
> That stir the spirit's inner deeps
> When one that loves, but knows not, reaps
> A truth from one that loves and knows?"[2]

He don't say anything of the feelings of the one who "knows" however. I suppose not *delight* but *patience* is as much as could be expected from that party in the transaction! I love you darling more than words can tell—As ever   Your own Eileen

ALS (WP, DLC).
  [1] New York *Nation*, xl (Feb. 12, 1885), 127.
  [2] From "In Memoriam."

From Thomas Dixon, Jr.[1]

North Carolina, House of Representatives.
Dear Wilson: Raleigh, Feb. 15 1885.
  Have just read the Evening Post's review of your book. Old fellow, you don't know how proud it made me. I just jumped up and yelled—"Three cheers for Wilson and the N E W North State!" I would give anything to be able to shake your hand and talk it over. Let me offer you my most heartfelt congratulations on your great success, which I trust will become daily more pronounced till your pocket becomes as full of filthy lucre as your heart is of just and commendable pride. I'll give your book a send off in the state press here in a few days. I am ever so sorry I missed you in Baltimore and New York Christmas, but it could not be helped I guess.
  I have met with a success in my little legislative career so far which is much greater than I had dared to hope for. I have appeared on the arena only on two bills—the Pension and Obscene

Literature but managed to stir up a considerable muss on both occasions. The salient points of my last argument on the Lit. bill will be published in next week's Register. My chief work as a legislator however has been on a bill which makes a complete and sweeping revolution in the Revenue laws of N. C. It is yet before the Finance committee of which I am a member, and I have high hopes of its becoming a law, and if it does, the immediate effect will be to increase the valuation of property in the state from $200,000,000 to $400,000,000 and decrease the rate of taxation from 25 cents on the hundred to 12 1-2. Not only this, but I believe that it will equalize the burdens of taxation as nearly as is possible.

Let me hear from you. Tell me what you are doing and intend doing next year. I am going to try to have a dept. of history and Pol. Sci. established at Chapel Hill, and if so, some one will have to take charge of it. It could be made the most attractive feature of the University in a short time—you know the temper of our boys. This Legislature is going to make a large increase in the annual appropriation to the University, which is now on a genuine boom.

Let me hear from you.

Sincerely yours,   Tom Dixon, jr.

TLS (WP, DLC) with WWhw notation on env.: "Ans. March 2, '85."

¹ Thomas Dixon, Jr., born Shelby, N. C., Jan. 11, 1864. A.M., Wake Forest College, 1883; graduate student in history and political science at the Johns Hopkins, 1883-84; LL.B., Greensboro, N. C., Law School, 1886. Member of North Carolina legislature, 1885-86. Ordained to Baptist ministry, 1886; pastor in Raleigh, 1887, Boston, 1888-89, and New York, 1889-99. Lyceum lecturer, 1889-1903; clerk of U. S. District Court, Eastern District, N. C., 1938-43. Author of many historical novels, including *The Leopard's Spots* (1902), *The Clansman* (1905), and *The Southerner* (1913). *The Clansman* was made into the film, "The Birth of a Nation," in 1915. Dixon died on April 3, 1946.

To Ellen Louise Axson

My own darling,   Balto., Feby. 16, 1885

I have just received a rather interesting note from Mr. Bradford, the *Nation* critic. He says: "You will probably have seen my notice of your book in the Nation and I trust that you will not be dissatisfied with it. I have a hope that you will be disposed to accept my view that it is best to push for the admission of the cabinet officers to Congress under the constitution as it is, rather than attempt the far harder and more uncertain task of getting the constitution amended." He sends me ("to show how long this has been a cherished hobby of" his) an address on the practical workings of our government which he delivered in Boston in

1873. I am glad to have an opportunity to tell him *why* I did not put what he would have had me put into my book, and, thus indirectly, why he should not have ridden his hobby into his review. I can point the same moral by assuring him that *of course* I agree to the advisability of the policy he advocates. I shall thank him for his generous praise of the book; but I need not say that I thought it judicious. But, why trouble you with what I am going to say to Mr. Bradford!

Your little note of yesterday seems to bring with it a breath of that perfect day's delicious atmosphere—into the damp and rather dismal weather of to-day. We must have had very much the same sort of weather that you had—except that with us the sun began very early in the day to melt the pure surface of the snow and thus stain and mar its beauty and symmetry. Whatever you have written, little lady, cannot fail to bring to me influences sweeter than any memory of the glories of nature. Your briefest notes— even when their brevity excludes the love passages which my heart is sure to miss sadly when they are absent—bring to me *the sense of being loved*: and that is life to me, for the love is yours and I love you with a love that seems to absorb all the strength and to constitute the whole joy of my heart! I like to talk of my love for you as one likes to talk of that which is best and purest in his nature; and I like to dwell upon your love for me as one likes to talk of all that gives him hope and courage. In heart, in life, in everything I am　Your own　Woodrow.

ALS (WC, NjP).

From Ellen Louise Axson

New York Feb. 16 1885.

I certainly did not mean to vex you or perplex you, my darling, by anything in my letter of the 12th; and yet when I recall what I said as far as possible, I begin to perceive that there *was* something rather foolish and unreasonable in my conduct,—something very well calculated to puzzle you. So I will lose no time in clearing up the matter as far as possible. In the first place I didnt *"plead*["] against an immediate settlement did I? I merely *suggested* that perhaps it would be better to postpone the decision. As for my "reasons," I think you know them dear, better than I! for they were those, and none other, which led you to make the same suggestion a week before. You asked me, you remember, if there would be time after the middle of May to decide on a plan and make ready to carry it out. I could not understand how the reasons which made that a wise course one week should have lost their force by the next. As I said above it was foolish in me because you had just been saying that as far as you were concerned it *was* settled; but still—I scarcely know how to explain. Perhaps you will understand, but probably *not*. I hardly understand myself[.] If there was in it a little lurking pride of the peculiar sort that used to possess my heart before love crowded it out, then we will proceed at once to dispossess it of this it's last stronghold. What have two people who love each other to do with pride? Mrs. Guerry has been telling us about some book which she said she liked because the heroine "let the man do most of the loving while she held her head high." (This was *not* the milkmaid story in the spelling-book! though it evidently resembles it!) She went on to say that she thought that was the way it ought *always* to be; she would never "give herself away" to a man, &c. &c. I might have thought myself once that maidenly dignity and pride, would suggest a course slightly resembling that, but now I only looked with something like contempt at a woman—a married woman too—whose thought about love was so small, and mean, and pitiful. That must be a poverty-stricken nature which has not learned that in the case of *love* more than of anything else it is *as* blessed to give as to receive. I would gladly suffer my darling to look into my very heart of hearts,—to read all the secrets of my love,—to know how entirely that heart is his, and how ready I am to give my *life* to him as well. But this is a long digression.

To return to the subject,—there is *no* reason, dear, why I cannot settle this question as well at one time as at another. I expect no "further developments"; the obstacles which undoubtedly exist, I have already decided can be surmounted "with some exertion";—an[d] of course the longer the time, the less violent the exertion! So it is really more convenient for me to decide now. And you cannot doubt now, my darling, what that decision will be. You can as soon doubt my love itself as doubt how I will choose between the sweet service of love and "a little longer freedom." If that is the simple issue uncomplicated by other questions of duty or expediency, and my consent alone is needed then I do "wish and will it" *settled*. Nor do I shrink from making the promise. If you wish you may come to me in June, my love. "With God's blessing we will fulfil our pledges and our hearts' desire" then.

There are many more things in these two letters to be answered, but I fear I *must* wait now until tomorrow. By-the-way it is quite true that this decision is'nt a proclamation to the world and I am *very* glad of it. But that suggests one of my chief grievances against the world. I believe it is totally depraved as concerns the keeping of secrets. It really is dangerous to make up your mind because someone, a mind-reader perhaps, is sure to know of it at once! The fact seems to be that in cases like the present one is obliged to tell two or three people for practical reasons, and you know *one* and *one* and *one* (111) are one hundred and eleven, which is the same as all the world. I am sorry to say that my own Grandmother, since she has grown old, has lost the power to keep a secret long. She is like her old friend Mrs. Porter; who *admits* that she can't keep one, she "forgets that she promised—forgets that it *is* a secret." So I shan't write to them even quite yet, but will give myself "a little longer freedom" from gossiping tongues!

I am so sorry the article in the "Nation" was a disappointment. I was keenly disappointed in it myself because I saw how it would to a certain extent, place the book in a false light, just at that point which you had so carefully guarded. I feared it would affect you just as it has done. It was inexcusable in such a man to be so *stupid*! But after all newspaper "articles are essentially ephemeral" and wont be of permanent injury to the book. But I *must* close. With all my heart, believe me, darling, now and forever   Your own   Eileen

ALS (WP, DLC).

To George Frisbie Hoar

Dear Sir: Balto., Md., Feby 16, '85

Your interesting and valuable letter reached me last week. I thank you very much for calling my attention to the error in my book in the matter of the Supreme Court appointments of 1870. I am very much chagrined that I should have fallen into it. I did *not* examine original sources upon the point. I found the impression prevailing so generally, in what had been written upon the subject, that the opinions of the new judges, as well as the decision of the Court, were known before they were selected for appointment that I thought it safe to accept the view at second hand.

Fortunately a mistake concerning the special motives for those appointments does not take away from the force of the instance as an illustration of the tendency which it was my object to point out: the tendency which brings the Supreme Court gradually to the political complexion of any party which long holds supremacy in the other branches of the government, and so makes it, without a suspicion of judicial corruption, an instrument of party policy—keeping it respectable at the same time that it makes it subservient.   Very sincerely Yours,   Woodrow Wilson

ALS (George Frisbie Hoar Papers, MHi). There is a WWhw draft of a portion of this letter attached to G. F. Hoar to WW, Feb. 9, 1885.

To Ellen Louise Axson

My own darling,   Balto., Feby. 17, 1885
    I am well aware that it would not be reasonable to expect you to *wish* to undertake the task of cheering and beguiling from his ill humour a man who is altogether out of sorts; but I can't help being selfish enough to wish that you were here to counsel and animate me to-day. The long-gathering storm of worry at my so far unavailing efforts to work off the arrears of my degree reading has broken upon me, bringing headache and dire discouragement in its train. I can't find anyone to give me sane advice. I can feel, from the strain of hurried, anxious work, that I am risking my health; and yet I know that if I don't take my degree, my position at Bryn Mawr will be one of just so much less estimation. The *name* of the thing counts for more than real preparation or genuine learning. I hate the principle, and yet feel compelled by it. If I break down next winter in health it will be because I didn't quite break down this winter. But I wont worry my darling about these things. It can't help me to distress her: it will only add to my disquietude to know that I have disturbed her peace of mind. If she were *here* I could tell her all, and in doing so dissipate the trouble; but since she is *not* here I must trust as before to my own not too certain strength. Sometimes I think, Eileen, that I have done you a very questionable service in preparing for you a life with a man of a sensitive, restless, overwrought disposition like mine! I hope that you will continue to be blind to the sacrifice you are making.
    I delight in your zeal for the new pronunciation, little sweetheart, and shall enclose the rules and lists you ask for. What a beautiful language it will be with the tongue of my darling's sweet voice lent to its most musical vowel!
    I wonder, little lady, if I ever do or say anything that gives you joy comparable with that which the slightest token of your love and faith and admiration gives me? It doesn't seem possible! But, for that matter, it never seemed possible before that I could love

anybody as I love my Eileen. She is incomparably the sweetest woman in the world, the most lovable, the most tender and loving. And how she inspired my life when she accepted me as

Her own   Woodrow.

The broad, Italian, sound of 'a' (as in father) seems to be most common

1. Before *th*: e.g., path, bath, wrath;
2.   ″ an 'l' whose sound is merged in that of some neighbour consonant: e.g., half, calf, calm, balm, palm, psalm, &c.
3. In *au* before an 'n' or 'f' sound: e.g. laugh, launch, vaunt, flaunt, aunt, &c.

The *intermediate* sound of 'a' (the Italian 'a' uttered with a very light touch) between the 'a' in *fat* and the 'a' in father, is most common before 'f', 's', or 'n.' Here are a *few* examples: advance, advantage, after, am*a*ss, answer, ask, basket, branch, brass, cast, chance, chant, class, contrast, craft, disaster, draft, example, fast, glance, glass, grass, grant, lass, last, pant, pass, past, pastor, plaster, raft, repast, sample, shaft, task, vast.

These will be enough to practice on for the present, wont they? I have given, as you request, only those that seem at least to follow a *rule*.   W.

ALS (WC, NjP).

From Albert Shaw

My Dear Wilson: Minn. Feb. 17, '85.
    I send you *Tribune* containing notice of "Congressional Gov't."[1] I was obliged to write it in great haste, & the proof-readers mangled it a good deal. Have had time to study the book with care, and am better pleased with it than ever. It will be read everywhere & will be *standard*. I reviewed it last night before the Pol. Sci. Club of the Minnesota Univ., and have written a review for the Chicago *Dial* to appear in the March number.[2] I was delighted last night to find that the *Nation* was able to appreciate the importance of the book. I see that Shinn's book has just appeared.
    Should like to know more about the School at Bryn Mawr. What is the endowment? and the general plan? Send me a *circular*.   Yours in haste   Albert Shaw.

ALS (WP, DLC) with WWhw notation on env.: "Ans. Feby 21/85."
    [1] It was a clipping from the *Minneapolis Tribune*, Feb. 15, 1885, which WW sent to ELA on Feb. 23, 1885. It is printed at that date.
    [2] Printed at March [1], 1885.

From Ellen Louise Axson

My darling Woodrow,   New York Feb 18/85

I was detained so long down stairs last night by Miss Comstock and the others, that when I came up my fire was almost out and there was no time to write. It is bitterly cold this morning and I suppose if I observed the letter of *that promise* I would not be writing this; but I have on my cloak so that I don't think it will hurt me to write a very few lines, besides I also promised to write you every day, and as I *can't* keep *both* promises, I choose the latter!

I am exceedingly glad that Mr. Bradford has given you an opportunity to enlighten him upon some points with regard to which he sorely needs it. I was wishing you could write him, but supposed it would hardly do; so it is well that he has himself made the occasion.

Yes, I received the "Life of George Eliot." I am so much obliged to you, dear;—and so glad you mentioned it, for I couldn't imagine where it came from; there was no postmark, and you had *printed* the address so that it gave me no clue. I have been reading it, by snatches, with deep interest. George Eliot—or rather Marian Evans, the woman,—has always been to me such a complete mystery—an entirely unknown quantity—and while these letters by no means clear away the mystery, they give us very pleasant glimpses of her personality; and tell us in short all one cares to know, or has a right to know. Did you ever see anything so odd and confusing as the way Mr. Cross runs the letters together, giving not even a hint of beginning or end, address or date.

God bless *you*, my darling, for the joy and strength you bring *me*, and may he help me to be worthy of your love;—worthy of it in more ways than that one of power to love you as well in return. With all my heart.   Your own Eileen.

ALS (WP, DLC).

To Ellen Louise Axson

Balto., Feby. 18, 1885

Oh, my darling, what a wonderfully sweet, what a perfect answer you have sent to my plea for that precious promise which means so much, which means everything, to me! Your letter of the 12th did not '*vex*' me, little sweetheart: nothing you might say could vex me—because you could say nothing to me that was not full of your love for me. I was *puzzled* because I did not know that you had understood as you did what I said about postponing arrangements until the middle of May. I thought that, to prevent all *possibility* of any miscarriage of our plans, it would be best to wait till then to fix upon a date and make active preparation; but I never for a moment thought that there would be any necessity for imposing a similar delay upon our private pledges to each other, made for our heart's ease. What I longed for was simply a loving covenant that we would do all we could towards a marriage in June: and, since such a covenant could be kept as one of our most sacred confidences, to be revealed only when our plans were matured, I was a little dismayed at your hesitation in consenting to it. I wanted to know that you felt just as I do, that, so far as you are concerned, it is settled. Maybe this is *over* caution on our part, little lady: for we have no *reason* to fear that any obstacle will arise; but, if it will really add nothing to the practical difficulty of your preparations, I see no reason why we may not err on this safe side. But, while I could wait for the perfecting of our plan, I could not wait, under the circumstances, for my darling's promise! And now, Eileen, how shall I thank you, how shall I tell you my gratitude for the precious words of this letter—which seems to me like my charter of freedom and of happiness! You have filled my heart to overflowing with joy and pride, my little queen. Oh, my darling, I am unspeakably happy at this last and best proof of your love! I would not for the world have you of that empty-hearted creed which Mrs. Guerry expressed. A man who "does all the loving" while the object of his love "holds her head high" is no man at all in my opinion; and I am sure that no true woman can love without making freest confession of it in everything she does and says to her accepted lover! I think that I can understand, and I know that I can honour, the shyness with which a modest woman makes her greatest promises and her greatest gifts to the man she loves; but I know that love will not be held back even by the strongest maidenly feelings: and my delight in your love seems to be enhanced almost in direct proportion as that love becomes more and more frank, and demonstrative. And your confessions are *so* sacred in my sight, Eileen. Each one is proof to me that you love me as I *want* to be loved, with a perfect love and trust, with open heart and free demonstration. You are mine and make glad acknowledgement that you are mine; and I am in every pulse and purpose

Your own   Woodrow.

ALS (WC, NjP).

From Ellen Louise Axson

New York Feb. 18/85.

I can't tell you, my darling, how distressed I am about this business of the degree. Indeed, this won't do,—it is *dreadful*! No degree can be so valuable a possession as health. And yet I don't undervalue the degree; I see just the advantage it will be to you. But please, *please*, dear, don't try to do all the reading—use instead that synopsis you spoke of. Surely there would be no impropriety in it! Everyone knows that *now* you are more entitled to the degree than most of the others *ever will* be however thoroughly they plod through the proscribed tasks. You should be able to answer certain arbitrarily selected questions (of fact chiefly?) Why not find the answers to said questions in the easiest way?—that's only common-sense! I should be perfectly *miserable* over this thing, if I did not see this way of solving the difficulty,—a way at once so simple and so perfectly right.

I believe they will give you the degree under *any* circumstances, and I wouldn't worry too much about it. Don't colleges give their degrees to scholars all over the world who hav'nt passed their examinations, whom they never even saw. By their *deeds* they are known, and judged and honoured.

Ah darling *don't* I wish that I could be with you to undertake "the task of cheering and beguiling." A great University would be no better than a grammar school if it's degrees merely meant that the persons upon whom they were conferred had committed to memory a certain number of lesson-books! But of course it means something more than that,—it means in the broadest sense thorough preparation for doing good and effective thinking and working in the chosen field. You have certainly more than fulfilled those requirements, for you have not only *prepared* yourself to work, but you have already *done* work of the most valuable sort. In short you would be conferring an honour upon the institution in taking their degree, and it is perfectly ridiculous that there should be any trouble about it! But if the rules of the institution require that—what greater happiness could be mine than to feel that I had the power to help and cheer you. And you fear you have done for me a "*questionable service*"! My darling, you have done for me the greatest service man ever did for woman in preparing for me a life with *you*,—you, just as you are, disposition included. "We live by admiration hope and love" says Wordsworth. Doesn't it follow then that if those be the animating impulses[,] that life in which there is most to arouse them, is the fullest, richest, truest, living. And—trust me darling—there is no one in all the world whom I could so love, admire, and believe in as you, no one who could so *fill* my heart and my life. So you see how you have blessed me with a double blessing when you give me the treasure of your love and give me also the right to love—to *identify* myself with—the one who is and will always be to me *the man of men*. With all my heart.

Your own   Eileen.

ALS (WP, DLC).

From John Wildman Moncrief

My dear sir,   Franklin Indiana, Feb. 18th 1885
    I wish to put a matter before you, and I am sure that you will at least sympathize with it. . . .
    I am Professor of History in our little college here at Franklin, and I undertake to find the truth and teach it regardless of party affiliations. . . . I take the Johns Hopkins studies in Hist. & Polit. Sci. and find much help in it. But we find much need of a special library of Polit. Science. Our general college library does not supply us with those books that are absolutely necessary, for more advanced work, such as is necessary in starting an Historical Seminary. So we decided to start a library. . . .
    It then occured to us that the eminent men who are making the books on Polit. Science, from a general interest in the subject, might each enjoy making a contribution. So to test the matter we wrote to the honorable and venerable Ex-Pres. Woolsey. He at once replied with a kind letter and his two vols. on Political Science, and his Communism and Socialism. So we have concluded to write to such men as write standard works, state our case, and request them if possible to assist us. I see in the last *Nation* a very appreciative review of your *Congressional Government*. If you are disposed to give it to us it will do great good and I believe cause many students to put it into their own libraries. . . .
    Believe me yours in the interests of Historical & Political Science and with great respect,   J. W. Moncrief.

P.S. omitted. ALS (WP, DLC) with WWhw notation on env.: "Ans. Mar. 4, 1885."

To Ellen Louise Axson

My own darling,   Balto., Feby. 19, 1885
    I have again been compelled to make a change of front with regard to the *degree* question. On Tuesday morning I was visited

by one of those ominous headaches of the sort I had last summer whenever I overworked myself with writing. It lasted throughout Tuesday and would possibly have been with me yet (for even
this morning an occasional throb reminds me of it) had your letter not come with its unspeakable gift of gladness to make me
forget all bodily ailments in the joy of the one absorbing thought,
that, God willing, I was to be wedded to my darling in June.
There is one sentence I have read which my heart seems to be
every moment repeating to me: "If you wish, you may come to
me in June, my love";—and that has *cured* me. I shall never forget that sweet sentence; and I will always treasure, as sacred, this
letter that contains it!

But not all the joy of being loved by my darling could *keep*
me well if I were to go on violating wilfully the laws of mental
and physical health: and I have given up—this time conclusively
—the struggle for the degree.[1] The Bryn Mawr people will be disappointed, of course; but I made no sort of promise to them about
taking it, and the sentimental disadvantage of not having it will
be very short-lived. But, whether or no, as a sane man I had no
choice. The cramming was killing me by inches, and I wouldn't
dare to continue it. I will do my class work, will complete my work
for Dr. Ely, and will make what special preparation I can for my
courses next year—and I shall find in these things all that the
utmost diligence can accomplish. It is this Ely enterprise that has
handicapped me in the race. I was a fool to take a hand in it,
if I wanted to win a degree; though I think that the reading I
have done in connection with it has probably done me quite as
much good as the degree reading would have done. Cramming
kills me; reading in development of a subject improves and in-
vigorates me. The one is mere filling to be full; the other is collecting material for new creations.

Good-bye, precious; I am the happiest man in the world because
you love me, and so give me leave to be heart and soul

Your own   Woodrow.

ALS (WC, NjP).
[1] As future documents in this volume will reveal, the decision was not as
"conclusive" as Wilson thought at this time. See, e.g., WW to ELA, Feb. 26, 1885.

From Ellen Louise Axson

My darling Woodrow,   [New York, Feb. 19, 1885]
I have been rather afraid that you could not read a word of my
last night's letter; and yet I dare say my fears are groundless,
for it is so absolutely impossible for me to do much worse than

usual that if you can read *any* of my effusions you can probably read all. At least I have the satisfaction of knowing that I can't *shock* you now. The truth is, I had such a blinding head-ache last night that I was hardly responsible for what I wrote. I had my first tumble yesterday, and it used me up for the time. You know I can never do *anything* in a half-hearted way!—if I make up my mind to fall I go about it with all my might, as though I had determined to go through to China once for all. The result of my efforts was that I struck my head—made a great knob, and stunned myself so that I couldn't get up at first;—don't know when I should if two or three men had'nt come running, which roused me most effectually and lent wings to my feet. That was just here on 4th St, but I thought I would be all right in a minute so I went on to the Met. When I reached there, however, I could scarcely see anything, felt like one walking in a dream; and the conclusion was that I spent the morning lying on the lounge there, with the girls teasing me almost to death talking to me. I was overcome by sleep, and they had a queer idea that they must prevent me,—it was *dangerous*. I told them that idea was as completely exploded as the one concerning the effects of water on fever. I knew all about it, for concussion of the brain ran in our family; my brother had it every holiday or so. By one, however the blindness had passed,—though my head ached quite badly—so I went down to the League and worked as usual in the "head" and sketch classes, which, I suppose, was imprudent for my head grew much worse and I was quite sick by night. But I slept it off, and feel almost entirely myself today,—not quite I imagine or I shouldn't have bored you with such an elaborate history of the case! That reminds me —(*what* does—guess!) that my friend Miss Case posed tonight in the most *delicious* old-time dress and bonnet. It was the prettiest pose we have had, and she looked *perfectly beautiful*! You saw her,—did you not? You know she is scarcely pretty on ordinary occasions,—so you see it proves the truth of what I said that people who are not *really* pretty sometimes *look* pretty. I must pose again a week from tomorrow—dont you pity me? I shall certainly *sit* this time.

By the way, I did not answer the question about little Jessie's picture. I am perfectly willing to do it now if they have a good photo, and I have only to make a copy; but if, as I fear, they have *not*, and the whole thing is to be an experiment, don't you think there would be much more hope of success if I *waited* until I could get suggestions in the course of the work from some one who knew her well. You know I saw her but once, and could scarcely trust my memory for making changes. Do you think your sister is very anxious to have it done now?

You don't tell me how you are feeling today, darling; I am anxious to hear whether you are a little more exhausted by the labours of another day, or a little more relieved because one more days burden is rolled of[f] your shoulders. How I *do* hope you will plan an escape from some of that reading! Believe me, darling, in every thought and feeling,　　　　　　　Your own Eileen.

ALS (WP, DLC) with WWhw notation on env.

From William F. Ford

Dear sir:　　　　　　　　Bradstreet's. New York, Feb'y 19 1885.

Can you not write for us something worth while in relation to the doings of Congress at the present session?[1]

Please let me hear from you.

　　　　　　　　　　Yours truly,　Wm F Ford

TLS (WP, DLC) with WWhw notation on env.: "Ans. Feby 24/85."
　[1] See W. F. Ford to WW, Jan. 7, 1885, Vol. 3, also requesting a contribution from Wilson.

Two Letters to Ellen Louise Axson

Balto., Feby. 20, 1885

My precious, my darling little comforter and counsellor! What a wonderful, true-woman's heart you have! If ever you ask me again why I fell in love with you, I shall show you this letter that I received this morning, I think: it is throughout such a proof of your genius for loving and thinking as a woman ought to love and think. Even in our separation, darling, you manage to cheer and beguile most wonderfully my unreasonable moods—to change the whole bent of my disposition by the sweet influences of your love. I *can't* be downhearted when I have such tokens as this precious letter gives that your heart is so bound up in my interests. Why, this is what I have been living for, to win love like yours: and now I shall find happiness in living to satisfy it. That is the thought to which I like again and again to return: that my heart's mission is found!

As you will have seen by my letter of yesterday, my resolve as to the degree reading had already run even beyond the limits of your advice. You see, my pet, if I gave up any part of the preparation I ought to give up all of it, because what was telling on me was, not the constant reading so much as the *cramming* of which it was, so to say, the menstruum, the medium. Cramming pure and simple, for me, would be one degree worse than the *diluted* cramming of full reading-courses. I sacrifice a great deal in giving up the degree, but I am as sure that I am right in doing so as I would be in guarding my lungs against the consumption. I don't wonder that you were distressed that I should even seem to count health of minor importance in the question. That state of mind was due to my temporary *want* of health, and could last only a few hours. I feel now as if I had recovered my senses! My friends utter all sorts of protests against my decision: but I know what I am about. My headache—brought back temporarily by the strain of taking notes on two very tedious lectures—reminds me of the necessity I am under. If I might go to see my darling for a few days, I should be quickly all right again; but, since I can't do that, I will treat myself to all sorts of indulgences and diversions here, amusing myself with such work as I *like* most to do, until I feel altogether myself once more. My little sweetheart need not feel the least anxiety about me any longer. I am only a *little* 'pulled down'; and she may rest assured that she has done worlds for me by her sweet sympathy and love—almost as much as if she had come to me in person and chased away my discouragements by her presence. It makes me *so* happy, Eileen, to know that you are *mine*, that you are already identified with me in life and in heart; and, if only June will hasten in its coming, that I may prove the gladness and the pride with which I give myself to you, I can promise not to let the 'blues' have any chance at all. Our bridal day, my love, will open a new life to me—a life in which it will be my heart's strength and my work's inspiration that I am alto-gether   Your own   Woodrow.

Balto., Feby 21, 1885

I cannot tell you how much I have been distressed, my darling, by this news of your severe fall and its very serious consequences: especially since, by refusing to be even temporarily invalided by it, you did what you could to make its bad effects permanent. I hope with all my heart that that single day of suffering *was* all the injury inflicted; but I shall be miserably uneasy until you can be *sure* that it ended there. I am *so* sorry, darling! It almost breaks my heart to think of my Eileen *hurt*, and nobody there that she loves to nurse and care for her. Oh, what would I not give for that privilege: how my heart rebels against this hateful separation which keeps me here, selfishly engrossed by my own cares and ailments! I hope that it is some comfort to my little sweetheart to know that my heart is wrapped up even in the least events of her life, and that when she *suffers* my whole heart yearns to lighten the pain by my sympathy and love, and by every service within love's power.

But what a wonderful little woman you are! It is scarcely credible by me that you could have written that precious letter of Wednesday night while your head was throbbing with the blinding pain of that fall! Why it was one of the sweetest, tenderest, most complete letters you ever wrote: I have kept it in my pocket to read and reread! Yet now I almost feel like upbraiding you for having written it. Surely, little lady, that terrible headache was a more imperative cause for putting me off with a few lines than—than having been detained so long down stairs "by Miss Comstock and the rest," for instance! Please, darling, never *sacrifice* yourself to my indulgence: *it* can wait, but care of your health cannot! This may sound like very ungracious blame, precious: but it isn't—it isn't blame at all—or, if it is, it is only *love* blame, which, if you were here, would be administered with a kiss. I trust my darling entirely—and I love her all the more for these unpremeditated proofs that she loves me perfectly because unselfishly. But, just because she is so unselfish, I must be selfish for her, and must insist that she shall take care of herself as if she were as precious to herself as she is to me—that she shall take care of herself as I would wish to take care of her! Are you quite sure, my pet, that you feel no ill effects *now* from that fall?

I am feeling very much better to-day—and with the return of sound health and the restoration of good spirits there comes, according to a perverse habit of my mind, a strong inclination not to give up the degree finally and altogether, but to try the shorter methods of cramming which you suggest—and which even Dr. Adams half advised. Shall I?

I wish I could go on, my love, with this letter: I'm in my Saturday writing humour. But there's an ominous pile of unanswered letters on the table before me—and I *must* set to work at once to reduce it.

With a heartful of love and sympathy,
Your own   Woodrow.

ALS (WC, NjP).

From Ellen Louise Axson

My darling Woodrow,   New York, Feb. 21, 1885.
   I am *immensely* relieved to learn your decision as to the de-

gree. Since your giving up some of the reading would not help you as much as I supposed,—since the choice was between doing everything or nothing (to that end) there was really *no* choice in the matter. It would have been madness to overtax yourself to such an extent. Of course, it is a great pity about the degree, but you are most undoubtedly doing right. By-the-way, what do you mean by "the sentimental disadvantage of not having it" being "very short-lived"? *What* friends of yours have so little sense as to urge your killing yourself? What does Dr. Adams say about it? Don't you think they will give you the degree "any-how," or is it against the law? I am sure they would if they could. You did not reach this decision any too soon, darling, I am distressed about those miserable head-aches, but I hope and trust that now you will very soon be altogether yourself. Ah! how I wish that you could be here—without the trouble of coming—for a few days! The people who talk about railroads having "annihilated time and space" talk preposterous nonsense,—don't they? Balt. and New York are so *dreadfully* far apart! But my hands are stiff with cold, and I must stop *trying* to write. I am altogether recovered from my tumble, by the way. You don't know, my darling, how happy you have made me by telling me that even in our separation I am able, to some extent, to cheer and help you,—that the love and sympathy, which I could no more withhold from you now than I could cease to live, are worth so much to you. You may well believe, dear, that my whole heart is bound up in your interests. I *myself* receive constantly fresh proof of that; in the every-day history of that heart. I am, my darling, believe me, altogether   Your own   Eileen.

ALS (WP, DLC).

To Albert Shaw

My dear Shaw,   Balto., Feby. 21, 1885
If I had not been overwhelmingly busy—and ill in consequence —if, in other words, I had not been for a time the most miserable of mortals, I should have answered your delightful letter of the 5th a week or more ago. Now your note of the 17th has put me doubly in your debt. And I'm in your debt in more ways than one: for it does me an immense amount of good, and gives me a tremendous lift of encouragement, to know that my book has met with your cordial approval.

The *Nation's* notice[1] was rather unpalatable to me—though of course I was exceedingly gratified by its high estimate of the work

—because it insisted upon supplementing the views of the book with the views of my *Overland* article, thereby making an *advocate* of me against my will; for you know how carefully I strove to keep out of the book anything like the tone of a political pamphlet. But the critic meant well and I don't suppose that the character he thrust upon it will stick to the little volume. The copy of the Tribune you sent lags behind your note—so that I have not seen *your* review yet. I am awaiting it with very great interest.[2]

Your paper on the economic topics and problems of the northwest is to be read to us next Friday night; Dr. Ely is keeping it very 'dark' till then, much to the trial of my patience.[3] But the little gentleman is in a very fever of enthusiasm over it, and *couldn't* keep it *all* to himself. He 'came to the bat' this morning with a lecture, in the Saturday educational course, in which he used Dr. Shaw and his interest in the coöperative coopers of Minneapolis as a notable example of the educational effect of the study of political economy in enabling men to see new meanings in their everyday surroundings. The only vitiating element in the argument was that Dr. S. is—according to my reading of him—a man whose intellectual eyes would be wide open anyhow—even without the anointment of pol. economy.

It is easy to tell you what you want to know about Bryn Mawr. The endowment is $800,000; and the plan of instruction is almost precisely that of the collegiate dept. of the JHU. Adams calls it "the Miss Johns Hopkins," for which Wilhelm[4] wittily suggests to substitute "the Johanna Hopkins." I will send you a circular as soon as I can get one; you will see by it that I am to have jurisdiction over a female "fellow."

As I intimated above, I've been very near a break-down in health in consequence of over-grinding for my degree. It looks even much as if I would have to give up the struggle—as both Levermore and Dewey have done.[5] The only men left to 'come up' would be Gould and Ramage.[6] The latter put in his appearance the other day—not perceptibly Germanized—on his way to visit his home, whence he will return next month to stay the session out with us.

Not a word from Shinn yet, since his dive into the West. His book is in the New Book Dept. and samples *well.*[7] The style has been greatly polished in the course of the various revisings, and I have no doubt that the volume will be a *permanent* success.

More anon when I have no headache!

All here send warmest greetings.

Affectionately yours,   Woodrow Wilson

TCL (in possession of Virginia Shaw English).

[1] Printed at Feb. 12, 1885.

[2] It is printed as Enclosure II with WW to ELA, Feb. 23, 1885.

[3] For a summary of Shaw's paper, see the Seminary Minutes printed at Feb. 27, 1885.

[4] Lewis W. Wilhelm, a fellow-graduate student.

[5] That is, to obtain the Ph.D. in 1885. Charles H. Levermore and Davis R. Dewey, like Wilson, received their doctoral degrees in 1886.

[6] Elgin Ralston Lovell Gould and Burr James Ramage. For a biographical note on Gould, see E. R. L. Gould to WW, Nov. 9, 1885, Vol. 5.

[7] See WW to ELA, Feb. 12, 1885, n. 2.

From Gamaliel Bradford

My dear Sir: Boston, Feb 21, 1885

I am much obliged by your letter of 17th, & admit, as you state it, that your reason for limiting your book to exegesis was a perfectly good one though I do not think that I could have had the requisite self control. But then the reform has been a passion with me for so long that I regard all else as subservient to it. I have interviewed Presidents & cabinet officers, senators and members of Congress & mean before next autumn to have a session with President Cleveland and try to urge him up to some action. The timidity of public men is very strange to me. I heard Benj. H. Bristow once at a dinner table argue the matter with as much earnestness of conviction as I ever had, yet all my appeals both by letter and in person failed to extract one public word from him. Even such a man as John Sherman once declared himself in my hearing as very strongly in favor of it.

I applaud your intention to make a thorough study of administration with a view to publication & only wish I had the courage & perseverance to put my own studies into shape. My theory of popular government for which I am an enthusiast is this. It has had hardly a century of existence and the whole course of that has been a series of experiments how to reconcile efficiency of administration with popular control through a representative body. The steady development in each nation & the parallelism of all is quite wonderful. In England since the Revolution the progress has been almost as regular as the growth of a tree. Most people regard the history of France since 1789 as a mere chaos of revolutions. To me it is a course of logical development of principles as consistent as any in chemistry, though of course with disturbing influences—and I believe that nowhere in the world has there been greater *relative* progress. The parallel in the working of principles between this country & France (modified by social & physical conditions) astonishes me constantly more

& more, and the beauty of it is that every town & city & state in this country is working away at precisely the same problems as Great Britain & France & Italy[.] The disturbing influence is the German empire which is about where it was 150 years ago, & threatens to throw all Europe back into the struggle for existence. I am moved to this outpouring by the sympathy in our lines of thought. In a day or two I will send you a pamphlet upon Municipal Govt. which you will see follows the same line, & I shall keep a look out for anything of yours which may appear.

Very truly yours   Gaml. Bradford

ALS (WP, DLC) with WWhw notation on env.: "Ans. Mar. 7/85."

From Ellen Louise Axson

My darling Woodrow,   New York Feb. 22 1885.

Again I write just after my return from church. It is another beautiful Sabbath day; my whole room is flooded with the sunshine,—though it is not quite so perfect perhaps as last Sunday for it is colder and the snow is not unsullied. Still it is warm enough to tempt out all the children and that is one of my chief reasons for wishing the Sundays especially to be bright. I saw a pretty little episode out on the avenue, which took my fancy immensely. Just in front of me was a young fellow leading by the hand the *sweetest* little toddler, she was just able to walk,—scarcely three,—and a perfect beauty. Suddenly he made a dash toward another young fellow who was coming from the opposite direction and who had with him a strikingly handsome little boy of four or five. The recognition was mutual and there were many cries of "how d'you do, old fellow! *so* glad to see you!" &c. &c;—then "is that your baby! why here's mine ha! ha!["] And then *such* a time as they had over the babies,—such boyish enthusiasm!—they were little more than boys. Then of course the children must make each other's acquaintance and it was charming to see how they went about it,—to see the little girl hold out her hand and smile shyly into the boy's face, while he, holding her hand in one of his, took her chin in the other, and raising her face, looked down into it with a grave, somewhat critical, yet approving smile,—at all of which the fathers were half beside themselves with glee. I of course *couldn't* resist lingering at a respectful distance to watch them, out of the corner of my eye, knowing that they were far too absorbed to discover that there was "a chiel amang them takin' notes."

But I really ought not to chat even so long as this now. I ought to look over my mission-school lesson, and it is nearly dinner time now. What a rush it is on Sunday!

By-the-way, Mr. Carter has just been warming my heart to him still more, by praising our Mr. Thornwell[1] in the most enthusiastic fashion;—actually comparing him to St. Paul!

I love you, dear heart, with all my soul, deeply, tenderly, passionately, and I remain as ever   Your own Eileen.

ALS (WP, DLC).
[1] Presumably the Rev. Dr. James Henley Thornwell, one of the founders of the southern Presbyterian Church.

To Ellen Louise Axson

My own darling,   Balto., Feby. 22, 1885

It is too provoking! I had promised myself a long, leisurely letter to you to-day, but Mrs. Bird has invited me to dine with her at two o'clock, and no decent excuse offers any chance of escape. A two-o'clock dinner of course means the greater part of the afternoon: and my letter has to be mailed by dusk. Mrs. B. is the Georgian lady of whom I spoke in one of my letters some weeks ago.

When I spoke of the sentimental disadvantage of not having a degree as of short-life, I meant simply that a degree was more essential for a young man than for a man of established position. No one ever thinks of inquiring (except from curiosity or biographical interest) whether a man of middle age who has made a distinct reputation for himself took his degree at a University; but a young man for a time needs some such stamp to pass current amongst boards of trustees. To lack it will be to start with a slight *presumption* against me: its possession would be *prima facie* evidence of ability and sufficient scholarly equipment. But a year or so of hard work will, I hope and believe, leave *that* disadvantage behind me—behind *us*: isn't that the proper pronoun in such a connection?

I am *so* glad, darling, that you are feeling no ill effects from your fall! I have been very anxious about its possible results. Did you feel no resulting aches and pains after that first day?

Yes, precious, New York and Balto. *are very* far apart! Separation by so much as a mile would be as bad as separation by these hundreds, if that mile could not be travelled every day, or if it might stretch its length between us for many hours. But June is coming, my love, and then—ah, how can I wait! My little queen!

Your reign has begun already; but it shall be infinitely more perfect some of these days. Every day my heart performs some fresh act of allegiance to its sweet mistress, for I am, darling, absolutely and altogether   Your own   Woodrow.

ALS (WC, NjP).

From Ellen Louise Axson

My darling Woodrow,   New York, Feb. 22/85.

I said to myself this morning that tonight I would *certainly* write to Mrs. Green,[1] but so much of the evening has already gone that I fear I am not going to accomplish it after all. I *must* try to write you a short letter and see if I cant do it once for all. How one does dread writing to a neglected friend!

And what do you suppose I have been doing all the evening? Why reading your old letters—the first ones; I used to read them every week last winter, but now there are so many between that this is the first time this winter that I have returned to them, so they were quite fresh again[.] How long ago it seems since those sweet letters were written! They *are* very, very sweet, my darling; yet these later ones are *more* sweet and precious, for we *are* more to each other now than we were eighteen months ago; are we not? Our love, a strong and vigorous young plant then, has had time now to strike it's roots deep down into our hearts, and "the boughs thereof are like the goodly cedars,"—it has filled our life. Yes, we have grown closer to each other in these months that have passed; and I cannot tell you, my darling, with what joy, and better still,—with what *peace* of heart I recognize that fact; for it not only casts its brightness backward across the past, but it gives me, ah, what sweet hope, what glad assurance for the future! There is but little left now of those misgivings which haunted me so in those early days and which these letters so vividly recall. I knew that your love must needs decrease or increase,—you see;—it *has* increased in spite of all the—well,—call them *limitations* of it's object; and having stood such tests, I believe in it entirely,—without waiting for it to pass all the ordeals that life prepares for it, I can believe that it is in the fullest sense "true love." How perfectly happy I should be if I only knew myself worthy of you! Ah that I might be all that I wish to be!—all that the woman you love *should* be! If God would only give me the power equal to my desire to satisfy that love!

You can't guess the immediate cause of my turning back to these old letters! I wanted to learn, from that letter in which you first told me your hopes and plans for the future, your exact thought on a certain point upon which you touched in one of this weeks letters, and to which my thoughts have frequently returned since. You say that "*since* you are shut out from realizing your first ambition, to become a public servant and actively participate in the direction of affairs, it is your heart's desire that you may become one of the guides of public thought." You do not mean that you would prefer that active participation to writing books of permanent value? But do you still wish to unite the two careers? Was that your *first* ambition in point of time only, or the first and dearest wish of your heart and is it still one of your ambitions,—even an ambition that has taken the form of a *regret* as for something from which you are "shut out"? I don't see why you should feel permanently shut out from becoming a guide of public thought, or policy either, in *any* way that seemed to you desirable. True, this is an age for division of labour; and if one were obliged to choose strictly between the two careers it seems to me there would be no room for hesitation even. Of all the world's workers, those which to my mind take by far the highest rank are the writers of noble books. Still I have often thought it a pity that your powers as a speaker should not find fuller scope than that afforded by the pr[o]fessors chair. Men of letters are constantly going into public life in England,—why not in America too, if it seemed good to them. But all this is doubtless very foolish; these are questions for the years alone to answer. Yet I could not but be sorry to think that there is in your mind that lurking sense of disappointment and *loss* as if you had missed from your life something upon which both your gifts and inclinations gave you a claim,—as if you had been cut off from one half of your inheritance, or in short were "shut out from your heart's desire." Nor can I help wishing to know, and seeking to know—even at the cost of many foolish words—*all* your thought about those things which most nearly concern you, and which therefore have the most absorbing interest for me.

But this letter isnt any too short after all. At any rate I need not stop to say at it's close that I love you darling, for I have said nothing else all through it. Believe me, dear love, to be *altogether*

Your own Eileen

ALS (WP, DLC).
[1] Aminta Green, widow of Charles Green, of Baltimore.

To Ellen Louise Axson, with Two Enclosures

My own darling,   Balto., Feby. 23rd., 1885

This has been, and will be to its close, a day of distractions: for, as you are doubtless aware (!), it is the day celebrated as Washington's birthday[1]—and Washington's birthday is also the birthday of "the Hopkins," and the day of our 'celebration,' consequently. We spent all the morning hearing addresses, seeing degrees conferred, and singing—or in getting ready for such entertainment. I aided, as I did last year, in serving up three Latin songs to the audience: so that I have been specially busy, first rehearsing, then shaving and getting on my best bib and tucker, then taking part in the tedious forms of getting into well-ordered procession of professors, non-resident graduates, fellows, graduate-students in residence, undergraduates, &c. &c. This evening we are to have *the* reception of the year—wh. will be simply the minor ones I have described from time to time intensified many fold. I shall have to get ready for *that* almost immediately after mailing this: for our dinner was pushed on well into the afternoon.

I enclose two notices. The longer one was sent me by the editor of the *Beacon* himself[2] with the information that it was his own production: I can't imagine why he wished me to see it. I knew that the American Philistine lived 'in large numbers' and was loose in our midst, but I did not know that he was quite so rampant in Boston. I thought that they kept him *chained* there at least. The other review was written by my friend Shaw,[3] and delights me the more because Shaw is *capable* of judging in such matters and is *in*capable of being blinded by personal feelings. He is the chief editorial writer for the *Tribune*, which is one of the largest and most influential papers of the northwest.

That's a *very* pretty picture you draw of the pretty episode you witnessed on the street on Sunday!

Good-bye, precious; there are several things I've been saving up to say: but they must wait till another time.

I love you with all my heart! I would give—anything for one word from my darling's lips—and one kiss that would claim me as

                         Your own   Woodrow.

ALS (WC, NjP).
[1] Because February 22 fell on a Sunday in 1885.
[2] Carl Wilhelm Ernst.
[3] See A. Shaw to WW, Feb. 17, 1885, in which it was originally enclosed.

The Boston *Beacon's* Review of
Congressional Government

[Feb. 21, 1885]

Mr. Woodrow Wilson's work on *Congressional Government*,
just published by Houghton, Mifflin & Co., is a critical study,
rather than a descriptive account. It presents a series of good essays about Congress and the Executive, draws a few comparisons
between our government and the English, and is strongly disposed to vote our system the less perfect of the two. "I know not,"
he says, "how better to describe our form of government in a
single phrase than by calling it a government by the chairmen
of the standing committees of Congress." This is not wrong.
Neither is it wrong in Mr. Wilson to say that "Congressional government is committee government; Parliamentary government
[as practised in the United Kingdom]¹ is government by a responsible cabinet ministry." But what of it? Does it follow that our
system is less good than the trans-Atlantic system? Mr. Wilson
falls into the singular error of comparing our system, viewed
practically, with the English system, viewed theoretically and
ideally. Such a comparison is bad in rhetoric; in the work of a
publicist or constitutional lawyer it is almost ruinous. There is no
reason whatever why our system of government should resemble
that of the country from which our fathers seceded for sufficient
reasons. If gentlemen wish to draw curious comparisons, they
may do so. But it is hardly worth while to inquire how far we meet
the pleasure of Mill or Bagehot, inasmuch as the point in issue is
simply this, "Do we succeed in governing ourselves to our own
satisfaction, and with reasonably good results?" We certainly do,
and that is sufficient. If Mr. Wilson had explained the practical
working of our government, including Congress, the Executive,
and the Supreme Court, or if he had simply explained the highly
complicated working of Congress, somewhat after the pattern of
Todd's classical work on Parliamentary government, he would
have enriched the public literature of our country more than he
has. But when he points out that we are not like England, and
that Congress is not like Parliament, he simply points out that
we have accomplished our object in seceding from British rule.
Again, when he points out that the lines between our federal and
State systems are not drawn very closely, he says simply that we
live under a practical rather than under a scientific government
—as do our good cousins, the English. To fancy the English sys-

tem perfect, is a pleasant dream in which some young Americans indulge. When one investigates that system, its limited suffrage, its absurdities in Parliament, and its coarse blundering as illustrated by Ireland and Egypt, it ceases to be an ideal, and becomes a subject suitable for criticism just like our own. Mr. Wilson is very unhappy in assigning to the debates of Parliament "an interest altogether denied to the proceedings of Congress." The debates in Congress are certainly more intelligent than those of the Imperial Parliament. It is only on exceptional occasions that the sessions of Parliament are attended by more than one-tenth of the members. Those who attend do not make good speeches. Congress is nearly always attended by four-fifths of the members, and they make good speeches. It is a little irritating, therefore, to read that Parliament is more interesting than Congress. "Congress," as Mr. Wilson himself says, "is fast becoming the governing body of the nation." He might have added that a United States Senator wields far more power than an English peer, and that the American President wields infinitely more power than does Queen Victoria or her prime-minister. Mr. Wilson cannot have gone very deep into his subject, as he imagines that "the editor directs public opinion, the congressman obeys it." If ever the press has induced Congress to pass one important law, what is it? Or if Mr. Wilson has ever managed a political sheet, what has he achieved? What he really hates, is the vast power wielded by the chairmen of the leading committees in Congress. What he would prefer is that we be a little more English. But on that point he is a hundred years too late. Well or ill, the cabinet consists simply of the President's deputies or clerks. Well or ill, our Supreme Court has powers far superior to those of the highest English Court. Well or ill, our Congress has ten leaders where Parliament has one. Well or ill, our system resembles the English system as a square resembles a circle, though Mr. Wilson tries to square this circle. His work is eminently readable and highly suggestive. But when it intimates that our practical system differs from his fanciful ideal of the English system, one need not mourn any more than one needs to shed tears because the Hudson is not exactly like the Thames, or the Rocky Mountains differ from the Scotch hillocks. What we need in this country is not a critique of our government, federal or municipal, but a little more understanding of its machinery and methods. Criticism and opinions are as cheap and plentiful as are strawberries in their season; an adequate interpretation of Congressional or municipal government does not exist. Let Mr. Wilson try to fill the gap in his next treatise, and let him take Todd for his model.

Printed in the Boston *Beacon*, Feb. 21, 1885.
1 Brackets in the text.

ENCLOSURE II

Albert Shaw's Review of *Congressional Government* in the *Minneapolis Daily Tribune*

[Feb. 15, 1885]

To state without qualification that the modest volume entitled "Congressional Government," which has just issued from the press of Houghton, Mifflin & Co., contains the best critical writing on the American constitution which has appeared since the "Federalist" papers, may seem extravagant; but it is true, and the book will mark an era in our political writing. The author, Mr. Woodrow Wilson, has given the public some taste of his good qualities in occasional contributions to the monthly periodicals; but the present masterly book could scarcely have been expected, and it gives Mr. Wilson an immediate and enviable place as an authoritative writer on the governmental machinery of the United States. Unlike the "Federalist" in purpose, scope, and method as this work is, it can hardly be compared with any other book on the constitution. The "Federalist" had, to be sure, an important object to gain and adopted the tone of advocacy. But its method was critical. It concerned itself with discussing, analytically and objectively, the framework of government which it was proposed to set in motion under the new constitution. Strange as it may seem, from that day until the appearance of Mr. Wilson's book, there has not been a single work which has contemplated, analyzed, and criticised our government as a concrete, objective fact. On the "literary theory" of the constitution there have been numberless books. Scores of commentaries have been written on the text of the constitution. Our wonderful system of divided powers, of checks and balances, of distributed responsibilities, has been dilated upon in whole shelves full of books. The dialectics and metaphysics of our constitutional literature surpass in their subtle refinements the most attenuated theological distinctions to be found in the writings of the medieval schoolmen. A strange superstition has haunted all these constitutional writers. They have dealt wholly with theories, and interpretations, and legal fictions. To not one of them has it occurred to doubt whether the written instrument were, after all, our real, living constitution. Not one of them has had sufficient immunity from the common fetish-worship of the written document, to institute an inquiry as to whether the machinery of government which we now operate, is just the kind of machine which the constitution makers of 1787 planned for. In other words, there has been no such thing as real constitutional criticism.

Mr. Wilson has found the new and true path. He brushes away the dialectical cobwebs and the absurd mysticism which have obscured what ought to be a comprehensible and accessible subject. He frees his mind from all preconceived theories, and in the direct and simple manner of the modern scientific investigator he proceeds to study our actual working governmental machinery of today. He pictures to us, not what the written constitution says he ought to find, but what in fact he does find. So much for Mr. Wilson's method; and now it may be in order to indicate his leading discoveries and leading conclusions. First, he finds the "literary theory" of "equal distribution of powers" and of "checks and balances" to be altogether overthrown by the facts. In place of that even balance of sovereignty between the states and the nation, he finds that the central government has taken things practically into its own hands, and that state sovereignty languishes. Instead of a government in which three "co-ordinate' and "independent" repositories of power, executive, legislative, and judicial, act as a check upon one another, he finds that congress, the legislative department, has gradually obtained supremacy over the other two departments, and that it really controls administration, while it suffers no permanent restraint in its career from the judiciary department. Thus we have developed a system of "congressional government." Mr. Wilson proceeds to analyze congressional government, and finds that it resolves itself into a "government by standing committees." How as a matter of fact the committees, the "forty-eight little legislatures" of the house do digest and formulate legislation, and how they push their authority into every detail of departmental administration, is shown with amplitude of evidence and illustration. It is in the disconnected character of these committees, their lack of correlation, their failure to respond to any unified policy of government, their subdivision and consequent destruction of responsibility, that Mr. Wilson finds the chief defects of the system. The book maintains, throughout, a series of parallels and contrasts between our congressional government and the cabinet government of the English house of commons and the French chambers. The advantages of a union of legislation with executive functions, and of a single legislative committee made up of the ministers of the executive departments, selected from the dominant party and thoroughly responsible for a government policy, are the lesson which Mr. Wilson evidently desires to teach. Many men, who would have rejected his doctrine two or three years ago, will be constrained to accept it in view of the striking manner in which the history of the Forty-eighth congress has borne out the argument which "Congressional Government" so amply elaborates. Those most conversant with our constitutional literature will be most delighted with this book, which inaugurates the "new criticism" of our constitution. What Mr. Bagshot [Bagehot] did for the study of the English system, Mr. Wilson has done for the American.

Printed in the *Minneapolis Daily Tribune*, Feb. 15, 1885.

To Ellen Louise Axson

My own darling,   Balto., Feby. 24, 1885

Mr. Wm F. Ford (of 'Bradstreets,' you know) writes again, begging for "something worth while" about the course of things in this last session of the Forty-eight Congress; so I have yielded and have been spending most of the morning in constructing an 'article' out of sundry sage remarks wh. it is quite easy to make on such a subject. I trust that Mr. Ford will find it "worth while." If he does not, I cannot take time to write another "something" for him.

This writing would remind me, if I needed to be reminded, of the contents of the sweet letter I received this morning, of its questionings with regard to my ambitions. For it *is* an exceedingly sweet and precious letter in my eyes, darling! I cannot tell you how much joy it gives me to have such proofs of the fact that we *are very* close together, with entire community of sympathy and thought; that we already stand heart to heart, in the complete union of perfect love! So you did not find a satisfactory answer to your questions in that early letter of mine? Well, my precious, it is very easy to supply the missing parts of the confession; and, although I would ever so much rather wait till I might *say* such things to you, when I could *feel* and *see* what you were thinking and what you were wondering upon the subject, and how much you were loving me the while, I will try to satisfy my darling now upon her points of doubt. These are *not* "foolish words," little sweetheart, into which you have put your questions, but very sensible, womanly words, which demonstrate your *right* to know 'all my thoughts about those things which most nearly concern me.' You have the title both of love and of understanding.

Yes, darling, there is, and has long been, in my mind a "lurking sense of disappointment and *loss*, as if I had missed from my life something upon which both my gifts and inclinations gave me a claim"; I do feel a very real regret that I have been shut out from my heart's *first*—primary—ambition and purpose, which was, to take an active, if possible a leading, part in public life, and strike out for myself, if I had the ability, a *statesman's* career. That is my heart's—or, rather, my *mind's*—deepest secret, little lady. But don't mistake the feeling for more than it is. It is nothing *more* than a regret; and the more I study the conditions of public service in this country the less *personal* does the regret become. My disappointment is in the fact that there is no room for such a career in this country for *anybody*, rather than in the fact that there is no chance for *me*. Had I had independent means of support, even of the most modest proportions, I should doubtless have sought an entrance into politics *anyhow*, and have tried to fight my way to predominant influence even amidst the hurly-burly and helter-skelter of Congress. I have a strong instinct of leadership, an unmistakably oratorical temperament, and the keenest possible delight in affairs; and it has required very constant and stringent schooling to content me with the sober methods of the scholar and the man of letters. I have no patience for the tedious toil of what is known as 'research'; I have a passion for interpreting great thoughts to the world; I should be complete if I could inspire a great movement of opinion, if I could read the experiences of the past into the practical life of the men of to-day and so communicate the thought to the minds of the great mass of the people as to impel them to great political achievements. Burke was a *very* much greater man than Cobden or Bright; but the work of Cobden and Bright is much nearer to the measure of my powers, it seems to me, than the writing of imperishable thoughts upon the greatest problems of politics, which was Burke's mission. I think with you, darling, that "of all the world's workers those which take by far the highest rank are the writers of noble books." If one could choose between the two careers, *with the assurance that he had the capacity for either*, "it seems to *me* there would be no room for hesitation even." But my feeling has been that such literary talents as I have are *secondary* to my equipment for other things: that my power to write was meant to be a handmaiden to my power to speak and to organize action. Of course it is quite possible that I have been all along entirely misled in this view: I am ready to accept the providential ordering of my life as conclusive on that point. Certainly I have taken the course which will, with God's favour, enable me to realize *most* of what I at first proposed to myself, and I do not in the least repine at the necessity which has shut me out from all other courses of life. It is for this reason that I have never made these confessions so fully before: I did not want even to *seem* to be discontented with my lot in life. I shall write with no less diligence of preparation, both moral and mental, and with no less effort to put all that is best of myself into my books because I have had to give up a cherished ambition to be an actor in the affairs about which only my *pen* can now be busy. The new *channels* of work shall not clog my enthusiasm, and nothing shall lower my ideals or make a pause in my effort to realize them! One thing there is which I have now that I did not have when I dreamed and planned about a career as statesman and orator; one thing that I had no conception of then, and which is more to me than the strength and inspiration of *any* ambition:—that one priceless, inestimable thing is *your love*, my Eileen! But continue to love me as you do now, and I shall stop short of the attainment of nothing noble of which my powers are capable! I accept your judgment: the writer's career *is* the highest: and you shall help me to write truely and worthily, to write so that every page shall testify, by its clearness, by its honesty, by its spirit, by its unsoured temper, that I have lived in the light of your love and am altogether

Your own   Woodrow.

ALS (WC, NjP).

A Letter to the Editor of *Bradstreet's*

[*Feb. 24, 1885*]

Sir—   Congressional Government in Practice.[1]

There are some obvious things that may be said about the last session of every Congress. There is, for instance, generally the same fertility attending the introduction of new measures of importance and always the same haste in passing deficiency and other appropriation bills. The appropriations committee ride rough-shod over all business that stands in their way, and both lack of time and lack of opportunity make the other committees hold back. By the time its last session is reached Congress is a superseded body and feels conscious of the fact. Its successors are elected and are waiting to take their places, and if their successors be not in large part their own reëlected selves congressmen sometimes hasten, with much human feeling, to forestall the action of the new Congress by casting fetters or creating embarrassments for it in the shape of some sweeping law not easily disannulled.

But there are some special things to be noted about the closing session of the Forty-eighth Congress. On this 4th of March not only are the House and Senate to receive the usual renewals of membership, but the executive is to be entirely renewed; and for twenty-four years there has been no change like the one now at hand. Whether by reason of these facts or because of an arrearage of unexecuted plans, the administration chose this session as a season for unusual activity. Longer or shorter courses of diplomacy culminated in an unwonted crop of treaties, and almost all political interest centered in executive initiative and senatorial consent. One could not reasonably desire more favorable conditions under which to study the operations of the federal government than have arisen at this critical moment of party history.

It has not often happened in times of peace, since the first half-dozen presidents left office, that the federal administration has taken energetic action in originating any vigorous and consistent line of policy, but President Arthur and Mr. Frelinghuysen conceived and sought to realize a very wide and important plan of commercial regulation and extension. Mr. Foster found the Department of State glad to accept the remarkable treaty which he had laboriously negotiated with the Spanish government.[2] A treaty with Mexico of very similar purpose was earnestly pressed upon the Senate by the Secretary of State,[3] and no conscientious scruples concerning possible consideration owed to England under the provisions of the Clayton-Bulwer treaty prevented the executive from seeking exclusive privileges and undertaking unlimited duties in Nicaragua.[4] But the moment the Senate came to act upon these treaties the sharp limitations of executive initiative in matters of national policy became very apparent, and it was at once evident why such activity on the part of the administration has become exceptional. The treaties with Spain and Nicaragua promptly failed of confirmation by the Senate, and the Mexican treaty, though ratified, was left inoperative by the willful inaction of the House of Representatives. It is not dead, but it sleeps very soundly.

We are not surprised or puzzled by such results in treaty negotiation; but we can readily believe that foreign governments are often greatly confounded by the discovery that in dealing with our federal administration they have been dealing only with titled individuals, not with governmental authorities; that the President or Secretary of State may exert a powerful lobby influence upon the Senate, but can hardly do more than that to secure a ratification of their engagements. This must be the more difficult of comprehension because of the open contradiction it gives to the apparent fact of party government. It would seem that the President is no surer of the support of the Senate when the majority of that body is of his own party than when it is not. He is in no way identified with the policy of the party he represents.

At the opening of this last session of Congress the President recommended in his message measures enough to have kept Congress busy through its longest session—through its entire term indeed. He would have had them modify the tariff and readjust the internal revenue; he urged opinions upon national education, upon the relief of the national banks, upon the regulation of the coinage, upon the control of the currency, upon every matter of present political interest. Of course he knew that Congress would not, and could not at that late hour, act upon his advice—it was a parting manifesto—he was putting himself on record. His single independent power was exercised and displayed, as his impotence had been, in the field of foreign affairs. He commissioned delegates to the Congo Conference. It was quite plain to everybody that representatives of the United States could have no legitimate business in such a conference, and that their presence in it was in direct contradiction of the foreign policy to which we had considered ourselves pledged ever since the administration of Washington, but apparently the Department of State wanted to do something, and this was what it did.[5]

The lesson taught by this session of Congress is very easily read. It brought into as strong a contrast as possible the powers of Congress and the powers of the executive. It confirmed the opinion now everywhere, even though unconsciously, being adopted, namely, that the policy of civil service reform centers in the character and opinions and will of the President, but that in other things his power and purpose are minor factors. It seemed to many persons, doubtless, a narrow and insufficient issue upon which to hinge a presidential campaign when the probable course of the candidates with reference to appointments to office was subordinated to the great questions of tariff and monetary reform, of national education, of bankruptcy laws and like vital concerns. But such a limitation of view was, nevertheless, eminently sensible, because strictly in conformity to plain political facts. In legislation, even in the determination of foreign policy, the

President counts for not half so much as he does in the capacity of chief of the civil service. He is master in a very real sense there; in other things he is only a very important servant of the governing powers of the state. It is proper to choose him primarily with reference to his power over the lesser officers of the state, and only secondarily with reference to his powers of guiding or gainsaying Congress. So long as President Arthur maintained his first modest rôle of chief civil servant he grew in favor with the nation; when he abandoned that rôle for the more ambitious one of an originator of legislative and commercial policy, he at once exposed himself to the sharpest criticism and to a most humiliating succession of defeats. And where he succeeded he was most blamed. The Nicaragua treaty was not quite so foolish as participation in the Congo Conference.

In discussing the treaties the Senate followed the custom, long ago discredited in other legislative assemblies, of going into secret session. It is quite conceivable—indeed, it is perfectly evident—that there are secrets of state which must be confided to the Senate, and which the Senate could not, without culpable neglect of duty, suffer to be divulged; and many delicate questions of diplomacy may require private debate. But there can be no good reason for closing the doors against the public when the general principles of such treaties as those acted upon this session are to be discussed, and the practice of doing so is quite bad enough to be discontinued. It does not identify the Senate with the executive; it makes the public anxious by keeping them in the dark, and it deprives the Senate of its proper privilege of being in such cases the authoritative spokesman of the nation. While the doors are closed the debate goes on in the newspaper press outside with great ardor and freedom, but often without any adequate foundation of official information; and the foreign countries concerned judge of the governmental action to be expected by the tone of the press. While the Nicaragua treaty was under consideration by the Senate the London *Economist* expressed the confident opinion that "the people" of the United States would not suffer the Clayton-Bulwer treaty to be so cavilierly disregarded; they were, it said, too honorably mindful of the solemn character and binding force of international agreements. This shows, on the part of the *Economist*, either a very vague notion of our constitutional machinery or a definite conviction that public opinion is in this country as distinct and ready a governmental force as any other. Policy is supposed really to proceed directly from the people, or, at any rate, as directly from them as from anybody.

Another uncontested presidential election has enabled Congress to leave open the delicate points which technical refinements have created in connection with the counting of the electoral votes, and Mr. Edmunds' language in announcing the result of the election is a very clear index of the extent to which very vital questions have been made subject to the subtle theories of hair-splitting lawyers, with the painful consequence of leaving the results of presidential elections dependent upon the chances of the state of opinion in Congress from time to time.[6]

But the session has been interesting in other ways besides illustrating very forcibly the subsisting relations between Congress and the executive; it has also furnished some curious examples of the methods of federal legislation. Inasmuch as Congress is sure to refuse to allow the President any effective initiative in legislation, it is natural and important to ask what sort of legislation is secured by its own initiative. For a test case, take the question of the silver coinage. There is certainly no question that is more pressing. Congress ought to spare time even amid the hurry of a brief final session to pass an act to stop the coining of 2,000,000 silver dollars per month; and Mr. [Aylett Hawes] Buckner, the chairman of the House Committee on Banking and Currency, did introduce a bill which provided for the suspension of this extraordinary coinage. But when he moved that the bill be referred to his own committee, it became at once evident that the House wanted decisive action postponed. It knew that the Committee on Banking and Currency had already declared themselves in favor of a suspension of this coinage, and that to refer the bill to them would consequently be to invite an immediate favorable report. This was not what the friends of the silver dollar wanted; they refused the reference Mr. Buckner asked for, and sent the bill to the Committee on Coinage. The nature and promptness of the action to be taken depended upon the initiative of the committee to which the bill should be assigned, and the House preferred having it go to a neutral or hostile or doubtful committee to risking an early consideration of a favorable report. The initiative of the committees was recognized as decisive. This dispute over a reference seemed a petty thing, but was really a matter of life or death for the bill. Refusing leadership to the executive, Congress has to choose as its leader, in each case, this, that or the other one of its forty odd standing committees, and in order to choose discreetly is forced to study the temper and opinions of the various committees.

The general results of the session have been negative results.

The measures of the administration were rejected or neglected; the measures of Congress itself have indicated a desire to wait for the new lines of party relation to be laid by the new executive. The value of the session has consisted in the illustrative material it has supplied to students of the Constitution.

Woodrow Wilson.

Printed in *Bradstreet's*, XI (Feb. 28, 1885), 133.

1 This essay bears a striking resemblance to portions of the editorial, "An Irresponsible Government," in the *Minneapolis Daily Tribune*, Feb. 15, 1885, a copy of which WW enclosed in his letter to ELA of Feb. 26, 1885.

2 See A. Shaw to WW, Dec. 19, 1884, n. 2, Vol. 3, for a discussion of this treaty.

3 A commercial treaty with Mexico was signed on January 20, 1883, and transmitted to the Senate on February 3, 1883. That body gave its consent to ratification on March 11, 1884, but the House neglected to pass an enabling act to put its terms into effect.

4 A Nicaraguan-American treaty, signed on December 1, 1884, and transmitted to the Senate nine days later, authorized the United States to construct an interoceanic canal, a railroad, and a telegraph line on Nicaraguan territory. The Senate refused to give its consent to ratification, and President Cleveland withdrew the treaty on March 13, 1885.

5 The Imperial German Chancellor, Bismarck, invited the United States to participate in the Berlin Congo Conference of 1884. Secretary of State Frederick Frelinghuysen accepted the invitation on the understanding that the meeting was to be a conference only, and not a congress, and that the United States reserved the right to decline to accept the decisions of the conference. The American delegates were John A. Kasson and Henry S. Sanford. The conference, which met in Berlin from November 15, 1884, to February 26, 1885, concluded a General Act providing for recognition of the Congo Free State and embodying a series of agreements concerning the navigation of the Congo and Niger rivers, suppression of the slave trade, etc. Contrary to Wilson's implications, the American delegates did play an important role in the conference. President Arthur submitted the protocols of the General Act of Berlin to the Senate, only to provoke widespread congressional and public protests against American meddling in European affairs, protests which Wilson was himself echoing. One of Cleveland's first acts as President was to withdraw the protocols. For a full discussion of this much-ignored chapter in American diplomatic history, see Edward Younger, *John A. Kasson: Politics and Diplomacy from Lincoln to McKinley* (Iowa City, 1955), pp. 322-37.

6 Wilson was referring to the questions, raised most dramatically in the disputed presidential election of 1876, of who should count electoral returns and which returns should be accepted in the event that more than one set of returns were sent in by a state or states. Senator George F. Edmunds of Vermont, President Pro Tempore of the Senate, in announcing the electoral vote for President and Vice-President on February 11, 1885, added the following comment: "And the President of the Senate makes this declaration only as a public statement, in the presence of the two houses of Congress, of the contents of the papers opened and read on this occasion, and not as possessing any authority in law to declare any legal conclusion whatever." A detailed discussion of the constitutional and political issues which prompted this statement appeared in the New York *Nation*, XL (Feb. 19, 1885), 150, 152. The Electoral Count Act, approved February 3, 1887, established definitive criteria and procedures for counting the electoral vote.

Two Letters from Ellen Louise Axson

My darling Woodrow,   New York, Feb. 24/85.

We are getting so very deep in that perspective business now that on the night after the lecture I have little time for anything else but to try and get those dreadful problems disposed of before they slip me altogether;—but I am glad to say we are almost through now, there are but two more lectures. Such an elaborate course was very unnecessary for most of us. We will have not the slightest use for a great deal of it, and we will therefore promptly forget it. But we will hope, at any rate, that it was "good exercise for the mind." But all this is by the way; I merely started out to explain why I did not write last night. I see you don't think these things as good an excuse as headaches! The *immediate* cause of my delays in writing is however always the cold room,— my promise on that point, combined with my experience that it is a great deal worse to sit in a room which is growing more chilly every moment than in one which was cold to begin with;—the one *always* give me a dreadful cold, the other I can do "with impunity." But I *would* have put off writing on that Wednesday night if your letter of that morning had been of less engrossing interest, —if it had not been on a subject which concerned you so closely and immediately. I scarcely dare advise you, dear, about the degree, for I haven't had the opportunity to learn by observation *just how much* cramming you can do without risk. That is something which I suppose only you yourself can know. Of course, I recognize the importance of the degree, and appreciate your "strong inclination" to do all that you would be justified in doing to win it. But did you not say that "cramming pure and simple" was harder than the full reading courses? Still I see that there might be much room for choice between a moderate amount of very hard work and an overwhelming weight of a sort less fatiguing in itself. Evidently the powers that be are ready to give you every advantage in *their* power. Would it be possible to relieve yourself in other ways?—put off Dr. Ely—lighten your class-work, or postpone your preparation for next year? But I must be on my way. Excuse haste. I love you darling more than life, and will be forever,   Your own Eileen.

My darling Woodrow,   New York, Feb. 24/85
    Of course I knew last year that Washington and the John's Hopkins were twins! but I had entirely forgotten it, and had no idea yesterday that you were having such a grand time;—I hope you enjoyed it all, and are not in any way the worse for wear today. I hope the glee club scored as great a triumph as it did last year; am glad it revived enough to take it's part, it seems to be

in a rather languishing condition this year, is it not? I never hear of it.

How did you enjoy the dinner at Mrs. Bird's, by the way; and how do you like her? I have heard of *her* all my life.

Mr. Shaw's article is *splendid* the best I have seen, I think;— he says just the right thing and he says it with such evident sincerity. I am very glad you have such a fine notice in an influential western paper. Mr. Shinn ought to write you one or two good ones for Cal. papers and magazines. It *is* astonishing that such a preposterous article as this other should be tolerated in a *Boston* paper. Both as regards manner and matter it sounds as though it might have come from a *Rome* paper for instance. I wonder if *he* takes Todd for his model! I dont think I ever saw in any article before so *much* assertion and so *little* argument. May you and the truth never have any more formidable enemies. I believe I would a little rather have such idiots as that against me than for me!

I have had a long pleasant afternoon at the water-colour exhibition. It is the best display of home talents I have yet seen here; there were really some charming bits. The exhibition included that of the American etchers club; and it was *splendid*. I liked the etchings much better than the water-colours,—some of them were perfectly lovely, and they were almost all excellent. But I must say "good-night" for I am so sleepy now I can scarcely keep my eyes open, and I have heaps of things to do yet. I love you my darling, ah! nobody knows how I love you! What would I not give for one glimpse of you tonight! You are all in all to

Your own Eileen.

ALS (WP, DLC).

To Ellen Louise Axson

My own darling,   Balto., Feby. 25, 1885

I think that I can tell you a secret of your own which possibly you have not yourself discovered, though it is revealed between the lines of one or two—perhaps of all—the letters you have written me recently. It is this, little sweetheart, that your love for me has received accessions of warmth and delight *since you pledged yourself for June*, because that promise has added definiteness to that sense of *identity* which is such a joy to us both. Isn't that the secret of that sweet "peace of heart" which you confess to feeling at thought of the fact that we have been drawn so close together, into such a blessed assurance of perfect union, as the months of our engagement have revealed us more and more perfectly to each other? Is it not true that this promise, by bringing you to a direct acknowledgment that your heart and will are ready, as mine are, for our marriage, has made you more vividly conscious that we stand together already in the closest and sweetest relations of perfect love and intimacy? I know that it has had such an effect upon me. It has given form and sanction, as it were, to that idea which from the very first moment of my love for you has been the idea which I most delighted to dwell upon, and to try to realize, the idea that you were to be absolutely mine; that love was to make us closer kin than blood could have made us; that every thing that was mine was to be yours and that you would feel that it was your chief gladness that it was so; that you were to be the presiding spirit and the light of my home, my heart's queen; that we were to be *one*, by free confession and joyful practice. Having promised, you are loving without reserve: and *I*—am living in the growing consciousness that my heart's sweetest dream has been realized: that I am all in all to the woman whom I can and do and ever shall love with all the powers of my heart! Love-making was very delicious in those first days, but how much *more* delicious—or, rather, how much more a matter linked with our *life*—it is now! We could not do without each other now! You see, little lady, I am still answering that wonderful letter that you wrote on Sunday night: I answered only one part of it yesterday. Now I want to return as full a response as I can to that part which contains you[r] most direct love-message. I hope, sweetness, that *all* your misgivings about the outcome of my love for you are dispelled now. There seems to be absolutely no limit to that love's powers of *increase*, and, if you will trust it altogether, it can, *I am sure*, satisfy even your loving heart. Love seems to be woman's special province, and my darling is gifted beyond other women in this regard; but you have, besides, the power of inspiring love as great as your own, and you have shown me that greater than any other power I have is my power to love my precious Eileen.

Your own   Woodrow.

ALS (WC, NjP).

From Ellen Louise Axson

New York, Feb. 25/85.

Your morning's letter my darling has given me much food for thought all day, as you can imagine. I *ought* to be satisfied with

so full an answer to my questions,—and yet I am *not* quite satisfied!—because you have not yet given me any good reason *why*
you have had to give up conclusively your "cherished ambition"!
I suspect that you have given me no such reason because there
is none!—and you *have not* given it up!—except for the present,
of course. It wouldn't be like you to give up you[r] birth-right so
easily;—and I don't see why you should,—unless you *know* that the
conditions of public life in America are—and are certain to remain for *scores* of years to come—such as no proud and honourable man can consent to be subjected to. And you *can't* be *certain*
of that, you know; they may have "cabinet government" before
you are forty—with your good help!—and you may be a member
of it. "The present state of things is too intolerable to last," you
know, and when the change comes there will be "room for such
a career as you wish." No young man of twenty-eight need begin
to talk of disappointed ambitions, for life is all before him, and
full of possibilities. True you can't enter on that career as early
as some,—you can't begin like *Jeab Wright* as an infant phenomenon "stumping the district" for the party candidate and as soon
as you are of age for yourself! But though the arts of the dema-
gogue, or at least of the popular local politician, seem to afford
the shortest cut to political prominence that surely is'nt the *only*
road thither. I can't think so badly of my country as that. You
will find a statelier entrance-way,—one more worthy of you. It
all comes to the same thing in the end, they are busy during the
first part of their career in making "a record" for themselves and
so are you,—such a record as they could not even dream of, or
hope for. You can indeed make your power to write a handmaiden
or a forerunner of your power to speak and organize. And people
can't say of you, as of some, that *because* you are a writer you
are man of theory,—and unfitted for practical politics;—for the
writings themselves are so practical that they are proof positive
of your fitness. And you can well afford to wait for your opportunity. Even some of those who take the beaten track, like my
cousin Ed,[1] say it is a great mistake to seek for office too soon.
Someday perhaps when you are in the thick of the fight, however
keen your delight in it, you may be very glad that your early years
afforded you quiet and leisure for doing your best in the other
direction in which your powers enable you to excel.

Fortunately you do know that you are on the right track and
that must ensure you peace of mind; that part of the path which
lies just before you is perfectly plain, and we need not be too
anxious as to the direction it will take later on. In fact *my* chief

concern just now is that you shouldn't "feel bad" as you go your way!—that you shouldn't suffer the pangs of disappointment and regret. I want you to believe as thoroughly as I do that your destiny will work itself out *all in good time*. And you have convinced me as to what that destiny really is,—or rather you have caused to crystallize, as it were, certain thoughts about you which have been long floating in my mind. That instinct of leadership, oratorical temperament and delight in affairs were given you, I am sure, for some great end.

But I must stop this at once. It is very preposterous in me to write so. I hope you won't draw from my sage remarks the inference that I imagine myself telling you something that you didnt know before! If my words have that *air* they greatly belie the feeling that prompts them. You know one must say just what one thinks sometimes if only to relieve one's own mind.

Whatever career is to be yours, of one thing at least you may [be] sure my darling, that whatever help you may derive from my *perfect* love and sympathy will always be yours.

With all my heart   Your own Eileen.

ALS (WP, DLC).
1 Edward T. Brown.

From Arthur Yager[1]

Dear Wilson: Georgetown Ky. Feb. 25 '85.

I write this note to send you my hearty, though somewhat tardy congratulations upon the successful appearance of your *book*.

I have ordered a copy from the publishers, but have not yet received it. I have seen the highly complimentary review of it in the "Nation" as well as one equally kind one in the N. Y. Examiner[2] et al.; and I have not the least doubt that the good things said of it are perfectly just.

When my copy comes I think I shall review it for the Courier-Journal[3] if I can find time.

Again I congratulate you, Old fellow, "Here's to the bravest! We pledge."

How is the "Glee Club"? and how are all the rest of you?
Very sincerely   Your friend   Arthur Yager

ALS (WP, DLC) with WWhw notation on env.: "Ans. Mar. 2/85."
1 Born Henry County, Ky., Oct. 29, 1858. A.B., Georgetown, Ky., College, 1879; Ph.D., The Johns Hopkins University, 1884. Professor of History and Economics, Georgetown, Ky., College, 1884-1913; president of same institution, 1908-13. Governor of Puerto Rico, 1913-21. Died Dec. 24, 1941.
2 New York *Examiner*, Feb. 12, 1885.
3 Printed as Enclosure II in WW to ELA, March 24, 1885.

A Biographical Note on Wilson in *The Nation*

[Feb. 26, 1885]

We have been informed that Mr. Woodrow Wilson, whose 'Congressional Government' we lately reviewed, has accepted the Chair of History in the Bryn Mawr College for Women. Mr. Wilson, our readers may be pleased to hear, is a product of the new South, a nephew of the Rev. Dr. Woodrow of whom we have recently made frequent mention, a graduate of Princeton (class of '79), and an alumnus (not a graduate) of the Law School of the University of Virginia. While yet an undergraduate he contributed to the *International Review* in 1879 an article of considerable thoughtfulness on "Cabinet Government in the United States," which was followed by the article in the *Overland Monthly* for January, 1884, to which reference was made in our review. These were the precursors of the recently published book, but, in addition to these, Mr. Wilson has made occasional contributions to the newspapers and to college magazines. While attending the Law School of the University of Virginia he was elected editor of the Magazine, and wrote for it two articles, one on John Bright and the other on Gladstone, which established at once for him a high reputation at that institution, and came very near securing its most coveted prize—the Magazine medal. Subsequently, while engaged in the practice of his profession in Atlanta, Georgia, he furnished to the *Evening Post* several very valuable letters on Southern topics. He has now been for two sessions at Johns Hopkins, pursuing a course of History and Political Science. We understand that in Washington his book is being eagerly read by Congressmen, and that its study is generally urged by instructors upon their pupils.[1]

Printed in the New York *Nation*, XL (Feb. 26, 1885), 183.

[1] For WW's reaction and attribution of authorship, see WW to ELA, Feb. 27, 1885.

To Ellen Louise Axson

My own darling, Balto., Feby. 26, 1885

I have just recommitted the folly of having an argument with my friend Levermore—on civil service reform this time—and I am now, consequently, in much the same condition as if I had been trying to talk the sea into silence. The best way in which to work off the chafed excitement will be to have a little chat with my darling!

I liked Mrs. Bird very much indeed, my pet. So long as one has no desire to say anything oneself, her bright, changeful, hearty, cultured talk is very delightful—and her dinner was very good! For one thing, the people she talked about most and best were people whom I know, or know about, and one enjoys *home* gossip.

I enclose two clippings. The review is from the Hartford *Courant*, and the editorial is from Shaw's paper (Bobby [Bridges] has marked it "Fruit," you see—and that is what it evidently is). The *Courant* also had a quotation from the book, and referred editorially to an article in the March *Atlantic* as "an interesting pendant" to "Mr. Woodrow Wilson's admirable study of the present workings of our government machinery"[1]

Yes, the singing passed off very nicely on the 23rd, the President's address was above his usual standard, and the reception in the evening was really brilliant, and quite enjoyable, much to my surprise. I met a large number of people and talked sense and non-sense, according to their various standards of age and mind, with the utmost diligence. You have'nt heard much of the Glee Club recently because the Glee Club (rest its soul!) is dead. The company that sang on the great birthday was a galvanized corpse, so to say. The Club died from lack of 'second tenors'—which is quite analogous to a man's dying for lack of *a body*. For some reasons I mourn its demise: it used to afford me an evening's diversion every week; but for other reasons I am glad it's gone: I can obtain as much and more various relaxation in other ways.

The degree question is settled, little lady. By Dr. Adams' advice, I am not to "come up" this year, but I am to wait until a year or two of routine work with my classes shall have enabled me to come back and stand the tests without any special effort—provided, of course, that I care to come back for a few days of examination then; provided, that is, that I find myself in need of a degree, or desirous of it, then. The work for Dr. Ely could not be postponed because I am under contract with him to finish my part of the treatise by the first of June: and it could be nothing but a burden and hindrance to me to have it on my hands after leaving here.

I am so glad that my darling had such a treat in the water-colour and etching exhibition! I wish that I could have been there with her! A few minutes with her would be more to me—more of delight and of lasting benefit—than weeks and months of these

tedious lectures! I love you, darling!—dearly, passionately—in our separation, almost *desperately*! I am altogether
Your own   Woodrow.

ALS (WC, NjP). Encs.: "An Irresponsible Government," clipped from the *Minneapolis Daily Tribune*, Feb. 15, 1885, and "Our Real Government," clipped from the *Hartford Courant*, Feb. 19, 1885.
1 Brooks Adams, "The Consolidation of the Colonies," *Atlantic Monthly*, LV (March 1885), 302-308.

From the Minutes of the Seminary of Historical and Political Science

Bluntschli Library, Fcby 27, 1885
The Seminary was called to order at 8.25 P.M., Dr. Ely in the chair. Absent: Messrs. Brackett, Lichty, McMahon, Morris, St[e]iguer, Wood, Worthington, and Levermore.

The Minutes of the last meeting, prepared by Mr. Brackett, were read by Mr. Randall.

Mr. Dewey reported the principal contents of the latest numbers of the *Banker's Magazine*.

Dr. Ely read a long and very interesting letter from Dr. Albert Shaw, of Minneapolis, Minn., upon the economic, political, constitutional, and social questions presenting themselves for study in the Northwest. As the principal of these questions Dr. Shaw enumerated:

(1) The municipal institutions of Minneapolis. It was pointed out that the unprecedentedly rapid growth of this city, whose population is now not less than 120,000, made the development of its municipal organization peculiarly interesting, because there had been crowded into its brief history all the difficulties elsewhere dealt with comparatively at leisure. As an interesting particular of administration in Minneapolis, it was mentioned that no liquor saloons were allowed outside of certain central patrol districts.

(2) The Coöperative Coopers of Minneapolis were referred to as affording a very remarkable example of voluntary productive coöperation. Of 700 coöpers in the city, 450 are grouped in seven coöperative shops. Two-thirds of the whole number have fallen in with the plan; and the credit and standing of their organizations are everything that could be desired, their success, moreover, exerting the very best sort of moral effect.

(3) The Milling Industry and Wheat Cultivation. Though there was no milling in Minneapolis 15 years ago, it is now the

greatest manufacturing point in the world for the chief food of the world; and the State of Minn. produces more than ten times as much wheat as is needed for home consumption. It is estimated that within two or three years we will export more flour than wheat; already the immense yields of the mills and of the wheat-fields have brought the prices of bread-stuffs lower than they ever were before. These facts must, of course, influence both agriculture and commerce both here and in England, and must, as Dr. Ely pointed out, have a direct effect upon *rents*.

(4) The Mississippi river, its history, politics, and economics.

(5) Transportation Routes. Dr. Shaw called attention to construction of the Pac. R. Rs. as probably more important than any other historical event for a very long period, the Civil War alone excepted, and laid great emphasis upon the influence of the great railroad systems in determining whither commerce shall run, and where, consequently, great cities shall rise. Nature intended the site of Duluth for a city: the railroads chose instead the site of Minneapolis.

(6) The economics of *Land*. It is in the West and Northwest that the completest tests of all the doctrines of economics concerning land and its rent are to be found.

(7) Political consequences of the Homestead Act, wh. has made of Iowa, Kansas, Nebraska, and Dakota prosperous and homogeneous agricultural communities.

(8) Society in the "Great American Desert"—that sinuous strip of country, from four to five hundred miles wide, which runs for 12 hundred miles along the Eastern side of the Rocky Mountains. This is the most novel field of study in all the West. This desert region, almost unwatered, constitutes the great grazing belt of the continent and is occupied by a nomadic people, possessing vast flocks and herds, ruled by a local confederation of shieks, obeying unwritten customs as strong as law, and settling their affairs in two great annual assizes.

(9) Land-ownership in the "Great American Desert." In this great section of country the Homestead Act has wrought nothing but mischief: it is meant to foster agriculture, and there agriculture can find no place. In Dakota there are cattle and agricultural lands both and there both the beneficent and the disastrous workings of this law are to be seen. The cattle raisers violate it and circumvent it; the farmers prosper by it. What laws are to be made for the Desert?

(10) Constitutional questions, such as *prohibition* in Iowa.

(11) Minority representation in Ill. Mr. Shaw attributed the

present deadlock in the Legislature of Ill. directly to minority representation. It was by means of this device that Mr. Haines obtained his seat.

(12) Criminal administration in the West. Lynchings are twice as numerous as jury trials; and the Iowa Constitution authorizes the Legislature to abolish the grand-jury system, as has already been done in several States.

(13) The ethical, social, and economical bearings of Exemption and collection laws.

(14) The taxation of Railroads, with comparisons of the systems obtaining here and abroad. In Minn. the railroads are exempted from local taxation but pay a large amount to the State in the shape of a tax on their gross-earnings.

After finishing Dr. Shaws letter, Dr. Ely read a brief paper upon Administration, prefacing the reading of it by calling attention to two points of interest in French administrative practice: namely (1) That over each administrative dept., large or small, a single officer is placed who is held strictly responsible for the workings of his dept., though he is often assisted by a council of advice. (2) Courts for the enforcement of administrative laws.

In his paper Dr. Ely dwelt upon the importance of administrative study; upon the special necessity for it in this country, in view of the fact that our administration is the worst in the world; and upon the strange apathy which has hitherto reigned in the U.S. with regard to questions of this nature.

Seminary adjourned at 9:30 P.M.

Woodrow Wilson   Scribe

WWhw entry, bound ledger book (MdBJ).

From Ellen Louise Axson

My darling Woodrow,   New York, Feb 27/85.

I was so desperately busy last night that much as I wished, I *could not* find time to answer your sweet letter. I won't pretend to answer it now either, when I am in such haste, but wait 'till tonight. It is especially important that I should be at the Met betimes this morning;—and besides I have taken so much time this week for galleries &c. We had a lovely time yesterday at Mr. Beckwith's studio. It was his reception day, and one of the girls who knew him invited me to go with her, and we also went by invitation to Mr. Flagg's studio.

I am so relieved, darling, about the degree;—this arrangement is very satisfactory I should think. I would not have you risk your health for *anything*, and yet I am very glad you are not to be cheated out of your degree altogether.

That is a splendid notice from the Hartford paper, is it not? And the other article is very encouraging, as showing that the leaven has begun to work. The "Nation" is "paying you marked attention"—I see they have a biographical sketch of you this week. Is that Mr. Bridges doing's?

Please excuse this scrawl—I write at breakneck speed. Believe me darling with all my heart   Your own Eileen.

ALS (WP, DLC) with WWhw notation on env.

To Ellen Louise Axson

Balto., Feby. 27, 1885

You certainly know, my matchless little sweetheart, how to answer my letters in the way of which my heart most approves—probably because your answers come so directly from your own loving heart! I want my darling *always* to open her whole mind to me as she has done in this sweet, womanly answer to my letter of Tuesday. I am afraid, however, that I cannot agree with the conclusions which she announces concerning the probabilities of my future career. I have not given up all idea of entering public life because I have given up all hope of seeing the conditions of public life bettered before I am too old to go actively into politics: but because I see very clearly (and entirely without regret, of course, so far as the single fact is concerned) that I shall all my life be under the necessity of *earning a living*. I expect to see a very rapid as well as a very early reform of our methods of party government—a reform which will open the doors to the most honourable and the most gifted; but I do *not* expect to inherit or to earn an independent fortune. The lawyer's office is much nearer Congress and the cabinet than a professor's chair, and money-making is possible in the former, impossible (or next to impossible) in the latter: I should have stayed where I was if I hoped to enter politics. But I saw that in every *electoral* system, and especially in ours, there are innumerable chances of defeat. It is often—particularly for a man of independent action—easier to lose than to gain a hold upon a constituency: and men in this country are, by long-settled policy, allowed to have no constituency but that which lives immediately around them, are suffered to represent no district but the one in which they live. And to lose his political place is, for the poor man, to find himself without *any* place. In his business—in his private profession, whatever it may be—he finds himself forced to begin all over again. Nobody wants a man who has tasted of political office, and so gotten political excitement into his blood, to manage the delicate details of his law business for him—and certainly no university or college board wants a politician in its faculty. For a man who has no independent means of support, the chances of defeat are the chances of *poverty*, are the chances of financial ruin. The youth who plans a one-day entrance into political life had better begin early to earn and to hoard, to acquire and multiply, money. He cannot afford to trust to the salary of political office for a livelihood: he cannot afford to be elected to-day unless he can afford to be defeated five or ten years hence.

Of course an unusual combination of fortunate circumstances may open a public career to me and give me a chance to find out whether or not I really do possess the peculiar talents which I have imagined myself to have; but that is an extremely remote contingency, and is by no means worth looking forward to. And you must not distress yourself with the belief, darling, that my regret at having been shut out from the life towards which my first and strongest desires drew me is accompanied with anything like *pain*, or with a sense of failure, of having taken that work which I can do second-best and missed that for which I was intended. As I said in my other letter, I am quite ready to believe that it was simply strong desire, not *instinct*, upon which that ambition was founded. I accept my new profession with a profound impression of being providentially directed, and accept it with pleasure, enthusiasm, and hope. If the circumstances which have shut me out from politics had been of my own making, I might feel differently: but, as it is, I obey cheerfully the plain dictates of prudence. I have not suffered defeat—I have not lost my proper birthright—I have simply been corrected in my views of myself and my talents and directed to the path which is the only one that leads to the successes I was meant to attain. A man of powerful muscle may regret that he is not a skilled athlete; but he will hardly *sorrow* for the loss by which he has gained some equally creditable skill to which his muscular strength is merely an underservant. I thought once that my ability to write clearly, my familiarity with the use of the pen, was merely to aid me as an orator and a statesman: it turns out that the latent powers of oratory and statesmanship which I possess—if indeed, I possess them at all—were intended to complete my equipment as a *writer* —on politics—in order that I might *see* as a statesman and might tell what I see with words that live and inspire. I am content; I am not baffled. Doubtless I have been pointed to my truest and best victory—provided, that is, that the *Nation* don't ruin me before the campaign is fairly opened! Did you ever see such absolutely ridiculous biographical details as those about me in the "Notes" of this week's number! Oh, "deliver me from my friends, and I will take care of my enemies"! 'Mr. Woodrow Wilson is a young man who has done some tolerable writing for the newspapers and reviews and came very near graduating at the University of Virginia, where he wrote some essays which just missed winning a college prize. Congressmen are eagerly devouring the book recently written by this dear young, mediocre, half-successful creature.' I suppose that Renick must be credited with the happy conception of that ludicrous piece of skilful damning. He supplies the *Nation* with items of various sorts: and no one else is so familiar with the points of my post-graduate biography. Of course he has the very kindest intentions: but the result is none the less fatal: fortunately such an item can't carry very far. It, too, is ephemeral and can be worked off!

But I have my hands full of work to-day, and had no business to talk on to such lengths! Good-bye, precious. Here is your message for Sunday's thoughts: nothing but your love could have made complete and joyous and full of promises of success the life of

Your own   Woodrow.

ALS (WC, NjP).

From Ellen Louise Axson

My darling Woodrow,   New York, Feb. 27/85

Well, my posing ordeal is over again, to my great relief! This time I passed it successfully,—indeed I only took one rest instead of the allotted three as there is nothing specially fatiguing in a sitting pose; it makes one's *mind* more tired than the body for it certainly is a strain to have fifty people stare at you for an hour. I posed this time, in a sort of Evangeline attitude, with my long white cloak and hood, and a plain white "Mother Hubbard" dress. I had quite a time trying to think of something that would do, for we have had almost everything practicable; I even went to a costumer's, as a good many of the class do; but I couldn't be paid to wear their gaudy things. By the way I didn't tell you of the remarkable pose we had yesterday. It was the Jewish high-priest, in a strictly accurate costume,—pomegranates, bells, breastplate and all,—and the man made it all with his own hands! We thought at first that he must be one of the actors in the passion play; but it turns out that he is only a lecturer who carries about with him for the public edification a tremendous model of the tabernacle and all it's contents.

I have just been re-reading less hurriedly the two articles received this morning; they are very good;—"something worth while";—and such editors as those will do some good in the world[.] I suppose the article in the Atlantic to which you allude was "The Consolidation of the Colonies." How do you like it?

By the way I have been reading "The Prophet of the Great Smoky Mountains" and am *delighted*; it is really a powerfully and beautifully written thing.[1] Is Craddock a Southerner?

I do not know, dear, whether or no you have surprised a heart secret of mine undiscovered—even by myself, it may be, I cannot tell. I only know and feel that we *have* been drawing closer together in the months that have passed and that in the same proportion I have been growing more happy in my love; so that now I can well believe that *anything* which serves to complete that "sense of identity" will be only an increase of joy. It *is* my chief gladness, darling, that I am to be absolutely yours. It is but reasonable that such a thought should add to my peace of mind. I have heard a great deal since I came here about "a woman's right to live her own life"! But that is a right from which one derives very little satisfaction unless one is sure that said life is worth living! The chances are that the woman is'nt sure of that. I don't speak of those who are society-women and fritter their lives away. Even those who work most earnestly and with the most definite purpose, are still not free from those uneasy questionings. There remains the doubt lest their work, absorbing as it is to themselves, should prove to be after all but a pretty plaything, of no real use to anyone and insufficient in the end to satisfy their own truest self. We havn't enough faith in ourselves, we women, to find contentment in living for ourselves, we must look beyond and away from ourselves to find something really worthy of our perfect faith and enthusiasm and untiring service. So the best way to still all doubts about the worthiness of our ambitions, and our power to achieve them provided they are worthy,—about the uses and meaning of our life, is to merge that life in *another* about which there *can* be no such doubt. So you see, dear, how much you have done for me, how you have made me at peace with myself, how entirely your love is able to satisfy my *whole* nature. Believe me darling, to be forever   Your own   Eileen.

ALS (WP, DLC).
1 Charles Egbert Craddock [Mary Noailles Murfree], *The Prophet of the Great Smoky Mountains* (New York, 1885). See WW to ELA, March 15, 1885.

From James E. Rhoads

My dear Friend,   Philadelphia. 2 mo. 27, 1885.

Thy favor of the 26th is at hand—and I am much obliged for its list of text-Books. I can easily understand the difficulty of selecting text-Books, every man's conception of the mode in which a subject should be taught differs from anothers, & the methods constantly improve. Thy work has produced so favorable an impression that I feel sure the Trustees will desire to make thee an Associate Professor, with corresponding salary upon the expiration of thy present engagement, if not before. But of this I can not write with any certainty: the working of the College will determine this and other questions.

I appreciate thy incessant labors, and hope thou will care for thy health. The necessity for the list for the Library is not immediate; take time so as not to overtax thy self.

We shall require a set of examination papers to be used in the June examinations, & also in the autumn.

There will be, unhappily, some lack of uniformity in preparation, some having studied the History of Greece & Rome & *most* of them that of England & the U. S.

I think the examination papers had better be made out for the History of England & of the U. S.

Berard's History of England[1] will be a fair specimen of the books studied by most of the students. The papers will *not* be published the first year. They should be a plain practical test as to whether the candidate has knowledge of the outlines of English & American History. The test should be honest not severe, nor should we use catch questions.

With regard, truly thy friend,   James E Rhoads

ALS (WP, DLC) with WWhw notation on env.: "Ans. Feby. 28, 1885."
1 Augusta Blanche Berard, *School History of England* (New York, 1861).

From William F. Ford

My Dear Sir: Bradstreet's. New York, Feb. 27, 1885

I have your manuscript regarding the work of Congress. I shall try and use it this week. It seems to me that you might have confined yourself more closely to the stating of conclusions, with considerable less manuscript as the resultant.

Yours truly   Wm F Ford

TLS (WP, DLC) with WWhw notation on env.: "Ans. Feby 28/85."

From Horace Elisha Scudder

My dear Sir　　　　　　　　　　Boston, 27 February 1885

Very likely you have followed the series which I have in charge of American Commonwealths, the enclosed circular of which will advise you as to the volumes yet to appear. I have not yet assigned North Carolina, yet I think the state one singularly fruitful in what may be called the social influences in politics. I should like very much to have one of my volumes do justice to the Scotch element which has been so vigorous in North Carolina and Tennessee as well as in Pennsylvania. I have somehow formed the impression that you are from North Carolina and very likely of Scottish origin. At any rate I know you will tell me frankly if you have not the special prerequisites for doing the work. Of your ability to prepare a good book I have no doubt, but I wish as far as possible to have each state written by a man who speaks the language of the people and does not approach the subject *ab actia.*

If you will write me on these points and indicate whether your engagements will permit you to undertake the volume I should be glad to write you further.

　　　　　　　　Yours very truly　　H. E. Scudder

ALS (WP, DLC) with WWhw notation on env.: "Ans. March 4/85." Enc. missing.

Albert Shaw's Review of *Congressional Government* in *The Dial*

　　　　　　　　　　　　　　　　　[March 1885]

Our Working Constitution.

Even if Mr. Wilson's book were of indifferent merit as regards its accuracy, its manner, and the pertinence of its conclusions,— whereas in all these respects its excellence is noteworthy,—it would, nevertheless, mark an era in our political writing by reason of its method. It is the first critical analysis of the mechanism of our living and working Constitution that has been published. From 1787 to 1885, a period of ninety-eight years, those masterly papers which collectively we call "The Federalist" have stood unique and solitary, as the only extended work which dealt with the machinery of our political system as with a tangible objective fact. "The Federalist" does not concern itself with the expounding or interpreting of a document; it discusses with critical nicety a proposed system of government, its diverse parts, and the correlations of those parts. "The Federalist" is like an architect's drawing: a picture of a house before the house exists, a projection from plans and specifications. And yet "The Federalist" has remained in vogue even to our day, because no subsequent delineator has given us a picture drawn from the object itself. Even assuming that the builders had succeeded in erecting a house which in its entirety and in every particular was the counterpart of the architect's ideal sketches, is it reasonable to assume that after a century's use no parts have fallen into decay, no additions or subtractions have altered the symmetry of outline, and no changes in modes of living have so remodelled the interior parts that the architect's drawings would no longer faithfully represent the building? The figure is a faulty one, because the real constitution of a country is a living and growing organism which is undergoing constant change by virtue of the vital forces inherent within it, and is not merely the passive subject of attritions and accretions, and of mutations wrought by the hand of time.

The first century of our constitutional literature will be a strange and puzzling subject for the political students of coming generations. It would not be in place here to discuss the curious conjunction of circumstances which led to the apotheosis of the written Constitution. It had become a fetish before Washington retired from the presidency. To question its sanctity and perfection was blasphemy; and the political parties were rival devotees. Its fundamental arrangements were deemed the very essence of political wisdom. Its division of power among three distinct agencies, executive, legislative, judiciary; its perfect and perpetual equipoise of federal and state government, "each sovereign in its respective sphere"; its elaborate system of "checks and balances," by which the equipoises and distributions should be automatically sustained;—all these arrangements constituted a system which was accepted as axiomatic in its universality and perfection. The blind worshippers of the paper instrument never thought of examining the every-day constitutional machine, to ascertain whether the plans and specifications had been carried out. No person doubted for a moment that the theoretical constitution was the actual constitution of the Government. The distinction was not perceptible. So long as this delusion should prevail, it is manifest that there could be no genuinely critical analytical account of our system of government as it was actually operating at any given period. Consequently, in all our voluminous constitutional literature we have had no book which was not based upon the paper instrument of 1787. We have scores of lesser commentaries, which are mere amplifications of the text, and contain the "literary theory" of the Constitution. In men like Marshall, Webster, Kent, and Story, we have a succession of great "expounders" and "interpreters" of the instrument, whose business it has been to develop it into a legal system and to apply it to the determination of specific problems. They deal only with the theories, conceptions, and fictions of law. But, above all, we have what may be called the casuists of the Constitution—the dialecticians, whose logical subtleties and whose refinements of theory and definition have no parallel except in the metaphysical theology of the schoolmen. It is undoubtedly true that up to the close of the late war a majority of our people were imbued with the belief that the nature of the Union was a matter of doctrine, of metaphysics, of political ethics, of logical interpretation, and not, as it really was, simply a matter of fact. It need not seem strange that our constitutional literature has been totally incomprehensible to European minds, when we reflect that John C. Calhoun is its most characteristic representative, and that so practical and objective a matter as the status of the South after the fall of the Confederacy was dealt with in thick volumes as a subject for metaphysical hairsplitting. Dr. O. A. Brownson soars through clouds of transcendental reasoning in his "American Republic," and tells us that he has discovered and proved that we are a nation. John C. Hurd, in an octavo volume of 550 pages ("The Theory of Our National Existence"), which is a marvel of erudition and incomprehensibility, grapples the question: "How do we know our political existence to be a fact?" It is, indeed, a strange spell which has bound the writers on our Constitution. They have bewitched and bewildered their fellow-countrymen into the belief that our political system is something absolutely apart and not comparable with any other system, nor susceptible of study by the matter-of-fact "observational" methods which the modern political investigator is learning to use in common with the whole modern scientific world.

From the superstitions and legal subtleties of the jurists, and the metaphysical dissertations of the political mystics, it is indeed a relief and a refreshment to take up a book like this by Mr. Wilson, which deals altogether with objective facts, and ushers in the new and rational constitutional criticism. Waiving preconceived theories, and rejecting documentary advices as to what he ought to find, Mr. Wilson approaches the constitutional machine of to-day, prepared to examine the concrete thing and to describe its working parts from the disinterested standpoint of a scientific observer. This is the same service which the newer writers on the

English Constitution, conspicuously Mr. Walter Bagehot, have rendered. Mr. Bagehot shows us that the literary theory of the British Constitution, if it ever agreed with the facts, is now obsolete. The central fact of the British Constitution is government by party, through the device of a responsible ministry which links together the legislative and executive departments. And yet the "literary theory" knows nothing of parties or ministerial responsibility to the Commons. Unhampered by rigid written documents, the British Constitution has been silently revolutionized within a century; and nobody fails to perceive that this is so, now that the facts have been pointed out.

But in a country whose constitution is reduced to writing, and where the written instrument is most scrupulously and ostentatiously respected, it is less easy to perceive those subtle but constant and inevitable changes which, behind the documentary screen, are taking place in that developing organism which is the real constitution. Mr. Wilson's opening chapter deals with this contrast between the written and the actual constitution. It describes what, in the main, are the departures from the "literary theory," or from the system which the convention of 1787 intended, and which "The Federalist" describes. It discovers that the elaborate system of checks and balances has practically broken down. The theoretical equipoise between the federal and state governments has no objective reality. The central government, being sole judge of the extent of its own powers, has made steady inroads upon the residuary sovereignty and jurisdiction of the state governments. Again, Mr. Wilson finds that the alleged equality and independence of the three "coördinate" branches of the federal government is little more than a myth. He finds that Congress is supreme. Practically, though of course not theoretically, the legislative department pushes its authority into the uttermost detail of administration. The President and his Cabinet are in point of fact only the heads of the civil service, for Congress forces its own policy upon every bureau and branch of the administrative system. And even the judiciary, in the ultimate analysis, has no independence as a political department of the Government. The Supreme Court acquiesces, and not even makes ineffectual attempts to check the career of Congress. In a rapid but massive array of facts, Mr. Wilson illustrates and pretty soundly establishes the proposition that we are now living under a system which the title of his book fitly defines as "Congressional Government."

Our author next proceeds to analyze "Congressional Government," with a view to discovering all its wheels and cogs, and its precise *modus operandi*. Beginning in the House of Representatives, he devotes 135 pages to a careful study of that body. He finds that the House does nearly all its work through its forty-eight standing committees. These committees claim his most profound attention. In their private meetings all matters of legislation are digested, and each one works for and by itself without any sort of coöperation or general understanding with the rest. Mr. Wilson's elaborate discussion of this committee system, and of the extensive code of House rules under which the system is operated, is the most valuable and original part of his book. As the English Cabinet, which is simply a committee of Parliament, is the centre and pivot of the actual British Constitution, although unknown to the theoretical Constitution, so the standing committees of the House, equally unknown to our "literary theory," are in Mr. Wilson's judgment the cardinal feature of our working constitution. These committees constitute so many "little legislatures," each having cognizance of a limited number of subjects; and they make possible that abnormal inquisitiveness which has given Congress ascendancy over the administrative departments. Some corresponding House committee overhauls and supervises the smallest details of every part of the executive service. And through the constant interference of the committees in the plans and conduct of the departments, Congress rules the President. The author's whole account of how Congress works is an exceedingly lucid and brilliant piece of descriptive and critical writing, and its value is much enhanced by the introduction of vivid parallel pictures of the House of Commons and the French Chamber. The contrast between the tangible and responsible operations of those single ministerial committees which have undisputed leadership in the English and French legislative bodies, and the hap-hazard, contradictory operations of our multiform committee system, is sharply drawn.

Mr. Wilson could not have chosen a better way to present the system concretely than by taking up the subjects of revenue and supply,—those ever-present topics in every legislative body,—and examining our mode of financial administration. There is certainly a painful contrast between the simple and efficient English way of making budgets, granting supplies, and devising ways and means, and our complex and wholly unbusiness-like methods. Twenty-four distinct committees of the two houses of Congress have charge of various branches of legislation pertaining to revenue, expenditure, and currency. By the time the original es-

timates of the departments have been whimsically mutilated by
the standing committees of the two houses, having been further
disfigured in running the gauntlet of the committees of the whole,
and have gone to a conference committee for the hasty compromise of egregious differences between the two chambers, the
session has generally drawn near its close, and the appropriation
bills are finally passed without any knowledge of their contents
and with slight reference to the exact needs of the departments.

A bicameral Congress is, of course, a part of our actual as it
is of our theoretical Constitution, and it does not belong to Mr.
Wilson's present undertaking to discuss the propriety of the arrangement. His chapter on the Senate deals chiefly with the relationship between that body and the Executive. It points out the
manner in which, by magnifying its functions of "ratification"
and of "advice and consent," the Senate has made large encroachments upon the appointing and the treaty-making prerogatives
of the President. "Senatorial courtesy," so-called, has practically
obliged the President to permit Senators to name the federal appointees for their respective states. And the President's treaty-
making power has come to be of very little account. If the administration is so audacious as to enter upon negotiations without having first received its cue from a Senate resolution or a
suggestion emanating from the august Senate Committee on
Foreign Relations, the chances for ratification are extremely
hazardous. The failure of the Arthur-Frehlinghuysen foreign programme readily suggests itself as illustrating Mr. Wilson's argument.

The chapter which treats of the Executive, and the actual position of that department in our system of government, is a masterly discussion. After an analysis of that machinery of parties
which has wholly superseded the theoretical arrangements for
choosing a President, the author proceeds to study the Cabinet—
another leading feature of our real Constitution which has no
well-defined place in the theoretical system. He finds that the
President's duties as an administrative officer practically end
with the appointment of his Cabinet, upon the members of which
devolve the duties and responsibilities of their various departments. These functionaries are selected from one party on the
theory that they have something to do in the way of formulating
a political policy; but this theory does not correspond closely with
the facts. The cabinet officers perform simply ministerial duties,
and they are the servants of Congress rather than of the President. The sort of clandestine and indeterminate relationship

through which Congress holds the departments in subjection is provoking and unsatisfactory on both sides. There is no frank and agreed coöperation. The departments resent Congressional interference, yet are powerless to prevent it. And Congress grows infuriated at the devices which the Executive officers invent for the purpose of evading the legislative will, as witness the controversy over the treatment of the silver dollar by the Treasury department.

Mr. Wilson holds it to be the "radical defect in our federal system that it parcels out power and confuses responsibility as it does. . . . The 'literary theory' of checks and balances is simply a consistent account of what our constitution-makers tried to do; and those checks and balances have proved mischievous just to the extent to which they have succeeded in establishing themselves as realities." Such divided responsibility admits of no governmental policy as the English or French understand that term, and renders it impossible that there should be much Congressional debating of a high order, for the reason that, as Mr. Wilson says, "there is no policy to be attacked or defended, but only a score or two of separate bills." And those bills have been reported from committees made up of both parties. There are no recognized leaders of policy, and none upon whom can be fixed any definite responsibility for things done or things neglected.

"Congressional Government" at once fixes its author's reputation as one of the foremost writers on American political institutions. He fairly deserves the credit of having inaugurated the concrete and scientific study of our political system. Thoughtful and learned essays in the reviews and magazines by Judge Cooley, Senator Hoar, and various others, have treated of the decadence of the presidential elector system, the failure of constitutional checks for the protection of state sovereignty, the subjection of the judiciary, and the complex committee system of Congress. But these articles have been written from the standpoint of the jurist, the legislator, or the practical politician. Neither singly nor collectively do they furnish a conspectus of that great objective reality, the working Constitution. Mr. Wilson is a relentless and unsparing critic, but he is an impartial and faithful witness. As the Forty-eighth Congress expires and the White House again changes occupants, it is scarcely possible for a reader of this book to take a retrospective view of the chaotic events of our recent legislative and administrative history without recognizing the accuracy of the picture drawn in "Congressional Government."

Albert Shaw.

Printed in the Chicago *Dial,* v (March 1885), 291-94.

To Ellen Louise Axson

My own darling,   Balto., March 1, 1885
    I did not write yesterday because I was feeling too badly to
write the sort of letter I like to write to you. I thought that I would
put the *force* of two letters into the one of to-day: but I am no
better this morning, so that I fear that, after all, you will have
to put up with a very dull epistle. My sickness is not such as to
cause you any uneasiness—it's a very small matter and will soon
be entirely gone. Its only considerable effect has been to put me
'out of sorts.'
    I am *so* much vexed at myself for having neglected to ask for a
sketch of this last pose of yours, darling! I had set my heart on
having one—and now I suppose that it's altogether too late, isn't
it? I would give anything I possess for a picture of *my* Evangeline!
I am delighted, little sweetheart, to know that the trial of the
pose is over, and that you came through it so well. I hope for your
sake that it is the last one that you will have to undertake.
    So I did not "surprise a heart secret" of yours after all? Well, I
had a half-confessed suspicion at the time I persuaded myself of
the discovery that my hope was father to the thought, that my
fancy was creating what my heart desired to believe! No reasonable man, however, could wish for more than you do confess—
and certainly I could have no greater joy than that which fills my
heart when you declare that it is your chief gladness that you
are to be absolutely mine!
    I don't wonder that you can have no sympathy with that false
talk about "a woman's right to live her own life." If it means the
right of woman to live apart from men, it is as untrue to the
teachings of history, to the manifestations of Providence, and
to the deepest instincts of the heart as would be the other proposition that *men* have a right to live outside of the family relation.
The family relation is at the foundation of society, is the life and
soul of society, and the women who think that marriage destroys
identity and is not the essential condition of the performance of
their *proper* duties—if they think so *naturally* and not through
disappointment—are the *only* women whom God has intended for
old maids. Their sex is a mere accident. In my opinion, a woman
proves her womanliness, a man his manliness, by longing for the
companionship of marriage, and for all the duties and responsibilities that marriage brings. I have no words in which to express
my contempt for the view which would have it that marriage
belittles a woman! It no more belittles her than it belittles a

man. If it be a marriage of love, it *ennobles* her as nothing else could. If she cannot preserve her individuality in the family—if she cannot make it more felt there than anywhere else—she simply has no individuality worth preserving. It is simply ridiculous to argue as if women were now what they once were, the mere drudges of the household: and, in order to make the creed, that women must take care, for the sake of their own independence, to live exactly the same life that men lead, a creed which will allow society to exist, it must first be provided that men be enabled to assume the sex and the duties abandoned by the mother and the housekeeper! Oh, it is a shame so to pervert the truth! For these people *are* very near a *great* truth—only their little souls are too soiled by selfishness to hold that truth in its *purity*. Women *have* a right to live their own lives. They have mental and moral gifts of a sort and of a perfection that men lack: but they have not the *same* gifts that men have. Their life must *supplement* man's life: and it cannot supplement man's life without being in closest wifely communion with it. This is not putting their lives in a position *subordinate* to the position allotted to men. The colours of the spectrum supplement each other, but without *all* of them we should not have the full splendour of the sun.

And here, little lady, we can find the true rule for analyzing our own case. You do not merge your life in mine from any doubt about your own being worth living separately, or because of any assurance that mine *is* full of the best uses and the best ambitions, but for that other, that glorious, reason, which makes our love for each other so sacred and so real, because neither of our lives would be *complete* without the other. I know that my life would be stripped of the great part of its worthiness and its power to achieve if I did not have you whom to love and to serve, and from whom to receive that love and sympathy which are the life of my heart! And our love warrants me in concluding that it is just the same with you, that it has been my privilege to make your life complete—and, my darling, you cannot know *what* a privilege, what an addition to my manhood, I esteem it!

An old German philosopher,[1] who used to search for—and in most cases *find*, it seems to me—the fundamental psychological facts of society, used to maintain the apparent paradox that no one ever fully realized his own identity until he lost it in the service of love for another, that duty performed at the promptings of the heart was the only true *freedom*. Just as a man realizes his muscular strength in *work*, so he realizes him*self* in *love*. A soldier is no soldier in peace; a heart is no heart in isolation and self-absorption. It is hard to express the idea without seeming to indulge in subtleties; but the *fact* is plain enough. We were not at peace with *ourselves* until we, in a sort, gave those selves away, pledged them in each other's service. Until you loved me I used to be tormented with "uneasy questionings" about *everything* in my future: *now* I am *uneasy* about *nothing* in that future. It is not peculiar to women, my darling, to fail "to find contentment in living for themselves." Men are quite as unable to satisfy themselves with self-service. True-hearted men are quite as far as true-hearted women from craving the privilege of "living their own lives." They all, consciously or unconsciously, testify to the truth of Hegel's beautiful conception, that they can find their true selves only in the love and devotion of family life.

And now, Eileen, you can see the true source of my impatience with the opinion which has served as the text for this long dissertation. It is a pernicious falsehood because it contains so much truth. Its untruth is unspoken. It lies in the implied judgment as to what woman's "own life" should be—in intimating that she has by right a *life apart*. Fortunately love asserts itself quite independently of such crude beliefs! When I come to lecture on the history of society, at Bryn Mawr, I shall make some remarks upon the principles lying at the foundation of the institution of the family which, mayhap, will be hard to forget.

I am quite conscious, little sweetheart, of having expended all this ink in proving to you what you have all along believed just as strongly as I believe it; but I hope that you will not grudge me the indulgence of thus setting forth at length what my love for you seems to make plainer to me every day, the truth of the *freedom* which love brings.

Yes, my pet, Craddock's story in the *Atlantic* is delightful, full of power and of beauty. 'Craddock,' you know, is a *nom de plume*, assumed by a one-time Tennesseean now living in Louisville, I believe. I know very little about him—even of these facts[,] that of the *nom de plume* is the only one I am sure about.

No, I have not read Mr. Adams' "Consolidation of the Colonies" yet, but I shall take time to do so very soon, seeing that it is just in my line.

I have been making some inquiries, my love, about summer resorts, and I am at present very much inclined to believe that we cannot do better than to go to one of the many little villages which nestle among the lakes of Vermont. A Vermont friend of mine at the Hopkins[2] has been telling me about the character and price of accommodations in that charming country, and from his uncoloured Yankee judgments it would appear that we could easily find there scenery, lodgings, and prices just such as we want. And certainly we should be as entirely 'by ourselves' in that far off State as we could be anywhere. At any rate, my inquiries have satisfied me that we can easily find a resort to suit us.

Dear me! what a letter I've written! But it has been splendid medicine: it has nearly made me well! My success in finding a tonic in writing to you has more than once served to corroborate my growing conviction that there is no personal ailment of mine which the thought of your love cannot drive away. Do you wish as much as I do, my darling, I wonder, that you could be present with me always to apply more directly the curative power of that love which is all in all to   Your own   Woodrow.

ALS (WC, NjP).
  ¹ Almost certainly Georg Wilhelm Friedrich Hegel, as Wilson implies in this same paragraph. A copy of Edward Caird, *Hegel* (London, 1883), is in the Wilson Library, DLC.
  ² Undoubtedly Davis R. Dewey.

Two Letters from Ellen Louise Axson

My darling Woodrow,   New York, March 1, 1885.
    As usual I am just in from church, and as usual I am exceedingly hurried. I failed to write last night not because I was so busy but because I was so lazy! Mr. Stimson took a party of six to the water-colour exhibition yesterday afternoon and gave us a sort of critical lecture; it was *delightful*—the best sort of lesson, but it kept us on our feet three solid hours, so that we were rather "used up" when we finally reached home, at half past six. I *actually* went to sleep reading over your letter!—after dinner, and was good for nothing all the evening.

    I did not tell you how artistic I find our bible-class. Miss Carter studies at Cooper's, and Miss Bevier is an old League girl who now has a studio of her own on 14th St.; which I have [been] intending to visit for some time but havnt had time. There are two Miss Beviers, the other being a teacher; they are young orphans alone in the city, and *lovely* girls,—exceedingly intelligent and interesting. They both teach in the Spring St. Mission school and I return with them, to church, every day, which you see does away with one half the "risk"; while I can take the 7th Ave car down, which takes me to the door.

    They have just been singing one of my favourite hymns at church, and it is still singing itself over and over so persistently in my head that I catch myself almost writing it's words instead of my own. "And in that light of life I'll walk—'Till travelling days are done." Oh dear! how I wish I could really sing it! I would give ten years of my life—provided I have so many—to be able to sing. You know you are a perfect mystery to me, I can't understand "a bird that *can* sing and *won't* sing"—except on set occasions and under the most favourable circumstances. I don't see how you can *help* it. If I could sing I should do it *all the time*, regardless of consequences! You don't live up to your privileges sir! But no more for the present. I love you, darling, as my own soul—and better,—and I remain as ever,

Your own   Eileen.

My darling Woodrow,   [New York, March 1, 1885]

I must admit that there *is* a great deal of sound good sense in what you say of the obstacles in the way of a political career for a poor man. And I believe too that you are wise in considering the matter as practically settled, you will thereby the sooner live down your regret and become entirely satisfied with the career which *is* open to you (and which, it cannot be denied, is great enough in its promise of usefulness and fame to satisfy any one man!) I suppose it might make you restless and impatient to dwell much on the other as something possibly within your grasp. If it *should*, after all, *prove* to be within your grasp,—as "it is often the unexpected that happens,"—why it won't be any the less pleasant for being 'unexpected.' I dare say you will find your hands full enough of work, as it is;—(one career is perhaps as much as a man has time for in one lifetime!) I believe that the channels of influence which *are* open will grow wide and deep enough to satisfy your highest ambition,—to answer *every* wish of your heart. And I believe too that whether you are an office-holder or not you will find occasion to make your *personal* influence felt,—to use your tongue as well as your pen. Congress is'nt the only place for oratory; indeed from your own account it is at present a singularly poor place for that sort of power to accomplish anything. After all, politics is a terrible business!—and I don't look at it entirely from the sour grapes standpoint! You know Sidney Smith says, "there is nothing so expensive as glory";—and it seems to me that sort of glory is the *most* expensive of all. What if it should turn out that one can wield as much power as an outside force without subjecting oneself to the miseries of candidacy or the irksome responsibility to a narrow constituency. I think there are many aspects of both office-seeking and office-holding

that must be well-nigh intolerable to a man like yourself. The
wear and tear on him must be terrible; he needs the hide of a
rhinoceros to begin with! You know how little to your taste you
found the struggles of the court-house[.] Ah well! I am sure it
will all come right in the end, and that you *will* "stop short of
nothing noble of which your powers are capable." You say you
will be *complete* if you can ["]inspire a great movement of opinion and impel the people to great political achievements," and
that is what you *will* do, and *are* doing already. As I understand
it, your *end* is the same in any case, and you will be content to
use to that end the *means* which lie nearest to your hands.

But I *wish* you were not to be forever hampered by the struggle for bread. It is *such* a pity! *Why* didnt you marry a rich girl.
That is such an easy way to make a fortune. But I did not mean
to perpetrate another letter of this type, but it is done now and
can't be undone.

Are you excited over the inauguration? Have you any idea
of running down?

That *was* a most absurd and unfortunate notice in the "Nation,"
—one that vexed me very much; but as you say it can't do any
great harm, it is too *small* a thing. And besides it won't probably
strike disinterested parties as offensively as it does us.

Good-night, my darling. Ah! if I could only see you for one
short hour tonight. It seems to me sometimes that my whole
self—thought, feeling,—*all*, is merged in one great longing for the
sight of your face. I love you, Woodrow, with all my soul.

Your own Eileen

ALS (WP, DLC).

To Ellen Louise Axson

My own darling,   Balto., March 2, 1885
    I am feeling all right again this morning, no ache remaining
anywhere. Contrary to usual Monday custom, I have been very
busy at the University to-day: Dr. Ely wants to get away to lecture elsewhere during the latter part of the week, and so takes us
now, in order to get his week's task off of his hands; and Mr. Eugene Schuyler, of the diplomatic service, is here to instruct us
about the organization and workings of the State Department.
I have just come from his first lecture. The lectures which are to
succeed this one will doubtless be more interesting and instructive than it was. To-day he spoke principally of the relations between Congress and the Dept. of State, and with that ground I

am, of course, sufficiently familiar. Indeed, he referred several times to my book as authoritative on the points which he could not stop to dwell upon. He is the author, you know, of that fine history of Peter the Great which came out in installments in Harper's Magazine,[1] and which we are all supposed to have read —though I am quite sure very few of us have!

Our book seems to be meeting with very substantial success in some quarters. I understand that the professor of constitutional law at the University of Maryland tells his classes that they cannot account themselves equipped in his courses until they have read "Cong. Govt."

I received a letter this morning from Horace E. Scudder, the editor of Houghton, Mifflin, & Co's series of "American Commonwealths" asking me to undertake the volume on North Carolina. I am very much afraid, however, that I shall have to decline the task. It is a great temptation to me to accept it—if I might be given abundance of time in which to do it—and I shall not refuse it out of hand. I shall first find out just what the conditions would be. But my necessities of class preparation at Bryn Mawr will be so imperative, and the inducements are so strong to devote all the leisure that I may have to pushing my special studies in administration (there is *some* prospect of my being offered a special chair of the sort I want in the Univ. of Mich.)[2] that it will probably turn out to be the best course not to saddle myself with any other work.

So you wonder at me as at "a bird that *can* sing and *wont* sing"? Well, little sweetheart, you know some birds wont sing till they get a *mate*! You shall teach me to sing for your own private benefit—tho' I never knew before that I *did* need a "set occasion" and "favourable circumstances." With love unbounded

Your own   Woodrow.

ALS (WC, NjP).
[1] Wilson was mistaken. Eugene Schuyler's "Peter the Great" was serialized in *Scribner's Monthly*, xix (Feb. 1880) through xxii (Oct. 1881). It appeared in book form in 1884.
[2] See WW to ELA, March 4, 1885.

From Joseph Ruggles Wilson

My precious son: Wilmn [N. C.] Mar. 2 85.

We are all more or less busily "packing up"—and have reached a point where we are embarrassed by *your* traps. What shall we do with the same?

The congregation met in large assemblage on last Thursday night (26th Feby) and with some grumbling (then & since) have *assented* to my going. The people—all—seem to be deeply grieved. Indeed they are, I fear, beginning to fall apart, at certain lines of division, into quasi parties, I, their gathering centre, being loosefooted and no longer drawing them together. It is a *"Wilson"* Church I am now disposed to think, rather than anything higher or more stable. It would be a source of bitter regret to me were my leaving to have a disintegrating effect—but things look that way. If Presbytery agree (it meets on Wednesday Mar 4— day after to-morrow) I will close my ministry here on the 1st Sabbath of April: and during that same week we will leave for parts as yet unknown—or not fully decided upon. My teeth necessity will detain me in Columbia fr. a couple of weeks. . . .

Your book has attracted a good deal of interest here—and both bookstores have it for sale. I met [T. B.] Kingsbury (of the Star) on yesterday (I mean Saturday) and found him enthusiastic in its praise. He said that there is no Senator or other public man now living who would not be proud to be thought its author! Well your dear mother and I *are* proud, and go strutting about now like peacocks with feathers all spread. Darling it is a remarkable production. One of the reviewing newspapers has, I am told, advised Congress to buy an edition of it for its own use! It is the very book that Cleveland needs, if he only knew it. I wish to thank you again for yr. graceful dedication. Please send me a copy of The Nation with your biographical sketch therein. None can be procured within this empty village.

Your dear mother will write "soon"—to enclose a letter from Jas Bones in which he agrees to square up (I believe, for I cannot bear to read what is written not in sincere heartfulness).

Dear Ellie sent me (by mail) for a birthday gift, a beautiful little thermometer tacked upon a surface of wood about the size of this page, at the left-hand corner whilst the residue of the space has on it a very, very pretty figure painted, of a girl jumping the rope. I felt quite complimented you may be sure.

Dearest boy, do *do* do guard your health. Even quit the Uy if so extreme a measure be thought *at all* necessary—and let study for the present go a-begging.

All send lots and lots of love

Your affectionate   Father.

ALS (WP, DLC) with WWhw notations on env.: "Mr. J. R. Spiegel" and "Ans. March 15/85."

From Alexander Johnston[1]

My Dear Sir: Princeton. N Jy Mch. 2. 1885.

You will excuse my writing you—for the reason that you are, I believe, a Princeton man and have achieved a success, according to the reviews, in a line in which I am much interested. You left Princeton before my arrival here, so that I must suggest to you as a stranger that, if you visit Princeton again in the future, as I hope you will often do, you should look me up and let me give you the welcome you may fairly expect from one who is as much interested in Congressional Government as you are.

Sincerely yours,   Alexander Johnston.

ALS (WP, DLC) with WWhw notation on env.: "Ans. Mar. 7/85."
    [1] Professor of Jurisprudence and Political Economy at Princeton, whom Wilson did in fact succeed in 1890.

To Ellen Louise Axson

My own darling,   Balto., March 3, 1885

I shall presently begin to suspect that *you* are the one who is politically ambitious. You are so constant in your belief that I am *not* satisfied altogether with my present opportunities, and so persistent in the hope that possibly the unexpected will happen and a way into active politics be opened to me after all, that I half believe that you would prefer the other career for me. Well, my precious, you need not wish it for the present anyhow. Nothing but manifest duty would induce me to take even a plain path to Congress—were such a path to be found—under the existing conditions of our public life. Until those conditions are altered radically and finally, I *prefer* outside influence, not only because its ways are more congenial, but also because its *power* is greater. The only difficulty will be in avoiding the danger peculiar to a professor's position, the danger of being accounted a *doctrinaire*. I must make all my writings so conspicuously practical that the sneer will be palpably absurd—a hard enough undertaking, but the better worth accomplishing on that account.

I can't tell you, darling, the feeling that comes over me when I realize that you are really so intensely interested in these things that *can* concern nobody but myself and those that love me! It is a feeling too exalted to be described! As a man could not, I suppose, put into words the consciousness that he is *great*, so he cannot, I am sure, put into words the consciousness that he is *blessed*. The strength and sweetness of your love and the ardour of your sympathy and trust give me a sense of completeness, a serene confidence in the future, which is beyond description, because beyond all comparison blessed! The life of the sweetest woman in the world, the life of my Eileen, the lovely little maiden whom I love with all my heart, is by her own heart's willing *bound up in my life*! Oh, what an unspeakably happy thought that is!

"Why didn't I marry a *rich* girl," Miss? Why because you are the only woman in the world whom I could love with *all* my heart, *and you are not rich*. No riches could have made me happy with a woman whom I did *not* love with a perfect love—and no poverty can make me feel poor with you, so long as you are happy and well. Wealth would be only a *means* of work, of free choice of work, and could never be an *inspiration*, such as your love has been, and always will be so long as it is given as it is now, with a full heart and a perfect faith as to

Your own   Woodrow.

ALS (WP, DLC).

From Ellen Louise Axson

New York, March 3/85

I am *so* delighted, my darling, to hear all these good things about your book—and yourself. You are indeed meeting with "substantial success" in some quarters!—in just the quarters where success is most valuable and gratifying. The people who are best able to judge of your work, and appreciate it, are the ones who invariably praise it most highly;—and that tells the whole story,—shows once for all, the place which your books will take and keep.

These publishers will keep your hands full to overflowing at this rate,—you are evidently to be one of the honoured few of whom it can be said that "the office seeks the man not the man the office." What is the nature of this "Am Commonwealth" series? Are they complete *histories* of the states? I suppose it would give you a great mass of work to do in the way of collecting materials; would it not? That is the worst of such undertakings.

I begin to believe, dear, that it [is] well you are going to a college for women, that you have a special mission to our poor deluded sisters of the north! You speak so wisely and well about those things on which they have gone so strangely astray. Your lecture on "woman's rights" is *excellent*—"apples of gold in pictures of silver"!

By the way, what is all this about the University of Mich? And could you take a chair there if offered, after having signed the contract for Bryn Mawr? Would your Quaker friends let you off?

I am *so* glad to hear that you are feeling "all right" today; I was worried lest your cramming had done you more harm than you thought;—how glad I am that all that is past!

I have a piece of a sketch, which I will send you, which gives some idea of my "pose" on Friday. It is a first attempt—unfinished—of Mr. High's, which I picked up that night. I will try to exchange with one of the girls and get something a little better.

Please excuse haste, I ought to be on my way now, so I am in a desperate hurry.

Don't forget, dear, to tell me all the nice things about your book, &c.—or as many as you can,—I suppose if you told me *all* your compliments [you] would be kept busy. But you don't know with what a glow of delight I read them. With truest love Believe me darling   As ever   Your own Eileen.

ALS (WP, DLC).

From Joseph R. Wilson, Jr.

My dearest brother: Wilmington N. C. March 3rd '85.

Mamma desires me to send you the enclosed letter—which is a reply to her letter—which she told you of. She wishes you to let her know if it is quite satisfactory. Mother says you may think from the letter that she has written Uncle James as to your affairs, but she did not say a word about your marriage. Of course he has heard of your engagement from other sources.

It is a shame that you do not hear from home more regularly. I will try to write oftener after this. I wish you would write to me sometimes. I am so sorry you misunderstood what I said to you in my last letter about your not accepting the professor. I only meant it in fun, and thought you would know it. I did know all about it besides, that is as much as you had told mother and father in your letters.

We are all busy getting things ready for moving. Dear mamma is just about worn out, and she *will* keep on working just as if she was as strong as you or I. Wont you beg her to "take it easy." . . .

We are all quite well, with the exception of mother who is almost worn out. Mama and papa join with me in unbounded love to the brother we talk and think about so much. *Please* write to me *soon*.   Your loving bro.   Joseph.

ALS (WP, DLC) with WWhw notation on env.: "Ans. Mar. 9/85." Enc. missing.

From James E. Rhoads

My dear friend   Philadelphia, 3 mo. 3. 1885.

Two ladies[1] expect to take one or both of the small cottages on the Bryn Mawr grounds,[2] and board professors. I feel assured that they will give satisfaction.

Wilt thou wish to take two connecting rooms at $20 per week —or one room at $9. per week—or two smaller rooms at $18. per week? During what portion of the year would thou wish to occupy the rooms?

Shall they be furnished or would thou prefer to furnish them? The charge would be nearly the same in either case.

Truly thy friend,   James E Rhoads

ALS (WP, DLC) with WWhw notation on env.: "Ans. March 4/85."
 [1] Addie C. Wildgoss and Lizzie R. Hawkins.
 [2] Two cottages that the college had built for faculty housing. See Addie C. Wildgoss to WW, July 30, 1885, n. 1, Vol. 5.

From Ellen Louise Axson

My darling Woodrow,   New York March 4/85

No letter for me this morning,—or at least none from you. I hope you are not worse again, I can't help feeling somewhat worried, remembering how unwell you were on Sat. But I shan't let myself get excited until I see what the night brings forth. Perhaps you have gone to Washington.

What a great day this is for us! I can scarcely realize yet that a thing so unprecedented in our experience is really going to happen. The boys at the League yesterday were mystifying us by offering to lay wagers that Cleveland would never see Washington alive! It was some time before any of us were bright enough to perceive that they meant the father of his country! But my enthusiasm over it all is kept within due bounds by Mr. Heiler's; when one is in sight and hearing of him one can't be *too* proud of being a democrat. He has been feeling "too good for anything this last week"; but happily he has gone to the inauguration now and the house has rest for a time.

I have obtained a sort of a sketch from one of the girls which I will send you. I am informed out of the mouth of two or three witnesses—of strictly unreliable character—that my pose was the prettiest (!) we have had yet! But you certainly would never have guessed it from the results they obtained. I will also send the

long promised perspective outline drawing of my room. You will
think it a queer looking thing, I imagine. I tried to add to the
strictly perspective part, a few details, of course in mere outline,
to make it look a little more as it really does, and the result, being a compromise, is neither scientific nor artistic,—but it gives
(me) a very good idea of the room and it's contents.

I like your Vermont scheme very much, dear; I have no doubt
there is beautiful scenery in all that region,—and that is the first
consideration in choosing a summer resort; the only *essential* in
my eyes. I had thought of New Hampshire. Conway Meadows,
for instance, which I have passed on the train, is almost the most
exquisite place I ever saw,—and of course the two states are very
much alike. Goodbye my darling, and excuse haste. I love you,
oh I love you, 'till my heart aches with loving!

Believe me to be altogether and always

Your own   Eileen.

I will send the unfinished sketch too because it gives a much better idea of the *pose*—the attitude—than the other. The girl who did
it, you see, could'nt get a place on the right—the proper—side.

ALS (WP, DLC).

To John Wildman Moncrief

My dear Sir: Balto., March 4, 1885
I have read with the greatest interest your letter of Feby. 18th,
concerning your efforts to collect a special library of Political Science. The undertaking has of course my very hearty sympathy,
and I am glad to have an opportunity to contribute my little volume to your collection.

There is certainly a very strong educational current setting
towards the study of Political Science in this country. There is
every reason, I think, to expect an early awakening of the fiduci-
ary consciences of boards of Trustees which will result in the
establishment of a great many special chairs for instruction [in]
its several branches. Meantime, we can, even with imperfect
facilities, pursue the study of it with sure promise of the very
richest intellectual reward. You are to be congratulated upon getting early into the field. With much respect,

Yours very sincerely,   Woodrow Wilson

ALS (photostat, RSB Coll., DLC).

To Horace Elisha Scudder

My dear Sir: Balto., Md., Mar. 4/85.

I am in receipt of your kind letter of Feby. 27, and I should like to be in a position to hesitate as to what reply I ought to make. The work you propose would be exceedingly attractive to me, and I should be eager to undertake it, could I be granted a rather generous allowance of time in which to complete it. Although the later history of North Carolina has had rather tame features, its earlier history is, as you say, singularly fruitful in the most interesting materials for a study of the formative social elements which played so prominent a part in the settlement and development of the South and the near Southwest.

But I have *not* the "special prerequisites" for doing the work. You are right in supposing that I am (nominally) from North Carolina and that I am of Scottish origin. But I have no really intimate connections with North Carolina. I lived there only for about two of the ten years during which my father's family has been residing in Wilmington; and my Scotch-Irish blood came to me, not from "the Old North State," but from Virginia (or rather directly from Scotland) and from Pennsylvania. I have lived in each of the South Atlantic States, and can claim a strong sympathy with those feelings and opinions which the original Southern States have in common; but I cannot claim to "speak the language of the people" of North Carolina, and I should probably unconsciously write somewhat "*ab extra*" of its history.

Both these disqualifications, therefore, and the fact that other engagements would render it necessary for me to be very long in doing the work make it for me a course equally of frankness and of prudence to decline an offer which my tastes and my ambitions so strongly incline me to accept.

With much respect,

Yours very sincerely,   Woodrow Wilson

ALS (Scudder Papers, MH).

From Richard Heath Dabney

Heidelberg, Haupt-str. 35, II. March 4th 1885

My dear "Tommy":

I am exceedingly pressed for time, and so will only drop you a postal to thank you for your most welcome & interesting letter,[1] and also, above all, for the copy of "Congressional Government," which I have just received. I read the glorious review of it in the "Nation," and lifted up my voice in a great shout of rejoicing thereat. I also went around to Harry Smith, and we gave each other "the grip" in vigorous style, to express our immense pride at old Φ. Κ. Ψ's possessing the author of "one of the most important books, dealing with political subjects, which have ever issued from the American press." I shall read it just as soon as possible, & shall doubtless enjoy it immensely. Three cheers for you old fellow! Hurrah! I reached here Monday.

Yrs.   R.H.D.

API (WP, DLC).
    [1] WW to R. H. Dabney, Feb. 14, 1885.

To Ellen Louise Axson

Balto., March 4, 1885

No, my darling, I did not "run down" to Washington to-day, though nearly the whole University has gone down, including all the men (4) from this house except solemn little Dr. [J. W.] Caldwell and myself. I wanted to go very much, of course, but I could spare neither the time nor the money. The stoppage of the cramming does not seem to have left me any the less busy. I am to make a report, at the Seminary on Friday night, upon my studies in American Political Economy, which involves the writing of something very like an elaborate essay—and that is what is driving me hard just at present.[1] I am not in the best trim for writing: my wits somehow seem jaded—owing to the low state of my health, doubtless: for, though I am not in *bad* health, I am conscious of not being exactly in good health either. Very little work is needed to make me feel weary, and a great deal of effort is required to keep my spirits up.

The "American Commonwealth series" is a series of state histories uniform in size with the "American Statesmen series," and is intended to do for the histories of the older and more significant States the same work of condensation and popularization that the latter series is doing for the great political biographies. So far there have been volumes on Va., Md., Oregon, and Ky. Some very distinguished men are on the list of writers announced.[2]

I received a delightful letter from dear father this morning in which he speaks with so my [sic] pleasure and admiration of the birthday present you sent him. It was *very* sweet in you, my darling, to think of and do that!—and you don't know how much, how deeply, dear father is touched by such attentions! Why wasn't I admitted to the secret, Miss? It is such a delight to *me*!

Of my book, dear father reports (besides the indulgent admiration of Wilmingtonians), "One of the reviewing newspapers has, I am told, advised Congress to buy an edition of it for its own use!"

The Univ. of Mich. affair amounts only to *this*, that Dr. Adams thinks, from a talk he had recently with the head of the History School[3] there, that they will want me to occupy a special chair of constitutional law and administration sooner of [or] later, when they have accomplished certain reorganizations for which they are now preparing. But it is all a secret (and a *vague* secret at that) as yet; and it would remain to be seen whether or not my Bryn Mawr contract could be annulled.

I am *so* glad, my pet, that you *have* secured a sketch of your pose for me! It was very thoughtful and sweet of you!

Notice how skilfully the enclosed article uses my own phraseology all the way through with only now and then quotation marks!

I love you, darling, with all my heart! I don't know what would become of me without your little love letters these low-spirited times!

Your own   Woodrow.

ALS (WC, NjP). Enc.: "Congress Government," clipped from the Philadelphia *Record*, Feb. 28, 1885.

[1] Actually, Wilson did not deliver this report until March 27. See Minutes of the Seminary of Historical and Political Science, March 27, 1885, and "Draft of a Report to the Historical Seminary" of the same date. Wilson explained the reason for the postponement in his letter to Ellen of March 9, 1885.

[2] Some of the authors announced for Houghton Mifflin's "American Commonwealth" series as of 1885 were John Esten Cooke, Thomas M. Cooley, Alexander Johnston, Josiah Royce, and Nathaniel S. Shaler.

[3] Charles Kendall Adams, Professor of History, University of Michigan, who became President of Cornell University later in 1885.

From Ellen Louise Axson

New York March 4/85.

No, my darling, if *you* are not politically ambitious I, emphatically, am not so for you! For as I have often told you the career which all my life long has seemed to me the greatest, the most honourable, the most desirable in every way is that of an author. And I have always felt more pity for statesmen than anything else; the wear and tear it entails on mind & body,—and alas too often on the spirit too,—is so great. But *of course* I want you to have the desire of your heart, and you had just been telling me in very earnest words that it lay in that direction,—that you craved a part in active life, that you thought your power as a writer was intended to be secondary to your power as a leader among men of action.

But I think that by putting your several letters together I know *exactly* how you feel about the matter, now, and I don't think that you are disappointed exactly or discontented with the prospect before you. And it is a thing in which I *can* have no wish other than yours. Indeed I wonder if there is *anything* left in which I could have a wish apart from yours. There may be such things but they havn't happened to come in my way of late! In great things and in small our *wills* have been as close the one to the other as our hearts. And yet I don't seem to have surrendered my right of private judgment at all! It is a strange power, this of love. What else has power to bring two natures so different as yours and mine (or say as those of man and woman) into such perfect union of heart, such full sympathy,—a sympathy all the more complete because of that difference,—for we could not give it if we were not "the complement of man." It is because my life *is* bound up in yours, my darling; I know well that it is impossible to any life revolving in a separate orbit of it's own. And it makes me more happy than I can say, dear, to think that I can give you something which you need, and which you cannot get from your dearest friends of your own sex; those whose intellectual sympathy with you is the strongest, who in that way are so much better fitted to be your *companions* than I can ever hope to become. They can't love you as I do. You may argue with them as much as you will, but when you grow weary of them (Mr. Livermore or any other,) you will still turn to me for *rest*. And you may be sure, my darling, that *you* shall never turn to me in vain for anything that woman's love can give. With all my heart

                                        Your own Eileen

ALS (WP, DLC).

From Annie Wilson Howe

My darling Brother,   Columbia Mar. 5th 1885.

   I am so sorry you have not been well. Do try to take care of yourself. I have been right sick with a cold—but am better. . . .

   Mr. Hemphill[1] has promised to send me some notices of your book to read. I am *so* glad it has been such a success. I am *very* proud of you. We have not quite finished reading the book yet, for the reason that George and I are reading it together, and he has been *so* busy that we can scarcely find time to read at all. I am not going to wait on him much longer, for I really enjoy the reading of it, and am anxious to finish it. I did not expect to find it so entertaining, I confess, because of the subject—but there is nothing dry about it. Everyone speaks of the dedication of it as being so handsomely expressed. Jimmi Woodrow[2] says he never saw anything he liked better. Don't be shocked with the last two sentences of mine. We are all pretty well, although of course we cannot feel like ourselves—the house seems so sad lonely and unnatural. It seems to me we miss our little darling more and more every day. Geo. unites with me in warmest love to our dear brother,   Annie.

P.S. omitted. ALS (WP, DLC) with WWhw notation on env.: "Ans. March 19/85."
   [1] Rev. Dr. Charles Robert Hemphill, Professor of Biblical Literature at the Columbia Theological Seminary.
   [2] James Hamilton Woodrow.

From Ellen Louise Axson

New York, Mar 5/85

I am so worried—so distressed, my darling, to read in the letter received this afternoon such bad accounts of your health. Can't *something* be done for you? don't you need a tonic? or better still would it not be well for you to take some regular exercise of a vigorous exhilarating sort, even though it does take time and is troublesome. If it really accomplished good,—if it proved to have, as they say, an invigorating, stimulating effect on mind as well as body you would save time by it in the end. It is distressing to think of you in such a "run down" condition already, with so much work and all the debilitating spring weather still before you.

That suggestion to Congress of which your father writes you is a very nice little compliment, I think.

Did you read that letter in the last "Nation" called "Congress in Paralysis,"[1] in which the writer, having before, in it's pages, opposed the admission of the Cabinet to seats in Congress, writes now to say he has changed his mind and wishes to take it all back! I wonder if that is more "fruit."

I am not surprised that you feel tempted to take a share in preparing the "Am Commonwealth" series. These series are so popular and so widely distributed, and the writers engaged upon them are known to rank so high, that I should think it would be of considerable advantage to you; perhaps they would give as much time as you want, since the series is only in it's beginning.

I have just been to a missionary meeting and "afternoon tea" combined at Mrs. Hamilton's;[2] she called the other day and invited me. I had a delightful time. I have entirely lost my heart to Mrs. Hamilton. She is a charming woman,—reminds me a little both in person and manner of your Aunt Marion [Bones]. She is very bright and clever and seems to be full of "business" of one sort and another, committee meetings mission "boards" &c., and yet she is not at all like the ordinary efficient managing northan woman. She is very feminine, and has a singularly sweet, graceful, winning manner. She has three lovely children who are always about her, and whom like the Dr. she frankly adores. Altogether it is a delightful household,—a sort of ideal home. They have an exquisite house by the way—almost too handsome for the pastor of the Scotch Presbyterians; there must be some money in the family.

Goodnight, my darling, I *hope* to hear tomorrow that you are feeling better and brighter. How I *wish* I could do something for you! I love you dear, with all my heart, and am as ever

Your own Eileen.

ALS (WP, DLC).
  [1] S. M. C., "Congress in Paralysis," New York *Nation*, xl (March 5, 1885), 198.
  [2] Mrs. Samuel M. Hamilton, wife of the pastor of the Scotch Presbyterian Church.

To Ellen Louise Axson

My own darling,   Balto., March 5, 1885

I am *very* sorry that my letter of Tuesday should have been so delayed as to cause you even temporary anxiety. You have Dr. Woods (Hiram) to thank for the mishap. I generally make a walk to the P. O. part of each day's exercise—in order that there may be no doubt of my letter reaching you in the morning (the collection from the boxes in this part of town being made at just the wrong hour for me); and on Tuesday I was on my way thither when I met Hiram who insisted that I should turn and walk up town with him, inducing me to drop my letter in a box upon which a collection was promised within a half hour. I don't know how the delay could have occurred, unless collected letters are postponed to others in making up the mails. It shan't happen so again!

I shall wait very eagerly, darling, for those sketches, of your room and of your pose. I have great *faith*, Miss, in the testimony of those witnesses who said that your pose was the prettiest they had had yet—but I am quite prepared to find the sketches quite unable to give more than a hint of how my darling looked.

I wonder, little lady, if all the weeks that must elapse between now and June are to be as long as these that have crept by since I saw you last? If so, I don't see what is to become of me. You have become so essential a part of my life, that I cannot much longer endure separation from you! Your love—and, above all, your love as manifested in your sweet *presence*—supplies, what without it is so lamentably lacking in my life, namely, *peace.* When I am alone—and so shut off from *active* sympathy, from communion with those whom I most trust and love, and who most love and trust me—I take life *too hard,* too seriously; *relaxation* of mind is next to impossible for me—because, without the presence of loved ones to whom I can open my heart, my *mind* is the only thing that has a chance to be exercised. My *heart* is repressed, subordinated. When alone, there is nothing to do but to *think,* no relief from one sort of work but in another sort! One can't hold affectionate intercourse with one's table or lamp. And when I am *not* alone there is nothing to do but to think. A man is expected to meet men and women alike mind to mind, not heart to heart. There is a laugh to drive away "sentiment." Oh, my darling, you cannot love me more than I *need* to be loved. My heart is *so* hungry, and it is hard to *feel* your sympathy through this miserable medium of pen and paper! Must *all* your notes be hurried, little lady? May I not now and then have one that stops to give me an hour, instead of ten minutes, of love? You see, the thoughts that your sweet letters bring me are the only *relaxation* I get!

My darling, I love you with all my heart!

Your own   Woodrow.

ALS (WP, DLC).

From William F. Ford

Dear Sir: New York, March 5 1885

I have received your letter of Feb'y 28th, in reply to my note of the 26th [27th].

I assumed that my judgment could be sent to you in the most direct and simple manner without giving offence. I had no thought of writing you in a censorious way. I believe that, had we been talking together regarding the matter between us, the words which I sent you would not have been taken in an unfriendly spirit. It occurred to me, in reading the article, that a closer classification of the points was possible, and that had this been done the resulting manuscript would have been considerably lessened. It is just possible that I erred in thinking that you would assume for me the many things unexpressed, but always in mind.

It had occurred to me that we had interests in common. I therefore undertook to aid in widening your audience, and I very much regret that you are not disposed to let me continue so great a usefulness. On the morning of receiving your complaining letter I was about to write you to ask the privilege of an interview, after a bit, in Baltimore regarding the bearings of the journalist's work on that of the politician. I had examined with care all your observations in "Congressional Government" on the newspaper. I have completed a fairly exhaustive examination of the state of publicity in the United States and the possibilities as to its further development. I had hoped to speak with you regarding the matter. In an experimental way, for the most part, I have been carrying out some of my notions with respect to a better reporting of the price-making facts of commerce. I am persuaded that the results of my studies have a most important bearing upon the great question which you are doing so much to elucidate. If anything has occurred, calculated to prevent our working together, I, for my part, shall be greatly disappointed.

Yours truly,　Wm F Ford　Editor *Bradstreet's*

TLS (WP, DLC) with WWhw notation on env.: "Ans. Mar. 6/85."

From the Minutes of the Seminary of Historical and Political Science

Bluntschli Library Mch. 6th 1885

The Seminary was called to order at 8-20 by Dr. Adams. The main topic under consideration was an essay entitled "The History of the Appointing Power in the United States," written by Miss Lucy Salmon,[1] of the University of Michigan, for the degree of M.A. The work was reviewed by Mr. Wilson. Great industry and carefulness are shown in its construction, and it will doubtless in the future prove an excellent hand-book. Little critical ability is manifested by the Essayist. E.G. the opinions of the various delegates at the convention for framing the constitution are all faithfully recorded, and then left, with the remark that much may be learned therefrom. No comparison is instituted between the appointing power as it is in this country, and similar institutions in other countries. English appointments are spoken of, but the only suggestion obtained by such investigation is, that English and American appointments have one characteristic in common, viz:—*corruption*. The conclusion seems to be drawn that the remedy for all the evils of our faulty administration is to be found in an application of the doctrines of civil service reform.

Much valuable material has been brought together in the footnotes. . . .

The Seminary adjourned at 9:45[2]

1 Lucy Maynard Salmon, born Fulton, N.Y., July 27, 1853. A.B., University
of Michigan, 1876; A.M., same institution, 1883. Fellow in History, Bryn Mawr
College, 1886-87. Associate Professor of History, Vassar College, 1887-89; Professor of History, same institution, 1889-1927. Died Feb. 24, 1927.

2 The modest scribe on this occasion, as on others, failed to sign the Minutes,
and it is impossible to identify him.

From Ellen Louise Axson

My darling Woodrow,   New York, Mar 6/85.

It evidently is not your fault that the letter of which you speak
was delayed in reaching me; it is probably owing to some change
in postal arrangements either in Baltimore or here, for it has
happened the last three days in succession. Your sweet letter of
yesterday reached me tonight. I am sorry to gather from it,
though you say nothing definite about your health, that you are
feeling no better as yet; but I suppose that as there is no positive
disease, no *positive* improvement can be expected all at once. I
only hope that you *will* improve, as fast as possible. Can't your
friend "Hiram" suggest something that will do you good? Ah how
I wish that I could be with you to do my little all to help and cheer
you! My darling, when I receive such letters as these, letters
which make me *feel* that you *do* need me, that I can, after all, be
of some real use and comfort to you, I long as ardently as even
you could wish for that day which shall end our separation. I
am conscious of but one thought—one feeling,—feeling and
thought being one,—and it is the desire to serve you, to be a comfort to you, to make life in some way easier and sweeter to you[,]
to be to you all that a wife, and only a wife, can be;—everything
else is lost,—merged in that one overwhelming desire;—so true is
it that "perfect love casteth out fear."

There is no *room* in my heart for fear or shame or pride or
anything but love. Ah how my heart yearns toward you, dear
love! My life waits for you, it will not be complete until—indeed
it can properly speaking be said to *begin* only when it has become
a part of your life;—and if you were here I should look you in the
eyes and tell you so,—see if I should not!—"in a voice as clear and
unhesitating as that of a young chorister chanting a credo!" I
want to belong to you altogether, and I am already too entirely
yours at heart to hesitate to confess it.

It is well I *suppose* that those to whom love has never come can have no idea of the *blessedness* of loving;—that in short they don't know what they miss, but think it after all but a light thing or disbelieve it altogether. If I had *known* in those old days how narrow and incomplete was my life without it,—without *you* it seems to me that I *must* have been dissatisfied,—must have longed to find myself by losing myself. And a young person who goes about pining for someone to love isn't an agreeable object to contemplate, you know!

I have been to the studio of my bible class friend Miss Bevier and I am completely fascinated with her work. It strikes me as better than that of any student now at the League. Indeed she seems from all accounts to have been one of Mr. Chase's best pupils; she is certainly very gifted, and then she has had six years of the best training here. She has a delightful studio, but she supports herself by giving lessons in a private school while she struggles upward. I should think she had a very fine future before her in her art, and she is certainly deserving of success—a delightful and interesting little person.

Goodnight, my darling, I love you more than I can express in *any* way. As ever   Your own Eileen.

Isn't this *delicious* weather we are having?
Mar. 7. Your letter has reached me on time this morning, dear.

ALS (WP, DLC).

To Ellen Louise Axson

My own darling,   Balto., March 6, 1885

I have been driven specially hard to-day with work, and must be hard driven till after the Seminary to-night—I have almost literally to *steal* this hour in which to write to you—but the work, for all its hurry, is not telling on me as it might some days, because such a fund of sweet love was poured into my heart this morning by the note that came to me from my matchless little queen! Oh, my darling, you don't know what you do for me when you open your heart to me thus and show me, what I am all the while so longing to see, your love, your wonderful and precious woman's love, for me!

But where, little lady, did you get this idea that my male friends are, because of intellectual sympathy, "so much better fitted to be my *companions* than you can ever hope to become"? That conclusion is quite contrary to the fundamental principle of my recent lecture on the relations of the sexes. The best *in-*

tellectual companionship that one can enjoy is companionship with one whose mind is *different* from one's own. *Here*, as well as in other things, women as [are] the best complement of men. I can find in my own sex no intellectual superiority over yours, but I every day recognize an intellectual *difference* between men and women, and I conceive that it is this difference which makes it tolerable for the two sexes to live together. Men suffice men for a certain sort of argument, for supplementing, as it were, the clearness, the colour, or the personal elements of the same general point of view. Carlyle differed from Gladstone, it seems to me, mainly in having the dyspepsia and living a life which confirmed and aggravated the disease: do not men differ only in *degree*? Lewes could not have lived with Marian Evans if she had *really* been *George* Eliot. Any intelligent woman who loves her husband and will take care to have a sympathetic *understanding* of his opinions and mental habits can supply just what he needs of *intellectual* suggestion—can give him what he can get from no man. He could not do without the stimulation he gets from other men: but, if he once feel the stimulation he can get from a woman, he will know that *still less* can he do without that. And, if my darling says that she is my intellectual inferior and cannot hope to give me such aid, I say simply that she is mistaken: and my proof is the fact that *already*, little as we have been together, I *have* received just such aid from her. I do not ask her to admit, or to believe, what I believe, that she is gifted beyond any of her sex that I have known: I ask her only to accept my testimony that her mind is the one that mine needs as its supplement: and to believe that her loving companionship will be not only my heart's ease but also my mind's strength. You are my equal, darling, in *every* way: only you rule as *queen consort*, not as king. And, if "Cong. Govt." was in part your own inspiration, what will you *not* contribute to what I shall write when you are always at my side! Oh, my darling, I love you, I believe in you, I trust you, I admire you: I could not be anything but
                                        Your own   Woodrow.

ALS (WP, DLC).

From Ellen Louise Axson

My darling Woodrow,   New York, Mar. 7/85
    It was *very* good of you to steal time to write me such a sweet letter as this before me when you were so busy; and I assure you I appreciate it.

Is this the Seminary meeting at which you must make your report concerning the American political economists? I hope so; —I am always glad now when you have gotten any one of your too numerous tasks off your hands. This is a wonderfully sweet and precious letter, my darling,—the one received this morning—and it has made me very happy.

I would *so* like to believe what you say about my power to give you the companionship you most need; why should I not believe it then? You ought to know best about it, I suppose! and I surely have every reason to put all confidence in your judgment. I remember that our friend Hamerton's opinion coincides with yours. "A woman helps a man, not so much by adding to his ideas as by understanding him," and she is his best helper because she best ["]understands him and sympathizes most truly with him."[1] Of so much at least I may be sure, dear, that your little sweetheart can have "a sympathetic understanding of your opinions and mental habits";—it isn't *understanding* that she lacks but *knowledge*. May she not borrow those words, which, in truth, become her in speaking to you so much more than they did the noble lady of Belmont in addressing the gay young spendthrift whom she honoured with her love—

> "but the full sum of me
> Is sum of nothing; which to term in gross,
> Is an unlessoned girl, unschooled, unpractis'd
> Happy in this, she is not yet so old
> But she may learn; happier than this,
> She is not bred so dull but she can learn;
> Happiest of all, is, that her gentle spirit
> Commits itself to yours, to be directed,
> As from her lord, her governor, her king."[2]

No my darling, I *won't* say that. I cannot hope to give you such aid as you need and describe; I *will* be "the cricket on the lyre."

But I have piles of things to do, and must write no more now. My darling I love you, I believe in you, I trust you, I admire you; I could not be anything but   Your own   Eileen.

ALS (WP, DLC).

[1] Ellen was quoting from memory. A passage phrased in similar language appears in Philip G. Hamerton, *The Intellectual Life* (Boston, 1873), p. 236.

[2] From *The Merchant of Venice*, Act III, Scene ii. Ellen made one significant alteration or error, substituting "nothing" for "something" in the second line of her quotation.

To Albert Shaw

My dear Shaw,   Balto., March 7, 1885

I must write you a few lines, at least, to express some part of my thanks for your reviews of my book in the *Tribune* and the *Dial*. They have given me the deepest sort of pleasure and the most genuine sort of encouragement. Your understanding of my aims is so sympathetic, that I feel like the ruler of a principality who has secured the alliance of a great power. It would really seem, from the tone of the best journals in speaking of my book, that the public mind is fast becoming ready for the 'new criticism' of our institutions: and, if that be so, it need not be very long before genuine and intelligent reform may begin. Anything like a combination of forces by the leading newspapers of the country in behalf of definite measures might, it seems to me, work wonders even now; and the editor of *Bradstreets* writes me in a way which seems to mean that he is in favor of such agitation.[1] The *Nation* has long manifested a leaning towards responsible Cabinet government.

Dr. Ely read your letter to the Seminary, as advertised, and, for my part, I enjoyed it altogether. It set me to wishing that I could go out and tackle some of those problems on their native heath. I believe that I was most attracted by the monographic possibilities, so to speak, of "the Great American Desert." I was made Secretary the night your letter was read and I took a full shorthand analysis of its contents, which I served up to the boys last night: so that you've gone on record.

We are having a brief course of lectures by Eugene Schuyler on the State Dept. and the consular and diplomatic services—a course which he is also delivering in N. Y., I believe. It is shrewdly suspected that Mr. S. is utilizing Univ. and other lecture-rooms as a means of indirectly advancing his candidacy for an Assistant Sect'yship of State!

Most of the Hopkins emptied itself into Washington on inauguration day; and the boys have not all recovered from the effects of the spree yet. At Friday morning lecture (we had no classes on Thursday) Dr. Adams could hardly leave the subject of what he had seen at the capitol.

You will be interested to know that at the exercises on Washington's Birthday we tackled the celebrated "Non nobis." Do you remember it? By 'we' I mean the galvanized corpse of the lately deceased Glee Club. We organized, but were killed by our second tenor—much like a man's being killed by his body going back on him!

Wright and Miss A. join me in sending you the warmest sort of greetings. In haste
                    Your sincere friend,   Woodrow Wilson

TCL (in possession of Virginia Shaw English).
¹ W. F. Ford to WW, March 5, 1885.

Three Letters to Ellen Louise Axson

My own darling,   Balto., March 8, 1885
    I was cheated out of an opportunity to write in the most provoking manner yesterday. I spent the first half of the day in writing letters to several professors and lawyers who have written me cordial thanks for my book and whom I felt it of the utmost importance to secure as co-workers in reforms for which they manifested so much enthusiasm—Prof. Alex. Johnston of Princeton, Mr. Simon Sterne¹ of N. Y., & others. But I promised myself a whole *evening* with my darling. I was engaged to dine at *five*, but I was sure of being able to get back to my room—and to the letter of which my heart was full—by half-past eight. And so I should, had the dinner been served on schedule time. To my great discomfiture, however, it turned out to be quite an 'affair'; dinner was not served till six; and nobody left before bed-time! May-be my little sweet-heart can imagine how I felt, being obliged to chatter away to mere acquaintances while all the time thinking of my heart's desire to send the letter my love would be expecting! I will tell you about Mrs Machen,² my hostess, and the people who were at her dining, some other time. Just now I can think of nothing but the letter I have just fetched from the P. O. Did you write that letter, darling, with deliberate intention of making me 'wild' with pride and delight—or did you write it just because you could not help it? I think I know. I think that my little queen is coming to understand my love and longing for her thro. her experience of the same feelings! Oh, my darling, how sweet these confessions are! They are the seal and sanction of our sacred pledges for June: they are so womanly, so like your own sweet self, so exactly what my heart desired,—the very medicine, and the only medicine, I need.

    I am not sick, precious; I am feeling altogether myself once more. You must not lay *too* much stress upon my complaints: I make them only that I may be indulged with your sympathy. My only disease is loneliness; the only thing that can effect a *per-*

manent cure I cannot have till June! Two years ago I could have endured present conditions with comparative equanimity; but to know that the woman I love with all the strength of my whole nature is waiting to give me her life—all the fullest riches of her heart—to know what it *is* to love and to long for the companionship of the woman in whose love I find my life—is to realize what a maimed, hampered existence I am enduring; and I take life too intensely not to chafe myself with the impatience of waiting. I realize my need to have my love satisfied as nothing but our marriage can satisfy it. My heart is nearly breaking with love—and mayn't one be excused for getting sick with eagerness when he has *such* a prize, such a lovely bride, promised him?

I will write again this afternoon, sweetheart. I must go to church now.

With all my heart   Your own,   Woodrow.

1 Wilson's letter to Johnston was in reply to A. Johnston to WW, March 2, 1885. His letter to Sterne was in reply to Simon Sterne to WW, March 2, 1885, ALS (WP, DLC), in which Sterne praised *Congressional Government* and referred to his own work on the same subject. Sterne was a member of the New York law firm of Sterne and Thompson and author of *On Representative Government* (New York, 1871) and *Constitutional History and Political Development of the United States* (New York, 1882).
2 Mrs. Arthur W. (Minnie Gresham) Machen.

My own darling,   Balto., March 8, 1885
I am just back from dining with Mrs. Bird. She captured me again to-day, by an invitation extended about a week ago: and would have had Dr. Caldwell too, but the little man was sick to-day. If it had not been for this engagement for dinner to-day, I should not have been so put out by my loss of an opportunity yesterday to write to my darling: I could have continued my letter of this morning after church and have had time to pour out the two-day accumulation of love thoughts, and to answer all at once that precious letter of this morning. I *can't* say half enough in answer to that letter! The only complete answer would be to take you in my arms and kiss you breathless—and even that would be insufficient, for it would express only my delight. The only complete answer must be that which I shall be all my life giving you—the daily evidence that I love you in a way that must satisfy even your loving heart and that I can give my whole heart to the endeavour to be such a husband as you deserve. Sometimes, Eileen, when I am talking to other women upon subjects upon which I feel very deeply I find myself holding back the expression of thoughts that come from my deepest heart with a distinct feel-

ing that the *first* expression, at any rate, of such thoughts is too
sacred for any ears but *yours*—that there are certain *best* thoughts
which must be rounded and stamped—approved—by your sympathy before I can bear to let other people hear them. It is part
of my incomplete feeling. It is the thought that is so constantly
in my mind, that I must wait for you before I can give the world
a complete expression of myself—that your companionship is to
open up the hitherto unused side of my nature and so *equip* me.
And when you write to me *thus*, darling, that you "long as ardently as even I could wish for that day which shall end our separation," that you are conscious of but one desire, "to be to me all
that a wife, and only a wife, can be, everything else" being "lost,
merged in that one overwhelming desire," my heart is filled with
an unspeakable peace, as at the assurance that my future is secure of all that is essential to it. My darling is won—what can I
not do with her love to inspire me!

The sketches came on Friday afternoon, precious, and the one
of your room has been a great delight to me. The others give me
an *idea* of your pose—which must have been beautiful—but the
failures to reproduce your face were ridiculous. What is the date
on the little affair hanging over the stand, my pet? I can form a
definite picture of my little sweetheart now—and it is *such* a pleasure: I get a perfect idea of the room from this sketch—but more
of it anon.

Wouldn't you like a kiss to-night, darling? Oh, if I could only
give you one to tell part of the love of

Your own   Woodrow.

I had a message from sister Annie about the picture, but I have
not been able to talk anything but love to you to-day.

Lovingly   W.

My own darling,   Balto., March 9, 1885

Sister Annie says that she has but one other photograph of
little Jessie, and that she is not satisfied with either it or the
one you saw. So her conclusion is, "If Ellie would rather wait
until you can be with her, of course I do not object. I would *rather*
wait, indeed, in order that the likeness may be as good as possible."[1] She is very grateful to you, my pet, for consenting to do
the picture—and she wants to know whether 'I know where you
are to spend the summer.' No, I *don't* know yet!—but I shall find
out! Little Maggie[2] will be Miss Axson then.

I was to tell you about Mrs. Machen, my Saturday's hostess; wasn't I? Well, she is niece to Mrs. Bird, and was a Miss (Minnie) Gresham of Macon. She married a lawyer of this place who is considerably older than herself, a man reputed of great culture and attainments. He didn't say anything on Saturday, confining himself to smiling. Mrs. Machen's father (Col. Gresham)[3] is an intimate friend of father's; and I was invited to dinner on Sat. as "an hereditary friend." Mrs. M. must have been either hurried or absent-minded when she wrote her note, for I was requested to come and dine *on* a few Georgians. These "few Georgians" were strangers to me, but very agreeable people: and one of them *did* look as if she would have been good to eat. The rest would have needed prolonged boiling, I am afraid.

Yes, it was last Friday's Seminary at which I was appointed to report on the American political economists; but Dr. Ely was away, and, inasmuch as he was anxious to hear my report, I was at the last moment given something else to report on which made it necessary for me to work at breakneck speed all that day. That was why I had to steal time for your letter. My report is now somewhat *indefinitely* postponed. A most provoking way of forcing a man into unnecessary rashes of preparation!

Of course you must believe, little sweetheart, what I say about your power to give me the companionship I most need: for it is true—I *know* that it is true! I have *proved* that it is true! And *you* have proved the same thing by your *desire* to be all that to me and by your ability to express, better than I had done myself, just what it was I meant. My darling, will you some time memorize that sweet "cricket on the lyre," so that you can repeat it to me the many times that I shall want to hear it? If I had any memory, I'd 'commit' the piece myself; but I should rather hear you recite it anyhow! Oh, my precious little maiden! What an exhaustless treasure and delight your love is to me! What a blessing it is to be

Your own   Woodrow.

ALS (WP, DLC).
[1] He quotes from an unpublished portion of Annie W. Howe to WW, March 5, 1885.
[2] Ellen's sister, Margaret, age four.   [3] John J. Gresham of Macon, Ga.

Two Letters from Ellen Louise Axson

My darling Woodrow   New York Mar. 9/85.

I vowed by all the gods last night that I would write to Anna Harris if it killed me! and I did it too. But as I was lazy about beginning, I found that after I had written fourteen pages it was too late for me to write you.[1] But you must forgive me, and give "place aux dames," for it is the *first* time this winter that I have written her! And you may be sure I dreaded it on that account, she is such an unrelenting sort of a person. How natural it is to put off a day of reckoning as long as possible, even when one knows that the interest is accumulating and one's case getting worse all the time.

I enclose another little sketch of myself which one of the boys made during a "rest" the other day. You are getting a large collection of them—are you not? I send this one, because it *flatters* me so delightfully. I saw a picture of myself the other day with a *title*! it was called "Perpetual Sunshine!"—and it was the crossest looking thing you ever saw!

That reminds me that I have at last seen a birthday book which gives me a motto that suits me;—at least the *first* part of it does. It is from Sheriden "Why there it is!—my distresses are so many that I can't *afford* to part with my spirits; but I shall be rich and splenetic all in good time!" That reminds me again of my motto for today on the "Holmes calendar"; you have sent me so many delightful ones from Ruskin that I will enclose it, by way of return. Don't you think it good?

I have just received a letter from Stockton[2] in which he says, "isn't it *glorious*, the way Mr. Wilson's book is taking?" He read the review it [in] the "Nation" it seems, and was delighted with it's praise. It is extremely gratifying that such men as you mention should show so much appreciation of your work. In fact, I think it *is* "glorious."

I won't pretend to answer this sweet letter of yours now, darling. Monday morning is such a busy time. Good-by until tonight. I love you, dearest, more than tongue can tell and am—with all my heart   Your own Eileen.

Please excuse haste

ALS (WP, DLC). Encs.: pencil sketch of ELA in profile and a page from a calendar with verse.

[1] ELA to Anna Harris, March 8, 1885, printed in George C. Osborn (ed.), "Letters from Ellen Axson Wilson to Anna Harris of Rome, Georgia," *Georgia Historical Quarterly*, XXVIII (Dec. 1954), 369-73.

[2] Her brother, Stockton Axson, then a freshman at Davidson College.

My darling Woodrow,   New York Mar 9/85.

I have just finished reading your sweet letter of last night. What precious letters are these two which today has brought me! No one *ever* wrote such wonderful letters as you, my darling, every one steals my heart afresh; or rather makes me wish it again in my possession that I might once more have the pleasure of *giving* it to you. I don't know what is to become of me if this goes on,—if you are to make me love you more deeply and passionately every day. But of one thing I am sure I can never love you more than you deserve to be loved,—by *any* woman whom *you* loved, but doubly so by me. No one will ever know what you have been to me. I feel sometimes as if you had made life itself possible. I have terrible days—or rather nights—now somctimes, when "the old sorrow wakes and cries"; but almost always I am *so* happy—so wonderfully happy; and it is all owing to your wonderful love,—as you well know, dear heart.

Yes, I do tell you these things because I "can't help it" now,—it will out. And because I don't *care* to help it too. I have grown so close to you—so identified with you,—that I no longer feel ashamed to tell you—or at any rate to *write* you—my inmost thought. It is because I am "won," even to the last strong-hold. Yours isn't a very great conquest but it is a complete one; I am even ready to believe in the "divine right" of such a king. That recalls the extract from "Sartor" which I tried to quote once. I have it now. "Can I choose my own King? I can choose my own king popinjay and play what farce o' tragedy I may with him; but he who is to be my ruler, whose will is to be higher than my will, was chosen for me in Heaven. Neither except in such obedience to the heaven-chosen is freedom so much as conceivable." To be sure Carlyle was not applying it to just this case, yet I am not perverting it *at all* from it's meaning.

We had a great time in sketch class this afternoon;—the model fainted "dead away" at the end of the first quarter. She fell down and had to be worked with quite a time and of course the class was broken up. One of the boys, a great strapping fellow, fell perfectly unconscious a few weeks ago, so you see I have someone to keep me in countenance now. It was a lovely pose this afternoon. It was an exquisite old Watteau gown of the richest gold brocade which was worn at the English court *two hundred years* ago;—so said the owner, at least.

I have just finished a study in textures of my velvet cap, *our* muff with the crimson lining and my silver-grey silk handkerchief. They made a very good study, and I shall always keep it to remember this winter. Now I am doing what Whistler would call "a harmony in browns"[—]some delicious old worm-eaten books an old brown velvet jacket and an antique brass pitcher. It is a very interesting study.

What good news this is! that you are "feeling altogether your-self again." It has made me very happy to read that, and I hope it will last. Good night—yes I *would* like a kiss tonight darling. I send you one here on you[r] name Woodrow.

With all my heart   Your own Eileen.

Mar 10 I have just received a letter from Mrs. Green. She says she will be *delighted* to meet you, and she is at home every eve-ning except Thursday. Her address is *447 Park Place*.

ALS (WP, DLC) with WWhw and WWsh quotation and citation of Goldwin Smith, "Organization of Democracy," *Contemporary Review*, XLVII (March 1885), 317, on env.

To Ellen Louise Axson

My own darling,   Balto., March 10, 1885
    I imagine that if the various theories I have advanced in the course of any continuous correspondence were to be collated they would constitute a queer fleet of unseaworthy craft! I am led to this reflection by what happened to me just before dinner. I sat down to write to you, and in the very first lines plunged into the exposition of a theory concerning the predominant powers of woman's mind—a theory which had just occurred to me and which promised, consequently, to prolong to inordinate lengths the epistle in which it was to try to get itself fairly stated and il-lustrated. But I had not gone on for very many lines when Mr. Wright came in, on his usual errand of waiting for dinner; and, for the sake of clearing my ideas up a bit, I broached my theory to him. Matter-of-fact discussions are terrible on theories, if they be only half true—only one side of the truth: so, when I sat down just now to finish that letter, I concluded that I could finish it best by beginning it all over again, *minus* the theory! It was in large part true, but it was much too imperfect to write about!
    These sketches are absurd caricatures, little sweetheart, though it is exceedingly entertaining to see them. Is Mr. Harwood the only one in the class who can draw something that looks like you? I prize very highly the sketch he made of your first pose. It occupies the central place above my mantel. It is well that I have convinced myself, by repeated failures of the most perfect sort, that *I* can't sketch faces or figures! Otherwise, I am afraid I should spend all the time next summer, for instance, trying to get such a picture as I want of your face and figure at certain angles. I would give *any*thing if I could but catch a certain ex-pression that my darling's face sometimes wears—if I could but

put upon paper some of the pictures of her that linger in my memory! If I were an artist, darling, I could draw or paint no form or features but yours. They have so taken hold upon my heart and my imagination that they would assert themselves in spite of me. It's well that you don't know what that charm is— well that *my* appearance is in no way striking, or capable of *possessing* any one—else you could never paint more than one portrait! Sometimes I have thought of studying art in summer vacations, under your unsuspecting guidance, just that I might some day paint my Eileen as she ought to be painted—with love to direct my brushes to the true meaning of her sweet face—the loveliest face in the world, because the face of the loveliest woman in the world—the face of the little lady who has brought perfect happiness, because she has given perfect love, to

Her own   Woodrow.

ALS (WP, DLC).

From Ellen Louise Axson

My darling Woodrow,   New York Mar 10/85

As I glance up at my calendar to see the date I am reminded that you asked me what date was on it in the sketch of the room,— and I must answer before I forget it again. It probably isnt *anything*, but it ought to be March 2nd, the night that I put in those little details. I am glad you liked the sketch so much. It will please me too to look at it hereafter, for I shall always love this room. Somehow I seem to have done an immense amount of thinking— of *living*—in it for five months. And of course that explains the fact that it has become inseparably associated with *you*. But I have already confessed—and found sympathy in—the feeling which I have in returning to my room,—the feeling that I am coming back to you. A very natural feeling indeed, for wherever and whenever the world is shut out, I am, in thought, alone with you.

And so you didn't like the other sketches!—and yet they were quite good—I mean artistic, in their way—and *I* thought the finished face quite like me!

We had my old blind Confederate veteran[1] this afternoon—and Sat. too,—and he was dressed in a *Yankee* uniform! I wonder if he found it comfortable.

There is great excitement at the League today over the grand yearly "costume party" announced today for about the first of April. They seem to be fine affairs; all the three floors are bedecked and bedraped and all the students of the League besides the two hundred members, among whom of course are all the younger artists of the city,—are expected to be present, looking as artistic or historic as possible;—all Bohemia on dress parade! I should like immensely to see it *from the outside*.

By-the-way, I am quite happy over my ticket for the painting class received today. I mustered up courage enough to apply the other day, though with very small hope of success, it is such a difficult class to get into; of course much more so than any other. So now I shall be obliged to leave the Metropolitan. The teaching there is almost as good, and the expense so much less, that I shouldn't have cared to enter at the League if they only had models. But I *must* paint from life. So I shall begin next week to spend all my time at the League again.

What a comical mistake was that of Mrs. Machen's! I suppose she is a sister-in-law of our friend "Miss Loula Billups" whom Papa married to a son of Col. Gresham, and who died some time ago; they—the Greshams—were all friends of his too, I believe.

Yes darling I will "learn by heart"—I like that queer phrase in this connection—the "Cricket on the Lyre"; in fact I almost know it now, I have *read* it so often,—and *by heart* more than by eye. I love you darling more than life. How great the blessing to *me* to be   Your own Eileen.

ALS (WP, DLC).
¹ See ELA to WW, Dec. 11, 1884, Vol. 3.

From Gamaliel Bradford

My dear Sir: Boston, Mar. 10th '85
    I am glad to receive yours of 7th, because it is discussion which leads to accuracy of thought. I start from two propositions—1st I am a profound, almost an impassioned believer in universal suffrage and leaving the management of their affairs to the people. It has faults, no doubt, but will bear comparison with the history of despotic & aristocratic rule. Improvement is to be sought in organization[.] 2d I am a strong believer also in local self-government, leaving to each state, city or town the utmost possible freedom from outside interference[.] Of course there must be a limit but it should be placed as far off as possible consistent with order and submission to law.

    Under both these heads I object entirely to foreign methods first in themselves and secondly because they are inapplicable to this country. At home they tend to crush out individuality and the popular sense of responsibility[.] I suppose Paris & Berlin

are the best examples. But Paris is powerless in the face of a mob
except through a standing army while Berlin has not spirit
enough even to make a mob but is the slavish instrument of the
rascalities of Bismark and the old Emperor, for both of whom I
have very little respect indeed. In fact with what you call a permanent civil service you must have somebody to run it, as it wont
run itself. The question is, will you have it controlled by the people, or by some external power, and the trouble is that that external power though it may preserve order & system will use these
for its own purposes, not only without regard to but generally in
defiance of the real interest of the people and, moreover, the
well to do classes feeling that there are bayonets to protect them
become utterly indifferent to the condition and the misery of the
poor. How different in this respect is even New York, almost the
cesspool of the world, from Paris & Berlin?

But even so far as the system is good in Europe, it is so because
there is a strong administrative power outside, but here there
is no such thing. Our state governments are just as weak & helpless as those of cities. There is no individual responsibility, and
of the efficiency not to say purity of State boards & commissions
I have a profound distrust. The state should make general laws
for the government of cities, but the whole personnel & detail of
administration should I think be left to the city itself, first because it is best in the long run for the citizens, and second because it is quite as likely to be well done by the city as by the state.

How then can the public opinion of the city be brought to bear?
How can the desire of the sober part of the citizens for good government be made effective as against the intrigues of politicians?
By so simplifying & concentrating the question they have to decide, that they can comprehend it, and take an interest in it with
a minimum of attention, & decide it with a minimum of effort.
For this there should be but one elected official the Mayor in
whom all the responsibility & credit for administration should
be centred. There is an abundance of first class men in every
city—either retired from business, or whose business can go on
without their personal attention, or who would gain in business
from a public reputation—who would be willing to hold the office
for a single year or any length of time. Such a man does not need
to be a technical administrator himself but only to be a sufficient
judge of men to appreciate those who are[.] An ordinary business
education proved by success is an ample qualification.

As to his staff or heads of departments he should have absolute freedom of choice, because thus only can he be held re-

sponsible and in his own interest he will retain or seek out the best men and for a well paid service in which merit can make itself felt there would be no difficulty in finding them. Civil service rules are well enough for the lower ranks and to prevent favoritism, but their chief value is against members of the legislative branch who are always seeking to bend the executive to their own purposes[.] But a single head, held to strict responsibility for administration can & will command enough of skilled labor.

I do not think that 'impeachment' or 'administrative courts' are the true check upon the executive, because the *selecting* process is much more important than the *rejecting* & the former must rest with the sovereign power whether people or prince. The function of the council is not to punish malfeasance still less inefficiency, but to keep the people informed as to the conduct of their servant. If the mayor has to go to the people annually, that is a sufficient tribunal. I know no higher provided you do not mix up the question by asking the people to decide upon details or to fill separate elective offices. The question should be simply 'Are you satisfied with the government as carried on by Mr. Jones?' and that after Mr. Jones has been held up to public criticism by the cross-examinations of the council.

It may be said that the population of a large city is too ignorant & vicious to be trusted. I reply make the better class feel that only by organization and education and proper institutions can they be saved from ruin. The moment you allow them to rely on the bayonet, from that moment they will relapse into a selfish indolence, which will allow the evil elements to fester & break out[.] I firmly believe that the events of the last twenty years will be the salvation of New York

I have tried to answer all your questions, but if I have not or you like to send a rejoinder I shall be very glad to hear from you

Very truly yours Gaml Bradford

ALS (WP, DLC).

To Ellen Louise Axson

My own darling,   Balto., March 11, 1885

No wonder I am continuing to feel 'altogether myself again' with such a tonic as these precious love letters from you supply! The very tonic I need, too: for, as I said, my only disease is loneliness, and the wear and tear of too great, or, rather, too morbid, self-consciousness which loneliness causes. No one can cure that loneliness but you—because it *consists of your absence.* I shall always, hereafter, be lonely without you—no matter who or how many of those who are near and dear to me may be with me —for you have become an essential part of my life, its centre and inspiration. These marvellous love-letters of yours are a perfect tonic, therefore, because they make me realize how near you are to me in thought and in spirit, though your lovely self *is* so far away—*so* far away!

Do you know, sweetheart, that it is only recently that I have been able to feel that you were completely won? Of course I have had perfect faith in your love from the first, and an exceedingly great joy in it; but until your lips were unsealed to speak freely of all, even the smallest, thoughts springing out of your love for me—until you confessed everything, as you do in these precious letters, because you wished to, because, instead of being an effort, it was a delight—I felt that there was some slight barrier between us—between my heart and the complete rewards of your love—yet to be broken down before our oneness, and our happiness, would be complete. Now! How can I tell the joy I experience in reading my darling's *talk* about her love! Wont you promise, precious, to *say* these things to me when next I have you in my arms?

And I can't help noticing another thing as proof of the same delightful conclusions: my little queen consents to-day to mention her *troubles* as well as her happiness—the other sacred secret of her life. It is an unspeakably sweet thought to me, Eileen, that my love has power to make you entirely happy, even to the exclusion of your great sorrows! Oh, if I could but *altogether* fill the places left vacant in my darling's sorely striken heart—if my love could but *establish* comfort and peace against the coming of the remembrance of her griefs! May God in his goodness and tenderness grant that in days soon to come she may be able to escape the *pang* of those griefs but [by] taking refuge close to my heart, to find that those she has lost are only happy now and that she has found for herself a love that can drive out all the terrors of sorrow! Oh, if I am worthy of this, may God grant it!

Yes, sweetheart, you must keep that picture of cap and muff and handkerchief: we shall frame it for our room—a token of those hours in which I grew to love you beyond all dreams before, and in which you found words for your love for

Your own   Woodrow.

ALS (WP, DLC).

From Ellen Louise Axson

New York Mar 11/85.

Oh my darling, my darling, how *glad* I would be if you were here tonight and I could cry all my troubles away in your arms! I have been trying it all the evening and I find it does'nt ease one's heart at all to dampen one's own sleeve with one's tears. But I am in a sorry mood for jesting, so I won't pretend to do it; —for indeed I am half sick with anxiety and distress about Stockton. In a letter received tonight Uncle Randolph [Axson] says "Stockton writes that he will be compelled to give up at college— his health has failed him. He has doubtless written you about his condition. Your Grandfather has written to your Uncle Will [Hoyt] about his case." And that is all—and the *first*—I have heard of it. Stockton with mistaken kindness, poor boy, has never even hinted at such a thing,—I had a letter from him on Monday too. And I have begged him so in *every letter* to tell me *just* how he was—*not* to keep anything from me;—for I found he had done so last winter, that he was unwell for some time and kept it concealed from us, and I have never been easy about him since. I fear it must be very serious for him to give up now as he has done, for he has grown so ambitious and determined of late. And he has no mother to nurse him, no home even,—and I am *so* far away and can *do* nothing! And I am so *utterly* in the dark about it all. It almost drives me wild. I shall telegraph him in the morning to send me word how he is and to write at once a full account of his condition, that the suspense may be shortened and I may know as soon as possible what to do; for if he is really ill I must go to him. I can't imagine why he should remain at Davidson if he has given up his studies. But it is all a mystery.

Oh darling I am ashamed of myself for writing so to you. It seems so selfish. I would not trouble anyone else so,—why then should I trouble you whom I love best—whom I am most anxious to see *untroubled*. It is because I can't help it—and because I know you would not wish me to help it, for I have learned now the quality of your love, and what a comforter you can be. And it has already comforted and helped me, darling, thus to unburden my heart to the one whose sympathy in my troubles is as much mine I know as if you were here to give it while I speak. And yet I fear that whether you wish it or not, I *ought* to refrain from so troubling you for your good.

Good-night my darling, I love you, I love you! why cannot I tell you how much I love you. Ah! words are powerless to do that, even actions fail to tell it all, at once. It will take a lifetime to tell it well,—to prove it.

With all my heart.   Your own Eileen.

ALS (WP, DLC).

From John Wildman Moncrief

Professor Wilson: Franklin Ind. March 11th 1885

My dear sir, your very kind and inspiring letter reached me Friday evening, the 12th, and your Congressional Government the following morning. Please accept my heartfelt thanks for both the book and the letter. The book instructs us and the letter greatly encourages us. I have given the book a pretty thorough examination and I do not hesitate to say that you have done for our Constitution what the lamented Mr. Bagehot has done for the English Constitution, and so I place them side by side in our library. This is a high compliment but I make it deliberately. If you so early in your career can do such work I am sure that we may hope very much from you in the future. I am glad that you are so situated that you can give your attention to authorship. In our young western colleges we have so much teaching to do that we have not much time for writing. I hope that your necessary work of teaching in Bryn Mawr College will leave you much time for original research.

You, I believe, are an alumnus of Princeton. Our Prof. of Latin is a Princeton man—class of 76—Arthur B. Chaffee.

I am sure that I shall be able to do considerable in extending the circulation of your book.

Believe me yours most faithfully   J. W. Moncrief.

ALS (WP, DLC).

To Ellen Louise Axson

My own darling,   Balto., March 12, 1885

Have your friends, the Carters, asked you if you know 'a Mr. Wilson who is at the Johns &c.'? If not, don't be surprised if they do.—Thereby hangs a tale.

I too am very happy, darling, over your getting the ticket to the painting class: I am happy at thought of anything that gives you pleasure; and this ticket is not only a source of pleasure but a source of gratification to you as well, being proof, as it is, of your title to take your place in this highest class—a title which no one but yourself could have doubted, however. I believe that I am glad, too, that you do not have to make any more of those long trips to the Metropolitan.

Why, little sweetheart, none but the upper part of the face in the sketch you sent me is *at all* like you! *Your* face isn't long, and doesn't begin at the cheek bones a projecting movement which is checked only at the chin. The artist has tried to make you look like *me* by drawing your features out immoderately and narrowing them rapidly towards the chin!

I hunted Mrs. Green's house up yesterday, in my afternoon walk—so that I could go to it at night without searching for numbers—and shall call upon her not later than next week. I should do so at once if it were not that I have three other calls that I am *bound* to make this week—on Mrs. Bird and Mrs. Machen, for instance.

I am coming in sight of the end of my reading and notetaking on the American political economists, and shall very soon begin writing my essays about them. I am anxious to reach that stage of the work, and yet it will unquestionably be the hardest part of it. Composition is no child's-play with me: in all constructive work I seem, so to say, to write in my mind's blood, to consume part of myself. It is a great, though in no sense an exhausting, strain on my mental system. I *can't* write just what comes into my head: I have to stop and perfect both expression and thought. Still there is a great deal of pleasurable excitement in writing: and *this* task will be like the preparation of that piece on Adam Smith,[1] not like the construction of the essays on Cong. Govt., plain and simple comment, not painstaking exposition. It's much easier to relate what other men think than to expound one's own opinions. I don't have to have any opinions of my own in doing *this* writing. I have simply to understand the writings of others, and appreciate their relations to each other and to the general body of thought in their science.

You don't know how glad I am that this is the last piece of writing I shall have to do *without you*—the last I shall have to do as only half myself! People will be puzzled to know why my future writings are so much better—they wont know that you have come to   Your own Woodrow.

ALS (WP, DLC).
[1] Printed at Nov. 20, 1883, Vol. 2.

From Charles Kendall Adams

Dear Sir: Ann Arbor, March 12, 1885.

I cannot resist the impulse to assure you of the great satisfaction I have found in reading your "Congressional Government." You have done a work for which every thoughtful student of our government ought to be grateful, & one which will be of great service to the rapidly inc[r]easing number of students of political science. I do not hesitate to express the opinion that as a critical study it stands quite above anything else that has been produced in our political literature.

I was pleased to observe that you have received the appointment to a desirable chair in the new University for women near Philadelphia. But I could not help feeling that the kind of talent you have shown in this work will not find there its adequate scope. I mean this as no disparagement whatever of woman's ability,—for I have had abundant reason in the course of my instruction greatly to respect it,—but after all it is of a somewhat different kind, & not of the kind that is quite at home in the acute analysis of political institutions. You ought to be in some school of Political Science where an opportunity for advanced work is afforded. I am not sure that the field for you is not at Ann Arbor.

We have a flourishing Law School of some 250 students, about 30 of whom, I suppose have taken a baccalaureate degree. There is considerable probability that at the end of this academic year, Judge Campbell,[1] who has been connected with the school from the beginning will tender his resignation. As Dean of the School of Political Science, I have hoped that a successor might be secured who could do considerable work in our school. For some years before Judge Cooley's[2] resignation he lectured in both of our Schools, & I hope that such an arrangement can be made in the future. My reasons for wishing it are somewhat as follows. At the present time we have in the School of Political Science no provision for instruction in the field of Administrative Law. Within the past two years we have accumulated at some pains a good library of what are supposed to be the best works in German, French, & English on Administrative Theories & Methods in England & in Continental Europe. I know of no other Collection equal to it in the country, & it has been gathered in the belief that there is a vast field that has never yet been cultivated in America & that may be turned to great practical use. There is no part of our governmental affairs that is more needing the thoughtful attention of our students than the government of our cities. My hope has been to find some one who could take hold of the opportunity here afforded & turn it to profitable account not only for himself but for the State & the Country. I despair of getting an appointment in the School of Political Science pure and simple; but if the place can be combined with the Law School, it seems to me not impracticable.

We have a Political Science Association before whom lectures and papers are frequently given; and if, as President of that Association, I had any fund at my disposal, I should invite you to visit us with a view to looking at the situation. I have no authority to grant any pledges, nor, to be frank, am I disposed to make any, but there is what seems to me a great opportunity, & it occurs to me that you may think it worth the while to come out here even at your own expense to see what there is. I should hardly venture to suggest this but for one reason. It is probable that Judge Campbell's resignation will be followed by an immediate appointment in June; and there is no probability that the Regents could be induced to appoint any one who had not been seen and heard. It need not be understood that you came at all as a candidate—that of course would be absurd, for the resignation is not yet presented—but I could easily manage to have such persons present as would make it certain that your name would not go before the Board as that of a person who was known solely through his writings. We have two young Law Professors here, who would give you all needed information concerning the work on that side. In this suggestion, for I intend it as scarcely more, I have presumed that your tastes are somewhat legal as well as political. Perhaps I ought to have said that Constitutional Law is the subject on w'h Judge Campbell has chiefly lectured.

While I should be very glad to have you talk the matter over confidentially with Dr. H. B. Adams, I trust you will regard the matter simply as a proposition on my part to put you and this University *en rapport* with a view to a better standing ground in case of possible contingencies.

I have the honor to be with much respect,

Very truly yours   C K Adams.

ALS (WP, DLC) with WWhw notation on env.: "Ans. March 19/85."

[1] James Valentine Campbell, a judge of the Michigan Supreme Court and also a professor in the Department of Law, University of Michigan.

[2] The distinguished jurist and legal scholar, Thomas McIntyre Cooley.

To Ellen Louise Axson

Balto., March 13, 1885

Oh, my darling, my *precious* darling, I have just read your letter of Wednesday night and my heart is full to overflowing with this news of your distress about dear Stockton! Try not to harass yourself too much with anxiety about him, my brave little pet. The blow has been in the *way* in which the news has come to you, without any explanation or particulars—in what you have been allowed to imagine about the dear fellow's condition—and I am almost sure that the facts, when you learn them, will go far towards reassuring you. Otherwise, little sweetheart, either your uncle or your Grandfather would have gone on to Davidson. The very fact that Stockton remains at college and Dr. Axson opens a correspondence with Dr. Hoyt about the case proves that there is nothing *critical* about it. The dear fellow has probably overworked himself and gotten his system out of order, as I did at the University of Virginia. It may be imperative that he should stop studying and yet comparatively easy for him to get well after he does stop—and his staying at Davidson would seem to mean that he hopes to go back to his studies again after all. At any rate, my precious, there does not seem to be any present cause for great alarm.

Oh, what would I not give to be with you—what an unspeakable delight it would be to me to have proof that you *could* cry all your troubles away in my arms! I would joyfully give my *life*, Eileen, my darling, my pride, to shield you from sorrow and anxiety—and it is *so* hard to be so far away from you, able to give you not even *words* of comfort when you most need them! I think that I *could* calm and reassure you in this case, if I could but hold you close to my heart and kiss the ears into which I should pour my thoughts about it. I am beyond measure distressed that dear Stockton should have suffered this break down: but I can't but feel sure, from the small evidence we have, that, now that he has given up, he will soon be all right again—and I wish I could make *you* feel so.

Of course, darling, you ought to have told me of these sudden anxieties. I should have been terribly hurt if you had withheld them from me. You could not wound me more than by withholding from me *any*thing that nearly concerns yourself. And, for all the pain that the news gives me, darling, I have the precious solace that you love me well enough to bring all your troubles to me and that you find comfort and relief in doing so. Oh, it is *such* a sweet thought that you find real comfort and strength in my love, that I am essential to you! This letter brings me precious proof of the fact that our love is bearing just the fruit that I have prayed it might bear. I shall be happy in proportion as I receive the title of your love to bear your burdens with, and if possible *for*, you. I love you, Eileen; I love you!—with all strength that I have of tender loving! I live for you—you are the centre of all my thoughts and all my hopes—and by bringing me into all your thoughts you enable me to live *with* you—you bless and delight   Your own Woodrow.

ALS (WP, DLC).

From William F. Ford

My dear sir: Bradstreet's. New York, March 13, 1885
    I am told that you have received the offer of a professorship in some Western college. Is it true? For some weeks I have had in mind to ask you if you would be willing to consider the matter of accepting the position of Washington correspondent for a New York newspaper. This on the supposition that such newspaper would stand for something far beyond the present newspaper methods. It seems to me that your studies have admirably fitted you for the field of activity indicated.
                    Yours truly,   Wm F Ford

TLS (WP, DLC) with WWhw notation on env.: "Ans. March 16/85."

From Edward Ireland Renick

My dear Wilson,   Washington, D. C., March 13, 1885.
    In reply to your recent letter I desire to assure you that I did not underestimate the importance of the College in which you have taken a chair. I had an idea—well founded—that you had a passion for public life, & I felt sure that your book would be likely to prove the open sesame to it. For instance, Senator Lamar was intent upon it at the time I wrote. He is now a Cabinet officer of considerable influence with Bayard.
    Two weeks since I heard Mr. Eugene Schuyler in his lecture on our Diplomatic Service, not only commend your book eo nomine in the heartiest manner, but appropriate its contents most liberally. Eugene Schuyler is apt to be our First Assistant Secretary of State. He would, most likely, want to get such men as

Ellen Louise Axson about the time of her engagement

East-Rome Oct. 2/83

My Darling,

Their messengers
brought me at once your two
letters — of the 27 & 28 — and therefore this day been like the demon
which, Aleeres last wrote,
"high Dalivering." "All its Immure,
lightly shaken, own them-
selves in golden Demals" —

I wonder if you would laugh
or what you would say, if
you knew how perfectly happy
your letters make me! More
best no one could be expected
to receive such letters, and keep
very cool. They are so like yourself, dearest —. As, I take it
all back! They are simply,

146 N. Charles St.,
Baltimore, Oct. 14th 83

My own sweet Ellie,

I have not forgotten that
scarcely two days have elapsed since
I wrote you a twelve-page letter: I
am quite conscious, on the contrary, that
I am carrying this matter of letter
writing beyond all bounds of reason.
But, then, I don't intend this to be a
twelve-pager, and I feel justified in
writing on this particular day because
it is a sort of mensiversary: just four
weeks ago to-day you were sweet and
imprudent enough to promise to marry
a certain respectable person whose life
has been brightened beyond measure by
that promise, and who has felt every
Sabbath afternoon since that memorable
16th that he had cause for special thanks-
giving that He who ordereth all things
had given him the love of such a woman

New York April 19/85

My darling Woodrow,

It occurs to me that I, in my turn, must lose no more time in "talking a little about a sub-ject in which we are naturally interested". I really am, at any rate end, that about it all—its den—

Balto,—April 21, 1885—

Well! my precious little sweetheart, I am thrown into an extraordinary, an almost droll, predicament by this sweet letter, this _precious_ letter of yours about "fixing the day" (for every word which recognizes the unity of our affairs is precious to me)! I am as eager, as

Savannah June 20/85

And can it really be possible, my darling, that this is my last letter to you! I did not realize the fact until just now when I began to count up, and perceived that a letter written tonight *[Columbia]* [?] & tomorrow would reach you leave on Thursday. How strange it seem to think that we will have no more need of letters

Columbia, June 21, 1885

My own darling,

It seems altogether too good to be true that our bondage to pen and ink is at ~~and~~ last at an end! Hereafter we can speak face to face whenever we please — this letter

Marriage license

Manse of the Independent Presbyterian Church, Savannah, Ga., where the wedding took place, with the church in the background

Honeymoon cottage at Arden, N.C.

you into the State Department or into the Foreign Service. He can send for you, it is true, to Bryn Mawr, but young men anxious to get in the service should, he may think, let it be known. I could, possibly, let him know that such is your ambition if you had so wished it (or if you *now* wish it), as I see him occasionally, without putting you in the position of an office-seeker. I saw a great many Atlanta folk & old college friends here during Inauguration week. Where in the thunder were you I wonder.

You will be glad to hear that Prof. Noah K. Davis[1] rapturously admires "Congressional Government."

If I continue in the present division of the 1st Compt's office (Consular & Diplomatic) for a short time longer (?) I purpose trying my hand on "Our Diplomatic and Consular Service."

We send kindest regards & hope soon to see you. Both wife & I I are sick with colds.   As ever,   Renick.

ALS (WP, DLC) with WWhw notation on env.: "Ans. March. 15/85."
[1] Professor of Moral Philosophy, University of Virginia.

From Ellen Louise Axson

My darling Woodrow,   New York Mar. 13/85[1]
Circumstances of all sorts seemed to conspire last night in the most provoking fashion to prevent my writing;—and I was most anxious too, to answer that precious letter the morning had brought me,—I won't pretend to do so now, hurried as I am, but will wait until tonight.

How glad I am that you are making such good progress with the political economists. I should think that while the writing is the hardest part of the work, the reading would be the greatest drudgery; and I am not surprised that you should be anxious to pass that stage. I hope with all my heart that the "wear and tear" which the writing will cost you won't prove *very* great.

What a *splendid* sentence this is that Ruskin gives us for May 11th! by-the-way—so well-put. I will tell you a secret,—one that you hav'nt even suspected(!) I shouldn't mind if it were May 11th either!

What is the tale about the Carter's? My curiosity is greatly excited.

I tried to send a telegram to Stockton yesterday, but found there was no office at Davidson; so as I had no idea where to send, I am forced to try and be patient until I can hear by letter.

But it is very cold this morning,—winter has come again with vengeance—and I *must* not linger in this icy room. I love you, sweetheart, with a perfect love and am altogether

Your own Eileen.

ALS (WP, DLC).
¹ The date 13/85 was supplied by WW.

From Henry Randall Waite

American Institute of Civics
Dear Sir: Boston, Mass., March 14th, 1885

Your advocacy of measures calculated to promote the public good leads me to believe that you will be interested in the plans of the American Institute of Civics, whose foundations have just been laid, and that you will take pleasure in giving to it the benefit of such counsel and cooperation as you mae find it convenient to offer. I believe that you will recognize in this institution an endeavor toward the realization of much that you have yourself hoped to see accomplished. In view of these facts I write to ask if you are willing to accept an election as one of the Institute lecturers? Those chosen as lecturers are expected to deliver an address before the Institute in Boston, once in the year,—expenses paid. It is expected that arrangements will also be made, if desired, by which the same lecture, or others upon subjects related to the purposes of the Institute, may be delivered elsewhere under its auspices, payment for services to be made to the lecturer.

You will observe that the duties of the position will not be more onerous than you choose to make them, aside from the lecture in Boston. These lectures will introduce you to a select Boston audience, in which there may be a possible advantage. I trust that you will think it expedient to accept the proposition.

You will observe by the prospectus that we are to commence, very soon, the issue of a publication especially devoted to the purposes of the Institute. We are not in position to offer compensation for articles at this time, but hope to be able to do so shortly. Our contract with the publishers is such as to guarantee the continuance of the publication for three years, and the basis of the arrangement is such as to encourage the hope that we shall soon be able to deal more generously with those who assist us in its successful establishment. Meantime may we not hope for at least one article from your pen, however brief?¹ The subject, and the time of contributing it, may be arranged to suit your convenience. I am well aware that you cannot afford to do *much* work of this kind, but you will perhaps think it best to make an exception in the present instance.

Very truly yours,   Henry R. Waite   Pres.

TLS (WP, DLC) with WWhw notation on env.: "Ans. March 18/85." Enc.: American Institute of Civics, printed prospectus, announcing its purposes and forthcoming publication of *The Citizen*.
¹ Wilson eventually responded with an article, "Courtesy of the Senate," printed at Nov. 15, 1885, Vol. 5.

To Ellen Louise Axson

Balto., March 14, 1885

God bless you, my precious little sweetheart, for this sweet, this charming secret, that *you too* wish that May had come and were half gone! You are a very witch for springing upon me new delights of your love, and keeping me constantly in such a rapturous state of mind that it is all that I can do to keep from going all the way to New York to overwhelm your sweet lips with kisses! When I see you next, Miss, I shall have to give you all the kisses and caresses I have longed to give you during these tiresome days of separation! (Do you regard that as a threat, or as a promise?) Oh, my darling, my darling! How unspeakably happy I am! You have found out how I have longed to be loved, and it is your delight to love me so—with a glad, irrepressible, playful, demonstrative love! Was ever man so blessed with his fullest heart's desire? Is it not the sweetest of all things, darling, to love each other with the simple, unconcealed ardour of children and yet with that added serious purpose and passionate devotion wh. children cannot know? How often have I had a naïve boy's desire to tell everybody I know that I have the lovliest, dearest little sweetheart in the world! I never feel old (as you do!), but I feel youngest when I let my thoughts dwell upon my love for you; and when June shall have fulfilled its promise I shall feel that youth itself has been crowned and perfected! Oh, sweetheart, if I could but hold you in my arms *five minutes*, to tell my love to your eyes, to your lips, to your checks—but really I must change the subject, for I haven't money enough to take me to New York!

Let's talk about that unexciting subject, myself: and there's nothing connected with myself worth talking about except my book. Renick wrote me some time ago protesting against my accepting a chair in a "female seminary" just at the time when my book was about to put me in the way of getting something so much better. I replied that Bryn Mawr was about as good a place as a fellow could expect to get into at first, &c. &c. Now he says:

"I desire to assure you that I did not underestimate the importance of the College in which you have taken a chair. I had an idea—well founded—that you had a passion for public life, and I felt sure that your book would be likely to prove the open sesame to it. For instance, Senator Lamar was intent upon it at the time I wrote. He is now a Cabinet officer of considerable influence with Bayard. Two weeks since I heard Mr. Eugene Schuyler in his lecture on our Diplomatic Service, not only commend your book *eo nomine* in the heartiest manner, but appropriate its contents most liberally. Eugene Schuyler is apt to be our First Assistant Secretary of State. He would, most likely, want to get such men as you into the State Dept. or into the Foreign Service" &c. &c. He mistakes the *sort* of public life I should want. Further on in the letter he says, "You will be glad to hear that Prof. Noah K. Davis rapturously admires "Congressional Government." Prof. N. K. D. is of the Univ. of Va.

Mr. Wm. F. Ford writes as follows: "I am told that you have received the offer of a professorship in some Western college. Is it true? For some weeks I have had it in mind to ask you if you would be willing to consider the matter of accepting the position of Washington correspondent for a New York newspaper. This on the supposition that such newspaper would stand for something far beyond the present newspaper methods. It seems to me that your studies have admirably fitted you for the field of activity indicated." I should like that infinitely better than a berth in the State Dept.—and what a chance such work would give me for my favourite studies, in Washington, the place of places for the purpose! But of course that's out of the question for the present.

Lastly, here's what came this morning from Prof. C. K. Adams of Michigan—a man of more than national reputation—: "I cannot resist the impulse to assure you of the great satisfaction I have found in reading your "Congressional Government." You have done a work for which every thoughtful student of our government ought to be grateful, and one which will be of great service to the rapidly increasing number of students of political science. I do not hesitate to express the opinion that as a critical study it stands quite above anything else that has been produced in our political literature." Coming from such a man, that's worth more to me by way of gratification and encouragement than all the newspaper notices put together!

And now, little lady, that's all the 'nice things' about my book that I have to tell—except that a Phila. gentleman writes me a long letter, putting me in the way of getting some very interesting information about the corrupt influences brought to bear on the Committees.[1] All these things make me feel very serious—almost anxious. So far from feeling any elation, I feel more and more a deep sense of personal responsibility. I have—almost unwittingly —taken the lead in a very great work. My book succeeds because I *have* taken the lead: and now, the opening having been made, I must come up to my opportunities and be worthy of them. That is enough to sober—as well as enough to inspire—anyone!

But with your love, darling, given to me as only you know how to give it, with June come and gone, I do not fear falling *behind* what I have already done. I have the best sort of strength so long as I am   Your own Woodrow.

ALS (WP, DLC).
 [1] R. Meade Bache to WW, March 13, 1885, ALS (WP, DLC) with WWhw notation on env.: "Ans. March 17/85."

From Ellen Louise Axson

My darling Woodrow,   New York Mar 14/85
I have been having my fortune told by a young (amateur) gypsy at the League, and I am very much pleased with it;—and the best of it is, that it is so *true*, as far as it has gone, that I ought to feel entitled to put confidence in that part of it which deals with the future! I am very much in love now, I am going to be very singularly happy in love,—I am not going to marry young (obviously!) I have one *very* dear friend—sex unknown,—I am going to have a very healthy life! &c. &c. Don't you think that indicates a satisfactory "fortune"[?] *I* am content with it at any rate.

The League is closed this afternoon, and will be tomorrow, out of respect to Miss Marsh, our vice-president, who died suddenly this morning of pneumonia. I never saw anything like the prevalence of that disease here,—but some lady was saying today that it was much more than usually fatal this season, "almost amounting to a plague."

I took the opportunity to call on Mrs. Hamilton but, much to my regret, missed her. Nearly all the girls seem to have taken advantage of the holiday to make visits, or engage in still wilder dissipation;—such is life! I have been running about so much in the strong March wind that as a consequence I have been quite overcome by sleep this evening, have spent a good part of it already actually napping in my chair; so you must excuse a very stupid letter.

It is a shame to write stupid letters, I must admit, in answer to such lovely ones as these before me. They ought to make me "feel altogether my—somewhat wide-awake—self." And yet again they make me feel that never again can I be "altogether myself" while separated from you. You have become an essential part of *my* life, darling, its centre and inspiration; so I must feel that it is at best an imperfect, mained [maimed] existence which I lead without you. How did I ever live without these daily letters? And even they cannot pretend to satisfy *one* of my many longings that concern you, cannot even tell me half I want to know about your daily life. I can't tell you, dear, how much my mind lingers about you in that daily life,—how constantly I am trying to follow you in all your in-goings and out-comings. I can imagine the keen though tantalized pleasure which the little imprisoned "Beauty"—in one of my old favourite *fairy-tales*—found in the magic glass through which she could constantly see,—as in a dream, the daily life of the dear ones in the far-away home.

Yes darling I think I can promise to say anything you wish when next we are together, and I am *sure* I could promise anything if I could thereby shorten your absence one day. Don't I *always* say what you wish though sooner or later? I am a very docile girl, I think! Yet don't flatter yourself too much, sir! you have never made me say or do anything yet *against my will!* Really, darling, I have come to think that you have been most wise in this, as in all things, that I am your humble debtor for forcing upon me, as it were, a happiness greater than I should ever have allowed myself;—for teaching me the full meaning and sweetness of love. But I suppose that in all cases it is the lover who determines the character of the love-making! we learn our lesson from you. For a sensitive woman could sooner give her love unsought, than she could give unsought, un-wished-for evidences of it; or continue to give them a moment after they had ceased to be desired or valued. As long as my darling cares to hear me say I love him, it will be my happiness to tell him so, freely, fully,—as fully as my poor speech will let me. There are many thoughts that lie too deep for words, there is a love too *great* for words and there are—dreams—shall I call them?—fair shapes which in the shining sunlit haze which hides the future seem ever forming, dissolving, and again forming themselves before me. These elude description. To attempt it is like tearing apart the half shut petals of a flower; let the blossom unfold of it's own sweet will,—that blossom on whose heart of gold lies the story of our life—only time can reveal that story. I can trust him, with his soft and quiet touch, to do the work well.

I have no space left and yet I *must* tell you that your wonderful love *does* suffice to fill *all* vacant places in my heart, my darling. You have filled my life full to overflowing with love and joy. And my pain, even now, lies not so much in *my loss*, or the change it has made in *my* life, as simply in the *memory* which *will* ever and anon make pass before me in too vivid detail the agonizing scenes which attended those losses. Good-night my darling. Believe me in every heart-throb   Your own Eileen.

ALS (WP, DLC).

From Marion Wilson Kennedy

My dearest brother: Little Rock, M'ch. 15th 1885.

I shall not try to tell you how glad I am, *we are*, of your well-merited success, and of your prospects. I am just as glad as—as *you* are, I verily believe. So glad that I make a goose of myself telling almost everybody I talk to of it all! Mr. W., the young lawyer friend I lent your book, compliments it quite eloquently—and seemed perfectly amazed when he was told you were no older than himself. I am not at all sure he is satisfied on that point yet. . . .

Do write very soon again. Ross joins me in warmest love and hearty congratulations.   Lovingly your sister,   Marion.

ALS (WP, DLC) with WWhw notation on env.: "Ans. April 21/85."

To Ellen Louise Axson

My own darling,   Balto., March 15/85

Of course your curiosity is aroused about the tale that hangs by the Carters' possible question; but why should I tell it before they have asked that question? That ought to be the preface to the tale. Mr. Robinson[1] was in college with me—and was quite a chum of Bridges'. The other day he was in N. Y., heard from B. about my book *and* my sweetheart, and, then, calling upon his friends, the Carters, was talking to them about me and about my being engaged to a young lady from the South who was studying art in N. Y., but whose name he could not recollect, when they said that they knew a young lady answering to that description in their Sabbath school, and declared that, if they got a chance, they were going to ask her if she knew a Mr. Wilson, &c. That is the tale, my pet, as Mr. R. told it to me last week while on a brief visit to Hiram. It was the only interesting thing I ever heard from Mr. R's lips: for he is one of those men whose opinions consist of prejudices and whose lives are correct because there's not force enough in them to accomplish a positive vice.

I suppose that you have of course seen in the papers by this time who "Charles Egbert Craddock" is? A *Miss* Murfree, of Murfreesboro, Tenn., once, but now of St. Louis. There is great astonishment in the *Atlantic* office at the discovery that this remarkable contributor is a woman—until recently a cripple!

And so you do like to let your thoughts "linger about me in my daily life," my precious little sweetheart? That must be because your love makes up so large a part of the heart side of that life, darling. You are its 'good spirit'; the sunshine that you are to bring into it seems to send a bit of its radiance on before to drive away shadows of anxiety and of discouragement. You are already the light of my home, my Eileen: and, oh, I am *so* glad that you love to be with me, even in thought, in my quiet home hours! Oh, my darling, my queen, how sweet it will be to have you always at my side! Would that time *had* wings!

Yes, sweetheart, you *have* always said the words of love that I wished, "sooner or later"—but I have almost always had to *plead* for them, to scheme for them, to coax—sometimes to dictate— them; and what has delighted me beyond measure of late has been the growing disposition my darling has shown to *volunteer* confession and demonstration. That was the crowning delight for which my heart was waiting—to see my lovely pet impelled in spite of herself to do some love-making on her own account. I have been trying to teach her that every word of love, every kiss, every caress that she might give unsolicited would fairly win my love anew, as the most precious proof conceivable that I am indeed, by her own joyous claim,

Her own   Woodrow.

ALS (WP, DLC).
[1] Probably William Andrew Robinson, A.B., College of New Jersey, 1881.

Two Letters from Ellen Louise Axson

My darling Woodrow,   New York Mar. 15, 1885.

Many, many thanks, darling, for the sweet letter of yesterday morning! It *did* comfort and reassure me more than I can say;—

I doubt not that I was unduly alarmed about Stockton's condition. A break-down is bad enough at best,—and this is a great disappointment to me also; for we have had a great deal of anxiety about Stockton all his life, but the last year or so he seemed to have been out-growing his troubles, developing into a strong and healthy boy; and I have been so much encouraged about him. Still I see that there is no reason to suppose the case critical— every reason indeed to think otherwise. It is probably the old story,—bronchitis or asthma. In that case he will be better as the weather grows warmer; or if it is over-work, the rest, I trust, will restore him. You see, love, how you can and do help me though we are so far apart; merely to write you about it did me great good and this sweet and, sensible letter has completed the cure.

But you are *always* my comfort and strength. Was there ever such a lover before! one so *all-sufficient*, so abundantly able to satisfy *all* the needs and yearnings of the many-sided woman's nature. Ah, darling, these letters of yours stir within me "thoughts that do often lie to[o] deep for tears";—what then can one do with *words*. But it is very late and I must pause, more tonight[.] With all my heart   Your own Eileen.

My darling Woodrow,   New York, Mar. 15/85.
   I have been laughing a good deal at those girls at the League who make such large collections of sketches of themselves, but I am almost as bad, this time, as any; I have *another*—number three!—and this I think you will like. A few days ago one of the boys came running to me with it, having just found it in another boy's book. He thought it so good that he wanted me to see it. The owner chanced to be a member of my class, one of the boys that I know very well, so when I found that he had two sketches, this and a full length, I sweetly suggested, after praising them highly, that my "family" needed *one* such good sketch of me more than he needed *two*. He didn't seem to agree with me exactly, but said that if I would sit for him again I might have this; and of course I consented, for I knew it would please you and I had made up my mind to get it for you. I don't know whether you will think it a good *likeness* or not but it is certainly a good *sketch*; it is well managed and the effect is picturesque. You would laugh to see some of the comical sketches of me that I have come upon! That is the heaviest price one must pay for attendance at the League;—*some* one is *always* sketching one, on

the sly. There are two among the young artists,—not League boys, —who come in to the sketch class who try their hand at me regularly every afternoon; and its an awful bore.

I don't think I thanked you for the "Dial" or told you how much I liked Mr. Shaw's review. Don't you think it about the most satisfactory of all? I would like to have a whole armful of "Dials" to send to my friends! None of the reviews satisfy me in one respect, but this comes nearer doing so than any other;—I mean they don't speak as they should of the singularly fine *style*. I suppose it is really a compliment that they find the *matter* of such absorbing interest that they have no thought for the *manner* of it,—as the greatest sermons, those which impress us most deeply are not those which send us away paying the preacher little compliments as to his "delivery" &c., but those which force us to think long and earnestly and to some purpose upon their great subject. But all the same, people *ought* to be told how delightful as well as "valuable" they will find the book. They ought to know what a *literary* treat they have before them, for quite apart from the interest of the subject, it is the keenest of pleasures to read such English,—to enjoy a style so fresh and vigorous yet so finished, so pure and clear, and powerful and brilliant. In the whole method of it, the way of handling the subject the book is a *masterpiece*!

Dr. Hamilton is away in Canada today, and we had a strange preacher,[1]—don't know who; but he gave us two excellent sermons. I never heard such a metaphorical style; yet it was not flowery in the least, on the contrary it was rather rugged—suggested Carlyle. They were rambling disconnected sermons but full of *such* good things, felicitous expressions or illustrations which one longed to remember word for word. His text this morning suited him exactly it was "the sword of the Lord and of Gideon." But it is time I said "good-night." Sweet-heart I am very lonely tonight without you, my heart cries out for you and will not be quieted.

> "What shall I do with all the days and hours
> That must be counted ere I see thy face"

Darling, you have indeed become the very *life* of
Your own Eileen.

ALS (WP, DLC).
[1] The Rev. Dr. William C. Roberts preached at the Scotch Presbyterian Church on March 15, 1885. A trustee of the College of New Jersey, Dr. Roberts was Corresponding Secretary of the Board of Home Missions of the Presbyterian

Church in the United States of America and became President of Lake Forest University in 1886.

To Ellen Louise Axson, with Enclosure

My own darling,   Balto., March 16, 1885

I know that you will agree with me that the enclosed editorial from the Wilmington *Star* entitles Mr. Kingsbury to at least a partial revision of my opinion about him. Certainly nothing could be more cordial. The review from the *Times* is a poser! After reading it twice, I have concluded that it was *meant* to be on the whole favourable; but it is a sort of calamity to the book that it should be so damned with faint praise by a paper which makes the opinions of so many of the best people in the country. I have ceased to feel any real anxiety about the fate of the book: but I can't help feeling some of that irritation, which all authors are said to suffer, at the thought that its success is so much dependent upon the diverse views of all sorts of critics. If a man happens to be a bit out of temper when he sits down to write about it, the author's chances of a just review are just that much diminished. I have, assuredly, no right to complain so far of the treatment I have received; but I can't help being made uneasy by what these fellows of the press *may* do. I imagine, however, that almost everybody has had his 'say' now, and that the trial of the thing is past.

I spent the morning in the alcoves of the Peabody library, seeing what it contained in the way of American writings on political economy—tedious work! One can spend a whole morning at it and come away with only fifteen or twenty lines of notes. I shall have to spend one or two more mornings of the same kind there, and then, probably, go down to Washington and see what the Congressional library contains. Not that I am to *read* what I find, beyond the title pages. This is for our *bibliography*, in which we want to include *everything*.

What did you do with your holiday (Saturday), little sweetheart? Did you make calls, or go to the galleries, or visit studios, —or what? I wondered all day what my darling was doing with herself—whether she was doing what left her free to think of me as much as I was thinking of her—and in the same way. I get perfectly desperate about our separation sometimes, Eileen. I don't see how I can stand it for three months longer! It is an inestimable comfort, an incomparable delight to me to know that my *letters* solace my darling's moments of anxiety and sorrow, and that I *have* been able to fill *all* the vacant places in her heart

with my love—filling them as much with *joy* as with love, besides
—but even to know these things does not make it easy to be parted
from her! I long to give my love *in person*, and to receive from
her every sweet personal acknowledgement that I am

Her own   Woodrow.

ALS (WP, DLC). Encs.: editorial clipped from the Wilmington, N. C., *Morning
Star*, March 12, 1885, and a clipping of the review, printed below.

E N C L O S U R E

The *New York Times'* Review of
Congressional Government

[March 15, 1885]

A statement of the actual character of the Federal Government
which dominates the States united; its machinery, the movement thereof and its results; the changes which in the course of
a century have taken place, either in accordance with or in spite
of the Constitution—a book of that kind would be a valuable addition to our political literature. More than one, indeed, has been
written with that aim, but they were rather descriptions of articu-
lated skeletons than of forms instinct with life movements; while
Mr. Wilson's book, without this being its special purposes, possesses in some degree that higher character. His main object,
however, is a comparison between a Government by Congressional committees and that where the administration of affairs
in a Parliamentary Government is intrusted to a Cabinet Ministry. To establish the proposition, which may be more or less true,
that ours is a Government by Congressional committees, there is
involved the necessity of a careful examination of the political
machinery and the practical operation of all its parts, and so far
as this may be done with candor and ability so far the book may
become of value aside from its direct aim. But it is not less true,
on the other hand, that an author whose main object is to set
forth an interesting political comparison is more than likely to
leave out of sight every aspect of the subject which does not concern his special point; and in so doing he may not admit within
his line of vision facts which, however essential they may be to
a clear comprehension of the general character of a Government,
may not strengthen the position he aims to establish, but may,
possibly, even weaken it. Nor does this necessarily indicate any
want of fairness. The object of the author is to draw sharp and
clear the lines of the contrast he wishes to point out; and, suc-

ceeding in this, he feels that there is no obligation incumbent upon him to follow those lines still further, though in that direction may be found other aspects of the subject not less interesting and in themselves even more worthy of consideration. For however instructive it may be to be taught wherein our own Government may differ from and be better or worse than other popular Governments in other countries, it profits us still more to understand the positive as well as the comparative merits or demerits of that under which we live. But as Mr. Wilson did not propose to write a text book upon our political system, but an essay, or series of essays, upon government by Congressional committees, which the system has developed, and as in this we find much of the value of a text book, so much the more is gained.

In another way, even less direct, but quite as positive, the volume is an addition to our political literature, and that is in the side light sometimes thrown upon questions which may be only incidentally alluded to. The reader is reminded, for example, without any direct intention on the part of the writer, of the old controversy upon the relative advantages and disadvantages of an unwritten and of a written constitution of government, because of the unquestionable elasticity of the one and the supposed rigidity of the other. In contrasting Parliamentary government under a Ministry and Congressional government under irresponsible committees, as both exist to-day, Mr. Wilson shows that the differences in the administration of affairs in England and the United States a century ago, though of another character, were not less marked than now. The change in the British Constitution is generally believed to be a growth for the better, and that growth, it has been assumed, was possible only because the Constitution, untrammeled by the written letter of the law, has gradually evolved from time to time as the exigencies of the people were made evident, and the increasing knowledge of their natural rights demanded. The result is undisputed; the reason given for the unhindered constitutional progress may not be quite so indisputable. It is not, it seems, "the letter that killeth" any more in the one case than in the other. The written charter of our rights and duties so carefully constructed by the "fathers of the Constitution"—and written that no change might be possible except of well-considered purpose and by prescribed form—has, nevertheless, been outgrown by the Government built upon it. The provisions for amendment, which they supposed would be insurmountable barriers to ill-considered and dangerous changes, have been avoided by approaches, the possible discovery of which was unforeseen a century ago. If this be true, as undoubtedly it is, it is clear that a Constitution need not be unwritten to be capable of growth. Whether, however, the change under the written letter of the law may not the more easily go on unseen and unsuspected, and, therefore, [be] insidious and possibly evil, is another question.

That ours is a Government by Congressional committees is the essential fact which, Mr. Wilson thinks, is not sufficiently considered and not even generally understood. The House of Representatives, as he says, "has as many leaders as there are subjects of legislation, for there are as many standing committees as there are leading classes of legislation, and in the consideration of every topic of business the House is guided by a special leader in the person of a Chairman of the standing committee charged with the superintendence of measures of the particular class to which that topic belongs." The *statement is involved and clumsy, as the style of the author almost uniformly is,*[1] but the purport will not be misunderstood. It is not Congress as a whole that legislates. Every subject of legislation that comes before it is referred to a committee appointed for the consideration of these subjects; an influential member of the House and of the dominant party is Chairman of that committee, and for the most part directs its decision. The rules of the House, which it is the will as well as the duty of the Speaker to enforce, are designed to secure an immediate hearing when the Chairman of the committee is ready to report; and the House, governed by rigid party discipline and the unbending rules, adopts, with little or no debate, the committee's report. The Representatives generally may be, and more often than not are, quite ignorant of the merits, or perhaps the character, of the measures before them; the country certainly is quite in the dark as to the arguments used or the principles accepted in committee which led it to a conclusion, whether wise, just, or otherwise. This government by committees not contemplated in this written law of the Constitution, nor provided against, because not foreseen by its framers, there is no power anywhere to withstand or modify effectively. It does not rest with the President, except in some extreme case, because of his relation to the legislative branch, nor with the Senate, because of its similarity in organization to the House, and the absence of that difference in character which the framers of the Constitution hoped and believed they had secured by a difference in the representative character of that body and the method of electing its members, and finally not in the Supreme Court, except where there has been some flagrant violation of fundamental law.

This analysis, which we only briefly outline, of the practical operation of this machinery of the Federal Government will probably commend itself to most observant persons, though they may not always see the force of Mr. Wilson's examination nor agree with all of his objections. It was not perhaps his purpose to suggest a remedy for an evil as yet not generally recognized, unless he meant to indicate it by the comparison with parliamentary government under a Cabinet Ministry. But, however this may be, the volume is a timely contribution to our political history, appearing at a moment when mere party ties are so universally loosened, and the minds of men are turned to the consideration of the essential end and possibilities of a popular Government.

Printed in the *New York Times*, March 15, 1885.

1 WW's underlining.

From Ellen Louise Axson

My darling Woodrow,   New York Mar. 16, 1885.
    Your letter received today is indeed a feast of good things[.] I have been so excited over them all the afternoon that I could scarcely work. The postman was late in the morning so that I came back at noon for my letters and then was ob[l]iged to rush back with them unread, in order to draw for my place. So it came to pass that I underwent the full effect of all your "nice things" at the League. I felt as if I were treading on air—as if I were altogether too buoyant to sit quietly on my high stool but must perforce rise to the ceiling! See how lucky we women are,—we have the full benefit of the music without paying the piper! It is *so* much trouble to win fame you know, but without having any of the hard work we enjoy the victory, sometimes as in the present case, ten times as much as the victor himself! Of course you *are* glad but your rejoicing is of a different quality; it is, as you so well put it that of "a strong man to run a race." Yes, you have a grand opportunity, and there is much in the very greatness of it to make one feel *serious*, but I am too entirely sure that my hero is great enough for *any* occasion to feel at all "anxious." But I did not dream that the book was not only so exactly the right thing, but was coming so exactly at the right time. "There is a tide in the affairs of men which taken at the flood," &c. You certainly struck the flood-tide! And what an opportunity that Washington post of

which Mr. Ford speaks would afford you to follow it up! What a chance it would give you, not only for devoting your *whole* time to your special work, but for making your personal influence felt! Is it your Bryn Mawr engagement which renders it so entirely "out of the question." Would they not excuse you if you were called away by "business of such importance"?—business that can't be kept waiting?

Oh dear! I have so much to say tonight, and so sorry that I *must* wait. But the weather has suddenly changed and this room is bitterly cold,—and so there is no help for it. Please excuse haste. Goodnight, darling. Can I ever tell you, sweet-heart, how much I love and honnour you?—how entirely I am

Your own Eileen.

ALS (WP, DLC).

From Janet Woodrow Wilson

My precious boy,   Wilmington, N. C., Tuesday [March 17, 1885]

Your sweet letter to papa was received this morning. I need not tell you, my darling, that we think of you constantly—and talk about you much every day. That we are inexpressibly proud of our beloved boy's success—unprecedented as it is. We are filled with joy & thankfulness.—We took tea last night with Mr. & Mrs. Wm. Phillips. He has expressed his delight in reading your book, of which he bought a copy, before. He is very particular to claim you as an old classmate[1]—makes much of that—and last night he was asking us whether you were really bound to go to Bryn Mawr. It seems there is to be a chair in your department established at Chapel Hill—and *he* hopes to be elected Prof. of Chemistry—will apply for the place. He thinks it would be so delightful if you and he could work together there—and wants you to apply for the "English" chair—or "History"—I am not sure as to the precise name of the new Chair.

My darling boy—are you *bound* in honour to go to B. M.? Of course we cant tell what will be for the best. But your father says he will advise you to accept an invitation such as Prof Adams of the Mich University proposes. But I will leave him to speak for himself as to that. Your father says he expects to be spoken of in future as *your father*! Mr Willard[2] said to papa this morning that your book is causing a regular "*furor*"—in his native section I suppose he meant. It would amuse you to hear what Mr Kingsbury has to say in public & private. He assures your father that he has predicted great distinction for you from the very first! . . .

God bless you, my sweet boy. Love unbounded to our sweet Ellie—from us each one. Josie is well & is helping us with all his might.

With love unlimited from us each

Yours as ever   Mother

P.S. omitted. ALS (WP, DLC) with WWhw notation on env.: "Ans. March 22/85."
¹ William B. Phillips and Wilson were classmates at Davidson College, '77.
² Probably one of three Willard brothers, prominent merchants of Washington, N. C., who also ran a large wholesale grocery firm in Wilmington, N. C.

From Joseph Ruggles Wilson

[Wilmington, N. C., March 17, 1885]

M[y]. R[evered]. S[on]., I enjoyed the review slips you enclosed. The writers are men of sense!

I hardly think I w'd break the engagement at *B. M.* A year or so there will be nothing lost; and, by keeping up a correspondence with yr. "big-bugs" here and there, you will no doubt find a first-class opening. "Festina lenti [*sic*]."

I wish *you* would persuade the dear mother to leave here at once. This spasm of packing will ruin her, else. You know how workful & unselfish she is. But I could do *all* that remains, with expert help.   Most affy your   F.

ALI added to JWW to WW, undated but postmarked March 17, 1885.

From Walter Emerson Faison

Dear Wilson: Clinton, N. C., March 17th 1885.

You have probably grown weary of the flood of complimentary notices and criticisms that have poured upon you since the publication of your "Congressional Government," but a simple expression of appreciation and of congratulation will not be unwelcome I trust from one of your Law classmates who joins with admiration of your book a sincere and long felt interest in the author of it.

During the ten days the volume has been on the table I have had scarcely an hour's consecutive reading in it and have read no further than to ch IV, for my partners (one of them has this minute come and asked "where is Wilson's book") and our loafing friends never let an opportunity slip to snatch it up and read till something compels them to lay it aside for the benefit of the next watcher.

The editor of our county news paper wishes, with your permission to publish a series of extracts from it for the enlightenment of his country subscribers who will otherwise remain forever ignorant of its existence and of its subject-matter.[1]

Mr. Minor[2] no doubt feels proud of the acceptance your book has received at the hands of the critics and the public, almost as much as much [sic] he would be if you had brought out a new edition of Coke on Littleton in six volumes. . . .

Now I will close and wait for my chance to begin the chapter on the senate. The papers say you have accepted the chair of History in a female college with an unspellable name. Your southern friends hope that you will enter upon your duties well fortified (by preoccupation of course) against the dangerous proximity of fair faces.

Yours very truly   W E Faison

ALS (WP, DLC) with WWhw notation on env.: "Ans. Mar 30/85."
  [1] The "county news paper" was the Clinton, N. C., *Caucasian*. No issues of this newspaper for 1885 have survived. The editor and publisher in 1886 was D. A. Nicholson.
  [2] Professor John B. Minor.

To Ellen Louise Axson

My own darling,   Balto., March 17, 1885
  It made me smile a grim smile to think of the *Times* review I sent you yesterday, while I read your praises of my *style* in the letter that came this morning. Strange that it should have escaped your notice that it is "uniformly involved and clumsy"! But oh, my darling, your praises of my work are *so* precious to me! Not unqualified commendation from Mr. Bagehot—were he living—could give me one tithe of the delight that these words—these sweet, generous words—of yours give me. I write to convince—and to convince partly through *pleasing*—the public—for pleasing is a part, an essential part, of *persuasion*; but there is some one else for whom I write—some one whom I would not only convince and please but also delight. I have told you already, more than once, who that is. My influence lives by the approval of the world; but *I myself live* by your love and approval and sympathy!

  I am finding out, sweetheart, the truth of the adage, that "nothing succeeds like success." I received a letter this morning from the President of the "American Institute of Civics" (an association lately formed by prominent men in Boston) asking if I would be "willing to accept an election as one of the Institute lecturers." "Those chosen lecturers are expected to deliver an address before the Institute in Boston, once in the year,—expenses paid. It is expected that arrangements will also be made, if desired, by which the same lecture, or others upon subjects related to the purposes of the Institute, may be delivered elsewhere under its auspices, payment for services to be made to the lecturer. You will observe that the duties of the position will not be more onerous than you choose to make them, aside from the lecture in Boston. These lectures will introduce you to a select Boston audience, in which there may be a possible advantage. I trust that you will think it expedient to accept the proposition." I will. I am also invited to contribute to the journal of the Institute, *"The Citizen,"* presently to be established. May-be so—if I have time *and something to say.*

I am *so* glad, my pet, that you have secured another sketch for me!—and I am immensely pleased and complimented to know that you already claim me as your "family"! It *is* very foolish in the other girls to make such collections of sketches of themselves, if they mean to keep them for their own gratification; but if they are securing them for *their* lovers—and their lovers are as eager to get them as I am to get sketches of you—I like them the better for it.—And you *do* beg them for your "family," sweetheart; for are you not related to me by the most sacred, and the closest, of all ties—the tie of love? I am never so happy as when I think that you *feel* that in deed and in truth I am

Your own   Woodrow.

ALS (WP, DLC).

From Ellen Louise Axson

My darling Woodrow,   New York Mar. 17. 1885.

Yes, I think it will be necessary to reconsider your judgment of Mr. Kingsbury. This is certainly generous praise, and better still it is *sensible* praise. Think of Mr. Renick's achievement in the "Nation" and then consider how you *might* be victimized by the local editors of your boyhood's home,—or homes. Most of those in the South are capable of it too; I wonder that some Columbia or Augusta news-monger hasn't already announced that you were "raised" there, and proceeded to give the world full particulars, from their point of view, of your "salad days"! As for the "Times," —well perhaps I had better not talk about the Times—I am too indignant! How I *should* like to tell that reviewer what I think of him. He is either a perfect simpleton who is incapable of knowing a good thing when he sees it, or he is a thoroughly dishonest and unprincipled critic, who, because he differs from you in opinion, tries to injure you by underhand methods and by telling what he *must know* to be a preposterous falsehood about your style. But then what *are* his opinions? He doesnt seem to have any. Was there ever such a yea-nay article? Not one *positive* or straightforward word in it. I dare say the poor creature is simply a fool. But it *is* unfortunate that such a paper as the Times should have entrusted the writing of a review to anyone so incompetent. But bah, let us not speak of him;—since by so doing I can do you no good and him no *harm*! I may as well keep my wrath to myself;—so we will change the subject.

Your "tale" about the Carters proved a *very* good story indeed —entertaining in the highest degree. How comical, when one thinks of it, that it should come around to me so soon!—as if this great New York, with Balt. and the intervening country thrown in, were but a little village. Am glad you warned me, for now I can be on my guard and ready to defend myself;—yet since I can't deny your acquaintance I am not sure that I can, after all, do much in the way of defence. But on the whole, it does'nt make any great difference; I am getting so *hardened* that I care very little who knows I am engaged.

No, I had heard nothing of Miss Murfree and I am utterly *amazed*. How could a girl—a cripple at that—gather the material for such a story, how could she know those rough fellows so well?—to go no deeper in search of surprises. Do you think there is *anything* in it so far to suggest a woman? But I am very sorry that she did not, or could not, keep her secret longer. See if people don't discover that it is'nt so good as it was, that it grows feebler as it progresses, that she is'nt capable of *sustained* effort! At best the verdict will be altered, for whereas it has been "a remarkable production," it will now be merely a remarkable production *for a woman*!

No, I neither made calls, nor visited galleries on Sat; I went on a greater "lark" even than that. In the morning I was busy at home over various odds and ends of work; at lunch time I went up to the Metropolitan, Miss Van Vorhis having promised me a sitting for an oil study, but just after my arrival some-one suddenly remembered that [Henry] Irving and Ellen Terry had returned and were going to play "Twelth Night" that afternoon, whereupon three of us, Miss "Van," Miss Farnsworth and myself simultaneously decided that we must see it; so off we went. Of course we went on the fifty cent schedule,—general admission to the gallery,—but never the less we got splendid seats and had a *glorious time*. She is perfectly lovely as Viola, and Viola was always one of my special pets,—while Irving as Malvolio was "immense," as the League girls say. I have heard *six* of Shakspere's plays now;—I begin to feel rich, for each one seems to me a *treasure* which will yield a perpetual interest of pleasure. It is certainly a large investment for fifty cents. We think of going next Sat. to see "Much Ado about Nothing"; Beatrice, we are told, is her greatest part. Isn't it queer that she does'nt play "As You Like It"? It seems to me that she was "cut out" for Rosilind; there is so much of that sweet archness about her even in acting Portia and Viola, where that quality is'nt conspicuous.

I began in the painting class at League yesterday, and am of course fascinated. We have a lovely little boy for a model, whom I want to kiss all the time because he reminds me of Eddie. I am on the fifth floor now you know, under the sky-light; yesterday I saw in the corner of the room another very steep flight of stairs, so I thought I would go on an exploring expedition and see where they led. So up I went 'till I found myself, to my great satisfaction, on the roof. It was really charming out there,—so much sunshine and fresh air, and *view*! But when I wanted to go in again I found myself *locked out*, and I had to do some very emphatic beating on the door before I gained admission.

I have received an answer to my letter to Stockton. It is reassuring but not as much so as I could have wished; he is a *great deal* better, so that the doctors don't think it imprudent for him to go on with his studies, dropping one only. But then the symptoms which he mentions are of so serious and alarming a character and so new for him that I am not altogether relieved even by the information that they are to all appearances a thing of the past. It began with a chill the day before Xmas; this was followed by great and increasing weakness, dizziness when he tried to run up the stairs, two pronounced fainting spells, and one night very acute pains in all the upper part of his body. He does'nt explain these symptoms at all,—gives me no hint as to what the doctors consider the probable cause of the trouble, so of course the letter is'nt satisfactory. But he says he is telling me the whole truth, and that no one thinks there is any cause for alarm or even for worry. Oh dear, I wish I could see them all for a little while and *satisfy* myself! It is a shame to have kept me so in the dark as they have *all* done!—and for nearly three months! I think deception about health is as wrong as about anything else.

I am so glad, my darling, that I can trust you in *everything*. With all the press of work that you have upon you, I should'nt be happy or at rest about you one moment unless I were *sure* that you would tell me *just* how you felt, and to what extent it was wearing upon you.

Yes darling I *do* think it the sweetest of all things to love with the simple, frank ardour of childhood, without thought of concealing either the love or anything else. I am sure one doesn't begin to taste the full joy of loving until one has learned that sweet secret. It *is* my delight to love you so, a delight great beyond the power of my imagination to shadow forth even on that day when believing, trembling, hoping, fearing, I first gave myself to you. Ah sweet-heart you have made *me* unspeakably happy! would that I *might* be in your arms five minutes to tell you so! Oh that I had wings like a dove for then would I fly to you and be at rest!

My! I am *shocked* at myself for perverting Scripture so, but I did it without thinking[.] After *that* I think it is time to close. Believe, darling, forever   Your own   Eileen.

ALS (WP, DLC).

To Ellen Louise Axson

My own darling,   Balto., March 18, 1885
Yes, my engagement at Bryn Mawr prevents my considering such propositions as that tempting one of Mr. Ford's. I am fully committed to the B. M. people, and cannot, therefore, coquet with these chances for other employment. I have been invited by Dr. C. K. Adams to go out to the University of Mich. and read a paper before the Historical Seminary there, with a view to impress the men who will presently be called upon to fill the chair of which I spoke a few days ago—and whom he would take care to have on hand to hear me—to go, that is, as an unannounced candidate. But I must refuse. It would not be honourable to *seek* another place. Possibly if such a chair as that at Ann Arbor were definitely offered to me, I could prevail upon the B. M. trustees to release me, rather than stand between a young man and a chance such as he could not expect to have more than once in a life-time; but I could scarcely ask their leave to go as a *candidate* for another place, however great that place. Without their consent, however, I cannot go. If Dr. C. K. Adams will make me some surer offer, I might think it best to sue for release from the Women's College folk. All this is terribly hard: but it's plain duty, and the only means of keeping a conscience void of offence. I seem to be losing much—everything—by it; but, since it is right, I can in the

end lose nothing by it! My ambition kicks against the pricks, but my judgment doesn't waver.

Yes, precious, Shaw's review in the 'Dial' was by all odds the best that has appeared. His attitude is so thoroughly and so intelligently sympathetic. I used to take him into consultation very often last year when I was preparing the essays and he knew just what I meant, and wished to be understood to mean, at every point. He had seen much of the argument of the book in process of manufacture. How many copies of the paper would to [you] like, to send off, little lady? I can easily order some for you—and would do so without more questions asked if I had any idea how many you want. "A whole armful" is too indefinite. By-the-way, have you been keeping the notices I have sent you? I should rather like to preserve the lot of them.

I shall call on Mrs. Green to-night. I wonder if she will discover my embarrassment?

I should like to 'punch' the heads of the two young gentlemen who annoy you by sketching you every day in the sketch class!

I love you, Eileen (the lines stand for the number of *kisses*)— every day seems to add *infinitely* both to my love and to my longing for your presence! Oh, my darling, what supreme joy there is in store for   Your own   Woodrow.

ALS (WP, DLC).

From Ellen Louise Axson

My darling Woodrow,   New York Mar 18/85
It seems to me that this last success—or rather this last evidence of your success is one of the pleasantest and most interesting of all. It will give you without any tedious waiting, the opportunity which I was sure would come sooner or later,—the opportunity to use your gifts as a speaker;—and to use them before an audience worthy of you too! I am indeed delighted, dearest, that you have such an opening—I wonder when I will have an opportunity to hear you speak!—I have always been so *wild* to do so, and this talk about it serves to quicken my desires, in that direction. How perfectly beside myself with excitement and delight I should be if I only could!

Yes it *is* strange that such conspicuous qualities in your style as those discovered by the *Times* should have escaped my notice and that of all your other critics!—but it required a great and *original* mind to make that discovery; we ordinary people can't hope to

follow him, but must needs keep the beaten track and agree with
"all the world" that ["] it is so good that it could not well be better,"
that it is "clear, luminous, well arranged," "lucid in statement,
philosophical in tone," &c. &c. But I won't fan into fresh blaze the
still glowing embers of my wrath towards that poor creature. How
strange it seems, dear that you should really care for *my* poor
little opinion of your writings,—and yet *not* strange, after all, from
love's stand-point. Well you may be sure that you *do* "not only
convince and please but delight" me. You make my life one long
delight,—or a succession of delights of all sorts,—delight growing
out of your writing and all your good gifts, and your successes,
and your precious love—and, in short, the the [*sic*] delight in *you*
yourself,—in the whole man. For you can't deny, sir, that you
are the most delightful person in the world! But I am belated tonight, and must now close. Goodnight dear Woodrow. Do you
know I am getting very *homesick?* there is no doubt but that these
long separations from ones "*family*" are trying[.] I love you, darling, I live by your love and approval, and always I am

ALS (WP, DLC).   Your own Eileen.

Draft of a Letter to Charles Kendall Adams

Dear Sir: [Baltimore, c. March 19, 1885]
    I thank you very sincerely for your kind letter of March 12.
Your cordial praise of my book is a source of the greatest gratification and encouragement to me. Through the success of the
book—of which such judgments assure me—I find myself put at
once in possession of opportunities for widely useful work such
as I had not hoped to have for some years to come. After coming
to Balto. to study in the Univ. I found that the signs of the times
in educational matters clearly justified me in yielding to my
strong inclination to make a specialty of administration, of the
study of practical govt., and it has consequently since that time
been my distinct purpose to seek ultimately a chair just such as
you suggest Judge Campbell's may be made after his resignation.
I did not expect, however, that such a chair would present itself
at once and I accepted a liberal offer from the trustees of B. M.
College with the idea of making several years' work in teaching
general history serve to supply me with a broad basis of historical
knowledge such as I might not otherwise acquire. I felt that I
could fill such a chair for a few years with pleasure and consequently with zeal; I hoped meanwhile, however, to keep my
special studies more or less actively afoot, with a view to prepar-

ing them for eventual mobilization and an aggressive campaign. I am now, therefore, fully committed to a two years' service at Bryn Mawr, and I should not feel justified in seeking, a position elsewhere without first obtaining a release from my contract there, a step which I should hardly be warranted in taking for the purpose of entering upon a candidacy wh. would be without assured issue. Probably, too, I should find in June that it was too late for the Trustees of B. M. to think of making so considerable a change in their arrangements.

I have been thus candid and unreserved in stating my motives in the course I have adopted and the circumstances wh. at present hold me fast because I am anxious that you should understand just why I feel constrained to decline the course wh. you so kindly suggest. Were I free to choose, there could of course be no doubt about my accepting your invitation to read a paper before your Ass. I should esteem it a privilege, under any circumstances, to be brought into contact with the life of your dept. But, as it is, I must deny myself both that pleasure and the tempting chances wh would just now go with it.

Believe me with great respect and sincere gratitude for your kindness

WWhw draft (WP, DLC) attached to C. K. Adams to WW, March 12, 1885.

To Ellen Louise Axson, with Enclosure

My own darling,   Balto., March 19, 1885

Look upon the enclosed clipping, from an Augusta paper, and recant![1] The "Augusta newsmonger"[2] has 'done himself proud' in this instance. His sentiments are expressed in a style of amazing extravagance, but he means well, and the praise is apparently quite spontaneous and sincere. I think that I shall have to ask President Gilman if he really did make that enthusiastic remark about me. It would not be quite like his eminently cautious self to say such things: but I believe he *does* think very highly of our little volume.

It *is* simply marvellous that Miss Murfree should have produced "The Prophet of the Big Smoky." There is certainly not a single touch in the story that reveals a woman's hand—unless my theory be true, that woman's mental powers are of the sympathetic sort almost entirely and that the great creations of fiction, springing as they do from a perfected capacity for the sympathetic interpretation of character, are the *natural* products of woman's genius; in which case *all* of this story illustrates my thesis, show-

ing *everywhere* a woman's hand. Were there not real genius in
the construction of the story, however, the woman's hand would
appear *in other ways*: and the least that can be said is that, all
things considered, it is amazing, that Miss Murfree should have
written it!

I am glad, my precious, that you are having such chances to
see Irving and Ellen Terry: I approve most heartily of such 'larks'!
And what a glorious long letter this is that you have sent me this
morning! I can't tell you what treasures I esteem these budgets
of news about your daily doings and adventures. I should like
to have a record of every trifling thing to which either my darling's hands or her thoughts turn. It is like an exile's eager desire
to know even how the grass looks in the little garden at *home*.
My heart's home is with my little sweetheart, and she cannot tell
me anything of herself that my heart does not delight to dwell
upon[.] Every strand of her hair is strong enough to bind me with;
every parting of her lips has in it for me memories of precious
words of love spoken and of precious kisses given; I envy the canvas that receives the light from her glorious eyes; I love a certain
great upper room at the "Met."; still more do I love *her* room,
which I have never seen, because there, for the time, is her
home, there my imagination has so often followed her about in
the performance of little house-wifely tasks, wondering about the
pretty white wrapper, about the thoughts of the sweet lady there
all alone, and about my fortune in winning her wonderful love
and precious allegiance! Oh, Eileen, darling, what can I not do
now that you have been won to *demonstration* in your love! You
are the sweetest, dearest little lady in the world: you are *everything* to your lover, to

Your own　Woodrow.

P.S. I am not through, after all. I wanted to tell you that I went
to see Mrs. Green last night, and enjoyed myself so much that
I stayed half an hour longer than I had intended, without knowing it. The only drawback was that she seemed to regard me as a
mere boy—actually asking me *if I had chosen a profession yet*!
She is going to take me to see her nieces.

I am so much relieved, my pet, to hear of Stockton's great improvement—so delighted that he is really well again. His symptoms were very extraordinary; but the doctors probably know
what they are about in allowing him to resume his studies; and
surely you can count upon him *now* to keep you advised as to his
condition.

Yes, indeed, darling, you *may* count upon me to deceive you in nothing—about my health as little as about anything else!

Here is an amusing extract from a letter just rec'd from Faison (Miss Kate Sprunt's husband) an old Univ. of Va. classmate of mine. He writes from Clinton, N. C., their home. "During the ten days the volume ("Cong. Govt.") has been on the table I have had scarcely an hour's consequetive reading in it, and have read no further than to ch. IV, for my partners (one of them has this minute come and asked 'where is Wilson's book?') and our loafing friends never let an opportunity slip to snatch it up and read it until something compels them to lay it aside for the benefit of the next watcher. The editor of our county newspaper wishes, with your permission, to publish a series of extracts from it for the enlightenment of his country subscribers who will otherwise remain forever ignorant of its existence and of its subject-matter."

Have I told you before, *Eileen*, that I love you with all my heart?   Your own   Woodrow.

ALS (WP, DLC).
    [1] Originally enclosed in Annie W. Howe to WW, March 16, 1885, ALS (WP, DLC).
    [2] James Ryder Randall, editor of the Augusta *Chronicle and Constitutionalist*.

E N C L O S U R E

[March 15, 1885]
Thomas Woodrow Wilson.

Mr. Woodrow Wilson, a graduate of Johns Hopkins University, has distinguished himself already by the production of a volume entitled "Congressional Government," which extorted the liberal praise of the "Nation" and other papers of the highest order. That a young man of 28 should have astonished the reading and thinking world by such a work is remarkable enough, but it is still more wonderful that he should have done so without having had any legislative training. It is an exhibition of pure intellect rarely displayed in any age or country. Very few Congressmen could have composed it at all, and it is much beyond the power of the average Representative or Senator.

Mr. Wilson is the son of the Rev. Joseph R. Wilson, who was once the honored pastor of the Presbyterian Church in this city. Of his already distinguished son, President Gilman says: "If the South has any more such young men, we would like to have them at our University. Woodrow Wilson is not only an honor to the South, but to the country. He would be an honor to any land and to any university."

Printed in the Augusta, Ga., *Chronicle and Constitutionalist*, March 15, 1885.

From Ellen Louise Axson

My darling Woodrow,   New York Mar 19/85.

I have been hearing all my life about "the embarrassment of riches" but never realized before how real a trouble it might become! I should say that is what you are suffering from at present, —is it not? Yes I must agree with you that the case is hard; *very* hard! But of course you are right in you[r] decision; it *would* be wrong for you to *seek* another position—and I believe that you are also right in your conclusion, that it will all work together for good. I am sure that if the fine position is offered you, the Quakers *can't* be so unreasonable and ungenerous as to put any obstacles in your way. That good Dr. Rhoads is too much your friend to permit it. Has this vacancy already occurred in Mich? Is it to be filled for the coming fall? By the way, what constitutes it such a peculiarly tempting offer? I seem to have heard oftener of the University of Mich. than of other Western colleges, but I really know nothing about it. Is it a very famous institution? Would the advantages of a place there be sufficient to compensate you for going so far away from the great Eastern centres of thought and action; and from Washington the grand focus of interest for you. Of course it seems much grander to be professor in a great University, than a newspaper correspondent; but wouldn't the latter post after all give you larger opportunities for doing your own special work—work that will live,—and also for exerting active influence? I remember your saying once that a place in a large institution was very undesirable for you because it would render your everyday duties so heavy and leave you no time for your private studies, for doing that which you have most at heart. These questions I, of course, merely "ask for information" as Rosa Dartle[1] says; I don't even intend them to be suggestions; they are simply prompted by my desire to know *all* about *everything* that concerns you. To know at least as much as is possible while we remain separated; I know one can't write *everything*, for want of time.

Yes indeed I am keeping the notices with the greatest care,— though there are one or two which it would give me immense satisfaction to burn; but I would not even distroy those on my own responsibility.

Many thanks, dear, for your offer to furnish me with "*Dials*["];—though I did not mean to give you a hint to that effect, but merely to express my delight with the article; but I should be charmed to have four or five of them if perfectly convenient.

So you called on Mrs. Green last night (I wonder Sir that *you* dont say called *for*, a l'anglaise!) I am curious to hear your account of your visit, and to know how you liked her.

I am sure darling that every day increases *my* love, and longing for your presence. I don't bear your absence with half the composure that I did. My love has far out-run my philosophy. I feel as though I could not bear it at all if I did not live more, in thought, in the past when we *were* together, and the future when we shall be always together, than in the darkened present,—darkened for want of you, darling, the light of my life. With all my heart   Your own   Eileen.

ALS (WP, DLC).
  ¹ A character in *David Copperfield* who was fond of saying, "You know how ignorant I am, and that I only ask for information."

To Ellen Louise Axson

My own darling,   Balto., March 20, 1885
  Many of your letters serve as a sort of standard by which I can tell the influence which you will exert upon me in the sweet coming days when you will be always at my side. Often, when irritating circumstances, small and great, have wrought in me the stern, indignant, defiant humour, the scarcely suppressed belligerent temper, for which there are abundant materials in my disposition, I have only to turn to my darling's sweet words of love and trust to be calmed and softened. They are like a tender caress, like a note of light-hearted laughter—chasing away discontent and making one instantly ashamed of anger. But, then, they do make me *so* homesick for my Eileen! I would give worlds for one real caress from her, for one eager kiss, for one tone of her dear voice! Oh, darling, you are all the world to me; I don't see how I ever lived without your love! The joy of being loved by you, my "rare and radiant maiden," grows every day: and I am beginning to see, Miss, that it is only of late that we have discovered the most joyous way of loving each other. That unfortunate circumstance of giving you a first impression that I was calm—if not cold—and undemonstrative made it necessary for you to go through a long and slow process of finding out that nothing could satisfy me short of free leave to give what extravagant demonstrative proof I chose of my love—and that nothing could delight me more—except to have my darling herself declare by every word and gesture that her heart could suggest how much she loved me in return. But my little queen *is* making that dis-

covery—and now we are free to love like children in our actions towards each other, and like man and woman in our thoughts of each other. I know that I have talked about this a great deal of late; but I can't help it: a fellow *must* rejoice when he's glad, *must* dance when he's merry, *must* speak out his heart's triumphant joy when at last his sweetheart of her own accord comes to him, puts her arms around his neck, looks with her sweet shy eyes full into his, and offers her lips to be kissed!—for does not such an action symbolize *every*thing to him—everything that his heart desires? But, dear me! I must not tantalize myself with such pictures! It's hard enough as it is to regard common prudence and not go to New York every time my loneliness threatens to become intolerable. I've had to pay a heavy bill for books recently, and there's no prospect of my being able to go to New York for some time to come without running partially into debt, by forestalling my allowance: I am kept here by an immovable anchor of *necessity*: and yet, when my darling declares that she is homesick for me—that she would promise any sweet bribe of love-making if only she could thereby shorten our separation a single day, it is all that my judgment can do to keep my heart from dragging me to the railway station! How I hate the distance and the expense that separate me from her! But think, sweetheart, what we are waiting for:—think *how* our separation will end! I would wait twenty years *for you*, if it were necessary!—and what are ninety days? When they are gone—well I shall be beside myself with delight! Eileen—tell me, sweetheart—do you wish that June, and the best day of June—*our* day in June—were come? Do you, precious?

In order to explain the enclosed letter, my pet, I must quote the following from the letter in which sister Marion sent it to me: "My letter to Ellie, which was addressed wrong, came back to me a day or so ago, directed to 'Marion, 506 State St.' As the direction came at the beginning of my letter and my name at the end, I presume the entire letter was read and suitably admired! [not a very *necessary* conclusion—skipping is a known art at the Dead Letter Office] "I will enclose you the troublesome epistle, and get you to forward to Ellie with explanations. I am afraid your P. card"—with the "New York address" on it—"is lost."[1] By her "warning" she means an eloquent picture she had drawn of the consequences of marrying a 'literary man.' She was anxious to be sure that you quite appreciated the risks you were running.[2] What a droll lot of nonsense that is about the "Song of the Shirt"![3] This dear sister of mine quite takes my breath away sometimes.

I had the unexpected pleasure of meeting Charles Dudley War-ner[4] this morning. He came up to "the Bluntschli" under Pres. Gilman's wing while I was taking notes under Dr. Ely—and presently Dr. Adams, into whose office the two had gone, came to fetch me, saying that Mr. Warner wanted to meet me. Mr. W. proved a most delightful, full-eyed man of frank address and unpretentious manners. He complimented my book most pleasantly —and said that he had sent a copy of it to Matthew Arnold, with the purpose of making him better acquainted with our government than he showed himself to be in his recent article in the "Nineteenth Century," "Onc Word More About America."[5] Mr. W. recommended the volume to him as "the best book on the subject"—so there's one more 'nice thing.' My chief satisfaction in these gratifying compliments, darling, is that I can repeat them to you, and make you *glad* with them. They would only *spoil*, if I had to keep them.

Dear mother, from the midst of her packing, sends "love unbounded to our sweet Ellie—from us each one." Dear father says he expects to be known hereafter a[s] 'my father'!

Good-bye darling. How I envy this letter its Sunday with you! But you won't be thinking of it—will you?—except as a messenger from　　　　　　　　　　　　　　Your own　Woodrow.

ALS (WC, NjP). Enc.: Marion W. Kennedy to ELA, Jan. 2, 1885, ALS (WP, DLC).

[1] From an unpublished portion of Marion W. Kennedy to WW, March 15, 1885.

[2] A reference to Marion W. Kennedy to WW, Dec. 10, 1884, ALS (WP, DLC).

[3] The reference is to Marion's letter of January 2 to ELA, cited above, with its account of housework and sewing and caring for four small children. "The 'Song of the Shirt,'" she wrote, "is, however, of very little variety, and consequently not entertaining."

[4] A leading American journalist, editor, and author. For example, he was editor of the "American Men of Letters" series, co-editor of the *Library of the World's Best Literature*, and co-author (with Mark Twain) of *The Gilded Age*.

[5] Matthew Arnold, "A Word More About America," *Nineteenth Century*, XVII (Feb. 1885), 219-36.

From Ellen Louise Axson

My darling Woodrow,　　　　　　　　　　New York Mar. 20/85.

I have just received a letter from Grandmother in which she says, "I begged your Cousin Loula [Axson] to answer your other letter for me, and, especially, to request you to tell Mr. Wilson how much your Grandfather thanked him for his book;—he doesn't know Mr. Wilson's address. I hope you delivered the message." No, I have not because this is the first I have heard of it! Strange! for Loula spoke of your book in her letter, expressing her delight at its success &c. and I should think that would have reminded her of the message. I have had letters from both Uncle Randolph and Aunt Ella since the book was received praising it, rejoicing in it's success, and saying how much Grandfather was pleased with it,—I never hear directly from him,—but neither did they mention that he had not been able to acknowledge it; I am *very* sorry the mistake occurred. And I suppose that Uncle Will too could not write you for want of your address.

Grandmother is of course much worried about Stockton, and says they are anxious to have him give up his studies and go to Sav. I do hope he will; it *must* be very imprudent for him to continue them. I wrote urging him to drop them when I received his letter. I am glad you enjoyed your visit to Mrs. Green;—but what an astonishing question for her to ask *you*! to think of a person of Mrs. Green's intelligence and culture being so ignorant!—living there in Balt. too! I am sure the most exalted piety doesn't demand that one should neither know nor care about anything that's a'doing in the world outside of hospitals and orphan asylums. But she seems to have reached that state. I think it would be *charity* for me to send her one of the Dials [—] that would show her whether or no you have "chosen a profession yet"!

I see in the new *Nation*, which I have just been looking over, that Cousin Marion, or as we call her Minnie, Reeves[1] has a new book just published by Houghton and Mifflin—"Pilot Fortune." Appleton has always been her publisher before. She and "Emily," her Aunt, have written it together, as has been their custom of late years. I hope it will be successful. Did you see the account of Miss Murfree in—or rather *from* a St Louis paper? It gave a good many interesting facts about her and some quite graphic touches, for instance her passion for small boys and negros, and the account of her favourite game as a child.

Yes I do recant! the Augusta paper has treated you right royally;—I ought to have remembered that the "Constitutionalist" and Mr.—what's his name—"Maryland! my Maryland"—oh *Randall*—I believe it is, are very respectable *institutions*. Hurrah for Mr. Faison and his friends! they are very worthy torch-bearers in your procession, and it is apparently a rather darkened corner in which they are making your light shine. I think you are very fortunate in your friends, dear, and they are all such *true* friends, for they are ready to give practical proof of their friendship. It proves that you yourself are a good friend as well as a good lover. I know the sort of friend you would be, but I venture to say that they don't know so well how you would play the other role! None of them can know you as well as I—and not all of them together can love you one hundredth part as well as I. Ah darling, my love and allegiance great and entire as they are are no more than you deserve—than you have fairly won from

Your own   Eileen.

ALS (WP, DLC).
¹ Marion C. L. Reeves and Emily Read, *Pilot Fortune* (Boston and New York, 1885). Ellen's relationship to Marion Reeves is unknown.

Two Letters to Ellen Louise Axson

Balto., March 21, 1885

Yes, my precious, the University of Michigan is "a very famous institution." It ranks with Harvard and the Hopkins. It has, I believe, a larger number of students than any other institution in the country. But the special fact which constitutes the chance of winning the chair which is about to be vacated a particularly tempting one is, that it is—or, rather, would be made, in case I were called to it—a chair of constitutional law and administration, my specialties: besides which, Dr. C. K. Adams has just finished collecting for his department the best library of works on administration (my *peculiar* hobby) in the country. A *general* chair in a large college—or a chair in *history* of any sort—*would* be a great disadvantage to me, by precluding all opportunity for prosecution of my private studies; but when one's lecture topics coincide with the topics he specially wants to investigate and write about his private and professorial work may go hand in hand—he can develop and test before his classes the principles and ideas he means to publish—it's his business to do what he wants to do. The great, the serious question, in case such a chair were offered me, would be, 'Am I sufficiently *equipped* for it?' An equipment of understanding, of ideas and energies, is not enough. There must be also large supplies of *materials*—manufactured stores, if possible; if not, *raw* materials in abundance anyhow. Otherwise, the work of preparing lectures would be tremendous, perhaps overwhelming. Nine months of it might wear upon one like nine years of less concentrated effort, of class-recitation and general sketches of long periods. I am inclined to think that dear father's advice is the best: "Hasten slowly. A year or so at Bryn Mawr will be nothing lost." Of course, if a definite offer were to come to me from Michigan, I should hardly feel at liberty to decline it, the B. M. folks consenting; because such things don't come to one often in a lifetime. But Judge Campbell, the present incumbent of the place, has not resigned yet—is only confidently expected to resign—and his successor, in case this expectation is fulfilled, will not be chosen till June, when, of course, it would be too late to ask the Quakers to release me— because too late for them to find a suitable substitute. So that my prospects in that direction don't seem to amount to a chance, after all, inasmuch as I have declined Dr. Adams's invitation to read a paper before the Political Science Association out there. I wrote him a plain-spoken letter, telling him, indirectly, how acceptable the place would be to me, but, at the same time, what considerations made it imperative for me to refrain from all efforts, open or covert, to secure it.

As for the newspaper correspondence, the more I think of it the more I question its being the ideally desirable thing. The best newspaper in the country when at its best would scarcely want to print letters embodying strictly scientific study of institutions; and, however that might be, what would lie beyond in the way of a career? The work would be thoroughly congenial and helpful from the first, but I should not want to keep at it indefinitely— whilst, on the other hand, I should not desire journalistic preferment and promotion. There is no other field of journalism that I care to enter ever. I decided *that* before I left the law, and have seen no reason to alter the decision. When the correspondence vein was worked out, where would I open a mine next. My letter (and, mayhap, book) writing would not have brought me in a fortune; I should have to take up some other trade. I confess that these objections are of the head rather than of the heart. I should *like* an occupation which would leave me foot-loose, living on my wits, as it were—free to take up any other task that offered to meet my ends better. But these are likings and suggestions at which prudence laughs. This excellent, conservative mentor says reprovingly, 'Wilson, keep your head! Don't let your love of active affairs tempt you to hover on their outskirts. You know well enough that you can't *enter* them ever. If you understood the practical side of government and extracted a bit of its philosophy as a college pupil, there's no reason why you should not hope to do more and better of the same kind as a professor, if only you keep out of scholastic ruts and retain your sympathetic consciousness of the conditions of the practical world, where prejudices never refrain from meddling, where passions never manage to keep out of mischief, where shortsightedness governs, where 'horse-sense' is always at a higher premium than learning, where practicable 'business' is everything.'

This sweet letter that came this morning, little lady, was quite a triumph of *pretty penmanship*—are you becoming artistic in *that* direction too?

Sweetheart, will you let me ask—and will you answer—an old question? You say, in the precious love-passage of this letter—which I have read till I can read it with my eyes closed—that you could not bear my absence at all if you "did not live more, in thought, in the past when we *were* together, and the future when we shall be always together, than in the darkened present"[.] Wont you tell me, Eileen, my matchless little darling, what you like best to picture about that sweet future? If I could get my darling to talk about that, I could almost forget the length of these days that keep us apart! Oh, my precious, I don't dare to think how lonely I am, how passionately I desire your sweet presence. It is a supreme delight, and yet just now a tantalizing suspense, to be   Your own   Woodrow.

My own darling,   Balto., March 22, 1885
I have a wretched cold in the head to-day—will you put up with a very stupid epistle? One is excusable for being *under* such weather as this!

Was it my own pulled-down condition, or was it sheer imagination, my pet, that made me fancy that the sweet letter I received this morning (the one that you wrote Friday evening) was written under a depression of spirits? Is it not part of our covenant, my darling, that such things shall not be covered up? Oh, my darling, promise to let me into the *moods* in which you write! Otherwise, this separation will be *altogether* intolerable: because our communion with each other will not be as perfect as even letters can make it. I want in all its fulness the precious privilege of sympathizing with you in *every*thing that affects you—even if it be only fatigue.

You need not feel badly, precious, about my having received no messages about my book from your Grandfather and "Uncle Will." It is so common for me to receive letters through the University office that it did not occur to me that they did not know to what address to direct a note to me; and yet I was not in the least degree hurt that they did not write. I *knew* that it was not because they did not appreciate my sending them the little volume—not an omission of the *heart*. I am not sensitive about the way I am treated in such things by people whom I know I can believe in.

By the way, I learn through our "New Book Department" that the first edition of "Cong. Govt." (one thousand, I suppose) has been exhausted. I don't know whether that is an unusually quick sale for a successful book or not.

You need not be surprised, little lady, that Mrs. Green knew nothing about me—I was not. Balto. knows less about my book than almost any other place of its size, I imagine. Mrs. G. knew quite as much as nine tenths of the people I meet. My *incognito* is altogether safe from danger of penetration here; and I am sure that it don't hurt my pride in the least. I should feel very cheap as a 'lion'! I met an acquaintance on the street the other day— a man who 'runs' with a 'reading set' of men—and he asked me 'what I was doing here now'—'he had an idea that I was studying for the ministry'—though I had seen him several times last year and told him just what I was doing! It's a capital drill in humility!

Didn't I tell you that I met Mr. Randall, of the Augusta "*Const.*," at Mrs. Bird's the last time I dined there? I had met men who expressed political opinions with which I disagreed; but never before had I met a man who held *all* the political opinions with which I most disagree.[1] I had to torture myself with silence to avoid getting into a violent controversy in a lady's parlour. And yet he probably wrote that notice!

I have no doubt that Stockton is out of the woods now in regard to his trouble; but it *would* be prudent, I should think, for him to stop his work for a time; and I hope he will be persuaded. Give him a great deal of love from me, my precious.

Good-bye, *Eileen*, my matchless little sweetheart! If you could know (if I could tell you in words) what I have been thinking about you to-day, you would be very happy—if supreme love, *my* supreme love, can make you happy. *I love you with all my heart.*

Your own   Woodrow.

I am waiting very eagerly for the *sketch*.

ALS (WC, NjP).

[1] One can only conjecture about the meaning of this interesting sentence. Randall, author of "Maryland, My Maryland" and other Confederate poems, was probably an "unreconstructed rebel." He was also closely identified with Joseph E. Brown, a member of the extremely conservative triumvirate that dominated Georgia politics during this period. Perhaps Wilson reacted against Randall's sectionalism and extreme conservatism in political matters.

From Ellen Louise Axson

My darling Woodrow,   New York Mar 22/85.

I must tell you what a scolding my boys at the mission school gave, they made [me] quite crest-fallen! They have been having a series of prayer-meetings there on Thursday nights, and they were taking me to task for my non-attendance. "Teacher, you warn't at prayer-meeting," said one[.] "No," said another, "she *never* is." "Yes" said I, I *can't* come, I have no one to bring me[.]" "Wha fer you want anybody ter bring yer?" "Why, I can't come alone," I answered. "Don't see why, *I* came alone!" was the severe reply! They evidently couldn't appreciate the situation, so greatly amused I abandoned all hope of justifying myself in their eyes. But I believe the funniest part of it from my point of view, was the sequel; I came home in the car with one of the teachers a very nice Scotch lady, and I was telling her as a good joke how I had "caught it," when to my surprise I found he[r] inclined to rebuke me too! She thought it perfectly preposterous that I should be *afraid. She* had been going for sixteen years and no one had ever spoken to *her*; "true" she added "I am too old now, but I was young sixteen years ago"; and her conclusion was that she was "*very* sorry for" me! I am afraid my dear grandmother would be inclined to call that good lady names if I should tell her that story. Really, I thought myself rather valiant when occasion demanded, but I am completely shamed and humbled and must e'en conclude that I was not intended for an "unprotected female."

By-the-way I would like, but I hav'nt time, to tell you all my experiences yesterday at the matinee,—how we three girls started together but were all separated in the crowd! Florence Young turned up afterwards at the League while I was in sketch class, but Miss Farnesworth has'nt been hear[d] from (by me) so far. But I saw and hcard the play perfectly and it was *superb*[.] I believe they say that Beatrice is her best part,—she was certainly exquisite in it;—while Irving made a *capital* Benedict. I shouldn't have thought it possible for him to play a light part so well, and he was so unusually free from affectations too. I believe I liked him better in that than in anything I have seen before. But that play always makes me *so* cross,—to read it even, while to see it acted was of course many times worse. The idea of having for its *hero* such a mean, base, contemptible ignoble wretch as that Claudio! When the young "puppy" said, in his mincing voice, "we had like to have had our two noses snapped off by two old men without teeth!" how I *did* want to throw something at him! And to think that Hero should marry him after all! *Why do* you suppose Shakspere made his men *such* poor creatures as a rule and his woman such paragons!

I didn't tell you of my other treat; I have been to see the Seney collection[1] and I am going again. We are admitted free on Thursdays. It is to be sold at auction on the first of next month. It was exceedingly interesting, of course, the best collection I have seen. All the great French artists are represented,—though on the whole not *very* well represented. But he has what was perhaps Jules Breton's masterpiece; and it is a *wonderful* picture!—the city ought to buy it, I think, for the museum. There is a strange charm about those quiet, dusky pictures with their simple peasant groups always *in the shadow* in more than one sense—they are so pathetic and so *true*, and they tell with such power their humble tale of "some natural sorrow, loss, or pain,—that hath been and shall be again."[2] By-the-way have you seen the Walters collection this year?

Please thank your sister, if you happen to write before I do—as is very likely!—for her sweet letter. I am *delighted* to welcome it after it's wanderings.

And now I must say "goodnight." I love you, I love you my darling! I don't see how *I* ever lived without your love; indeed it was but half living. Yes, I think we have of late found the most joyous way of loving. Perhaps I did think you calm—and cold (?) but at least, made quite as great mistakes about myself. I have discovered in myself too altogether unsuspected depths of passion. I knew I could love well and truly, you know, but not—not this way. My darling, I believe it is literally true that my life is bound up in yours. It would be infinitely worse than death to live without your love. Believe me, love, to be forever

Your own   Eileen

ALS (WC, NjP).
   [1] The extensive collection of the banker, George Ingraham Seney, was at this time on view at the American Art Association in New York. It was sold at auction in late March and early April 1885.
   [2] From Wordsworth's "The Solitary Reaper."

From Janet Woodrow Wilson

Wilmington. N. C. Monday night [March 23, 1885]

My precious boy,

Your father thinks that I neglected to tell you, in my note written a few days ago, what I had written your Uncle James B. as to money matters. I wrote accepting his offer of payment as follows—"$100, on the 1st of April—$100, on April 15—$100, on May 1st—& $200, with the interest on May 15th"—and directed him, as you wished, to send it direct to me. Now, dear, dont fail to send me the note that I am to send him at the proper time—and dont fail to give me full instructions as to every particular in the matter.

We are as busy as can be, packing. We have gotten pretty well through with the little things—which is decidedly the most tedious & vexatious part of the packing you know.

You asked me about your *present* for sweet Ellie—and I wrote in such haste that I neglected to say—that I want to get dear Annie to suggest as to the matter—she is apt to know more of what is new and appropriate than I am—for she has been in a position to see & hear more about such matters. I will let you know what I hear from her as soon as possible.

We are constantly hearing something new of the wonderful success of your book. *Do you take it in*, dear boy, that you have made yourself *famous*? We are so proud—but more *thankful*, than proud.

I scribble this note in haste, & amid much confusion & discomfort. Love unbounded from us each one to dear Ellie & your sweet self.   Yours as ever   Mother.

I received yours of the 22nd this morning (Tuesday) Dont be anxious about me, my darling. The worst is over. Your father & Josie are busy boxing the large pictures. I am not permitted to come near. The main part now left, is the packing of the *furniture*—which your father will employ experts to do. I have only to pack the clothing—and the odds & ends left—and the carpets & bed clothes now in use. It is possible that I may leave next week —but I long for a little interval at home—for rest—and then there are some visits that I feel bound to make. How long must it be before I can see *you* my darling! What would I not give for a sight of my sweet boy. I never needed you so much in all my life before! You are my own dear boy still—and nothing will ever separate you from me, thank God. In haste
                              Yours most lovingly   Mother.

ALS (WP, DLC) with WWhw notation on env.: "Ans. March 29/85."

To Ellen Louise Axson

My own darling   Balto., March 23, 1885

If I were making a separate collection of those letters from a certain little lady in New York (the sweetest lady that ever man loved) which most thrill me with love and love's delight, I should certainly consign to that collection the little note that came this morning—and which, when once I had opened it, I read five times before ever I could fold it up again! It would be next to impossible to make such a collection—so precious are *all* her letters in my estimation—unless I were to adopt some arbitrary standard, such as the actual number of lines of spoken love each one contained. Even *that* wouldn't answer in all cases, though, because sometimes in just a line or two this little bewitcher of mine says things for which I would not exchange all the riches of the world: as, for instance, when she says in this dear note before me, that she wishes with all her heart that June were come —the time when my life will begin, the time when she will be my bride! It is just as if she had laid a deliberate plan to make me forget everything but just the supreme happiness of being loved by her—as if she had said to herself, 'Do my letters rest him when he is tired, cheer him when he is downcast, calm him when he is irritated and disturbed, carry joy and contentment into all his moods? Yes; he says they do. Then I'll write him one that will make him beside himself with delight, that will make him forget that he *can* do anything but smile and love: I will tell him that my love for him has attained its *perfect* work, has overcome timidity, has conquered all things that stood between us, and that now my single wish is to make him happy by becoming his wife! *I* know the young gentleman! I know what delight will spring into his eyes when he reads such a confession: I know that I *can* make him unspeakably happy by such words. Why shouldn't I, then? They are true!" Ah, my darling; plot or no plot, you *have* won my heart afresh by this sweet, sweet confession! It almost makes June seem nearer. It *does* bring it nearer! For it proves that we are already one in heart, that not even my darling's shyness now conditions the outspoken joy of our love for each other. All my life I shall strive, Eileen, my queen, to make you increasingly sure that June did not come too soon. I hope, sweetheart, that you will find in your husband more to love than you have found, or could ever find, in your lover. Your lover can only love you; your husband can love and serve you. And, then, there are lots of secrets which you can know only as my wife. Only then can you know the great, all-inclusive secret, how entirely I am

Your own   Woodrow.

ALS (WC, NjP).

From Charles Andrew Talcott

My dear Woodrow: Utica Mch 23 1885

So long as you have put it on a title page I may as well write 'Woodrow' but I still think 'Tommy'. I was casually looking through the New York Times at the house of a friend yesterday afternoon when my eye lit upon a paragraph which informed me that one Woodrow Wilson was the author of a work entitled Congressional Government which had been very favorably received. I am at present anxiously awaiting the arrival of the book and from my knowledge of the author and his previous work, I expect to find this book much more interesting than any I ever read. You know you have my congratulations in this success of yours as you will have them in every other, and I feel certain that there will be many others. I had not before understood why my letter of last summer had remained so long unanswered.[1] The veil is lifted now. If you expect, as seems reasonable to suppose, to confine your correspondence with me to communications in book form as one of the general public, I shall never the less treat them as altogether personal and sit down and write you an answer privately. You may now therefor consider the burden of the correspondence upon your shoulders, and I have no doubt that, in time, the press of Houghton & Mifflin will turn out a very substantial and effective answer. In the meantime if opportunity offers, just keep me posted once in a while about yourself and your whereabouts and especially as to whether you will attend the 'Sexennial' of '79.

Yours very sincerely   Chas A. Talcott

ALS (WP, DLC) with WWhw notation on env.: "Ans. Mar. 26/85."
[1] C. A. Talcott to WW, Sept. 4, 1884, ALS (WP, DLC).

From James E. Rhoads

My dear Friend,   Philadelphia. 3 mo. 23. 1885.
Estes & Lauriat of Boston are publishing Victor Duruy's History of Rome profusely illustrated; Edition deluxe, at 14 sections at $10. per section.[1] 1000 copies of 1st Edition, with all original plates of the French Edition. Please see if it be worth our putting on lists for the future. At present it is of course beyond our reach.
Thine truly,   James E Rhoads

ALS (WP, DLC) with WWhw notation on env.: "Ans. March 25/85."
[1] Victor Duruy, History of Rome and of the Roman People, from Its Origins to the Invasion of the Barbarians (8 vols. in 16, Boston, 1884-87).

To Ellen Louise Axson, with Two Enclosures

My own darling,   Balto., March 24, 1885
My cold, I am bound to tell you, is treating me most shabbily. Like some of its immediate predecessors, it is sending out harass-

ing scouts from my head, its headquarters, to all parts of my
body. I am confident of routing it before many more hours have
passed: but, meantime, I am in a sad humour over my temporary
discomfiture. I will of course keep you posted concerning the fortunes of the campaign.

I am at a loss whether to laugh or to be vexed over your story
of about the Thursday evening mission prayer-meetings. I suppose that it would be foolish to get vexed; and yet I *cant* be
amused. I am a great admirer of your sex, as you know; but
there is a section of it which has been put into the world without
the sligh[t]est endowment of sense, and this 'pleasant Scotch
lady' evidently belongs to that section—the only section of the
human race for which I have absolutely no tolerance! Of all the
nuisances which the world holds, in the shape of silly women,
the worst is a woman, old enough to be a mother, who is devoid
of all trace of motherly judgment! It is that 'pleasant' person, my
darling, not you, who is to be pitied—because she *was* intended to
be an "unprotected female." I am glad that you are so well balanced in your exercise of sweet womanly sense as not to be irritated by such impudent reproofs. I should be compelled either
to keep silence or to make a flaming reply.

I am delighted, my pet, to hear that you have had opportunities to see the Seney collection. I thought of you as soon as I saw
the advertisement of the exhibition and sale; and wondered if
you would have a chance to see its treasures. It's astonishing,
the vicarious interest I take in exhibitions that are within your
reach! What would I not give to have the Walters collection
within your reach! I have not been to see it this season simply
because I did not want to see it again *without you*. I laugh to myself sometimes now—with a tingle of pain in the laugh—to think
of the time last year when I bought several tickets under the
impression that you were coming all the way from Savannah,
with Mrs. Green, to visit the gallary. I had to visit it myself often
enough to know its contents like old friends, in order to use up
the tickets!

I wish I could watch your face as you read the enclosed extract
from the *Tribune*! The book is not at the mercy of *that* sheet, my
darling—so you need not mind too much what it says.

Arthur Yager is a friend—a last year Ph.D. of the Hopkins.

Don't be worried about the *cold*, sweetheart. I shall cure it in
a trice, I hope—as quickly as all ailments would go if *you* were
but with   Your own   Woodrow

ALS (WC, NjP).

The *New York Tribune*'s Review of
Congressional Government

[March 20, 1885]

Mr. Wilson's object in publishing this essay is to show that our
Constitution has proved a failure, that the ideal system of checks
and balances about which we hear so much exists only on paper,
that the English, or Parliamentary, plan is a great deal better
than ours, and that, further changes in the spirit of our institutions being inevitable, we ought promptly to "apply with the unhesitating courage of conviction all thoroughly tested or well-
considered expedients necessary to make self-government among
us a straightforward thing of simple method, single unstinted
power, and clear responsibility." He maintains that Congress has
steadily encroached, and is still encroaching, upon both the co-
ordinate branches, the executive and the judiciary, while the
federal authority has practically subjugated the States; yet that
increase of power has been accompanied by diminishing responsibility, so that Congress is at once meddlesome and inefficient,
an obstacle to the carrying out of any positive policy, either the
Executive's or its own. The government cannot be said to follow
intelligible lines of action when the legislative and administrative
departments are inharmonious, as so often is the case; nor is
there even any policy or accountability in Congress itself, because
business is so conducted there that legislation is not controlled by
the majority, but proceeds generally by a series of compromises.
This brings us to the most important and most interesting part
of the book, a description of the system of law-making by committees. The business of the House of Representatives is distributed
among forty-seven standing committees, and the operation of
the rules is such that the forty-seven chairmen have practical
control of all bills. Legislation is thus shifted from the floor of
the House to the privacy of the committee-rooms; party responsibility is taken away by the representation of both parties on every
committee; and party vigor is made impossible by the lack of
concert among the forty-seven chairmen, each of whom is in fact
anxious to promote his own bills at the cost of all others. The
anomalies and defects of this curious system have been pointed
out before, and Mr. Wilson has a somewhat familiar theme. He
amplifies it, however, with zeal, and with an eye for all its weakest points. Perhaps his description would be more effective if it
were less rhetorical.

It is not quite clear what substitute Mr. Wilson would propose for a method which has great merits as well as great imperfections, and which has grown gradually out of a general sense of the public needs. His aim is not to suggest a remedy, but to demonstrate the disease. His preferences, nevertheless, are obviously for some such approach toward the English system as would make the majority party in Congress absolute in its control of all legislation and also of the administration of the laws. The majority would then be responsible for the entire conduct of the government, and the President and his Cabinet would hold office only at their will. Mr. Wilson apparently does not see that his plan would mean the complete obliteration of the federal principle, which is the characteristic note of the American system, and the principle which has been most signally vindicated by our century of successful experiment. It would mean also of course the obliteration of the Senate as well as of the States; and how the inconvenient necessity of dividing and distributing the onerous business of the House of Representatives would be removed by increasing the mass and variety of that business, we fail to see. It is hardly worth while, however, to enter upon a defence of a system of government which almost every competent political student knows to be the only system which could hold this country together. Mr. Wilson starts with the assumption that there has recently been a change in the general feeling toward the Constitution, and that "our generation" has "serious doubts about the superiority of our own institutions as compared with the systems of Europe." This is quite wrong. Our generation has no such absurd feeling. And Mr. Wilson is also grossly deceived in imagining that the Constitution, with its balance of powers, has been changed from the original pattern. It is a wonder to us that any man can read the history of the last twenty-five years without perceiving that the constitutional "checks and balances" are as effectual to-day as they ever were, that the form of our government has developed only in the line of growth marked out for it from the beginning, and that the boundaries of federal and State authority, instead of becoming confused, are steadily getting more and more distinct—the judiciary (which Mr. Wilson thinks that Congress has subjugated) having especially vindicated its independence and its superiority to party prejudice by overturning a whole series of enactments passed during the reconstruction period in forgetfulness of those limits of jurisdiction. The fact is that Mr. Wilson is so careless and contradictory in his statements and so hasty and short-sighted in his conclusions that to answer him in detail would take more time and room than we can afford for such an easy but unnecessary enterprise.

Printed in the *New York Tribune*, March 20, 1885.

Arthur Yager's Review of *Congressional Government*
[March 20, 1885]

—*Our Federal Government*—Nothing is now more clearly established and more generally understood among modern scientists than the fact that the actual concrete phenomena of nature constitute the only proper subject matter for the student of natural science. If men would make of themselves biologists they must enter the laboratories and study real animals, not spend their time in simply reading books about animals. Young students are transformed into trained chemists by personal experimentation with real chemical apparatus and with real chemical substance, not by studying learned expositions of chemical science. This is not simply the best way; it is the only way in which the severe demands of modern science can be met.

But the world is now beginning to learn that this method of investigation, so universally applied in the natural sciences, is, after all, the only perfectly trustworthy method in any department of inquiry. Everywhere it is facts that we want, and not theories. And especially in the study of government has there been shown of late a disposition to abandon the old-time custom of literary essay-making, and apply the more rigid and modern methods of scientific investigation. This is certainly much to be commended, for no branch of human knowledge stands in greater need of just this sort of study.

In the volume which forms the subject of this article, and which the author calls *Congressional Government*, Mr. Wilson has made a notable advance in the application of this method to the study of our governmental institutions. In this respect, indeed, it is an altogether unique book—a book stonding apart by itself, and constituting an entirely new departure in our political writing. It is indeed strange, almost incredible, that in the ninety-six years of our constitutional life no author has come forward to tell us from knowledge gained by actual observation of the facts what sort of thing our actual working constitution really is. The fact that we have a written constitution, and that this document lays the foundation of a Government which, in some important respects, is quite peculiar, has cast such a potent spell over our political writers that they have uniformly neglected to examine the actual workings of our governmental system, in their anxiety to give their interpretation of this document, and point out these peculiarities. We have no end of philosophical treatises setting forth the importance of the three-fold distribution of governmental powers, extolling the beauty and harmony of the theory of checks and balances, and explaining the delicate nature of the relationship between the national and State governments. We have, in addition, great commentaries like those of Story and Kent, which have developed the Constitution into a complete system of jurisprudence and applied it to the solution of specific cases.

Yet from no one of these works, nor from all of them combined, can one who is not already acquainted with the subject derive any adequate idea of what our Federal Government really is, or how it performs its work. The question [as to] the nature and limits of the powers of Congress has evoked the most passionate and perennial discussion, but the question as to how Congress should exercise the powers which it possesses has scarcely been touched. And yet it is easy to see that this last question is infinitely the more important—is indeed the only one which the student of political facts will require to be answered.

This is the question which Mr. Wilson has proposed to himself, and to this question his little volume forms a most admirable answer.

The first fact which he observes is that the theory of checks and balances, which is the very corner-stone of all the literary expositions of our Constitution, has in practice completely broken down. The right which the Federal Government has now definitely established of being itself the sole judge of the limitations of its own powers, and the resistless force of that potent doctrine of the "implied powers" of Congress, have slowly but surely overborne the barriers which the Constitution erected around the independence of the separate States. In like manner the three-fold distribution of powers into independent departments, legislative, executive and judicial, has in practice proved a delusion and a snare.

In all important matters Congress has always succeeded, and, from the nature of the case, always will succeed in appropriating to itself the supreme powers of government. The absolute control of its "standing committees" over the Executive Department, its power of enlarging the Supreme Court at its pleasure, and the powerful executive functions of the Senate will always enable it to impose its will upon both the other departments of the Government. It is impossible to convey, within moderate compass, any adequate idea of the masterly array of facts with which Mr. Wilson supports this proposition, but the conclusion is irresistible of all the political powers, which the Constitution parceled out among the different institutions of our Government. The powers of Congress alone have grown with our growth and strengthened with our strength.

Having established the fact that, in spite of the "literary theory" of our Constitution, our Government has, in practice, become a Government by Congress, Mr. Wilson devotes a large part of his volume to a graphic description of the internal machinery, by means of which Congress exercises its vast powers. He takes us into the heart of the Capitol at Washington, conducts us through the committee rooms, the caucus chambers, and into the hidden recesses of law-making machinery, with a view to explaining what actually goes on there. He observes faithfully and intelligently, reports accurately and criticizes unsparingly.

Turning first to the House of Representatives, it is found that all of its vast powers are parceled out in a somewhat indefinite way among its forty-eight standing committees. About everything that comes before the House is referred to one or another of these committees, and each committee is, within the scope of its own jurisdiction, almost omnipotent in its control over legislation. All the rules have, from the necessities of the case, been so devised as to secure and strengthen the influence of the committees over the destinies of the bill which come within their powerful grasp. Moreover, each of these committees has its own organization, consisting of chairman and clerk, and meets and collects evidence and deliberates according to rules of its own. Everything that is done in committee may be done in the most absolute secrecy, the public being at any time excluded, and the strictest injunctions being laid upon the members to reveal nothing that transpires. In addition to this each committee is quite independent of all the others, owing no sort of allegiance to any power whatever, except the uncertain deference which it may be constrained to pay to the party caucus. It is in these dark corners, in their powerful and irresponsible little councils, that all of our legislation is begun and directed, and the entire policy of our government determined. With a few slight modifications, the same methods are applied in the Senate, and therefore it may be said that in the ultimate analysis "Congressional government" is government by some sixty or seventy semi independent and totally irresponsible committees.   •

This is the quintessence of our American Government as contrasted with the government of all other great nations of modern times.

The form of government which is being universally adopted, with more or less completeness, by all the leading nations of Europe is that form known as "Parliamentary Government," which has been so strikingly portrayed in Mr. Walter Bagehot's "English Constitution." One of the main objects of the present book seems to have been to trace a continuous contrast between Committee and Parliamentary Government. The distinguished characteristic of the latter form of government lies in this: The powers of the governing legislature, instead of being distributed among numerous committees, are concentrated in the hands of a single committee, called the "Ministry" or the "Cabinet." The Ministers are chosen by and from those members of the Assembly who belong to that political party which is for the time being dominant in the Assembly. To this Ministry, compact, harmonious and disciplined, are intrusted for the time all the powers of the Assembly itself, so that it may control the entire policy of the country, both foreign and domestic. But, on the other hand, this Ministry is immediately and completely responsible to the party which created it, and can not retain office for a day longer than it can so lead and mold public sentiment as to maintain its majority in the Legislative Assembly. In direct contrast to this is our own system of government by committees, which parcels out authority and divides responsibil[i]ty amongst numerous inharmonious committees, and places the legislation of the country and Congress under the joint control of the Speaker of the House and the several dozen chairmen.

The substance of the whole distinction may be summed up in the two words *party responsibility*.

In the Parliamentary form the parties face each other squarely upon every issue both in Parliament and in the country. One party at a time has entire direction of the Government, and is responsible for everything that takes place. If Parliament do not like the way things are going, one vote is sufficient. If adverse, the Ministry must resign. If the people do not like the Ministry one general election settles the whole matter. But under the Committee system, responsibility may be divided among the various committees of the two Houses in such a confusing way, that the parties do not seem to be amenable to the people for what they do, or do not do. Who can say, for instance, which party should be held responsible for the sins of omission and commission of the last Congress? Somewhere between the two Houses, or among the innumerable wheels and cogs which make up their working machinery, many important and needed measures were lost, and much costly time was wasted; but which party is to be blamed for it? Each party blames the other, but so bewildering is our Congressional apparatus with its committees, caucuses and conferences, that the people can not find the man or men with whom to reckon.

Who has any doubt as to what would be the fate of our present tariff, if a plebiscite could be taken upon that one question alone? Yet, the Protectionists, sheltering themselves behind the inherent weaknesses of our Committee system, have succeeded in so complicating the situation and perplexing the public mind that the old war tariff has stood almost intact for twenty years, and no one knows how much longer it is to last.

The history of Congress, since 1875, when the Democratic party first got control of the Lower House, has been a continuous proof of the clumsiness of the Committee system, and its want of adaptability of party government. As Mr. Wilson says, in another connection, it is "too clumsy and clandestine to last."

We hail this book as the first attempt to study our Federal Government in the concrete, and predict that it will not be the last, nor will it be without effect. Arthur Yager.

Printed in the *Louisville Courier-Journal*, March 20, 1885.

Two Letters from Ellen Louise Axson

New York, Mar. 24 1885.

The fates were unpropitious last night, my darling, and I was forced to postpone answering those two delightful letters of the morning. Now of course I must still postpone, for since I have entered the "paint class" it is very important that I should be at the League in time,—that is by nine o'clock, and it is something very hard to accomplish these cold mornings.

I am altogether fascinated with the class by the way, it is *so* much more interesting than black and white,—we have a splendid model this week, a burly old Dutchman dressed as a burgo-master. Last week we had a charming little brown-eyed, rosy-cheeked boy who won my heart by reminding me of Eddie; he turned out to be named Eddie too.

I had almost forgotten the sketch! I will try and send it tomorrow, I waited to get something to do it up with.

And what was it, darling, that made you think me low spirited on Friday? You are altogether too "cute," sir! I believe I *was* blue that night, Grandmother's letter, just received had served to quicken my anxiety about Stockton, but it was scarcely worth while saying anything more about that. How can I ever tell you darling how I prize this tender, watchful love of yours. Every smallest proof of it is treasured up in my heart of hearts and will be, all my life. What a happy little woman I am and shall *always* be. I can scarcely believe sometimes that it is really I who am so blessed,—blessed more than I ever thought to be, even in my dreams   Yours *forever*   Eileen.

ALS (WC, NjP).   *excuse haste*

My darling Woodrow,   New York, Mar. 24/85
While I am more than ever inclined, after reading your account of the University of Mich. to agree with you that it is "hard" to be obliged to let such an opportunity slip, I am almost equally inclined to agree with your father that it would be wiser to hasten slowly[.] There certainly does seem to be great doubt as to the advisability of accepting such a chair even were it offered you. How would you *answer* the question, which you raise, as to your equipment for the place?—your supply of raw material? It would be terrible,—it would be wrong—to accept a place which you knew or even feared would demand any sacrifice of your health. Could you or could you not find out enough about the requirements of the place beforehand to settle all such doubts? But why speak of it,—since from what you say there would seem really to be no chance—if they can't make you the offer until June and that will be too late for you to accept. I was about to ask you if you could not sue for a release from your Bryn Mawr engagement *now*. I don't think you would run the least risk in so doing for even if the Mich. scheme fell through there would be no lack of offers in other directions, as the past few days have abundantly proved. Not even prudence herself could object to your trusting fortune to that extent;—and of course our plans, unformed as they are, could easily wait upon that fortune. But I am so frightened at the thought of the work wearing upon you so, that I don't dare

even make any such suggestion until you are *sure* that the labour of preparing lectures will *not* be "over-whelming." And perhaps it would not be possible to ask the Bryn Mawr people to release you except for stronger reasons than you can give at present. After all it is such a very hard question that perhaps it will contribute to your peace of mind—and save you much trouble and anxiety to feel that you are not altogether responsible for the decision. I see the objections to the newspaper correspondence, it could be only a temporary thing, and then, as you say, what next? To trust time alone to answer that question would perhaps be imprudent.

And so you must have an answer to that "old question," you inquisitive youth!—and yet, sir, when I ask *you* that same question I fail to get a very *definite* reply,—and so you ought to appreciate the difficulties which such questions present[.] But yes I will tell you, darling, what I "like best to picture about that future" of ours. The question, as you put it tonight, is easily answered because the picture which I love best is a simple one and easily described. I find that the thought upon which I dwell most lovingly;—which comes back to me most frequently and spontaneously in thinking of that coming time is of evenings like the present—yet how unlike! evenings spent—not as we are spending this in solitary confinement—but together,—close together—by our own fireside,—talking, reading, working together;—or in a communion of heart so entire—so full and deep that *silence* renders it none the less perfect; and which, even when you are most absorbed in your work, will still suffer me to be in a very real sense your *companion* by right of my ever present though quiet sympathy. How happy I should be *now* if looking up from my page I could see your dear face just over against me—or could *feel* it there without looking up! But sweet-heart, I dispair of materializing my visions! to attempt it is but to prove what I knew before, that it is impossible; I would "compass you round with sweet observances," but what is there to *say* about them? Can one describe the atmosphere in which one breathes? Not though we know it is our very life. Do you ever think of our future when we are grown old together? Doubtless you have for "the thoughts of youth are long, long, thoughts." Sometimes I seem to be for the moment transported to that far-away time by a *flash* of the imagination so vivid that the present only seems unreal. I am actually living in that future and looking back on my foolish young self from those calm and peaceful heights by an effort of memory only, and in the spirit of old age, contemplative, tolerant sympathetic yet half amused. But enough! May I conclude with an adapted quotation from a certain no longer "*obscure*" writer? I shall strive, Woodrow my king to make you increasingly sure that June did not come too soon, for your sweet-heart can only love you, but your wife can love and serve you. And then, there are lots of secrets which you can only know—then! Only then can you know the great, all-inclusive secret, how entirely I am

ALS (WP, DLC).   Your own   Eileen

From Harold Godwin

The Commercial Advertiser [New York]. March 24, '85
Dear Tommy:
If any of your professors feel interested enough in the Bryn Mawr College to give us some account of it we should be glad to make use of it.[1] Have written for one to Vassar which seems sadly on the decline. We'll boom you when the appointment as Minister to England falls in your hat. Congratulate you on the book!
Every sincerely   Harold Godwin

ALS (WP, DLC) with WWhw notation on env.: "Ans. March 26/85."
[1] Wilson responded with the article printed at April 20, 1885.

From Addie C. Wildgoss

Haverford College P.O.
Mr. Wilson,   Penna March 24th/85
I have taken the cottage on the Bryn Mawr College grounds for the purpose of accommodating the professors connected with it, and Dr. Rhoads the president having handed me among others your name and address, I write to know if you would engage one or two rooms. The terms per week for each room will be $9. or $10. according to desirability.
Respectfully   Miss A. Wildgoss

ALS (WP, DLC) with WWhw notation on env.: "Ans. March 26/85."

To Charles Andrew Talcott

My dear Charlie,   Balto., March 25, '85
When your welcome letter of the 23rd. came this morning I felt heartily ashamed of myself, that you should have been compelled to write again, out of pure goodness of heart and magnanimity, before I had answered your delightful epistle of last summer! And yet there was no real *ground* for my feeling ashamed of myself: for, if self-sacrifice, if preferring duty to pleasure, is

a virtue, I have deserved all commendation for not writing to you. Ever since I came back to Balto. last Oct. your letter has lain here under my eyes and I have *wanted* to write to you; but just could not do it without letting some part of pressing, and for the moment imperative, University tasks go by the board. Last summer my time and energies were both consumed in the composition of the fourth, fifth, and sixth chapters of "Congressional Government."

But, my dear fellow, my having put 'Woodrow,' without introduction of 'T,' on a title page, or anywhere else, gives you no good excuse for dropping 'Tommy' in converse with your chum, who values the nickname as a badge of that old fellowship which is amongst the treasures of his memory, and which it is his ambition to perpetuate in spite of separation and the thousand other ills that college friendship is heir to. You would not call me 'Woodrow' to my face with impunity: and you should pay me the delicate compliment of seeming not to notice my modest efforts to compact my name and avoid the awkward device (so happily characterized by one Ridgeway Wright) of 'parting my name in the middle.'

One penalty you have to pay for not having heard from me for several months (odd that *you* should have to pay the penalty for my misdeeds!) is the reading of a large budget of personal news. And first, about the sextennial. I am mightily afraid that I can't be there—and that for a very important reason: I hope to get married at just about that date. I hope that you will hold this a sacred secret, because it is as yet a hope only—though a strong, well-founded one—and not a definite plan. My justification for getting married is that I have secured a 'place' for next year. I am to teach history and political economy at Bryn Mawr College, the new University for women which is to be opened in September next, under the auspices of the Society of Friends (it having been endowed by a wealthy New Jersey Quaker) at Bryn Mawr, just ten miles from Philadelphia. I do not mean to identify myself with the higher education of women, much as I sympathize with it, by spending my life at Bryn Mawr; but the work there will be of the most liberal sort, the place being planned as a sort of "Miss Johns Hopkins," and will be as good a berth as a fellow could desire for those few years of foundation-laying which it behooves every man who aims at filling a special chair some day to preface his career with. Since my little volume has won its astonishing success numerous opportunities to step at once into higher posts such as are the ultimate goals of my ambition have opened up before me, and have made me regret for a few days at a time the engagements which bind me to the good Quakers of Penn.; but, on the whole, I am convinced that it is wisest to hasten slowly in approaching the special work in *administration* which I want to do eventually. In teaching the demure Friendly damsels I can ground myself in history as I would not otherwise be grounded, and can, I hope, at the same time, at least keep the rust off my special studies, against the day when they will need to be bright for present use. I must have a period too, for the accumulation of raw materials such as a chap must gather before he can venture upon the manufacture of formal lectures.

And that's about the sum and substance of the news that has accumulated about 'the present writer' since last summer; except, of course, the (for me) great event of the publication of "Congressional Government." I hope that you can find time, Charlie, not only to read the book, but also to write and tell me just what you think of it, without choice of considerate words. You know that I value your opinion most highly; and my first wish is to learn where the book is at fault. Of course you will recognize in it the fruits of the studies which began in that *International Review* article of August 1879.

I shall not give up all hope of attending the sextennial, especially if you are expecting to go. I will try to make anything possible that will reunite the old gang. But first let me know what you are going to do in the matter. I guess that Hiram will certainly be on hand, and Doc. Mitchell (who is as German as Vienna could make him—and yet as American as his blood could keep him), and I expect to spend the vacation in the North anyhow; so, I wont say yet 'for certain' *what* I'll do. I got a brief note from Pete[1] the other day—but only to ask for matter for his paper —and Bob.[2] every now and then sends me a roll of notices of my book. I saw Bob Xmas—because Miss Axson is studying art in New York! With the old-time love,

Your sincere friend,   Tommy.

ALS (photostat, RSB Coll., DLC).
  [1] Harold Godwin.   [2] Robert Bridges.

To Ellen Louise Axson

My own darling,   Balto., March 25, '85
    I am feeling better this morning. My cold has withdrawn most of its scouts from my body and limbs and is snugly and safely confined to my head once more—supremely uncomfortable and

stupifying, but quite harmless. It does not give one very cheerful views of the world to feel that one's head is stuffed with *cotton*, or some such unnatural, uncerebral substance; in fact such a feeling affords the most favourable conditions conceivable for downright *crossness*, sans philosophy, sans everything. But, somehow, ever since a certain 16th of September[1]—that is to say, for the past eighteen months—I have found it a very difficult matter to get *altogether* cross under *any* circumstances. There's a sort of silent, pervading influence running, subconsciously, as it were, through all my moods which compels me, in spite of myself, to be light-hearted. And, strangely enough, that influence seems to be in some way connected with next June, growing stronger as that charmed month approaches! In a word, my darling, your love has the wonderful power of diffusing itself through every conscious moment of my life. Infinitely lonely as I am without you, I am not *altogether* lonely. You are with me in a sense. Your love is a sort of companion—a sweet companion sent me by my queen as a temporary substitute for her lovely self—as an earnest that she means not to keep me waiting long before coming herself to make me glad—oh, so supremely glad—by her loving, wifely presence! That love seems to be my good, my guardian spirit, making me ashamed of everything mean or small or unworthy, making me love life and all my fellow creatures.

There is one feeling with reference to your love for me, my darling, which I'm sure you'll laugh at me for having, but which I must confess to having had from the first, that is, the feeling that it is a wonderful *free gift*—a gratuity—given for no merit or attractiveness on my part whatever, and calling, therefore, for supreme gratitude, as well as supreme love, from me in return. As I have told you before, I am quite conscious of being capable of giving such love as a woman might feel inclined to make considerable sacrifices for, if she could but know my heart; but it does seem *so* queer that the loveliest woman in the world, who might take her choice from amongst the delightful men of the world, should wish to spend her life with me—notwithstanding the fact that I am sure that nobody else *could* love her as I do. Still, self-contradictory as my wonderful good fortune seems, it has come and has made me the most exaltedly happy man in the world[.] Eileen has wrought wonders by acknowledging, by loving, me as   Her own   Woodrow.

ALS (WP, DLC).
  [1] September 16, 1883, the date of their engagement.

From Houghton, Mifflin & Company

Dear Sir: Boston, March 25th, 1885

We have your favor of the 23rd inst., and shall probably have no objection to the editor of the paper in Clinton, N. C. copying some extracts from your volume on Congressional Government,[1] but as we have to watch and protect our copyright property pretty carefully, we must ask that he will first submit to us an exact statement or memorandum of the portions which he desires thus to use, that we may give our definite and explicit assent.

We shall be happy to send copies of the book to Prof. E. A. Freeman, and Prof. James Bryce, as you suggest, and we are glad to report that the sale of the book, while by no means rapid or enormous as yet, is quite steady and satisfactory thus far, and we trust and believe that it will continue to have an ever increasing circle of readers. You will observe in this week's Nation, that we have given an especially noticeable advertisement[2] of the work, with quotations from some of the very satisfactory notices which it has received.

Yours very truly, Houghton, Mifflin & Co   F. J. G.

TLS (WP, DLC) with WWhw notation on env.: "Ans. Mar. 28/85."
  [1] See W. E. Faison to WW, March 17, 1885.
  [2] It was a notice of a "Second Edition" in the New York *Nation*, XL (March 26, 1885), iv.

From Ellen Louise Axson

New York Mar. 25/85

I am *very* sorry, my darling, to receive such bad accounts of you[r] cold;—it seems to me that they are using you rather hardly of late. Take good heed, dear, to those warning "scouts"; remember that this is "pneumonia weather" and discretion is the better part of valour in dealing with such enemies.

But I must not abuse the weather unjustly for it has been lovely today. There really has been at last a hint of spring in the air. Surely it is time! I can scarcely realize that April will be here in a few days, and I will have only as many weeks at the League as I once had months. I received a letter from my Cousin Hattie[1] tonight reminding me of my "promise" to visit her as soon I finish here. Her deep interest in you remains unabated, or, I should say, increases. She is delighted with your book; and asks a great many questions about your prospects, &c;—and in conclusion she says, "God bless you both and keep you always lovers!" Mr. [Robert] Ewing says that Hattie wont give him space enough to tell all *he* thinks of the book, he means to write me himself about it.

The article from the Louisville (?) paper was very good, was it not. I must try not to talk of the Tribune, for if I do the result will be a cross, disagreeable letter; but I do *feel* very wickedly towards it. Though I ought to feel pity rather than anything for *I* believe that poor paper is literally in it's dotage. The three wise men of Gotham must be the authors of it! Who else could have concocted such drivelling nonsense. Bah! I do pity them, almost as much as I despise them. But I must keep my word, I *wont* discuss it. Did Mr. Bridges send you these?

By-the-way, one of my new comrades in the painting-class told me today, that she had heard of me through Mr. Bridges, with whom she boards. She is not the one you met however, but she had heard of you too. I was curious to know *what* she had heard of me from him—if anything special. I imagine not; at any rate she made no sign—though it *was* odd that she should mention your name, and the nature of my acquaintance with Mr. B. She says he seems to be so exceedingly exthusiastic about his friend Mr. Wilson, is always talking about his book and giving them extracts from various papers praising it.

I have been dreadfully extravagant today and though I know I "hadn't ought to" have done it, I am highly elated over my purchase! It was a bargain of course,—my extravagance always takes that shape—a slightly rubbed copy of "Modern Artists and their Works" for $1.49. Did you ever see it? it is *delight*ful. I have been wild to possess it, but of course it was far out of my reach. It contains sketches biographical and pictorial of about thirty-five of the most famous living artists, with several specimens of the work of each. There are four or five of my old friends of the "Watts Collection." I have been so busy with my new toy all the evening that now it is high time for me to think of saying "good-night." If I could only *say* it indeed! When you are well my darling, I long with an inexpressible longing to see you but when you are sick I feel as though I *must* see you. Believe me sweetheart to be now and ever   Your own   Eileen.

ALS (WC, NjP).
  [1] Harriet Hoyt Ewing to ELA, March 22, 1885, ALS (WP, DLC).

To Ellen Louise Axson

Balto., March 26, '85

If I had been in search of proof, my darling, of that long ago proved and accepted truth, that we were *meant* for each other, I could not have wished for more or better than this sweet, this precious letter of this morning has brought me. My Eileen's picture of the future as she likes to think of it is also a picture of what my own day-dreams have promised me. It means, it is summed up in, just one thing: *being together*, and doing for each other just what love and duty prompt,—and that is the thought which is of all others the most inexpressibly sweet to me. Yes, my little treasure, I have often thought of that far-away time when we shall have grown old together, and thoughts of that time are a great delight to me; but somehow I rather hope that we will never be so old that we must *stop* to look back upon our lives. I have a great love for the *harness*, and I want to die in it. I want to the last to be the *active* centre of my family, its prime-minister, not merely its aged counsellor. I want always to be *serving* those whom I love, not as one who has gotten beyond them and must look back to lead, but as one who is *one of them*, a comrade, though the oldest, the leading comrade, in a common life-under-taking. I want never to be made, but always to be a-making—to have my head growing clearer and my mental sinews readier, as well as steadier, as my hair grows greyer—to have the dust of the road always in my nostrils. And the joy of the thing is that I know that my darling's heart is of the same temper, that her sympathy will ever be my spur! I have seen into my darling's heart, and I know that it was made for my home. It has been my increasing delight to find out how near kin her spirit is to mine. It is a very *different* spirit; it has taught me to wonder at and to love many things that I never knew of before; but it is none the less a kindred spirit—a spirit that seems to understand me with-out interpretation and to be native to the same tastes and im-pulses that I possess. But it is not relationship of *blood*; she is not my sister. She is nearer to me than that; she is my pledged wife!

Oh, Eileen, if you knew the keenness and the character of the delight it gives me when you try to tell me your thoughts about me—about our relations to each other—I think that you would try something of the kind in every letter you write! It is the purest, most perfect joy that my heart knows. You always touch the chords which—which nobody but you *can* touch—the only draw-back is that you make June seem *so* far away! You give as much happiness as it is possible to give, so long as you must withhold yourself, to   Your own   Woodrow.

My cold is better, my pet—i.e. *I* am better, for having got partially rid of it.

ALS (WP, DLC).

From Ellen Louise Axson

My darling Woodrow,   New York, Mar. 27 1885

Yesterday afternoon I spent at the Seney collection, it being our free day, and at night Mr. and Miss Carter called for me to go to the Spring St. prayer meeting; and the consequence was that when I returned from the latter I was to[o] tired and sleepy even to write to you—unless I had covered the sheet with repetitions of "I love you, I love you," for that was the only idea I had left in my head!

By the way, my friends the Bevier girls with Miss Petingill set me a fine example last night, and themselves reaped the reward of well-doing. They went down to the chapel alone, or perhaps I should say *too well* attended, their companions, the only ones in the car besides two coloured women, being three drunken men who were singing at the tops of their voices when they were not making pleasant advances to them.

I am very glad, dear, to know that your cold is better in some respects and trust you will soon be better in all; this beautiful weather will perhaps help you in throwing it off. I have another letter from Stockton answering some of my questions about his case. The doctor says it is partly the result of overwork and insufficient exercise and partly malaria. He says he was confined to his room for several days last week, but is now at work again. I think it is *madness* for him to go on in that way. He ought to be *made* to leave, at once.

I shan't pretend to answer this dear letter before me now, my darling, for it is "criticism day" and I must be at the League betimes. I ought to be at breakfast now. But I *must* take time to tell you sir, that I think you do my love great injustice! I know that a great many women seem to give it where there is "no merit of attractiveness," and their incredible folly in despising the best and noblest and doting on fools and rogues has become a proverb. But I have a profound respect for my love, sir, because it has shown such sapience and fine judgment;—it is so well able to render a *reason* for the faith that is in it. I have never seen anyone— there *is* no one—who can be *compared even* with you for good and great and *delightful* qualities. So when head and heart unite in telling me that this is the man of men, the one of all others whom I can most honour, admire, look up to, as well as the only one whom I can love, it would be strange indeed if I did not wish to spend my life with him—and for him. The *really* strange thing

is that you should choose to spend your life with *me*. You know
Carlyle says that "let but the rising of the sun or the creation of
a world happen *twice* and it ceases to be marvellous." But this is
one great mystery which even use and event cannot make less
marvellous. "Oh wonderful, wonderful and once again wonderful!"

With all my heart   Your own   Eileen.

ALS (WC, NjP).

From Houghton, Mifflin & Company

Dear Sir: Boston, Mar 27th, 1885
    We have already sent a copy of your book to Prof Freeman,
but not to Prof Bryce. We will see that the latter receives one.
The copy for Freeman, together with one for Prof. Seeley,[1] was,
we believe sent at your request.

Yours truly   Houghton, Mifflin & CO.   D. B. U.

ALS (WP, DLC) with WWhw notation on env.: "Ans. Mar. 28/85."
    [1] John Robert Seeley, Professor of Modern History, Cambridge University.

To Ellen Louise Axson

My own darling,   Balto., March 27, '85
    Whenever I *begin* a letter to you with expressions of the love
that is always forcing itself to my lips, all other subjects are shut
out—none is *big* enough to interrupt it—and the consequence is
that I am in arrears on one or two little points: for I *have* begun
with love the last day or so—and would like to to-day, if doing so
would not prevent my telling you how delighted I am that you
find the "paint class" so satisfactory. I don't believe that even
you, my Eileen, can have any idea how much I am wrapt up in
your studies—for your sake, of course, above everything else, but
also for their own sake in a measure. You know what I believe
with regard to your powers in portrait-painting: I believe that you
can do some really *great* work in that, which seems to me one of
the very highest departments of art; and I am *so* glad to see every
technical obstacle taken out of your way: so that, if you *want* to
paint hereafter, you can be free to realize the very best results—
so that you can satisfy yourself. I am just as much interested,
darling, in your work as you can be in mine; and I am sure that,
if you find subjects that you choose to paint, with all your heart
in the painting, you can leave some immortal portraits. Of course
there's that fact which sometimes makes me feel so guiltily selfish,

that marriage will take away almost all your chances for work of that kind; but my heart will be in any arrangement you choose to make by which time may be found for your studies, even after I have appropriated you to myself. Do you know, Eileen—yes, of course you *must* know—that I have often wondered what you thought on this point? Wont you tell me, darling? That is now the only point of importance upon which my little sweetheart has never said *any*thing to me—the interference of love with her profession—the sacrifice of that profession involved in giving herself to me; and I have longed inexpressibly, without knowing how to confess the longing, to know just what my darling thinks, and has thought, about it. In that sweet talk we had about my stealing gold to be foil for my silver I learned only the wonderful perfection of her love, which made no sacrifice made for me seem a *sacrifice* at all: but has she no plans concerning her art studies after June? Ah, sweetheart, this thing has torn my heart more than once! I *hate* selfishness, it hurts me more than I can tell you to think that I am asking you to give up what has formed so much of your life and constituted so much of your delight. And yet that is what is involved in becoming a wife: we shall want to go to housekeeping as soon as possible. My darling, my unspeakable love for you cries out to know what your feelings are about it all! I would give my life for you, and yet I am asking you to give your life to me—for me, to be merged in mine. Does my darling want that—does she want to belong to no thing as well as to nobody but   Her own   Woodrow.

My cold still hangs on—but promises to go.

ALS (WC, NjP).

From the Minutes of the Seminary of Historical and Political Science

Bluntschli Hall. Friday evening, March 27, 1885
... The paper of the evening was by Mr. Wilson, who presented a review of recent American political economists. He stated in brief the economic doctrines of Amasa Walker, Perry, Bowen, and Francis Walker, choosing the cheif [*sic*] works of these writers as types of the recent works published in this country.

Remarks were made by Dr. Ely, justifying the method adopted by Mr. Wilson: Dr. Ely also called attention to a late letter of Mr. Bryce to Dr. Adams, in which he calls attention to the subject of laissez-faire in the U.S. as a fruitful one for investigation. Articles in the Christian Union on topics connected with socialism were noted as illustrating signs of the times.

At 9.20 P.M. the Seminary adjourned.   [Davis R. Dewey]

Draft of a Report to the Historical Seminary

[c. March 27, 1885]

It may be said broadly that the development of economic thought in America since the middle of the present century has held to the same general direction as that taken by English writers during the same period and has accompanied English thought with a pretty equal pace. Not that American text writers have merely reflected the thoughts of writers accross the water. It would be fairer to say that thought in the two countries has had a common history, that it has all been in the broadest sense English thought. Still the greatest names connected with political economy during the period have belonged over sea and writers on this side have followed rather than led. Until very recent years at any rate the lustre of American political economy has been like the light of the moon rather than like the light of the sun. Henry C. Car[e]y and those who have followed his lead, though adhering to a few doctrines peculiar to themselves, have been seekers after new articles for the old creed rather than after a new creed.

It is at the same time true, however, that the American writers have been characterized by much wideness of view and much freshness of comment. The old doctrines have received from them liberal interpretations, wide-viewed illustrations, and applications as large as America itself. And in being thus cast afresh these doctrines have of course undergone considerable modifications. American goods have been made out of English raw materials.

So independent, indeed, and so individual have our text writers been that it is very difficult to make any satisfactory grouping of them. Each has had his special point of view and his special idiosyncracies of belief. There have, however, been certain broad tendencies common to most, if not to all. All except the most recent have been inclined to take very optimistic views of the economic life. They have seen little but promises of blessing in the unrestricted operation of the principles of their science. However much reason they may have found to doubt the wisdom of this or that legislative interference with what they regarded as the course of nature—that is, the course of the fundamental principles of their teachings—they have seldom criticised unfavourably the existing order of society. Writing in a country where vast, almost unprecedented, developments of industry and movements of population were taking place their imaginations have been impressed, of course, and they have realized the scientific importance of the rapid economic progress proceeding under their eyes; but they have not seen in it all much to arouse grave questionings as to the future; these great movements have seemed to most of them as propitious as a holiday procession. "In this country the general and extraordinary prosperity has spread a sort of poetic haze over the whole machinery of society, and made all enquiry into the laws of its working seem a kind of idle speculation," or like the ingratitude of looking a gift horse in the mouth.

One natural result has been a very general rejection of the darker tenets of the British school of writers, notably of the tenets which bear the name of Malthus. A world too fruitless to sustain every human being that might come into existence has been very hard for an American to conceive of. His own boundless continent with its still untaxed resources has seemed a palpable refutation of all the Malthusian forecastings. Facts all about him have seemed to speak for the unlimited capacity of nature to feed all her children.

Cliff Leslie's "Political Economy in the United States"—Fortnightly Review. 28 (n.s.) 448-509.
Characteristics of American writers:
(1) Reject Malthus.
(2) Introduce a great deal of theology
    "Children used to have a way of classing books as 'Sunday' or 'week-day books' by looking over the leaves for sacred names. According to this criterion several American treatises on political economy would be set apart as Sunday books." p. 497.
(3) Absence of long chains of deduction. Rejection or ignoring of the assumption that competition equalizes the wages of labourers and the profits of capitalists in different occupations and localities throughout a country.
(4) "Systematic teaching of protectionism in colleges and text books as a scientific doctrine."

As to (2), above, many of the earlier writers on political economy in the United States (as well as some of the later ones) were ministers of the Gospel who taught p.e. along with the moral sciences, or something of that sort.

If we were to accept Prof. Bowen's division of American political economists into those who for the most part follow Adam Smith and those who for the most part follow Henry C. Cary, we should have a very simple and in some senses convenient grouping of the writers whom we have to consider; but the progress of the science can be marked satisfactorily only by looking more closely into the methods of individual authors and grouping them according to their particular points of view. It requires no very particular examination to discover a general tendency to use less and less the strictly and exclusively deductive method and to adopt more and more exclusively the opposite, the inductive, method. Probably at no time would a Ricardo have been a possibility in this country. The industrial facts furnished ready to the hands of our writers by the history of almost every American community were much better than any supposititious cases which they could frame for themselves. They lived, so to say, amongst object-lessons in their science. They would have had to be without neighbours to have been without illustrations of the topics upon which they were writing. The experiences of actual life thrust themselves into their speculations and by their very presence affected those speculations, preventing their becoming mere library theories, mere fine-spun threads of logic. Our writers therefore have all of them, though for the most part orthodox, had strong latitudinarian tendencies, and none of them has hesitated upon occasion to venture as far as actual dissent.

Still, some of them have been fonder of theory than others; some have taken much more kindly than others to abstractions wh. excluded a careful examination of concrete economic facts; and it is quite practicable to to [sic] classify their methods upon this basis. Prof. Arthur L. Perry may be taken as a type of the extremer theorists and the gradual decline of the fondness for the *a priori* methods may be traced through Prof. Francis Bowen to Prof. Francis A. Walker, the most rationally inductive writer our economic literature has yet produced.

WWT MS. with hw emendations (WP, DLC).

From Ellen Louise Axson

My darling Woodrow,   New York Mar. 28 1885

What a very pleasant and appreciative review this is from the Chicago Times![1] I am charmed with it. Do you know who wrote it? And from what paper do you take the short comment? What a comical mistake!—that about "the class of undergraduates"!—

doubly comical because of the positive air with which the statement is made.[2] But at least they give you credit for the wisdom
which comes with age and experience.

Today's extract from Ruskin *is* fine. How well and truly it describes the difference between the self-conceit of a little man and
the self-reliance and self-respect of a great man. I believe it is
true that only men who are *great*—in soul at least—can look at
themselves in that calmly impersonal fashion and make a full
just estimate of their powers yet without any touch of vanity as
to the result. It must be because they are able to rise above self-
consciousness. With "the majority of people["] there seems to be
small choice in their attitude towards themselves; they are either
consumed with self-conceit or they are the victims of a paralysing
self-distrust. It may be that the distrust is well founded. And yet
I don't know, we were all given *some* work to do, and the problem is simply to find out what our portion is, and then, whether
great or small, to quietly "go ahead and do it.["] And I suppose
that if we knew the commission to be Heaven-sent and if we did
it to God's glory rather than our own, we would be content with
the work whatever it's nature. I imagine that the ministering
spirits feel equally honoured, in their *great* humility whether
they are sent on the humblest or the grandest of missions. And
then of course if we could be sure that God had set us the task
we should be no less sure of our power to do it. But there's the
rub;—the problem isn't a simple one after all. It is very easy to
say that to "know thyself" and then—*forget thyself* comprises the
whole secret of living, but it isn't so easy to *do*. Strange that it
should be so hard to find oneself out! But how I run on;—what
I started out to say was merely that I think these words of Ruskin's describe *your* spirit exactly, my darling, and it is one of the
things which I admire and love most in you, that rare combination of power and modesty. One must be conscious of his power
to *use* it effectively,—you *know* your power and it spurs you on to
great deeds yet leaves not a trace of self-conceit.

How I have wasted my few short moments this morning! I had
a great deal to say and a very short time to say it in,—and now I
must leave it all unsaid a little longer, for the time has flown.
I wanted to tell you, darling, that our spirits must be akin because
all your words so surely find their echo, full and clear, in my
heart. Your words of love, for instance, I am often tempted to repeat to *you*, because they express so exactly *my* feeling, my experience. How well I know that silent pervading influence running
subconsciously through all my moods and making me always

light-hearted. How true it is that *your* love has the wonderful power of diffusing itself through *every* conscious moment of *my* life. I can no more forget it than I cease to feel and breathe this balmy spring air and sunshine, and be made happier for it. In short, dear, you are my life; and I am altogether

Your own Eileen

ALS (WC, NjP).

¹ Clipping from the Chicago *Times*, Jan. 31, 1885 (WP, DLC). It is not clear in which letter Wilson enclosed this or the other clipping which she mentions next.

² Unidentified clipping (WP, DLC). Ellen refers to the following sentence: "The volume evidently has been delivered in lectures to a class of undergraduates."

To Ellen Louise Axson

Balto., March 28, '85

When it rains as it is raining this afternoon, sweetheart,—as if just to keep people at home—with a gentle, leisurely, protecting downpour—my little den here seems particularly cosey and homelike, and consequently particularly empty without you! Its similitude to homelikeness seems almost a mockery so long as it lacks the only thing that can make my heart feel at home, your presence. It is only a home for my body; my heart is far away with the precious little lady whose presence could make the strangest country in the world seem like home to me. What an afternoon for a chat!—an afternoon in which to sit snugly and feel safe from the intrusions of the rest of the world—a *home* afternoon, for home secrets, home plannings, home caresses, home frolics. I should so like to say to my queen some things that I don't know how to write. What a chance to broach some of my half-conceived ideas, which dare not bloom without encouragement from the sunshine of her sweet sympathy! What an opportunity to read to her tid-bits which have delighted me, but which cannot be perfectly enjoyed unless there be a loved one to share the enjoyment! On this particular occasion I might laugh into her sunny eyes and ask her what she thinks of the consistency displayed in a letter I received this morning in which my correspondent first takes me to task for doing injustice to her love by the suggestion that she could find nothing attractive in me to justify it, and then immediately declares it a mystery why I should ever have fallen in love with her. But then it might make her desperately *jealous* to read her *that* letter; mightn't it? I could talk about myself, though, and avoid all embarrassing mention of the love letters I had received. I could tell her about the reading of my paper on the American Political Economists last night to the Seminary;

about the harassing difficulties of articulating with a nose and a throat both stubbornly unwilling to coöperate—difficulties to be compared only with those of making even a group of students listen with interest to the discussion of a dry subject. Or, if she tired of such topics—as she well might, were she anything but a loving woman—I could take her in my arms and tell her that one kiss of hers was sweeter to me than the greatest success of oratory, that I would rather fill her eyes with the light of joy and love than win the plaudits of all the world, that life and love are one and the same for me so long she is altogether mine! And maybe I could persuade her to tell me of those things that are sweeter to my ears than the sweetest music, when her voice utters them— her own thoughts of me, her love, her hopes, her dreams—all the precious confidences which belong only to me, which *can* be spoken only in her lover's ear! And then, too—But dear me! dear me! what am I thinking about to be writing these day-dreams down! The rain beating against my window-panes seems to be laughing at me. It's time to stop tantalizing myself, and you, with these reveries of one who is a bachelor sorely against his will. I have accomplished one thing, however; I have drawn a companion picture for that one, that charming one, that my darling gave me from *her* reveries the other day. And the joy of it all is, sweetheart, that it is only as many weeks as it once was months— scarcely more months than it once was years—before we can realize these things we now delight to dream of. For our dreams are not extravagant dreams: their realization will be complete in our being *together*—and within twelve weeks we will be together, in the sweetest, most sacred, most lasting, and, as it seems to me, most inspiring of all unions—and Mrs. Wilson shall be the happiest woman in ten kingdoms if the life-long love of her Woodrow can make her happy. As long as the bitter cold was upon us time seemed to me to stand still, to hold me as far away from summer and my hopes as I was when winter began; but now that spring seems at hand, my hopes and my spirits are quickened, as if they were flowers, and I begin to realize with surpassing surprise and joy that June is at hand, that my long waiting is almost over, that my darling holds out her hands to me and soon I may go to her—not to come away any more! I could almost cry out for joy when these thoughts come crowding upon me. They are like some blessed influence to turn me away from pain and anxiety and fatigue and discouragement. They make me feel it a pride and a privilege to live, to inherit such an estate, such wealth of womanly love. Henceforth all life will be doubly mine because my Eileen will share it with me. Do you wonder, darling, that my pulses are so quickened by the first promise of spring? Why, *this* season has but to go and I have my heart's desire! How hard it will be for me to behave myself when I get to Savannah! Will you be very strict with me, and compel me to preserve some *appearance* of calmness and dignity until we get safely away? You will have to give me careful instruction in deportment, and will have to give Palmer [Axson] and Randolph [Axson] stern injunctions on no account to consent to play with me! But, all the same, I shall expect you to confide to me in private that you share to the full the joy of   Your own   Woodrow.

ALS (WC, NjP).

From Ellen Louise Axson

New York, Mar. 28/85

No, my darling, I did *not* "know"—it never occurred to me that there might be any question in your mind as to my course with regard to my work hereafter, yet now that such a thought is suggested I can easily understand your uncertainty—and I am *very* glad you have asked the question; am sorry we have not talked it over long ago. But, as I remarked above, the omission was merely owing to the fact that it did not occur to me that there was anything to say; the case being to my mind so simple and clear, and having been so entirely settled from the day that I pledged you my hand. Sweetheart, I would never give you a divided allegiance; I owe you my little *all* of love, of life and service, and it is all my joy to give it. Believe me, dear, it is an absolutely pure joy—there is in it *no* alloy, I have *never* felt the *slightest* pang of regret for what I must "give up." *Don't* think there is any sacrifice involved, my darling, I assure you again there is *none whatever*[.] If at desert just now I had exchanged my banana which I like very well, for an orange which I like a great deal better, would I have been entitled to letters of condolence because of the loss of the banana? Is it a sacrifice to give up a *thing* which one *likes* more or less, for a *person* whom one *loves* more—infinitely more—than all the world beside? I wish that it *were* a great sacrifice, or that I could make *any* sacrifice which would prove how much I love you,—how much I value your love. Suppose, for the sake of argument, it were as great a sacrifice as even you imagine, my darling *must* know that it would be a pitiable price to pay for such love as his, for the love of such a man as he, for the wonderful happiness with which he has filled my life to overflowing. And to think that he should feel "guiltily selfish" for having done all this for me!—oh wonderful! Was there ever anything so *un*selfish as this letter that lies before! Was there ever such a man—such a *gentleman* as this one! I am sure I don't know why I should have cried over this letter—but cry I certainly did!

But to answer your questions more in detail,—I must remind you that I never had any ambition, and that I can't give up what I never had! Nor had I ever any faith in myself; I never even dreamed of painting "immortal portraits." My experience and observation since I have been here have driven me to the conclusion that I *have* talent, above the average among the art-students. It is *barely* possible that my talent for art combined with my talent for work *might*, after many years, win me a place in the first rank among American artists—who don't amount to much *anyhow* you know! But "art is long";—it would take years of steady effort to do any *really* (not just *comparatively*) *good*—to say nothing of "great" work. And I am firmly convinced that it would not have *paid*, that I could be much more *profitably* employed[,] that if I had chosen to *sacrifice* to such an object my woman's heart with all it's natural impulses and cravings I should have cried bitterly in [the] end that it all was vanity and vexation of spirit. And then, as I said before, I have never felt the slightest desire to be prominent as an artist. I worked partly to gain a means of support and chiefly for pure love of the work for it's own sake I believe. I do love good work in that way,—as an *end* even more than as a means.

So there are very few reasons why I should, and a great many reasons why I should not entertain such an idea as that of doing "great" (!) work or of pursueing my studies seriously after this spring. Art is a severe mistress; she demands long and constant service before she will give the smallest reward, and I am the merest beginner now,—for I feel that nothing *counted* before this year. True, I have made a *good* beginning; I have accomplished what I came here for, I am quite thorough as far as I have gone,—prepared to work in the "humbler walks" of art without the disturbing sense of being a humbug imposing on a confiding public; and that shall suffice me. Except that I wish if possible to take some lessons in landscape painting, partly because some knowledge of it is necessary to that practical equipment, which you know is the hobby upon which I rode to New York, and partly because I think it must be one of the most delightful and healthful of recreations; and one for which I shall probably have some time, in summer vacations! &c.—since it is everyone's *duty* to spend a portion of their time in the open air. But the chief reason why it is best—and easiest too—to give up, once for all, every thought of art as a serious study lies in my disposition. You don't know *yet* what a curious disposition that is, though I have tried to tell you several times! I am not at all well-balanced, I have entirely too much badly regulated energy and concentration; it is well-nigh impossible for me to divide up a day into bits as other women do;—I must do one thing all day long. It makes no difference whether it be something I *like* to do or not,—for that matter I like,—I grow interested in any work when I have once begun it,—but I may not have wished to begin it and I may be dreadfully tired, physically and mentally, yet all the same I want to *go on* to the end, and to leave it before, is nothing short of a great *wrench.* I am altogether too one-idead, and it is a terrible quality for a woman. I imagine it would be rather useful for a man. I used often to wish myself a man just on account of it; and I must admit that while it is my greatest weakness it has also been my greatest strength in some respects, and has enabled me to get through with work which I could not possibly have managed without it. I am not without hope of learning some self-control in this matter; this winter has helped me, for the working with models has *forced* me to divide up my day,—to observe times and seasons and *common-sense*! But you see how it would work if I tried to cling to anything so absorbing as art with one hand and to you with the other. "We shall want to go to house-keeping as soon as possible," of course, and if I did not forget then that I had ever thought to be an artist, I should be a *caution* as a house-keeper!— that is I should be all house keeper one day all artist the next!— and you would be the most uncomfortable of men! Of course it would be very unwise and wrong to drop it so completely as as [*sic*] to lose what I have gained and defeat the very purpose which brought me here; but I could accomplish so much as that in my leisure moments, were they of the briefest;—and to keep it in such a subordinate place as that is very different from following it with serious purpose and not at all dangerous—I hope. I have thought that I might for a time at least, while my "leisure moments" are many, do a few portraits for my Sav. "connection." I might begin by raising my price to the regular city standard for work of that sort and then of course my "orders" would be few and far between, but if one did happen to come in occasionally it would be really worth while.

Well I believe I have told you all my thoughts on this weighty subject, though in so rambling and disconnected a fashion that I fear you will be more dazed than anything else.

In conclusion let me beg you once more, darling, never to let this trouble you again. It is too bad that it should "hurt" you when it doesn't hurt me in the least. If you were a woman you would understand that at once; of course it would be a great trial to a man "to give up what had formed so much of his life and his delight" but with a woman—a sure enough (!) woman—it is *nothing*, because however much of her life it may have constituted, it was not her *true* life, the life for which she was made. As compared with the privilege of loving and serving you and the blessedness of being loved by you, the praise and admiration of all the world and generations yet unborn would be lighter than vanity. If *now* I held such *greatness* in my hand I should toss it away without a second thought that the hand might be free to clasp in yours. Indeed I should probably drop it without even the *first* thought simply because, having something better to think of, I had forgotten all about it,—had forgotten to hold it.

My darling, it would not be a sacrifice to *die* for you, how then can it be one to live for you? Believe me my love, to be even to the uttermost   Your own Eileen.

ALS (WP, DLC).

From James E. Rhoads

My dear Friend,   Philadelphia 3 mo. 28. 1885.
Thine with list of Books received. I think we had better buy the books on the list sent, and add others next year. If it appears during the year 1886 that we need more they can be added by special order. Most of the works required are in the English Language, and hence can be had promptly. Please accept sincere thanks for thy kind care in this matter. My own judgment about Duruy's work corresponds with thine. Perhaps it or one like it, can be had a few years later.

When time and strength will permit, please make out an examination paper for English & American History, & then thy special work for Bryn Mawr will be off thy mind for this year.

With sincere regard thy friend   James E Rhoads

ALS (WP, DLC).

To Ellen Louise Axson

My own darling,   Balto., March 29, '85
The enclosed cutting is from Shaw's paper, the Minneapolis *Tribune*. I send the letter whole because the reference to our little

work is made more intelligble by the context. Mr. Schouler's history is unquestionably the best we have had so far, and it is, consequently, immensely gratifying to have one's name mentioned in such a way in connection with his.

No, my pet, I don't know who wrote the notice in the Chicago paper; but it is certainly amongst the most satisfactory that have appeared. And I don't know what paper the short extract was from. It was sent to me 'plain so.'

I hope that I *will* have a chance, through you, to hear what Mr. Ewing has to say about the book: I feel that he is one of the men one can *trust*. As for 'cousin Hattie,' I have fairly fallen in love with her, for her sweet sayings and for her cordial love for my little queen. But, much as I love her, she shan't have that visit just when she is counting upon having it.

Speaking of Tenn. folks reminds me to ask, sweetheart, if you have heard anything this winter about "the Prodigy."[1] Wasn't he expecting to be in New York before this?

I share your anxiety about dear Stockton, my darling, but I hope that you will not distress yourself too much about him. He is not the sort of boy to neglect advice recklessly and wantonly, and he has had advice both from the doctor at Davidson (who is doubtless familiar with just such cases) and from home. I have no doubt that "uncle Will" also has given him full counsel. And Stockton is not wilful, is he? *These* are the reflections which serve to reassure me, and I hope that my darling may see some force in them.

My pet, may I give *you* a piece of advice, with my love for justification? Please don't let any change in the weather tempt you to make a change of underclothing until you can be absolutely *sure* that summer is come[.] And now imagine that you've kissed me and forgiven my impertinence!

And so your sweet, surpassing love prompted you to apply to *me* Ruskin's fine judgment about greatness and humility? Ah, little sweetheart, if you knew how precious these loving judgments of yours are to me, what an unspeakable joy it gives me to have this tender, whole-hearted admiration accorded me by my Eileen, whose love and trust are very life to me, I think that you would be almost repaid for the gift you make of these priceless treasures of your heart! What a wonderfully blessed man I am—what marvellous love I have won! But I have a great deal to give in return. I give that unmeasured love, that perfect trust, that glad homage, that delighted admiration, that *all* of heart and soul that make me altogether

Your own   Woodrow.

ALS (WC, NjP). Enc.: "Men and Books," clipping from the *Minneapolis Daily Tribune*, March 25, 1885. This was a review of current books in which a notice about the third volume of James Schouler, *History of the United States Under the Constitution*, followed a notice of *Congressional Government*.
¹ Thomas Frank Gailor.

From Ellen Louise Axson

My darling Woodrow,   New York March 29/85.

I wonder if this morning brought you as great a surprise as it did us in New York when we awoke and found the ground thickly covered with snow. I don't think I was ever more astonished at a freak of the weather—for yesterday the air was so soft and warm that one could have fancied it time to go a-hunting May-blooms. After all I am rather glad that the Spring weather *is* slow in coming; it is delightful if one can take time to enjoy it, but otherwise it is tantalizing to see so much to tempt one out of doors and yet to feel obliged to stay in. It is unfavourable to hard work for other reasons too, for it makes one feel so lazy and good for nothing.

I had a letter from Eddie last night written on the 15th of Mar. and he says they had a heavy snow-storm there that morning; which seems to me very late for that latitude. Eddie's letters are very amusing, he gets off so many unexpected words and phrases; —he say "I sit at the window and look out on it, (the snow) but with me on account of my throat it is touch not, taste not, handle not!" He also says that he saw a very "complimentary notice of Mr. Wilson's book in the Presbyterian."¹ I wish my brothers were "more account"! We seem doomed to perpetual anxiety about them. Uncle Henry writes that Eddie is having a great deal of trouble with his throat, and that he had an attack of croup a few days ago. He mentioned a slight throat trouble before, and it seems to have become considerably worse; it is something new for him. Eddie writes that the doctor says he must spend next winter in a *warmer* climate! That sounds serious, but I hope from the rest they tell me that the case in [is] not painful or alarming in any way, but simply troublesome.

But I must go back to that precious letter of yours which came Friday, and which I have never had an opportunity to answer. I wanted to tell you, for one thing, how much I liked what you say about the sort of old age you covet, and how entirely I agree with you. We havn't enough of Teufelsdrockh's² "excellent passivity" to look forward with much pleasure to being laid on the shelf; and we are too young, and I hope will always remain too young to "long for rest" as the chief of blessings! I grow so tired of hearing people talk of heaven as if it were nothing but a place of *rest*. It is a genuine Irish Roman Catholic ideal—"Sure and the Virgin will make a bed in heaven for ye—bless ye." Of all the imaginings of heaven which I have heard or read, I think I like best that of the noble woman, who when asked how she best loved to think of it, answered quickly, "as a perpetual service without weariness."

And, my darling, I want to tell you too that when you speak of ours being kindred spirits you touch one of the deepest sources of the ever-growing joy which fills my heart to over-flowing. I too have had an ever-deepening sense of the inborn sympathy there is between us in all matters of importance; we look at life in the same way, our ideals and aspirations are in harmony, and our thought is so often the same about those things that make it a great and sweet though solemn privilege to live. And it is this sympathy which, together with the greatness of my love, makes me hope now that in spite of all my unworthiness I was indeed "meant for" you,—that I may do you good and not evil all the days of my life. I do indeed seem to understand you, dear, without interpretation[.] Not even the services of love himself are needed *as an interpreter*, because it is my native tongue you speak. And when I reflect how little of that community of thought and feeling I have found in any other man whom I have met—how constantly for want of it, I have been obliged either to suppress my real self, my more earnest thought, or to utter it only as a protest, I am lost in amazement at the wonderful way in which God has blessed me, blessed me beyond my very dreams. And I am *so* undeserving! Would that the blessing could make me as good as it has made me happy. It *has* filled my heart more full of love toward the great Giver of all good things. But I must say "goodnight." I love you darling as my own soul, and am now and forever.   Your own Eileen.

ALS (WC, NjP).
   1 This may refer to a brief notice of the publication of *Congressional Government* in the Columbia *Southern Presbyterian*, Feb. 5, 1885. This notice was reprinted from the Wilmington *North Carolina Presbyterian* and quoted favorable comments from two other North Carolina newspapers.
   2 Diogenes Teufelsdröckh, the protagonist of Carlyle's *Sartor Resartus*.

To Ellen Louise Axson

                                        Balto., March 30, '85
   Oh, my matchless little sweetheart, what a prodigal I have been in superlatives to have none left with which to crown the expression of my unspeakable delight over this precious letter that came this morning! It is an inexpressibly precious letter to

me—it was too sweet to read with dry eyes! What with admiration of its wonderful womanly sense and delight at its still more wonderful womanly *love*, my heart is even yet almost too full to trust itself to speak. Oh, Eileen, what a happy, God-sent inspiration it was that made me love you at first acquaintance! My heart knew at once the treasure it had found, and ever since my slower head has been daily discovering, with increasing amazement and delight, fresh proofs of my heart's instinctive wisdom. Why, this incomparable little lady cannot, it would seem, choose so much as a single word, whatever she talks about, that does not seem to me just the word that I should have chosen to use in seeking to speak most tenderly and most justly my thoughts to her. But one thing she lacks—and that for the time only adds to her charms—she does not recognize her genius for thinking and loving in just the right way. It shall be my mission to lure her away, by love and trust, from her self-distrust and make her see some part of the discovery that I have made, that her powers are as great as—as her *love*. I shall not fear to destroy the *beauty* of her humility: I shall hope to remove its *blindness*. My darling's heart is too great for anything but humility, and too true to hold anything but the truth: and the truth is, that her gifts *both* of mind and heart are such as *any* man might be proud to do homage to. I admire her as I could admire no one else in the world, and I love her—oh, I love her as if to love her were the only exercise in which my heart could be satisfied—as if I had been created to love her! No, darling, I will never let thought of what you may be giving up for me trouble me again. How could I *now*? I do not understand this marvellous woman's love; I simply *accept* it with boundless joy and gratitude. Oh, sweetheart, *why* have I no *words* in which to love you—why must your tenderness and love bring to my eyes these tears that can find no language for their joy? If we were but together to-day, how we could laugh into each others eyes to think how *ready* our hearts are for the sweet ceremonies of June, my Eileen! If *we* are not ready for marriage, who ever was? Who were ever closer together as lovers than we are? Have not our hearts yielded up to each other their utmost allegiance? Am I not the happiest man that was ever loved by woman? God bless you, my darling, my queen, for all the sweet gifts you have brought to   Your own   Woodrow.

ALS (WC, NjP).

From Ellen Louise Axson

New York Mar. 31/85

Why cannot I tell you, my darling, how sweet and precious I find these letters of yours? They are *wonderful* letters, my *heart* answers them as neither pen nor tongue can ever do it. The only trouble is that these sweet pictures which you paint make me— shall I say it?—*homesick*; for where ever you are, *is* the home of my heart. And my heart is *at home* too, it has gone before me;— and gone to *stay*!—so as it cannot come to me I will—ah gladly!— go to it. It would be strange—would it not?—if the little wanderer, far from home, amongst aliens, were not glad that the days of her exile are shortened. Yes dear, that *is* the sweetest part of it all, that the dream will come true—that sweet dream which has in it nothing extravagant or unreal, the dream of being together. I *will* be the happiest woman in the kingdoms, my darling.

I did really dream of it, all last night, and it has made [me] long, this morning, more than ever, if that be possible, for a sight of your dear face. But as you say, why should we tantalize our- selves so? Yet it is a sweet pain, and one that we would not be without; one that brings with it a joy that swallows up all else. Twelve weeks! I had not thought of it as so soon! and I am not startled by the thought, as I should once have been;—my darling I *do* love you with a perfect love.

I am glad that you have fallen in love with dear Cousin Hattie; and you will love her still more when you know her, as I am so anxious to have you do. No, I have heard nothing of the "Prodigy," I didn't expect to see him. He don't like engaged girls!—he said so; —his own somewhat overweening self-love and—I beg his pardon —self-conceit, craves from the young ladies whom he honours with his society a deeper interest,—a keener sense of his impor- tance than he is likely to get from such as I! for Rose[1] let him into the secret.

That is a *very* pleasant and gratifying little mention of your book—the one from the [Minneapolis] Tribune.

How is the cold? You say nothing of it in this letter, am sorry it hangs on so long. Yes, you may consider your "impertinence" forgiven, and your advice taken! But I *must* close,—excuse haste. Believe me darling, with all my heart

Your own Eileen.

ALS (WP, DLC).
[1] Rosalie Anderson.

To Ellen Louise Axson

My own darling,   Balto., March 31, '85

Dear little Eddie must have gotten under the influence of that wonderful literary cousin[1] of yours to write in so 'polite' and high-ly-flavoured a style. How delightfully amusing! I am sincerely grieved to hear about his throat troubles. You *have* an unreliable pair of brothers. We shall have to keep them supplied with hy-gienic literature and with books on 'how to get strong.'

This is a wonderfully sweet letter that came this morning with its loving, delightful words about our kinship of spirit; but I have a great mind, Miss, to read you a lecture about persisting in de-claring so vehemently that my darling is 'undeserving' of the blessings that have come to her with my love, after I have given it as my deliberate conviction that she deserves infinitely more than I can ever give her. It is very impolite of you to reject my judgments with so little show of respect! I am surprised that you should say such things to my face about the lady whom I have chosen to be my wife and to receive from me all the honour that man can pay woman! You must remember, Miss, that I have, in one way and another, seen a bit of the world; I have met all sorts of 'woman-kind,' from the gauky, simpering Miss just out of the unnatural life of the boarding-school to the accomplished woman of the world—to 'Aunt Saidie'[2]—from the shoddy, new-wealth damsels of Atlanta to the stiff-backed culture-daughters of Boston —and the simple fact is that I know a genuine woman when I find one. Most women, like most men, *tire* me before very long. They have a certain round of feelings and ideas wh. one gets to know almost at once. Women are much less tiresome than men be-cause their wonderful sympathy enables them to reflect the senti-ments and opinions one pours into their ears; but with most of them the reflection is imperfect—as if from a defective mirror— there are blank, dull spots in one's intercourse with them. But I met a lady once who thrilled me with a strange discovery. To my soul hers was like a mirror without a flaw! Never a feeling or an opinion did I speak, did I confess, to her but I saw it returned to me by her wonderful eyes with a woman's sweet sanction and blessing upon it. She helped me to think by showing me in the clear depths of her woman's mind what I had thought! She loved me passionately because she found in me a spirit the counterpart of her own—and this was my Eileen, my rare, my matchless dar-ling! And *do* you think she was undeserving of the happiness of

a perfect love? No, no, little lady: she fulfilled the promise of her own sweet nature—and conferred an unspeakable blessing upon
Her own   Woodrow.

ALS (WC, NjP).
1 Marion C. L. Reeves.
2 Mrs. Thomas A. Hoyt.

From Ellen Louise Axson, with Enclosure

My darling Woodrow,   New York, April 1/85
I am extremely sorry that I did not or could not write last night, for I had a great deal to say, and now it must *not*! (postscript)[1] all remain unsaid, I fear. In fact I succumbed, I think, to the sweet influences of spring last evening; for while I was reading the Tribune's sage remarks about sending Confederate Brigadiers to represent the country against which they had fought,[2] I went fast asleep, to wake no more till nearly midnight!

Are you, in Baltimore, kept as busy discussing "appointments" as are my boarding house friends?[3] Poor Mr. Heiler! the "Phelps" appointment filled him with amazement, and the Pearson business with inexpressible consternation;[4]—while Mr. Finlayson's glee over his discomforture is beautiful to behold! "*Phelps!*" he cried a score of times on the night when that news came, "who *is* Phelps can't *anybody* tell me," with the deepest anxiety in his voice[.] "Yes the newspapers can," said Mr. Brigham shortly. I am very glad he *was* chosen from a Republican state for he must have had a dreary and discouraging time of it all these long years and I suppose his loyalty to the democratic party is the only thing which has prevented his being more famous. What a *stone wall* Cleveland is! My respect and admiration for him increase daily; —and to tell the truth I didn't like him very much, except by comparison with Blaine; I never liked his "looks." But this Pearson appointment has made me really enthusiastic over the man's strength of character, his stern regard for principle before all things. People must believe in him as a reformer now; that seems to have been a great test case. But it was an *extreme* case too— do you think it *will* "dismember" the democratic party?

But enough of politics. You have not told me yet how your cold is,—if this glorious weather has enabled you to throw it off entirely. *Isn't* it delightful?—the weather I mean, not the cold. One of the girls who come in from the country yesterday brought her hands full of the beautiful "pussy-willow" twigs, and I knew by that sign that though "spring comes slowly up this way" it was time to give her welcome. Nothing that grows could have made me so happy,—except it had been a branch of peach blossoms. How I should like to be in the country now! It fills me with such speechless delight to see and to feel "the green things a' budding everywhere you pass[.]" Is'nt the winter's chill atoned for by such a spectacle? Who would choose to live in a land of perpetual summer, and miss the rare delight of seeing, once a year, a beautiful, young world created, as fair and fresh "as if our Lord but yesterday had finished it." I wonder if one never hears the birds sing in New York? I dare say one could at the park;—by-and by I shall take a half holiday and go and see. Do you remember Coleridge's pretty "Lines in answer to a childs question"? I am reminded of them just here, and they are so "cute" that I think I will write them down for your amusement. Now these things are an allegory in which *I* am the lark! only *this* lark has sung all winter, as you know,—though perhaps with the coming of spring her note grows more jubilant.

Sweetheart I won't try to tell you now with what thoughts I read that dear letter which came yesterday, because it would all be in vain; but perhaps your *heart* will tell you how my *heart* answers to your every word,—with what unspeakable joy I bask in the sunshine of your love and approbation. I won't stop to question whether that "admiration" is due to your love or your judgment, since whatever the cause of it, the joy which it brings me remains the same. My darling, no treasure could be so great to me as your generous praise,—except your love. I am *very* glad that you *like* as well as *love* me. With all my heart

Your own Eileen.

ALS (WC, NjP).

1 "*not*! (postscript)" written above the line at this point.

2 The New York *Tribune*, March 31, 1885, in an editorial entitled "The Latest Nominations," commented on President Cleveland's latest group of diplomatic nominees as follows: "A better way to show the magnanimity of the North toward former rebels could hardly be devised than by sending them abroad as representatives of the Government they tried to destroy."

3 That is, Messrs. Finlayson, Brigham, and Heiler.

4 Cleveland, determined to assert his independence from office-seekers, in a surprise move appointed Edward J. Phelps as Minister to England. Phelps was relatively unknown. He was a Vermont lawyer and had been president of the American Bar Association. Henry G. Pearson, Postmaster of New York City, a Republican who had won acclaim for competence, was reappointed by Cleveland in spite of opposition from office-hungry Democrats.

E N C L O S U R E

Answer to a Childs Question

Do you ask what the birds say? The sparrow, the dove,
The linet and thrush say, "I love and I love"!

In the winter they're silent—the wind is so strong;
What it says I dont know, but it sings a loud song.
But green leaves and blossoms, and sunny warm weather,
And singing, and loving—all come back together.
But the lark is so brimful of gladness and love,
The green fields below him, the blue sky above,
That he sings, and he sings; and forever sings he—
"I love my Love, and my Love loves me"!

Hw MS. (WC, NjP).

Two Letters to Ellen Louise Axson

Balto., April 1, 1885

Oh, my little bewitcher, I never knew what it meant to be *tumultuously* happy until you began to confess your wish that our wedding-day might be speeded in its coming! These sweet confessions seem to teach my heart a gladness such as even you never gave it before. This *demonstrative* love from my shy darling fills my heart so full of supreme joy and exultation—with so solemn, so pure, so unspeakable a delight—that I imagine everybody about me must *see* the new light in my face, the new pleasure in my life. Ah, sweetheart, I wish that I could coin for this letter some phrase of love which would delight you more than the sum of all the things that have made you gladest in all my other letters, that it might repay you in part for this single golden sentence, which I may adopt and send back as my own heart's message to my precious Eileen: "And my heart is *at home* too, it has gone before me,—and has gone to *stay!*—so, as it cannot come to me, I will—ah gladly!—go to it." If my letters are "wonderful," as you say, little lady, it is no wonder! I do not write them with my old-time faculties: they are creations of my new self—the self which your love has made. They are inspirations of this wonderful new life into which I have come by your sweet guidance. You don't love now the same man, sweetheart, that you pledged your hand to eighteen months ago—but you are responsible for the change: and I have a sort of suspicion that, if you knew what the change had been, you would be quite willing to assume that responsibility! So, you see, as a matter of fact, you yourself, not I, *really* write the letters I send you. The authorship is, at least, *ultimately* your own. You created the love and are mistress of all the thoughts that are in them. They are just the mouthpieces of my heart—and my heart *is yours.*

I may tell you, as a secret, that this transformation wh. your precious love has effected has some curious results. It gives me, for one thing, an odd sense of identification with you, so complete that I now and again find myself about to forget that it is an identification as yet only of love, not of marriage, and about to say certain things which I am sure that you will let me say after sweet June has come—and which I believe that you would forgive me for saying now—but which you would open your pretty eyes at if I were to say them as I think them! Is it wonderful that my one heart-thought is of the time when *every* barrier shall be taken from between us, and you can find out just how unspeakably precious you are to   Your own   Woodrow.

ALS (WC, NjP).

Balto., April 2, '85

No, my darling, my cold has *not* gone, I am sorry to say. Not even this delicious weather is able to charm it away, and I am just at this moment suffering from a throbbing headache which only this loving, lighthearted letter of yours could have kept from being intolerable. This does not mean that the cold is worse; it is not; it is only persistent and persecuting. I am to dine with Hiram this afternoon and shall make him give me a prescription. Hitherto I have done next to nothing to cure myself. I almost wish I did not have to say anything to you about it! What's the use in *two* persons being made miserable about one small ailment? But you must not *allow* yourself to be concerned about me, my pet; I am taking the best care of myself.

Yes, Cleveland is certainly acquitting himself most creditably in the matter of appointments. Phelps is, I feel quite sure, just the man for the English mission—though scarcely the man, as far as I can make out, for anything else. He is not the active citizen, whom I admire, but the *passive* citizen whom I have small affection for—save as a pattern of culture and integrity, as a courtly gentleman. But I have not quite made him out yet. His fault, apparently, is not that he was not widely known, but that he has never cared to exert himself to make his talents widely useful; a political *dilettante*.

It is impossible to say *what* the effect of Pearson's renomination will be—or whether it will have *any* considerable political consequence. The dismemberment of the Democratic party is a consummation devoutly to be wished, and, if this appointment, which must delight every true advocate of civil service reform, every wisher for good government, is to have any influence, let us pray that it may effect that dismemberment. Then my November hopes, for the rise of a new party to which one could belong with self-respect and enthusiasm, might be realized.

I send you a little volume, my precious, to read in *moments* of leisure.[1] I am sure that you will enjoy it. It seems to me as full of good things as anything I know of—except Bagehot.

Yes, sweetheart, this *is* glorious weather—worth all the pains of bitter winter. And oh! I am so glad to see my darling's—my *lark's*—sweet joy at the coming of the Spring. It makes me so happy to feel her happiness. It makes me see doubled beauties in this best of the season's, this heyday of the year's life, to know of the laughter it brings into my pet's lovely eyes. But, sweetheart, when you go to the Park you wont go alone? Oh, my darling, my queen, my precious little lark! I love you, I love you! I love you!!

Your own Woodrow.

ALS (WP, DLC).

[1] [Augustine Birrell] *Obiter Dicta* (New York, 1885). Wilson inscribed the book on the title page and flyleaf, respectively: *"Ellen L. Axson"* and "From Woodrow Wilson, to a young lady whom he would delight, and who will, he knows, be delighted by the rare good things of this book." The volume is in the possession of Robert Reidy Cullinane, Washington, D.C.

Two Letters from Ellen Louise Axson

My darling Woodrow,   New York April 2/85.

Not being able to write last night, I thought I would try, this morning, my yesterday's plan and rise a little earlier to secure the time; but the scheme came to grief from the simple fact that I didn't wake up,—and the result is that I can only send a few lines this morning.

So you are disposed to take up the guantlet in defence of your lady-love, and like the knights of old give battle to all who don't see her in the same light as yourself,—who fail to recognize her trancendent merits! Well, if it comes to that I must at least hold my peace about her, being like Viola an arrant coward and not caring "who knows my mettle." So you may brag of her as you will, Sir Knight! I will carefully stand out of the way!

There is one thing that puzzles me darling,—*I* know that I do very deeply and fully sympathize with and understand all the thoughts and feeling which you have confessed to me. But how do *you* know it since it is so often a speechless sympathy? How I should like to possess your power of saying always just what you want to say! Truly, I can chatter fast enough upon occasion about indifferent subjects; but the very matters upon which I feel most deeply and think most earnestly and constantly are those upon which I am most tongue-tied. I so often struggle in vain even to *write* you my deeper thought, and finally leave it unsaid, and scribble a letter full of trivialities instead;—because I won't talk *at* it; if I *can't* say what I mean, I *won't* say what I don't mean.

It reminds me of the despairing way in which some of the girls at school[1] used to say "oh, I *know* it, but I can't *say* it! I can't *express* myself!" And Mrs. C.[2] would answer in her severest tone, "then you *don't* know it, one *never* knows a thing until they can tell it to someone else." True—perhaps! and yet it seems to me a rather narrow pedagogue's view. I am *sure* I know *many* things that I can't express,—not to speak of what I *feel*. There is one difficulty;—with ardent little people like me, feeling and thought are so inextricably interwoven that the problem of true and adequate expression becomes very complicated. I am sure that *everything* my darling says to me calls forth some strong feeling, as well as an answering thought. But time flies—there *must* be no more of this; excuse haste! I love you, sweet-heart, more than tongue can tell, and I am as ever   Your own Eileen.

[1] The Rome, Ga., Female College.
[2] Either Kate Pearson Caldwell or Caroline E. Livy Caldwell.

My darling Woodrow,   New York, April 3/85
    I send this morning the sketch which I have been "going to" send for so long,—whenever I did not forget it I was too hurried to do it up, and vice versa.
    I wish you could have seen our pose yesterday, it was the lovliest thing I ever saw;—the dear little model about whom I have raved to you before perhaps, with her sweet, innocent face for all the world like one of Sir Joshua's little ladies;—and she had on a wide green velvet hat and a delightful old Vandyke gown of green velvet, which exactly suited her style. As she stood there holding back a crimson curtain she was the prettiest, quaintest little figure, and the most perfect picture I ever saw. You never saw anything so delicious as the curves of her cheek and throat and mouth. I could scarcely try to sketch her for looking at her. Isn't it pitiful that the lovely little creature with her pure, sweet, face, should be a *model*.
    I am *so* sorry, dear, about the cold! I do hope your friend "Hiram" will be able to conquer it;—to have it hold on so long is enough to wear you out,—and I know how hard it makes one's work. How is it about the work now? are you able to take it somewhat more easily, or are you getting "used up" as the spring

weather approaches. How I wish you could take a complete holiday until you recover from your cold and headaches!—and spend it here of course! Oh, *are* you going to be able to come this month? How the mention of it in this letter makes my heart dance for joy! When I spoke of going to the Park in search of spring, I almost wrote down my wish that I might not go alone, but then I thought I wouldn't!—tisn't *proper*—is it?—to urge young gentlemen to visit you!

By the way,—there is nothing like being practical!—if you can tell beforehand when you will be able to come and if, as seems likely, it is near the end of my month in the paint class, I won't begin another until your visit is over, and thereby I will save fifty cents a day!

But I am desperately busy this morning and ought not to have written so much I suppose,—though it certainly doesn't take long to scribble in this fashion! I am staying at home to *move*,—downstairs! I havn't told you the various ups and down's of my boarding house experience. Miss Beatty told me a month ago that people were beginning to enquire for rooms and she would like to show mine, as of course the arrangement with me, as I understood, was only to last until she could rent the room at her regular price. She said nothing of the sort to me, by-the-way when she made the arrangement, but of course that makes no difference. I wouldn't wish to keep it as a favour. I thought at first I would seek another place at once,—indeed I found one,—but I finally decided that I would stay until she did rent it, and perhaps I could tide over the cold weather here. As it turns out I was wise to stay, for the room isn't rented yet, though there have been a number to look at it. But the painters are coming to do it over for the summer on Monday, and I am to take Miss Comstock's room—she having just left—until they finish. She told me the other day that the hall room on the first floor, which has an extension behind, and is very much nicer and larger than most hall rooms, would be vacant in a couple of weeks, so I decided to take that, for the same price as this. Now here's another complication. Miss Farnsworth, the girl from Atlanta,[1] whom I like very much, thought of coming to room with me several weeks ago, but she was *holding* a room for another lady and could'nt honourably give it up until her return; she has returned suddenly, and just now while Miss Beatty was preparing my little room for me, Miss F. came to see if she could get in with me. She is wild to come,—afraid to go among strangers, &c—almost crying in her distress and uncertainty. But Miss Beatty won't let us have the room,—says she must rent it now permanently, for when we leave in June she can do nothing again 'till fall. "But the large hall room had often been occupied by two," if we wished we could have it for six dollars apiece. Miss Farnesworth caught at that, she ["] would be only too glad if I were willing";—and I *couldn't* say that I was unwilling especially as she was in such despair! and so anxious to come. I have no doubt we will [be] very comfortable, for it is like two small rooms and we shall have a cot in each, and she is a very nice and interesting girl. But I am really blue about leaving this room;—as Carlyle says, we don't like to leave our old house 'till it falls about our ears, and though I *am* young I have already learned to dread change of any sort—or at least of *most* sorts!—more than I crave it.

But this won't do,—I *must* stop. I will try and answer those two sweet letters of yours tonight, my darling, and in the meantime remember that your little sweet-heart loves you more perhaps than you even yet know, and longs for you every moment of her life.   As ever   Your own Eileen.

Excuse haste. I hav'nt time to look this over.

ALS (WC, NjP).
¹ Ellen wrote "Atlanta" by mistake. Antoinette Farnsworth was a Westerner, as ELA to WW, April 13, 1885, makes clear.

To Ellen Louise Axson

My own darling,   Balto., April 3, 1885
And so you want to be told *how* I know that I have your deep sympathy in everything—in all my greater thoughts and feelings? Well, I learned it first of all from the loveliest, most eloquent eyes in the world—eyes that can say so much that is sweet that they are the most *tantalizing* eyes, too, that ever a lover was privileged to look love into: for the thought that they suggest is, 'Ah, if this little lady could but speak the one half of what her eyes hint, how could a fellow contain himself for joy!['] Then, too, what she *has* said—the confessions, more precious than gold to me, that *have* come from her lips—have all corroborated her eyes; she has written me letters, full of self-revelation, that have seemed to make my heart bigger and lighter by half; and there is another language, which neither lips nor eyes speak—and which no pen can write—which has told me that my darling's heart beat quicker and her breath came and went faster—that all her soul answered

me—sometimes when I wispered my most sacred heart-thoughts into her ear! Ah, sweetheart, I have *felt*, and *thus* known, that your heart and mind were both in tune with mine

Besides, my pet's pen, if *not* her tongue, has acquired new powers of speech of late—has been able to tell me secrets which have made me rich in a happiness I never felt before. The trouble is that self-expression is still a new thing with my little lady—and for one of her nature it is one of the hardest things in the world to learn. If I knew the secret of it myself, I would spare no pains to reveal it to her—for my happiness in her love will not be complete until she can tell me every syllable of it that is translatable into words. But I know that she will learn—that she is learning—just as I am learning; and, if, as she thinks, I am learning more rapidly than she, it must be because I work harder at it! Does my little sweetheart suppose that the love letters I write her satisfy *me*— or that they run off from my pen with an easy flow of phrase, as if I were simply chatting the thoughts uppermost in my mind? Not a bit of it! They *never* satisfy me—and they cost me, often, supreme, concentrated effort. Four pages written to my Eileen have more than once cost me a headache! My whole heart seems ready to burst with one absorbing, passionate thought of love; I realize at once that no words will contain that great love: and the *struggle* to put some shadow, some suggestion, some type of it into some at least partially articulate phrase, or illustration, or figure constitutes the hardest, most hopeless task of composition that I ever conceived. But the effort is worth all it costs! No matter how incomplete and imperfect the result—no matter how *little* of my thought I have translated—I have done *something* towards liberating me heart from its intolerable prison of silence, and the pleasure is exquisite! I wouldn't give over *trying* for anything! And every trial makes the words come easier next time—seems to aid in collecting a sort of love's vocabulary which becomes richer and richer in words which serve the heart for messengers. So I never give up! I know always, when I take up my pen, that I cannot say one tenth—one thousandth—part of what I feel, and that what I write will seem to me bald, or overstrained, or flat—*cold* in comparison with the fervour that runs through my thoughts. But I write all the same. I try to imagine myself close by my darling's side and, with *that* thought guiding me, I pour out every thought of her that is in my heart, coining every phrase that I can devise that will serve as any sort of a vehicle for my feeling. I endeavour to open my mind to *myself*, and then to tell her everything I find there. And oh! it is such a revelation of

happiness to be able to say *anything*. It is such a relief from bondage to find that I am not altogether speechless, after all! The
voice fails on all but a few notes; but a single string of the harp
will respond: but I will sing and play what I can till I learn to
fill out in fuller compass and richer melody my answer to the
sweet carol of my joyous little lark, "I love my Love and my Love
loves me!" If what I sing charms *her* ear—as every note of love
that she utters charms me—what need I more to satisfy my
heart and make me gladder than all the gladness of the Spring?
Sweetheart, read this wonderfully beautiful passage of Ruskin's about the birds, and then imagine what my song would
be to you if it could take up and interpret all the silent voices of
my love as the birds 'knit together' in their songs all that is wild
and sweet, yet formless, in the speech of the wind, 'interpreting
all intense passion,' and gathering into single strains of complete
melody all the scattered harmonies of silent nature! I am lonely
without you, darling, but my love is like a song in my heart all
the same—and I would make it like a song to you, that it might
ripple like laughter in your ears when you are sad; that it might
serve as your language when you are light-hearted; that it might
make you wish always for June, till June be come, and delight
always in June's gifts, when June is gone; that it might surround
you and bless you, as do the thoughts of
Your own   Woodrow.
ALS (WC, NjP).

From Ellen Louise Axson

My darling Woodrow,   New York, April 3/85.
   The little book has arrived safely and I have just been dipping
into it,—have read with absolute *delight* the essay on Carlyle.
Many, *many* thanks for it, dear! No, I havn't seen for a long time
anything "so full of good things," so racy, brilliant, pithy;—there
is so much sparkle to it that one is kept in a perpetual *flutter* of
enjoyment as one reads. And then too it strikes me that his estimate of Carlyle is singularly just and true. Is the book as anonymous as the title-page indicates? I hav'nt thanked you yet for the
Dials either,—I have been so hurried in writing the last two or
three days. I am delighted to have them and shall make good use
of them. By-the-way, have you heard anything more from Michigan?—what did you decide finally to do about it?—or did you decide to do nothing; perhaps it would be more correct to ask what
you finally decided to *think* about it?

I am very glad to find that I agree with you about Pearson. Being such a good thing in itself it can't result in any real evil, be the consequences what they may. So we—of Sav.—are not to have two foreign ministers after all! Well, if I were Gen Lawton I shouldn't care a thrip.[1] I can't imagine why he should wish to go, *anyhow*. Is there any great good to be done or glory to be gained by going? He can make as much or more *money* at home, —and then too his wife and daughter, who are delicate in the extreme, couldn't live there four months.

I am writing from my new little room, in which I can just turn around. Won't it be fun when Miss Farnesworth is in here too, as she will be for a few days, until the room upstairs is ready for us. We are to occupy it until it is rented; and I am afraid I am selfish enough to hope it won't be rented soon.

My darling, what is there left to say to you in answer to this precious letter received yesterday. I too *would* but cannot coin for it a phrase which would say more to you than aught I have said before. There is *no* sort of happiness which you have not made *me* feel,—"tumultuous" joy, sweet peace too deep and still for words[,] irrepressible gaiety and light-heartedness, and the passionate heart-throb which is almost akin to pain,—I know them all,—and more than all else a solemn, prayerful, awed feeling at thought of the way in which God has blessed me, and of what he demands of me in return;—of all that it means to be a true wife, —and to such a man as you, my darling. You must admit, sir, that in the case of some men I know, it would have been a much simpler affair, because their conception of a *wife*, as of a *man*— and of life itself, are all lower and narrower. Such a man deserves less of a woman too, because he gives so much less. She *couldn't* be so in debt to him as I am to you. But there is one thing I *know*, darling—I have yet to learn whether the most perfect love, the tenderest service, the most passionate loyalty, can make me, without certain qualities which love cannot give, such a wife as yours should be,—but I *know* that notwithstanding the demand is so much greater, I will be a better wife to you than I could ever have been to a smaller man, because no other but yourself could have so stirred my nature to it's utmost depths, could have inspired me with such passionate longing toward my own ideal of womanhood, or have given me so strong a motive for earnest, unflagging effort for its attainment. I am afraid all this is very wrong, it sounds almost as if I were putting the human love above the divine as a motive for well-doing; but you will know I don't mean *that*; I am sure that my love for God and desire to serve him hav'nt grown *less* in these two years. But it would be strange if a great love did not exert some great power upon one's life and nature. Neither do you love the same *woman*, sweetheart, whom you knew eighteen months ago. Your love has changed me in many ways, either by infusing something new into my nature or developing what was latent there, or by crowding out some things that were best away;—we have all read Chalmers great sermon on "the expulsive power of a new affection,"—and Tenneyson tells us in two beautiful lines how

> Love took up the harp of life and smote on all its chords with might
> Smote the chord of *self* that trembling passed in music out of sight.[2]

But you understand that what I mean to say is that this love of your—and of mine—has made me *long* more than ever to *be* good, it has'nt succeeded in *making* me good in any respect, and probably never will, my heart being more than commonly deceitful above all things and desperately wicked. So don't imagine that you will *ever* have a saint for a wife any more than you will have a beauty or a genius. You will simply have a very loving woman, one who is with all her heart　　　　Your own Eileen.

ALS (WC, NjP).
[1] President Cleveland had just nominated Alexander Robert Lawton, former Confederate general, as Minister to Russia. The Senate Foreign Relations Committee reported adversely on the nomination on April 2, 1885, on the ground that Lawton's disability for federal office had not been removed by President Andrew Johnson's pardon. Cleveland thereupon withdrew the nomination.
[2] From "Locksley Hall."

To Ellen Louise Axson

Balto., Md., April 4, 1885

Alas, my darling, nothing was further from my thoughts, when I spoke of your going out to the Park alone, than a suggestion that *I* might be able to go with you. I simply wanted to be sure that you had not forgotten, what you had yourself told me, that it was necessary for a lady to have some one with her there—and that you would get some one of the League girls to go with you. I would not for anything have hinted at the possibility of my coming, because I have known for some time that it would not only be impossible for me to go to N. York this month, but that I could not afford to go there again until we pass through on our way to New England. It almost breaks my heart to have to tell you this! I have been trying to believe that it was kindest, and therefore best, to let you continue to entertain the hope that it has cost me so many hours of keen suffering to give up; but, since I have to tell you part of the truth, I must, of course, tell you all of it. Of course the reasons are *pecuniary* reasons. My fellowship stipend is not more than sufficient to meet my expenses here, and the allowance from home, upon which I have hitherto been able to depend, of course ceases of necessity now, because dear father's salary from the Wilmington church stops with the close of his pastorate at the first of this month; the salary of his chair does not begin till September; and, in the mean time, there are great expenses of moving and of the summer sojourn in the North to be met. I have nothing, therefore, for the present but my salary as Fellow, and am bound to accept the fact that a stay of twenty-four hours in New York (counting in the travelling expenses) would swallow up all the surplus I can expect for these two months. All this involves no *hardship*. On the contrary, I am beyond measure glad that I *can* just at this time relieve dear father of *all* charges for my support. The sore trial comes from the longing to see my darling with which my heart seems sometimes nowadays about to break—and, even more (if possible) from the knowledge of the disappointment it must bring to my Eileen, whom I would so gladly, at *any* cost to myself, shield from anything of the sort! But I know whom I have loved; and I know that she is full as brave as *I* am to accept any disappointment that is necessary—that it may bring tears to her eyes—as it has done to mine—to think of the long waiting—but will be loyally submitted to with loving patience. It is just one of those cases, sweetheart, in which we are called upon to exercise the highest powers of our nature, the power to forecast the future and the courage to wait for it. We are buying, by present sacrifice, unembarrassed enjoyment of the sweet summer that is before us! When I think of what I am waiting for, *any* sacrifice seems insignificant! Within two months I shall catch a glimpse of my darling, as she goes South, and within *three* months—in *less* than three months—I shall go to her *not to leave her again*, to be with her always, to be continually glad because of her sweet presence, to live in the *visible* light of her love! I don't try to conceal from myself the trials, the *bitterness* of waiting: I make no pretence of offsetting against my eager, impatient longing desire to see my little queen the sour-grapes reflection that I could under any circumstances be with her just now for only a day or two—only to suffer immediately the pangs of parting again. I should be willing to pay even that price. The pain of our partings has been

cruel enough: but how compare it with the delights—brief as those
delights have been for us—of being together? The stern, unalter-
able necessity which keeps me from paying even a day's visit to
my darling is like a knife in my heart. I could not, if I would,
tell what it has already cost me: and I dare not think what it will
cost me before our waiting is over. It is one of those terrible things
that excludes hope! It might seem a diverting comedy to any indifferent third person that two lovers should make such ado about
being separated for a few weeks just before their marriage; he
would doubtless think it absurd to speak of it as being 'terrible';
but the very circumstance that makes my anticipation of our
marriage full of unspeakable joy makes our present separation
a real heart's tragedy. My darling's love has become so much a
part of my life that my separation from her simply makes that
life stand still. It could not be otherwise with my peculiar, intense
disposition. If my heart *had* no home, it could feel a calmness
something like content; but, having a home—the very home of
sympathy and love that it needs—it is intolerably homesick. Nothing could be more *dangerous* for a man like me to *have* to be
alone, shut off from all that he passionately loves, from all in
whose enjoyment he can *forget himself*, just at such a stage in his
career as that which I have reached. My bane, my worst enemy is
self-consciousness, self-criticism,—that communion with my anxieties, that impatience of my own weaknesses and faults, which
fills my life when I am alone. I am too self-analytic; and it is only
in the love-intercourse and love-services of home that I can forget, throw off this too morbid tendency. My darling is preparing
greater blessings, greater strength, greater liberty than she knows
for   Her own   Woodrow.

P.S. I am feeling *much* better to-day, my precious,—and I am
quite sure that I can very shortly report myself perfectly well
again. So you may dismiss *all* fears concerning your sweetheart—
inasmuch as he is far away: for, if he were present, he would
proceed to pick a crow with you; because you have disappointed
him twice a day (at every mail delivery) ever since you told him
that you had a certain *sketch* for him.   Lovingly   W.

ALS (WP, DLC).

From Horace Elisha Scudder

My dear Sir   Boston, 4 April 1885
    You will think I have taken ample time to consider your letter

of 4th ulto. and I am really ashamed to find that I have let it lie a month unanswered. I had my answer ready as soon as I had laid the letter down, but I waited as I sometimes do, to see if my second thoughts were the same as my first. One matter after another has pushed the subject aside, but I hope the delay has not been prejudicial.

As regards the time when I ought to have North Carolina, there is no date which is final. Judge Cooley's Michigan is in press, and Kansas and California with perhaps one or two others are so advanced that I confidently expect to publish them in the Fall.[1] Of course I should like to close the series promptly, and not let it hang on indefinitely, but even after I have published all the volumes for which I have planned, I shall be very likely to be haunted by the possibility of working in some state of minor interest, if I fall upon an exceptionally good writer. So, there is really no reason why you should not do North Carolina, even if you can not see your way clear to doing it for a year or two yet. Only, if the time is likely to be so long, I should perhaps wish to withhold the announcement, as I think it works against a book to have an appearance of indefinite delay.

Upon reading your letter, this question of time seems to me the only one of importance. The relations which you hold to the state are sufficiently close and natural. Moreover, in the case of North Carolina, the effect upon the sale in the state itself—a matter sometimes of importance—need hardly to be taken into consideration, as we must depend upon a general interest in the book and its treatment, for a remunerative sale. I should be glad if you would keep as near as possible to the limit of Dr. Browne's Maryland.[2]

I hope you will see no further difficulty in the way of accepting the appointment under these somewhat free conditions.

Yours very truly   H. E. Scudder

ALS (WP, DLC).
    [1] Thomas McIntyre Cooley, *Michigan, A History of Governments* (Boston, 1885); Leverett Wilson Spring, *Kansas, The Prelude to the War for Union* (Boston, 1885); and Josiah Royce, *California, From the Conquest in 1846 to the Second Vigilance Committee in San Francisco. A Study of American Character* (Boston, 1886).
    [2] William Hand Browne, *Maryland, The History of a Palatinate* (Boston, 1884).

From Janet Woodrow Wilson

Wilmington, N. C.

My darling boy: Sabbath afternoon [April 5, 1885]
    I have been so busy that it has been *impossible* for me to write

sooner—as I intended, & so much desired. So, my darling, it has been that I could not write to James Bones in time to instruct him to send the 1st of April remittance to you direct. I *hope* I will find it awaiting me in Columbia. In any case you shall be provided with the funds you need[.] I will write him as soon as possible after we reach Columbia—directing him to send directly to you the remaining payments. Perhaps he may feel obliged to remit to you more promptly than he would be to me. I hope he may.

Monday. I was interrupted here, and was not able to finish. Yesterday was a hard day for dear papa—but he got through perfectly[.] Oh how I wish you could have heard his two wonderful sermons! the morning being a Communion Sermon—the night sermon a farewell. But we are having a trying time these days—at least *I* am—for they come to *me* with all their moans. But I will not write of that.

We start for Columbia tonight and I have yet much to do so I must say good bye my dear precious boy till tomorrow or next day—when I hope to write you more satisfactorily. Please let me hear particulars as to your plans for the summer.

In haste, with love inexpressible

Yours lovingly   Mother

ALS (WP, DLC) with WWhw figures on env.

From Ellen Louise Axson

New York, April 5/85.

A happy Easter day to you, my darling!—as happy a one as it is with me. I hope the day is as bright and beautiful with you as with us and that you are enjoying it as much. I have loitered so on my way home enjoying the air and sunshine and I blush to add watching the endless procession on the Avenue that the time has slipped away unawares and left me none at all for writing. But I shall have another chance later.

We had an unusually good sermon from the Doctor on a rather unusual text,—though Mr. Finlayson says those quaint old-testament texts are very much affected in Scotland,—"I did but take a little honey on the end of my staff, and lo! I must die[.]" He says that if Jonathan had been offered a whole land flowing with milk and honey as a bribe for abandonning the pursuit he would have rejected it with scorn; but the trap was baited more skillfully, —it *seemed* such a *little* thing; he turned aside but for a moment.

But I am entering on too large a subject for this brief interval of time—I am overjoyed, my darling to learn that you are feeling *much* better! Has the troublesome headache entirely gone?

I love you sweet-heart more than tongue can tell; it is and shall always be the study of my life to prove to you how entirely I am

Your own   Eileen.

ALS (WC, NjP).

To Ellen Louise Axson

My own darling,   Balto., April 5, 1885

I would give a great deal to know what you are thinking as you read that letter I wrote yesterday. I know that you will accept the disappointment with bravery and loyalty, with the wish to help me bear it—like the true, loving little woman that you are —and that you will see that it will be all the more worth while to trick the time into seeming short by keeping as close as possible to each other in our letters. But I wonder if you will be able to see in it all from the first the *good*, the satisfaction, that I have schooled myself to recognize in it? My heart laughs to itself to think what a zest this waiting will add to the delights of our summer: it will be like going home to each other not only, but like going home from *exile*. If anything *can* make that time more precious, it will be made more precious by just such sacrifices as we have to make now. It's like starving oneself the more to enjoy a meal, like living in a mine to learn how to rejoice in the sunlight and the open air. At any rate, such are the fancies with which I cheat myself into partial contentment. Think, darling, what sweetness is being *stored up* for our next kiss by this long waiting! The next time I take you in my arms it will be—as the boys say—'for keeps'! If these ideas are as sweet to you, my pet, as they are to me, try to live on them, as I am doing. I try to *skip* the next ten weeks in my thinking, and when I succeed I dance about this little den of mine as if professorial dignity was a thing which must always be out of the question with me—with capers which I am quite sure would secure me an engagement with a minstrel troupe, could I repeat them in public. When I manage to forget that I want to go to New York and to fill my thoughts with the wish to go towards Savannah and with the certainty that I shall be going *very soon*—to find there a little lady waiting with a new light in her eyes—a light telling of that love, that trust, that loyalty which a true wife gives to her husband—I shall be the most distractedly delighted man in the world!

And, in the meantime, what a feast of sweet letters I am having! The idea of your being puzzled to know *how* I could have

found out what your heart contains for me when you can and
do write such letters as this of Friday night! You dear, innocent,
bewitching little girl, you! Maybe you don't know how much you
do tell—or perhaps you imagine that I can't read the English
language. If your love and sympathy *are* 'speechless,' as you say,
how are you going to account for the fact that when I read a letter like this one before me all my pulses are quickened and I can
hardly see the writing for the—well, *something* that comes into
my eyes, seeming to relieve my heart a bit of its burden of joy?
I assure you I have *not* imagination enough to read into what
my darling writes all that I want to find there—and yet that's
just what I find. And I *don't* imagine, sweetheart, that I am "*ever*
going to have a *saint* for a wife"; I should be very much frightened and discontented if I did! I could not get along with a saint
for twenty-four hours; and I want a wife who can understand and
even *sympathize* with my own *badness*, as well as my love and
any *good* qualities I may have. What a terribly unsympathetic
person you would be if you *were* a saint! Don't you remember,
Miss, the *first* thing that attracted me towards you, before ever
I had spoken a word to you or even knew who you were? It was
the joyous mischief, the *roguishness* in your pretty eyes! I recognized in you a kindred spirit in that—and thought to myself
'a half hour's romp with that young lady would be a half hour's
delight.' But alas! I have reminded myself of one of my standing
perplexities: which is that there's one whole side of me whose
acquaintance you have never made, and to which I have always
been awkwardly unable to introduce you—though I *have* had
sense enough to speak of it once or twice in my letters. It may
shock you—it ought to—but I'm afraid it will not, to learn that
I have a reputation (?) amongst most of my kin and certain of
my friends (the Boylston family in Atlanta,[1] for instance) for
being irrepressible, in select circles, as a maker of grotesque
addresses from the precarious elevation of chair seats, as a wearer
of all varieties of comic grimaces, as a simulator of sundry unnatural, burlesque styles of voice and speech, as a lover of farces—
even as a dancer of the '*can-can*'! How you have reformed me I
can't divine; but I know that I *could* not so much as imitate the
sound of a cornet in your presence in Savannah, and that not a
single trace of the comical vein which used to make my letters
so dear to sister Marion's heart has found its way into my correspondence with you. I am not conscious, however, I assure you,
Miss Eileen, of having been at all *saddened* by my acquaintance
with you; and, though it's natural that an engagement of mar-

riage and the experience of a love which seemed like a revelation of all that was deepest and most lasting and most manly in my nature should have made me realize as never before that boyhood's irresponsibilities were behind me and that all the highest strivings of manhood were at hand—though my darling's love inspired me as I had never been inspired before with a "passionate longing toward my ideal" of manhood, just as my love inspired her with "passionate longing"—so sweetly confessed—"toward her own ideal of womanhood"—I did not feel robbed thereby of boyhood's *gaiety*: I received, rather, a notable augmentation of *that*. It must be that most of my letters to you, and all of my thoughts during those brief, precious weeks when we have been together, have been full of my love for you, which has seemed too holy, too wonderful a thing in its perfect joy to be *played* with. I have been a little *awed* by it—and afraid, consequently, even to seem to make light of it. Besides which, you must remember, Miss, there was the embarrassment, in the beginning, of our short acquaintance! You had not *seen* me make a goose of myself (Miss Jennie Hall says she can't keep her face straight now while I am in the room!) and I was afraid that you would not understand any pranks I might indulge in in my letters. And so the thing has gone on! But you'll find out soon enough what an overgrown boy you have taken as your 'lord and master.' I suppose that I shall not *always* be awed by your presence!

I am *very* sorry, my pet, that you have had to give up your room and go into such different quarters! I suppose you could not have managed without a row to keep the big room, but it seems to me that you have allowed the Thing to impose upon you most outrageously in giving you only *conditional* tenure of the hall room. She does it, I am sure, only because she thinks you will stay anyhow! In spite of the drawbacks to having Miss Farnsworth with you, I am rather glad to see such an arrangement effected: for I know that if *I* had a room-mate to occupy my attention, even to *worry* me a bit, I should think less of my own concerns and June would come more rapidly!

Yes, sweetheart, the author of "Obiter Dicta" is quite anonymous to me. I am *so* glad you enjoy his delicious originality. I was tempted to keep the book till I could read it to you!

As to the Michigan affair, I frankly wrote Dr. C. K. Adams substantially what I said to *you* about it—so that nothing can now come of it unless—as is extremely improbable—he wants me so much that he will try to have me invited or, at least, assured of election, before June—immediately

Many thanks and kisses! for the sketch, my darling! It *is* beautiful. It's no *likeness,* unfortunately, because the artist has failed altogether in the lower part of the face—but it's a lovely picture and has my darling's *eyes.*

Good-bye I love you a thousand times as much as you think and a thousand times less than I will when you have revealed a wife's love to   Your own   Woodrow.

ALS (WC, NjP).
    1 The family of J. Reid Boylston, with whom Wilson lived in Atlanta in 1882-83.

From Ellen Louise Axson

My darling Woodrow,   New York April 5/85

I begin to believe that we really *can* sympathize with each other in *everything*!—so you even understand and appreciate my difficulty of "self-expression," because you "know all about it yourself"! Sweet-heart, I will prize your precious letters more than ever now; and I will also take fresh heart myself. I know that I cannot say what I *would,* but it has come to pass that I *must* say something to relieve my own heart as well as to satisfy yours. And I believe, my darling begins to understand me so well that he can read my *real* thought through the poor words, which seem some times merely to serve Tallyrand's purpose of *concealing* thought;—that he knows what I would say about our love and on all those other subjects "which alone are of perennial interest, 'on man, on nature, and on human life' "! I am quite sure dear, that you have other means of reading my heart than is given you by my words; I should be very unhappy if I thought otherwise, if I thought you knew no more of me than you could give verse and chapter for. Do you suppose it is possible for *any* human soul fully to reveal itself even when it most wishes to do it? I fancy that our knowledge of that great mystery never comes from tracing step by step its hidden processes, but from inferences judiciously drawn from telling facts gleaned here and there,— from hints and suggestions;—that we pursue the same process that the scientist does in trying to unravel the secrets of nature; only of course in our study of *human* nature we have great advantage in that it is our *own* nature,—our knowledge is an intuition. And when to that we add the knowledge which comes from great love and perfect sympathy we need not dispair of fully understanding one another in spite of the difficulty about *words.* By that light of love we cannot *but* see plainly. When we were but friends (was there *ever* such a time!) it may have been that we saw through a glass darkly, but now that we love, face to face.

But—query!—if you know a woman so well that you are sure beforehand what she is going to say, or what she would *like* to say on any given subject, what special interest do you find in hearing her try to say it? Why isn't she an unmitigated bore? When you have "seen through her" even down to the "vacuum" which somebody says lies below all our talking and thinking, what next? That is a question which seems to have disturbed even so sensible a man as [Philip G.] Hamerton, who in discussing "the intellectual marriage" suggests, I believe, as the only remedy that they "renew themselves" constantly for each others benefit. I am inclined to think it would be hard to find anyway to ward off that danger from a *purely* intellectual marriage. I believe a marriage should be that of course, but a true marriage is a great deal *more* than that. If one married a Macaulay simply to hear him *talk* one would grow tired of it in course of years if one didn't exhaust his resources, the novelty would wear off, and the "flashes of silence" would be like balm to the suffering. But I know *now* that a true man and woman never weary of true love and sympathy. It is a possession which time doesn't cheapen. I remember when such questions as those I asked you above seemed to me among the greatest difficulties in the way of marriage. What *do* they talk about! I should think they would wear each other out! or suffer from a most embarrassing dearth of remark! What a foolish school-girl's idea it seems to me now! as if marriage were like an evening call where long pauses are awkward and must be avoided at any cost, and as soon as both feel themselves "talked out" it is time to part;—only in the former case the inability to *part* renders the situation truly deplorable!—a *never-ending* evening call!—*horrible*! But enough! it is too bad to parody myself in this fashion, not to speak of Mr. Hamerton.

What an exquisite thing this is about the birds! My darling your love does make such a song in my heart, it does surround and bless every moment of my life. It does make me wish for June 'till June be come and it will make me delight always in June's gifts when June is gone; it makes me in short *altogether*
Your own   Eileen.

ALS (WC, NjP).

To Ellen Louise Axson

My own darling,   Balto., April 6, 1885
    It seems that Mr. Scudder, the editor of the "American Com-

monwealth" series did not take my answer about the volume on North Carolina as final after all. That was mere negotiation: now comes a definite proposition that I undertake the work, with leave to use two years at it. But, hard as it is to do it, I must, I think, decline: I am beginning to see that my health will not allow it. I must not overload my *vacations*: I must not load them at all: they must be *real* vacations, with no work in them except such as I am led to do by natural gravitation. Otherwise, I am of opinion, my darling would not have me for a husband very long—except, perhaps as an invalid, which, from my point of view, would be worse than death. Don't be frightened at my talking so, sweetheart: you may be sure I wouldn't write of such terrible 'ifs' were they possibilities *now*. I shall take good care to make them impossibilities—as I can very easily do,—as, for instance, by declining to have anything to do with Mr. Scudder's series.

I am finding to-day very long because no letter has come for me from my darling. I am not uneasy—I know that it was a mishap consequent upon her Saturday night tasks and her numerous Sunday engagements—but the disappointment is none the less on that account, and I shall feel very much better after the postman has been his rounds to-morrow morning.

I was so well yesterday, my precious, that I forgot to tell you that my ailments were gone. To-day I am not feeling altogether bright and serviccable—but there's no *cold* to blame. I have probably been worrying myself a little to[o] much about this offer of a tempting piece of literary work. I clearly need a little wife to chccr me up and make me quit thinking forever of the *responsibilities* of life. I could be gay, were you by my side; but without you it's clearly 'no go.'

Do you know, my Eileen, that there are two words in your Friday night's letter that contain for me a sweeter essence of delight than any other words that were ever written? They are, "passionate loyalty"—and they have been running in my head all day. They seem to me to sum up more woman's love than any other words could possibly convey: and it gives me a strength such as my darling—not being a man—can hardly imagine: but which was explained in a letter written to her in August 1883 which, possibly, she has kept.[1] My darling *believes in me*, and therefore her love is a tower of strength to   Her own   Woodrow.

ALS (WC, NjP).
[1] WW to ELA, Aug. 12, 1883, Vol. 2.

From Ellen Louise Axson

Yes, my darling, I will accept the disappointment bravely and patiently, and I will *try* to accept it *cheerfully* too, though of course I could not prevent it from bringing tears to my eyes, and I must confess that I have been very heavy-hearted all day. But it is so evidently *right* and necessary that I should be no better than a spoiled child if I did not submit with loyalty and "loving patience." Indeed the case is such a clear one that I am not even greatly surprised. If I had not so stupidly misunderstood your words about going to the Park alone I would not have been taken by surprise at all, for I had feared before that it would prove to be impossible, both because of the expense and the press of work toward the close of the term. Of course, I cannot deny that it is hard,—is not separation from my Love the hardest thing—the sorest trial that can befall me now? But there is comfort to be had for the seeking without trying to make it, by any such poor device as that of disguising the truth from ourselves. There is more than *one sort* of separation and while any sort must make my heart ache, there can be no *bitterness* in that which is only a waiting for the end of separation. Nor is it even a *long* waiting, "the days are gliding swiftly by,"—and I a pilgrim stranger, would not detain them as they fly!—those two lines really ran off the end of my pen unaware, but they are very true and very appropriate. And then think how many sweet thoughts we have to beguile us on the way and make it seem shorter;—how many messengers of love pass between us as we journey *toward* one another. It were strange indeed if I could not live for so long on such food as my friend the postman brought me today. Nothing but your presence can *satisfy* me, yet I cannot starve while you provide me with such wayside refreshment as this! And how sweet the end of the journey; it grows sweeter to me every day, my darling, as it draws nearer;—this is not a case where "distance lends enchantment to the view"!—the distance is too short to play such tricks as that! Only three months and my darling is with me to leave me no more! Think!—there will no more,—not *one* more such parting as has torn our hearts so often! How strange to think that when *next* you come, you come to claim your little wife,—when *next* you leave, I follow. Why, darling, this disappointment ought to make it seem nearer! I believe it does—because there is *nothing* between to hide the view. It is the same principle which moved Agnes [Tedcastle] to wake earlier one Sunday that she might the sooner say,—"*this* week Arthur comes back." Oh yes, it *is* sooner than it was this morning! it is not disappointment that has power to make my heart beat so high with hope and love. The many happy thoughts almost crowd out the thought of the present disappointment;—only the sweetest of all the thoughts recalls it again and gives me another pang. My darling needs me,—needs me now—he says he does, and says it in such a way that he had made me believe it *true*—not that he merely *thinks* he does! I suppose all *true* men feel the need of a home; but he has shown me that he more than many others, is dependent for happiness and health, of mind at least, upon the influences of home;—that home which it is the God-appointed mission of a loving woman and of her alone to make;—that is the *real*, exclusive "woman's right." Ah wonderful to think that it is *my* right and precious privilege to make that home for *you*! That is, I trust, for *me* a God-appointed mission; and with His good help I *will* fulfil it.

I have, I see, spent all my time answering the first of todays letters, and now I have none left for the delightful one of yesterday. But it can wait. I am expecting Miss Farnsworth every moment and *must* close now. Believe me darling in very truth

Your own Eileen.

Excuse this *terrible* scrawl, I am in great haste.

ALS (WP, DLC).

From Addie C. Wildgoss

Mr. Wilson   Havcrford College P.O April 6th [1885]

Your polite note of March 26th, would have been answercd long since had I not waited to give you if possible deffinite information. I can only say now that the rooms can be seen after July 1st, the cottage being at present occupied by other parties. As I shall rent it from the Bryn Mawr Coll. trustees for the exclusive purpose already mentioned, the number of rooms being limited, each room must bring its fixed price. There is only one very small room, which, in connection with a good double room would be $18. per week for yourself & wife. I should be glad to have an interview with you either in July when you could see the rooms or before.

Very truly yours   Miss A. C. Wildgoss

ALS (WP, DLC) with WWhw notation on env.: "Ans. April 9/85."

From Charles Howard Shinn

Dear Woodrow,   San Francisco April 7th [1885]

I *won't say* I am sorry. But if you knew how resolutely I've put personal things aside of late! I have watched your work, & read your book, and the reviews of it, and been made very very happy over your transcendent & well-deserved success. You are going straight to the front. God bless & keep you, and your dainty, loving, genius of a wife-to-be. Won't there be a wedding this year, Woodrow? There was a review of your book in the *Overland*. It was written by Prof. Moses of the U. of Cala. .[1] My sister always sends that sort of thing to him. *I* think, & so do others, that he made a botch of it—& I shall write an article on the subject for the *Overland* soon. I wrote the article on "Recent Hist. Monographs" in April *Overland*. I have been made very unhappy at not having the *Overland* review of your book a more *understanding* one. Prof. M. is of the old northern school, not the American one. . . .[2]

Love to you—Charlie.

P.S. omitted. ALS (WP, DLC) with WWhw notation on env.: "Ans. April 14/85."
  [1] [Bernard Moses] "Congressional Government," *Overland Monthly*, Second Series, v (April 1885), 444-45.
  [2] Moses concluded his review as follows: "A considerate judgment of this book must recognize in it an analysis of our Federal institutions in their existing form, which is excellent; and suggestions as to reform in methods and practice, which are of no special value."

To Ellen Louise Axson

Balto., April 7, 1885

No, my sweetheart, I do not "suppose it is possible for *any* human soul fully to reveal itself even when it most wishes to do it," if its *purpose* be self-analysis and self-revelation; but if its purpose be to love as it would be loved and to speak that love as it would have love spoken to it, it *may* succeed, if the purpose is such as guides all its life. Love lives not in oneself but in the object of one's love. What I strive to show my darling when I write to her is not my heart itself, but *her image* in that heart; and what I try to *say* to her is what I think will best serve to show her how completely that sweet image has excluded all others. She may draw what inferences she pleases from such pictures as to the quality and powers of my heart; it is not my object to supply her with those inferences—I want only to supply her with such love as will satisfy her heart to the utmost: it is my study to love her as she most desires to be loved. The misery of *correspondence* is, that *words* must serve as the *only* proofs, the only earnest of that love. Words are precious beyond measure; one's heart would starve if one were doomed to be loved in silence; every syllable of love's confession seems to renew youth and joy—life itself— I know that it is so with me when my darling speaks her love. But, for the *complete* contentment of a loving heart, there must be leave and opportunity to supplement words with acts of tenderest, self-denying service. I have hardly defined to myself the special guiding purpose with which I write my letters to you: but generally the thought is something like this: 'My darling sits all the day at her drawing and painting; there is very little movement and incident in her life to occupy her thoughts with things outside of her; she will be thinking of something her own heart supplies—maybe she will be making herself anxious about Stockton or Eddy; cannot I send her some love-message that will take a predominant place in her heart's-memory, inviting her thoughts to dwell on it—some message that will seem like rest to her when she is tired, like light-hearted laughter when she is sad, like all-sufficient solace when she is grieved? And, even if I cannot make it all that, cannot I put some note of delight into it, some phrase that she will like to recall, some word that will seem sweet to her? It's worth striving for—if it *does* take a big piece of my morning in which to do it—and it will be *such* a relief to my own heart to interpret—though it be never so poorly—some of that infinite love which it holds for her—and which has made a new hope, a new joy, a new life—which has made *everything* new for

Her own   Woodrow.

ALS (WC, NjP).

From Ellen Louise Axson

My darling Woodrow,   New York April 7/85

Miss Farnsworth did not come last night after all, or rather only "a piece of her" came, namely her trunk. But she has come at last and we have just finished settling ourselves in our—or my —old quarters. By-the way, we are to keep the room three weeks longer. Mr. and Mrs. Guerry are coming back the first of May to take it. I believe it is pleasanter to be sure of it for three weeks than to have the chance of keeping it for seven, with the expectation of being turned out any day. And that reminds me, that I could not have expressed myself clearly about my plans; it is this room only that we occupy conditionally, the hall room we keep as long as we choose.

Isn't it odd that on *Sat.* I should have received a letter from Cousin Allie[1] asking me if possible to get a room for her here, or to let her room with me, for two or three weeks?—and I had taken a room-mate just the day before. But I found a place for her at my prize boarding-house, Mrs. Seaman's; she engaged it today by telegram and is coming on Friday. I am not sorry that she can't come here for she wouldn't be satisfied with this house; she must be feeling a *great* deal poorer than she would like to condescend to a boarding-house at all!

Did I tell you that Florence Young had been summoned home on account of the desperate illness of her father? I learn today that he died on Friday before she reached him. He had been ill for two or three months but died of a congestive chill at last. How *very* sorry I feel for that family! Mrs. Young is a perfect invalid and almost blind besides, and Mary is in exactly the same condition; you know that in addition to the trouble with her eyes she has now a spinal disease—hasn't been able to walk all winter. I don't know what is to become of them all,—it makes my heart bleed.

The spring exhibition is open at the Academy now and I have been spending the afternoon there. I didn't intend to be in such a desperate hurry about going, but I could do nothing better;— careless girl that I am, I lost the key to my padlock and couldn't get into my paint box; we couldn't pick the lock, or break it or do anything with it; so I had to wait for the shopman to get me, if possible, another lock just like it, or failing that to have a key made; so I am reaping the reward of my evil ways. But to tell the truth I was rather glad of so good an excuse to take a holiday, for I was doing little good at my work, and felt even less *like* working. You remember laughing at what you call my dread of *words*, which, you thought, seemed to be far greater than my fear of what the words represented! I think that must be the explanation of my disquietude today[.] You said nothing but what I had long ago realized,—that my darling's health is not *poor* exactly, was what might be called "uncertain,"—not very strong; that his constitution is one with which he must not dare take any liberties. In fact *safty* lies in our knowing and realizing that and *never* forgetting or ignoring it. What was there then in your simple *statement* of the fact, the knowledge of which is so valuable, to render my eyes, all day, so blinded with tears that I could scarcely see the model,—to so preoccupy me indeed, that I hardly knew there *was* a model but sat gazing at her like one in a dream. Such conduct is decidedly foolish and unreasonable—extremely reprehensible! How glad I am that you have rejected Mr. Scudder's offer! And I cannot be sorry that you were prevented from going to that great, hard place in Mich. My darling are you *sure* that you tell me *all* about your case? do you sleep well? how is your appetite? Remember that my only comfort is in the thought that I at least *know* just how it is with you, though I can do nothing to help. You must not give my imagination *any* play in the matter —as you love me, *dont*! How glad I would be if I were not obliged to trust even you but could see for myself! Ah darling, these are the things which make the separation well-nigh unbearable! my heart is almost breaking with the longing to help you to do some-thing—*anything*—to make life easier for you. I love you, sweet-heart, with a perfect love, and I am forever

Your own Eileen.

ALS (WP, DLC).
¹ Alice Hoyt Truehart.

To Ellen Louise Axson

My own darling,   Balto., April 8, 1885
    You are a sweet, brave, splendid little woman to take our dis-appointment as you have! You don't know how much it helps me to have a little sweetheart whom I can depend upon to look at things in just the right way: to accept disappointments with a sweet womanly courage—as well as hail pleasure with unfeigned girlish delight. Indeed I *do* need you, my peerless little pet; no-body in the world knows so well how to help me with love and love's perfect sympathy. Why, this precious letter that came this morning has done me untold good: for, to tell the truth, Miss, my longer knowledge of the necessities which would keep me away from New York had not resulted in taking the edge off of my dis-appointment, and I needed comfort as much as you can need it. But this letter has converted me to its own delightful way of think-ing. It has made *me* see how giving up all thought of seeing you sooner has made June seem nearer. The *next* thing we have to look forward to is our wedding—that taking possession of my prize the mere thought of which makes all my pulses fairly dance—makes me forget that I am not *worthy* of such happiness and re-member, with gleeful delight, only that I am to have it. And ah, sweetheart, what shall I say to *your* joy in the same thought: what *can* I say when you declare that it seems each day a sweeter thing than it ever seemed before that you are to be my bride, my honoured, cherished, adored wife! I cannot *say* anything in reply

to such words—words sweeter to me than any others that ever were or ever can be uttered! I can only pray that you may continue to have such thoughts in stronger and stronger currents until June comes, in the hope that then I may be able, as your husband, to pay you some part of the debt of love and gratitude which I now owe, but know not how to pay, you as your lover. Maybe I can invent a language for my precious when she is my wife such as I know not how to frame now when she is only my sweetheart,—a language which will make her thrill with a complete knowledge of what she is to me

So, it's agreed, isn't it, darling, that we will be gay, and not sad, in this *little* interval of waiting that keeps us away from our wedding-day? I shall expect you to smile all the day long over your work; and, for my part, I promise to work at my tasks as if I could see that smile and were living even now in its light. And then, when the waiting is over, who will be happier than

Your own   Woodrow.

ALS (WC, NjP).

From James E. Rhoads

My dear Friend,   Philadelphia. 4 mo. 8, 1885.
     Herewith I send testimonials of Clementine L. Houghton, as an applicant for a fellowship in History at Bryn Mawr for 1885-86. I understand that she *graduated* in 1884 B. L. at Michigan University; and has spent the past year in the study of History, but has given most of her time to Physics & Chemistry in order to broaden her culture. As her admission to a fellowship is equivalent to conferring the degree of M. A., it is to be regretted that she has apparently no knowledge of Greek. I do not forget that she or rather a future student might secure the degree of M. A. at Bryn Mawr with only a half-year's study of Greek. I do not infer that her success in French & German has been unusual from her testimonials. She has had five years of University study, however, and has been a diligent and at least fairly successful student. I infer that the Mich. Univy. catalogue is at J. H. U. or would send it by mail. Please examine the papers and state whether thou thinks we shd encourage C. L. H. to even look towards receiving the Fellowship & oblige

truly thy friend   James E Rhoads

ALS (WP, DLC) with WWhw notation on verso of letter: "Letter accompanying application."

From Janet Woodrow Wilson

My darling Boy,   Columbia S. C. April 8th 85.
Josie and I arrived here yesterday morning. Papa will follow tomorrow I hope. I have only time to scribble a hasty note to enclose the accompanying draft. I found James B's cheque for the amount (on the Rome Bank) awaiting me here. I wrote giving him my receipt and asking to send the remaining payments to you in Baltimore. Giving as a reason that I cannot be sure of my movements (which is true, as I will explain again) and you will be in Baltimore long enough to receive it. . . .

Will write before many days telling you about everything[.] God bless you my sweet boy. Much love to dear Ellie.

ALS (WP, DLC).   Lovingly yours   Mother

From Ellen Louise Axson

My darling Woodrow,   New York April 8/85
I didn't mean to do it, but I find that I have put you off tonight so long that now there are only a few moments left you,—and they are really not worthy of you, so sleepy and stupid are they. But it is all Mr. Browning's fault! We feel that our hard work entitles us and almost forces us to rest and read a little after dinner; so tonight I went on an exploring expedition into Mr. Browning's pages, being of course inspired thereto by "Obiter Dicta's" enthusiasm. Recognizing the fact that I had never taken the poet seriously enough, but like the "British paterfamilias" had been too partial to the short poems, I resolved that I would bring to the enterprise tonight some courage, energy, and determination. I would give him as fair a chance as if he were Prof. Huxley![1] (though to be sure I havn't given *him any* chance!) My labour was abundantly rewarded; indeed I struck a veritable goldmine; and you know people are apt to be somewhat carried away on such occasions so that is the reason I failed to mark the flight of time. Did you ever read Caliban?—if so can you give me any good —or bad—psychological reason why men should "not unnaturally prefer it" to "Saul" or to *anything*? Have you read "By the Fireside"? It is lovely I think;—indeed there are *so many* good ones, and yet after all they *are* frequently "hard reading." You remember Beaconsfield's comment "I like Robert Browning and I wish some one would translate him into English!" but the curious part of it is that they *are* in the simpleist, homliest English,—good honest Anglo-Saxon words, but so strung together that they don't

give you the ghost of an idea;—"we wonder if it is all the fault of the punctuation!"—that is a capital hit.

But why should I spend my time on such matters as this which can so well wait, when there are other things which cannot wait. And all the time I have is not half enough to tell you what infinite tenderness and love wells up in my heart as I read these sweet words which describe the purpose with which you write your letters. You have your reward, my darling! never did anyone so fully achieve the object of his labour. I cannot find words to tell you all that these letters are to me,—how they *do* "rest," solace, delight me; I cannot even tell you how many times I read them over in the course of the day, or how constantly my thoughts hover about them. Those sweet words are a perpetual refrain running, soft and low, through all my life,—setting all my days to music. How could I frame for you a greater wish than that all your "literary labours" might be as successful in accomplishing the end proposed? But unfortunately they don't fall upon ground so well-prepared as is the heart of the woman who loves you; it is more like the good seed cast upon the highway. But you will gather a harvest even there. We read how "a traveller on a dusty road strewed acorns on the lea, and one took root and sprouted up and grew into a tree!"[2]

But I must say good-night,—remember sweetheart that your love "has made a new hope, a new joy, a new life—*everything new*" for your own   Eileen.

ALS (WP, DLC).
[1] Probably Thomas Henry Huxley.
[2] From Charles Mackay's "Small Beginnings."

To Ellen Louise Axson

Balto., April 9, 1885

Yes, my precious little sweetheart, you may be quite certain that I tell you the *whole* truth about my health—everything that is at all essential. I did not tell you that week before last, when my recent cold (which I had very stupidly done nothing to cure) was at its height, Hiram and my other friends declared that I was *looking* wretchedly—worse than they had ever seen me look before—; but that was not part of my malady. To have told you of it would only have tortured your imagination without in the least enlightening you about my condition. *Now* these same friends say that I am looking *ever* so much better. And I *am* ever so much better—and taking the most indulgent care of myself imaginable. I have never lost either sleep or appetite (though I have nothing to tempt the latter); and I am taking my work only in such amounts and at such times as suit my inclination. Isn't that a satisfactory report? I had no idea that my letter of Monday would distress my darling so much! I thought, on the contrary, that she would find its contents rather reassuring, because of its testimony that I recognized the necessity of taking care of myself for a while and was acting accordingly. Oh, sweetheart, it made my heart ache to think of my precious Eileen sitting there before her easel, her eyes blinded by tears because of her anxiety about me! Sometimes I have wished that you could cry more than you do, instead of *containing* your grief and letting it tear your heart in silence—*but not away from me*, not away from my arms—not all alone with nobody to whom to go for whole-hearted sympathy and loving comfort! It's *that* thought that brings the pain to my heart. And, though it *is* sweet to know that you care so intensely for me, I have never wished you to cry about *me*, little lady. *Don't* let yourself be so anxious. I will always tell you all about myself—and there is no longer anything to be anxious *about now*! I am quite on my feet again, and can easily realize my purpose of staying on them. And I am, besides being as full of health, as full of mirth as the sunshine outside my window here, for thinking that I am nearer to-day than I was yesterday to the time which is bringing *you* to me, my darling, my peerless little sweetheart! You must not let yourself be sad these days, little lady! I shall be very much offended if you do. You must accumulate, as I am accumulating, a fund of light-heartedness for our wedding day. This time don't count: we will date everything from *that* time, when you will come, as a bearer of all love's sweetest gifts, to   Your own   Woodrow.

ALS (WC, NjP).

From Ellen Louise Axson

My darling Woodrow,   New York April 9/85
    I received such an appealing letter the other day from my dear little Cousin, Minnie [Hoyt], that it was impossible for me to put off writing her any longer. Of course she wanted to know about all my "doings," and it would have been adding insult to injury to put her off with a few lines after my long neglect. So I have just finished a fourteen page letter, and am now in a state of utter exhaustion. Do you think you can forgive her for almost crowding you out for once? She thinks she has a great deal to forgive you in that line.

Dr. [Basil L.] Gildersleeve last summer was very witty at the expense of poor Sappho who according to him was the mistress of a boarding-school and wrote wildly intense poetry to her favourite pupils full of such passion as no modern woman would ever think of bestowing upon her lover! My dear little poet cousin resembles her illustrious predecessor (!) in that respect if no other. What will the dear child have left to say to her lover! all words will sound flat and stale to her. And yet she is so perfectly in earnest in all she says. By-the-way I had a dear little letter from Uncle Tom yesterday; and I believe I will enclose it—to eke out your short rations! I want you to know some of my relatives better and to read their letters, you know, is an excellent means to that end. I have been thinking I would send you one or two of Cousin Hattie's. I had one from Cousin Allie today, she is coming —to Mrs. Seaman's—tomorrow. She says she has a great deal to tell me about her summer arrangements, "they are perfectly charming,—a perfect *dream*"! I'll venture to say it is not half as perfect a dream as *mine*! But there are tastes in dreams as in everything else, I suppose. Yes, sweet-heart, it's a bargain, we will be "gay and not sad" though we are separated from one another. I will try to "charm the interval that lowers" in that best of ways described in a little poem I sent you a year ago,—by making it "a noble task-time." If I thought that I could by *waiting* grow more worthy of your love—better prepared for the sweet, the solemn though happy duties of wifehood, I would "kindly but firmly"—as people say when they are most disagreeable—make you wait until June had come and gone and come again. But I perceive so little progress in that direction that I am disposed to think in my despair that the only way to learn the duties of *any* station is by trying with all one's might to fulfil them when the time comes. So I go bravely and joyously to face them with all my imperfections on my head. Good-night sweet-heart

With all my heart   Your own   Eileen

ALS (WP, DLC). Enc.: T. A. Hoyt to ELA, April 7, 1885, ALS (WP, DLC).

To Horace Elisha Scudder

My dear Sir: Balto., April 9, 1885

I am in receipt of your very kind letter of the 4th of April and am exceedingly gratified by the liberal and very complimentary offer which it contains. I had taken it for granted that, in view of my rather unattached and nomadic life hitherto, my disabilities for undertaking the composition of one of your series of local histories were conclusive, and had, consequently, hardly expected any reply to my answer to your former letter. And, now that my disabilities are removed, I find myself obliged, much against my will, to decline for other reasons this work which I would, under favouring circumstances, be so quick to take up. Since I last wrote to you I have experienced something very like a breakdown in health—sufficiently like to render it imperatively necessary that I should add nothing—but should subtract as much as possible—from the work which I have already undertaken for the next two years. This partial breakdown is the result of my having worked during past 'vacations' as I should have to work during future vacations, were I to accept the appointment you offer.

I need not add that I am extremely sorry to have to make this reply to your proposition—any man would be sorry to be handicapped by precarious health, and any young man would be sorry to lose a chance to enter the "Commonwealth series"—but I may add the hope that my declining will not inconvenience you, and that it will not exclude North Carolina from the series.

Very Sincerely Yours,   Woodrow Wilson

ALS (Scudder Papers, MH).

From James E. Rhoads

My dear Friend,   Philada. 4. 9. 85.
Enclosed I send letter of H. C. Adams about C. L. Houghton. I think the extent of her general culture as indicated by her five years' course at Ann Arbor will justify us in accepting her, *provided* she has given sufficient attention to *historical* studies and has made adequate acquirements in them. Of this thou must judge.   Thine very truly,   James E Rhoads

ALS (WP, DLC).

To Ellen Louise Axson

My own darling,   Balto., April 10, 1885
I was engaged last night, have been engaged this morning, and shall probably be engaged till time for writing to-morrow, upon Bryn Mawr business. For one thing, I am making out entrance examination papers in English and American history—the most perplexing task I ever undertook; and, for another, I am giving earnest consideration to the testimonials &c., &c., accompanying the application of Miss Clementine Lord Houghton, of Michigan

University, for the 'fellowship' in History. How is one to form any sane conclusion from these testimonials—except that Miss Houghton is a young woman of twenty-three, possessed of abounding physical vigor and intellectual energy. I shall ask for a thesis from this aggressive young person—and shall hope for other applicants with whom to compare her.

I can readily understand, Miss, that I have small chance of your attention when I have Browning as my competitor—but I must protest that it is not fair to put me to such an unequal contest—though you do soften my defeat by saying, not that reading the great poet made you forget all about me, but only that it made you cease "to mark the flight of time"! I must be comforted by knowledge of the fact that you read what I write *oftener* than what Browning has written.

No, sweetheart, I have read neither "Caliban" nor "Saul," and so cannot venture "any good—or bad—psychological reason why men should 'not unnaturally prefer' " the former to the latter; but I will read both as soon as may be, and then possibly I shall have some very problematical explanation to offer. You will doubtless wait in great suspense! But, meanwhile, I may say that I *have* read "By the Fireside" and agree with somebody else in thinking it "lovely."

Well, my pet, the parsonage in Wilmington is empty and closed by this time and the three dear people who lately occupied it are in Columbia. I received a brief note from dear mother this morning written from Columbia on the 8th. She and "Dode" had arrived there the morning before and were expecting dear father to follow the next day. She sends, as always, a great deal of love to "dear Ellie." I can't help feeling a little sad about the breaking up of the home in Wilmington. It wasn't much of a home, outside of the house itself, because there were in the community almost no companionable people for us. But still it was a home *place*, such as can't be found, for a time at least, in Clarksville; because houses are so scarce there that the dear folks will have to *board* for some time, and so feel unsettled. It is all *right*—and every way for the best—I am sure, but it makes me feel "kind o' blue." It aggravates the homesick longing I so often have to *see* them all. There can be no doubt about the correctness of the judgment early passed upon me: I am clearly a 'home boy.'

Still, I read something this morning which wonderfully—with an unspeakable sweetness—beguiles my loneliness and takes the sting out of everything that threatens attack upon my spirits. My darling says that my poor letters, at whose composition my heart works so hard, do carry to her the rest and the gladness with which it is my dearest wish to fill her thoughts. And this precious news suits so well with our new agreement, to enjoy what we have of each other, even in our present separation, to the top of our bent, as a school for our hearts in the infinitely greater joys that we are to have in the near future. You see, Miss, you must be training your lips for the smiles which your *husband's* lips will be aways tempted to blot out with kisses! I shall expect you to be as openly delighted at finding yourself wedded to this not too attractive man as I shall be at finding myself the husband of the loveliest little woman in the world. I shall *exact* gayety from you; I shall insist upon seeing all the depths of laughter which your heart contains—all the sweet mirth—not of shallow amusement, but of deep heart-joy—that your pretty eyes promise! By the way, Miss, you have made no reply to what I said in my letter of last Sunday about what I first saw in those eyes and about my own proneness to love the mischief I seemed to find there. I thought that you would take pity on me and tell me what your feelings are concerning the revelations I insisted upon making of my fondness for extravagant fun. You see I don't want you to be too much disturbed when you discover that you cannot be continuously dignified in my presence. Oh, darling, I wonder what you will think of me when you know me in *all* my moods—some of which are so capricious that, when they come, I feel as if I hardly knew myself? Will you promise to put up with even my pranks? Will you promise to do nothing but love me even when I am most outrageous? I promise to be moderately well behaved in public; but there's no telling *what* I'll do in private when the awe with which your presence at present fills me has worn off! I assure you that I can *be* as nonsensical as my talk! But then, henceforth, even my frolics cannot but be full to overflowing of that love which makes me so absolutely   Your own   Woodrow.

ALS (WC, NjP).

From James E. Rhoads

My Dear Friend,   Philadelphia. 4 mo. 10, 1885.
  The enclosed from Professor Adams is full upon the point of special preparation in History on the part of Clementine L Houghton, & I think meets all objections upon this point. I see no objection to recommending her to the Trustees, so far as her training is involved.

                       Thine truly,   James E Rhoads

When prepared to give thy judgment please return the papers & oblige thine truly   J E R

ALS (WP, DLC).

From Ellen Louise Axson

My darling Woodrow,   New York, April 11/85

Your enemy, head-ache, was serving me so ill last night, that I concluded that it would be wise for me to go to bed and sleep it off,—since it was the result merely of fatigue. So my writing was postponed,—better I thought a hurried letter in the morning than one beyond measure stupid, or worse, at night. I am most happy, my darling to hear that you are feeling and looking so much better. It is a comfort even to know that there is "nothing to be anxious about *now*," and we will try to devise means of security against any cause for anxiety in the future. You yourself will have to study the books about "how to get strong" which you prescribe for Stockton! Yes I have already admitted that it was very unreasonable, very illogical in me to be so distressed by your letter of Monday, but I couldn't help it. I begin to perceive that certain lessons which I learned long ago for myself and have practiced so assiduously that I thought they had become second nature, I have to learn all over again in their application to *you*; and inasmuch as I love you much better than myself, it is going to be an infinitely harder task to learn them. Do you suppose I shall ever be able to take your troubles and vexations with as much equanimity as I do my own?—which I conquer simply by a strong effort of the will *forbidding* them to trouble or vex me,— unless thought be necessary *commanding* myself not to think of them at all. Of course I refer to the smaller ills of life—it's *passing* troubles. I really think I have acquired a good deal of philosophy for a "young person"! Nor did it altogether fail me in the greater troubles of life. I had almost learned in whatsoev[er] state *I* was therewith to be content. Suppose it *wasn't* a very happy estate!—what difference did it really make after all?—the purpose of life isn't to be *happy*. "There is in man a higher than love of happiness; he can do without happiness, and instead thereof find *blessedness*[.]" Besides it seems to me that happiness is a perverse nymph,—pursue her and she flies you, turn from her, treat her with indifference and contempt, and she follows you;—literally throws herself in your arms. But all these wise and *original* reflections give me no comfort where you are concerned; I *can't bear* for *you* to have any of the ills that flesh and spirit are heir to. I want you to be *perfectly* happy and fortunate, and can't accept with my usual serenity the fact that as you too are mortal the thing is manifestly impossible.

But this won't do. I am not keeping my appointment with that charming model of ours,—such a fright I never saw before. It is hard to get up much enthusiasm in working from her.

By-the-way Antoinette Farnsworth is very much puzzled over me, she don't see how anyone *can* work so hard and so enthusiastically at a thing which she is going to give up almost immediately; the thought would paralyze her energies, it would seem like spending her labour for naught. I told her I worked for *love* of it, and love, not hope of gain, is the mother of enthusiasm. "Yes" she said "Mr Stimson always said that the best work, the only good work, was that which was a labour of love," but she couldn't "stick at it" so without the additional spur of ambition—and I hadn't "a grain of it"—she "never saw anything like it!" Ah! but I *am* ambitious! and the best of it is that *mine* is *gratified* ambition, for I am ambitious for *you*—and for *myself* too, dearest, I hardly dare too say how *great* is my ambition,—I would be the best and truest wife that ever man had. There came to pass one sunny September day something which glorified my life in a way that would satisfy the aspirations of any woman under heaven.

> "I am named and know by that moment's feat;
> There took my station and degree
> So grew my own small life complete
> As nature obtained her best of me—
> One born to love you, sweet!"

That was a charming little poem in yesterday's letter! *Many* thanks for it, darling,—may *our* "love's summer be for life"!

And so the home is actually broken up and the dear one's in Wilmington are gone. I am not surprised that you feel sad at the thought, most changes are more or less sad even when we know they are for the best.

Believe me darling with all my heart

Your own Eileen.

ALS (WP, DLC).

To Ellen Louise Axson

My own darling,   Balto., April 11, '85

I want to talk to you to-night upon the very novel topic of an event, in which you and I are very much interested, which is to take place in June. I received the other day the first installment of the payment on the *note* upon which I have told you I am depending to defray our expenses next summer; and of course that payment is a further earnest of what I was morally sure of before, that the whole amount will be paid, as promised, by the 15th of May. So that I think that my darling would be quite safe in consulting "Aunt Ella" when she pleases about making arrangements and fixing a date for my deliverance. I guess that "Aunt Ella" has wondered sometimes what has become of the wish you expressed to her so many weeks ago, that it might be possible to humour your impatient lover by fixing an early day for the crowning of his hopes—don't you? And I can say for that lover that he has the eagerest sort of desire to know at least the *week*, if he may not know the day, in June to which he may look forward, as to the beginning of his real life! Of course, sweetheart, you will know when and how it is best to act in taking the dear folks in Savannah into our confidence: I just wanted you to know that, so far as my affairs are concerned, there is no reason why you should not do so now.

April 12.

I stopped at this point last night, precious, because I was too tired and thick-headed to go on. I had had one of my nervous headaches all day, and so had waited until evening to write; but when evening came I found myself overcome by sleepiness, resulting from the fatigue of the long walk of the afternoon by means of which I had gotten rid of the headache, and from the fact that I had stayed very late at Hiram's the night before. My visit to H's, though accidental, had been long as usual. I happened to pass the house about six o'clock, just before their dinner hour, and Daisy [Woods], Hiram's sixteen year old sister, who is one of my chief playmates, banged so lustily on the window at which she was sitting, in her efforts to attract my attention and make me bow to her, that I of course went in to give her a lecture on dignity—and then in came Miss Nellie [Woods] and Hiram and I was made to stay to dinner and didn't get away till after eleven o'clock. I never do get away from that house much sooner than that: I am made to feel so thoroughly at home and have such a jolly time that I don't realize, until I notice that all the children of the family have been sent off to bed, that it is high bedtime for older folks.

To-day I am feeling all right again, except that I am very anxious about my darling. Eileen, is it only now and then, when you go to some exhibition or take some irregular half-holiday, that you take any exercise except the little scrap you get in walking once or twice the distance between Eleventh St. and the League? If so, I wonder that you do not oftener have headaches from fatigue. ("Merely of fatigue" indeed!) I am constantly haunted by the thought that you sit all day at your easel, doing all that it is possible to do to drive the bloom out of your cheeks and to bring dark lines under your eyes. And, if that is what you do, I must say, my darling, that I think that it is very wrong. It is not right to presume so on present health at the risk of *future* failure of strength. No one can break the laws of health with impunity—least of all a woman who is expecting soon to become a wife. I need not tell you, my pet, that I am not conscious of so much as a single touch of selfishness in saying this. I say it altogether for your sake: for, if I know my own heart, I should—aside from the unspeakable anguish of seeing you suffer—esteem it a sweet privilege to nurse my darling through a *life-time* of ill health. And you will see how great a proof it is of my perfect faith in your love's power to understand me that I should venture to put the warning as I have put it. I don't want to exaggerate the danger of letting your system get run down, as it inevitably must without plenty of regular exercise and an abundance of fresh air; but you know, little lady, that you have neglected my earnest advice on this score in every *other* form in which I have put it. I dare not neglect plain speaking when I hear so often of my Eileen's finding herself worn out by her day's work. Let me *beg* you, my pet, for the sake of your love for me, if not for your own sake, to give up your work in black and white, or *some* part of your daily appointments, in order that you may spend the time so gained in taking exercise in the open air and in some sort of diversion. I have been a very long time in making up my mind to make this request, because I have felt the greatest reluctance to interfere with your plans, knowing how much store you set by this opportunity to study in New York; but I can't hesitate any longer: I must urge the request with all the earnestness possible, hoping that you will be willing to accept my judgment in the matter—unless I am altogether mistaken about the facts as to the length of your confinement at your work every day. No matter how little of a *task* that work may be to you—no matter how much you may enjoy it—it *does* confine you all day in close rooms, and so leave you with less strength for the future. You cannot help me more, darling, than by taking my advice in this matter. If I could sacrifice *myself* to save you any sacrifice that may be involved, I would do so gladly—oh *so* gladly and eagerly—except as my sacrifice might distress my loving little sweetheart; but *I* can do nothing, so I must appear selfish and ask you to do this *for my sake*. No amount of rest and care and diversion can enable me to get robust again so long as I feel that *you* are overworking yourself. When I am with you and can watch over you I shall be content, but until then I cannot be, unless you will let me watch over you a little bit now.

You see what an impatient fellow I am, in spite of all my resolutions. I want to anticipate the duties—and even the authority!—which our love is bringing me. I know that my darling *will* "be the best and truest wife that ever man had"; but I want her to be, besides, the *happiest* wife that ever man had—and she cannot be happy without health. I have an unbounded ambition for you, my darling,—not an ambition for things that the world shall know, but a *domestic* ambition, to crown my darling with such *home* happiness of satisfied love, of perfect companionship, of loving co-work, of tender, cheery service, as will make her think it blessed to be my wife—even if I *am* often irritable, often hard to understand, and sometimes hard to please. If *any*thing can cure me of unreasonable and selfish ways it will certainly be the infinite love I bear to you, my queen, my precious heart-treasure. What a wonderful part you have played in my life these last two years!—for it is two years, just two years, this month, you know, since we made each other's acquaintance! And that reminds me of a parenthesis in one of your recent letters: "if there ever was such a time"—when we were 'only friends.' For my part, I doubt if there ever was—at least, if my darling felt as strangely in my presence during that first visit of mine as I did in hers. I had even then a strange, passionate desire to know you better, my sweet love, because of a vague, half-formed consciousness that intimacy would reveal sympathies and beauties such as I would give the world to discover in *some*body—such as I have since discovered, as a source, an inexhaustible source, of delight and happiness, because as an irresistible motive of love, in the little lady whom within ten weeks (if God will) I am to call by the sweetest, most sacred name that a man's lips could utter. That was a strange time! I like to go back to it in thought and try to penetrate its mysteries. That is the reason I have asked you so many questions about it one time an another—beginning with the one 'what did you think of me that first day?' which you evaded by telling me what you had *said* of me—'quite an infant'—to some one. Since we were so manifestly *meant* for each other from the first—drawn

together as if by a fate which we could not and would not resist—
I thought that your first feelings towards me, added to my first
feelings towards you, might form a more complete picture than
I yet have of that time about which I *would* know and understand so much more than I do. Even if your feelings were much
less positive than mine—as they of course were—even if they were
altogether *negative*, they would at least serve for the neutral tints
that would make mine the more distinct by contrast. If you *could*
recollect the sort and the degree of interest you took in the
stranger that day, it would doubtless serve as a much less *biassed*
judgment of his bearing and his character, Miss, than you can
give to-day—unless, as you may think, his character lies in his
heart, which you had yet to discover. How odd it is to remember
the cold chills that used to come over me in my conversations
with you whenever I used to imagine (like the love-smitten fellow
that I was) that the pretty interest you used to take in our talks
was rather in the topics themselves than in the person with whom
you were discussing them! That was the whole tale in a single
feeling, my dread of being kept at arm's length. Not that I had
any immediate design of coming nearer to you than a literal arm's
length! but I had the feeling that, if only you would let me show
you how near of kin I felt to you, you would maybe some day recognize in me, or grant to me, a right to take you in love as close
to my heart as I chose and tell to your *lips* what I could not frame
for your ears; and every sign that your interest was *impersonal*
of course baffled that feeling and made me feel the space between
us very big and cold

But how I have been running on! This epistle is threatening to
grow too large for the mail! I wish I could close it with some
word of love half as precious as these you have sent me about
your ambition to prove that you were born to love me! You were
born to *bless* me, you matchless little maiden! Else, why does it
make me so proud and happy to declare myself

Your own   Woodrow.

ALS (WC, NjP).

Two Letters from Ellen Louise Axson

My darling Woodrow,   New York, April 12/85

I find my little interval between church and dinner in which I
usually write to you almost entirely gone today in consequence of
it's being Communion Sunday. But I won't try the plan of finishing
after dinner as I did last Sunday, for I find it don't work;—you will

have *no* Monday letter again. So I will,—because I *must*—put you off with a hasty line at present, and wait 'till tonight to answer the sweet letter which came yesterday.

So you wish me to be training my lips to smile! do you sir? Why I had been thinking that it would be well for me to train them— and the rest of me—to greater sobriety and dignity of demeanor. I have been so teased (?) for always smiling, even to myself, that I once vowed I would never smile again—and I kept it too—for half an hour! "Mademoiselle est toujours sourire" my old professor used to say, himself smiling very benignantly; and I felt as though some serious reflection had been cast upon my intellectual powers!

I don't think you need to be reassured to any *great* extent as to the way in which I will accept those "revelations" of yours! A young lady who habitually *sits on her foot* in her most *serious* moments don't stand or sit either—on her dignity! and can't afford to be "shocked" at any pranks indulged in by her friends in *their* hours of *relaxation*! Nor should I think she would inspire any one with *awe* in her presence. I dare you to any prank which I can't with the *greatest pleasure* "put up with." And I promise to love you in all your moods, and with all my heart,

As ever   Your own Eileen.

My darling Woodrow,   New York, April 13/85.
   That room-mate of mine[1] proved so irrepressible last night that I found it impossible to do anything at all until I had put her to bed —as a punishment. And then there are so many duty letters that I am *obliged* to write on Sunday night that when I had finished it was almost if not quite Monday morning. So I concluded that my darling would rather have me *dream* about him than write to him at that hour of the night, and I forthwith proceeded to do it.

   You will want to know more about this delightful room-mate of mine but I must not take time for details now. She really is a charming girl, I like her "better'n-better." She says that if she were a man she would be desperately in love with me! She is a real Western girl,—much more warmhearted and impulsive than the Yankees, and yet more matter-of-fact than than [*sic*] the Southerners. She is a wee bit Western in her manner,—free and easy, you know,—but not enough "to hurt." It makes her seem more original. She is really a fine girl, and a very interesting one; there is a great deal *in* her. She is intelligent, and something more;

for she is one with whom you *can* talk,—and talk with real pleasure—on matters of deeper interest than either books or art. I think we are very congenial;—we *think* of the same things at least, though often we think very *differently* about them. We have a great many quarrels, in which she accuses me of being "an incorrigible little Southerner" and I deplore her benighted condition and predict that the scales will fall from her eyes some day. She is a very handsome girl, large and well developed, with a rich complexion, sunny blue eyes, brown hair, and superb teeth; she has a very bright face and a very bright manner and is a good talker. I shall make a slight sketch of her and send [it to] you as soon as I have time.

That reminds me that I never expressed my surprise at learning that the last sketch I sent you was not good of me! I thought the lower part of the face especially *perfect*. How true it is that one doesn't know and *can't* know anything about one's own appearance! I had a curious instance of that the other day when I went to Mrs. Seaman's. She asked me if I had seen the Seney collection, and if I had seen a picture there which looked like anyone I knew[.] "Why no" said I. "Think" she said you *must* have seen it! "Is it any one in this house," said I, all in the dark. "Why it seems *incredible* that you shouldn't have noticed it!" she said, "it was as much like *you* as if you had sat for it. We were all astonished at it, it was the most singular resemblance I ever saw, I was going to write you to be sure and see it, but then I thought you would certainly do it anyhow." Unfortunately I can't recall the picture now, for she could not remember the name of the artist and it was only called an "ideal head."

But I am indulging myself too much for Monday morning, and must close now much against my will, for I had ever so many things to tell you.

I wanted to tell you that I *should* be frankly delighted to find myself wedded to a man of whose attractions I am the best judge, sir! This separation, darling is doing its work well,—since there is but one way for it to end, it has made me look forward to my wedding day with a joy which one year ago I should have blushed to think *possible*. My love I am without any reservation,

Your own Eileen.

ALS (WP, DLC).
¹ That is, Antoinette Farnsworth.

To Ellen Louise Axson, with Enclosure

My own darling,   Balto., April 13, '85

This *is* a "dear little letter" from your uncle, and I most cordially approve of your sending me such letters as introductions of those of your relatives who are dearest to you. I love "uncle Tom." because he loves you: I don't *need* any further evidence in favour of "cousin Hattie," but I should be delighted to see her as she appears in her letters.

I enclose Mr. Scudder's answer to my last letter. It seems to me an unusually gratifying episode in a mere business correspondence, and I have just written him in return a brief note of cordial thanks for his "personal concern in my fortunes." I do like a man with a heart!

Mr. Gamaliel Bradford (my *Nation* critic) writes me from Old Point this morning that he will be in Baltimore for a few hours on Thursday and would like to have some conversation with me. So we will meet and discuss oppressively heavy topics, doubtless, much as if all the weight of government were on our mental shoulders. Verily there are penalties connected with writing a book! The penalty of having to pose as if one really knew something and were quite at home with sundry profound thoughts unfamiliar to the rest of the world has its droll, and therefore redeeming, side, however. There's rather more comedy than tragedy in it, on the whole; and in this case I can amuse myself by putting Gamaliel, old boy, through *his* paces. I can see what sort of feet he has to sit at. He is to be in Washington to-morrow and next day, to induce the President, I suppose, to command Congress to open its doors to his Cabinet. Good luck to the enterprise!

Yes, Miss, I love your smiles: I am not willing that any one of them should be forbidden. There's a precious store of sunshine in them—and, were they to *cease*, I should fear that my darling had grown weary of me—had ceased to find cause for smiling. But I am very selfish: I want you to reserve all the sweetest of them for me—to keep them as messengers of the happiest thoughts of your love, and as special deputies to receive and welcome the warmest demonstrations of my love. Ah, Eileen, my darling little sweetheart, it makes me nearly wild with delight sometimes, often, to think that *all* your charms are *for me*; that the smiles, the kisses, the caresses, all the words, all the most precious gifts and tokens of love that can be given to man by woman are to be given me by the loveliest, most lovable, and most loving little woman in the world; are to be given by *you*, my Eileen, to

Your own   Woodrow.

ALS (WC, NjP).

From Horace Elisha Scudder

My dear Sir   Boston, 10 April 1885

Of course there is nothing more to be said except that I am sorrier to hear of your reasons for declining to write North Carolina, than I am to lose your work, much as I regret that. I sincerely trust that you have heeded the warning in good season, and that an uncompromising adherence to your self-imposed rules may result in greater freedom hereafter. I took so warm an interest in your little book on Congressional Government that you must allow me to feel a personal concern in your fortunes.

Sincerely yours   Horace E. Scudder

ALS (WP, DLC) with WWhw notation on env.: "Ans. April 13/85."

To Horace Elisha Scudder

My dear Sir: Balto., April 13, 1885.

I cannot refrain from returning you my very warm thanks for your cordial note of April 10, which I received this morning. That you do feel a personal concern in my fortunes is, I assure, a source of genuine gratification and encouragement to me. I have good reason to hope that I have taken the care of my health in hand in season; and I trust that, with restored health, I shall be able to realize my ambition to do honest work in thinking and writing. Through prudent *physical* administration I hope to aid myself in getting into the heart of that governmental administration which it is my purpose first to understand myself and then to assist the reading public in understanding.

Very sincerely yours,   Woodrow Wilson.

TCL (RSB Coll., DLC).

From Ellen Louise Axson

New York, April 13/85

The long letter received this morning was a delightful treat, my darling, in spite of the terrible *scolding* it gave me! You see I have the consolation of feeling that I am not half as naughty as you think me!—there is nothing like a good conscience to enable one to "bear up" against such things! I assure you, sir, that I can't remember when I ever worked so little as I do now,—only six hours a day!—you surely don't think that too much! You see I am entirely at the mercy of the models here, when they stop posing I *must* stop working, whereas heretofore it was always from—no, *not "early* morn to dewy eve"! The morning pose is from nine to twelve, and the afternoon from one to four; and a half hour of each the model and we with her spend resting, so that even counting the sketch class which is from half past four to half past five, we have only six hours of work, and the intervals of rest I have been disposed to think entirely *too* numerous: there is a whole hour, you see, at lunch time. I do plead guilty on one point, except the walk to and from the League I havn't been taking *regular* exercise,—yet I take a great deal of exercise, there is scarcely a day that I am not obliged to tramp somewhere,—across town to Mericks, the art store on fourth Ave., if nowhere else. Would it satisfy you if I took a regular walk every day at noon?—or do you still wish me to work only half the day? If you say the word, my lord, it shall be so!—but I can't promise not to *think* it very absurd, sir!—and what would I do with myself? I would be obliged to be busy about something else, you know. It would certainly make me ill to do nothing,—and besides I don't know how. I assure you I am not at all "worn out." Mrs. Seaman says I am looking a great deal better than I did two months ago, and you know I was not exactly in a decline *then*. I am *only* tired at night when I have been *standing* a good deal (and I shan't do that to any extent hereafter) during the day either in galleries or at my work; that was the one thing that *always* tired me greatly. And I very, very seldom feel anything like *over*-fatigue; you know a certain amount of weariness,—is a good and pleasant thing, it makes rest and sleep all the sweeter. Indeed, dear, *I* think I am making wonderful progress in learning to take care of myself,—and all for your sake;—"for if I be dear to someone else, then should I not be to myself more dear." Now that I look back on it all with my eyes open, I know that I used to be *outrageous* in such matters, and I almost wonder that I am alive. Uncle Will says it is a phenomenon which he can't understand;—but I thought it was my *duty* and that I could not help it. And I seem to have an excellent constitution, not *iron* by any means but *india-rubber*,—like Grandfather's. Yet though I perceive that I am still stronger than the majority of girls with whom I have been thrown, I know that I cannot bear quite as much as I once could. I have never altogether recovered from the terrible strain of that last fall and winter in Rome. Before that I scarcely knew the meaning of the word "fatigue," except when I had been standing all day, and now I am some times really very tired.

But though I have been very imprudent and foolish in the past, I have come to my senses now; I fully realize that one of my first duties to *you* is to take care of my health, and I *am* trying to do it. But you don't know how dreadfully hard it is for a woman to take care of herself,—to keep the matter on her mind; and then too however well she *knows* it to be her duty she can't help *feeling* that it is selfish and self-indulgent to be always "sparing herself." You are quite right to exercise that "authority," sir, for I don't believe any woman *ever* performed that duty without some such strong moral support!

By-the-way all this reminds me of my "well-nigh blunted purpose" formed last summer;—said I to myself said I, "when I go to New York where there are plenty of *doctresses*, I will find out all about myself and if I am not quite sound I'll break off my engagement!" But I *feel* so well all the time that I forget all about it. I think perhaps I had better do it before we talk any more about "fixing the day" &c! What do we girls know about ourselves?—why absolutely nothing! We can manage to tell when we have a headache, and that is about all! My lungs might be as seriously affected as my heart—that is to say, entirely gone,—while I continued in blissful ignorance!

But I must close;—so far as I know I am guilty of but one imprudent practice, viz., sitting up late, as I am doing now, to write *you* when I am in any way prevented in the early part of the evening.

Remember, dear, that I will do anything you wish about the work; if you still want me to give up one class I will do it, though I am sure your fancy has been deceiving you as to the facts. I am no longer in a black and white class, by-the-way, but am in both morning and afternoon painting classes. In the one I pay by the season having been simply transferred, in the other by the month. My first month is out on Wed. and then I propose to take a few half holidays to see about Spring work &c. &c. Don't you think *that* all that is necessary? Goodnight my darling; I must close now in haste. Believe me, dearest, with all my heart.

Your own   Eileen.

ALS (WP, DLC).

To Ellen Louise Axson

My own darling,   Balto., April 14/85

You certainly know how to write a sunny letter that brings with it an air of having come from a little maid who harbours cheery contentment—and likes to talk about, not herself so much as her room-mate, her new room-mate whom she half loves already. I believe that I was right in being glad that you were to have a room-mate—and now that you have introduced me to Miss Farnesworth I am sure that she was the right one for you to have —that she will be *good* company—will keep you from feeling lonely without making you feel uncomfortable—will divert you without jarring upon your tastes. She must be very nice; and she is evidently a person of discerning mind—for I find myself agreeing excellently well with the only two opinions of hers that you have reported. Certainly if she were *this* man she would be desperately in love with you: and one of my reasons for loving you is that in all sweet womanly qualities you *are* "an incorrigible little Southerner." Is it only since she came to room with you that Miss F. has fallen so much in love with you? You may give her my respects, or my regards, or my love—since you are the messenger, you may choose the message.

Ah, my darling, what would I not give for that "Ideal Head" in the Seney Collection! I do so long for a good, an adequate picture of you. I pinned the last sketch you sent me on my wall, but the more I looked at it the more dissatisfied with it did I become, so I took it down this morning and put it carefully away. It contained for me no secret of the lovely face that is before me in all my day's thinking and all my night's dreaming. By the way, Miss, it is very cruel of you to speak of dreaming about me and yet say never a word of what forms your dreams take!

At last I have heard from Shinn! He is in San Francisco working for the *Overland*; he may return East in June,—and he may remain out there for two or three years: that's all he tells about himself.[1] His letter is just an overflowing expression of his interest in us—in all whom he left behind on this side the continent. Isn't this like the dear old fellow: "I have been made very very happy over your transcendent and well-deserved success. You are going straight to the front. God bless and keep you, and your dainty, loving, genius of a wife-to-be. Wont there be a wedding this year, Woodrow?" Yes, my dear fellow, and I wish you could be present at it! Ah, sweetheart, if *you* look forward with such joy to our marriage, what do you suppose *I* feel about it, who am to be the chief gainer! Oh, I *long* for you, Eileen! I shall be *so* happy—*so* proud!—when I can show you in every day's increasing love how completely I am   Your own   Woodrow.

ALS (WC, NjP).
   1 Wilson is referring to unpublished portions of C. H. Shinn to WW, April 7, 1885.

From Ellen Louise Axson

My darling Woodrow,   New York, April 14/85
    This is an unusually pleasant business letter—one that gives me a warm liking for the writer. I suppose, of course, you have never met Mr. Scudder personally,—have you? I am glad you are to have the opportunity of meeting Mr. Bradford,—hope you will enjoy it as much as you *anticipate*! It will be an advantage to you to have some personal friends of influence in Boston, especially if you are going there to "lecture" the "Civics";—is that the name? But I must in conscience postpone writing further until the morning for Antoinette has gone to bed with a nervous head-ache, and I *must* follow, for this light, which is unfortunately quite high, is keeping her awake. She has made herself sick *crying*, poor child! she has been at it three or four hours because of something cross Mr. Stimson said to her. What a girl she is! I tried to console her by telling her that Mr. S. didn't really mean it for her, all the facts showed that, and she had done *nothing* to irritate him; something or other that she knew nothing about had put him out of temper; he was ready to go off half-cocked and she had happened to come within his range,—that was all—(poor comfort, I must admit myself, but the best I could invent) "Yes," she said between her sobs, "he couldn't treat me worse if I were his wife—that's the way men *always* treat their wives,—the cowards! some *man* makes them angry and they don't *dare* have it out with him, or else they think it policy to control themselves, so they vent all their spite on the unfortunate creature—weaker than themselves —who is in their power!" "But," she added "I'm *not* in his power and I won't stand it, I'll never speak to him again!" What do you think of that severe judgment, sir?—*is* that the way men treat their wives?—but to be sure you are not in a condition to know.
    Wed. morning [April 15].—Alas the day!—I am dreadfully late this morning, having had a number of little things to do, and it is after nine now, so there is nothing for it but to close at this point. So you would like to know what I dream about you! Why my dreams havn't enough method in them to bear telling; the begin-

ning and the end is simply this—that "in my sleep to you I fly—I'm always *with you* when I sleep, the world is all one's own,—but then I wake and where am I?—all,—all alone." Can you wonder that I should be tempted to sleep as long as possible. That with your image to occupy me, such trifles as "rising bells" should fail to attract my attention?

I love you—I love you, darling, truly, tenderly, passionately. I am with all my heart   Your own   Eileen.

ALS (WP, DLC).

To Ellen Louise Axson

My own darling,   Balto., April 15, 1885

I doubt if you knew how hard your Monday night letter would be to answer. I have just destroyed an eight page epistle in which I tried to answer it; this is my second attempt. It was easy enough to say that if you *are* taking care of your health—and are sure that you are succeeding—I have, of course, no more inclination than I have right to ask you to give up one of your classes; but it was *not* easy to say even that while my mind was full of the other part of your letter that I wanted to answer, and when I came to answering that second part I had to give over trying, before I had fairly made a beginning, as it seemed, for fear that my heart would break before I got through! I mean the part in which you spoke of consulting a physician with a view to breaking off our engagement, should it be thought that anything was wrong with your system. I had no fear that anything would be found to be wrong with *you*; but there came crowding in upon me thoughts of my own precarious health. Had I a right to ask you to marry me? And what if the engagement *should* be broken! It's a matter of life and death with me. If I am not to have my darling, I can have neither love nor hope to aid me in my work and it would grind me to death. I could perform my duty bravely without her—but I could not perform it long! It is too late now to think of drawing apart, if she still loves me. She has become the most essential part of my life—my heart is given her in marriage already, and it must die if we are to separate now—unless she has ceased to love me. In that case my heart must turn to stone. But how foolish I am! I am repeating the attempt to answer that part of the letter! How I wish I knew how to *cry* that I might *spend* these feelings somehow. You can scarcely have been in earnest about inviting a doctress to find defects in a perfectly well person! *I* am the one that has been sick; shall *I* go and have myself examined, to be sure that it would not be best for me to die of a broken heart?

According to your own reckoning, precious, you have but a single hour in the day which is free for exercise out of doors. Rests in doors are of no sort of account *for building one up*. I should be very glad if you would take what walks you can regularly—if they will not be *tasks* to you—and if you will eat your lunch *besides*. Remember that every moment spent gladly out of doors is a love gift *to me*! Will that make it easier to be regular? And oh, my darling, *please* keep your promise not to sit up late at night! Put me off with a line—do *any*thing rather than break that promise! I don't care a rap for myself, but I do care everything for you. By taking care of yourself you are doing the *greatest* kindness to

Your own   Woodrow.

ALS (WC, NjP).

From Joseph Ruggles Wilson

My precious Son,   Columbia, Ap. 15, 1885

Your request for advice was received last Thursday or Friday: and the question you proposed has been simmering in my thoughts without coming to a decision & concentrative boil. This morning I had, however, resolved upon writing to you what views I had formed. But meanwhile yours to dear mother came containing your own decision. What was in my mind to say to you was about this, in the fewest words (1) it is important that you should keep yourself before the world (2) History-writing is in your line (3) *but* health *first*. So that you are wise in declining. What you now need more than aught else is to build up *your* constitution, let what will come of the country's.

As to our plans we have them before us only in general outline. We will remain here until after 1st May. Then go to N. Orleans if your mother can: I must at any rate on my way to Gen Assy at Houston. Meanwhile I shall procure a set of new teeth, if the throbbing & butchered nerves which the awful pulling of last Friday will permit. After Assy I am due (3d June) at Clarksville to deliver my inaugural. Upon leaving Clarksville I had thought to arrange for meeting your mother in the North, say at N. York, in view of a couple of months stay & study. But we can almost as well meet here in Columbia, and be ready for going to Savannah by say June 7 or thereabouts. June 7 was the date of *our* marriage. Yet if you, on account of Johns Hop. cannot get married so soon as this—then we will accommodate our movements to yours.

Mrs. Howe, Sr., died in Augusta last night at 11 o'clock. The funeral will occur to-morrow—so that every thing here is once more in mourning and in confusion. Annie will accompany the remains from A. to-night, along with Dr & Mrs Green[.] Geo. was over to see his mother yesterday.

Your mother & Josie & Geo.—all send love such as only such true hearts can feel, for your darling self

My own affection for you I shall not try to put into words.

Father.

P.S. I enclose R. W. Hicks' mem. of yr. goods in his hands, and subject to your order. There is an additional box (important) which was sent to Univ afterwards[.] There is no mark on the goods *except yr. name.* Hicks thinks they had better be ensured for $200 or $300—but I forgot it. He charges nothing for storage.

ALS (WP, DLC) with WWhw notations on env.: "Incloses *Hicks' mem.*"; "Ans. April 21/85." Enc.: R. W. Hicks to JRW, hw receipt signed, April 8, 1885, for household goods "to be shipped as directed."

From James W. Bones

Dear Woodrow   Rome Ga Apr 15/85
At your mothers request I inclose check for $100. to be credited on my note in her favor. I have already sent her $100. (on Apr 1st). Please credit both amts. It distressed us all greatly to learn of your dear sisters great loss.

We have all be[en] much pleased to hear of your great success & of the bright prospects which seem to be opening up before you. . . .

Yours affectionately uncle   James W Bones

ALS (WP, DLC) with WWhw notation on env.: "Rec'd and Ans. April 18/85."

From Ellen Louise Axson

My darling Woodrow,   New York, April 15/85
I have just returned from prayer-meeting, Miss Farnsworth and I having escorted each other tonight. Was in time to hear the last, or next to the last, of the series on the hymn-writers. It was *delightful,*—how I wish I could have heard them all! We had to-night Keble and Faber and Newman, and several others including the women who wrote "Nearer my God to Thee," and "Just as I am." Odd that nearly all the great hymn-writers should have been Episcopalians, most of them high-churchmen,—a number of them,

indeed, converts to Romanism! I wonder if there is any plausible explanation.

I am truly delighted that you have heard from Mr. Shinn at last. I was quite concerned about him; was beginning to wonder if it was not time to advertise. Yes, the letter is just like his "dear old" self. Does he tell you *nothing* of his own affairs? I was very anxious to know if he succeeded in extricating his sister from her difficulties. And doesn't he mention his own book—his own success,—for it is *quite* a success; is it not? Am *so* sorry he will probably remain West. I am afraid we will never see much of him again and I know of no friend who is more to be missed. I consider his having been called away the only serious misfortune that has attended my winter in New York. Please send him my warmest regards—nonsense!—I mean my *love*, for such it really is, and why shouldn't I send it to my "brother adopted"?

By-the-way I gave Antoinette your message and she says I must send you back whatever—and as much of it—as I will let you have. I think I will let you love each other if you wish; though I suppose that if I expressed her feeling exactly I should send you for her a very *keen interest* in you and all that concerns you.

We have the beautiful little model this week who posed in the green velvet. She isn't "a'wearing of the green" however, and she is'nt quite so "paralyzing" divested of that old-world charm. But she is *lovely* in any costume. She interests me extremely; I would like to know all about her—poor little thing! In fact I believe I would like to know all about every body! I am afraid I have a good deal of curiosity about my neighbours affairs;—ought I to blush to confess it? All these people at the League, for instance,—what are they really? what are they thinking and feeling? what does life mean for them? We are all there together, and yet how far apart! —our circles barely touch at the outer edge. I am forever speculating over them,—wondering,—wishing I could understand. How they would laugh if they knew some of *my* thoughts of them; for instance I constantly catch myself pitying them because they don't know and love you, and because you don't love them. Of course I laugh at myself when I become conscious of what I am thinking, but I go on thinking it, all the same. I *do* feel sorry for them,—poor things!—because there is only one Woodrow Wilson in the world,—and he belongs to me! what singular good fortune is mine! It is almost too wonderful to be true that you should so love me, that we should belong to each other forever and ever; yet, oh sweetest of thoughts! it *is true*! Ah my darling, you don't know how happy you have made me—what sweet and wonderful new meaning you have given to my life,—you don't know, you *can't* know how I love you, how entirely I am

Your own Eileen.

ALS (WP, DLC).

To Ellen Louise Axson

My own darling,   Balto., April 16, 1885

I ought in conscience—and I must as a gratification of my own feelings—make this letter a tribute to Mr. Bradford. I have spent most of the day with him—so much of it, indeed, that I am afraid that this letter will be late in getting to you—and I have enjoyed him more than I should have enjoyed an old friend. I felt as if I had seen him before because he resembles Dr. [Jacob A.] Lefevre so much. He is like a larger, fuller, more robust image of the doctor. But the good things are *inside* him. He is natural, he is earnest to the pitch of enthusiasm in things worth thought, he is full of knowledge *and* full of affairs, he is cordial,—he is delightful. His nephew, who is with him, evidently has the warmest affection for him—and one can see *why* he has. His sympathy and his power to stimulate thought have done me as much good as a week's vacation! I feel that I've gained a friend worth having and that I have had my thinking apparatus loosened and lubricated again just as it was in peril of growing rusty. I have met a *man*, and I am excited over the event

Ah, sweetheart, if I could only have come back to talk out my enthusiasm to the *woman* who seems to me the one woman in the world! My heart cries out for her sweet presence every hour of the day—and weaves vagrant fancies about her every hour of the night. Now and then I get a feast for my mind such as this I've had to-day, but all the while my heart grows hungrier. That is why any, even the slightest, suggestion of the possibility of my losing my matchless darling—such as that contained in your letter of yesterday—draws from me, in spite of myself, such a cry of anguish. It is a suggestion that my hunger may run on into starvation—and such starvation would be the *quickest* death for me! You have taken possession of the central, the largest and most vital part of my whole nature. Ruling my heart, you rule my life, my *mental* life as well as the rest—my *all*; and if its queen be taken away, the kingdom must be ruined: its *motive* power is taken away. I used to laugh, like other people, at love rhapsodies: but that was when I did not know what it was to love; and for my darling's eye I can write the full meaning of my love for her. *She* will not think the words extravagant! Does she not love me in the same way, with the same faith, the same life-dependence, the same ardent longing for the time when our lives shall be as much one as our loves, and she shall know

Her own   Woodrow.

ALS (WC, NjP).

From Ellen Louise Axson

New York April 16/85

Ah! my darling, my darling, what would I not give for one little hour with you tonight! It seems to me that never before did I so rebel against "that ring of necessity whereby we are all begirt." Ah it is well for us that we must begin *early* to recognize the fact that "*would* in this world of ours is a mere zero to *should* and the smallest of fractions even to *shall.*" It is only because we have been *well grounded* in that stern lesson of self-control that we avoid doing desperate things sometimes;—that I, for instance, have been able to resist today the wild desire to *go to you*, cost what it would. How is it possible with this slow pen to answer *this* letter to express any portion of the tumult of thought and feeling with which I read it. What answer is possible except one which would *show* you how close I am to you in everything, how utterly and irrevocably I am yours.—"If we are to separate now"! —"unless she has ceased to love me"!—"is my lord well that he doth speak so *wild?*" Yes, thank God, it *is* too late now for such questions,—we are already *one* in heart;—my very life is bound up in yours, does not your heart tell you that? Oh, sweet-heart you did not,—you *could* not really doubt me!

You *must* know how much more eagerly I have longed to be your wife since I have seen that you had in your "precarious" health a special need for a wife's loving care and service;—you must see that you are indeed all the world to me. "Entreat me not to leave thee, or to return from following after thee; for whither thou goest I will go and where thou lodgest I will lodge; thy people shall be my people, and thy God my God: Where thou diest I will die, and there will I be buried: the Lord do so to me and more also if aught but death part thee and me."

And to think that it was something that *I* said which gave you that so unnecessary pang. How can I ever forgive myself! and yet how could I have thought that it would suggest such an idea to you? The case is so different—you must see that it is different. You have your work to do in the world,—your race to run, and if you married a very delicate woman you would be "hanging a millstone around your neck"; but by no abuse of language could a woman be said to hang a millstone about *her* neck though she married the most confirmed invalid, it would only give her fuller scope to perform her woman's mission. If a man's steps are feeble it simply means that he more [than] ever needs an help-meet, and he has a God-given "right" to ask that help of the woman who loves him.

If there is no difference in the two cases why is it that we require a man whether married or not to have a professon, while of the woman we say "that marriage itself is a profession"!—and if possible it should be her *only* one[.] Is it not that she may keep he[r] mind and heart "at *leisure from itself* to sooth and sympathize"? If you had nothing to do in the world but to make me happy,—if you were never to be anything but my husband it probably would never have occurred to me to raise such questions as those in my letter; but I must confess that a great terror seizes me sometimes when I look about me and see two thirds of the women I know invalids to a greater or less degree, for I think, "and what if that should be the end of it all with me,—if I should be only a life-long burden to him," and then I think of your disposition, of how hard it would be for you to take such a thing easily as some men do,—and as they should,—not allowing it to distract or interrupt them, and I feel as though I would give half my life if the veil that hides the future could be lifted as regards that one thing. But since that is impossible it is, of course, very foolish to make oneself unhappy over evils that may never come to pass. It is a risk that all must run;—you would take it with someone, so you may as well take it with me as with another, better indeed since you happen to love me! My chances for health are as good as most others; and better than many.

So we won't raise such questions again, will we, dear? If my heart were not so full now I could laugh at the absurdity of the thought that anything could come between us now—between me and the lover who has been *my* help and comfort in so many dark hours.

Good night, my darling; I send you "a score of kisses" to seal our compact afresh. Do you remember, sir, when you first threatened *me* in that way? By the way I have been studying the calendar, with a purpose, and I imagine that any day between the 24th and 31st of June, would work as far as I am concerned. But more of that—anon. Believe me, dear love, always and altogether   Your own   Eileen

ALS (WC, NjP).

James Bryce to Houghton, Mifflin & Company

My Dear Sirs   April 17/85
Permit me to thank you for your kind present of Mr. Woodrow
Wilson's "Congressional Government["] which has duly reached
me. I have begun to read it, and find it full of interest and instruction

I hope to have opportunities of calling the attention of some
English friends connected with politics and history to so valuable
a contribution to those subjects. Believe me to be
                              Very truly yours   J Bryce
ALS (WP, DLC).

To Ellen Louise Axson

My own darling,   Balto., April 17, 1885
How does this suit you as a "plausible explanation" of the fact
that most of our best hymns have been written by ritualists? Our
creed is essentially an intellectual creed—theirs a much more contemplative, sentimental creed. Their forms of worship are full of
symbolism; from our forms almost all symbolism is excluded.
Their ritual is, so to say, embodied, materialized poetry; with us
no ritual comes between God and the heart. We are students of
living; they are students of expressions of worship: they live in
a sort of Lake region of religion. Is there any motive power in
all this?

Yes, Shinn told me this much of the affairs of the *Overland*,
that he had succeeded in working up abundant financial support
for it and in interesting some very 'solid' men in it, and that
everything would be all right with it, if only they could get some
legal snarls disentangled, as they hoped to do within a month.
But of his own personal plans he says nothing except that his
cash is very low and he will have to do some journalistic work out
there to replenish it. The flowers that California has had for a
couple of months don't make him want to stay: he longs for the
East again. But I can make out nothing as to the cause of his discontent. Of his book he says only that he has not seen many notices of it (tho' he hears of one in a London journal) but that he
has no time to worry about that.[1]

I am happy to say, sweetheart, that I have a fresh and important argument to offer in favour of "fixing a day." I received a
letter yesterday from dear father from which it appears that the
little party will be ready to start northwards early in June. They

are anxious to know, therefore, how soon after the 7th, or thereabouts, you will let them go to Savannah. After that date their movements must wait upon our wedding day, inasmuch as they are strongly and naturally desirous of being eyewitnesses of the ceremony by which I am to be made happier than I ever was in all my life before. So you see, darling, that a good many things besides my contentment depend upon the setting of the day when I may come to you to claim the fulfilment of those precious promises in which my whole life is bound up—and thoughts of which seem nowadays to reign in my heart to the exclusion of every other power but their own sweet power to delight. Do you often think, sweetheart, as these days run by (April is already more than half gone—in eight weeks the middle of June will have come!) how rapidly we are drawing near to the sweet day for which our lives seem to have been made? It seems to me, Eileen, my matchless darling, that I never knew what it was to have an inspiring hope until this was given me, to make you a happy wife: to prove to you by something infinitely better than words that *I love you*, that it is the crown of my manhood, the meaning of my life that I am   Your own   Woodrow.

ALS (WC, NjP).
    [1] Wilson is paraphrasing an unpublished portion of C. H. Shinn to WW, April 7, 1885.

From Ellen Louise Axson

My darling Woodrow,   New York, April 17/85
    I am truly delighted that you have found such a congenial friend in Mr. Bradford. Your description of him is *charming*, I have never heard of one who seemed to be in *all* respects better worth knowing—better worth *your* knowing. I can well believe that the day with him did you good, and I am *so* glad you had the pleasure.
    I have had a lovely time time [*sic*] today; Antoinette and I took our lunch and our sketch books and spent the morning in the Park;—it has been a glorious day here—the sort of day when it is a luxury merely to *breathe*, and we enjoyed our "outing" immensely. This holiday you see was among the first-fruits of your appeal;—and I have found another way of taking frequent draughts of fresh air,—I spend every "rest," when the wind isn't too high, on the *house-top*. It is only to run up one flight of stairs and you are there,—and nicely hidden from the street by the tall sky-light. It was delicious out there yesterday and today. Some of the girls

were sketching there the other day; they had gone over to another roof where the view was better, and had put their basin of water on a low sky-light. Suddenly the basin turned over as the sky-light opened and a man appeared looking as frightened as if he had seen a ghost.

By the way, I have *two* free hours in the day from twelve to one and from half-past five to half past six,—it isn't dark now until seven, and I walk after school.

We are all very much amused at a new law the League managers have made viz., that there is to be no more falling in love at the League!—how they are going to enforce it is another question. But as one of the girls expressed it "they say this sweet-heart business has got to be squelched some-how or other,"—some parents have taken their daughters away on account of it,—couldn't run the risk of their falling in love with the young Bohemians. It is probable that the views of such parents on the co'-education question are not very advanced!

By-the-way, *I* have a new admirer—in the person of Dr. Hamilton's little six-year old daughter;—she says she does *wish* she were a man so that she could marry me! She is a little darling; I was there on Thursday,—went to another of Mrs. Hamilton's afternoon teas. Had a delightful time.

But I am *very* busy tonight and must close now. I love you, dear, as much as you could wish me to,—with all my soul,—with the same faith, the same life-dependence which is my darling's precious gift to me. You also rule the heart, the life the *all*, of

Your own Eileen

ALS (WC, NjP).

To Ellen Louise Axson

Balto., April 18, '85

No, my darling, no indeed, I did not, I *could* not "*doubt*" you for a moment! I could not doubt *you*, my precious, my loyal, my darling little sweetheart, without doubting all that is true and sacred in the world. I don't believe that I could *live* after doubting my Eileen. *That* was not what I meant by saying "unless she has ceased to love me." I was searching for the strongest possible form in which to express the *impossibility* of our drawing apart *now*. It was as if I had said 'unless all light and trust be gone out of the world forever.' No indeed, darling; the only fear that your words had prompted concerning your own attitude in the matter was lest you had, in the very warmth and loyalty and unselfishness of your devotion, conceived a false idea of your duty towards me;

that because you found yourself more delicate than you once were, or because you fancied some defect in your constitution, you might bring yourself to believe it right to break your own heart and (unintentionally) mine in the effort to spare me the "burden" of an invalid wife! And that such a course was at least *possible* on your part I could not but for the moment believe because of the terribly real questionings in my own mind as to what would be my duty towards you were my health actually to break down as it threatened to do a month or so ago. I see now how futile and how unreasonable such questions were. To end our engagement now would certainly break both our hearts: the blow of separation would be infinitely more disastrous than any life-long burden, however real, could be! And, besides, there is not the slightest foundation now for fearing that my health will fail—no more than there is for fearing that *yours* will. A woman of your constitution has ten chances of continued health where the stalwart, muscular woman has one.

Still, my precious one, I don't admit the validity of your argument about the superior right of a man, so to speak, to impose himself as an invalid upon a woman. He must in any case, if he is really a man at all, be the bread-winner of the partnership. On the same supposition—that he is a true man—it will be no more of a "burden" to him to spend his life in caring for an invalid wife than it would be to a woman to spend her life serving an invalid husband—that is, it would be no burden at all. Such service would *exalt* a man, would draw him out of himself, would force him into the blessing of unselfishness. But, if a woman had both to serve and to *support*, the physical strain would be too tremendous—the *mental* strain would be overwhelming, because she could not make her husband happy so long as he felt that the care of him was wearing her life away—it would kill her! Of course a man with merely delicate health needs a wife's loving services more than any other man—and I am sure that *my* sweet wife's love and service will establish my health as nothing else can; but it would seem to be criminal for a man with *broken* health to marry—and if I felt that mine was likely to break—but "we wont raise such questions again: will we, dear?" And oh, what a royal compensation for the anguish of having had them raised for a brief moment is this letter here on the table before me, in which my darling has so poured out the priceless love that her heart contains for me that I can scarcely read the lines for the tears of joy and thankfulness that come into my eyes at the call of her sweet words! It seems to me that all that I have been living for is summed up in the passionate love of this letter. And oh, how my heart laughs with delight at the thought of the marvels love has wrought! My shy little sweetheart no longer loves me from behind a veil: she volunteers to send me 'a score of kisses'! Somehow it seems to me that the sun shines brighter to-day than it ever did before. For does not this precious letter close with one of those "By-the-ways" which often serve my little lady instead of a P.S. to introduce the most important things she says? "By the way, I have been studying the Calendar,—and I imagine that any day between the 24th and 31st of June would" &c! Do you think, Miss, to escape in that way the embarrassment of fixing a particular day? To say that means that we will be married on the 24th: —for I shall certainly take the earliest date you offer—the 24th if I can get no earlier! Oh, how passionately I love my little sweetheart—and when she is something *more* than my sweetheart— when she has been *installed* as my queen—how shall I ever make enough of the opportunities I shall have to reveal the breadth and depth and power of my love? The days that follow our wedding day will be too short for the happiness they will contain! And it seems to me when I write to you nowadays, darling, that I *cannot* write about anything but my love for you. It seems to be my heart's *necessity* to spend this time of waiting in renewing my declaration of love, so soon to be sealed by my bride's coming! Every time I use the words 'I love you' they have fresh meaning for me. Their meaning grows with my ever-growing love. It is all of life to me that I love you and that you love

Your own   Woodrow.

ALS (WC, NjP).

From Ellen Louise Axson

My darling Woodrow,   New York April 19/85

Just in from church as usual, and as usual suffering under the necessity of sending you a short and hasty note. Such a perfect day as it is again! How I should like to spend it in the Park; or better still in the country,—with you (it is as easy to *wish* for great things as for small!). I was reading in the *Atlantic* a queer scheme for changing the climate of North America, making it correspond with that of the opposite shores of the Atlantic. I believe the idea was to make an artificial Gulf stream by cutting a channel in the Arctic regions for the warm waters of the Pacific; the man had a little of Jules Verne's talent, for he actually made the scheme sound plausible, and it struck me as a very laudable undertaking!—but after all I don't believe it is necessary. This really is a *delicious* climate. How delightful it must be in Cal. now! It is odd that Mr. Shinn is'nt contented there. I should think it would be more congenial to him in many ways; indeed when he was *here* he said he liked it best. I am *very* glad that they are working out of their troubles so well. I am very much interested in that wonderful sister of his. I saw a notice of the last volume of "Stories by Am. Authors" in which her's was praised very highly and at length—the others not being mentioned at all.[1]

I should like to see some English notices of your book, wouldn't you? I have no doubt but there have been some.

You will be glad to learn that I am going to take "lots" of half holidays, perhaps a whole week of them in order to go shopping, &c with Cousin Allie. Lily [Hoyt] is coming up on Wed. to be here with Allie the rest of the time. Is'nt that nice for me? —only I fear I shall get dreadfully demoralized.

But no more at present. I love you,—I love you with all my heart, Woodrow, my darling, my first and last and only love! It is with a joy more full and sweet than words can tell that I write myself   Your own Eileen.

ALS (WC, NjP).

[1] Ellen was referring to a notice of Milicent W. Shinn's "Young Strong of 'The Clarion,'" in *Stories by American Authors* (10 vols., New York, 1884-85), IX, 93-138, which appeared in the New York *Nation*, XL (April 2, 1885), 286.

To Ellen Louise Axson

My own darling,   Balto., April 19, 1885

I am delighted to hear of your and Miss Farnsworth's expedition to the Park, and you are a sweet, loving little girl to take two walks and spend your "rests" in the open air for my sake. I can't tell you, sweetheart—my private opinion is that there are no words in the English language that would serve to tell you—what feelings crowd into my heart when I think of your doing any thing *for my sake*! The thought that you are gladly willing to do what I wish *because* I wish it is unspeakably sweet to me. Not because I love to direct and control, however; but because I prize, as I would priceless treasures, every evidence of your love and trust, and your desire to be guided by my wishes is the best evidence my heart could want.

I received a letter from dear sister Annie this morning in which she says, "If you will come and stay with us until the time for *the* wedding"—I have confided to her the June secret!—"we will all go

to Savannah with you—and then I want you to bring Ellie to Columbia. She can make us *all* a visit at one time. Wont that be
nice? It will be for *us*. I am going to keep dear Father and Mother
just as long as possible.”[1] What do you think of *that* proposition,
little lady?

Had I told you of old Mrs. Howe’s death, my pet? She died on
Tuesday last in Augusta, where she was visiting Mrs. Alexander.
I can hardly regard the news as sad. The dear old lady had, sister
Annie says, “longed to ‘go home’ for so many months. She was
getting so feeble that death was a relief to her.”

My darling, isn’t it a blessed thought that there is one sure, one
infallible means of making our love and our married life, which
will be the proof and crown of our love, unbrokenly happy—that if
we but love God as much as we love one another, He will be ever
present to bless our union? Our love for Him is the best earnest
that our love for each other will have a perpetual summer!

I wonder, my little treasure-trove, whether you quite realize
what you are saying when you declare that you love me ‘as much
as I could wish you to’? Have you any idea, Miss, how much that
is? Why, I want you to love me as if I united in my single self
every quality that commands a woman’s most passionate; most
spontaneous, and most irrepressible love—as if I deserved every
thing your heart can give! That is one way of saying that I want
you to love me *blindly*; but we wont put it that way. This is better
—and equally true—: I want you to love me as much as you would
if I were as lovable as you are—and as lovely. I want you to love
me as you are loved by   Your own   Woodrow.

ALS (WC, NjP).
[1] Annie W. Howe to WW, April 17, 1885, ALS (WP, DLC).

From Ellen Louise Axson

My darling Woodrow,   New York April 19/85
   It occurs to me that I, in my turn, must lose no more time in
“talking a little about a subject in which we are naturally interested”! I really am at my wits end, dear, about it all,—in consequence, of course, of what you tell me of your father’s plans. It
seems *dreadful* to keep them waiting so long just for me, I can’t
bear to think of it. I feel as though I *must* not;—and yet it seems
impossible to help it, at least with all my thinking I have found
no way out of the difficulty so far, no arrangement which will
enable me to be ready before the twenty-fourth. You know that
when you first spoke of the last of June, that seemed to me im-

possible,—quite out of the question,—and it *is* a tight squeeze I assure you. That will give me barely three weeks at home. Being a man it is probable that you think three weeks more than time enough for *anything*! Perhaps I should make some little concession to masculine ignorance and explain more fully; there is a good deal of sewing which I really *must* do, I can't afford to have it all done for me; here in New York the materials for an inexpensive dress cost just *half* as much as the making of said dress, —and in Sav. it is almost as bad. It is positively ruinous to 'put out' anything but a handsome dress. So you see my predicament—one must have some time to prepare even the most modest "trousseau." And yet I feel that I *must*, "somehow or other," avoid keeping your parents waiting two weeks and over on me. I will puzzle over it a little longer and try to devise some scheme which will make it possible to push it forward to the 17th. By-the-way, do you propose to come back by steamer or rail? The former is a great deal cheaper, you know, and much more pleasant—*or* unpleasant as the case may be. I am, of course, going South in that way on account of the great difference in expense; I am more than sorry that I feel obliged to do so, for it will prevent my getting that little peep at you as I pass Balt. But what I began to say was that I think the steamers always leave Sav. on Saturday so that if you chose that route it would be necessary to decide on the twentieth —or twenty-seventh! I think I could arrange for the twentieth. Will your parents be in Columbia until they go to Sav. Will they go direct from there to N.Y.?—by steamer? Well darling I have explained sufficiently for the present. How I wish we could talk it over. Do you think you could find out, dear, exactly what you[r] parents wish, and I will use my best exertions to make my plans conform with their's, for their convenience is certainly of a great deal more consequence than mine. I can't tell you how *delighted* I am that your mother will be able to come too. I *need* not tell you how much more glad I will be to see her there than any of my own relatives who are not already on the spot. I had so hoped she could come yet feared at the same time that she would not, knowing that she was not fond of moving about. You don't *begin* to know how much I love them both, or what an unparalleled piece of good fortune I feel it to be for *me*, as well as *you*, that you should have such parents.

Yes, sweet-heart, I *do* think very often how rapidly we are drawing near to that sweet day for which *my* life too has waited. And because I think of it with no other feeling but deep peace and joy, I know by that sign that I am prepared in that one respect if no other to be a wife,—to be *your* wife. I *must* repeat these beautiful words of yours, my darling, for no others can express so exactly my heart's message to you;—it is *so* true that I never had an inspiring hope until this was given me, to make you happy, to prove to you by something infinitely better than words that I love you; that it is the crown of my womanhood, the meaning of my life that I am yours,—all yours. Ah, if you *can* be happy with me always, can remain as unreasonably satisfied and pleased with your little bargain as you are at present how little cause you will ever have to fear my being less happy!

With truest love to your dear parents and as much as you want for yourself I am forever   Your own   Eileen.

ALS (WC, NjP).

From Albert Shaw

My Dear Wilson: Minneapolis, Apr. 20. 1885.

I have not time to write a letter today, & this is merely to enclose a review of "Congressional Government" which I find in the Chicago *Daily News* of Saturday.[1] I think you will like to read it.

You ought certainly to feel some complacence over the recognition you are getting. Of course your friends are delighted.

In great haste   Yrs as ever—Albert Shaw

ALS (WP, DLC).
[1] Clipping from the *Chicago Daily News*, April 18, 1885 (WP, DLC), which Wilson sent to Ellen either in his letter of April 23 or of April 24, 1885.

To Ellen Louise Axson, with Enclosure

My own darling,   Balto., April 20/85

The enclosed letter is 'all of a piece,' so I wont try to tell its news in brief by extracts, but will send it entire to speak for itself. I am delighted, but I am not surprised. There was something in the odd impersonality, the unusual exclusion of everything but "matters in general," of the first letter he wrote me that made me suspect that something of this kind was behind. I *feared* that, the rival being somehow disposed of, his relations had been renewed with that very extraordinary young woman about whom I told you Shinn's story. I'm immensely pleased to find that I was mistaken and that things have taken just the turn they have. It strikes me as very strange, however, that a man of Shinn's make, who speaks so enthusiastically about other people in whom he is interested, should speak in so unimpassioned, so business-like a way of the woman with whom he is in love, concluding that he is "satisfied." There's a decided anticlimax in a man's saying that he is "perfectly satisfied" in such a case! Maybe, however, it's just an effort on his part to "keep his head" which has resulted in this rather featureless picture of Miss Fisher.

Yes, darling, I am indeed glad that you are to have cousin Lily within reach for a while and that her coming is to result in "lots of half holidays" for the shopping. I believe in half holidays: but I hope my little sweetheart will be careful not to wear herself out with *standing* in the stores. Is it *your* shopping, darling, or cousin Allie's, that you are to do? Maybe it's both.

I have secured another delightful Boston acquaintance, my pet, —or, rather *Cambridge* acquaintance: for Dr. Ross[1] is from the Harvard town. But his attraction consists in his opinions (about true methods of study, about literary art, &c) and I must not undertake to introduce him to you in a letter. I must wait for some time when I may have a quiet interview with you, when we shall be free from interruption and I can expatiate upon the views that claim my enthusiasm. Ah, how many thoughts and parts of thoughts, how many schemes and parts of schemes, how many fancies and parts of fancies, how many secrets that are partly of my mind and partly of my heart I shall have to confide to my darling little wife! I look forward to those conversations, and to all sorts of snatches of speech with her as I can imagine the trees looking forward to the spring time! Then all the possibilities of my mind and heart shall burst into bloom and fruit—and I will lay the fruit at my darling's feet as token of my homage for her wife's blessings to   Her own   Woodrow.

ALS (WC, NjP).
  [1] Denman Waldo Ross, Ph.D., of Harvard, who read a paper entitled "Study of History in Colleges and in Universities" to the Seminary of Historical and Political Science on April 17, 1885.

E N C L O S U R E

From Charles Howard Shinn

Dear Woodrow—   San Francisco, April 14th 1885
    I wrote you the other day about matters in general—now I write you, with a new gift & story—to you, beloved friend, and dearest of all my brothers . . . and you can tell Miss Axson, and no-one else. The past of which we spoke once a time is forgotten & wiped out —& I am actually a proof of some of your philosophy, the which I used to think rather hard. It happened yesterday—my engagement

I mean—and I don't just know as yet, exactly how it all came to pass except that I am perfectly satisfied. The young lady is Miss Lucy B. Fisher, New England & southern parentage. I used to know her when she was a little girl and our families have always been intimate, but she went away to school, and I had not seen her for ten years. She is twenty-one or two, quiet, gentle and as lady-like as possible. About high school education with a good deal of study at home since & lots of housekeeper faculty. I've seen a good deal of her this last few months in the most careful way—and it was a foregone conclusion for both of us. In social standing the family has no superior in the region, tho not at all wealthy. They belong to the literary & University circle, Berkeley Club & all that. We can't possibly be married until I get a good strong foothold, either east or west, in Journalism. . . .[1]

You may tell my dear little "sister Ellen," that Miss Fisher has studied art, water colors &c. for two years, and hopes to keep it up. And if you still think I've neglected *thee*, let this letter, written before, yes, actually before my own mother has been informed of the incident . . .[2] be my atonement.

Love to you.   Charlie.

P.S. omitted. ALS (WP, DLC).
    [1] Shinn's engagement proved to be short-lived. See C. H. Shinn to WW, July 18, 1885, ALS (WP, DLC).
    [2] Shinn's elision.

A Newspaper Article

[c. April 20, 1885]

Bryn Mawr College.

The opening of the College for Women at Bryn Mawr, Pa., next September, will be a sort of object lesson in modern educational ideas. It will be the most decided step yet taken in this country toward the higher education of women, and will therefore seem a notable consummation in the eyes of many people—an interesting and important experiment in the eyes of everybody. The freedom and range in choice of studies which are to be accorded the young women who attend the college are such as were not until very recent years offered to young men on this side of the water. A very cursory examination of the program, issued a few weeks ago, shows that the institution is meant to be for women what the Johns Hopkins University is for men.

This appears most conspicuously in the "group" arrangement of studies in the undergraduate courses. This group arrangement —which has worked admirably at the Johns Hopkins—may be called a device for reducing the elective principle to a system. It enables the student to choose very freely as to the main line of study to be pursued, and yet at the same time compels the choice of a harmonious, symmetrical combination of subjects. In most of our American colleges the elective principle, as a modification of the old-time hard and fast curriculum, allows at some stage of the student's four-year course a partial specialization in this, that, or the other branch of the required courses, or in some brief side course. The elective studies follow and supplement the predominant required studies. The idea of the "group system" is just the opposite of this. In it the required studies are subordinate to the elective. The latter are, so to say, permitted to set the pace, while the former enter only to make up "the field." The student may, for instance, select two languages, or a language and mathematics, or mathematics and physics, or physics and chemistry, or chemistry and biology, or history and political science, as chief, or "major" courses to which to devote most time and attention, in which to seek a special training; but there is a common ground of English and philosophy upon which all must meet; those who do not choose to give chief attention to a language must give some time to linguistic studies in a short required course; and those who give most of their time to history or to languages cannot exclude science altogether, but must take some branch of it as a "minor." In a word, each one is free to indulge a bent, but the requirements come in to fill out the special courses where they are too one-sided. Science must be let in to give stamina and largeness of view to the humanities, and the humanities must be let in to soften and brighten science.

These undergraduate courses lead to the degree of A. B., and are so grouped that that degree can be earned in the usual four years but no limit of time is prescribed, and special students are admitted who are applicants for no degree at all. In these particulars the Bryn Mawr College is not to differ essentially from others already established, but it is to differ very essentially from others in going beyond the degree of A. B., and offering facilities for post graduate studies leading to the degrees of M. A. and Ph. D. As a separate degree, the M. A. is to be open only to graduates of Bryn Mawr itself, who can earn it by one years's post graduate study at the college, but is to go with the Ph. D. as part of one, and the same degree, the M. A., which will be open not only to graduates of Bryn Mawr, but also to "graduates of other colleges who shall have satisfied the Faculty that the course of study for which they have received a degree is equivalent to that for which the degree of Bachelor of Arts is given at Bryn Mawr College, or who shall have attended such additional courses of lectures as may be prescribed." As a special inducement to graduate students, five fellowships are to be offered each year, one in History, one in English, one in Biology, one in Greek and one in Mathematics. "All candidates for the degree of Doctor of Philosophy and Master of Arts," says the program, "must pursue for three years, after having received their first degree, a course of liberal (non-professional) study at some college or university approved by the Faculty, and spend at least two of these years at Bryn Mawr College. They must be examined in two, and may at their discretion be examined in three subjects (the examination being of equal difficulty in either case); and must present a satisfactory dissertation on some topic included in their first or principal subject. They may be required to pursue certain auxiliary studies in connection with the subjects which they have elected; and the degree of Doctor of Philosophy, like that of Bachelor of Arts, will be given to no one who cannot read Latin, French and German, or who is wholly unacquainted with Greek. The dissertation must be printed. The degree of Doctor of Philosophy will in no case be conferred by the college as an honorary degree." Besides the resident fellowships, there is to be, in the course of time, so soon, that is, as the college has any graduates of its own, a "Bryn Mawr European Fellowship," which is to be conferred each year upon a graduate of the college, "on the ground of excellency in scholarship," in order that she may be enabled, by the aid of its allowance of $500, to pursue her studies for one year at some English or Continental university; her choice of a university being subject to the approval of the Faculty.

The village of Bryn Mawr, in which the college is situated, and from which it takes its name, is just ten miles northwest of Philadelphia, and is one of those comfortable, picturesque little suburban settlements for which the neighborhood of that city is celebrated. The college buildings stand back upon high ground with ample space about them, out of which lawns and tennis courts are in sure course of being evolved. The founder of the college, the late Mr. Joseph W. Taylor, of Burlington, N. J., had the work of building begun some years ago under his own supervision, but he did not live to see it completed, and the three buildings now erected have been finished under the direction of the trustees to whom he left the management of the fund of $800,000 which constitutes the endowment of the institution. One of these buildings, called Taylor Hall, contains the library, recitation rooms, etc. Merion Hall is a very complete and very modern dormitory, and the third building, the gymnasium, which is so large that one expects to find it a smaller dormitory at least, is doubtless one of the best fitted as well as one of the largest structures of the kind in the country. It is certainly the most elaborate and complete gymnasium that has yet been provided for women. It is to contain a full set of the apparatus which goes by the name of Dr. Sargent, of Harvard, and instruction in physical culture is to be given by a lady director who has taken Dr. Sargent's full course of training. The large hall which contains the apparatus has also a running or walking track for use in bad weather, and about this central hall there are grouped all the usual dressing and bath rooms which one expects nowadays to find in such buildings.

Altogether the material side of the equipment of the college is so attractive that the male visitor is almost inclined to wish that he might be a young woman long enough to enjoy a course of study amid such surroundings. It is natural to expect that Bryn Mawr will become a favorite winter resort for study as it has already become a much frequented summer resort for pleasure.

Among the most significant signs of the progressive nature of the institution is the composition of its Faculty, which is made up entirely of young men and young women, who have received either in this country or abroad—or, as in most cases, both in our own and in European colleges—the fullest instruction both in modern views of things, new and old, and in modern methods of education. Laboratory work is to go along with theoretical instruction in the sciences, and in all branches lectures are to supplement text-book drill, and individual investigation by the students themselves to be added to both. The prime object of the whole system is to direct and develop individual talent. The purpose is to substitute rational instruction for the old and now almost worn-out methods of dynamic, rule-of-thumb cramming, and everything done in this direction must, of course, be watched with the utmost interest and sympathy by everyone who is truly well affected toward educational reform.

Printed in the New York *Commercial Advertiser*, April 29, 1885.

From Gamaliel Bradford

My dear Sir: Cambridge Mass April 21, 1885

We reached home safely after a very pleasant trip, & I write to say how much we enjoyed our visit to Baltimore. My nephew Mr Clark desires me specially to present his regards, and to express his pleasure at meeting you. I wish also to correct an omission in taking leave, namely to beg that if you ever come this way, you will be sure to let me know as early as possible so that I may have the opportunity of contributing to the pleasure of your visit.

Very truly yours   Gaml. Bradford

ALS (WP, DLC) with WWhw notation on env.: "Ans. April 25/85."

From Addie C. Wildgoss

Mr. Wilson   Haverford College P.O. April 21st [1885]

Your polite letter of the 9th would have been answered earlier had I not been away from home at the time. The only two rooms in the cottage that connect, and are the very best, being on the S.E. side are those I spoke to you of at $20. pr. week. One of them would be furnished the other not, such furniture as you have going towards either. Fuel and light will be extra. The small room adjoining in connection (not communicating) with one of these large ones would be $18. pr. week, the fuel and light extra. The dimensions of the small room are 2 yds 34 in by 2 yds 16 in. That has a southern exposure.

These rooms are on the second floor. On the first floor under the two first mentioned rooms, is a long parlour, which will be divided by a curtain into a study and chamber. This will not be as desirable for you as the ones on the second floor. I think the house is calculated to accommodate not more than five professors. I should be glad to hear from you at an early date as I am in communication with others.

Very truly yours   A. C. Wildgoss

ALS (WP, DLC) with WWhw figures and notation on env.: "Ans. Apr. 27/85."

To Ellen Louise Axson

Balto., April 21, 1885

Well! my precious little sweetheart, I am thrown into an extraordinary, an almost droll, predicament by this sweet letter, this *precious* letter of yours about "fixing the day" (for every word which recognizes the unity of our affairs is precious to me)! I am as eager, as longingly and impatiently eager, as you can well imagine any one's being to have as early a day as possible chosen, and, since there is no sewing that I *can* do, but I must buy everything I need 'plain so' in making up *my* "trousseau" (!), every day of postponement will be for me simply a day of *waiting*, after my jobs here are finished. But I fully recognize the necessities of your preparation, and I just *wont have* you rush yourself to death and sew your fingers off and your eyes out for the sake of suiting either my wishes or the plans of the dear home-folks! I shouldn't have any right to say that I love you if I did not argue against my own ardent wishes in this matter. No doubt mother and father can wait till the 24th without *serious* inconvenience (and sister Annie wants to keep them "just as long as possible"); but even if they couldn't, *they* would not want you to sacrifice too much to their convenience, and it would be worse for you to hurt yourself hurrying than for us to miss having them with us in Savannah altogether. I should be willing to do a great deal to escape that sore disappointment, but neither they nor I would consent to have *you* run to death in order to escape it. Make all the haste you *can*, sweetheart,—not a bit more than you can make with perfect safety to your health and comfort—and I am quite sure that they can wait the day you set—even if it be the 24th. Of course I shall write them very fully about the whole matter, to-night, and tell you what *they* say, just as soon as they say it.

Don't it take less time and trouble, darling, to make straight skirts with perpendicular pleats, or like devices, and bodies of the same style, than to make flounced skirts with skewed over-skirts (you must let me use my own terms, however untechnical) and bodies with stiff necks? You know, as I confided to you "when we were only friends," I have very decided tastes in ladies' dress (else I would not dare to venture into this department of inquiry, where I don't know the language, and where it almost takes my breath away to be!) and I have—as I *didn't* say before—most positive convictions as to what best becomes the lady who is the first of all ladies in my eyes. I couldn't, if my life depended on it, give any clear and definite description of the costume I should like most to see you wear; but I know that for some reason the close-fitting, high-necked body of your black silk dress is not at all becoming to you, while the body of the black dress in which you came to Wilmington was *very* becoming, and you could not look sweeter than you do in such skirts—or, for that matter, in such costumes— as the 'mother hubbard' I used to ask you to put on last summer. Is it because you are best suited by square yokes, open necks, simple pleated skirts, and—but dear me! I must get out of this just as fast as I can! What temerity! You had better mind your own business, Wilson, and confine yourself to things you understand! Maybe you will go down to Savannah and offer to superintend—or even to *do*—the sewing! I know that you think that you could choose just the bonnet your sweetheart ought to have, but my private opinion is that you don't know what you are talking about—so you may shut up!

So you are going to Savannah by *steamer*, are you, my adventurous little lady? Do you know of any one else who is going on the same boat—or do you think yourself safe without escort? It frightens me a little bit, sweetheart. Those boats carry very few passengers and not always passengers of the most gentile sort— I had supposed. How is that—do you know?

As for our coming North by sea—that will bear thinking about. *You* can *practice*, Miss, on your way down, and will be able to say whether it will be pleasant or unpleasant for you; but *I* shall have no such preliminary training. I am morally certain that I should be very sea-sick—and you would not like your husband to be in that distressing condition during the first days of your intimate association with him, would you? Yes, there will have to be a very *great* difference of cost to justify that risk. The difference between *Baltimore* and Savannah is only about $3.00, I believe.

And so I am *not* to catch even a glimpse of you before that unknown day of June? Ah, sweetheart, even that glimpse of you (I could surely have managed to go as far as Washington with you) would have been exceedingly precious; but, after all, maybe it would be only tantalizing. It is much better to make *this* separation serve for all—to merge in it all the pain of being apart and not expose ourselves to the keen pang of another *parting*. At any rate that is the best philosophy I can devise for the occasion— and no man could have the face to be *blue*, whatever his disappointments, with such words as these of my darling's lying before him—these in which she declares the deep peace and joy of her expectation sure proof that she is prepared to be my wife! 'My wife'! Oh what sweet thoughts are in those two words! When Eileen is my wife she will know, perhaps, what love there is for her in the heart of   Her own   Woodrow.

ALS (WC, NjP).

Two Letters from Ellen Louise Axson

My darling Woodrow,   New York, April 21/85

I am afraid I shall have to give you tonight a very short and dull letter in return for those two precious ones received this morning. After my much tramping around today I found myself overcome with sleep tonight, the lounge was a temptation which I could not resist, and now I have just waked up at bedtime

sleepier than ever. I have been doing my—ah!—spring! shopping
today with Cousin Allie's assistance. It is a great piece of good
fortune that I have her to help me, for she is famous through all
the family connection for her *genius* for shopping. Indeed it
seems that she has gone into the business of shopping on commission; it is that which has brought her here. We have had a
comical time today,—have done nothing but quarrel; she wants
me to have everything so *dreadfully* "stylish," while I want them
"picturesque." I *hate* the word *stylish*,—am not surprised to hear
that in England "it is used only by the most vulgar."

By-the-way, I think I must tell you about a most ludicrous thing
that happened today—it is "too good to keep." I have been at my
wits end for a dress-maker who would consent to take into some
little consideration the fact that I am not a millionaire. So today
I appealed to Miss Case, the only one of my "chums" who lives in
the city. She knew of one but was not sure that she could be engaged. I told her she *must* get her for me, and finally, knowing
her to be trustworthy, I decided to enlist her more fully in my
service by telling her *why* I must have her. But imagine my
amazement when at the first hint I gave, this singular girl burst
into a passion of tears. She kept it up for half an hour declaring
repeatedly that it was "too perfectly dreadful!" &c. &c. She made
me laugh until I cried too. Of course I was anxious to discover
the nature of her objections, but she seemed unable to control
herself sufficiently to state them. At last she said there were more
than she could tell and I ought to know them,—in the first place
I was "too young to know my own mind"!! but at that I went off
into such convulsions that I lost my opportunity to hear the rest
of the objections. What a gay deceiver I am! All these people here
who hav'nt been told better have settled it that I am nineteen!
But did you ever hear of anything quite so "funny" as Miss Case's
behaviour. Whenever I think of it I have a "relapse"! This afternoon I got my "unlimited ticket" to the painting-class (you know
in every class the students are put on trial for one month;—and
sometimes for a good many more than one) I was quite beside
myself with delight, not having dared hope for it at *all*, and as I
went rushing down the hall to tell my "set," I met Miss Case; and
she, as soon as I had told her, began to cry again, saying, "what
do you want with *tickets*, pray? What good will it do you?" I
didn't expect anyone save perhaps Grandmother, to waste any
tears over *this* affair!

I "think" very well indeed, my darling, of the invitation which
that sweet sister of yours extends us. I shall be most happy to go

if you wish; it will be delightful to see them "all at one time." It is exceedingly kind in her to want all at once. And how charming that she too will go to Sav.

I can't tell you, darling, how happy I am to know that you feel so encouraged about your health. I have felt; in very truth, like a lark today chiefly on that account. Chiefly on that account!—yes—but I have so many causes of happiness that it would be difficult to classify them; to say which is first or second. But you say well, darling, the sweetest of all thoughts is that with the blessing of our God upon our love, we will not—cannot fail of the true marriage; and that if we truly strive to love and serve Him as we do each other, we may go to Him for blessing "as children to a Father able and willing to help us." Ah, dearest, I can never feel grateful enough that there is between us this blessed bond of sympathy on the greatest of all subjects. Believe me sweet-heart with all my life's love.   Your own   Eileen.

My darling Woodrow,   New York April 21/85
I am *very* glad to hear this good news from Mr. Shinn; to know that the past is forgotten and he is happy—if indeed he be happy. I must confess that I am *not* "perfectly satisfied" with his letter on the subject. In fact I read it with something like dismay; it is so unlike him to write in that cold-blooded fashion. I hope that New England streak which he has somewhere about him in spite of his poetry and his Bohemianism hasn't gotten the upper hand, and betrayed him, against his true nature into making a "suitable arrangement," merely. But it is very possible that the queer fellow thought it would be more—dignified—perhaps, to announce it coolly, and so has overdone it. We will hope for the best at any rate; and please give him my warmest congratulations and tell him I hope it won't be *very* long before I will have the pleasure of knowing "Lucy."

I am delighted to hear of the other pleasant Boston acquaintance, dear; it always give me *real* pleasure to hear of such episodes. They give a sort of variety to your life which I am sure will do you good.

But I *can't* make Antoinette stop talking to me, so I think I had better stop writing until she finishes, for I am getting more than a little mixed.

April 22nd
Have just finished reading your delightful letter of yesterday, dear. Would your feelings be deeply *hurt*! if you knew how I have

been laughing over it? You have Bible authority for not liking "stiff-necked" people but what *is* a stiff-necked "body"? I *believe* I catch the idea about the "skewed overskirts," thanks to your illustrations! I perceive that you, like myself, like picturesque dresses rather than stylish ones. I have a special weakness for plain skirts and "peasant" or "Mother Hubbard" bodices, but what would the city people or the Bryn Mawr people say if the professor's wife dressed always like a peasant? I am afraid you won't like my best dresses—that silk "body" for instance was considered a great success. But those that I make myself for summer or the house are to be simple and artistic and I hope you will like them; —though for that matter they are all to be simple enough,—perfectly quiet! Do you like my "surplice" waists for white dresses? but I forgot—you won't understand technical language!—they are such as I took to both our "*picnics*["]; a little low in the neck and crossed over after the fashion of a kerchief. And you didn't tell me what sort of hats you like! Pray write a full description of them! You do it *so* well! It will afford me such exquisite delight to read it! Really I think it *very* nice in you, dear, to take an interest in these things, and since I find you *have* some decided opinions about them I am more than anxious to have them. All suggestions thankfully received! Do you like little bonnets tied under the chin or broad-brimmed hats or "turbans" or "pokes"? And perhaps I had better take your opinion on the colour question. My relatives are almost at war over that. Allie and Lily with the dress-maker to back them say it is "perfectly preposterous" for a bride to wear black, while Grandmother and Aunt Ella with their Charleston ideas think it wouldn't "look well" to have anything else, even brown. What say you? They told me here that I *ought* to ask you about that; they didn't "believe you would like it at all["] for me to wear nothing but black. *I* prefered brown and greys for practical reasons—they will last me longer. But I have an engagement with Allie and *must* close in great haste; please excuse this dreadful scrawl. I have *so* much more to say! It is hard to wait until tonight. I love you, darling, as if I were born to do nothing else but love you. I am forever

Your own　Eileen.

Excuse mistakes haven't time to look this over.

ALS (WC, NjP).

To Ellen Louise Axson

My own darling,   Balto., April 22/85

I hope that you wont wear yourself out with your shopping. If these warm days take 'the starch' out of you as they do out of me —for I don't dare to risk wearing lighter clothing yet—a very little "tramping" will be as hard on you as four times as much would be in winter.

What an extraordinary creature Miss Case must be. That *was* an exceedingly ludicrous experience you had with her!—but there surely must be something behind it all—some secret of her own— to account for her behaviour! I can't conceive of any one's being *such* a—goose without some special cause or provocation! Did she refuse to engage the dress-maker for you in order to save you from your terrible fate?

There is a touch of poetic justice, Miss, in your being taken to be only nineteen: you *feel* so very old! I don't wonder a bit at the mistake, though; my darling don't look a bit more than nineteen. The idea of a young lady who is so well, so *glowing* with health that she can't get any one to believe her as old as she is, thinking of having herself tested to see if she was strong enough to get married! Do you know, sweetheart, that I find myself very much non-plussed when my friends who haven't seen you ask me 'what you are like'? I don't want to tell them that you have brown eyes, because I can't tell them how gloriously yours differ from *other* brown eyes; I don't want to say—and yet what other description will do?—that your lips look as if they were meant to be kissed—that is their secret *for me*! I wont show them what I have in my pocket-book in order that they may see the colour of your hair—and yet I can't describe it. I can't describe *you*—that's the long and short of the matter! I can *love* you—I can *love* the beautiful depths of your eyes that reflect so many treasures of love for me; I can love the sweet lips whose precious messages, given both in word and kiss, have made my heart throb with a delight such as no words can utter—such as nothing but a life-time of love-service can express; I can love the pretty silken hair—I can and do love *all* my darling's beauty: I love her very walk, her very gestures: I love her *voice*, her *self* and everything that *belongs* to that self—but how can I describe her to a stranger! He would *smile* were I to try to tell him about the image of her that is in my heart—I *couldn't* tell him of it without sacrilege: and yet that's the only true picture of her I have. Sweetheart, I love you with all my life's energy! To your love is entrusted everything that is best in   Your own   Woodrow.

ALS (WC, NjP).

From Ellen Louise Axson

New York, April 23/84 [1885]

How I hate, my darling, to be obliged to postpone writing until morning, when at best I am hurried and can't write half as much as I would, and at worst I can write but a line as now!!!! (postscript)[1] But sometimes it can't be helped. My! how hot it was yesterday, and how "collapsed" I was when night came! When Antoinette and I got back from prayer meeting I don't think either of us could have signed our name for a fortune. I had been shopping all day for Aunt Emmie [Hoyt] chiefly and the state of mind to which it had reduced me was pitiable. She wanted me to buy her fifty, or it would be more correct to say a hundred, dollars worth of goods for twenty-five; so you can imagine the situation, —trying to make a square foot of carpet cover two square feet of floor. Then this morning I was obliged to rush off and get them packed and expressed as soon as possible, she being in a desperate hurry for them; and the final consequence of that, with other interruptions, is that it is now after lunch and I am very much afraid your letter won't reach you at the usual time.

I am so sorely tempted to go South by rail for the sake of seeing you, that I mean to enquire as soon as possible about the difference of cost, and steal that precious "peep" if I can. I had an idea that there was a very *great* difference, and in that case I suppose I *ought* to go by steamer whatever I *want* to do. I don't think there can be any objection to the steamer; the Savannah people never *think* of going and coming in any other way; and you know the boats are simply superb in every respect so that they *must* be intended for people who are at least "genteel." Young girls come and go alone constantly; Eva. McNulty did so at Xmas. They say it is a particularly safe way for us to travel because the captains are always so nice and they act as your guardian. But I don't succeed as well as I could wish in making the sour grape mode of reasoning cover the case[.] I suppose it *is* much better to—make this separation serve for all, but—I'd rather not! I would chose the bliss of meeting even at the cost of another parting[.] It seems so strange that that last visit *was* the last, and I *didn't know it*; there is in my mind a little curious lingering regret about that which I cannot at all understand. But neither can *I* have the face to be blue whatever my disappointments.

I love you, my darling. I love you as one that unites in his single self every quality that commands a woman's most passionate, most spontaneous most devoted love,—for you *do*. My love *does* deserve everything my heart can give. The wonderful part of it all, my darling, as I have told you before is that you *should* so unite everything in your single self,—that your love should leave no part of me unsatisfied, repressed. I have seen some wonderfully thoughtful, considerate men like Charlie Gilbert; me[n] who surround one with a tender care, an *atmosphere* of love which gives a peculiar sweetness to a woman's life like that of a flower in the sunlight;—we might know right well that we were loved but if we did not *feel* it in that way there would [be] a great sense of loss; —such men I am sure win a very true, warm, grateful love. Then I have know[n] phenomenally good men like "the missionary" who would make it very easy to obey the Bible injunction which bids the wife reverence her husband. I have know[n] intellectual men—though none to compare with you—who would inspire a strong and loving pride and admiration. And I have seen one man in whom there was a power partly that of sympathy partly that of his own great love, partly something else indescribable,—I know not what—to *command* a woman's lifelong *devotion*, her perfect, heart-whole, passionate love; one for whom it would be a joy to dare all and bear all that life *could* bring[,] whom it is blessing beyond words to love and serve all the days of my life. But I never thought to meet one who combined in his person *all* those good things. I imagined they existed only in a school-girl's dreams. And yet I *have* met him and he is mine and I am forever

His own   Eileen.

ALS (WP, DLC).
1 She wrote "(postscript)" above the line in reference to the exclamation points.

From Charles Robert Hemphill

My dear Sir: Columbia, S. C., April 23, 1885.
Amid the many congratulations that you have doubtless received in recognition of the merits of your book, it may not be amiss to let you know that you are not without honor in your own country. Having been nourished on the *Nation* for ten or twelve years, I felt a strong appetite for your book, and read it with unceasing delight and instruction. You may feel confident you have

rendered a notable service to your country, and you have opened a vein that I trust you will continue to work.

Accept my thanks for what I have learned from you, and my best wishes for your success and happiness.

Sincerely yours,   C. R. Hemphill

ALS (WP, DLC) with WWhw notation on env.: "Ans. Apr. 25/85."

From Harold Godwin

The Commercial Advertiser
[New York]. April 23d 1885.

Dear Tommy

I am very much obliged for your prompt reply as to article on Bryn Mawr which came a day or two since. Will set it up tonight and use as soon as we can. Trust you are well & that we shall see you in the city of N. Y. again before long.

Ever affy   Harold Godwin

ALS (WP, DLC).

To Ellen Louise Axson

My own darling,   Balto., April 23/85

So I am to write another essay on the dress question? Well! You display a splendid temerity in asking me to do this: but I'll do it, whatever the cost—even at the risk of getting laughed at again and poked in the ribs with such sentences as "you do it *so* well! it will afford me such exquisite delight to read it!" There is such a thing as doing one's duty in spite of ridicule—and in this case of course the duty is plain! And I *have* devoted some study to the question. Since my experience in writing my last epistle on the subject revealed to me its inherent difficulties of treatment, I have made extensive observations of dresses and costumes during my afternoon walks, with a view to discovering some philosophical ground for my dislike of the pattern of your black silk "bodice" and for the preferences which I have avowed, without attempt at explanation, for certain other dresses of yours. I find that I do not like *any* close-fitting silk bodices. The material is so stiff that it gives, when so fitted, a *rigid, stayed* appearance to the figure—and the straight round of military collar with which such a fabric is usually crowned suits only persons of military fulness of bust, for whom a suggestion of *drill* is not out of place. Consequently what seems to be needed is relief of the stiffness by means of some perpendicular arrangement (how language does fail me in this great undertaking!) of some more pliant material in front, shirred, or something of that sort, at the throat and at the waist.

A *basque* form that goes below the waist and is reinforced with whalebones, or the like, is terrible to look upon. There is the real beauty that delights my eye only in those fabrics out of which bodices can be made which *suggest*, rather than severely outline, the figure—fabrics which lend themselves to soft folds kindly and which have a capacity for drapery in them. If I were framing fashion aphorisms, I should say, for one thing, however, that 'capes are hideous.'

I like 'surplice' waists very well, except that they have almost too *little* suggestion of the figure. I don't think that you need give a thought to what city or Bryn Mawr folks will say. I have noticed that people admire any costume that is becoming—and you can make your things becoming without going outside the fashions. I hope that you wont have anything unbecoming just because it is conventional!

I am afraid that I had better not say very much about colours —because I am conscious of holding very radical opinions about them. I *don't* like *too* much black, I confess; but neither does my taste approve altogether of browns and greys *for you*. Of course, since I have never seen you dressed in *any* colours, it is impossible for me to be sure of my own opinions in this matter. My imagination prompts me very strongly to the idea, however, that very deep blue or a rich marroon, purple or (for the heresy will out!) crimson, would suit you best. At any rate, I am quite sure that the colour of what you wear must have depth and body to it—must not be pale or undecided. I am sure, too, that I should like to see a touch of crimson or yellow at your throat.

And this brings me to the great bonnet-hat question,—for in the trimming of your hat, also, a dash of bright colour seems to me a consummation devoutly to be wished. Let me begin negatively: I do not like turbans very well; I do not like bonnets that tie under the chin at all. To turn to affirmatives, I do like broad-brimmed hats, on occasions—you looked as sweet as possible in the one trimmed with the feathery grasses—but my preference for you would be for, what I *suppose* is a "poke"—a bonnet which (how in the world shall I describe it!)—a bonnet which fits pretty snugly to the crown and sides of the head but which forms a slightly projecting frame for the upper part of your face, much as a lace "fascinator" or shawl would when thrown over your head from behind so that the point of one of its corners will lie almost touching the centre of your brow. The effect I have in mind (oh that I could *draw*!) is pretty much that of the upper front part of a *hood* such as you wore at your last *pose*, only with a little more of the projecting *poke* effect about the temples. Height of *crown* is an abomination—but a sort of "peek-aboo" effect for the upper part of the face is charming, for some faces.

Well! Miss, isn't that quite enough to mix you up completely—to mix you as much in idea as I've been mixed in description? I have the proud consciousness of having done my duty, however, no matter what confusions may result in the minds of those who cannot understand untechnical language! And you have only yourself to blame for this second dose.

Of course I am *much* interested in "these things"—I want my darling to look as pretty as possible. The sum of this letter is that she can't look prettier than in fabrics of rich colour simply made.

I didn't tell you, sweetheart, in my last letter (so full was I of your *self*) *my* delight at your 'unlimited ticket,' for wh.—(like the dear little goose that you are)—you didn't "dare" to hope. I am *so* glad, darling! I am so glad for all your successes, because I love you with all my heart and am altogether—and oh, so glad-ly—   Your own   Woodrow.

ALS (WC, NjP).

From Ellen Louise Axson

My darling Woodrow,   New York April 24/85

Once again things have gone wrong with me as regards the writing to you; I dined at Mrs. Seamans with the girls last night and didn't get back until late. Then this morning I had an engagement with the dressmaker—at half past nine, and was too lazy to write as I expected before I went,—was obliged to rush off immediately after "doing my chores" to make connection; so it is again after lunch.

I have just been shopping for a *bonnet*—so your letter came in good time, you see. I had told Cousin Allie before that I didn't want a bonnet, they were unbecoming, but she said I was beside myself. I *must* have it, &c. &c. and as she is *very* determined I at last yeilded. But this morning I told her I *wouldn't* have it, I was going to have a "poke"; and a battle royal ensued in which I came off conquerer; that is, I secured a mild form of poke which I hope will be pretty, but that remains to be seen; it seems impossible to get what one really wants. I must congratulate you, sir, you are progressing wonderfully in your new course of study! Who told you what "shirring" meant?—and you have learned all about basques now! Your ideas—always excepting those concerning col-our—are *very* good indeed, my dear, and as concerns both dresses

and hats they are mine exactly, which is fortunate, is it not? As
I understand, it is the material rather than the pattern to which
you object in the silk since both it and the other black were, of
course, made to fit as trimly as possible; a heavy silk *is* a stiff in-
artistic material. But for all the common sense in your letter we
were not cheated out of our laugh! Think of *me* in crimson or
purple! oh my! Do you take me for Rose Yeiser, sir? If you saw me
in purple you would speedily change your mind. I can wear no
colour brighter than golden brown and soft greys, dove colour or
fawn. I told Miss Farnesworth what you said and I thought she
would bring down the house with her expressions of amusement.
She told me a great rig-a-marole which she said I must write you;
I told her I would do nothing of the kind upon which she sprang
up declaring she would write it herself, and forthwith she scrib-
bled off the enclosed production. I had promised beforehand to
send it so send it I must.[1] What a case she is! I told you she was a
Western girl, you know, but 'not to hurt.' But this won't do. Time
is very precious today, for I want to start out again and finish up
this tiresome business once for all. So good-bye until tonight. I
love you, sweet-heart, more than tongue can tell, I am for life and
death,   Your own   Eileen.

ALS (WC, NjP).
  [1] Ellen forgot to enclose the note, but sent it with her subsequent letter, written that evening.

To Ellen Louise Axson

My own darling,   Balto., April 24/85
    I don't suppose that I *ought* to be anxious because no letter has
come from you this morning; but it is only the second time that it
has happened so since we have been writing daily—for this is Friday, not Monday—and I can't for the life of me help feeling sick
at heart. I depend on your daily letters not only for my heart's delight but as earnests of your welfare, and a tumult of ugly fears
and anxieties rush into my mind when they fail me. Your life is
already part of mine, through these letters, and were they to cease
now for any length of time I should feel like one bereaved! What
can have delayed my darling's letter to-day? But what a fool I am
to be torturing myself thus!—the afternoon's mail has not come
yet. 'My private opinion is, Wilson, that you are more desperately
in love than any other man I ever saw! Why can't you take things
more calmly, instead of always stretching your thoughts of your
lady-love to such a terrible, wearing tension?' 'Oh, go away with
your preaching, Alter Ego; I'd a thousand times rather be hotly,

passionately, restlessly in love than have your cold, critical disposition; and when one's in love with a little maiden like Eileen how can he help giving her his whole life with all its thoughts and energies—how can he *help* being so wrapt up in her that he forgets *himself* altogether and thinks only of her welfare, her happiness, her smallest interests? Don't demand impossible things of a fellow!' 'Oh yes, I know all that, and I make liberal allowances for a chap in your condition; but I think that you yourself will admit that you are not *helping* Eileen by being so anxious about her, and that there never was a little woman better equipped with that rare combination of independence and discretion which enables those who possess it to take care of themselves. Besides, she thinks about *you* now and then, and if anything serious were to happen, she would get some one else to write or telegraph to you, if she could do neither herself. Be as wildly in love as you please—I don't wonder that you *are* wildly in love with *her*—but be reasonable, be just a little sane, about it!' 'Thank you, Alt., you're as sage as ever—but your advice don't *work*, my dear fellow: it has a sad lack of practicability! So shut up, wont you?—and let me write my letter in peace.' 'All right:—but *don't* bother the dear little woman about the terrible consequences of this single failure to write to you!' 'Mind your own business! You're more provoking than any other likeable fellow I ever knew!'

I've been *trying* to write you a letter, sweetheart, for the last half hour or so, but have been so interrupted by a persistent roommate of mine, that I am only now able fairly to begin! First of all, I must propound a postponed question. Is it only 'if I wish' that you would like to go to Columbia for a few days after the wedding?—or would your own independent inclination prompt you to make the visit? This is the quandary I am in—and I have just made a frank statement of it to sister Annie.[1] I declined sister Marion's invitation[2] on the ground that, as *wise* newly-married folks, we had to be a bit selfish, and felt it best to go off somewhere where we could be practically alone together for a while, and so free to enjoy, and become familiar with, our new relation to each other without too much self-consciousness—and sister Marion is an excessively *sensitive* individual. If father and mother and 'Dode' are to be in Columbia *after* our wedding—or, for that matter, whether they are or not—it would be delightful, in spite of the embarrassment, *for me* to visit dear sister Annie (she knows that, and I quoted to her what *you* said about it) and we could go to Columbia—unless we return North by sea—without *any* of the additional expense that would be involved in going to

Arkansas (an imperative consideration, of course)—but I do not want to hurt sister M's feelings; I don't want you to make any visits which *you* would rather make some other time; and—well, we had better think about it for a while. Tell me *just* what *you* think, sweetheart, and *all* that you think. We shall probably be obliged to do nothing else *but* visit *next* summer, I suppose. Then, however, we can do it with exemplary dignity and mature equanimity.

Speaking of visiting reminds me that Mrs. Caldwell arrived this morning from New Orleans to be in Balto a few weeks (?) with her husband. The latter went over to Washington to meet her and returns a transformed man—as "chipper" as a sparrow, supernaturally vivacious for his usual taciturn self—at least, for the self he has suffered *us* to see.

Sweetheart, do you know that I wish with all my heart that I could write poetry—that familiar expression, 'with all my heart,' exactly weighs the wish, for it is for my heart's uses that I want the poetic faculty. I can't write songs to my Love in *prose*, and so all the wonderful song themes which her sweet love stirs in my heart must remain forever unsung, and there can be for me no forms of speech adequate for telling her of the delights which thrill me whenever she speaks the sligh[t]est word of love to me or addresses me with *any* term of endearment. Oh, darling, into what a new world your love has brought me! How that single, all-inclusive privilege of loving you with all his heart has enriched and glorified the life of   Your own   Woodrow.

ALS (WC, NjP).
 ¹ Wilson wrote in reply to Annie W. Howe to WW, April 17, 1885, ALS (WP, DLC) with WWhw notation on env.: "Ans. April 24/85."
² Extended in an unpublished portion of Marion W. Kennedy to WW, March 15, 1885.

From James E. Rhoads

My dear Friend,   Philadelphia. 4 mo. 24, 1885.
Thine of the 22nd. came duly. I will reply to it more fully soon. Meanwhile I send some essays of Clementine L Houghton & her note which accompanied them. Another lady has expressed a desire for the fellowship but I think that although she is fairly intelligent, she is not prepared for the position. She is a graduate of Wellesley. When done with the essays please return by express at my expense & oblige
                    truly thy friend   James E Rhoads

ALS (WP, DLC) with WWhw notation on env.: "Ans. Apr. 27/85."

From Ellen Louise Axson, with Enclosure

My darling Woodrow,   [New York, April 24, 1885]
    I hadn't time this morning to tell you about my novel experience yesterday. I went to Mrs. Hamiltons tea and found there a live Turkish nobleman! dressed in costume, who gave us a wonderful account of his own life, and of the manners and customs in his country. Indeed it was such a very steep talk that I was disposed to be incredulous, but Mrs. Hamilton and the rest consider him a saint and martyr, it seems he is a member of the Scotch church and they have known him for twenty years; so I presume I must believe it all. He is a native of Bethlehem; his father was governor of India; he became a Christian early in life and was imprisoned bastinadoed and finally exiled and disinherited on account of it. He was driven away with nothing save the clothes he wore—he had had an income of eighty thousand dollars. He wasn't even permitted to tell his wife and child goodbye, and he has never heard of them since. After that he was a missionary for some time in Egypt but now he is almost blind, and helpless; he teaches Arabic a little but he is chiefly supported by Mr. Peter Carter. Of course, he doesn't wear his native costume all the time but he put it on yesterday for our benefit. By the way he told us what his wedding dress cost, four thousand, I believe, it consisted chiefly of cashmere shawls and pearls; his wife's cost about twenty thousand. I forget what the wife herself cost, but I remember that his uncle paid about sixty thousand for one of his; she was a very handsome sixteen year-old Circassian. He, by-the-way, was seventeen when he married; he gave us a full account of the affair from beginning to end. His mother was also a Circassian; she was an Arminian in faith and in secret taught him her belief though outwardly she was obliged to conform to her husbands religion. He was a very strict Mohammedan. But though it is a good story I must not devote quite *all* my letter to it.
    I enclose Miss Farnesworth's remarkable note now; forgot it today. It occurs to me that you may think we were a little hard on you about the colours. But of *course* you understand that I didn't mean what I said,—I was only laughing. I know your idea is that dress should be "not expressed in fancy, *rich* not gaudy." Still I really think even rich colours are more suitable for people who are more or less Oriental in their style,—and you know I haven't a trace of that about me; they don't become a "little puritan[.]"

So you think there is "poetic justice" in my being *thought* young because I *feel* old? Oh, but I *don't* feel old except when I deliberately call to mind the fact that I am nearly twenty five; the rest of the time—except when I think too hard—I *feel* nineteen or less; —but I am a queer mixture you know, I am always either a little child or an old woman[,] *never* a "young lady" exactly, in feeling.

Have just received a letter from Stockton, from which the following is a extract—"Well, *isnt* Mr. Wilson's book making a stir? On all sides I see the most flattering notices of it. I happened to be on the committee for purchasing new books for our Library the other day. We got Dr. Hepburn and Prof. Martin[1] both to make lists for us; and on each list we found "Congressional Government" by Woodrow Wilson." So you see this prophet is not without [honor] in his own country. But I must close and write to Aunt Emmie.

That little letter which came yesterday, darling and which I hadn't time to answer last night was a very, very sweet one. Yet it is a pity that you can't be cured of that hallucination about my beauty (!) before it is too late. But I suppose that ["] what *can't* be cured must be endured." How unfortunate that I could never get up a severe headache for your benefit, in order that you might see how I *can* look;—what a perfect fright! But *you* would perhaps simply say that I did not look like *myself*! Such is your hopeless condition! I wonder whether our best or our worst self is our *real* self morally and physically. I have heard it said that no one ever knows either the best or worst of us. I have scarcely left myself one little corner in which to say 'I love you,' but my love knows it *so* well already! There is no *need* to tell him again how entirely I am   His own   Eileen.

ALS (WC, NjP).
  [1] The Rev. Dr. Andrew D. Hepburn, President of Davidson College; Col. William J. Martin, B.A., Professor of Chemistry at Davidson.

E N C L O S U R E

From Antoinette Farnsworth

Mr. Wilson,   New York City—Apr 24th 1885
    Our mutual interest in Nellie's new finery has induced me to write and try to persuade you that crimson, purple etc, would be entirely out of place on her. Do you want her to look like a walking kaleidoscope? A womans clothes should serve as the back ground to herself. With her sunny hair, brilliant eyes and rosy

cheeks, Nellie needs no other brightness than her own bright face. Everything else about her should be subdued. Some pictures need a warm back ground, *never* a brilliant one, so some people need warm colors but one dash of conflicting color, be it red, yellow or blue, on Nellie would be at open war with her face. Were it even a trifle too warm it would be rank heresy to her whole nature. Let her dress be harmonious; like her—soft and gentle, yet leaving the crowning point, the warmth, to herself. Hoping that my lame argument will have a little effect I am—

Sincerely your friend   Antoinette Farnsworth

ALS (WC, NjP).

From Lizzie R. Hawkins

Dear Sir   Bryn Mawr Pa Apr 24 [1885]

Yours of the 22nd was received, and in answer would say that we will accommodate you at the terms you mention including fire & light, and also with the two *back* rooms. But you could not have them before Oct as they are now rented up to that time, though as I told you, we could give you a room in the cottage till you could get them. The exposure of the rooms is East, South & West. The size of one is 14 ft. by 11 ft[,] the other, 14 ft. by 7 ft 8 inches[.] Three windows in one and two in the other.

Please let me hear from you as soon as you decide, as there have been others here from the Collage, for rooms.

Hoping for a favorable reply I am

Respectfully Yours   Miss Lizzie R Hawkins

ALS (WP, DLC) with WWhw notation on env.: "Ans. Apr. 27/85."

To Ellen Louise Axson

My own darling,   Balto., April 25, 1885

I went to our annual fraternity supper on Friday night,[1] and of course the feasting, toasting, singing, &c. continued till midnight—and, equally of course, I felt utterly good-for-nothing all day yesterday in consequence. I concluded, therefore, that you would hardly enjoy such a letter as I would write under the circumstances, and that I had better wait and say all that I had to say to-day. There's really no reason why I should ever make Saturday's letter separate from Sunday's, except that my heart is not satisfied without *daily* permission to send some message to you: for I am painfully conscious that all my letters to you are alike; no particular day has any special news or any special meaning that can be put into a letter; each letter simply repeats, with more or less variety of form and some range of stupidity, what all its predecessors have contained. My darling somehow manages to reflect her life in her letters; she has a woman's genius for finding news to tell and incidents to describe. I can do nothing of the kind: partly because my life is just now little else than a mere *mental* life, whose only incidents are thoughts and feelings, but principally because I don't know *how* to use in my letters the few things that do happen to me or around me. But what a fool I am to be talking thus, in direct conflict with my imperative determination to get rid of my morbid habit of thinking about myself, of examining and chastising my own short-comings and defects! You see, sweetheart, the truth is that I have not the same command of myself—the same repressive control of erring habits— when I am writing to you that I usually have at other times. When I sit down to write to you nowadays my heart is, as it were, opened wide. *All* its secrets, its sensitive pride, its morbid self-consciousness, both its strivings after things that are noble and worthy and its inclinations towards things that are unworthy, both its lights and its shadows, both its musics and its discords, as well as the love and loyalty, the admiration and passionate devotion which are specially yours—altogether and exclusively yours—*all* its secrets are yielded up to you—they *will* tell themselves *to you*—and with the rest there run out to you those of which I am a bit ashamed, the things which prove me little, petty, weak; small irritations, transient doubts and discontents which ought never to be spoken—ought, indeed, ignominiously to be driven out, suffered to speak not even to me, much less to you. If I can but write long enough, I can generally write myself *out* of a dark mood when I write to you, my sweet confessor, but I cannot for the life of me prevent the shadows of such a mood from getting into the first sentences. I should not like to tell you how often you have received a comparatively short letter because I had deliberately destroyed the four or five pages which I had written first, and which contained some such dark lines, and had begun afresh at the point where the brighter mood began! It was *too* bad to make *you* feel the influence of a passing cloud which would probably be superceded by abundant sunshine before the letter could reach you! I have most unreasonable, vagrant ups and downs, though I manage to conceal them from most persons—why should I reveal them to *you* whom I love with all my heart and whom I would *shield* from all distress! I *can* do it, surely; it must be only selfish self-indulgence that prompts me to worry you with my small ills. See how much kinder I was to other people on Friday night, for instance, at the supper! My heart has seldom been heavier, because all the day had gone by without bringing me a single line from you—my heart was fairly sobbing to itself: and yet I masqueraded as a merry fellow; I told droll anecdotes in mocking of my mood; I even made a jocose speech in response to a toast—a speech which "set the table in a roar"—I was voted a jolly companion! And, of all the toasts in the world, to give me 'The Ladies'! No wonder I was good for nothing all day yesterday and had to go to bed early last night—it would kill me to be a player for many nights together! By-the-way, sweetheart, *you* were toasted that night. "Congressional Government" brought *me* a toast, and as they were about to drink to my success at Bryn Mawr, friend Hiram got up and proposed to include the health of the one who was to go with me—and the double sentiment was drunk standing. It was as if Hiram had divined what things were in my secret thoughts. I wonder if he could guess how much my success depends on the love and sympathy, and upon the companionship of 'the one who is to go with me'?

I am glad, my pet, that you will follow your own tastes on the question of colours: I want you to follow your own taste in *every* matter of dress, and of course I gave my own ideas on the subject without any wish that you would regard them as in the least binding,—the second time, indeed, only because you asked me to. Miss Farnsworth has read the most vulgar tastes conceivable into the opinions I expressed—I must have made a greater botch than usual of expressing myself if she really thought I should like to see you dressed in flashy colours and gaudy stuffs. If I *had* thought that you could make a "Rose Yeiser" of yourself in the matter of dress, I should have wished to go blind before marrying you! I knew that my darling would interpret my meaning aright, as she *has* done, and that she would consult her own artistic preferences rather than my awkward guess-work. I was writing, indeed, under the full persuasion that you had already chosen all the dress goods you were going to buy; and I named the colours I did simply because I did not know the names of the shades I meant—and because I knew that if I said *pea-green* there would be no danger of your *getting* pea-green if it was not suitable. In a word, I knew that you would read *sense* into my words,—not the vulgarity with which Miss Farnsworth has credited me! But why trouble *you* with what is really an answer to *her*, when I have put all that I wish her to hear from me into the enclosed note?

I must turn to answer *you*, Miss, for there is a sad heresy in your last letter! It is to the effect that I know so well already that you love me that there is no need to tell me so again and again. There is no need to tell it *for proof*, but there *is* need—with which my heart keeps *me* constantly acquainted—that you should repeat the sweet truth *for the sake of my happiness*. The letters in wh. you dwell upon your love for me are my most precious possessions, darling! I go to them again and again, when my spirits burn low, to set my heart on fire with joy. Each fresh expression of your love seems to me to bear in its heart all the precious meaning of all the words of love that have come from my darling before! It is as if my heart were a harp which loves its mistress more for every touch she gives it. The nature of her love for me *frightens* me a little sometimes: it frightens me to find that she fancies me possessed of virtues and attractions which I am all too conscious of lacking; but at the same time it exalts me! If anything can make me worthy of your marvellous love, Eileen, my precious, inspiring little sweetheart, your sweet, unquestioning faith in me will do it: for it does fill my heart so full of the resolve and the hope to be everything that I should be to my pet, my life's queen, my wife. If anything can exalt my life to what it should be for your sake, surely your love can do so. It *has* exalted my life. The new meaning which it has given it is a meaning of good—of pure ambitions and of hopes wh. bless. Oh, darling, our wedding day is coming!—surely *then* I can tell you what love I give you in return!

What you say of the Savannah steamers somewhat reassures me upon the question of your going home by sea, but I can't help hoping that you will find that a land journey would not be so *very* much more expensive. At any rate, I wont conceal my delight in the fact that my darling longs as much as I do for the "precious peep" we should have of each other were she to go by rail. I want you to take the *safest*, easiest way of travelling, darling—and of course I appreciate your reasons for chosing the least expensive —and yet oh I *do* want *so* much to see you—if only for a moment! I feel very much as you do about not having *known* that my last visit to New York *was* my last—for I did not know it then any more than you did. I was hoping—though even then almost 'against hope'—that I could come again. But, sweetheart, think of the time when we shall be together for a 'visit' which will have no more real partings till death shall have come between us! Oh, sweetheart, I love you, *I love you*! and I live to prove as your husband that I am in all things   Your own   Woodrow.

ALS (WC, NjP).
    [1] Of the Phi Kappa Psi Fraternity, held at Guy's Hotel on April 24, 1885. The Baltimore *Sun*, April 25, 1885, noted only that "The occasion was enlivened by toasts and college songs" and went on to mention members present.

From James E. Rhoads

Dear Friend,   Philadelphia. 4 mo. 25. 1885.
    Thine came duly. Dr. Hopkins[1] has been here; he saw A. L. Wildgoss and found he could make better terms with Mrs. Hawkins, which he will do. A. L. Wildgoss also called today. She thinks she cannot furnish two rooms for less than $18 per. week for two persons & supply such a table, &c, as she feels necessary to comfort & health. I should be extremely sorry for thee to have to board in the city. It is very desirable that the Resident Professors be near the college. I learn that $15. per week is as low as two rooms & respectable board can be had for two persons in the city; & it would cost 40.8 cents a trip to Bryn Mawr by rail, or $2.04 a week. I think therefore that if thou can either with Mrs. Hawkins or A. L. Wildgoss get board—two rooms for two persons at $17. per week [—] it will be as cheap as in the city. This I think may be done. Try Mrs. Hawkins when on in June to the Examinations. History comes on the 25th, and we will pay thy expenses on & while at the College. These will be held at Merion Hall, & thou can lodge at the Hotel.
                          Thine very truly,   James E Rhoads

ALS (WP, DLC) with WWhw notation on env.: "Ans. Apr. 27/85."
    [1] Edward Washburn Hopkins, Ph.D., Associate Professor of Greek, Sanskrit, and Comparative Philology at Bryn Mawr.

From Ellen Louise Axson

My darling Woodrow,   New York April 26/85
    It seems to me that the Western people are treating you especially well. This review from Chicago is *very* good and appreciative; is it not? The writer seems actually capable of appreciating not only your ideas but your manner of expressing them.
    I am reminded that my acknowledgment of the Bryn Mawr catalogue was crowded out. I was, of course, much interested in it; truly they have a masculine standard "sure enough." Oh dear me! what a little goose I am! This brings it home to me afresh. I think I had better go to school there!—only I couldn't get in. By-the-way I was quite amused to find that "Sesame and Lilies" was included in their course of study![1] What have they to do with such a book as that! As you said the other day, a'propos of an

extract from that very book, it would be difficult to construct a
Bryn Mawr programme in harmony with those ideas.

I am so sorry, dear, that you were made anxious about me by
the failure of my letter to reach you. It seemed unavoidable but
it shan't happen again;—I don't think it shall at least.

A few words about the visit to Columbia, and then I must close
for the present. I hav'nt the slightest objection to going, dear;
indeed I am sure I should enjoy it. Of course it is impossible to
avoid feeling some little apprehension about it; but I know from
experience that such things never are as embarrassing when you
come to the point as you imagined they would be beforehand;
because then you sit down alone and think about yourself and
how you will feel and behave; but when the time comes you *cannot* think about yourself; because there is always something so
much more interesting to occupy your attention; and things seem
to move on quite naturally.

I don't think there would be any trouble about your sister Marion's *feelings*; she must see what a great difference there is between going half across the continent and stopping a few days
on our direct route to the north. So decide the matter, dear, just
in the way that will be most agreeable to you, and I will be equally
pleased whatever you do. But the dinner bell has already rung
and I must close abruptly. I love you, my darling, truly, tenderly,
passionately,—I am forever   Your own Eileen.

ALS (WC, NjP).
  1 Ellen referred to a statement in the *Bryn Mawr College Program*, *1885-86*,
p. 8, to the effect that candidates for matriculation in the English Department
should be familiar with Ruskin's *Sesame and Lilies: Two Lectures*, among other
works.

To Ellen Louise Axson

My own darling,   Balto., April 27/85
  I have been forgetting to tell you that Mrs. Caldwell brought
direct news of your uncle Randolph. He was in New Orleans
when she left, the week's stay his ticket allowed him being then
about half over. Mrs. C. told this news at the dinner table, adding
that she often told Dr. Caldwell that she had 'taken a fancy to
him' first of all because he looked enough like "cousin Randolph"
to remind her of him.(!) Dr. C. seemed to enjoy the reminiscence
very much!

  Sweetheart, I shall agree with you, that you are a "little goose,"
if you bemoan the fact that you don't know as much as the Bryn
Mawr girls are expected to know! What do you think of *my* case?

I am to be one of their instructors, and yet I not only could not pass the entrance examinations without special preparation, but could not even be an advanced student, much less a Fellow, in my own department—because I can't read German at sight! But that by no means indicates that I am not infinitely better educated than my pupils will be. Both you and I have what is immeasurably better than the *information* which is all that would be needed for passing Bryn Mawr, or any other college, examinations! We have the power to think, to *use* information. For my part I want to have to carry as little *information* in my head as possible—just as (to use some one else's illustration) I want to forget the figures in the column whose *sum* and *result* I have ascertained and want to keep. I must *scan* information, must question it closely as to every essential detail, in order that I may extract its meaning; but, the meaning once mastered, the information is lumber. It is enough if I know where to find it, for corroboration, for illustration, &c. Of course one *can't* make himself familiar with facts for such a purpose without remembering some of the more essential of them: but it is sheer, barren, ignorant waste of energy to try to remember a fact *for its own sake*. It is like eating for the sake of eating. If you mean, Miss, to get into sympathy with my mental processes, you must learn not to feel at all disturbed about the small amount you 'know.' Be glad, rather, that you are *past* that—that drill, that *exercise* at digestion, that preparation for the period when memory's *burdens* can be —and should be—thrown off, and the mind be brought into the glorious liberty of *choosing* what it shall know—the liberty of exchanging plethora for *health*! But more of this anon—I cannot write more to-day

I love you, darling, my true, my precious, my peerless little sweetheart!   Your own   Woodrow.

ALS (WC, NjP).

Two Letters from Ellen Louise Axson

My darling Woodrow,   New York April 27/84 [1885]

Antoinette has gone into the business of letter-writing tonight and I must make haste to take advantage of the unusual quiet to do the same. I have hard times trying to write now-adays, for that charming young person *won't* or I should say *can't* keep silent five minutes; and I don't like to write after she has gone to bed because the light keeps her awake. She is perpetually trying to get up an argument with me; I never saw a girl so fond of that amusement. She has been trying to engage me all day on the simple subjects of "fate, free-will, foreknowledge absolute"! but I politely waive such topics as that. I think that for most people and on most occasions, nothing could be more unprofitable than such discussions. But her favourite subject of controversy—next to the "life class" of course, is "woman—her duty and destiny"! *She* is an "incorrigible northerner." I have positively refused ever to be drawn into the subject again. But she is an odd mixture—the other day some expression of my views made her turn from me apparently in deep disgust, saying that I was too much in love to have any sense at all. But after a long silence she suddenly put her arms around me, kissed me tenderly, saying very softly: "you little wife! you *are* already one in heart."

Did you ever see anyone to equal Cousin Allie? She as coolly as possible told all those people at Mrs. Seaman's that I was to be married in June! Says she thinks it perfectly absurd to mind when it is so near;—as if one wouldn't mind all the more because it *is* near! But it seems she did it in the first place from "a sense of duty" to Mr. Clapperton! He is a very nice Englishman who is, in a small way, an admirer of mine. He happened to ask her incidentally if she knew me; "yes" said Allie, "she is my cousin"; then he began to rave, as the manner of man is, but in a way that has disappointed me in him, for I thought him remarkably sensible. He "heard her voice ringing in his ears, hovering (!) about him all day long"; it was "the most wonderful voice" he ever heard! &c. &c. (Isn't that too good to keep? Of all the absurd things people say, nothing strikes me as so exquisitely ludicrous as their selecting my *voice* for praise,—a voice which isn't equal to "Yankee Doodle." Did you know that according to another young man I have a wonderfully soft cooing (!) voice?

But to finish my tale;—"Yes!" said Allie, ["] she and I are very busy at present selecting her trousseau." "The dickens, you are! Why[,] is it a sudden thing." "Oh, no, she has been engaged *two* or *three* years[.]" "Then I should like to know what business she had coming to New York,—or to this house! Why did she want to waste her time studying so hard? Where was the good &c.["] And so the murder's out; and as there is a League girl boarding there I suppose the whole crowd will know it soon. But I presume it will be all the same a year hence—or two months hence.

Cousin Allie has been telling me her troubles. She is really separated from her husband. Such a miserable story as it is! He turned out dreadfully in every respect, treated her, as well as others very badly,—actually tried to kill her twice. Just before he went away he put a pistol to her head saying that he "might as well do it then as anytime." And she didn't move an inch, but told him she would be rather glad if she [sic] did; and she looked at him so calmly and steadily that the madman dropped his arm and crept away. But I won't begin on the story. I like Allie better than I ever did before, I think she has improved. She *has* a great many faults of the sort that are least to my taste, but she has some singularly fine qualities too.

So my darling wishes that he could write me love songs! I wonder if he wishes it as much as I long sometimes to sing them! I certainly wish that "with all my heart," for I am sure that nothing else would give that heart *such* relief as to be able to express in that way its overflowing love and joy. "Oh life and love, oh happy throng of thoughts whose only speech is song." If that be the only speech for such thoughts, then I must remain speechless, which is of course a deep affliction!

I love you, I love you darling, if it makes you glad to hear such words, your own heart can tell you with what joy I, in my turn read them. I am *very* glad, dear, that you did not turn out to be as undemonstrative as I once supposed you. I shall be a much happier little woman because of it. Though I should have loved you well in any case, there would have been a great deal of repression about it—would there not? Some of the strongest needs of my nature would have remained unsatisfied; and I *never could* have let you know how much I love you. Ah sweetheart, I wonder if you know even yet how much that is. As ever

Your own   Eileen

My darling Woodrow,   New York April 28/85

I have just received *such* a kind letter from your sister Marion which I must enclose for you to read. Is'nt it sweet in her to speak so of our marriage. I can't tell you with what a full heart I read such messages. They are all *so* good to me. How wonderfully fortunate I am to have gained their love; how miserable I should be without it!

Oh dear! how sorry I am that your pleasure at the supper should have been so marred by that unfortunate mishap about the letter. *Nothing* shall be a sufficient cause for such a delay again if it is to have such consequences; but I will accuse you, my dear, of loving "not wisely but too well" if you take it so "hard" as that. You may be very sure, sweetheart, that I will let you know at once if all is not well with me. Ah well! I am not selfish enough to be

anything but sorry that you were so disturbed, yet it is sweet to
know that there is one who cares so much,—and I think it is
doubly sweet to an orphan girl. How shall I say how sweet it is to
know that it is *you* and no other who cares! My dear, if there
was "sad heresy" in my letter how shall I describe the enormity
of that in yours; that is to say of your conduct in deliberately
destroying letters to me because they *truly* reflected your mood.
There is nothing which I prize so much in your letters as the feeling which promps such confessions, because nothing else could
give such clear proof of your confidence in my entire love and
sympathy. That perfect confidence is the most blessed privilege of
our present relation. However closely our hands are clasped if we
deny that to each other we must ever be "strangers still." Did you
never say anything of that sort to me, sir? Out of your own mouth
I will condemn you if you take the position that it is "selfish indulgence" to "worry" me with your "small ills." My darling knows
that my one great wish now is to give him that perfect helpful
sympathy which is impossible without a *full understanding* of
him; and how can I attain to that if he shows me but one side of
himself, or if he keeps from me any of his "moods"[?] So remember darling that you will "indulge" *me* by telling me *all* that is in
your mind;—especially since the inclination you feel to do so
proves that it would be for your own hearts ease.

I feel highly honoured to have had my health drunk in such an
august company as that of Friday night. But was it not calculated
to embarrass you? However I suppose "friend Hiram" knew what
he was about.

I am glad that Mrs. ~~Anderson~~[1] Caldwell has come to bring her
husband good cheer; how do you like her? She is a sort of cousin
of mine you know.[2] I have never seen her however and I don't
suppose she is aware of *my* existence.

I assure you Miss F. did not mean to read a "vulgar" taste into
your opinions. We both knew that you meant only deep rich colours, which certainly have nothing of that sort about them; they
are the *royal* colours. She wrote the note altogether as a joke; but
I thought when I read it that it was a failure in that respect;
it's tone was too grave. I think her slight awe of you got the better
of her merry insertions, and yet she would not give up her scheme.
And so her production took the *form* of a jest but lost its spirit.

Yes I had bought all my materials before your letter came, and
even were they becoming I could not have gone directly out of
black into *decided* colours, without outraging the feelings of my

Sav. friends more than I dared. Some of these days I will see how you fancy a crimson wrapper for winter!

Where *am* I going to sign my name on this epistle? *Believe* me darling as ever

Yours most lovingly and faithfully   Eileen

ALS (WC, NjP). Enc. in second letter: Marion W. Kennedy to ELA, April 21, 1885, ALS (WP, DLC).

¹ For Wilson's comment on Ellen's crossing out, see WW to ELA, April 29, 1885.

² Mrs. Caldwell's grandfather, Edward Palmer, and Ellen's great-grandmother, Sarah A. Palmer, were brother and sister. Hence Ellen and Mrs. Caldwell were second cousins once removed.

To Ellen Louise Axson

My own darling,   Balto., April 28, '85

What a blessed little charmer you are! The idea of your longing to sing because without song you can't speak your love! Why, sweetheart, the simplest of your words of love—even of these *written* words which lack the charm of my darling's sweet voice and the emphasis of her tender eyes—seem to *me* as satisfying as any song you could sing. I don't wonder that you want, for *your own* delight to be able to have such an outlet for your thoughts of love and joy; but you need not wish such powers for my sake, precious. I would rather hear you say 'I love you' than hear the most glorious song ever sung! You have that way of keeping my *heart* full of music, if you *haven't* any way of filling my *ears* with music: and if, whenever, in the sweet future, you feel as if you would like to sing of the love and happiness that are in your heart, you will come to me—whatever I may be doing—and tell me as much, or as little, of your thoughts as you can, looking with your own wonderful eyes into my eyes, I promise you that you shall receive instant proof that you have done more for my delight than you can ever do by singing. And it shall be the reigning thought of my life to be such a husband to my peerless little wife that she shall *often* have such impulses—that she shall not lack for thoughts of love and happiness such as she would sing, 'an she could, for lack of being loved tenderly, devotedly, absorbingly!

And what a dear little ignoramus you are about yourself! If you were not, you certainly couldn't wonder at people who praise your voice. See what Shinn says in the letter I enclose—and it's true, every word of it! This is the letter Shinn wrote just after meeting you for the first time, last October. I believe I quoted some sentences to you from it at the time. I didn't send the whole of it to you then because—shall I confess it?—because I was a little bit *jealous* that another man should so admire you—should "rave" over you so nearly as if he had himself fallen in love with you. The feeling is one I do not pretend to be able to explain or justify—though I have several times *tried* to explain it to you. I have only to confess it, and be ashamed of it.

I cannot refrain from smiling, sweetheart, whenever you recall your early impression, that I was undemonstrative: it seems to me such an *impossible* thought, that I could *help* being demonstrative towards you—that my love for you could by any means be kept from showing itself in everything I do in your presence! The truth of the matter is that you do not yet know how much *less* demonstrative I am in my love for you than I feel constantly impelled to be. Does that frighten you? It need not: for I shall never tell my darling more than she wants to hear or caress her until she tires of my caresses—shall never show her more of myself than she wants to see. But my words and actions can never exaggerate—can never fully express—the ardour and transport of my affection for my precious Eileen, my joy and pride!

That was a *very* sweet thing that you report of "Antoinette"— her coming a[nd] kissing you for your wife's feelings—and it serves to confirm my liking for her. I don't wonder, though, that you decline the extraordinary controversies to which she challenges you. I should assuredly do the same: for there's no possible profit in them.

What a sad, sad story this is of your cousin Allie's separation from her husband! It is not wonderful—because it is common— for a man to be desperately wicked; but how *can* a *man* be *despicably* wicked: how can he be so mean, so low a *coward*! I believe that I can understand a man's being driven into desperate things by an exasperating woman—a silly rattle-pate, a sullen virago, an icy prude, any woman whose disposition denied or disgraced her sex—but that he should ever attempt the cowardly purpose of doing her personal violence is simply inconceivable! And of course your cousin's case stands a world's distance from any I have suggested. Even if she *was* worldly and frivolous, without the noblest part of a true woman's earnestness, *that* could not offend such a creature as he seems to have been! It makes me ashamed of my sex to hear such histories of marriage.

Well "cousin Allie" did 'do herself proud' in the Clapperton and Seamans case! I am sorry, pet, if it caused you annoyance; but that conversation of hers with Mr. C. would have been spoiled, ruined, without that delightful dramatic turn in it at the word 'trousseau,' whereas *with* that turn what an excellent story it makes! Mr. C. *does* seem to have been *quite* an admirer of yours "in a small way." 'What business had you going to New York or to that house'! Phew!—what *sublime* 'cheek'!

I think that your *last* remarks on the subject, darling, about settle it that we will stop over a few days with sister Annie—it will be such a delight to her, and I'm sure it will be a very great pleasure to me—if my darling little bride will enjoy it. Oh, Eileen, how my heart beats to think of that time—how full of sacred delight is the thought that you will be my wife—will have given yourself to me in sacred trust. And oh, how I shall strive to prove worthy of the trust! with what joy shall I repay love with love till you *know* that I am   Your own   Woodrow.

ALS (WC, NjP). Enc.: C. H. Shinn to WW, 11 p.m., Oct. 25, 1884, ALS (WP, DLC).

From Ellen Louise Axson

My darling Woodrow,   New York April 28/85.
What a delightfully consoling letter is this of the morning! Please accept my most sincere thanks for it, sir. I have such profound respect for your opinion that I must perforce accept your judgment in this case, however surprising the conclusion to which it leads me. When you have, now and again, expressed a very charitable opinion of my mental powers and acquirements, I have thought,—"oh but you *could* not think *that* if you had any idea how ignorant I am!" But now I learn from the best authority that I am "not to feel at all disturbed about the small amount I know";—that the matter of real importance is something very different from that. But then I am so *painfully* ignorant; and I fear I never had "the preparation for the period when memory's burdens can be thrown off."

Ah me! how much I was going to do in the way of self-education when I left school and how little,—or nothing—I ever did! But my daily duties were always so many and so pressing that self-culture seemed little more than self-indulgence, and my craving for it merely created a necessity for rigorous self-denial. You would have a good laugh at my expense, I suspect, if you knew how much political economy and constitutional history I was "going to" read after our engagement in order to be more of a "companion" for you! And, of course, I hav'nt read a word; for never in all my busy life have I had so little time for reading as in these particular eighteen months. I have had indeed, absolutely *none* for serious consecutive reading. You had better make up your mind, dear, once for all, to avoid future disappointments, that you are going to marry a little girl who is'nt in *any* sense *educated*; one who has everything to learn from you, as your mother says she learned "everything" from her husband. I hav'nt forgotten that, you see! it was such a great comfort to me. I daresay I have as bright a mind to begin with as the average girl, and I have a very intense appreciation for some good things;—I suppose, of course, there are others, equally good, which I don't understand or appreciate at all. I don't believe I even have as great a thirst for knowledge as I once had!—for then I wanted to know *everything* (!) but now I am so discouraged, that I fancy I should be almost content if I could read and write,—and talk,—and, of course, understood something of *history* and *political economy*!! But it grows late and I must curtail my letter tonight. I love you, my darling, my true, my peerless sweetheart, I am with all my heart,   Your own,   Eileen.

ALS (WC, NjP).

From Addie C. Wildgoss

Mr. Wilson   Haverford College P. O. April 29th [1885]
  Yours of the 27th was received last evening. In engaging the Bryn Mawr cottage, I was lead by all circumstances to suppose that the best rooms would bring $10. pr week, and made my calculations accordingly, and this must explain my asking higher at first and dropping in price.
  The two only communicating rooms seem to suit your purpose better than any others, and if $20. pr week including furniture fuel (furnace) & light is still too high for you, I must ask you to let me hear again from you before making other arrangements. The long parlor on the first floor immediately under these two rooms, would have to be curtained off. That you can have inclusive of furniture, fuel and light at $18. pr. week. Hoping to hear from you immediately, as others are dependent on the result.
I am   Very Sincerely Yours   A. C. Wildgoss

ALS (WP, DLC) with WWhw notation on env.: "Ans. Apr. 30/85."

From Thomas A. Morris

Dear Sir: Arden, N. C. April 29th 1885
  Your letter of the 25th recd. We should be glad to have you and your wife with us this summer & can give you a nice double room for $80. per month, provided you take it from the 1st of

July. We have several new cottages added to the Hotel & have every reason to believe our rooms will be filled as we had many more applications last year than we could accomodate. Hoping to hear from you soon and with kind regards from us all,

I am, Yours respectfully   Thos. A. Morris.   (per S.)

HwL (WP, DLC) with WWhw notation on env.: "Ans. May 5/85."

To Ellen Louise Axson

Balto., April 29, 1885

Eileen, my sweetheart, wont you tell me what was the *matter* when you were writing your letter on Monday night?[1] *Something* must have affected my darling's spirits: for, in spite of its sweet, loving words, the letter was so *sad*. It made me feel as I felt that morning at home, last September, when you received news of Mrs. Killough's desperate illness[2] and would not take any breakfast, but went to your room to be alone with your sorrow. I thought my heart would break that morning, because I felt that I was of no *use* to you; that you could not come to me when you most needed sympathy and comfort, but must wring your heart in silence; that there were times when you must be separated even from me. There was a point at which my love had failed you! Had I, then, failed to do for you the very thing that you most needed? Was my love to fall short in the very thing which it had been sent to accomplish, the opening of my darling's heart to full communion and sympathy? Your disposition is very different from mine, you know, sweetheart. My impulse is to tell *every*thing, even the trivial ills of my experience, to the one I love—to make my mind an open book to her. But your life has been one of self-withdrawal—one long effort to wear smiles for those you have loved and keep your tears for yourself alone. You have, as I know from your own lips, schooled yourself in self-repression, for the sake of others—and because you thought so to command your sorrows. It was only the other day that you were wondering if you would ever learn to bear the ills that affected *me* with the same 'philosophy' which you had compelled yourself to practice with reference to your own. I pray God you never may! It shall be my life-long effort to convert you to a different philosophy with regard to *yourself*: that to keep sorrow kills, while to *share* it, with those whose love makes them capable of sharing it indeed, is to change it from a poison into a blessing. I never felt more joyfully grateful, darling, than I did when I received your letter about dear Stockton's sickness; for it admitted me to your sorrow: and

I shall never feel that you have really accepted my love in its fullness until you have learned to cry in my arms! Is it anything this
time, sweetheart; or am I only imagining? Has bad news come
from Suwanee (you wrote 'Mrs. [H. M.] Anderson' when you
meant Mrs. Caldwell, in this letter)?

Of course you see that what I have been writing, though meant
to be only a lover's heart-plea to you, is also a condemnation of
myself for the very thing for which you so sweetly and gently
take me to task in this letter of yours which has been my text.
I *was* wrong, my pet, in destroying those letters which reflected
my heavier moods—though they were not essentially different
from many others which I have sent you—and I wont do so any
more. My idea was that my moods were so momentary, passing
away in the very act of writing, that it was not right to perpetuate them. Of course I should never have dreamed of keeping from
you any real distress; but to colour my sentences with a transient
humour seemed weak. To wait for a brighter moment brought
me quite as much heart's-ease, and would take sweeter thoughts
to my darling

And I fancy that my letters often misrepresent me. They are
grave when I am gay; their sentences seem almost like stern
rebukes when the feeling that prompted them was one of overflowing tenderness; they prose when my heart is full of the most
passionate sentiment. Oh, what an unspeakable joy it is that they
will not much longer stand between me and my Love! The time
is almost at hand when my precious little sweetheart shall see my
love face to face—and when I shall be able (shall I not, my Eileen?) to coax every secret of her heart from either her lips or
her eyes! Darling! you have already given me the best proof possible of your wonderful love for me—for you have already learned
to tell me *much* that is in your heart—much more than you would
tell anyone else—and all that I meant just now was that you had
not learned to tell me *all*. Oh, how I hope that in the days to come
my love can make it an *easy* lesson for you to learn!

What a wonderful month June is, Eileen! It is not yet *May*, but
through all the weeks that separate us from it June is making
my spirits merrier than its own sunshine! No, it's not *June* that is
doing this—June comes every year!—it's not even *this* June which
for joy has never had a predecessor—it is my darling herself who
is bringing me this glorious happiness that is stealing so sweetly
upon me! June will be the *first* month crowned with this new joy;
but the same crown will rest upon the months that follow, and it
will grow brighter for the wearing! June after June will see the

joy of that first June grown sweeter and sacreder: for the wonders of this love that is between me and my Eileen cannot but grow as it receives time's sanction and life's proof! I have never yet *begun* to tell you, precious, what the wonders of that love have already been in my heart. I have had a happy life—no man's life was ever richer with blessings—but I never knew the *meaning* of happiness until my darling loved me! Did you know what wonders you were working for one man in the world when you came into the life of   Your own   Woodrow?

ALS (WC, NjP).
    1 Actually, Ellen dated the letter April 28, which was a Tuesday.
    2 While Ellen was visiting the Wilsons in Wilmington. Helen Porter Killough died in November 1884 after a lengthy illness. See ELA to WW, Nov. 13, 1884, Vol. 3.

From Ellen Louise Axson

My darling Woodrow,   New York, April 30/85.
    We went last night to the closing exercises of the Metropolitan school and returned rather too late for letter-writing. The programme consisted of an exhibition of the year's work, a very surprising speech from Mr. Stimson, the delivery of prizes, and a vast deal of leave-taking. You have heard of the famous $100.00 prize, about which they have been so "exercised," and for which Mr. S. managed so cleverly to exclude the League girls from competing. Another fifty dollar prize was also offered for the second best drawing, and we are very indignant because it was given to "the Bowery-boy" instead of to our favourite "4½"! I think it ought really to have been offered for the greatest improvement and then Antoinette herself would have gotten it without doubt. She has really done wonderfully, for she was a mere beginner when she came, and yet her drawing was almost as good as the best. Then our "sculptor," young Conkling who models so exquisitely was given a "prize" on the spur of the moment by one of the company;—we are all so interested in his future;—and isn't it delightful?—Mr. Stimson has gotten some rich man interested in him who will probably send him to Europe and educate him.
    Was there ever such a piece of extravagance as this letter of Mr. Shinn's? It seems as though he tried himself to see what [he] *could* do. The *audacity* of his applying to *me* that compliment of Steele's!—"the greatest compliment ever paid to woman," as someone says. I am more than ever surprised at his coolness in speaking of "Lucy" now.
    I have found the price of a passage to Sav. by steamer $20.00[.]

Am going to find out today what it will be by rail. If only there were some chance of *really* seeing you if I went by rail I would do it at almost any cost. But to see you merely on the cars where we could speak of nothing but the weather and the company, would be more tantalizing than anything else. What do you think of it. But I am in a perfect rush this morning and *must* close. No, my darling, you never *will* show me more of yourself than I want to see,—because you never *can*. And I could as soon "tire" of that love which is my very life as tire of the expressions of it. Sweetheart, I can never tell you with what joy it fills my heart to hear you [say] "I love you."

With all my heart   Your own Eileen.

ALS (WC, NjP).

To Ellen Louise Axson

My own darling,   Balto., April 30, '85

This *is* a very *sweet* letter of sister Marion's, and is written in the little woman's best vein. You may be sure, too, that what she says in [is] *genuine*: she means every word of it. Yes, darling, it is a thing full of sweet happiness that you have gained the love of all the dear ones of my family; and yet it seems to me so much a matter of course that everyone should love you that I should hardly have recognized the blessing as a blessing had you not spoken of it as a thing to be wondered at and to be thankful for. I am deeply thankful for it: but it seems to me part of that crowning blessing wh. is the crowning glory of my life—the blessing of having won you—a little lady to be loved by everybody who knows her! The real *test* of the case will come, Miss, when your relatives pass judgment on *your* choice. But I feel wonderfully untroubled on that point: for, in my estimation, nothing could counterbalance the sanction of your blessed father's blessing on our engagement. *He* gave you into my keeping with his benediction, and that suffices me. Your love came to me with his blessing—and now you have come into fullest share with me of the love of *my* parents, as well as of all who are dearest to me! Sweetheart, haven't we every *reason* to believe that blessings will come with the wedding in June?—for we are also of the children of the Father of blessings! How could we be nearer kin, precious?—kin thro. the love of husband and wife, and kin by reason of our common love for the God who has given us to each other!

I like Mrs. Caldwell very much indeed. She is a bright, wide-awake person who compels you to be interested in her; and she seems to have a very sweet, gentle, lovable disposition. She has found out more about Balto. and Balto. affairs in the six days she has been here than her husband would have found out in six months. Of course she knows all about you. Our engagement was one of the very first things Dr. C. spoke to me about when *he* came, and there are infallible signs that Mrs. C. has not spoken of it to me only because we have had no conversation except at meals. She told me of your uncle Randolph's visit to New Orleans as she would have told me a piece of family news. "I forgot to tell you that cousin Randolph Axson" &c. Pray, Miss, by what line of reasoning were you led to the conclusion that Dr. Palmer's daughter did not know of the "existence" of a young lady whom Dr. Palmer specially loves?

I had intended, sweetheart, to postpone further exposition of my favourite views as to what constitutes education, and as to the wherein of the comparative uselessness of 'information'—that information which is by most people supposed to be the content of knowledge—till our future *talks*; and I am still of that intention; but my darling's letter of Tuesday night leads me to anticipate in a word or two that part of the discussion which most immediately concerns her own dear little self. I want to deny two statements made by my precious little mischievous, self-depreciatory mistress, whom I should so like to punish with half a hundred kisses for talking so! In the first place, then, my lady, I would have you understand that the opinions which I have expressed concerning your "mental powers and acquirements" have never been "charitable"; they have been founded upon sober truth. And, in the second place, I would have you understand that I am "going to marry a little girl who is," according to what I hope some day to induce all who know me to accept as the true standards, in a very *true* and *large* sense educated; one who has, I trust, a great deal to learn from me, but from whom I have quite as much to learn of such things as are worth learning. Why, my artless little lady, you yourself prove my case for me in this very letter: for you avow your thirst for the good things of the mind, your earnest curiosity as to all things worth knowing. That is the very thing that made me love your companionship before I was conscious that I loved your *self*. If you are not educated, then I am not: for I have always found you quick to appreciate the things that constitute the staple of my thoughts—of such thoughts as I could not think were I not educated. Cultivated tastes may be said to be almost synonymous with education; and my darling has gotten from her friends, the poets, the painters, the essayists—from all her book companions—as great—nay, a much greater—power of sympathy, of *stimulating* sympathy with my work than she would have had if she had spent a score of years systematically reading history and political economy. Education is gotten much better in the reading prompted by one's natural tastes—so it be *sober* taste and earnest reading—than in going thro. *any* task *against* one's tastes at the bidding of a task-master—after the initial drudgery of school is gone through with. I know my own mental needs, sweetheart, and, if marriage were a mere business partnership, to be determined by the sort and amount of capital (pecuniary for the merchant, mental for the student) contributed by the partners, I should chose to add to my own capital just what *you* have to contribute—even if you did not know that the U. S. has a Constitution. That is my *head's* conclusion, just as it is my heart's conclusion that I love you as I could love no other woman in the world. There is *every* proof that I am

　　　　　　　　　　　　　Your own　Woodrow.

ALS (WC, NjP).

From William F. Ford

My dear sir:　　　　　　　Bradstreet's. New York, April 30, 1885
　　How are you to put in the summer vacation? I am thinking to go on to Baltimore in a few weeks. Will you probably be there then? Have you anything further in mind for *Bradstreet's?*

　　　　　　　　　　　　　Yours truly,　Wm F Ford

TLS (WP, DLC) with WWhw notation on env.: "Ans. May 5/85."

From Ellen Louise Axson

　　　　　　　　　　　　　New York April 30/85
　　How I wish, my darling, that I *could* write you an answer to your morning's letter such as it deserves. I could not at best write you half of what my heart says in answer, and I fear that if I tried to reply at all tonight you would be more impressed than ever with the "sadness" of my letter;—and yet I am not sad at all, only tired. I fancy my letter of Monday night "misrepresented" me, sweetheart; I can't recall much about it or about my mood at the time, but I am sure there was nothing the matter; I had had no bad news from anywhere, nor was I at all depressed, I was, if not "merry," as "glad" as usual. And no one knows better than my darling how much that is;—how full of joy he has filled my life. I am one of the few who are most fortunate—more fortunate even than children, for I am not only happy but I *know* it. Ah,

dearest, your love falls short of *nothing*; if you ever know, your heart must tell you, for words cannot, what "use" as well as joy your love has been to me in all things. I do not believe that there is any barrier now between our hearts,—I *would* tell you *all* that is in my heart; if I do not it is partly because I cannot find the words,—and partly from that life-long habit of "self-repression." But I think I have learned to tell you my deepest, most constant and earnest thought; it is only the little flitting fancies grave or gay, especially the passing *clouds*, which I have not learned to seize as they float by; and I know not how to give them or even *attempt* to give them substantial form. But as I said I must not try to answer this precious letter because I am so "awfully" tired and I must get up early in the morning to *pack*! Yes, we are going to move tomorrow! We only found it out at eleven this morning, and we have tramped "all over creation," as Antoin. says, this afternoon looking for a boarding-place. We succeeded splendidly at last and are going to join the Miss Beviers at 95 *Seventh Ave.*— very near 10th St. They like it exceedingly;—it is a *very* pleasant looking place, and we got a very comfortable room on the fourth floor for $12.00. No time for details now. Will tell you all about it tomorrow. It is all right; we have had no "fuss," but Miss Beatty didn't keep her engagement with us, and as there were two of us we felt strong enough and, after our winter here, experienced enough to refuse to be imposed upon. So direct your next letter as above. Believe me darling with all love and faith

Your own Eileen.

ALS (WC, NjP).

From the Minutes of the Seminary of Historical and Political Science

Bluntschli Library, May 1st., 1885

Seminary called to order at 8:10 P.M., Dr. Adams in the chair. Twelve members present.

As the principal contribution of the evening, Mr. D. R. Randall read a paper on "The Puritan Colony at Annapolis." This paper was an attempt to give, in a continuous and detailed form, the history of a Puritan colony of Va. a part of which was, in the year 1648, forced by stress of persecution to leave that Province and seek a settlement in Maryland. Puritans had come to Virginia as early as 1614, but the Puritan church which was in course of time organized did not become a factor in Virginian history until about 1642. It slowly increased in size and importance, and had become strong enough to send Delegates from three or four counties to the Assembly, when, in 1648, it was suppressed by an Act of Assembly, which banished its ministers and elders. One congregation of this colony, from the Nansemond river, went up, by indirect invitation from Ld. Baltimore, into Maryland and settled all that portion of the State now know[n] as Anne Arundel Co., but which was at that time called by the new colonists "Providence." There the colony rapidly grew strong and united, and was able, from 1652 to 1658, virtually to control the government of Maryland. Becoming displeased with their supremacy, Ld. Baltimore's officers sought to wrest it from them in 1655; but in a battle fought near the Severn river between Baltimore's forces and the adherents of the Puritans, the latter confirmed their power by a complete victory. In 1658, however, the government was by aggreement peaceably surrendered to Ld. Baltimore's representatives, and after that date there was a speedy decline and disappearance of the influence of the Puritans in Maryland politics. "Providence" soon became the centre of a Quaker element, and remained a stronghold of the Friends from 1660 to 1690. In 1692 the Church of England was established in Maryland, and Annapolis, then a mere village, was made the capital of the Province.

The importance of this Puritan colony in the religious, as well as in the political, history of Md. has always been underestimated by historians of the State, who have been accustomed to stigmatize the Annapolis Puritans as factious and rebellious. Rebellious indeed they were, but only against unlawful oppression; and their triumph in the Province was a triumph of democratic ideas and institutions over the aristocratic govt. framed by Ld. Baltimore.

Dr. Adams called attention to the fact that the slights which Md. historians have put upon the Puritan influence in the early history of the State have resulted in a wide-spread distaste amongst the intelligent people of the State for any opinion which seems to ascribe importance to the part played by the Puritans in shaping the destiny of the Colony.

Dr. Adams reverted to the special element of personal interest in Mr. Randall's study in view of the fact that it was possibly in this early Puritan settlement that the family of the late Johns Hopkins originated. He then read an outline of the facts so far brought to light concerning the descent and life of the founder of the University. He spoke of the probable incorporation of this material in a projected series of brief biographies of representative Md. men.

Dr. Ely read a brief review of Mr. Jno. Fiske's book entitled "American Political Ideas, Viewed from the Standpoint of Universal History," characterizing Mr. Fiske as a serviceable mediator between scholars and the public.

Mr. Dewey made an informal oral report upon the sources of information upon the history of economic thought in the U.S. to be found in the libraries of Philadelphia.

After some minor things of interest to the Seminary had been noticed by Dr. Adams, the Seminary adjourned at 10:10 P.M.

W. Wilson, Sec'y

WWhw entry.

To Ellen Louise Axson

My own darling,   Balto., May 1, 1885

May has come—and *next month* we are to be married! Think of it, sweetheart! Are you glad?—are you *very* glad? How I wish that I could take you in my arms for—oh, just the shortest time would bring full delight!—and tell, on your sweet lips, how glad *I* am.

> "Oh! Eileen dear, that you were here
> With your brown eyes bright and clear,
> And your sweet voice like a bird
> Singing love to its lone mate
> In the ivy bower disconsolate;
> Voice the sweetest ever heard! . . .
> Eileen dear, come to me soon,
> I am not well whilst thou art far;—
> As sunset to the sphered moon,
> As twilight to the western star,
> Thou, beloved, art to me."[1]

And you actually promise never to tire of the ardent speeches and passionate caresses in which I will, when our wedding-day is come, always be telling you how much I have needed you all my life and how full my heart is of joy, of love for you, of *you* and all that concerns you? Rash little maiden! you can't know what an overwhelming rush of demonstration you are inviting! But what would I say—what would I think—if there were any signs that you *would* grow weary of the manifestations of my love!

"Nor I can *live* if thou appear
Aught but thyself, or turn thine heart
Away from me, or stoop to wear
The mask of scorn, although it be
To hide the love thou feel'st for me."[2]

If I seem sometimes, precious, to think it possible that you should ever feel inclined to receive any expression of my love with coldness or indifference or impatience, it is only because I am so sure of the contrary. I pretend half to believe what it would kill my heart really to believe, only to provoke my sweetheart to these sweet declarations which are so precious to me—to make occasions for her to speak words wh. I treasure as my heart's most precious stores of memory! Yes, darling, *I believe in your love*—wonderful as that love seems to me, I believe in it, I trust it as I would trust nothing else in the world—and that sums the whole matter up! I know that my life is in your keeping, my happiness, my all—and, because I know whom I have loved, I am as sure that you will keep that all with a true woman's steadfastness of love and singleness of devotion as I am—that I love you! And, oh, sweetheart, can you guess—is there anything in your own experience that enables you to guage—the blessedness of that assurance—the strength and joy that it has given me? It fills the greatest, the all-inclusive, need of my life. For all my life long I have needed *you*, my queen—have needed such love as yours from such as you—and there is none other such in the world—my Eileen is the only woman who *could* love me as I need to be loved, and—but I'll *break* my heart trying to write it down thus! Is not the whole of the sweet truth summed up in this, that you have accepted me as   Your own   Woodrow.

P. S. I have found it so slow and uncertain a matter so far, sweetheart, getting the addresses I want in Vermont that I have been writing to find out whether Arden Park were still in the same hands. To-day comes a letter saying that it is, and offering bearable terms. Would you think with any degree of allowance of spending part of our vacation within nine miles of where—where it all began? Tell me just what you think. Of course I've not given up Vermont. This is as a possible alternative.

I hardly know *what* to say, dearest, about steamer vs. rail. Give me a day or two in which to think about it. Even if it *were* in the cars, an hour's time together (it would be a little more than that) would be a very precious experience—to look forward to, and back upon—and we *could talk* of what we pleased; but it

would be terribly tantalizing in other respects—in its other restraints (you would be *obliged*, Miss, in mercy, to let me *act* your
brother at meeting and parting!) and if going by sea would really
be both safer and more comfortable for my precious little lady—
I want her to go by sea. We will think of it!
　　　　　　With love unbounded,　Your own　Woodrow.

ALS (WC, NjP).
　¹ A paraphrase of Shelley's "To Mary———."
　² From Shelley's "To Mary Wollstonecraft Godwin."

From Lizzie R. Hawkins

Mr. Wilson　　　　　　　　　　Bryn Mawr Pa May 1 [1885]
　In reply to your letter of the 27th I would say that the rooms
are rented until the 1st of Oct. but of course it would take a few
days to have them cleaned and in the meantime you could be ac-
commodated elsewhere. Also you can have till the 3rd of May to
decide.　　　　　　　Respectfully yours　Miss Hawkins

ALS (WP, DLC) with WWhw notation on env.: "Ans May 9/85."

Two Letters from Ellen Louise Axson

My darling Woodrow,　　　95 Seventh Ave. New York May 1/85
　Well here we are snugly ensconced in our new boarding house
—odd that we should have happened to move on the general moving day, May 1st;—is it not? We have been here only about an
hour, have just finished getting settled, and are feeling very comfortable. Our room is *very* neat and pretty—not quite so large and
"stylish" as the other, and of course without the dressing room;
but it is altogether "desirable." My report must end here for the
present as we have taken no meal as yet, and seen none of the
people except the Beviers, the land-ladies, Miss or Mrs. Pope and
Martin are very nice-looking; the latter is quite pretty with a fine
clear complexion and curling grey hair. They look much more
amiable than Miss Beatty.
　By-the-way, I forget that I did not tell you the cause of all this
commotion;—our agreement with Miss B. was that [we] were to
keep our room until it was rented, and she in the meantime was
to have a larger extension put to the lower hall room and then
we were to move down. But the extension proved a castle in the
air; the workmen have been about the house for weeks, but there
has appeared no sign of such a thing. But yesterday morning she
sent word that the room below was ready, the bed made, and she
would like us to move at once,—no further explanation of any

sort. We sent word that we *couldn't* move, "at once" we were expecting company; and then when the company Allie and Lil. had
left, we put on our hats and went house-hunting, with want
[what] success you know. *Then* we went to Miss B. to know what
it all meant. It seemed that the lady below stairs had taken a
fancy to our room and was going to move up; the room she at
present occupies—with three others all remaining vacant! We respectfully enquired for the extension and were told that it wasn't
to be; the authorities objected to wooden structures. So we expressed our polite regrets, but would find it impossible to stow
ourselves and our "things" in such close quarters, and we would
therefore accommodate her by leaving the next afternoon. I don't
think she realized how much we have grown in knowledge; the
first part of the winter we probably *should* have been so terrified
at the thought of a change that we would have paid without a
word the double price for a single room,—the same price for which
we get this. So this morning Antoinette came and engaged this
room, and tonight just after dinner we left; it is raining heavily,
but A's "golden youth" as she calls him brought a close[d] carriage for us,—as well [as] the wagon for our trunks—so arrived in
good order. We meant to leave before dinner but I *couldn't* leave
without telling Mr. Finlayson good-bye;—it all happened after
dinner last night, you know, and he always breakfasts alone at
some unearthly hour, so dinner was my only chance. It is astonishing how sorry I am to tell the queer little Scotchman "good-
bye." I asked him to come and see me;—he said he wouldn't, of
course, but as the ladies said, they had never seen him so delighted at any thing;—indeed he made his pleasure apparent, in
a very comical fashion. I told him I should be very much hurt if
he ignored my invitation. By the way, I must tell you the neatly
turned compliment he made me; I was never more amazed that
at such a thing from *him*. "You know" he says ["] Mr. Obiter Dicta! (I had lent him the book,) speaks of the advantage of 'keeping
an atmosphere.' Now be *sure* always to keep *your* atmosphere.
It will be of great advantage to yourself and everyone around you
—*never* lose it!" So I told him if he really thought it worth keeping, I wouldnt!

I find I have occupied so much of my space with my boarding-
house story, that I have none left for all the other things I wanted
to say tonight. What a wonderful art you have, dear, of saying
the right thing to me,—the thing which will best quiet my doubts
and fears. Well if you think you have made such a good invest-
mcnt, I suppose I have no good reason for trying any longer to

persuade you to the contrary. And the conclusion of *my* head as well as heart is that I love you, darling, as I could love no other man in the world. I am very happy tonight, dear heart, to think that it is *next month* our separation ends. I have more to say about that but I *must* not say it now. With truest love believe me darling as ever   Your own Eileen.

What put it into your head, sir, that Mr. Palmer "specially loves" me? I have never seen him in my life. Cousin *Edward* Palmer and I are great friends.[1]

[1] "Mr. Palmer" was the Rev. Dr. Benjamin M. Palmer of New Orleans, brother of Edward P., who was also a Presbyterian minister. Benjamin M. and Edward P. Palmer were Ellen's first cousins twice removed. See the genealogical table in Thomas Cary Johnson, *The Life and Letters of Benjamin Morgan Palmer* (Richmond, 1906), facing p. 16.

My darling Woodrow,   New York May 2/85
    Upon my word, I am inclined to agree with Mrs. Gummige (?)[1] that everything is "contrary." I mean about these plans of ours. I thought a day or so ago that I had settled matters (in my own mind) satisfactorily, and now here is another difficulty. I believe I told you last night that I had something more to say concerning the event which is to take place next month. Have been *trying* to say it for two or three nights but, as you know, have been so hurried in writing you that I had no time to broach the subject.
    The thought of keeping your parents waiting on me,—or of risking the loss of their presence either,—has been weighing on my mind greatly as you may imagine. I felt that something *must* be done to avoid it; so I concluded to write you that we had better decide at once on the 18th. Then if I found that I *could* not get ready in two weeks, as would probably be the case, I could leave New York a week before the school closed;—a very simple way out of the dilemma as it seemed. Of course, I thought of that at first, but was prevented from deciding it at once in that way merely by the fact that I had paid to the close; and one hates to throw away nine or ten dollars (I shall be obliged in any event to leave the League a few days before I leave the city;—especially if I go by steamer since they start only on Saturdays—so I *must* lose some time.) But of course one can ignore such material considerations as that when there are such important matters at stake. But here is another serious "hitch";—Stockton writes "I am sorry to hear that you think of settling on the eighteenth;—that is the very day our college closes!" And so I am all at sea again, I had thought the school closed earlier. I suppose it would almost break

his heart to miss his first college commencement, and the earliest chance after that Thursday seems to be the next Tuesday or Wed. But I don't know what to say about it;—your father's convenience *must* be considered first, and we will do *anything* to ensure their presence. Have you heard from them yet on the subject[?] I think I will leave you to decide the matter, dear, for you will know better than I how the delay will affect their plans. I fear they will make light of the inconvenience to me. You know, I *could* if it were necessary have it as "soon after the 7th" as the 10th by leaving here the middle of May;—but if I decided on that it would be necessary for me to do so *immediately*. So now you know all the facts, and must decide this troublesome question; and remember darling I am perfectly willing to do *anything* to suit your dear parents.

As to the question of a summer lodging. Of course it would be *perfectly lovely* to go to Arden Park, it is the sweetest place I ever saw, and the associations would not make it *less* so! But I would not think of going, dear, unless the terms were something more than "bearable," unless they were almost if not altogether as reasonable as can be had at the North. I wish I could help you in this perplexity, darling;—the place Miss Blanchard spoke of in Mass. I find is out of the question; but I mean to ask Miss Granger next week; she is a particular friend of mine at the League who lives in Vermont; her father is a Cong. minister. This reminds me of an odd little coincidence which came to pass today;—but I must wait till tomorrow to tell you of it,—we have had enough of such matters for one letter.

To think of your speaking as if there *could* be any doubt as to the judgment of my relatives on *you*! They, all of them, have already, the profoundest admiration for you, to which those who have met you add a strong affection. That information *I* have obtained from head-quarters, though I regret to say that those of them who are Axsons will take particular pains never to let you discover it if they can help it, so dreadfully undemonstrative are they.

Yes, it is a sweet thought, darling, to remember how gladly my dear father gave me into your keeping. My eyes grow blind with tears, not all of sorrow, whenever I think of that last evening I had him with me, of his words of ardent admiration and respect, and tender affection for you. Ah yes, we will have his blessing at our marriage as truly as if we had his dear presence among us. He took a deep comfort in our engagement, darling, from the first; he felt as we did not that he was soon to leave us forever; and to know that he left his little girl in the care of so true a *man* as you, gave him a joy such as none but so tender and anxious a father can feel. May the Father in Heaven give us His blessing in equal measure! May he make me less unworthy of the over-flowing cup of blessing which he has already given me! Oh my darling I love you, I *love* you! I may truly say that I am *altogether* yours for there is no one to dispute your claim. Can I *never* tell you what you have been to me or how dark this fair and beautiful world would be without you. You are in very truth 'all the world to me.' I suppose I do love "harder" than many, but even aside from that there is small wonder that I should love you more than most girls love their lovers. With all my heart

Your own　Eileen.

ALS (WC, NjP).
¹ Ellen refers to Mrs. Gummidge, a character in *David Copperfield* with a lugubrious view of life.

To Ellen Louise Axson

My own darling,　　　　　　　　　　　　　　Balto., May 3, 1885

Again I had to forego writing yesterday. I am ashamed to say that I began the day with a terrible case of 'the blues,' and in my energetic efforts to exorcise the evil spirit I walked so much, so hard, so far, I stayed in the stiff, cold wind so long, I tired my attention with so many things, that by the time evening came and I felt sufficiently in command of my mood to write to my darling I found that I was no longer master of my *body*, that I was so completely fagged out, so overwhelmingly sleepy, that the only thing I *could* do was to go to bed. There had been no good reason, of course, for my depression: its only immediate cause was a sneering review of my book in a small local sheet of no circulation.[1] But no *good* reason is needed in my case for low spirits: not even an appreciable pretext can always be discovered by searching. My loneliness—heart-loneliness—seems to accumulate and then with its gathered force to spend itself upon me during some single darkened day. It almost always takes the form of blank discouragement. It shows me every defect in my work, dwells upon the insignificant results of that work, and emphasizes the conclusion that I am a shallow, thought-barren fraud, boundlessly ignorant, absurdly weak! I am filled with disgust for myself and with pity for all who love me. But, my blessed little sweetheart, you see the sweet conclusion to which all this leads. I am sure that I am right in attributing the recurrence of these days of gloom to the almost unbearable strain of heart-loneliness—and next month is to cure that! My darling is to come, with that blessing of blessings, her precious, loving, wifely presence! My heart is to have the sweetest of all companions, is to have daily evidence that it is loved as much, as passionately as it loves. *Are* you happy, darling, "to think that it is next month our separation ends"? May God bless you for that confession! That *you* are glad that our wedding-day is near is more to me than all my other hopes and ambitions combined. *I* am *more* than glad, more than *happy*: I am profoundly, unspeakably thankful! What would become of me if I had many more months to wait? Sometimes I tremble at the power and conscious meaning of my love for you, my Eileen: it makes me guilty of the folly of torturing myself with the terrible questions, 'what if I should *lose* her!'—'what if God should say 'no' to our plans!' But of course it is *only* 'sometimes' that I admit these morbid, groundless fears. Most of the time it seems to me that everything about me is as full as my own heart of the joy that comes with the thought that you love me and have promised to love me always. Oh, my pet, my sweetheart, my lovely darling, my Eileen, will you—*can* you—be made as happy as I shall be made by our marriage? I live to make you happy—will simply living with me do that!—but I *must* change the subject: it is fairly heart-breaking to *fail* to say half of what I feel! Wait until we *are* married, sweetheart; *then*, if there be *any* way of telling you, you shall know how love for you and delight in your love for me make up the whole of my life! You say in this morning's letter that you have something more to say about next month—is it to bring the day a little nearer?—oh! how I hope so!

I should have been very much disturbed about your having to move, my pet, had not the news of the necessity been accompanied with the statement that you had found entirely pleasant and satisfactory quarters elsewhere. I hope that you will find the other boarders pleasant and the table comfortable; for then I shall be altogether satisfied with the change—for I am *so* glad to have you out of the power of that outrageous fraud, Beatty! Her conscience and heart must be as lean and ill-favoured as her ugly person. How delightful that you *could* act independently! Tell me all that you can about your surroundings, dearest—because you know how my heart likes to go with you in imagination wherever you go.

I enjoyed ever so much your account of your parting with Mr. Finlayson. I don't hesitate to say that he is a *brick*: I wish I knew him myself! I shall be curious to hear whether he accepts your invitation to call.

I received a letter from Dr. Rhoads the other day in which he suggested that I could see about certain boarding arrangements 'when I came up to the [entrance] examinations on the 25th of June'! I informed him that on the date specified I should be otherwise engaged—very sorry to disappoint him &c., but really could not attend.

The Dr. also sent me three essays written by the candidate for the fellowship of whom I spoke some time ago. Alas for the poor Queen's English: the woman's style is abominable! I suppose, of course, if there are to be no other candidates, this person must be appointed: but any other girl who wants the place would find this a golden chance to apply, if she but knew it!

But I must not write any more now, precious; this room is much too cold to sit in: my hand is stiff! I love you—I love you as much as you can wish or *imagine* and I am oh *so* gladly

Your own   Woodrow

Regards, or what you please, to Miss A. F. Who *is* her "golden youth"?

ALS (WC, NjP).
¹ Not found.

From Ellen Louise Axson

My darling Woodrow,   New York May 3/85
I have just returned from Dr. Taylors church, where we had a *magnificent* sermon. He certainly is a grand old man if he does hold some objectionable ideas. I went under the escort of the Bevier girls, but I don't know that I will try going so far again without stronger protection; even one of Dr. Taylor's sermons scarcely pays one for being frightened half out of one's wits by drunken men stumbling all over the sidewalk in front of you. I may as well give up trying to get myself converted to northan ideas on *some* subjects. There turns out to be three *Miss* Beviers. The oldest one evidently isn't so much of a church girl and for that reason I have never seen her before. She is a teacher too. They are *all such* nice, bright, intellectual girls, and the little one, the artist, is "too sweet for *anything*." Their only brother I learned today is a Johns Hopkins man,—took a fellowship in Greek there and afterward studied in Germany and *walked* all over Greece. He is now professor in his own college, Rutgers.

He is Louis Bevier—the sixth; the first of the name was a French Hugunot who came to New York (state) and settled in the spot where they now live. The girls are almost demented over *Louis the Seventh* who is now a very small baby and their first nephew, —or niece either! so to speak!

What *do* you think! We actually have a *baby* in this house!— and the *sweetest, prettiest, lovliest* of babies! Isn't that *delightful?* But unfortunately he is going away in two weeks to the Sandwich Islands!

We have a very nice looking crowd of people here, much more attractive in appearance than those at Miss Beatty's. But I am not likely to meet many of them as, the long table being full I am at a little side table tete-a-tete with one gentleman and his wife. There are two married couples, two other young ladies, in addition to the Beviers and their friend, and about half a dozen gentlemanly looking young men. It is a *very* nice place—exquisite-ly neat,—meals as good or better than Miss B's, and remarkably well served. By the way, do you remember Mollie Ives the friend of Helen Porter's—and of mine—who was nursing her last fall? You met her once in the hall at Miss Beatty's. I find that this was the very place where she boarded!

Yes darling, I *am* glad, I am *very* glad that *next* month is June. Don't you know that I *must* be very glad to confess it so frankly? And I confessed it even before you asked me, did I not? Is not your victory complete? Do you think I could be more entirely yours? Ah, darling it would be very strange if I were *not* glad! I fully agree with you now that I would not be ready for that new life if I were anything else than *very* glad at thought of it. And to be unwilling to confess to you that I am glad would be un-worthy such love as ours.

I well know that if this love of ours is to fulfill it's sweet prom-ise we must see to it, first of all, that it be "without dissimula-tion." My love has no secrets from you, darling. If I have not told you *all* the story of my love, and joy, and faith in you, it is only because I cannot;—I am ever seeking that great heart's-word which will say to you all that my *heart* says,—vain search, for only a life-time of love and service can tell the tale 'aright.' With God's blessing, love, I *will* keep that which you have com-mitted to me with a true woman's steadfastness of love and sin-gleness of devotion. You may well trust my *love*,—as I trust *yours*; for I *do* know the blessedness of that assurance—the strength and joy it gives. I often think with uncontrolable regret of what your wife should be which I am not, but "I'll *love* you more, more than e'er wife loved before Be the days dark or bright."

Your own   Eileen.

ALS (WC, NjP).

From Thomas Dixon, Jr.

Dear Wilson: Shelby, N. C. May 4th 1885.

Just returned from New Orleans. Your letter rec'd. I'll give it prompt attention. Several of the new trustees were my associates in the last Assembly & I am sure they will give my recommendation a considerate hearing—I'll write to them at once. I sent you yesterday a copy of "*Western Sentinel*" containing a cruel cut of my gloomy visage but a very handsome sketch.

I am terribly busy now[.] Have to deliver three commencement addresses and the memorial ad. at Charlotte 10th & have not done anything on them yet.

Wilson, old boy, I completely lost my heart away down South in Dixie—just gone beyond all redemption & don't care if I am—its made a man of me—she's the brightest, smartest handsomest, sweetest little woman in seven states. You remember that picture—tis she.

Don't forget to tell Mr. Murray to send me one of your books *immediately*. Let me hear when you can.

Sincerely yours,   Dixon.

ALS (WP, DLC) with WWhw notation on env.: "Ans. May 13/85."

To Ellen Louise Axson

Balto., May 4, 1885

Oh, my cruel little sweetheart! You must have wonderful confidence in my powers of self-control and sober judgment to tempt and try me by leaving the "fixing of the date" to me—by saying, in effect, 'if you wish, it may be the 10th'! And the temptation to listen to my heart is all the greater because I have nothing definite but its suggestions to go by. Those dear home-folks have evidently done as I feared they would do: have evidently accepted the 24th and taken no thought of suggesting any modification on their own account of the provisional plan I outlined in writing to them. I have had *not a line* from any of them since I told you that I would consult them at once—nearly two weeks ago—yes, more than two weeks ago!

But, darling, I *must* look at the *objections* to the dates you name—if only to ease my conscience. Would not Stockton be in the midst of his final examinations on the 10th, if the closing day is to be the 18th? He *could* forego the final exercises, but he could scarcely neglect the examinations. As for the 18th— well we must not cheat him of his commencement enjoyments, unless it be very plainly necessary. I feel as if it *would* be plainly necessary on my *own* account to make the day earlier than the 24th—but I will make one more effort to hear from Columbia before I venture a final judgment in the matter. I'll stir them up this time!

Your endorsement of Arden Park is so warm, sweetheart, that I have a great mind to write at once to secure board there—for my own heart inclines in that direction, and the charges are so nearly what we should probably have to pay in New England that the relative travelling expenses would about balance the account. We cannot have the choice for very long, either; because we can get a room at Arden only by writing very soon.

Did you call for the letter that reached 11th St. on Saturday, my pet?

'What put it into my head that Dr. Palmer specially loves you'? Why, Miss, nothing but his own letter, which you were good enough to show me last summer in Rome. Amongst lawyers, written evidence is accounted the very best evidence.

I *hope* to get a letter from Columbia this afternoon; and in that case I can write to you again to-morrow about these plans of which my head and heart are both so full; but I've been hop-ing the same thing for very many afternoons: so I will stir them up all the same—and you may be sure that I shall let you hear immediately of the answer I receive. Meantime don't bother your little head about the perplexities of the case, precious. I don't want you to be anxious: I don't want you to be anything but happy—and happier and happier as the sweet time approaches when you are to give yourself to

Your own   Woodrow.

ALS (WC, NjP).

From Ellen Louise Axson

New York May 4/85

I am so *very* sorry, my darling, that you had such a black day on Sat. It makes my heart bleed to know that you have had such experiences; and that I can do nothing to help—am so far away that I can't even know about it until it is over. Ah me! how I wish that all that much walking could have brought you to me. You ought not to spend those darkened days in lonliness, my darling;—yes you *do* need the loving sympathy at such times of the woman who loves you, for I have seen before this—at home—that it is the power of love which will soonest sooth such moods and drive them away;—*argument* does no good, for my darling knows as well as I that his discouragement is "without reason." Wouldn't it be well to avoid if possible reading such articles as the one you mention; certainly you can derive no sort of *good* from reading the stupid senseless things. But I suppose that it would be hard to accomplish; one gets "into it" before one knows. But I must protest vigorously against one phase of your darkened mood;—even that shadow shan't excuse you, sir, for feeling "pity for all who love" you,—pity indeed! and I love you best of all, and am *because of it* the happiest woman in the world. Yes, love, I can and will be made as happy by our marriage as you can be. My darling knows well the worth of love;—what can *prevent* a woman's being happy who is given such love as yours, and whose own heart is so filled to overflowing with a happy love, a love which makes it a blessed privilege to live, which sheds a glory over the smallest "meanest" details of daily life if only I may do them for your sake. I will give you an unerring standard, dear, by which to gauge the measure of my happiness; it is the measure of your love for me; when it grows cold my happiness dies, but not before.

I finally succeeded in finding a ticket-office today and enquired the price of a through ticket to Sav. It is $24.00 and the sleeping-car five dollars more;—so that the difference in price as compared with the steamer would be about ten or twelve dollars. Oh dear me! what a simpleton I made of myself this afternoon! I went to the office on my way from the sketch class and then stopped to see the girls a moment on an errand;—and my heart was growing heavier at every step as I pondered the matter and felt myself being forced to the conclusion that I *ought* to go by steamer. And then, as fate would have it, Allie asked me when I would see you again, following it up with several other questions on the subject, which I tried to answer bravely but—finally shall I confess it?—broke down and *cried* like the great baby I was. I am dreadfully ashamed to confess it, but I couldn't help it! They were very sympathetic! and strongly advised me to go "anyhow." If I could be sure of having my usual luck in the way of missing connections in Washington, I think I should go;—nothing would please me better than to be stranded there for two or three hours; —but I *must* not yield to temptation just for the sight of your face and nothing more, for *I* can't talk on the cars if you can, sir. It is too public and too noisy for anything but the smallest of small talk.

Miss A.F. sends her regards,—or what you please! I don't know anything about her golden youth except that his name is Blaney, and he seems to have more money than he knows what to do with. She says he can't talk about anything but stocks and bond, and clubs,—to half a dozen of which he belongs,—and he "bores her nearly to death" but the mercenary wretch cultivates him all the same because he is "so convenient." I never saw him except on the night when he brought us here; he is very nice looking. By the way she received a note from him yesterday in which he declares that I am the image of Mary Anderson![1] Just to *think* of his comparing my classic features with *hers*! outrageous! In what *can* the resemblance consist? Oh I have it!—it *must* be the *nose*! I'm *sure* it's the nose!

Good-night, my darling. I hope before this reaches you, you will be quite well and happy again—I trust you are so already. I love you sweet-heart more than tongue can tell. I am forever
Your own   Eileen

ALS (WP, DLC).
   [1] A popular young actress of that day.

To Ellen Louise Axson
Balto., May 5, 1885

Yes, my precious little sweetheart, you not only can but *have* told me 'what I have been to you'—are you not glad to hear that? *I* should be to know that I had enabled you to see as well the love that is in my heart for you, my queen! How have you told me? Why the sweet story is in daily course of telling. Its most wonderful and most significant chapters are these precious confessions which my darling makes of the joy and eagerness of her love for me. Is it not perfect proof, and full history, of that love that it has now no secrets concerning itself to keep from me? Ah, my peerless sweetheart, how could my heart *fail* to be satisfied with the demonstrations of your love? But I don't want you to misunderstand me, Miss. I don't want you to suppose that I am ready to excuse you from all further efforts to find that single heart's-word that will tell me all! Because the sweet love-messages in your letters are all-sufficient to fill my heart to overflowing with perfect gladness, I would not have you suppose that anything has been abated from my constant lover's wish to see the love passages encroach morc and more upon the other matter in your letters as you learn more and more the habit which it is my love's object to teach you, the habit of talking to me about yourself, about *all* the secrets of your inmost heart—about the trifles light as air, as well as about the graver affairs—about the shadows, as well as about the delights. *That's* the proof I want, darling, that I am 'all the world to you'—*that's* the proof I want that my love can make you, and has made you, altogether mine. And my shy little mistress *has* made *wonderful* strides in this direction. I often go back to the letters you wrote me long ago, and when I notice, what they show me, how your heart has been gradually opening more and more to admit my love to its treasures, I am unspeakably happy and grateful! Oh, little lady, you are my delight, the light of my life!

I am so glad to hear such favourable accounts of your new boarding house, my pet,—of all its pleasant inmates—especially the 'delightful' baby! Do you love all babies, sweetheart?

I am also glad to hear that you can't learn the northern practice of going out at night without a man's escort. I shouldn't try very hard, if I were in your place.

No letter came from Columbia yesterday (*wont* I blow those dear folks up when once I get hold of them!), but I wrote a letter which *ought* to bring a reply double-quick.

Will you allow me, Miss Axson, to remark that I think you the loveliest woman in the world and love you with all my heart? I *live* for the time when you shall *not* be Miss Axson, but I shall be *in law* as well as in fact　　　Your own　Woodrow.

ALS (WC, NjP).

From James W. Bones

Dear Woodrow　　　　　　　　　　　　　Rome Ga May 6/85

I enclose check for $100. which you will please credit on the note. It should have been sent on the 1st but great pressure of business caused me to overlook the matter. . . .

Dr. Hoyt kindly lent me recently the copy of your book you sent him & I have been reading it with much pleasure.

Marion & my mother are both quite well.

　　　　　　　　　Your affect uncle　James W Bones

ALS (WP, DLC) with WWhw notation on env.: "Ackn'ge May 11/85."

From Ellen Louise Axson

My darling Woodrow, New York May 6/85

Yes I perceive that the 10th would be more inconvenient even for Stockton than the 18th. I was thinking that he might go back to commencement, but of course the examinations are of most importance. So that date won't work at all; it would have given me a frantic scramble to have accomplished it, besides, so that unless it is very important for your parents to be free to come north near the first of the month we won't consider that. I hope you *will* manage to get an opinion from them this time. They are too generous in leaving it all to us young folks.

What about these entrance examinations? is it very important for you to attend them? Odd that they should have them so long before the school opens, making the poor girls take two journeys where one would do. By the way, your mention of making boarding arrangements then, reminds me of the "coincidence" of which I was going to tell you! You have heard me speak of Saidie Stewart, my special friend at the League. She is the one from Maryland; and a bright and shining light among the Leaguers, there is so much sweetness, refinement, real womanliness about her. I told her our plans the other day, and she was delighted to learn than [that] Bryn Mawr was to be our home, for she has cousins living there and is often there herself. I told her it was possible we would be obliged to remain in this city for lack of a boarding place; and she then told me of some other cousins Wildgoose! by name living at Haverford (?) within the college grounds, about a mile from B.M., who took boarders, in summer at least; —and she offered to write and ask their terms and if they would keep them all the year. But when she told her family in Astoria about it, (she lives with her grandmother) they said that their cousin, when here a few weeks ago, had mentioned receiving "such a nice letter from a young man at the Johns Hopkins who was to be professor at B. M. asking for board"—so it seems you have already applied, I suppose it didn't fill the bill or I should have heard of it. Miss S. said she was afraid their terms were quite high. I am "awfully glad["] that she *has* cousins there, whether they take boarders or not, so that I shan't lose sight of her entirely. But it is very late and I must stop. I hadn't an opportunity to write last night, and as usual I am exceedingly hurried this morning. I love you, I love you darling, as my own soul;

sleeping and waking I dream of you and long for the sight of your dear face. I am with all truth, and faith, and love,

Your own　Eileen.

ALS (WC, NjP).

To Ellen Louise Axson

My own darling,　　　　　　　　　　　　　　　Balto., May 6, 1885

Again I must insist that the English language is marred by a sad lack, the lack of an adjective which carries in its single self all that is included in those insufficient adjectives, 'delightful,' 'lovely,' 'sweet,' 'womanly,' 'delighting,'—an adjective, in short, which would describe *you*, as you appear in this precious letter that came this morning, for instance! Yes, indeed, sweetheart, my dark mood of Saturday is gone and forgotten, I *am* "quite well and happy again"; and, if I had not been before, I should have been after reading the unspeakably sweet words of this letter! And oh, darling, *what* would I not have given for the privilege of kissing away those tears which you shed because you could not see me till—till the day of days! You *may* have been a "great baby" to cry so, Miss, in the presence of the two cousins: but I'll venture the worth of a kingdom *they* did not think so, and I know that to me those seem the sweetest tears ever shed. The story of them brought tears of *joy* to *my* eyes—was that *very* heartless?—and—"shall I confess it?"—I kissed the paper on which that story was told!

And so you *will* go by steamer, after all? I dare not offer any objections, for you "cannot talk on the cars" and you have about convinced me that the return by sea would be safest. It would not be feasible to start in time to precede the through train by an hour or so in reaching Washington, and so have a chance to stop there? But no! I take it back; I wont tempt you. Wont you consult "uncle Randolph" about the safety of the outside passage, though?

Never mind, precious, on the 24th I shall see you, by God's will, and shall kiss you as my peerless bride—the most loved little wife in the world! For I suppose I *shall* have to wait till the twenty-fourth. My letter *did* stir up the Columbia folks with a vengeance! My letter was answered to-day by a *telegram*, which says, "We considered the twenty-fourth as settled: it suits all.—Mother" —So it *is* settled, unless my darling thinks Wednesday the *only* day for weddings and will not give me the 23rd! I am *so* eager that *one day*'s gain of time will delight me.

And, sweetheart, we shall be due at Arden Park on the 1st of July. Yes, I have actually engaged a room there for that date —are you satisfied?[1] If not, I can still withdraw. We shall have to pay just about Bryn Mawr prices.

How near this concluding of arrangements seems to bring the day! I could conclude a thousand if by so doing I could really hasten the dragging time that keeps us apart. I *love* you precious, passionately, *altogether*, and I am with all my heart

Your own   Woodrow.

ALS (WC, NjP).
[1] See the photographic section for a picture of the cottage at Arden Park where Ellen and Wilson stayed.

From Ellen Louise Axson

My darling Woodrow,   [New York, May 7, 1885]

This concluding of arrangements *does* seem to shorten the time, somehow; by giving it a definiteness I suppose. Your parents are *very* kind about it, and I *do hope* it won't inconvenience them. It seems too bad to make *them* wait on us; but I suppose it can't be helped. So we too will consider the 24th as settled, I suppose. Tuesday, of course, would suit me as well, but I thought perhaps the middle of the week would be more convenient to persons coming from a distance, your sister, for instance.

Another "coincidence"! The 24th of June last year was Janie Porter's wedding day! It did not occur to me when we first spoke of it, but in thinking of it afterwards; it was my impression that it was the same day, so I looked at her invitation, and so it is.

That reminds me that in our dress discussions I am surprised that you did not give me your ideas as to a wedding-dress, sir! Would you have me a *bride* or a *traveller*? Rather an unnecessary question I imagine, unless you are *very* different in your ideas from other men;—most of them like Miss Georgia's "Mr. Wilson" "*hate* this travelling-dress business!" However Grandmother settled that, for when I thought *all* my things were to be black, I got a black travelling dress, and at the same time gave up the idea of marrying in it, for of *course* I wouldn't *marry* in black. So I shall have a *very simple*, but I think very pretty, white dress.

Yes it *would* be feasible, *perhaps*, to stop over in Washington if I went South by rail; the through tickets allow for "stop-overs." We must think it over; how delightful a quiet talk in Washington would be! Ah, you don't *need* to "tempt" me, dear! I can do that for myself. I really think it is *necessary* (!) for us to see each other again to complete arrangements and get a clear understanding of our plans! don't you? I am delighted, darling, with the Arden Park arrangement, and yet not altogether satisfied, for I have a great horror of "Bryn Mawr prices"; but more of this tonight, excuse haste for I am very busy this morning.

I love you, my darling, passionately, *altogether*. My heart is flooded with a deep, sweet, wonderful joy, when I think how rapidly the days are putting an end to our long separation. I think my darling would be satisfied if he could look into my heart and see how everything which even *seems* to bring us nearer, so surely brings also an increase of happiness to

                                          Your own Eileen.
ALS (WC, NjP).

To Ellen Louise Axson

My own darling,   Balto., May 7, 1885

I received a letter from dear mother—or, rather, *two* letters, one of wh. that rascal "Dode" forgot to mail a week or so ago—by which the telegram of yesterday is indirectly explained.[1] These letters were evidently mailed just before mine arrived, and the telegram was meant to supplement them as speedily as possible: for they said nothing about the date. It plainly *was* considered "settled," just as I at first surmised.

Dear father has gone to Clarksville to consult with the "Executive Committee" of the Board of Trustees concerning the arrangements for the new "Divinity School" of the University. Thence he will go to the Gen. Assembly in Houston, Texas, stopping a day or so with sister Marion in Little Rock on the way; and, then, when the Assembly closes, he will have to go all the way back to Clarksville to deliver his "inaugural" at the Commencement.[2] He will *need* a couple of weeks' rest before starting out for Savannah!

Yes, I have been carrying on a somewhat protracted correspondence with Miss A. C. Wild*goss*, of Haverford, about board, and shall probably come to terms with her before very much more paper and postage is spent. She is to take one of the cottages on the college grounds at Bryn Mawr, specially with a view to accommodating the college instructors; but she apparently thinks that the salaries paid by the College are to be very large, and I have found some trouble in undeceiving her on that point. It will not be exactly to my taste to form one of a household of instructors—there'll be a scandalous lot of "shop" talked, which will take much of the satisfaction out of life—but that will, I am beginning to think, be about the best we can do at first.

No, there is really no need of my going on to the entrance examinations to be held next month. They are held only for the convenience of such applicants as live in the neighborhood of Bryn Mawr and wish to get these examinations, or some of them, "off" before vacation. There will be other entrance examinations held in September, of course, for those who did not care to take advantage of the earlier ones. I knew of these June examinations long ago, but I never had any intention of attending them. I sent on my questions to Dr. Rhoads several weeks ago.

No, sweetheart, you never, so far as I remember, spoke to me before about Miss Saidie Stewart; but, now that you *have* introduced her, I am as delighted as you are that you are to have opportunities of seeing her at Bryn Mawr. How I wish we could have a house of our own to which to invite your friends! There are several *other* reasons why I wish that we could from the first have a house of our own!—but this is the only one I'll mention in this connection.

I am writing steadily now every day on the American political economists and am kept very busy at it indeed.[3] The stage of composition has at last been reached, and in one sense it is much the hardest stage. It certainly involves longer stretches of sustained effort; and, since I have, for hygienic reasons, to do my writing in the morning, I have of late been pretty well fagged out by the economists before I could think of the love-task of writing to my precious little mistress. So remember, Miss, that, if you find your lover's letters particularly dull or provokingly hasty these days, he is writing hard against time, so as to escape as soon as possible from Hopkins thraldom and prepare himself for the happiest days of his life—his days with the little lady whom he loves with all his heart, the little lady who is his joy and delight, his peerless darling. He sees in all his writing pictures of the sweet days that are to come after it is done, and if there should be found any light in that writing, *he* will know that it was a reflection from the brightest dreams he ever had.

I was *so* hurried in writing my letter yesterday, darling, that I did not *half* answer the precious letter that came in the morning. I wanted to congratulate you, Miss, on your prospects of happiness! If the measure of that happiness is indeed to be guaged by the measure of my love for you, you are the most fortunate of women: for, since my love for you is boundless *and ever growing*, so that my heart can scarcely find room to contain it, your happiness must be boundless and ever-growing! Ah, sweetheart, my *precious* Eileen, how shall I ever repay you for these wonderful tokens of your love? By loving you as much in return? I *do*! I love you so passionately that I am actually afraid to write down the words in which my love sometimes offers to express itself, for fear you might think them overwrought and extravagant. But no more to-day, sweetheart! I love you! I love you!! All my heart goes out in love to you! You are my darling, my pride, my strength, my *all*, and I am altogether and forever

Your own   Woodrow.

ALS (WC, NjP).
¹ JWW to WW, April 28 and May 6, 1885, both ALS (WP, DLC).
² Joseph Ruggles Wilson, *Inaugural Address Delivered Before the Board of Directors of the S. W. P. University, in June, 1885* (Clarksville, Tenn., 1886).
³ See the Editorial Note, "Wilson's 'History of Political Economy in the United States.' "

From Addie C. Wildgoss

Mr. Wilson   Haverford College P. O. May 8th. [1885]
    I must apologise for so long delaying a reply to your last. I was waiting for answers from Dr. Hopkins, with regard to the long parlor on the first-floor in order that I might say whether it was still at your disposal. You can have it at $18. pr. week inclusive of heat, furniture & light. The other two rooms that we have been corresponding about, I will put at $19. inclusive of the same. I will thank you to say the price is $20 if inquired of respecting them as I shall have ten for a single room of the same disccription. These are the only rooms excepting one on the third floor of like dimensions (& exposure) with the parlor, which would be $18.   Very truly   A. C. Wildgoss

ALS (WP, DLC) with WWhw notation on env.: "Ans. May 9/85."

From Thomas A. Morris

Dear Sir   P. O. Arden, N. C., May 8th 1885
    Your letter of the 5th inst. to hand. It was our intention to reserve a room for you in the 8 room cottage. I suppose you remember the situation of it. The rooms are all pleasant in it and we cannot allow children in it which will insure, as far as we are able, quiet for the occupants.
    Mr. Walker, the artist, prefers his room there and will install himself in it the 1st of June. Do you remember the room up stairs that Dr Howe's family had for a day or two? That is the most quiet room on the place and if you like we will keep it for you but if you prefer a room downstairs we will reserve one of the most desirable ones there. I am of course speaking of the 8 room

cottage. The cottages built this year are all 3 rooms & are intended for families of children. We are glad to think of your coming & with kindest regards I am,

Yours Respectfully   T. A. Morris (S)

HwL (WP, DLC) with WWhw notation on env.: "Ans. May 16/85."

From Ellen Louise Axson

My darling Woodrow,   New York May 8/85

You will have to forgive me for spending all last evening writing to other people to the total neglect of your claims! But I find that if I *begin* with you I never reach anyone else; and almost all my friends have been transformed into enemies, this winter by reason of my neglect of *them*. I think they would be inclined to scoff if I gave as excuse the fact that I am obliged to write you *every day!* I had a letter from Rose, Wed., asking when she was to expect me, "for *of course* you are coming here on your way South, and you *must* stay several months!" I knew she would feel dreadfully aggrieved if I kept her in the dark any longer. I am *so* anxious for the dear girl to come to Sav. and so afraid she can't. Ah me!—when we were children, and thought that if we were only "grown up" we could do whatever we pleased, it would have seemed utterly inconceivable to us, that one could be married without the presence of the other!—and now I hardly expect anything but that she will say it is impossible,—can't afford it &c.—especially as it is so late in the season.

You say you can still withdraw if you wish from your Arden Park engagement? Do you think that it be best then to go to such an expensive place? True there will be a decided difference in travelling expenses—but still—how would it do to write to someone at North Conway, New Hampshire,—the postmaster,—the railroad agent!—who *is* the proper person to ask for information? —and get the addresses of some private boarding houses there. It is quite a "community," you know, and they nearly all take boarders in summer; and I should think that among them all there *must* be some cheap places. But I must ask you to excuse haste again this morning, dear. Good-bye my love, my joy, my pride. I love you till my heart aches with loving—I am in every thought

Your own   Eileen.

ALS (WC, NjP).

To Ellen Louise Axson, with Enclosure

My own darling,   Balto., May 8th/85

Of all the days of the week this is the day on which I least like
to be limited in the time available for writing to you, because this
is, as I said once before, the day on which I *want* to write you a
letter that will *last through Sunday*; but, as hard luck would have
it, things have crowded, and are crowding, upon me to-day so
thick and fast that I am left with scarcely *any* time for my letter. Maybe the sweet letter from dear mother, which I enclose,
will please my darling enough to make up for what haste may
exclude from mine. Dear mother's arguments against Arden
Park overlook the fact that we are looking for scenery and associations, and that, consequently, the towns about New York
would not suit us.

What a delightful exhibition my two letters of this morning
afforded me!—a contest in unselfishness between my sweet mother and my "dear little promised wife." "I *do hope* it wont inconvenience them. It seems too bad to make *them* wait on us." "We
would not on *any* account add to her anxieties or sacrifices." If
I am not the most blessed man that ever lived, to be loved by
such people as these two ladies, I wish somebody would write the
biography of the other man, that it might bring a fresh light of
love into literature!

I did not offer any suggestion about the wedding costume,
sweetheart, simply because it never occurred to me that it was
'any of my business'; and somehow I had taken it for granted that
you were to be married in travelling dress. Are we to start for
Columbia on the day of the ceremony, or are we to spend the
first night in Savannah? In other words, is the pretty white dress
(I am sure it *will* be as pretty as can be—or, at any rate, that it
will seem so to me) to be changed immediately, or—what? But
how daft I am (I can't for the life of me think *straight* about *that*
day!)—of course all that depends on train-time, and a dozen other
things. And of course this is one of the questions which make it
necessary (!) that we should have that consultation in Wash. I
have an idea that the through train South leaves New York about
11 o'clock P.M. In that case you could leave in the morning, according to our scheme, and board the 'through' in Washington
in the wee sma' hours, *next* morning. But I can find out all the
facts about trains &c. here.

Darling, do you realize how happy you make me by telling
me of your delight at the flight of the time which is now the only

thing that separates us? I have been wonderfully happy to-day—because the words of this sweet letter before me have somehow made me more than ever *conscious* how supremely glad and proud—with a sacred, lover's pride—every day's passage is making me. How I love to tear the leaves off my Calendar! And oh! how I love my darling—and how I delight in her love for

Her own   Woodrow.

ALS (WC, NjP).

E N C L O S U R E

From Janet Woodrow Wilson

My precious boy—   Columbia, S. C. Wednesday [May 6, 1885]

My letter written yesterday will explain, in part, our silence. Yours of "May 4th" was received a little while ago—we are all greatly distressed that you have been made to suffer so unnecessarily—in consequence of not hearing from us. We have just sent you a telegram—to relieve your mind as to the most important point in question—*the date of your marriage*. Dear, sweet, Ellie! How lovely she is! We would not on *any* account add to her anxieties or sacrifices—in any case. But, indeed, I think it is *perfectly* convenient for us to fall in with her plans & yours. You know your dear father has a way of being a little *"previous"* in his plans. He has been in too much of a hurry in his present journey —as he found by the time he reached Augusta—he might just as well have remained here till tomorrow. At first he thought that he must go North immediately after his return from the Assembly. But before he left he was quite satisfied to remain here till the time appointed for your marriage. You need not be anxious as to Annies capacity in way of *room*. They have been making considerable improvements of late. George has added a room to the house—so that now his office arrangements are complete— and they now have five bed-rooms—*without* the "attic" so that they have a "spare" room, even now that we are here. So please bear that in mind in making your plans. However your movements *after* the marriage you have plenty of time to arrange for—even after you come to us. As to *Arden Park* I will only suggest, at present—1st It is too much like "visiting" a family of acquaintances —now that we know them. 2nd You can go pretty much where you please for the same amount of money—certainly to places where you would have comfort and freedom. In the towns around N. York City, you can get nice boarding from seven dollars a week up—according to the number of steps you are willing to climb.

But I will not write more now. I think I answered your former letter in mine sent yesterday as to everything except the date of your marriage. That I had considered as settled. I did not see your fathers last letter to you—but supposed he had written with regard to that. Annie, George, Josie, and the little boys[1]—all join in love unbounded to you, my sweet boy. God bless you & your dear little promised wife. She seems to me a part of my precious son already—and I love her accordingly.

Lovingly   Your Mother

ALS (WP, DLC) with WWsh notation on env.
  [1] Annie's sons, James Wilson Howe and George Howe III.

From Ellen Louise Axson

My darling Woodrow,   New York May 8/85.

So you are now in the thick of your task on the the political economists! And how is it agreeing with you, dear? Do you continue to improve in health and strength in spite of it? You must not write *too* hard against time. When do you propose to finish it? You never told me by the way, how *large* a work it is to be;— though to be sure that isn't in any sense a measure of your task. I imagine that it is often much harder to write a small book than a large one, since it takes so much time to select and condense;— like Pascal, you know apologizing for the length of his letter because he hadn't time to make it shorter. How has Dr. [Richard T.] Ely performed *his* part of the work?—to your satisfaction?— and I have heard nothing more of Mr. Dewy (?) [Davis R. Dewey] Did he contract for a third as was at first proposed? I wish you much success in the work, darling, and that it may be pleasant labour to you. My heart is with you in it, as in everything you do. I must assure you that there was no evidence in your letters of there being anything of that sort on hand. They are certainly anything but "dull"! nor do they ever show any marks of haste; they are in all respects the sweetest and most delightful letters ever written. There is but one thing to be compared with them and that is your dear presence, the voice and smile and the beautiful eyes to give their full meaning to the precious words. Ah how I love those wonderful eyes!—and admire them too, as every part of that dear face! How *did* it come to pass darling, that you are in *every* respect, heart head and person, just the sort of man that I admire most?

How glad I am that there will in all probability be a place found or rather made for the professors at Bryn Mawr. I do hope Miss Wildgoss will come to terms without more ado. It would have been *very* hard to have had you ten miles away so much of the time; though of course if it is necessary we must do it with a good grace. Saidie was rejoicing over the plan today—she had just gotten word of it from them;—though she is very sorry that it is'nt "Cousin Mary" instead of "Cousin Addie"![1] Cousin Mary is perfectly lovely; but Cousin A. though very bright and nice is too much inclined to speak her mind regardless of consequences. It seems that the former will continue to keep the house at Haverford. Surely, I must have told you about Miss Stewart! I remember when you were here the first time telling you of the two lovely Southern girls, Miss Stewart and Miss Randolph, and of what a shame it was, that Miss Arnold should be considered the "type" of our class when they had such fine specimens as those to judge from. We have been planning to go South together if I go by rail (!) but now to my great disappointment, she finds she must go next week; tomorrow is her last day at the League. I shall miss her exceedingly for she is, by far, my dearest friend there, but it isn't so bad now that we are to meet again.

How would you like to spend the summer in a regular New England farm house? After trying for several days I managed to see Miss Granger today, and she told me of a place at Mt. Mansfield, where she was born, and where they have beautiful mountain and lake scenery. She says they are very nice plain people who have delightful country fare, cream &c. and that they are very kind and good natured,—the old farmer will "hitch up" at a moment's notice and take one all over the country. It might turn out to be the ideal farmhouse of which we have all read, and then again it mightn't! She says she is afraid the accommodations would be very rough. But of course it would be *very* cheap, and I think it would be fun. If we didn't like it, I suppose we could leave; she thinks that in or about Burlington one could do well for about a dollar a day. The girls leave tomorrow for Phila., I shall miss [them] a great deal now, especially Lil. She and I went on a regular "lark" yesterday[.] She went shopping with me and I went to look at thoroughbred dogs with her, then she took me to lunch at the Brunswick and after that we went to the artist's prize fund exhibition.

I am afraid I must close; I had so much today that I thought I would spend the evening writing you, but the light flickers so dreadfully, that it is making my eyes and head ache. Yes, you do well, my darling to congratulate me on my prospects of happiness; I *am* the most fortunate of women and the happiest because of your wonderful love. If I did not believe in that love, dearest, as I believe in *you* [,] if I did not know that it [is] strong [enough] to *endure* through all the ordeals of life, I should be of all women most miserable;—the very greatness of my love for [you] would but make my trouble greater. But now it is no less a joy to love you than to be loved by you. I am—ah how *gladly*!

Your own   Eileen.

ALS (WC, NjP).

[1] "Cousin Addie" was Addie C. Wildgoss, with whom Wilson had already had much correspondence. "Cousin Mary" was presumably her sister and lived with her in Haverford.

From the Minutes of the Seminary of Historical and Political Science

Bluntschli Library. May 8, 1885.

The Seminary was called to order at 8.10 P.M., Dr. Adams in the chair. Mr. Wilson read the minutes of the last meeting.

Mr. Worthington reported upon the Socialist magazines and papers; Mr. Sato, upon the Antiquarian Magazines; and Mr. Wilson upon "The Dial," "The University," and "The Nation." Dr. Adams called attention to a review, in The Nation for Apr. 30th, of a recent work upon Psychology by David G. Thompson.

Mr. Bancroft,[1] a member of the Columbia School of Political Science, was introduced to the Seminary, and read an essay entitled "The Negro in Mississippi Politics." . . .

The Seminary adjourned at ten o'clock.

C. H. Levermore.

[1] Frederic Bancroft, American historian, who was then completing work on his Ph.D. at Columbia. The paper was undoubtedly a portion of his dissertation, *A Sketch of the Negro in Politics* (New York, 1885).

To Ellen Louise Axson

My own darling,   Balto., May 9, 1885

Another arrangement is concluded. I wrote to-day engaging board at "the cottage" with Miss Wildgoss. We are to have the two best rooms in the house—they are the only two that would at all suit our purpose—and are to pay $19.00 a week for them. This is—if my long correspondence with Miss W. and with Miss Hawkins (the only other candidate for our patronage) proves anything—the best we can do. It is considerably cheaper than what Miss W. was at first inclined to charge. She wanted $20.00, fuel, light, and the furniture of one of the rooms *extra*. Miss Hawkins did not come below twenty; and Miss Wildgoss still begs that I will say to others that her price is twenty, since she expects to get ten dollars apiece for rooms like ours. It would cost very little less to take only one room: and I had determined not to do that unless it was absolutely necessary, because the rooms there are small at best and it would be unhealthful, as well as uncomfortable and inconvenient, to 'live' and sleep in the same room. We must have a work room—and it must be *your* shop as well as mine—because I want my darling to be with me while I am studying as much as at any other time. It is then that I most need sympathy. To make study easy and delightful, I need the presence of some one to whom I can speak from time to time of what I am writing or reading. I will know that my precious little wife will lift her bright eyes to mine and smile if I should happen to think or read aloud—and that she will volunteer a caress and a kiss when she learns that she can rest and delight me most in that way in the intervals, the recesses, of my work. Don't you know what it is, sweetheart, to *feel* a loving, sympathetic presence? It will be worth inestimable things to me! My darling will add power to my work simply by being at my side when it is in progress; and if we don't have jolly romps—mental romps of course included—when that work is *not* in progress, my name is not Wilson but Dull! If you expect, Miss, to get a sedate husband, whom you will not have to reprove for outrageous jokes, you are 'awfully' mistaken; and, if you are not prepared to have him talk and act nonsense whenever sense is not *imperative*, you had better be preparing— the time is short! But, dear me! how I have wandered from the subject! We were speaking of Arden Park. Well, if we were not, we *will* speak of it now—and I was about to say that, unless my sweetheart *prefers* New England, I am very much inclined to stick to my engagement with Mr. Morris in Buncombe Co. According to my calculations, it will not be more expensive than the other plans we have had in mind. I am assured that it would be quite impossible to get comfortable board anywhere near the mountains in New Hampshire at any price within our reach. The only likely places are in out of the way parts of Vermont or New York: and the mischief of it all is that all the decent places must be spoken for *early*. We can't risk going and *looking* for board such as we want; neither can we take the recommendations of people we don't know; the only thing left seems to be, to go to some place where we *do* know that we can get what we want at prices we can pay. If mother finds a cosey retreat in New York, we can leave Arden and join the family party, sometime later in the summer.

I have been studying the schedules, darling, with reference to our Washington scheme, and find them most unsatisfactory. To avoid staying all night in Washington, you would have to pass through here at night. You will see that the enclosed schedule seems to limit us to this plan: that you should leave New York at 9 P.M. and, reaching W. about 6 the next morning, wait over there until 11.01 A.M.—in other words, that you should leave N. Y. on the *slow* through train, and then wait in W. for the fast one. You will see that the train which leaves W. at 11.01 A.M. reaches Savannah at the same time as the one wh. leaves W. at 6 A.M., having overtaken the latter at Florence, just below Wilmington. Unfortunately, there are no through trains leaving Wash. in the afternoon or evening; so that you could not start from N. Y. in the morning—and the 9 P.M. from N. Y. is the only train that would get you into Wash. at a decent hour. I could, of course, board the train here easily enough at 4.40—and you need not wake up to receive me—but could you get proper escort to the train at night? Alas! alas! this schedule has put me sadly out of sorts!

Yes, indeed, sweetheart, I will forgive you for having stolen time from me in which to write to Miss Rose. I would not be-grudge her anything, because you have made me see her with your eyes, and, consequently, love her as you love her. I do hope that you *can* persuade her to come to Sav.—for your sake—*I* don't expect to see or think about anybody while I am there but you. I shall have to meet the people I meet there all over again some other time. If I am beginning to grow excited and elated already over that little 'experience,' what will be my state of mind when it is actually at hand? Oh, sweetheart, you are to be *mine*, and I would rather have you than anything or everything else that the whole world holds! I am to win the prize which is to crown my whole life with gladness—I am to win for good and aye my love-ly, my peerless Eileen, whom I love with a wonderful, joyous, un-speakable love wh. makes me altogether

Her own   Woodrow.

ALS (WP, DLC). Enc. missing.

From Ellen Louise Axson

My darling Woodrow,   New York, May 9/85.

That "dear sweet" mother of yours! how lovely,—how *perfectly* lovely she is! and how I *do love* her! I can never be grateful enough for her love and kindness. Ever and again "it comes all over me" afresh, and makes my heart, and my eyes, too, full to overflowing. Surely I am the most blessed of girls to be loved by such people as these two. And then think how I should feel if they were not my friends,—if they looked upon your marriage with disfavour. A thing of that sort would break my heart. It is even so, sir, that not even a longer letter from you could have pleased me more than this sweet letter from her!—is it possible to say more?

Thank you, dear, for offering to find out about trains there; it will be quite a convenience to me. Do you suppose there is but one through train. It did not occur to me that I should be obliged to spend the night in Washington.

Some of those other questions, I suppose I shall scarcely be able to answer until, I reach Sav. and learn more about the trains &c. there; but I take for granted it would be best and pleasantest to leave Sav. at once, that is in an hour or so; suiting our convenience to that of the railroad schedule. The train by which you left Sav. last winter started at quite a convenient hour. But you know your sister must be consulted about our going at once to Columbia. If she is to be at the marriage—and you must *make* her keep that promise,—some other plan may suit her better;—and of course *any* plan will suit me. I honestly do think there is need for us to see each other before the 24th! don't you? otherwise what an endless amount of writing about details we must do. But I have a great deal to do tonight, sweetheart, and must close for the present. I must echo certain words of yours, dear, for I too have been "wonderfully happy today";—and *I* can give proof of it too, for one of the girls asked me today, why I had been looking "so exceedingly happy all day, really *beaming*." I evaded in a cowardly fashion I fear, but I was really obliged to decline telling her that it was because I had the good fortune to be loved by the truest, noblest and most lovable man in the world, *and* his mother!

By-the-way, I didnt give you Miss Granger's message. She said I must tell you that she had "been wondering all winter how such a girl as you happened to be *floating around loose*! your sort are not generally permitted to remain very long undetached!" It really seemed to relieve her mind to know that at any rate I was not un*att*ached. She bore the news with much more fortitude than Miss Case,—said she was *very* glad to hear it and she is an old maid too. But this won't do, I must close. Goodnight, my darling, I love, *love love* you—I am as gladly as I am completely

Your own Eileen.

ALS (WC, NjP).

To Ellen Louise Axson

My own darling,   Balto., May 10, '85

Who should turn up last night but 'Ned' Webster, one of my most loved class-mates. He lives in Belair, Md., and at last, after numberless invitations, Hiram has got him down here to spend Sunday. They came to see me last night *at bed-time*, and I am to dine with them to-day. I am *delighted* to see 'Ned' again and expect to enjoy, this afternoon, a regular old-fashioned college talk, wh. will do me as much good as a week's rest.

In the meantime, however, I have time enough to write a little love letter to my darling, in answer to this sweet letter of Friday night which I have just fetched from the office.

"How did it come to pass that I am in every respect just the sort of man that you admire most?" Maybe I could answer that question, Miss, better if I knew whether you loved me, first of all, because you admired me, or admire me now because you love me —whether the love or the admiration came first. Until I am informed on that point, I can say only that it came to pass in just the same way that it happened to me that the little lady of whom I had been dreaming all my life came to me at last in your own sweet person. How did *that* come to pass? Sweetheart, if you do admire this homely face of mine, in which my mirror finds so little, I will never say again that it is ugly: it shall be respected— I will try to like it—because you love it. As for that lovely face and that dear little form which seem to me the prettiest in the world—not only because they are pretty, but above all because they are my darling's—I cannot find words in which to tell my admiration of them. I saw a little lady in church to-day about whose hair there was a light, and in whose cheeks there was a touch of colour—about the pose of whose figure—there was something which reminded me of you—and I wondered if the people about me—if she—could hear the beating of my excited heart! I must confess, sweetheart, that I never dreamed that it would be this way, that I should be carried to such a pitch of love for every line of your face and figure—but so it is. It is but one side of the great, the sweet and glorious fact that you have filled my heart with your*self*, and that my darling's beauty is just the image of that self. I don't love the beauty itself—it might fade and my love not be so much as touched—but I love whatever form *you* wear— I love *you*. That's always the sum of all I write to you and of all I think about you: and what a wonderful, glad, blessed sum it is —*for you love me. That* it is which transforms my love into strength! Otherwise it would be despair. Oh, Eileen, darling, sweetheart, my promised bride, I love you with a love beyond all power of words, and I am—oh with what delight—

Your own   Woodrow.

ALS (WC, NjP).

From Ellen Louise Axson

My darling Woodrow,   New York May 10/85

What do you suppose I have been doing. Reading an old sermon of your father's, preached before I was born! A commencement sermon, on the training of women preached at Greensboro.[1] It is *splendid* too,—I have but one objection too it, viz that he calls women "our females"! I read it with real pleasure—for it is as "timely" now as then, and not at all too "old-fashioned" to suit us. I found these *two* pamphlet sermon's of his when I was breaking up in Rome and shipped them in my trunk to read at my leisure, but in consequence of putting them under several layers of drawing paper, &c. I overlooked them until a week ago.

Oddly enough when I came across them last Sunday I found the text of one of them was our bible lesson for that day—"Servants be obedient to them that are you[r] masters according to the flesh"; &c.[2] Of course, a thoroughly *Southern* sermon, and a very strong presentation of that side;—and though it *is* an outworn subject now, I read it with peculiar zest because of a little episode in the Bible-class that morning. When the words "bond or free" were read one of the girls asked Mr. Carter if Paul's exhortation was addressed to *slaves*;—and his expression was a study as he answered in a curious, nervous, *scared*, tone of voice, ["]why ye-yes, my dear, yes!"—hastily changing the subject. I derived much quiet amusement from the scene.

We have had such a *perfect* Sabbath day. We walked all the way down to Spring St. and back and enjoyed it greatly. Somehow I have been very happy all day, with such a peaceful, restful, *Sunday* happiness. One reason, I think is that now the days are longer, I have a quiet hour or so in spite of my engagements; until recently I have been occupied until dark and I missed the Sabbath calm. For some unexplained reason the long evening of quiet did not satisfy; doubtless it was the sunshine I missed, for when I am able to *feel* disengaged,—that is to say on Sunday afternoons alone—I enjoy basking in it almost as much as an Italian begger.

I didn't tell you what a great advantage we have here;—we

actually have a horizon,—an extensive view! We even see a little patch of green hills which show purple in the evening light;—for—rare good fortune—the *sun* sets just opposite our windows, so that we have a grand matinee every afternoon if we reach home in time;—it was superb this evening. The homely explanation of all this is that just opposite us is a large *coal-yard*! which being only one story or so in height is no obstruction to the view, we being in the "attic." I can easily reconcile myself to having the words "Lehigh and Wilkesbarre coal" staring at me all day long for the sake of this treat in the evening. But I fear I must follow Antoinette's example and "give up trying to *see*" tonight[.] Our light has been terrific for the last few nights and it is flickering so now that it is making my eyes "jump" too in a bewildering fashion, so I must close abruptly. I will sit and dream of you a little longer as I have been doing this afternoon—instead of writing more. That is a more satisfactory process to *me* because I *can't write* the love and tenderness which fills my heart to overflowing, but in dreams one does whatever one wishes,—even to cheating time and space. For I can dream that my love and I are together in fact as we are in heart. Goodnight sweetheart ever faithfully and lovingly

Your own   Eileen.

ALS (WC, NjP).
    [1] At the Synodical Female College of Georgia (later the Rome Female College), of which Ellen's grandfather was president from 1853 to 1857. Dr. Wilson's sermon is missing.
    [2] Cited in Vol. 1, p. 4.

To Ellen Louise Axson

My own darling,   Balto., May 11, 1885
    My health does not seem to be suffering at all under this labour on the political economists. There is not very much thinking of one's own to be put into the work—interpretation and quotation are, of course, immeasurably easier than strictly original development of a subject—and I write only in the mornings when I feel fresh, stopping when I begin to feel fagged or nervous. Sometimes, as this morning, for instance, I write a little too long—up *to* the headache point, though never beyond it—but even then I am never affected as I was a month or so ago. For I have just now a wonderful fund of high spirits, of gladness, because of my relations with a lovely little maiden in New York, which seems to be daily receiving marked accessions and which seems to render all my faculties as buoyant as my heart. Yes, Dewey is to do his full third of the writing, if not more than a third, and he is doing it excellently well. Dr. Ely is waiting for vacation to put his

portion into shape, so that I don't know what it will be like—though I can easily guess. I imagine that the volume, when printed, will be not very much larger than my "Cong. Govt."—about 'a dollar-and-a-half book,' as the publishers would probably say.

I remember now that you *did* speak to me of Miss Stewart before, but only in connection with Miss Randolph—and so she did not make any impression on me *by herself.*

I am a bit afraid of such experiments as that would be with the New Hampshire farmer, darling. Don't *you* think that it would be risking a good deal? And, unless we knew beforehand *where* to go, it would not be easy to escape. Besides, we should have to act *as part of the family* under such circumstances!

Yes, precious, I believe it *is* my *head,* as well as my heart, which tells me that there is a real *necessity* that we should see each other before the 24th! But how can my little queen manage to start at night? Will she collect an escort of young ladies? Oh, how desperately impatient it makes me to know that I am her natural protector and yet that I can't help her even in these *little* things!

I appreciate Miss Granger's message thoroughly! It is a remark of great force! It *would* be altogether against the rule that a little maiden like you should be allowed to go through the world so long with such a wonderful wealth of power to love and to attract love without being captured by some rapacious man like myself—and that the prize *was* kept for *me* is one of the most marvellous pieces of gracious good fortune that ever a man didn't deserve! Oh, darling, precious, my sweetheart, "I love, *love, love* you!" How can I *help* being   Your own   Woodrow?

ALS (WC, NjP).

From Ellen Louise Axson

My darling Woodrow,   New York May 11th/85.

And so you have actually completed all your arrangements for both summer and fall! Do you always take time thus by the forelock, sir? I am glad it *is* all settled, for I doubt not it will be a relief to your mind not to be obliged to keep on thinking about it from now till the time comes.

That is one *very* strong argument in favour of Arden Park. You won't be worried with finding a place, and wondering how it will "turn out" after it is found. No dear, I don't "prefer" *any* place to Arden Park, and since you think the plan a wise one I am *wholly* delighted at the thought. But you have your mother to answer also since she was like myself somewhat dubious about it. But I agree heartily with you that we don't want to go to any *town*.

I am *so* glad that you have succeeded in making arrangements at Bryn Mawr, dear,—that we won't be obliged to put that ten miles between us so often. I suppose the terms Miss Wildgoss offers *are* as good as one could hope to get for two rooms even in the city, and you do need the two rooms it is true,—a student without a "study" is in a deplorable condition. And what a delightful picture you paint of life in that "workshop." I should like to volunteer a kiss and caress for it now, darling; indeed I shouldn't stop at *one*. I wonder if you know how supremely happy such words make you[r] little sweetheart,—happy partly because of the many glad thoughts and sweet hopes which they suggest to me, and happy most of all to see how entirely we are of one mind,—to know that we dream the same dreams.

Ah darling, we ought to be happy together it seems, for not only our hearts, but many other things, our tastes and sympathies, our hopes and aspirations are in sweet accord. Yes, I hope we will have "all sorts of good times" including the "jolly romps" in that little work-room which I already begin to love. You are *very* good, love, to let me *live* by your side. You could not grant me a privilege which I should prize more. I shall hold it in due esteem, and be as still as a little mouse when you want me to—when you are busy,—so that I shan't be sent away like a naughty child for 'making a disturbance'!

How are you getting on with your task now darling? I am somewhat uneasy about that "writing against time"; you must not forget to report how *you* are faring in the meantime.

Alas, this schedule has put me too "sadly out of sorts." I fear I must let this impediment combined with the others decide me finally to give up the plan,—to yield to what seems to be inevitable. I *can* get an escort but none that I would not much rather do without. But no more of this at present. I must dream over it before I decide. Believe me darling in all faith and love.

Your own   Eileen.

ALS (WP, DLC).

From William Battle Phillips

My dear Woodrow—   Wilmington, N. C., May 12th, 1885

If hope deferred maketh the heart sick there is very little left for duty-deferred to do unless it slays you at once. As soon as I could secure a copy of Congressional Government I divested myself of hat & coat & went to work on it. That was some 2½ or 3 months ago & I survive, after having read & reread it until I think I have a fair notion of it as a whole. I am free to confess that it was to me a complete eye-opener. In common with most men of my age, experience & education I thought I knew some thing of the manner in which our national government was conducted. Your admirable treatise showed me that I knew nothing. I have read it several times, & each time find some new feature unnoticed before that illuminates the subject as with an electric light. The work is exceedingly well done, & I offer my sincere & hearty congratulations.

You recall the pathetic picture of the author of a dead book in "The Guardian Angel."[1] Authorship seems to me the next most sacred position to that of Father, involving as it does so much of influence which can not be amended, it must stand as a whole, good or bad. You have nothing to fear from this book, it is alive, is good, & will grow. What more can a Father demand? If my book meets with half so cordial a greeting I shall be happy. Not that I am about to publish, but I hope to do so some day. I see where there is a gap to be filled & I want to try my hand.

I am sorry you will not, can not, send in yr. name to Chapel Hill. I had hoped that you could & would, for we are in terrible need of such names, & such men hereabouts. It will afford me pleasure to do any thing I can for yr. friend.[2] I have heard of him. There is a rush for those places, & from so many a first rate man can be chosen for each position. Yes, I am applying for the chair of Agric. Chem. & Mining, & Dr. Noyes,[3] an old Johns Hopkins man, is also, & several more, so it will be lively. My voice is raised in behalf of the *best* man, whoever he may be, & if I fail why I will conclude that I was *not* the best man. The converse is hardly so true! The Johanna Hopkins with the unpronounceable name is a kind of annex to the Johns, is it not? A female annex where the future mothers can be instructed in any thing. Good luck to you, & may your shadow never grow less! The departure of your Father & Mother was and is a great loss to us, & to me especially. I had anticipated both pleasure & profit from intercourse with so genial a scholar & man of God as is your Father. His example is a living epistle known & read of all who see him. His place is not to be filled. The garment he left behind will have to be reefed & tucked so much for the next man that he will have to cry aloud as a sign that he is actually in it.

The hour is late, in fact I could date this 1 a.m. May 13th, but I was always somewhat of an owl having the solemn visage & look of infinite wisdom.

With kindest regards

I am very truly yrs—Wm B. Phillips

Yrs. 29th. Thank you!

ALS (WP, DLC).
    1 The author of the "dead book" was Byles Gridley, A.M., a character in Oliver Wendell Holmes, *The Guardian Angel* (Boston, 1867).
    2 He was probably Richard Heath Dabney.
    3 William Albert Noyes, who had taken his Ph.D. at the Johns Hopkins in 1882 and was then Professor of Chemistry at the University of Tennessee.

To Ellen Louise Axson

My own darling,   Balto., May 12, '85

I have not been feeling at all well to-day, not well enough to work or to do anything serious. I don't know what is the matter. It is not a return of the trouble of a few weeks ago. It must be that slight malaria and decided dyspepsia have combined to produce this provoking lassitude and good-for-nothing-ness. I am, however, already feeling very much better than I did during the first part of the morning and I shall doubtless be quite rid of the trouble by to-morrow. I should not have mentioned it, if I were not bound by our contract to do so. And, after all, I profit more by that contract—I mean I profit more in fulfilling it—than you do; because all the *distress* of being unwell or out of sorts seems to vanish when I have told *you* about it! My heart seems to catch beforehand the influence of the tender sympathy you will feel, and I forget that I am sick in the consciousness that I am loved. I suspect that when my little wife has come to me I shall almost wish to be sick for the pleasure of being nursed and petted by her. I can be indifferent to bodily ailments then, because in those sweet days my *heart* can never get sick! *That's* the present horror of being unwell: it intensifies my loneliness and distracts me with a *full* view of how much I *need* you, my precious, my lovely little comforter. The very fact that I can take solace in anticipating your sweet sympathy only serves to quicken my consciousness of the delightful fact that soon I wont *need* to use this poor device, and to put a quicker pulse into my unspeakable longing for your presence.

Six weeks, Eileen! Had you counted the time recently? Just think! this miserable bachelor, of whose company I am so *terribly* tired, can be dismissed in six weeks, and in his stead I shall

have the loveliest, most satisfying companion that ever a man
had—a little lady beyond compare! You have professed, Miss, a
strong liking for this bachelor's company; but I think that I can
safely assure you that, little as there can be in him under any
circumstances, you will like him a great deal better when he is
married:—that is, if you like—as I am sure he likes—to be loved
joyfully and without reserve.

Tell me, sweetheart, do you really think that you know how
much, how passionately you are loved?—when you stand before
the mirror, do you think how much somebody loves that face
and form?—when you wish somebody were at your side, do you
realize how much he would give to be there?—do you think how
constantly his thoughts hover about you and all that he can
imagine you doing?—do you think that you can guess—have you
any means of guessing—what the next six weeks mean—and what
their *end* will mean, to   Your own   Woodrow.

ALS (WC, NjP).

From Ellen Louise Axson

My darling Woodrow,   New York May 12/85
   I sat up rather late last night writing duty letters, and for that
reason I suppose, I can imagine no other, I have been fast asleep
and dreaming for an hour already, though it is but half past nine;
—and am still asleep in fact as this letter will doubtless prove.
I have been partially roused but not at all effectually by the stale
episode of refusing one of Mr. Goodrich's numerous appeals to
"see" me. He is below stairs now entertaining? Miss F. who
though she calls herself my friend was pursuaded to bring up
one of his notes!
   I too am 'delighted' that you have had an opportunity of seeing
your old friend and having an old-time talk, for I can well believe that such a treat will do you good. Do I know anything about
Ned Webster by the way? The name seems to be familiar but I
can't place him.
   Are you not afraid that you will spoil me, dear, by giving me
so many compliments as this letter contains? However there is no
special danger at present for I have a particularly good antidote
in the shape of my mirror; *all* mirrors indeed serve that purpose
admirably well for me; but this one is especially useful in that
way,—in fact 'tis the only way in which it *is* useful. It makes our
faces look as long as if we had been drawn through a key-hole
besides turning them green, blue, yellow all colours but the nat-

ural one. Such glasses are exceedingly bad for the disposition—of a girl! It keeps us in a perpetual ill humour over our own exceeding ugliness. A woman should if possible always have a glass that flatters her for the general benefit of all about her!

You propound a rather puzzling question, my dear, when you ask me to define the exact connection between my love and admiration for you. *Did* I love you *because* I admired you? Not exactly that, of course, for we don't fall in love with everyone whom we admire; and yet I could not love anyone whom I did not admire and look up to and believe in *wholly*;—faith must come before love. And the admiration, of course, came before love for I admired you extremely the first day that I met you; you seemed to me even then "a Saul, than your fellows taller and stronger," and I certainly had not fallen in love with you *then*, though I did begin that process with such rare promptness as was only equalled by your own! Of course I loved you partly too because of that love of yours,—yet we don't love all who love us, so we must add to the admiration and faith, and the love which begets love that other reason that it was my most blessed *fate*. You were the one for whom my heart had waited, the only one in all the world who could altogether satisfy it. It is very well perhaps that love refuses to let us "pluck out the heart of his mystery." I should greatly prefer you not to know exactly *why* you love me;—I should be in despair if I thought you loved me *because* you admired me. Love me still you *know not why*, so that you may be sure all your life of having as good reason for loving me as you have now. Oh darling, I have every reason in the world to love *you* but I want you to continue as you do now, to love *me un*reasonably. Believe me, sweetheart, now and always in perfect love and trust

Your own   Eileen.

ALS (WC, NjP).

To Ellen Louise Axson

Balto., May 13, 1885

I *hoped* that my precious Eileen would like that little sketch of mine of our life in our workshop next winter—and she *has* declared her approval of it, in words that have made me glader and prouder than I know how to say! I am 'very *good* to let you live by my side'? I'm glad you think so, my darling little sweetheart; but it is not so, Miss: I am only very self-indulgent. If you were to stay in the other room while I was studying, how could I make any progress in my work? I should be constantly having my thoughts wander off to my little wife in the next room; I should be forever stopping to wonder what she was doing, and ever and again getting up to go and see! What a sad lot of fatal breaks there would be in the continuity and coherency of my work! *She* cannot disturb me; the closer by my side she is the better. I have even dreamed of an hour or so now and then of *special* indulgence when she would come and—if she could find ease in such a position—sit on a low seat at my feet, her arm upon my knee, nestling close to me as she read by the same light by which I should be writing. Could I *write* under such circumstances? Why of course I could—never better! My mind is never so generous of thoughts as when my heart is full of a sense of completeness such as would come from having that little form so lovingly near. The *interruption* to my thoughts would come from *not* having her near—from *wanting* her! I know that most of the time I must be content with something less perfect than this—I certainly do not intend to make her a slave to my heart-hunger for her sympathy and close companionship—no wife was ever freer than she shall be: but I want her to know what her presence will be to me, and that she cannot make me too conscious of it.

You would "like to volunteer a kiss and a caress now" and you "wouldn't stop at *one*"? Ah, sweetheart, you *can't* know how glad you make me when you say such things! *Will* you volunteer to kiss and caress me when next you get a chance?—'When next you get a chance'!—alas, sweetheart, *must* it be by steamer? It gives my heart a terrible tug to have to give up the hope that the Washington plan might prove feasible. And yet what an utterly unreasonable chap I am! Can't wait for six weeks, when waiting for *such* a prize? No; I confess it. Maybe it *ought* not to seem hard; but six weeks are like six months to a heart waiting for what mine is expecting!

My precious, will you let me tell you a secret—a *deep* secret? *I love you* with all my heart! I think that you are the sweetest, loveliest, truest, most delightful little woman in all the world; and I *know* that you shall be the making of me when you acknowledge me before the world as   Your own   Woodrow.

I am feeling very well to-day, sweetheart—symptoms of yesterday all gone.

ALS (WC, NjP).

From Ellen Louise Axson

New York, May 13/85.

I am *so very* sorry, my darling, that you are feeling so unwell again; I have been afraid that this "writing against time" would result that way. But I know that you *are* conscientious about over-taxing yourself; that you know it is wrong and have strength enough to resist temptation; so I try not to worry about it need-lessly. I trust it will prove a passing trouble;—that you *will* be "quite rid of it tomorrow." You are very wise, sweetheart, to tell me all your ailments if it affords you any gratification, "to put a quicker pulse into my unspeakable longing for your presence"— if you want to make even six weeks seem long to me. Ah, darling how my heart yearns toward you when I hear of your suffering from pain or lonliness or discouragement,—*anything*! This sepa-ration would be a heart-breaking business indeed, at such times were it not for the sweet thought that the end comes.

But, dear, *don't—please* don't say,—don't *think* that you will have "the most satisfying companion that ever man had"—un-less indeed you can boast, like some Scotchman I heard of, that you "*never* change your mind." I should by no means object to your thinking me "satisfying" if I could ensure your *always* think-ing so! But if you allow your expectations to rise so high now, the fall will be all the deeper and more disastrous. Choose some safer level for your hopes, sir, so that *I* too can hope—that you may be able to keep it. Instead of life with poor little me, my dear, you are describing heaven,—

> "And of it's bliss is naught more wondrous told us
> Than in those words 'I shall be *satisfied*' "

Darling, I would gladly give my *life* to satisfy you but I know that my nature and the nature of "things in general"! forbids that;—and with all my faith in your love I am almost frightened at it sometimes, at the character of it, I mean. But whatever, the natural limitations! of your little love there is one thing at least which you *shall* be able to say of her, viz. that "she hath done what she could."

I have just received a letter from Rose tonight[1] and I think I must give you the benefit of a scrap of it;—am sure you will laugh at it's "lamentation and weeping and great mourning." Indeed, I feel like weeping too that she can't come to Sav, though it is just as I expected. I am in almost as great dispair as she about your ever meeting each other.

She says she don't think she will marry until a year from this summer. It seems these high-church people think it wrong for a deacon to marry; Mac[2] as I knew when I was there wanted to break the rule, but Rose's principals (!) were stronger. He isn't to be ordained until Dec. and Rose won't marry in the winter because it is impossible for the girls to be there. Don't this model couple put you to shame, you impatient youth?

Did you ever go into the Historical Library here? And if so how did you get in. I think it is "too mean for anything"—and selfish— to keep such a treasure house as they say it is hermetically sealed. We are perfectly *wild* to go before we leave the city, and we can't do it without a permit from some member; and though they say nearly all the literary men in the city are members we havn't the luck to know one. I presume of course young men like Mr. Bridges however 'literary' are not likely to be members?

But I must say 'goodnight.' Yes darling I do know,—my heart tells me that when I wish for somebody here at my side the wish is sure to find a full echo. I know,—ah how wretched I should be if I did *not* know,—that my Love is mine as I am

His own   Eileen

ALS (WC, NjP).
  [1] Rosalie Anderson to ELA, May 10, 1885, ALS (WP, DLC).
  [2] McNeely DuBose.

To Ellen Louise Axson

My own darling,   Balto., May 14, 1885
    How shall I write you a birthday letter? How *can* I content my-self with wishing *you* all joy in the anniversary? It ought to be a day specially for *my* celebration—and yet how can I celebrate it away from you! How much the 15th of May means to me, my peerless little sweetheart! What would my life have been if you had not come to give me your priceless love? There was a real poetical fitness in your being born in May, precious, for you have brought into so many lives the sweet influences which May rep-resents—but above all into the life of your lover. No, Miss, I am not in the least 'afraid that I will spoil you by giving you so many compliments' as some of my letters contain—for I am not afraid that you will take them as 'compliments.' I pay 'compliments' to people whom I don't love: to those I love my praise is just a new form of love-making. In either case I mean *just* what I say: in the latter case perhaps even more literally than in the former. But what I say to those I love has an additional sincerity: it bears the sanction of love—of a love that would not for all the world

deceive. I speak my admiration for my darling because love gives me leave to speak it freely—and I am no more afraid of 'spoiling' my little queen by confessing my admiration for her than I should be afraid of spoiling her by confessing my love for her! I know that my praise will go to her heart, not to her head! I know that she will return to it, as she does to my caresses, an answer of love, that she will not keep it to make her *vain*! I *love* her simply because I can't help it; because my heart goes out to her as if she were *born* to be absolute mistress of it; because—oh, I don't know why—I know only the strength and delight of it; because somehow she brings more light and help and satisfying gladness into my life than could any other woman in the world. And *therefore* it is—that I love her and she loves me because of some unfathomed heart's-necessity, passionately and without discovered reason—*therefore* it is that I am at liberty to admire her as if my admiration were the sole *source* of my love; as if it were the sum and meaning of my love. I admire my friend (?) [William Cabell] Bruce's striking face and brilliant talents, but the words would stick in my throat if I were to try to *tell* him so, because I thoroughly dislike the man. I admire beyond measure dear father's gifts and I love him with my heart of hearts; but I can hardly manage to tell *him* so because of the sort of reverence which might restrain one who is an artist from praising his master's work. But a lover's devotion, sweetheart, if it be true, has a touch of *worship* in it. It is his *necessity* to express his homage to the woman he loves

Darling, will you accept—and value—a fresh declaration of love as a birthday present? I cannot do *more* than give myself to you all over again—and there's nothing sweeter in my experience than the privilege of dedicating to you all that is best in my heart. I want you to regard the parasol I have sent as a special bearer of this love-message[.] I want it to be a sort of earnest of my thoughts of you. It is not much in itself—I confess that the handle is too big (I *hope* it wont be too long to get into your trunk!) and that the colour of the lining don't suit me, though it *was* the most tasteful parasol I could find—but it means a great deal, as you would know if you could but see into my heart when thoughts of your birthday crowd into it. Ah, darling, my Eileen, it means that I love you and think of you all the time. I like mementoes wh. one can *use* constantly—don't you? That is one reason of my delighted satisfaction in this beautiful screen that serves me so well every night! By-the-way, I found a poem the other day which fits the case of this screen exactly (may-be you remember it?)

"she sate and stretched
The silk upon the frame . . . .
That, forced to wander till sweet spring return,
I yet might ne'er forget her smile, her look,
Her voice (that even in her mirthful mood
Has made me wish to steal away and weep)
Nor yet the entrancement of that maiden kiss
With which she promised, that, when spring returned,
She would resign one half of her sweet name,
And own thenceforth no other name but mine!"[1]

Do you realize, Miss Axson, that this is your last birthday—that on the next 15th of May you will be *somebody else*? So I don't wish you 'many happy returns,' but hope with all my heart—hope with all my life's purposes and wishes in the hope—that to that little lady whom I shall love and honour as my blessed little wife, when she owns "no other name but mine,"—that to Mrs. Woodrow Wilson may come as many happy birth-days as a life of love and of joy can contain—that to her there may come a long succession of mid-May days, each seeming sweeter and more hallowed than the rest because of life-long love and devotion. And oh, sweetheart, I pray God that I may never do aught to bring even the least shadow upon the memories of the birth-days that shall come to you; that my love may always be able to add brightness to the course of your life; that it may lighten the trials to come, ease the pains, dispel the anxieties! I would bring my love to its perfect work, that you may always find strength and delight in the devotion of   Your own   Woodrow.

ALS (WC, NjP).
[1] From Coleridge's "The Keepsake." WW's elision.

From Ellen Louise Axson

My darling Woodrow,   New York, May 14/85
    I begin to think that there is something like enchantment in all this, and that you are the sorcerer! When I think that it is utterly impossible for me to love you more than I have done,—that the outermost limit is reached[,] you straightway create new worlds for my love to conquer. What is that but wonder-working? You are ever, by means of some delightful letter, making me fall in love with you afresh, by showing me some fresh gladness and sweetness in loving.
    I don't know whether to attribute the little coincidence in this

letter to magic or to our inveterate habit of thinking and wishing for the same things,—or what! But no—the very fact of it's being such a small *detail* makes such an explanation as the last impossible. I *must* have told you, though I don't remember it of my peculiar weakness for sitting in low chairs, and especially at the feet of those I love best. It has always amused the children immensely to see Cousin Ellie always sitting in their chairs; and if the older ones were called upon to describe my idiosyncrasies they would be sure to mention that among the first as one of the strongest and most characteristic. Moreover when after a true day-dream; one of the perfectly involuntary sort,—I suddenly arouse myself in time to catch a glimpse of it as it fades away, I find that almost always we have been not merely *together*, but together in *just* the position which you describe! As I say, the fact of it's being such a trifle makes this oneness in thought more remarkable. "Our hearts ever answer in tune and in time, love, As octave to octave and rhyme unto rhyme, love.["]

I honestly do not believe, darling, that there is another woman in the world so happy, so blessed, tonight, as the one to whom you have given this priceless treasure of your heart. What can I do to show at what worth I hold that wonderful gift? What would I not do to make you happy;—and you tell me I can do it best simply by being at your side, by being myself the happiest little wife in the world.

Truly it is well that the girls who are not in love don't know what love is, else how unhappy, how discontented they would be. How is it possible for anyone to say they "loved once";—I could as well walk abroad in my grave-clothes and say I *lived* once.

Tomorrow is my birthday! I naturally avoid discussing the subject further, seeing that I shall have had twenty-five of them, —in fact that I shall be an old maid tomorrow! If I *am* at a boarding house I am going to have my birthday dinner—the Seamans have invited me to dine with them;—of course not knowing that it was an anniversary.

I am *so* happy, dear, to know that you are feeling well again. I hope it will prove a thorough recovery. Believe me, love, with all my heart   Your own   Eileen.

ALS (WP, DLC).

From Henry Marquand[1]

The Commercial Advertiser [New York].

May 15, 1885

Dear Mr. Wilson,

The election of a Senator in Illinois is apparently reaching a final stage, illustrated by Mr. Morrison's withdrawal.[2] I do not know whether you have followed the course of the extraordinary farce played at Springfield. It strikes me as something unique in our history & yet that may be repeated some time when far more momentous results may be at issue. The exact balance of the parties is unusual—the presence of an equal (or nearly equal) number of Knights errant on each side, the absence of any regularly recognized representatives of third & fourth parties, the popular apathy of the State, which satisfies itself in vague & general ridicule—but brings no pressure to bear on its legislators— as is frequently done in N. Y. vide election of Evarts[3] &c.—all combine to make the case one of value as illustrative of the 'typical' in American politics & to commend it to the philosophic historian as an example & a text. Has the subject come in yr. way at all and does it strike you as important or only as a tiresome burlesque? If you would care to utter any words of comment in a general review of the situation[,] its causes & consequences, we shd. be glad to give them to the public—perhaps using them as editorial (say about 1200-1500 words) or letter over yr. name— about 2500 words to a column. It strikes me that such an article wd. be timely & interesting if printed when an election occurs— if that event is to be! The editorial cd. only be used *directly* upon the election, the letter a reasonable time after.

Yours truly   H. Marquand

ALS (WP, DLC) with WWhw notation on env.: "Ans. May 16/85."
  [1] An editor of the New York *Commercial Advertiser*.
  [2] For an account of this affair, see A. Shaw to WW, May 24, 1885.
  [3] He had been elected to the United States Senate on January 20, 1885.

To Ellen Louise Axson

Balto., May 15, 1885

It is scandalous, my little queen, that I should have to *scold* you on your birth-day; but really, Miss, you deserve a scolding, which can't be put off, for what you say in to-day's letter. "Don't, *please* don't say—don't *think*—that I will have the 'most satisfying companion that ever man had,'" when I have you? And why not? Because, if I allow my "expectations to rise so high now, the fall will be all the deeper and more disastrous"! Oh sweetheart,

sweetheart! this will never do! It will break my heart if you are to go on looking at my love askance, expecting it to *change*! Have you so soon forgotten the many, many words in which I have tried to tell you what sort of companion I want in my wife—and do you think that I have required anything that you cannot be? Have you forgotten your own quotation from Hamerton: "It is not by adding to our knowledge, but by understanding us, that women are our helpers"? "The intellectual life is sometimes a fearfully solitary one. Unless he lives in a great capital"—and generally even when he *does* live in such a centre—"the man devoted to that life is more than all other men liable to suffer from isolation, to feel utterly alone. . . . Give him one friend who can understand him, who will not leave him, who will always be accessible by day and night—one friend, one kindly listener, just one, and the whole universe is changed. It is deaf and indifferent no longer, and whilst *she* listens, it seems as if all men and angels listened also, so perfectly his thought is mirrored in the light of her answering eyes."[1] Now, sweetheart, is there anything in 'your nature' or in the "nature of things in general" to forbid your being that sort of companion to me, or to frighten your faith in my love because I want you to be that sort of companion to me and am sure that you will be? It requires only love and just the sort of education and sympathetic intelligence that you have to enable a woman to realize *that* ideal. I have not built castles in the air which the first slight breath of experience can blow away. I don't expect the unalloyed 'satisfaction' of heaven anywhere, in anything, this side of heaven itself. I am too sensitive, too intense, too anxious, too selfish, too open to any influence that stirs anywhere near me, to escape having a great deal of acute suffering at every turn of my life. But, darling, isn't there some *reason* for the 'satisfaction' of heaven, and isn't that reason *love*? Love, *your* love, is to keep the experiences which cut me from cutting to the quick. If I find in you a love that is boundless, which is altogether mine, which is unquestioning and ever ready to respond to the utmost claim that can be made upon it, I shall have found "the most satisfying companion that man ever had"! Does *that* frighten you? Is there anything in your nature or in the nature of things in general to forbid my expecting that sort of love from you?

Darling, I am not a creature apart; I am like other men! Does Miss Rose tremble for fear she will not satisfy "Mac."? Did Miss Janie feel that Mr. Chandler was running a great risk? No, the cases are not different. "Mac." wants Miss Rose's perfect love, her life-long devotion—wants Miss Rose, *for his heart's sake.* I want *your* perfect love, your life-long devotion—I want *you, for my heart's sake*! Hamerton has not sketched the picture merely, he has *completed* it. Have I not often told you the sort of persons I most delight to converse with—that my enjoyment is proportioned, not to their wit or learning, but to their sympathy, to their pleasure in understanding me? Your imagination has endowed me with a great mind, and you have frightened yourself with the idea that your companionship can never satisfy that *mind*! That's not the question at all. The question is, can you love me and can you take pleasure in trying to understand me? We speak of the mind and the heart as if they were two separate things, but of course they are not and the companion who satisfies one's heart satisfies all of the mind that companionship is meant to satisfy. There's no companionship between teacher and pupil or between scholar and scholar until complete *sympathy*, complete oneness of *heart*, comes in to create it. So remember, darling, that your love for me and your power of sympathizing with me are the tests of your companionableness as my wife. The rest will take care of itself: and of the rest I can judge—and *did* judge before ever I loved you. My darling has a power of sympathy with serious thought which was once my wonder and is now my delight. "She is not bred so dull but she can learn," and her willingness to "commit her gentle spirit" to me is plentiful inspiration to her "lord and king."

You see, sweetheart, for your sake I have taken only the *selfish* view of the question. I have said nothing of the satisfying delight which I shall derive from serving you by aid of perfect love, and loyalty, and sympathy. I shall have you to live for—and *that* shall be my happiness, as well as that you are living for me!

And now, precious, my joy, my little comforter, what say you? Can you match my *love*—will your love never let your delight grow less in being my companion? Then you *can* satisfy me, you *can* answer all my needs; you will come with *all* the best gifts of happiness to   Your own   Woodrow.

P.S. I am unspeakably distressed and indignant, my darling, to learn that that spiritless fellow Goodrich is still troubling you with his attentions. His 'attentions' indeed! They are *insults* now— because they indicate a hope that you will sooner or later consent to see him. Because you had not mentioned him for a long time I had hoped that he had at last made up his mind to act the gentleman. How terribly my estimate of his character—my suspicion of his character—has been confirmed. Of course, love, you do not read the notes he sends. To receive them would be as compromising as to receive his visits. If he persists in his efforts to see you, I shall come on to New York and take some means of delivering you from the intolerable annoyance. It will be my *duty* to do so—and I beg that you will not fail to tell me of his actions. You owe it to me and to yourself to let me act as your protector in this case. Did he dare to say anything more to you at Miss Beatty's? Why does Miss Farnsworth see him? Please tell me all about it—I had no idea that my darling was still suffering from the fellow's insults!   Lovingly and anxiously,   Woodrow.

ALS (WC, NjP).
1 Philip G. Hamerton, *The Intellectual Life*, pp. 236-37; WW's elision.

From Ellen Louise Axson

New York May 15/85.

Many, many thanks, my darling, for the *beautiful* birthday present, which was safely received tonight. It is perfectly lovely, as well as elegant, in *every* respect. *I* like the lining exceedingly and charming to tell it matches the colour of my light summer suit. Yes I do like mementoes that I can use constantly, and it is needless to add that I shall never use this without thoughts of the dear giver. I can't thank you enough for your lovely gift,—if you were only here that I might give you for it as many kisses as,—I was going to say, as it is *worth*, but that is too tremendous,—at any rate as many as you want. How shall I even try to thank you for this precious birthday letter and its priceless gift of your love,—of yourself? What can I do more than pledge you once again my little all—my *great* all of love in return! I know right well the rare worth of this treasure which has been committed to my care, and with God's help, my love, it shall be safe in my hands. I pray God to give me wisdom equal to my love and then I shall be sure to guard my treasure well. I trust that there *is* a wisdom which is the direct result of love, and of my absorbing desire to serve you well,—to be a true help-meet for you; otherwise there would be something terrible in the thought of such a life as yours, with all it's wonderful possibilities for good, being at the mercy of one foolish little woman. Ah! you must believe in us, you men, before you trust us with such power to work you weel or woe;—a power which even the most thoughtless,—though she may not recognize it cannot escape from exercising.

Darling if I am to have your life-long love and devotion you need have no fears for my future birthdays; their happiness is ensured, for there *is* no trial, pain or anxiety which it cannot lighten or dispel. I hope "with all my life's purposes and wishes in the hope" that my darling's life may be as rich in blessings as his love has made mine.

The little lines you copy are lovely, dear; they are so very familiar yet I can't place them;—can they be from Coleridge? I am sorry sweet-heart to write you such a short note on my birthday. But I have just returned late from Mrs. Seamans where I had a lovely evening;—and the excessive heat all day makes it *feel* later than it really is. So, as I have an engagement at nine in the morning, I must close now 'for good.' Am *so* glad you are feeling better. Goodnight, my love. With all my heart.

Your own   Eileen.

ALS (WP, DLC) with WWhw notation on env.: "I love you, sweet: how can you ever learn how much I love you."

To Ellen Louise Axson

Balto., May 16, 1885

No, my precious little sunbeam, there was no sorcery in the picture I drew of the little lady sitting lovingly at my feet in our workshop—and no *memory* either! I won't let you detract from my originality by attributing my choicest bits to memory! I do not remember ever having heard you speak of your fondness for low chairs and—the uses to which low chairs may be put; and my delight at finding from your delightful letter of this morning that my dreams of those sweet days to come are not only like yours in substance but even in detail is simply the crowning delight of all our intercourse. For I was putting into words thoughts from my very heart of hearts when I wrote what was to prompt this precious letter which lies here before me. Oh you delightful little girl! How reckless you are in giving me fresh cause for love—and what a blessed thing it is that I need not resist! Twenty months to-day since you gave me leave to love you as my own, and here I am loving you more than I expected to learn how to love in twenty years! And *you*!—why you precious, innocent little girl!— if these small bits of my *dreams* make you more in love with me than before, what will become of you when you find out the full meaning of my love for home-life and for the queen of my home-realm? When you discover that, no matter what I am doing, you can quicken, not interrupt, the train of my thoughts by coming and whispering in my ear just the three words, 'I love you,' and that to add a kiss will but give the more efficacy to the words— when you discover such things, will you—profit by the discovery? Why often *now*, when the stillness of this little den of mine makes me, and keeps me, so conscious of being a lone and lorn bachelor,

I pause in my work and, leaning back in my chair, dream that I feel your arm put about my neck and that your head is close enough to mine for your ear to catch a very soft whisper—and I break my reverie by actually whispering words of love as if you were really there! Maybe you *are* there in thought, and my heart is only going out to meet yours. Can you form no idea, Miss, of a fellow both desperately and delightedly in love—delightedly *be-cause* desperately, for the desperation is to take flight at his next glimpse of his darling's eyes, his next touch of her sweet lips? When next you dream, dream of that sort of lover—no, dream of what he will be after he has been welcomed as something more than lover—dream what you will of your intercourse with your husband, and I undertake to fulfil the dream, if it demand only delight in that intercourse: for on that side my capacity is boundless.

'Am I not put to shame for my impatience by that model couple in Sewanee?' No, Miss, not in the least! But I am sincerely sorry for poor "Mac." I think that Miss Rose is just a little bit hardhearted in the matter, whatever force of high-church principles and principals there be to excuse her. But "Mac." ought to know how to fight his own battles: I'm not half so sorry on account of his disappointment as I am on account of yours, in not having your sweet chum at our wedding. My heart is very sore about that, because I know how much the disappointment means to you. But, sweetheart, I don't see any reason to dispair about Miss Rose and I having chances to make each other's acquaintance. It will be easy enough some time, when we are visiting sister Annie in Columbia, to search Miss Rose out in her "corner of S. C."[1] It seems very odd to me that she should be so anxious to meet me, unless it be altogether out of curiosity, and anxiety, as to the sort of man you have chosen. Maybe she has learned to like me through you —just as I have learned to admire and love her. I am sure that I am as anxious to meet her as she can be to see me. We'll manage it sooner or later. We will try to go to *her* wedding—*that's* the scheme!

Why was I vouchsafed only a scrap of her letter? This part made me wish for all

Have you definitely settled on your plans yet, precious,—when you will sail, &c.? Oh those fatal schedules—what havoc they have played with some very precious hopes! If you are going by steamer, you will be off *next week*, wont you? May will have run out before the next week closes; and *then*—June! Oh, sweetheart, it is almost too good to be true that the time is so near at hand!

I am going to try my best to get through with these economists by the first of June, so as to start for Columbia on the 3rd.—though of course I sha'nt overtax myself in order to do it. I've finished with the three principal writers and I don't think that the minor ones will be hard to dispose of in short order.

But it's late, my little pet, and I must say 'good-night'—must go dream about you. You are a very capricious maiden in my dreams often, disappearing when most I want you, tantalizing me with just a glimpse now and again of your sweet self; but, for a' that, I'd rather have you capricious than not have you at all; and sleep has gained a fresh charm for me since it has proved the way to you. Ah, Eileen, my peerless little darling, I love you with all my heart—I love you as   Your own   Woodrow.

ALS (WC, NjP).
   [1] Rosalie Anderson's fiancé, McNeely DuBose, was soon to become rector of the Church of the Nativity in Union, S. C.

To Albert Shaw

My dear Shaw,   Balto., May 16, 1885
   I am anxious to get at the true inwardness of this extraordinary Senatorial contest in Ill. and I write to ask if you can send me any material that reveals the said inwardness. There's nothing at hand here that touches it. I have an idea that minority representation is in some degree responsible for the opportunity given our friend Haines to play the trickster and that Haines is at the bottom of much of the mischief; but whether this idea is well-founded or not I have no means of finding out unless you befriend me.[1] Of course I should take good care of any matter you might send me and be diligent to return it in condition as received.

   I have had a long tug with ill health these last two months and most of my work has, of course, been turned topsy-turvy in consequence. But I am on my feet again now and am dishing up American economists at the rate of about one *per diem*, for the great history, which is beginning to scent printer's ink. I hope to be through with the job by the end of the month, and then 'good-bye Johns Hopkins'—I shall be off home to wonder at my leisure what I shall talk about to the Bryn Mawr girls. But another part of my program is a little more definite than that. I am going to be married, my dear fellow, on the 24th of June, and this is to invite you to be present, in Savannah, Geo., at the ceremony on that date. It is to be a private wedding, to which no formal in-

vitations are to be issued; but *this* invitation means a great deal
more than any other sort would, and it would delight me immensely if I could hope that you would find your way to the Southern coast about that time!

I received, in quick succession, two notes from Shinn a few
weeks ago—the first word from him since he crossed the continent—but they were so brief that I don't know much more about
him or his movements now than I did before. He may come back
this summer, and he may remain out there two or three years!
But doubtless you have heard from him too.

There's *absolutely* no news in the Seminary. Having known it
last year, you have known it this!

Miss Ashton and Wright unite with me in sending much love,
          Your very sincere friend,   Woodrow Wilson

TCL (in possession of Virginia Shaw English).
  ¹ Shaw answers Wilson's question in some detail in his letter of May 24, 1885.

From Ellen Louise Axson

My darling Woodrow,   New York May 17/85
    It is worth my while to give you the benefit of *all* my little mis-
givings about myself if I am to be rewarded for it with such letters as this. If you put such a premium upon doubts, sir, you may
tempt me to suggest some that I don't feel, merely to "draw you
out"; doubtless I *should* pursue that course if you had not added
that it will break your heart to have me "go on" so! In that view
of the case, I must promise, I suppose, never to express any fears
that I don't feel,—and that means *now none whatever*, my darling;
You are the most satisfying lover that ever girl had!—satisfying
in every sense, for you leave me nothing to fear and nothing to
desire. You even reconcile me to your fate! those questions shall
vex me no more, you have answered them well and I believe truly,
—and I am satisfied. You see, I have even made friends with the
word which startled me. For I well know that in my nature and
yours, and the nature of things in general there *is* nothing to forbid your expecting from me such love as you wish. It is these
very things which *compel* me to love you, for it is now as much
my necessity as it is my joy to render you a love that is boundless
and altogether yours, unquestioning and ever ready to respond to
the utmost claim upon it.

    But I must send you only a little love-message now, dearest,
for I am very late today, the dinner bell has already rung and if

I don't hasten down I will be behind time for my class. Excuse desperate haste; and believe me, sweet-heart, now and always

Your own   Eileen.

ALS (WC, NjP).

To Ellen Louise Axson

My own darling,   Balto., May 17, 1885

I am *delighted* that you think the parasol tasteful, and everything that it should be. I have no great confidence in my own taste—positive as that taste is—and I was afraid that the lining (the sales-girl called it écru) would not suit you as well as some I might have chosen. Will the long handle suffer itself to be put into your trunk?

And do you think, Miss, that in offering me as many kisses as I *want* for the gift you are offering fewer than the gift is worth? In *my* opinion, my little sweetheart, *one* of your kisses is more precious than many such gifts could be;—and you can *never* give me as many kisses as I want! I challenge you to *try* some of these days!—if you succeed, I'll—give you as many as *you* want,

> "Thy mouth's culled sweetness by my kisses shed
>   On cheeks and neck and eyelids, and so led
>   Back to thy mouth which answers there for all."[1]

Ah, precious, you don't know what your kisses mean to me! They are tokens of that complete surrender of your*self* to me which has made my happiness, and shall keep it ever fresh.

> "Your voice is not in the air,
>   Yet, love, I can hear your voice:
>   It bids my heart to rejoice
>   As knowing your heart is there,—
>   A music sweet to declare
>   The truth of your steadfast choice.
>   O love, how sweet is your voice!"[2]

If it were *not* so, if my darling's love were silent, if there were none of these sweet letters to stir my heart with fresh gladness, what would become of me! The weeks move with such a leaden pace this time of year!

How delightful it was that Mrs. Seamans should give you a birth-day dinner unawares!—and how very glad I am that you enjoyed your evening there—even if it *did* result in my getting a very brief note just when it seemed as if my heart were most longing for a *long* letter. A long letter could not have contained more precious words of love than this short one has brought me: but—don't *you* sometimes feel that your heart hungers for *long* messages of love—words upon words of the sweet import—from—somebody? All the same, I am gladder by far that my little sweetheart was made happy at the dinner than I could have been made by any blessings brought to me. What would I not give to see her *always* happy!

"I love you, sweet: how can you ever learn how much I love you?" If I could write you the love letter my *heart* contains, you would know better than you can know now how completely I am

Your own   Woodrow.

ALS (WC, NjP).
¹ Adapted from Dante Gabriel Rossetti, Sonnet XIII, "Love-sweetness," in *The House of Life*.
² From Rossetti's "Parted Presence."

From Ellen Louise Axson

My darling Woodrow,   New York, May 19[17]/85.
I think the fates have been very unkind to me the last few nights; everything seems to conspire to prevent my writing;—and I have been more than usually anxious too, if that is possible. We were entertaining the Beviers last night until it was too late for me to do anything but scribble off a letter which it was absolutely necessary for me to write Grandmother. And there is truly a 'poor chance' to write Monday morning. At any rate I will answer your questions about Mr. Goodrich and get him off my hands, so that when I do have an opportunity to write a letter again it may be about something pleasant. I thought I wouldn't vex you with that name again, as there was nothing worth telling; don't know how I happened to do it the other night. Of course he never said anything objectionable to me again, but he did continue teasing me to forgive him and be his friend until he wore me out completely, —until I was obliged to "insult" (!) him—send back his notes unread, &c. Of course I tried at first to treat him as though nothing had happened,—as I would any mere acquaintance. But he hadn't sense enough to take that course. He took Miss Farnsworth into his confidence, and to a certain extent secured her friendship for a time; that is, she said she thought I was too hard on him, and too "prudish," and that she was sorry for him. But she too has grown so disgusted with his want of manliness and self-respect, that she thinks I am altogether right now. There is nothing to

worry about, dear; now that I have left the house I am rid of him, of course, and while there I could manage him perfectly—except on one point! He thought it perfectly *dreadful* for me to go to Spring St. unprotected; and do what I would, I *could* not prevent his watching the cars at Washington Square until he found mine and then going down in it. He would not speak to me or notice me unless I bowed to him. So now I don't go down in the car but walk with the Bevier girls. So don't disturb yourself about the poor baby any more, dear. If if [*sic*] I were utterly selfish and inconsiderate, I should be tempted to *pretend* that I did need to be delivered from an "intolerable annoyance," by that suggestion that you would in that case "come on to N.Y."! But my conscience won't let me do that, since I have your interests at heart as well as my own,—since yours and mine are one! But now that I feel I *must* go by steamer you can understand how even that is a temptation.

But I *must* close for the present

Yes my darling I *can* match your love. What shall I say of the satisfying delight which I shall derive from serving *you* "by aid of perfect love and loyalty and sympathy," of the happiness I shall have in living for you. Never was there a promise more sure than the one I make when I give you my pledge that my love *shall* never let my delight grow less in being your companion. I am always and altogether Your own Eileen.

ALS (WC, NjP).

From James E. Rhoads

My dear Friend, Philadelphia, 5 Mo. 18. 1885.
Thine of the 16th is at hand.

Of the papers presented by C. L. Houghton I read only the one on the English Poor Laws. I noticed its defects of style and spelling and want of logical clearness. But I was impressed by Dr. H. C. Adams rather strong commendation of the lady's historical work. We will arrange to keep open the Fellowship until autumn, & I hope some qualified candidate may offer.

I observed the reference in thy previous note to thy expected marriage next month and heartily congratulate thee upon its near approach.

With kind regard thy friend, James E Rhoads

ALS (WP, DLC).

From Ellen Louise Axson

My darling Woodrow,   New York, May 18/85

I have just come in from church where we have been to hear
one of Dr. Hamilton's lectures on "the Gospel notes in modern
poetry." This time he gave us Tennyson, and it was *delightful*.
He seems to be almost as great an admirer of Tennyson as Prof.
[Hiram] Corson (?)—I *should* say *Lord* Tennyson[.] The doctor
shows his British birth by the extreme care with which he always
bestows the title. It never once occurred to me to call him by it.

By the way, we were told that "In Memoriam["] was the greatest product of the nineteenth century! What do you think of that?
I was inclined to open my eyes rather wide at it, though I am such
an extravagant lover of poetry—and Tennyson and "In Memoriam."

What good people—what fine workers they are in that Scotch
church! The reports &c. read tonight show a fine record. I am
very glad I attached myself to them; it serves to keep my courage
up. At the League I feel sometimes as though all the world were
turning aside to infidelity, and I am really disheartened; but when
I think of these good people I am convinced that the battle is'nt
lost yet;—and won't be. The state of affairs at the League is terrible in that respect; every other person seems to be some sort of
a "free-thinker["]; and what seems specially shocking to me is
that the girls are as bad as the men! With them, I fancy it is one
form of that folly which is demoralizing so many of the northan
women; they are just as clever as the men and the latter shan't
be more "advanced" than they in any respect! For the arrogant
young simpletons, of both sexes, plainly think it an evidence of
a superior mind to rise above the old prejudices,—to take *broad*
views.

I have just received one of Beth's motherly letters.[1] She gives
me even more sage counsel than usual in view of the new life
before me;—and also the benefit of her experience which she even
hints, for *my* good, has not been that of *unalloyed* happiness,
though she gives a favourable report, on the whole. But she
warns me against starting out with the idea that you are fault-
less. I must give you a choice extract—"How I wish I knew the
man you are going to marry—I would like to know who it is my
little girl is going to love so blindly,—to be sure that he will be
true and staunch. . . . You have always had pretty much your
own way, and now will this will of yours bend to his easily?—for
bend it must to that *chin!*" All this probably was not meant for

your eye, as she of course could not know upon what confidential terms we are,—what a perfect understanding there is between us, but it was too good to keep! I shall tell her that I am going to be a perfect Griselda!—that I am already so "broken in" that she wouldn't know me!

She is very anxious to hear that we are going to Arden Park,— "for of course you would not be that near me and not spend some time with me." She says if we don't come *she* don't expect to see me—"perhaps forever"! What a gloomy view of the situation as it affects them my friends take! But neither do I feel at all hopeless about seeing Rose since her father's home is at Sewanee, and your father's will be at Clarksville but a few miles away. She will be sure to "go home" sometimes in the summer. I am more surprised and pleased my darling, than I can say at this delightful coincidence in our dreams;—you may be sure dear that I *shall* profit by all such discoveries. It is a serious question that of what will "become of" me if I find out much more that is lovable in my Love. I am sure I don't know. But Carlyle says there is "an infinite in man," so I presume my capacity for happiness will turn out to be as boundless as your power to make me happy. There surely is something infinite about *that.* And so you dream sometimes that I am near you,—near enough to hear your whisper—ah, darling I believe *I* am there then. If our senses were keen enough "to hear the grass grow" for instance, you might catch the answering whisper, for I too have often unconsciously broken the silence in the same way when, as it were, my heart has grown full to overflowing. Ah love, it is sweet to think of you—to dream of you, but there is something sweeter than dreams, and my heart is flooded with a great joy to think how soon that something —the substance of all the dreams will be ours.

With all love and faith   Your own   Eileen.

ALS (WC, NjP).
¹ Elizabeth Adams Erwin to ELA, May 13, 1885, ALS (WP, DLC).

Two Letters to Ellen Louise Axson

My own darling,   Balto., May 18, 1885
I must content myself, and ask you to be contented, with a very brief note to-day, because my head is so full of a wretched cold I've caught that I've already used up all my sense in working up the political economist whose turn it was to be 'treated' to-day, and have now absolutely none left, for letter-writing or anything else. I am doctoring the cold in season this time and

don't expect that it will tarry with me long or trouble me much; but for the time being it is making me very thick-headed and uncomfortable.

Your sweet little note of Sunday has made me very happy, precious. I am glad to see that my 'scolding' did you so much good! Ah, sweetheart, no one ever had less reason for misgivings than you have in regard to our marriage, so far as its effects upon me are concerned. I am sure of happiness so long as you love me as you do now, and are yourself happy in my love. And it *would* break my heart if you were to go on expecting my love for you and my delight in your love for me to change. That would be terrible. I love you—I *must ever* love you—I cannot help it—my love for you has become part of me—the very centre and spring of my life.   Your own   Woodrow.

My own darling,   Balto., May 19, 1885
My cold is less troublesome this morning, and Hiram has given me a tonic which *tastes* as if it had every possible 'virtue' in it, so that you may count on my being in a fair way to achieve the utter overthrow of this oppressive force which is campaigning in my head. A cold in the head is all the more irritating because it is a *small* ailment, not a big disease worthy of one's mettle.

I have 'dished up' another political economist too this morning (these are the small fry I have come to now) and feel better on *that* account.

I am *very* much relieved, sweetheart, to hear that you have found a way of ridding yourself of Goodrich. I was afraid that he was unmanly enough to thrust himself upon you in ways which a woman would not know how to thwart. Since he had altogether lost all self-respect, I did not know what he might *not* attempt. But your letter of this morning has taken away all my fears, and leaves only a keen regret that you should still be made to suffer the annoyance of having to be watchful to avoid him.

On what days do the Savannah steamers leave New York, precious,—on Saturdays? And on which one of those sailing days will you leave? Don't forget, my pet, to send me before you go a ring that will fit your marriage-ring finger; and, sweetheart, do you care to wear ear-rings? They make ear-rings so much more beautifully nowadays, it seems to me, than they do any other pieces of jewelry that I am sometimes tempted to ask you to wear some of the dainty little things I see. Ear-rings don't catch in one's coat, or one's mustache, do they, and hurt little lady's ears? But *don't forget the ring,* Miss, if you want to escape a scolding. Do you remember, my little queen, how I ran back from the 'bus in Asheville to borrow a ring? What a sweetly purturbed little lady took that piece of gold from her finger that day, and with what a blaze of blushes she handed it to the young gentleman whom she had not long since been trying to dissuade from loving her— as if he could help it! Ah, my peerless little mistress, what a wonderful experience that was—how it opened my heart to you!—and I had thought that my heart was open before! And to what delights was that experience the sweet prelude! And *now*, darling, my blessed little promised wife, *only five weeks* and my heart will be fuller than it knows how to hold with the inexpressible happiness of knowing that those sacred promises are fulfilled and that our lives, as well as our hearts, are united! Darling, love has cast out all fear—hasn't it?—and you will come with *only* gladness— wont you?—to   Your own   Woodrow.

ALS (WC, NjP).

From Ellen Louise Axson

New York May 19/85

I am so exceedingly distressed, my darling, about that heavy cold, for they are peculiarly wretched things at this season, I think, when they combine with the first heat; which, by itself, is apt to make one feel a little under the weather. With all my heart, I hope you will succeed in breaking it up at once, for if you are oppressed in that way your work will seem so much harder for you. I trust you will find release from the latter the first of June. I shall be relieved as much as you, dear, when this spring, which has been so hard upon you, is finally over, and safely over, for you. Even the pleasant work at the League is beginning to seem a little "trying" in these very hot days so that I shan't be as sorry—as broken-hearted—as I expected to see them end. There are very few feelings which are not more or less mixed,—while this "breaking up" at the school *is so* hard, I can't forget that it is bringing me nearer to *you,* long enough to be as sorry as the situation demands!

We have been having a gay time there last week and today having our fortunes told! Our old model turned out to be a professional fortune-teller, and you may imagine the sensation she created in the school. She was the most deliciously funny old soul I ever saw, with her quaint turns of speech, her broken English, her "nods and becks and wreathed smiles," and the utterly indescribable expression of her face. Oh it was rich! And there really seems to be some method in her madness, she has *some* system about it,—and a fine sense for mystery;—her oracles are truly Delphic in that respect. She told me, by the way, that I was going to get a present, and I did get one the next day, that exquisite parasol; also that I was to go on a journey the last of June, so in view of those "coincidences" I am disposed to believe her, when she says that you (or rather "he") always mean what you say and say what you mean, and do what you promise, and that I am to have a happy married life. But I know more about my fortune in those particulars than all the—other—witches in the world don't I dear? And yet *anyone* who knows my lover would be wise enough to forecast the future happiness of his wife;— would know that she *must* be blessed among women who wins his love. But no one but myself can know *how* blessed she is. It is most wonderful how entirely you 'satisfy' *me* in everything. I have seen a great many men whom I liked more or less, but they all jarred upon me in one way or another. There was always some quality which they possessed or some other which they lacked or at best some want of sympathy, rendering intercourse imperfect, a constant compromise. But with you how different! It will be easy for us to grow together, dear, for there are the same tendencies in us both, and our roots are in the same soil. I am *very* glad that my love happened to behave so reasonably so that it will be spared the task of making me all over again the better to fit into your life! I am glad there are no barriers for it to burn away. I suppose that sort of achievement proves the strength of love. But I hope to find some less destructive way to prove to you the strength of mine. But I must say goodnight or I will leave myself no place wherein to say it. Goodnight sweetheart, I love you more than words can tell; I am altogether and always

Your own   Eileen.

ALS (WC, NjP).

To Ellen Louise Axson

My own darling,   Balto., May 20, 1885

I must begin by reporting my cold less troublesome to-day—if I did not *begin* with that report, I should probably forget to put it in at all. Hiram's tonic is doing me good, and I am really not *sick* at all—only uncomfortable.

That must have been a very *sad* letter—the one from "Beth"! In a true marriage—a marriage, I mean, not of fancy but of genuine love—how could there be so much as a thought of a contest of wills, of the will of the wife bending, almost to breaking, under that of the husband! The idea seems to me a *terrible* one. The love of those who are meant to be married means *mutual help-fulness*—means identification of heart and interest—or it means nothing noble. If, in looking forward to our marriage, my thoughts were principally, or at all, concerned about what I should give up to you, how far I might expect you to yield to me, what would be the proper limits of command and indulgence, and other like questions—I don't want to mar the sheet with any more such ugly phrases!—why then I should know that I ought not to marry you, that my love was not such as I had any right to offer you;—*and I should not offer it*! True love lies at the opposite pole from selfishness. Its blessedness consists in delivering us from selfishness. Oh, it makes my heart ache to think of such a marriage as Mrs. Erwin's, where to give up for love's sake is bitter! She doesn't know—does she sweetheart?—that, when two persons love each other as we do, 'having one's own way' consists in serving, with a glad love-service, the interests and wishes of the loved one

Oh, my sweetheart, my precious darling, *I love you*—and it does seem to me such a sacrilege for anybody to make such suggestions about our future relations as man and wife! The profound pity and repugnance which such views excite in my mind cannot be measured by anything but the delight which I experience when I see with what opposite feelings my darling's heart is filled, how utterly incapable it is of such thoughts, and how naturally and sweetly it chooses to learn, not from such counsellors, but rather from cousin (mayn't I call her cousin *now*?) Hattie Ewing, and those who have discovered wedded love. Eileen, my little bewitcher, I am the happiest man in the world—for I have found the love I want—I have found *your* love, which makes my heart feel so rich that—surely there is no other heart in the world that can call such love *all* its own! Think, darling! Only five weeks, and then we can daily prove to each other what those sweet dreams we have been dreaming mean—what we *mean* by love—what the bond *is* between my Eileen and

Her own   Woodrow.

ALS (WC, NjP).

From Ellen Louise Axson

My darling Woodrow,   New York May 20/85
   I am *very* glad to receive today so encouraging an account of

your cold. "Hiram" is a friend worth having; indeed it is always of advantage to number a physician among ones friends; you can consult him, by-the-way, when it would seem unnecessary to "call in" a doctor. Am glad too that you are getting on so well with the work; at this rate you will soon dispose of the economists unless their name is legion.

The Savannah steamers leave on Saturdays at three o'clock,— and when I say that I have exhausted my fund of information on the subject. I have been studying papers so far in vain to discover where I am to go to get my ticket, where the wharf is, &c. &c. This thing of getting myself transported by steamer is a new experience for me and I don't know exactly how to begin. I shall leave next Sat. week I think, though there is a bare possibility that I may stay over to the next steamer, if I can find a cheap sewing-girl here!—a remote probability! I need the time at both ends, there for sewing, and here for all sorts of odds and ends, *so* that if I could combine the two here, I *might* stay over; but I I don't think I shall.

I will be sure to send the *ring*, dear,—the same ring which I gave you on that memorable day in Asheville. Ah, *don't* I remember how you came back for the ring and the fresh "turn" which your asking for it gave me; when I had not begin to recover from all the other shocks! What a blessed impluse [impulse],—instinct, —what shall I call it—that was which led me to behave so unreasonably that day! For it was unreasonable you know;—my want of commonsense was equalled only by yours. Neither of us would advise any young and inexperienced friend to act in so precipitate a fashion. But [?] I have discovered so much that is noble and lovable in you since then. I was as sure that I knew *you* then as now; I would have staked my life on your being all that I dreamed as freely then as tonight. And as for the doubts about myself, my heart and your love left me no choice but to let them pass. I hope love has an intuitive wisdom of its own above that which is the product of reason, for all the days which have followed that one have united to prove that our hearts were safe guides. Of what a happy love was that the beginning! Truly it has blessed me with "blessings beyond thought" for then, in the first flush of first love, I could not have *dreamed* of the great flood of happiness which is filling my heart today, of the deep—the perfect joy with which I look forward to life with you and for you. Yes, my darling, love *has* cast out all fear. I will welcome the day which gives me to you with purest most unmixed gladness.

Yes, sweet-heart, I like the very small dainty earrings very

much, like a tiny ball, a single pearl. I have ceased wearing them
at all, merely because I had nothing small. Though by the way
I can't wear the smallest of all those that *screw* into the ear, they
always inflame them; the holes were made only large enough to
accommodate "drops"! But I don't know that I ought answer inquiries on the subject of jewelry. I have no *need* of such things.
Beware, you extravagant youth, or I will give you a scolding instead of thanks. I advise you to eschew all such vanities—to keep
away from jewelry stores.

Good-night darling. Believe me with all my heart

Your own   Eileen.

ALS (WP, DLC).

To Robert Bridges

Dear Bobby,   Balto., May 21, 1885

I am *very* sorry to have kept you waiting so long for an answer
to your notes about making arrangements for the 'gang' at
Princeton; but I have been quite unwell for the last few days and
found it difficult to get around to see Hiram and the little doctor[1]
any sooner. And now to explain my telegram: Cow[2] and the little
doctor will certainly come, but I cannot because my marriage is to
take place on the 24th of June and it is imperatively necessary
that I should go south just as soon as I get through with my work
here, which will be, I expect, about the 1st. or 2nd. of June.
There's no need to say that I am desperately disappointed at not
being able to join the gang on the 15th. I've been looking forward
to and counting on the sexennial for a long time, and I'd give anything I know of to see our crowd together once more. I believe that
I love the fellows of that crowd and value the genuine friendships
existing amongst us now more than I ever did before. But I *must*
be in South Carolina about that time, and it will of course be
out of the question for me to make the trip from thence to Princeton, for the few days of the reunion. I haven't the money to spare
for the purpose now. There's one comfort: I wont be so far away
another time!

But about the wedding: We are to be married in Savannah on
the 24th, and the wedding is to be a private, family affair to
which no formal invitations are to be sent out. I want, therefore,
to invite each one of our gang over my own special sign-manual.
It would make me gladder than any additional circumstance I
can imagine if all or any one of that crowd could be present! And
as for your single self, Bobby, I need not say what I would give

to have *you* come; for, if you don't know now the special value I set upon your friendship and the deep pleasure I have derived from the fact that my intercourse with you has been more nearly continuous and unbroken since graduation than with any of the other fellows, nothing I can say in this connection will enlighten you.

Tell the other fellows that they may expect to hear from me before the 18th and that Sav. is a delightful place in June!

Miss Axson will be in New York until next week, Bobby—at 95 *Seventh Ave.*—and, if you *can* go to see her, I know she would be delighted—and so would,   Your sincere friend,   Tommy.

Much love to Pete.

ALS (Meyer Coll., DLC).
 1 Charles W. Mitchell.
 2 Hiram Woods, Jr.

To Ellen Louise Axson

My own darling,   Balto., May 21, 1885
My cold is comparatively light to-day. It is manifestly losing courage as it loses ground, and I am in the same proportion gaining in comfort and satisfaction.

What a funny little girl you are not to say a word about your plans when the day for sailing must be so near! Are you waiting till you get your trunk off, then to write 'good-bye' and be off? I *suppose*, from what slight indications I have to judge by, that you will leave on the 30th. Of course you will take a carriage to the steamer, precious? Ah, how my heart shall stand still while all its treasure is on the ocean! May God keep my darling safe!

And you too sometimes break the silence, in spite of yourself, whispering to me across these two hundred miles? Ah, my precious little sweetheart, my delightful little pet, I am so glad, so unspeakably glad, that you too have the love-habits and the love-fancies that seem to me so sweet. You don't know how much store I set by these little things! When you promise to 'profit by these discoveries' you add an almost infinite amount to my already over-flowing treasures of joy at the approach of our wedding day. But how strange it seems to me that these should *be* 'discoveries' to my Eileen. Why, sweetheart, how little you have known of me! It must have been my fault, for I have been dreaming such dreams ever since first you gave me leave to dream of living with you,—dreams of twilights when all my heart's, all my life's, secrets should be told to my darling, and when, sweeter still, all her most sacred confidences should be given to me, as she nestled close at my knee and never chided me however often I might lean over and interrupt the sweet words for a kiss;—dreams of stealing up whcn she least expected it, when she thought me at work or sleeping, and leaning above her dear face to tell her with laughing eyes a story of growing love deeper than if it had been spoken with tears;—dreams of little *pranks* of love which would make us like glad children to each other, of every syllable of the language of nestle and caress. Why, Miss, what else did it mean that I always wished to walk *'hand in hand'* with you when I could—if it didn't mean that my heart was full to overflowing with that tenderness for my little sweetheart which is the real essence of these 'discoveries'—of these delightful dreams we've been telling? I shall believe more than ever hereafter, darling, that you *are* here when these strange impulses come upon me to turn and speak to you with my whole heart in the speech. Maybe you will hear! You can't wish for any more of love than those involuntary words contain. Be sure to send as much back to

Your own   Woodrow.

P.S. I have just written to Bridges to say that I can't go to the class reunion at Princeton on the 15th of June (how I wish I could— all my dearest chums are to be there!)—and inviting him to come to Sav. on the 24th. I told him your present address and that you would probably be leaving some time next week, so maybe he will find time to call. If he should, you will be 'posted' hereby as to what he knows.

With all love and faith,   Your own   W.

ALS (WP, DLC).

From Ellen Louise Axson

My darling Woodrow,   New York May 21/85

I have been *so* busy all day, with the two classes in the morning and afternoon, the dress-maker at lunch time; and the American [Art Association] exhibition from four o'clock until dinner time, that I feel rather collapsed now; my eyes insist upon shutting do what I will;—so if this letter is utterly unintclligible both as regards form and substance you will know the reason why! Havn't you noticed a peculiar inanity about my letters of late, a singular confusion of ideas and eccentricity in my mode of expressing them? The explanation is that when I write them I am too nearly asleep to know anything, except that I love you. My busy days and the sudden heat together reduce me to a state of imbecility in the evenings. And oh dear me what piles of letters I ought to write!—but can't! I think I will take a dose of morphine to keep me awake (it would do it most effectually,) and spend a whole night writing;—finish it all up at once, and get it off my mind! It is a perfect shame that I have not written to your sister, for instance.

Yes, I think Beth's letter was a sad one,—a *very* sad one. It was written for *my* benefit, with reference to my case, but as affecting me, it all passed by like the idle wind since there was absolutely nothing in it all that had aught to do with a love like ours. It only set me thinking once again about *her* and that unfortunate marriage. But it is an old story now;—poor girl, she could hardly confess anything which I had not seen for myself. It does seem a sort of "sacrilege," when one thinks of it seriously for anyone to connect with *our* love such ideas as those she suggests; but that she should think *her* experience as the wife of that creature could be of service to *your* promised wife struck me as too absurdly preposterous for anything but laughter. As if the wife of Caliban, if he had had one, should undertake to tell Miranda after her betrothal what she was to expect in a husband! Yes, thank God, we have nothing to do with such questions as those! Our love would indeed be of little worth if it did not even raise us above such mean small thoughts as those. I had forgotten that such things could be, or ever had been a source of trouble in married life. What is there in all the world for which I wish, as I wish to make my darling happy? How then *could* I have a will directly at variance with my very reason for living. And since it is my will to do all in my power to make you happy, I should be thwarting *myself* if I chose to do what did not please you;—and certainly I am not quite so illogical as that! If love did not even emancipate us from *self*, we would in truth do well to cast it away. You have taken my answer to Beth out of my mouth, dear. I *shall* always have my own way because your way and mine will be one as our lives are one,—our interests one. We who have learned the meaning of love so well can afford to pity those less blessed. May God help me to *prove* that I know what it means;—to be as true a wife as I should be if my character were as perfect as my love. May He, in short, give me my *will*—the desire of my heart!

Believe me darling With truest love   Your own   Eileen.

I am truly glad, dear, that you can still report progress in curing the cold.

ALS (WP, DLC).

From Robert Bridges

Dear Tommy: New York. My 21 '85
   Your telegram just received. *You must come.* There is no other
way. Lee, Henderson, Talcott, Webster, Woods, Mitchell, Pete and
Myself will all be there. I cannot bear to think that you will not.
Can't you move several acres of earth and a wee bit of heaven to
accomplish it? The whole gang expect it. Don't give us a disappointment. Come if only for Monday night. Pete will only be
there on that eveng. Come.   Yours   Bob Bridges
ALS (WP, DLC).

From Charles Andrew Talcott

My dear Tommy: Utica, N. Y. May 22d 1885
   The interest which I took in your book at first was not a whit
abated by the perusal of it. I enjoyed it thoroughly and regarded
it with a sort of personal feeling which I concluded must be
quasi-fraternal. I almost deprecate your somewhat flippant allusion to Utica's illustrious Son;[1] I hope in your future works, when
you mention any product of Oneida County, it will be in terms
of unstinted praise. Although I knew you had given the subject
much thought in times gone by I never realized how deeply you
had gone into the question nor how many avenues of thought it
laid open. . . .
   Please remember me to Hiram & the doctor; I hope the 15th of
June will find us altogether—
                    Yours Very Sincerely   Chas. A. Talcott

ALS (WP, DLC) with WWhw notation on env.: "Ans. June 9/85."
   [1] Roscoe Conkling, United States senator, 1867-80. For Wilson's reference to
"Utica's illustrious Son," see *Congressional Government*, page 132 of the present
volume.

To Robert Bridges

Dear Bobby,   Balto., May 22/85
   Thank you *ever* so much for your note in answer to my telegram.
I would give the world to come, my dear fellow: the disappointment can't hurt you and the others of our dear old chums half as
much as it will hurt me. But it is a case of clear necessity and I
see no possible way out of it. Think of me as much as you can at
P.——get the boys to drink my health as a token that they all remember me, and I'll try to get along with that.
                    Affectionately Yours,   Tommy.
ALS (WC, NjP).

Two Letters to Ellen Louise Axson

Balto., May 22, 1885

My sweet, sweet darling, it seems to me that every letter I receive from you nowadays is more precious than all its delightful predecessors. *All* the letters you have written to me—from the first, to your "dear Mr. Wilson," to the last, to your "darling Woodrow" (my name never seemed pretty to me until you used it with that adjective before it!)—have been charming—Miss Rose don't know how 'charming' you can make your letters!—but of late—what has loosed my darling's pen?—you have taken to talking, all your letters through, about your love, about *our* love, and as I read I can't for the life of me tell whether I am sitting still or standing on my head! Don't pretend to be astonished, Miss, at this extraordinary effect of your letters. Think of what this change in their character means for me. Think of the shy little maiden who used to confess to hot blushes whenever she so much as wrote a single sentence of her heart's thoughts to me and who found it hard in my presence even to *whisper* 'I love you'; think of the old-time thoughts I used to have about inventing love-artifices, after our marriage, wherewith to beguile my little wife into being demonstrative in her love; think of the almost innumerable only half-successful attempts I have made, when my little queen was in my arms, to get her to talk to me about her love; think of the unspeakable longing I have felt to have her talk to me so—and then think of what I must feel when I read, with eyes that swim with tears of pure delight, such sentences as this: "Yes, my darling, love *has* cast out all fear. I will welcome the day which gives me to you with purest, most unmixed gladness!" And then to have whole letters overflowing with expressions of love, of joyous, perfect love! Why, darling, it's *enough* to make me lose my head with delight!

Yes, indeed, Miss, our hearts *have* been safe guides—and, for that reason, you will, if you please, confine your uncomplimentary speeches to yourself! If *you were* "unreasonable" in Asheville that day, if *you did* show a "want of commonsense," *I* did not. I knew perfectly well what I was about; *I* wasn't frightened at my own conclusions. I admit that I felt a little bit sorry for *you.* You *were* a little goose to give yourself to such a chap! But I knew that it was the biggest piece of good fortune that had ever fallen to me. I *knew* that you were the most lovable little woman in the world (for hadn't you made yourself the centre of every hope and purpose of my life?), and I knew that if you would love me and give yourself to me I should be richer in happiness than the love of all the rest of the world could make me. What I did not know was *how much* more lovable you were than others and *how much* richer in happiness I should be with you than I could be with anyone else. So, if you please, Miss, you'll confine your strictures to yourself. *You were* unreasonable—though maybe you have reason on your side *now*: for you *do* know now—don't you, sweetheart?—that I love you more than anyone else in the world could: —and love is what you *want*, isn't it, precious? And I am a *better* chap than I was then—made better by loving you! Nobody could love you—and know that you loved him—and be *very* bad, or bad very long! I am so glad that I am young so that I can give my youth to you; I am so glad that I am likely to be in a position to be useful so that that usefulness may deserve sympathy from you; I am so glad that God has given me a big heart so that I can give you such love as you deserve; I am so glad that in everything I may be entirely yours, my matchless darling! Yes, sweetheart, you *do* 'know more about your fortune' in respect to all that concerns our love "than all the—other—witches in the world"—but you don't know yet what your wonderful love is to me; and I can't teach you until—until we have gone on our journey together. Will it be a sweet discovery, precious, to find that your love *constitutes* my happiness—and will you let that love grow, and grow *visibly*, that you may see my happiness grow?

Ah, my pet, how long these weeks are growing! It is five weeks now, *less two days*, and yet that seems a longer time than six weeks did! Is it to go on seeming *longer*, do you think, dearest? Tell me, Eileen, don't you think that a kiss will be sweeter on the 24th than any other kiss ever was? I dreamed of you last night— of course—and you put your hand over my mouth and stopped my kisses, 'not because you objected, but for *discipline*'—I dont approve of such discipline, Miss, and I overcame it in the dream! If you had *really* been here you would not have done so—*would* you? For I love you with all my heart and am altogether and forever,   Your own   Woodrow.

P.S. Somehow I *skipped* this side of the sheet without knowing it: so I'll use it to report my cold still better—and to say, what I had it in my heart to say about these letters of yours, but (apparently) didn't have space enough to say,—that they seem to me sweet beyond expression because the explanation of them must be that June is near and that my darling's heart is *feeling* its preparation for what June is bringing. *Is* that the explanation, dear? I know that that cause is operating to make it impossible for me to write about anything but that theme of themes—our love and its fulfilment. With gladdest love   Your own   Woodrow.

ALS (WP, DLC).

Balto., May 23, 1885

Let me beg you, my precious little sweetheart, not to tire yourself as you confess to having been doing the last few days. If you feel so "collapsed" at night it is proof that you have been overtaxing your strength—as you promised not to do—and it is a much more serious matter, a much more dangerous thing, to overtax your strength during this debilitating spring weather than it would be in the winter or even in the real summer. Remember, my darling, that you are going from New York to Savannah—not to a cooler climate which would brace you up—and that you don't want to be a *jaded* little woman when the 24th comes. Wont you be careful, pet? Don't try to do both your League tasks and your "odds and ends" of preparation at the same time. I shall be intensely anxious unless I can know, through your own promise, that your are sparing yourself, no longer feeling jaded at night. What if you were to make yourself sick? I believe it would throw me back six months in *my* recovery! If you have piles of letters to write, let mine go, and write them—one every evening, as you would mine—and in the morning send me ten lines, or five, or three: say 'I am quite well, darling; I love you and shall not be happy till I can tell you so, with as many kisses as you want, as —as *in law* your own Eileen';—send any love message you please, but don't steal from your sleep when you are sleepy. I would rather a thousand times have a lump come into my throat from disappointment at finding your letter so short than go all the day nearly crazy with anxiety about you. These letters are part and heart of my happiness just now, because they are, for this time of separation, the only possible substitutes for you; but *you* are my real treasure. *Please*, darling, give up *any*thing—my letters, one of your classes,—anything to avoid this overexertion. It makes me miserable to think about it.

I have already answered your question about your recent letters: they certainly have *not* seemed anything but delightful in style and thought—and they have been *full of love*: that has made them seem to me the most precious letters ever written.

I have put my plans about leaving into shape, sweetheart, and think that I shall get off on either the first or second of June—

Monday or Tuesday. I have only one or two economists on hand now. I can dispose of them in a day or two, and be free to begin active preparations for leaving. So, if you leave New York on the 30th, according to your present plan, I shall not be so very far behind you. Possibly I may reach Columbia about the time you reach Savannah. How intensely glad I shall be to get away! Principally, of course, because it will seem a distinct move towards *you*; but partly, also, because I have suffered a good deal here of late (in the last few months, I mean) and the burden of that suffering seems now and again to rest on me still in this little den of mine and in these University surroundings. Except for this cold, which is now insignificant, I feel well enough *now*, but, in order to spare myself, I have kept away from all University lectures for the last six or eight weeks, attending only the Seminary meetings on Friday nights, and this program has served, as it were, to suggest to me, to keep me reminded, that I have been for some time a quasi-invalid—and I want to get away from all such suggestions. Recuperation will be easy now. All the alarming symptoms—the nervous head-aches, the inability to work, &c.— are gone, long ago, and there remains only a slightly 'played out' feeling—a relaxed condition which makes me liable to catch cold &c. in the most absurdly unreasonable manner.

But such reasons—at bottom sentimental rather than hygienic —are as nothing when weighed against that other greatest reason for my joy at the prospect of getting away: that it will seem like going, part of the way, to you, my peerless darling, my queen! Those three weeks in Columbia will, I know, be terribly *long* weeks, even spent, as they will be, with those who, next to your precious self, are dearer to me than I can say; but they will make a sort of golden progress, all the same. They will be, for my heart, the road *near* home, and it will see nothing but beauty all about them!

Probably I shall spend my last Sunday in these parts—the Sunday after you sail—with Ned. Webster, my college chum. Hiram and I half promised to return his visit when he was down here, and, since I am not to be at the class-reunion at Princeton, I am afraid he would feel hurt if I went off 'for good' without making an effort to see him. And it will not cost a very *great* effort. His home is distant only about twenty miles from here. Hiram will go with me, of course, and we shall of a certainty have a jolly time—since Ned. has a delightful home and a delightful family, as well as a delightful *self*. By-the-way, I did not answer your question as to whether or not you 'know anything about Ned. Webster.' Not from me, I think, precious. I don't remember ever to have made him in any way one of your acquaintances.

I love you, sweetheart, loyally, tenderly, passionately, alto-gether—with a love which makes me *in everything*

Your own   Woodrow.

ALS (WC, NjP).

From Ellen Louise Axson

My darling Woodrow,   New York, May 23/85

I especially dislike to be prevented from writing on Friday night, and thereby forced to give you only a hasty line for your Sunday letter;—but circumstances are sometimes beyond ones control. Now I *must* make haste for I have an engagement with Miss Granger to go to the "Historical."

That reminds me,—I cant stop to explain *why*,—of our old for-tune-teller. I must tell you the rest of that story, she did not finish mine before because they "called time" and interrupted her; so she told it all over the other day. She said that some lady was ex-pecting me soon over the water, and when I reached there I would find someone sick, but not fatally. Then she said a gentleman was going to take me to a certain place in six weeks,—he had already written to the place to see about going—and she added "he will have a right to take you." "Why what *do* you mean?" said I. "There is only one way for him to have the right" she said mysteriously. "Why["] exclaimed one of the girls "you don't mean she is going to be married then?" And she nodded her head adding, "Is next month June? Well June will be a gay (!) month for her." Was'nt that a queer chance?—for *positively* no one had told her about me; I should feel somewhat *impressed* if she hadn't made such great mistakes about other people; for instance she did not know that one lady was married already. By the way, she gave me as-surance on one point which was very encouraging, viz. that the place which I was to fill would be "very becoming" to me! Of course the spirit of mischief prompted me to tell my fortune in class; and how you would have laughed in your sleeve at the scene which followed; the young men were *so* amused at the absurdity of it, and her audacity in putting the date so soon; they shouldn't think she would risk her reputation in that fashion. Then they bade me an affecting farewell and asked for cards, which I demurely promised to send. But I am spending all my few precious moments in nonsense.

I find there are *three* steamers a week, whereas I supposed there was only one. So I have about decided to wait until the middle of week after next, that will 'work' much better for me. I have found out all about my steamer now,—where to go for my ticket, &c.

Am *so* sorry that you can't go to the reunion; don't you think you could manage it? It is too bad for you to miss such a rare pleasure.

But I must close. I wont try to tell you now, darling, hurried as I am, my thoughts about this precious letter of yesterday— of the gladness with which *I* discover more and more fully that we have the same "love-habits," "love-fancies,"—that we are each sure to love the other as we most wish to be loved. Ah dearest, I have no words to tell you the inexpressible tenderness which fills my heart when I read such letters as these. I love you—*love you* my darling, as I could not have thought it possible to love[.] You are in very truth all the world to   Your own   Eileen.

ALS (WP, DLC).

To Ellen Louise Axson

Balto., May 24, 1885

Why is it, my darling, that Sunday is always with me a day of special, of almost desperate, longing for your sweet presence? It can hardly be because my heart is simply unconsciously answering yours, for you are so hurriedly busy on Sunday that you can hardly have time to think about me more than usual. It must be because of the feeling of which I have spoken before, the feeling that Sunday is beyond all other days a *home* day—and on such a day my heart must of course be specially full of home-sickness. It is homeless without you—and its homelessness seems specially dreary on this home-day. Only four more Sundays, though, and then my heart will be so full of home-joy with my little wife that I can look back with the calmest sort of content, even with a touch of mirth, maybe, to these disconsolate intervals in the week's work when it was all fighting against loneliness and 'the blues'!

Maybe, my little queen, because you can't be lifted like a feather but are demonstrably a maiden of solid flesh and bone, of active blood and all the delightful substance of a real, blooming woman, you will be inclined to laugh at me if I call you a *fairy* with all the earnestness of a real belief; but you *are* a fairy all the same. Else, how could you weave all these spells about me—spells alternately of gladness and of sadness, seeming to come, not from my own heart, but from some ever present influence out-

side of me, as if from someone whispering to me, now that there
has been given me freely and without stint the most precious
love in the world, and again that I must yet wait a long while before I can enjoy that love? Else, how could you mould my daily
life as you do, as if I were guided by a fancy that you are always
by my side, reminding me, when despondent, to smile for your
sake, and prompting me, when gay, to imagine that your eyes
are full of laughter too? Is not all this a fairy's work? Ah well,
anyhow that is a convenient explanation of real facts. I am led
captive by *some*body—that's certain!—and she holds me captive
all day long, and even in my dreams. It's a sweet captivity of
thought presaging a sweeter captivity of life soon to come. My
thoughts serve her now as my actions shall serve her then. Ah,
how I wish that I could *see* my little fairy sometimes! I think that
I could then teach her to carry back to her real self in New York
infinitely more satisfactory messages of love and loyalty than
these poor, stupid, half-intellig[i]ble letters can ever carry! *They*
cannot give my darling *any idea* of the depth and strength and
fulness of the love of   Her own   Woodrow.

ALS (WP, DLC).

From Ellen Louise Axson

My darling Woodrow,   New York, May 24/85
    I lost so much time after church, dear, telling my friends 'good-
bye' &c. that I have no time at all left for writing. Will you excuse a little bit of a note until tonight?
    I feel rather heavy-hearted, at taking leave of dear Mr. Carter
and the rest; in fact, I would rather enjoy a good cry. I wish I did
not get so attached to people;—I havn't really seen so much of
them; I feel a great deal more badly than the circumstances furnish excuse for. However I shall see them all once more, Mr.
Carter this afternoon, and Dr. and Mrs. Hamilton on Wed. when
I lunch with them.
    You perceive I have changed my plan again, or at least I have
settled upon one at last and am going on Sat. The extra days will
do me more good there than here I think, and besides I fear I will
be bankrupt if I stay any longer. Ah me, if I only could go by rail!
—but we won't speak of that; we will try not to think of it.
    There is the dinner bell, as I expected,—I *must* stop.
    Am so glad the cold is still better. Take good care of yourself,
love, and let me [see] you looking *real well* a month from today.
One month!—and then nothing in all the world can separate us

again. What a wonderful thought it is! With that precious thought to dwell upon, I can say "good-bye" to everyone else and still be happy beyond measure.

With all my heart   Your own   Eileen.

ALS (WP, DLC).

From Albert Shaw

My Dear Wilson: Minneapolis, May 24, 1885.

Although I have read whole floods of literature on the Illinois deadlock in the Chicago papers, there is nothing I have preserved. Have probably written half a dozen articles myself since it began —the only essential points are that the legislature was originally tied (or almost exactly tied) between the two parties on joint ballot. Senate had Republican majority of 1, House Dem. maj. of 1, —counting Haines Dem. When it came to choosing speaker of house, Dem. caucus hit on another man. Haines didn't like this, & refused to vote for either caucus nominee. Hence an exact tie. Meanwhile, Haines had been made temporary speaker & used tactics to prevent the election of a permanent speaker. He was master of situation for days—until tired out when he voluntarily withdrew & allowed another man to be made temporary speaker. Finally the Democrats held another caucus & made Haines their candidate for speaker. He was elected by receiving one or two Republican votes if I remember rightly. All this, of course, was in January. It took, I think, some 3 wks to elect speaker. With the subsequent attempts to elect a U. S. senator on joint ballot, Mr. Haines had no such conspicuous relationship. I think there never was a time when his vote would have elected a Senator. There was one recalcitrant Repub. (Sittig by name) who refused steadily to vote for Logan. Morrison, I believe, never rec'd every Dem. vote. To elect, it was necessary to have a clear majority, and neither side was able to get it. The death of a member or two on each side did not break the dead-lock, but finally the unexpected election of a Republican to fill the seat of a Democratic senator who had died, made it possible for the Republicans to elect if they could muster all their men. Sittig had once said that if the time ever came when his vote would avail to elect Logan, he would waive his personal antipathies and vote for L. in order that the Senatorship should be kept in Republican hands. Sittig's vote was accordingly given for Mr. Logan & the deadlock was broken. Haines himself gets to the legislature by cumulative voting in Lake County (adjoining Cook County—Haines' residence is suburban). The legislature would have been closely balanced under the ordinary system of representation, I think; but of course minority representation is always advantageous to the minority party. It is my impression that the closely balanced legislature which sent Judge David Davis to the Senate some years ago owed its painful equilibrium to minority representation. I have written all this very hasily and inaccurately as to exact details, and probably you knew it all before. If you want definite knowledge, state your precise points and I will get them looked up for you.

And now let me congratulate you on *the* approaching *event*. A man who teaches in a girls' college ought by all means to be married. But then, even if he doesn't teach in a g.'s c. it is the right thing to do. My theory is that a man does'nt fairly begin life till he has a wife. Possibly you remember my frank confession in Miss Ashton's dining room that I should be married at the age of 31. Nothing has yet occurred to bring the date any nearer. Really, I haven't found her yet. She exists, subjectively; and I hope to find her objective counterpart.

I am sure you deserve all your good fortune and happiness, and I wish you no end of it. Should be delighted to accept the invitation to your wedding, but of course it isn't possible. I shall be attending "commencement" at Iowa College at the very time. I give the address before the Alumni this year. Am not certain as yet what I shall read on the occasion. . . . Have heard only once from Shinn since he went to California. He sent me his Northern Pacific pass to have time extended.

Shall be glad to know of your relief from the disagreeable ordeal of examinations. Have no doubt whatever, of course, as to your honorable survival!

With warmest regards for Miss Ashton and Wright and the family circle in general,

Your Sincere Friend   Albert Shaw.

ALS (WP, DLC).

From Ellen Louise Axson

My darling Woodrow,   New York, May 24/85.

I have just been busy writing to your sister and two or three others whom I *could not* put off any longer; and it hasn't left me half as much time as I wish to write you on this 24th day of May and in answer to this wonderful letter of yesterday morning. It seems to me, love, that each of your letters too, is more precious than that which went before,—adds something more of sweetness and joy to my love; they fill my heart so full to overflowing that I *must* seek whatever relief can be found in words. I must try to tell you that so far as heart-treasures go you have had no advantage taken of you; that I match your love with love as great. I am not one of those who think love should be in any of it's aspects one-sided. I would like to satisfy the cravings of your heart as you satisfy mine;—to render you equally happy in loving.

Don't you think those reasons are sufficient to loosen my pen? —that I can't help it, and that I would like if possible to make your cup brimming over with gladness as you have made mine. Then too I am naturally making progress in the lesson which my master admits he set himself so patiently to teach me; it would reflect greatly upon his abilities as a teacher if it were otherwise. I am fast gaining courage to *write* my deepest thought,—whether I can *speak* it yet or not, I do not know. It is a difficult lesson to learn and you have proved yourself a good teacher for with most men one could never learn it. But you are *such* a perfect *gentleman*, as well as *man*, that you never say or think anything at which a woman's pride and sensitiveness could take alarm. There is *no* reason why I should *not*,—there is every reason why I should show you how entirely I am yours, how my whole life is bound up in yours, how utterly dependent I am upon your love. You know it is pitiable when a woman so reveals herself to the wrong man!— one who does not understand her woman's heart or who holds the gift of it lightly. One is apt to despise the woman as well as pity her,—for example Marcia in "A Modern Instance."[1] But, thank God, I have known from the first whom I have loved, my heart has always said what my pen says now. It was not faith but works I lacked. I *would* have said it all but *could* not. No doubt one of the causes why I can now *is* as you say that June is near and my heart is feeling its preparation for what June is bringing. In the fullness of my heart I too cannot linger long on any other theme. But I must say goodnight, sweetheart. I love you, dear, as much as you would have me, I am forever   Your own   Eileen.

ALS (WP, DLC).
   [1] William Dean Howells, *A Modern Instance, a Novel* (Boston, 1882).

From Robert Bridges

Dear Tommy: [New York] May 24 '85—10 pm
   I have just finished writing my usual screed for *Life* and am

not in the humor for the long letter I had in mind. It has been a hard pull to say anything bright tonight even with the $5 inducement. . . .

I am heartily glad to hear of your happiness and the near coronation of it. The only thing I regret is that you cannot be with us at Princeton, and that I cannot be with you in Savannah. I had somehow always hoped to see the boys of our crowd married, but have been disappointed both in your case and Pete's. . . .

I want to call Tuesday eveng to see Miss Axson. . . .

Not long ago I had some photographs taken and send you one of them. The most noticeable feature is the side-whiskers.

Good night   Your friend   Bob Bridges

ALS (WP, DLC).

To Ellen Louise Axson

My own darling,   Balto., May 25, 1885

What a dear, affectionate little girl you are! I had no idea that you would find it so hard to part with your friends at the Scotch church. I am sorry, sweetheart, that you have to suffer so much at the parting—I would give a great deal to help you somehow. I am afraid that I must be a bit hard-hearted; certainly I am as compared with you: for, intimate as are some of the connections which I have formed here in Baltimore, I am quite certain that I shall go away with sincere regrets but with no suggestion of *grief* at leaving my friends. My friendships are strong and lasting, but only my loves are passionate. And, in leaving Balto. *this* time, it would be very hard for anything short of a genuine calamity to distress me: for I feel as if all my *life* were ahead of me and as if leaving Balto. were a distinct step towards all that it contains of joy and promise! I have a longing, impatient *eagerness* to be away, and feel myself nearer my precious Eileen, whose love is my charter of liberty. Oh, how happy I shall be! *I love you*, sweetheart; you are all the world to me! You are my queen, and all my happiness is in your keeping: it is dependent on your love and presence. It will be *perfect* when you are my bride!

So you *are* going on Saturday, after all? Oh, my love, may God keep you safe through your journey! What would I not give to be able to go on and see you safely off—or to *go with you*! But I wont talk about that: that's a dangerous subject! It's hard enough for me to be content, anyhow, unreasonable fellow that I am. As if it were not enough to know that after only four weeks "nothing in all the world can separate us again"!

Yes, darling, I *will* try to come to you "looking *real well*"—if that will make you just so much gladder to see me. I am feeling better to-day than I have felt for more than a week, and I mean to get just as well as ever I was in my life, before another 24th of the month comes around. You see I'll have fine mental help—my mind will help my body. I shall be very happy when I get with the dear one's in Columbia, and that will give a sort of equable pace to the rise of my spirits as the sweet days of our marriage draw nearer. My bodily ailments wont have any show, so triumphantly pre-dominant will be my heart at the prospect of receiving its crown.

By-the-way, pet, dear mother quite agrees now that the Arden plan is delightful.

"Dode" was delighted with your letter—and they all rival each other in sending love to you,[1] whom *I* love beyond all power of words to say. I cannot tell you *half* of what makes me altogether

Your own Woodrow.

ALS (WP, DLC) with ELAhw notation on env.
[1] Letter or letters missing.

From Ellen Louise Axson

My darling Woodrow,   New York May 25/85

I suppose I must prove by my deeds tonight my regard for your wishes and send you but a short letter, for it is after ten o'clock and Mr. Bridges, who has been making a very pleasant visit, has just left, and I *am* decidedly sleepy;—though I am only going to work half the day this week, I must devote my afternoons to running about.

I went away down town almost to the "jumping off place" this afternoon all by myself—wasn't I brave?—and secured my passage. My boat is the "City of Savannah."

But I must keep my promise to Mr. Bridges, and as I have but a few moments to write, I must do it at once. He is *keenly* disappointed that you think you can't go to the reunion; he can't reconcile himself to it,—says you *must* come, all the other fellows —eight of them—will be there and it will spoil it all if you are missing. Don't you think you can go, dear? It hurts me to think of your losing it, because I know you *want* to go. Mr. B. says you must come up and stay with him here until the time and amuse yourself writing items for his papers. I think he will make you enjoy that too—not the items but the visit to N. Y. And they have made delightful arrangements for the Princeton frolic. Indeed you will have such a good time that you will be left lamenting the fact that your bachelor days are so nearly over! But I am even willing to run *that* risk, for the sake of the pleasure you will gain from it. Well, I think I have pleaded the case strongly enough to please Mr. B.—more strongly perhaps than I ought for of course you are the best judge as to what is best,—as to which you would prefer, to have the two weeks longer with your parents or spend them here. How I wish that you could eat your cake and keep it too, so to speak;—or that the reunion came the first of June.

But I must close abruptly, dear, for I must get up early tomorrow to fill an engagement. So good-night sweetheart. I love you more, infinitely more than all the world beside. I am in every heart-throb   Your own Eileen.

ALS (WP, DLC).

EDITORIAL NOTE
WILSON'S "HISTORY OF POLITICAL ECONOMY IN THE UNITED STATES"

Richard T. Ely, in February 1884, invited Wilson and Wilson's fellow-student at the Johns Hopkins, Davis R. Dewey, to collaborate with him in writing a history of American economic thought. What Ely had in mind was a brief compendium to be used as a textbook tracing the development of American economic thought through the writings of principal authors. Ely said that he would prepare the chapters on the leading American economist, Mathew Carey, and that they would constitute about one third of the book. Dewey should devote his third to economists before Carey; Wilson, his third to economists since Carey.[1] Ely, as editor and senior author, also undoubtedly planned to write the introduction and concluding chapter.

Although Wilson was at this time deeply engrossed in writing *Congressional Government*, he seems to have accepted Ely's invitation with alacrity, not only because it was difficult to refuse, but also because he regarded collaboration with a leading economist as a means of enhancing his own reputation. By June 1884 he was beginning to regret his impulsive decision because, he explained, he knew that he was not properly equipped for the task. He had about decided to withdraw, he wrote to Ellen Axson. "I could write something altogether *readable*, doubtless," he continued, "but it would not be thorough or profound; and no chance of getting my name before the public shall tempt me to do what I should some day regard as beneath my reputation, as weakly done."[2] Perhaps other reasons for his second thoughts were fatigue, lack of interest, and, above all, dread of having to do the work involved. In any event, he soon decided to defer decision until he had had a talk with Ely. "May-be he can show me how I can do what he wants," Wilson wrote to Ellen, "without doing sham work,

[1] WW to ELA, Feb. 19, 1884, Vol. 3.
[2] WW to ELA, June 5, 1884, *ibid.*

all talk no knowledge. I wont do what I can't do honestly, even to keep peace with Dr. Ely."[3]

Relaxation of tension after the completion of *Congressional Government*, and perhaps a reassuring conference with Ely, caused Wilson, soon after his return to the Hopkins in September 1884, to abandon his tentative decision to withdraw. He began research for his section on about November 17 and, as he put it, "waded through" all the principal economists of his period between this date and about March 27, 1885.[4] Wilson began writing his section afterward, and his letters enable us to follow his progress almost from week to week. On May 7 he indicated that he had begun writing a few days before and was now gaining momentum.[5] His letter to Ellen four days later makes it clear that he had seen at least a part of Dewey's section and suggests that he had found it helpful.[6] His last reference to composition was in his letter to Ellen of May 23. In it he said that he had only one or two economists to go and expected to finish within "a day or two."[7]

Wilson wrote his manuscript out by hand on seventy legal-size pages. He wrote it in sections, each dealing with a single economist; and he numbered the pages of each section independently in order to be able to rearrange them easily. His sketches of economists and analyses of their works were based entirely upon the references, notes, and digests that he had earlier set down in two notebooks.[8] For footnotes, Wilson used asterisks and other signs at the bottom of each page.

This manuscript was obviously Wilson's first draft. He wrote it in a great hurry and then made a number of interlinear changes. But the numerous misspellings that remain indicate that he did not tarry while revising the copy. His letters to Ellen at this time make one reason for his haste clear enough. But it seems reasonable to conclude that he did not prepare this manuscript with his customary care because he regarded it as a first draft. He gave it to Ely, expecting him to make suggestions for revision before he, Wilson, prepared the final copy.

It is still something of a mystery why the book was never published. It is not possible to comment on Dewey's contribution, since it has never turned up; but Wilson's letters to Albert Shaw of June 8, 1885, and of November 11, 1885, Volume 5, indicate that Dewey had not completed his section by the latter date. Insofar as is known, Ely was pleased by Wilson's section. At any rate, he made only one minor change in Wilson's text when he went through it. The foregoing indicates that the main reason why the book never saw the light of day was simply that Ely, for some reason, failed to do his part.[9]

[3] WW to ELA, July 3, 1884, *ibid.*
[4] See the Editorial Note, "Wilson's Research for a 'History of Political Economy in the United States,'" *ibid.*
[5] WW to ELA, May 7, 1885.
[6] WW to ELA, May 11, 1885.
[7] WW to ELA, May 23, 1885.
[8] Described at Nov. 17, 1884, Vol. 3.
[9] Ely, while writing his memoirs at an advanced age, gave a garbled and inaccurate account of the collaboration. For example, he named Burr James Ramage instead of Dewey as the third collaborator along with Wilson. He also erred in saying that the separation of the collaborators in 1885 was a cause for the

Only William Diamond, in *The Economic Thought of Woodrow Wilson*, has ever subjected Wilson's section to much review and analysis.[10] He characterized it as "a colorless . . . description," and observed that it both "contained little of Wilson himself" and suggested that Wilson *might* have been familiar with the classical economists and German historical economists. Except for Wilson's research notes for his lecture on Adam Smith, the documents relevant to Wilson's education in economics and his thinking about the subject were all available when Dr. Diamond wrote his monograph. They have been printed or described in this volume and the two preceding ones, and there is no need to summarize their contents at this point. However, the editors feel constrained, in view of the importance of the subject, to suggest that the time has come for a new and more adequate review. And they believe that such a review would emphasize the following points, among others:

1. That Wilson had a very rigorous introduction to the literature and science of economics by Dr. Ely, one of the founders of the new economics in the United States. Wilson took both Ely's undergraduate and graduate courses in political economy in 1883-84, and Wilson's lecture notes taken in these courses, along with individual items like his report on Adam Smith, references in other notebooks, and comments in letters, make it clear that he had a thorough exposure, not only to the writings of the classical school, but also to the work of the newer school of German historical economists up to that time.

2. That there is abundant evidence in the documents and descriptions mentioned above to reveal Wilson's reactions to and opinions about various economic theories. Dr. Diamond, after saying that the section for a "History of Political Economy in the United States" revealed little about Wilson himself, went on to point out the significance (which will become evident to the reader as he goes through Wilson's section himself) of Wilson's reactions to particular doctrines and interpretations. Even more revealing are the remarks that Wilson set down in his research notebook[11] after reading his economists, and the general summary and interpretation that he presented to the Historical Seminary on March 27, 1885.[12] This evidence indicates (a) that Wilson had positive disdain, if not contempt, for classical economic theory as expounded by Malthus and Ricardo, and considerable suspicion of all theory *per se*, particularly theory allegedly based upon theology; and (b) that he was himself, at least to this point, very lati-

---

failure of the project. But he also said that he had found it far more difficult to gather materials for his own section than he had anticipated, and he intimated that he never completed it. Richard T. Ely, *Ground Under Our Feet* (New York, 1938), pp. 112-13.

Interestingly, Dewey was also later unable to offer any "distinct recollections" about the collaboration, or, indeed, much about his relationship with Wilson during this period. See D. R. Dewey to R. S. Baker, Sept. 24, 1925, and Sept. 23, 1926, RSB. Coll., DLC.

10 (Baltimore, 1943), pp. 30-32. Dr. Diamond had access only to a typed copy with many typographical errors, which Dr. Ely had sent to Ray Stannard Baker. The fact that the manuscript was badly typed did not, however, affect Diamond's evaluation.

11 Diamond cites this notebook but apparently did not give it close analysis.

12 His report is printed at March 27, 1885, in this volume.

tudinarian and open in approach and believed that economic theories and policies were the product of local situations and historical development—in other words, that he had assimilated the assumptions of the new economics.[13]

3. That it does not suffice to characterize Wilson's ability at economic analysis only on a basis of his section for a "History of Political Economy in the United States." Whatever one thinks of this section, it is important to remember that the plan and scope of the book were determined by Ely, not by his junior collaborators. It is also important to bear in mind that Ely had no doubt promised to provide the generalizing and interpretive parts in the introduction and concluding chapter. This is not to argue that Wilson had either any *fundamental* interest in economics as a discipline or superior talents at economic analysis. It is only to say that in his section he simply did what Ely had asked him to do.

The text printed below is from the original manuscript, presented to the Princeton University Library by Margaret Hale Ely in 1965. Consecutive numbers have been substituted for Wilson's asterisks and other signs. Wilson's text has been reproduced exactly as he wrote it, without any repairs. All brackets, words in brackets, and ellipses are Wilson's. Full bibliographical information about articles and books to which Wilson referred, both in his notebooks and manuscript, may be found in Volume 3, pp. 449-50.

[13] For additional evidence on this point, see "Socialism and Democracy," printed at Aug. 22, 1887, and the two lectures on the functions of government, printed at Feb. 17, 1888, and Feb. 18, 1888, all in Vol. 5.

Wilson's Section for a "History of Political Economy in the United States"

[c. May 25, 1885]

One of the strongest and most interesting representatives of the older school of economists was Henry Vethake, L. L. D. (1792-1866), a native of the colony of Esquibo, Guiana, S. A., who came to the United States at the age of four years, received his collegiate training at Columbia College, New York, studied law, and finally became known as one of the leading teachers of the country. He seems to have been a man of extraordinary versatility. He taught, apparently with equal facility, mathematics, natural philosophy, chemistry, intellectual and moral philosophy, and political economy, from time to time filling chairs, now in one, again in another of these branches, in nine of the principal schools and colleges of the middle Atlantic States.

His "Principles of Political Economy," which was published in Philadelphia in 1838 and subsequently passed into a second edition, is an admirable exposition of orthodoxy. Its style is lucid and straightforward, and its thought has everywhere a thoroughly modern air. He seems to claim originality in making the "bold innovation" of including under the terms "wealth" and "capital" immaterial as well as material products; and after stating the doctrine of diminishing returns together with the consequent theory of rent now known as Ricardo's, and calling attention to the undoubted tendency of population to press against the means of support, he is careful to add that these doctrines had been similarly set forth in his class lectures so early as 1822. It is impossible to determine, by means of the evidence available, how much he was indebted to Ricardo; it is hardly possible that he had not read Malthus. He insists, however, partly in modification of Malthusian views, "that the command of the great body of every community over the necessaries and luxuries of life is determined in a much greater degree by moral than by physical causes; and that its enlargement depends, therefore, in a much greater degree on the general diffusion of education, of morals, and of religion, among the people, than upon the particular system of legislation that may be adopted by the government."[1]

Francis Wayland, D. D., L. L. D. (1796-1865), an eminent Bastist divine, and for many years a leader of education in this country as President of Brown University, has probably heretofore exercised as much influence upon college instruction in economics as any other American writer. Dr. Wayland was a man of great intellectual strength, but little originality; and his "Elements of Political Economy," first published in New York in 1837, was in no sense an attempt to recast the doctrines of the English writers who had preceded him. It was, rather, an attempt to mediate between those writers and a public who needed that everything in the least recondite should be made very simple and plain for the benefit of its ordinary, workaday, unanalytic comprehension. It seemed to him that the works on political economy in general use, "while they presented its doctrines truly, yet did not present them in such order as would be most likely to render them serviceable either to the general student, or to the practical merchant."[2] This more serviceable order, consequently, he set himself to supply; and the very great vogue of his "Elements" as a textbook, both in this country and in England, would seem to attest his success. It not only passed through several London editions, but was finally translated into the Hawaiian language.

Important as Dr. Wayland's influence has been, however, his

---

1 *Principles of Pol. Econ.*, p. 404.
2 Preface, *Elements Pol. Econ.*, ed. 1866.

place in the history of economic thought is one of no very great prominence. He was simply a great organizer of education. His book is the work, not of one who would develop a science, but of one who would impress its tenets upon others, of one who would organize and facilitate instruction in it. It is just the 'orthodox' creed, wages-fund and all, analyzed, and illustrated by means of every-day cases of trade and manufacture "with which every person is familiar."

Dr. Wayland was Professor of Moral Philosophy, as well as of Political Economy, and these two branches of instruction seemed to him very nearly allied. "The principles of Political Economy," he says, "are so closely analogous to those of Moral Philosophy, that almost every question in the one may be argued on grounds belonging to the other"; and, although he has not "thought it proper, in general, to intermingle them, but has argued economical questions on merely economical grounds,"[3] there is throughout his writings a strong theological flavor, a constant tendency to call all seemingly established principles of the science laws of Divine Providence. Still, the 'orthodox' economy has received not a little of clearness at his hands, and his vigorous commonsense and keen appreciation of practical educational needs have combined to make his Elements a very excellent compendium of the views which he represents.

George Tucker (1775-1861) was born on the island of Bermuda, but came in early youth to Virginia to be educated under the supervision of his relative, the well-known Judge St. George Tucker. He was graduated from William and Mary College, studied for the bar, and entered public life, to serve first in the legislature of Virginia, and afterwards, from 1819-1823, as a Representative in Congress. He soon turned from active politics, however, to accept the chair of Moral Philosophy and Political Economy in the University of Virginia, which he held for twenty years, from 1825 to 1845. After 1845 he lived until his death in retirement, most of the time in Philadelphia.

He was a most voluminous writer on philosophy, history, and economics; he even ventured into fiction, publishing a novel which was thought worthy of republication in England, and which even found its way into a German translation. His chief economical works are, "Principles of Rent, Wages, and Profits" (1837), "The Theory of Money and Banks Investigated" (1839), "Progress of the United States in Population and Wealth in Fifty

---

[3] Preface, *Elements*, ed. 1866.

Years, 1790-1840" (1843), and "Political Economy for the People" (1859).

All of his economical works give evidence of literary skill, of great sagacity, and of full information; but they contain few positive contributions to the development of the science. Tucker's writings were but some among the many mirrors held up on this side the water to reflect the doctrines of the English writers and their French interpreters; and, though these mirrors caught upon their surfaces, along with these foreign objects, a good deal of American scenery, that scenery was evidently present only accidentally. In their special works such writers bring these common doctrines to bear upon American questions, American banks, huge American profits, unstable American currency; but the staple of thought is all the while as much foreign as domestic, and such works belong quite as much to a history of English economic thought as to a history of American contributions to the science.

In his "Political Economy for the People" Professor Tucker sums up his economical views in a series of short chapters which, as he himself says, constitute a sort of compendium of his University lectures. The usual grand divisions of Production, Distribution, &c., are omitted, and a most extraordinary range and variety of topics are laconically treated within the two hundred and twenty-six pages of the volume. "By omitting the arguments which have been urged on contested questions, as well as all historical details," the author "flatters himself that he has set forth all the principles that are important to the national welfare."[4] In regard to all questions of public economic policy he adheres to that rigid *laissez-faire* school who regard "the forbearance of government" as "one of its highest attributes." Like so many other American students of political economy, he seems to have learned his Adam Smith for the most part through Say, and to have received, along with the English thought thus derived, some of Say's own opinions. He gives to Say's theory of *gluts*, for instance, his unquestioning adherence. He turns, in one of the most interesting portions of his work, to discuss the economical aspects of slavery in the South; and here, of course, he is in a strictly American field. But he does not even here subject the question to any but very general tests such as might properly be applied to slavery anywhere.

"Notes on Political Economy, As Applicable to the United States," by a Southern Planter, was published in New York in

4 *Pol. Econ. for the People*, Preface.

1844. Though unsystematic and fragmentary, and in no sense a methodical treatise on the principles of the science, this book is remarkable as a plea for the extremist doctrine of protection coming from the South at a time when free-trade sentiments were almost universal there. The beginning, body, and end of the Notes is protection. The treatment is striking, for a certain practical sagacity which runs through it, and which, though narrow, is broader than a mere farmer's shrewdness. The author enunciates, moreover, with some force the principle that, in economy, as in other practical affairs, the facts of history and the circumstances of each case, rather than *a priori* conclusions, should be the determining premises in every discussion. In spite of the fanatical nature of the book, its dissertations are touched here and there with a sort of historical spirit. It contains no really scientific induction, but the author has at command a vast miscellaneous collection of the facts connected with the economic history and condition of the United States and a considerable familiarity with the trend of economic policy abroad; and he makes constant, and often skilful use of his information in the construction of his arguments.

He takes a rapid general view of the past economic policy and existing economic condition of some fifteen countries of Europe, Asia, and the American continents for the purpose of showing that their prosperity has been in direct proportion to the care with which they have fostered manufactures and the commerce which springs out of manufacturing industries. He sees, in whatsoever direction he looks, the utmost inequality existing between nation and nation. "Some nations stand on the vantage ground in every respect, as regards labor, capital, ships, productions, manufactures, and skill. . . . They have gotten the start of others in a way that cannot be mistaken. Whether this be the effect of long time, superior skill, more capital, greater activity or wisdom in their counsels, matters not."[5] The nations which which have gained this lead and these advantages will keep them unless extraordinary means for overtaking them and driving them from their ground of vantage; and "this single fact seems to render half the reasoning of these [the English] writers of no practical use."[6]

Everything, consequently, must be done to nurse and develop national resources. The forces of the nation must be "scattered" by an extension of territory which will bring all soils and all physical conditions within the control of a common government, that

[5] *Notes on Pol. Econ.*, pp. 18-19.
[6] *Notes*, p. 207.

the nation may in all respects be sufficient unto itself. "I would go so far on the principle of protection and bounty," declares the author, "as to assert, that there are cases that do arise in most countries, where a government should use money or credit in loaning the means, or giving bounties to enterprizing citizens, to enable them to start some branches of business, such as iron and the woolens, that are so necessary to the independence and comfort of all countries. When it is pretty clearly ascertained that these branches would not be developed by individuals, government funds must be used in bounties, in order to ensure their production, and the consequent wealth, comfort, and independence, that would be realized from them."[7]

Regarding economic self-sufficiency as the proper aim of each nation and its only safe-guard against inferiority, and perhaps annihilation, in the struggle for national development, this 'Southern Planter' looks forward with complacency and with confident expectation to a gradual extinction of almost all international trade and the all but complete economic isolation of the nations. "The trade and commerce of the world," he stoutly predicts, "are destined to be confined, in the nature of things, to the interchange of such raw materials and productions as cannot be raised or produced by any people at home. The time is coming, if not now at hand, when no article of manufacture will be purchased from abroad, in any civilized country. There will be labor and skill enough in all to produce each and every article, whether of necessity or luxury, and it will be their interest and duty both to do it. . . . But one tariff law or regulation will be known to the statute books, that of the total and absolute exclusion of all and every article fabricated or produced which the nation in question can make or rear. Until that day arrives, the nations of the world will struggle to undersell and overreach each other."[8]

Writing amidst the rise of those party struggles which prepared the war between the States, the author of the "Notes" cries out with alarm at the low ebb of national feeling and prays for a foreign war that, by the rallying of all parties to meet a common danger, the federal power may be lifted out of "the dust where it lies" and given "a character, a name, and perhaps a glory that would cause it to be respected, and impart to the people some pride in it." "Nothing but a war," he urges, "can save us—can brighten our escutcheon, lift us above all this meanness and local feeling, and make and preserve us a nation."[9]

The book closes with a series of odd, desultory, vague, dogmati-

---

[7] Notes, p. 67.   [8] Notes, pp. 190, 191.   [9] Id., pp. 219, 220.

cal remarks upon banking, population, education, internal improvements, representation, public opinion, the suffrage, State debts, city defences, licenses to sell spirits, &c. But even these discussions are made subservient and tributary to the main thesis of protection and a *national* economic independence.

Francis Bowen, late "Alford Professor of Natural Religion, Moral Philosophy, and Civil Polity" in Harvard College, was born in Charlestown, Mass., in the year 1811. He was graduated from Harvard in the year 1833, and passed from college almost immediately into a literary career of great activity. Ten years after graduation he became editor of the *North American Review*, which he continued to conduct for eleven years. After entering upon the duties of the "Alford Professorship," he published his "Principles of Political Economy," which has been very widely used as a text-book and has given him a prominent place amongst economic writers in this country. He did not confine himself, however, to economic writing. The studies of his chair included much besides political economy, and he has given to the literary world "Gleanings from a Literary Life," to the philosophical world, "Modern Philosophy from Descartes to Schopenhauer and Hartmann."

The "Principles of Political Economy" was first published in Boston in 1856, and various editions of the work appeared subsequently under that title until 1870, when its name was changed to "American Political Economy."

In Professor Bowen we have a most interesting example of the best American contribution to the elucidation of the doctrines of Adam Smith. He has little sympathy with Mill, Ricardo, and the other economists of that ilk, whom he groups and rejects as "Malthusians"; but he rejects their orthodoxy only to return to the father of the church. His methods are untrammelled and his views clear. He goes back to the open-eyed methods of Adam Smith, dwelling much on actual economic conditions and keeping his 'principles of human nature' well in the back-ground. Not that he denies *natural laws* a place amongst the foundations of the science. "There is," he says, "a general science of Human Nature, of which the special sciences of ethics, psychology, politics, and political economy are so many distinct and coördinate departments." But he thinks that "these universal principles are comparatively few and unimportant," and that, "if the science were limited to them, it would be of narrow compass and limited utility." "It can be fully and profitably set forth," he declares, "only in the inductive method, by observing and analyzing the phenomena in a particular case, and tracing these up to their sources, the circumstances of the people *and* the principles of human nature in which they originate."

It is, he affirms, only the science of political economy as taken in its broadest sense, as a branch of the general science of Human Nature, "which such writers as Ricardo, Malthus, McCulloch, and J. S. Mill have endeavored to develop and teach; though," as it seems to him, "with very limited success." They have even assumed to treat it deductively, deriving its principles from their knowledge of human nature, and tracing these down to the outward conduct of men and to the social phenomena which these general motives produce or influence." He himself, on the contrary, joins hands "with Mr. Samuel Laing"—and, one may add for him, with Fredick List—in the opinion "that 'every country has a Political Economy of its own, suitable to its own physical circumstances of position on the globe,' and to the character, habits, and institutions of its people."[10]

This, then is Professor Bowen's creed: He would establish for each country its own *national* political economy. There is a political economy which is universal: there *are* a few principles which assert themselves everywhere. But this universal science is a mere outline map: national political economy must fill it in with its details of mountain and river and plain, must add to it a text concerning climate, soil, and natural resources, and must recite the history and aptitudes of its peoples and their institutions.

In his view, political economy "is no *art* at all, but a *science*; for its immediate end is knowledge, not action or the guidance of conduct. . . . The general principles of any science are obtained only by abstraction,—by leaving out of view many of the details and particulars which actually belong to the case, and thus so far simplifying it that we can reason about it with facility. The conclusions at which we arrive by this process are very comprehensive, but do not admit of immediate application. *They are true only with certain qualifications and restrictions.*"[11] "In order to obtain a broader field of inquiry," the subject which he proposes for his own discussion is *"the general wellbeing of society, so far as this is affected by the moral causes regulating the production, distribution, and consumption of wealth.* It may be doubted

[10] These quotations are taken from the Preface of "*American Pol. Econ.*" (1870)
[11] *Am. Pol. Econ.*, p. 11.

whether the whole of this theme is included within the limits of political economy properly so-called; and therefore" he proposes "to consider not only the science itself, but its application to a particular case, the circumstances and institutions of the American people. . . . The social economy of different states has now become the chief object of interest, even to the historian."[12]

There is, consequently, in almost all parts of Professor Bowen's work a certain breadth and appreciativeness of view. Following the methods which he has thus laid down for himself at the outset, he often pauses to notice the influence of laws and institutions upon the operation of social and economic laws, attributing, for instance, the marked industrial contrasts existing between England and the United States to the fact that in England only the middle or trading class is free to get unobstructed gain, the noblemen and labourers outside the cities being in his view *castes*; whilst in America all are of the trading class, and land is one of the free commodities of commerce. His induction is not always quite of a scientific sort; it is often mere generalization based on a wide but rather miscellaneous *personal observation*. But it is far, on the other hand from resembling the narrow deduction from which he has revolted. His *spirit* in almost every inquiry is strongly historical. He does not seem to have been familiar with the writings of the German economists who first directed economic method into the same historical channels into which historical research itself had been turned by Savigne and Niebuhr, and his work, in its first form, preceded the cis-Atlantic fame of the Continental historical school; but he is thoroughly of their way of thinking. Much more controversial than most of the writers of the deductive school, who are for the most part too sure that they are right to turn aside to correct those who err, his attacks are directed generally against those too broad theoretical doctrines which seem to him to leave too much out of view very apparent historical truths and very evident practical limitations. He carefully adjusts his own principles, when he comes to apply them, to the circumstances of each case. He has a strong grasp of practical conditions and unhesitatingly trims his theories at every point at which they seem to rub against facts for lack of proper adjustment. He is constantly leaving the theoretical development of the science for the discussion of such practical questions as strikes, taxation, banking systems, debt-funding, joint-stock and coöperative companies. Indeed, most of his space is given to the consideration of such questions and of the general

12 *Am. Pol. Econ.*, pp. 13-14.

principles of currency and finance, "which," he affirms, "are the most interesting, because the most practically important, portions of the science of Political Economy."

"Professor Cliffe Leslie has very clearly shown the powerful influence exerted upon the economical views of Adam Smith, who, as Professor of Moral Philosophy in the University of Glasgow, had occasion to teach both Political Economy and Natural Theology, by the assumption of a natural order of society, to the disturbance of which by human institutions are due all the economical evils that afflict mankind."[13] And on this side the water Professor Leslie has found theology itself playing a very prominent part in political economy. "Children," he says, "used to have a way of classing books as 'Sunday' or 'week-day books' by looking over the leaves for sacred names. According to this criterion, several American treatises on political economy would be set apart as Sunday books."[14] This fact is naturally accounted for by the facts, that many of our economic writers have been ministers of the gospel who had turned from their first-chosen profession to undertake the not dissimilar duties of class-room teaching; and that in many instances they wrote from chairs which, like Adam Smith's and Professor Bowen's, kept their occupants as much concerned with moral as with economical and political questions. And it should be said, besides, that in the use of such writers theological tenets are not often made really to carry the weight of the argument. 'Providence' plays a large part on many of Professor Bowen's pages; but he never introduces it to make reasoning easy: he never shifts upon it any burden of his subject.

As has already been said, though Professor Bowen follows Adam Smith, he does not follow the professed followers of Adam Smith. Like most American writers, for example, he rejects the Malthusian views as to population. His issue with Malthus is an issue of fact. "I begin," he says, "with the proposition that the power of the earth to afford sustenance is now so far in advance of the actual numbers of mankind, that no probable, and in fact no possible, increase in those numbers, not even by geometrical progression, can create a general and permanent scarcity of food for centuries to come."[15] "Looking merely at the capacity of the earth to afford sustenance, it appears that the most densely peopled country in Europe, and one by no means richly favoured in respect to the natural properties of its soil, is not yet more than

13 Quoted from Prof. F. A. Walker
14 "Political Economy in the U. S.," Fortn. Rev., 28 (n. s.) p. 497.
15 *Am. Pol. Econ.*, p. 134.

half populated; and still several centuries must elapse before all Europe can be as densely populated as Belgium."[16] "If there are more mouths to feed, there are more hands to feed them with." "We can now see with sufficient distinctness the two great facts which afford a complete refutation of Malthusianism. The *first* is, *that the limit of population, in any country whatever, is not the number of people which the soil of that country alone will supply with food, but the number which the surface of the whole earth is capable of feeding.*" Second, *"The practical or actual limit to the growth of population, in every country, is the limit to the increase and distribution, not of food, but of wealth*; and it is certain that, in every civilized country, the increase in the number of its inhabitants is attended by a more than proportionate increase of its wealth."[17]

He conceives the *true* theory of population to be, that, "in a normal state the inclination of people to marry is controlled by their opinion of the effect which marriage will have upon their position in life."[18] For he finds that, in the old world, "the numbers of the poor increase most rapidly, of the middle classes more slowly, and of the upper or wealthier ones, either not at all, or so slowly as hardly to be perceptible."[19] "Whatever tends to keep men hopelessly poor is a direct encouragement, the strongest of all incentives to an increase of population. Take away the causes of misery, remove the insurmountable barriers which now keep the various classes of European society apart, and educate the people,—and there will be no fears of an excess of numbers. Take away the lower weights which keep down the spring, and the lever will never rise high enough to meet the upper check. . . . It is not the excess of Population which causes the misery, but the misery which causes the excess of Population. The Malthusians say that the rise of wages encourages marriages among the poor, and thus augments distress. On the contrary, it is the fall of wages which, by inducing recklessness and despair, causes the poor to multiply faster."[20]

Professor Bowen regards the Ricardian doctrine of Rent as a fallacy rooted in the peculiar conditions of farming in England under the corn laws. Under normal conditions, increase of population should lead, not to a resort to poorer soils, but to importation. "The original and inherent powers of the soil, as an element of *rent*, are wholly insignificant in comparison with nearness to market," and it is a great mistake to suppose that "popu-

[16] *Am. Pol. Econ.*, p. 136.   [17] Id., p. 140.   [18] Id. 143.   [19] Id., 146.
[20] *Am. Pol. Econ.*, p. 143.

lation, as it increases, necessarily remains stationary, or on the same spot." "Instead of the food coming from a distance to the population, the population go to the food." "Rent depends," therefore, "not on the increase, but on the distribution of the population. It arises from the excess of *local* demand over *local* supply, and is, therefore, ultimately determined by the expense and inconvenience of bringing the food from a distance; or by the discomforts and privations which attend the removal of a portion of the people to a new home."[21]

Skeptical on other points of the orthodox creed, Professor Bowen still adheres to the old wages-fund theory. He says, "the aggregate of capital or wealth devoted to the payment of productive or unproductive labor may be termed the wages-fund of a country; but the measure of it which each laborer receives will evidently be determined by its amount, divided by the whole number of persons seeking employment. Thus explained, the doctrine is a mere truism."[22] He holds, consequently, that "the true mode of raising the rate of Wages is to alter the relative number of employers and employed, not to diminish the absolute amount of population." "If the policy of the English law had favored the distribution as directly as it has actually encouraged their aggregation, the laboring classes of England, like the peasant of France and Switzerland, and the inhabitants of our own land, would be free to follow their own inclinations without incurring the charge of imprudence."[23]

In discussing Money, Professor Bowen advances the opinion that we can do without money *as a medium of exchange*, but not as a standard or measure of value.[24]

Amasa Walker, for more than twenty years professor of political economy, first in Oberlin and afterwards in Amherst College, was born in Woodstock, Ct., in 1799. He died in 1875 after a most active life spent in business, in the service of the State, and in teaching. He was for fifteen years a merchant in Boston; when the controversy over slavery grew warm, he became an active Abolitionist; in 1843 and 1849 he went abroad as a delegate to the Peace Congresses of those years; entering political life, he was successively State representative, State senator, Secretary of State, a member of the State constitutional convention, and, from

[21] *Am. Pol. Econ.*, pp. 162-4 *passim.*
[22] Id., 173.
[23] *Am. Pol. Econ.*, pp. 175, 177.
[24] Id. p. 293. See Prof. F. A. Walker's views, p.

1862 to 1863, a Representative in Congress; from 1842 to 1849 he held the chair of political economy in Oberlin College, and from 1861 to 1875 a similar chair in Amherst.

His principal economic works are "The Nature and Uses of Money and Mixed Currency" (1857) and the "Science of Wealth, A Manual of Political Economy, Embracing the Laws of Trade, Currency, and Finance (1866). Professor Walker's chief strength lay in the discussion of questions of finance. In most other branches of the science he is content to follow with very little variance the teachings of the English masters of the first half of the century, but in considering all matters of finance and money he exhibits much sturdy independence of judgment and is consistent in the use of a really scientific statistical and historical method. His attention is devoted principally to the problems connected with a "mixed currency; and, if his method in dealing with these problems had not been for the most part carefully inductive, the conclusions at which he arrives might fairly be called his hobby, so often does he turn to ride them. He defines a "mixed currency" as consisting of "promissory notes issued by individuals or corporations legally authorized to do so, in excess of the actual specie held for their redemption"; and the position which he maintains, and maintains with great force and skill, is, that such a currency is not governed by the ordinary laws of value, by the laws, that is, of demand and supply, but that its expansion is always in excess, because it creates speculation, and a feverish demand. In consequence of such speculation, *contraction* takes place, from any cause which affects credit, whether that cause be an adverse balance of trade, a demand for specie, stringency in the money market, or any of the manifold forms of suspicion. He gives tables and diagrams of "Mixed-Currency Fluctuations." Considering *inflation* the irresistible tendency, and consequently the inevitable and invariable result, of a mixed-currency, he discusses at length the fatal evils of an inflated, a really inconvertible, paper currency.

"The panic of 1873," he declares, "was as certain, in the light of science, as the succession of day and night. It came, because under such a currency as existed it must come; and it will come again, and yet again, so long as our present [1875] monetary system exists. Expansion, rise of prices, speculation, over-trading stimulated by an inordinate circulation, will follow each other until another and more frightful catastrophe shall give additional evidence of the essential weakness and viciousness of a currency consisting of mere credit, issued in the form of promises to pay money by the government and the national banks."[25]

Professor Walker is inclined to demand astonishingly little of the teacher of political economy. In offering his "Science of Wealth" as a text-book, he says, "Although desirable that the instructor should be familiar with the subject himself, it is by no means indispensable. With a well-arranged text-book in the hands of both teacher and pupil, with suitable effort on the part of the former and attention on the part of the latter, the study may be profitably pursued. We have known many instances where this has been done in colleges and other institutions, highly to the satisfaction and advantage of all parties concerned." But his view of the province and functions of the science do not, of course, attribute to any such second-hand perception of its truths any authority in the discussion of economic questions. Broad investigation alone can give authority to those who labor in the development of the science. Since political economy is "founded, like every true science, upon the observation of facts, its purpose is to show what these facts teach." The facts at its foundation, however, are only universal facts. It "can recognize no party interests, no national boundaries, no prescriptions, no assumed antagonisms between the industries of different countries or between the different parties to production in the same country." "It pays no deference to the opinions or prejudices of mankind. Its only inquiry must be, 'What is true?' assured that in answer to that question will be found the highest interests of humanity."[26]

In his conception of Value Prof. Walker follows Bastiat. "Value," he declares, "always expresses precisely power in exchange, and no other power or fact."[27]

In his classification of Wages, he offers a somewhat new statement. "Properly considered, wages are paid for three different kinds of *power; viz:*" (1) Physical power, (2) Mental power, (3) Moral power, for "as man advances in civilization it becomes more and more necessary that important trusts should devolve on individuals occupying particular situations."[28] His discussion of the relations existing between variations in the rate of wages and fluctuations in price is very suggestive. "Although wages rise and fall with the general rise and fall of commodities, they do not in equal proportion." Prices are constantly being carried up, sometimes are carried up for long perids together, by *speculation*; but

25 *Science of Wealth*, Pref., pp. viii, ix.
26 *"Science of Wealth,"* Pref. pp. v, vi.
27 *Science of Wealth*, p. 23.
28 Id., p. 289.

no one speculates in wages; wages must depend, not upon future sales, but entirely upon that which is immediate and actual. "Therefore it is that a general rise of prices, so far as covered by speculation, may operate against the laborer, or the persons employed on salary or on wages." Wages never rise so high or so soon as the price of commodities, consequently, and they *fall sooner.* "The fall of merchandise is broken by the disposition and ability of the owner to hold on, and, as far as possible, prevent loss; but the laborer cannot do this, he must sell his labor at once for the most it will bring."[29]

Professor Walker finds in the "mystery and terror" which characterize the treatment of the subject of population by British writers—"Malthus," he says, "exhausted the direst horrors of the subject"—these three fallacies: "(1) That subsistence is not progressive, (2) that population necessarily increases, (3) that, even if these were granted, there would exist between them any such melancholy relation as is assumed." His most interesting remarks in this connection are made with regard to the laws which govern the increase of population. "The rule of geometrical increase," he laughs, "is a favorite weapon in the defence of certain theories; but it is wonderfully far from the truth of nature. Boys have frequently exhibited, on the black-board, the immense wealth they could acquire if they should lay by a penny a day, at interest, for so many years; and the result seems very alarming, as if that particular school would eventually become the owners of by far the greater part of the earth's surface. So much for mathematics. . . . Contemplating certain positive, unquestionable facts in history, great instances of depopulation, ages of decline, the slow advances of reviving production, we may fairly begin to doubt whether propagation is a permanent force irrespective of conditions. We may not unreasonably inquire whether it ever appears without *a special reason in the case*; whether the rule is not the other way; *viz.*, not that population does not proceed in spite of adverse influences, but that it is never called out except by physical circumstances, which, in all their contradiction and bewilderment to us, really form the condition precedent of human reproduction. Why not? We do not say that individual *growth*, either vegetable or animal, is a constantly operating force, irrespective of circumstances. We recognize the necessity of heat, moisture, and special properties of the soil to educe the latent powers of expansion. Similarly, though more remote and perplexed, are the influences which bring out reproduction in the animal or vege-

[29] *Science of Wealth,* pp. 280, 281.

table. It is therefore more correct to say that population, instead of being limited by adverse, is only developed by favorable, conditions. We are deceived in this matter, since propagation acts almost universally. That happens simply because the favorable conditions are nearly universal."[30] Even granting the first two points, however, he thinks the interchange of products through the means of a world-wide commerce sufficient safeguard against the "melancholy relation" assumed to exist between the slow increase in the means of subsistence and the rapid growth of population.

Professor Arthur Latham Perry, author of "Elements of Political Economy" (1865) and "Introduction to Political Economy" (1877) was born at Lyme, New Hampshire, in the year 1830. In 1854 he became professor of history and political economy in Williams College, Mass., from which institution he had been graduated in 1852.

Before he himself undertook to write a treatise on political economy he had taught his classes in Williams College for many years from the works of Adam Smith, Ricardo, Senior, and John Stuart Mill, asking himself all the time, however, these questions: "What is Political Economy about? Within what precise fields do its inquiries lie? Is it possible clearly and simply to circumscribe that field?" It was only when these doubts were at last resolved that he felt the impulse to write. He tells us that when, after these years of questioning, his mind "had almost reached the conclusion in which it has now rested for many years with perfect composure," his friend, Professor Amasa Walker, recommended to him Bastiat's "Harmonies of Political Economy," and here at length he found a position with which he could be altogether satisfied. "I had scarcely read a dozen pages in that remarkable book, when the Field of the Science, in all its outlines and landmarks, lay before my mind just as it does to-day. I do not know how much I brought to that result, and how much towards it was derived from Bastiat. I only know, that from that time Political Economy has been to me a new science; and that I experienced then and thereafter *a sense of having found something*, and the cognate sense *of having something of my own to say*."[31]

Professor Perry's principal work, "Elements of Political Economy," was published, in New York, first in the autumn of 1865. Having quickly proved a very acceptable text-book, it has passed through a large number of editions, receiving from time to time

[30] *Science of Wealth*, p. 431 *et seq.*
[31] *Political Economy*, ed. 1883, Preface, pp. viii, ix.

various additions of matter and undergoing, the while, sundry changes of doctrine more or less important and extensive. Each edition has contained an introductory chapter on the history of the science, and as this chapter has received the largest additions in the course of the successive revisions so it also illustrates very forcibly the character of Prof. Perry's work. Here, as everywhere, his treatment is full of matter and wide in view, constantly growing fuller in matter and wider in view; but here, as everywhere, he remains *unhistorical* in method to the end. In the latest edition of this work—which has now dropped the "Elements" of its first title and become simply "Political Economy"—this chapter is made valuable by a very clear and full recital of the progress of opinion, in which Prof. Perry follows the rational and satisfactory method of hanging the history of economic thought upon the history of economic policy and of legal institutions. He considers the development of trade; he analyzes Roman laws of trade and of property; and he dwells upon the influence of the political work of such men as Sully and Colbert. But all the while he rigorously applies modern standards—the standards of his own system—to ancient, mediaeval, and modern policy alike. The recital is historical in form, the treatment unhistorical in spirit. He seems scarcely to be conscious what true historical criticism is when applied to philosophical questions. The generalizations of his own speculative creed are unhesitatingly used as standards for the thought of all past time, as measures of the excellence of every departed system.

This is the key to his method throughout the work. His whole effort is after an absolute speculative creed which can be applied indifferently to every problem of the science and nowhere be found to fail in a perfect resolution of all difficulties, theoretical or practical. His search is for perfect definitions and unimpeachable generalizations. He must remind every reader of that characteristic declaration of Sydney Smith's to one of his correspondents: "Political Economy has become, in the hands of Malthus and Ricardo, a school of metaphysics. All seem agreed what is to be done; the contention is, how the subject is to be divided and defined." Prof. Perry virtually declares himself of the same school in his suggestive strictures upon the method of Adam Smith. "A strange lack of precise definitions," he says, "a want of consistency in the use of terms, and consequently an absence of scientific generalizations, mar the 'Wealth of Nations,' and have given rise to endless controversies." If Dr. Smith "had organized his matter around *this* point [Exchangeability] as a centre, instead of around

the 'annual produce of land and labor'; if he had widened his discussions so as to include all exchangeable things as such, instead
of narrowing them to 'what is fixed and realized' in some vendible
commodity; and if he had given his mind more to definitions and
thus to generalizations; his book would never have become, as it
has already become, antiquated."[32]

Much, however, as Prof. Perry insists upon this progress by
definition and generalization, the scope and content of the science, the "outlines and landmarks" of its field, are more to him
than its method, although it is manifestly upon its method that it
must depend for the acquisition of truth. His grouping of the
writers who have preceded him is proof of this. After speaking
of the Physiocrats as constituting the earliest of the schools of
thought which he recognizes, he divides all subsequent writers
into a "Commodities School" and an "All Sales School," according
as the scope of their definition of the science is broader or narrower. According to this division, Adam Smith founded the "Commodities School" by excluding all but material commodities from
his definition; the "All Sales School," to which Prof. Perry himself
ardently adheres, received its life from Condillac's definition:
political economy is the "Science of Commerce" or Exchanges.
Thus "the third school happily escapes the limitations of the two
others, namely, *that material things alone are saleable.*" It includes within its view all exchangeable things, services and
claims as well as material commodities. Indeed it seeks to simplify its discussions by discarding 'distribution' as a division of
treatment and regarding commodities as merely materialized
services.

Had Prof. Perry separated his several schools according to their
scientific method, he would undoubtedly have been compelled to
rank himself where the historian of economic thought must of
course rank him, with what we nowadays call the English classical school. Only a disciple of that school could write thus: "To
unfold this science in an orderly manner will require an analysis
of those principles of human nature out of which exchanges
spring; an examination of the Providential arrangements, physical and social, by which it appears that exchanges were designed
by God for the welfare of men; and an inquiry into those laws
and usages devised by men to facilitate or to mediate exchanges.
The science of value will be soundly based and properly unfolded
when its propositions systematically arranged are shown to be

32 *Pol. Econ.*, ed. 1883, pp. 66 & 67. All quotations are from the ed. of '83
unless otherwise stated.

deducible from acknowledged principles of human nature, and consonant with the Providential structure of the world and of society; and when, in the light of these propositions, human institutions and laws relating to exchanges are explained and correctly estimated."[33] But it is not differences of method, it is differences of definition, which determine his allegiance and guide his examinations of the progress of the science. He is in nowise conscious of his nearness of kin to the English writers of the Ricardo type.

The premises from which he sets out are laid down with the utmost confidence. "No man has ever denied the great facts that lie at the basis of exchange. That men are possessed of desires, that efforts are necessary in order to meet these, that these efforts are exchangeable, and that mutual satisfactions are the result of the exchange, are propositions universally admitted. *From these simple truths spring all the laws of our science.*"[34] In carving the laws of the science from these simple truths, "Induction, Deduction, introspection, feigned cases, and results measurable in numbers, are the tools with which economists work."

Prof. Perry excludes from his definition of the science the "bad word, *wealth*," as itself not susceptible of scientific definition. "Political Economy is the science of exchanges, or, what is exactly equivalent, the science of value," value being "a definite relation between two things, though one somewhat hard to be caught and held."[35] As distinguished from the exact, or physical, sciences, "Political Economy is a Moral Science, and possesses all the conditions of a scientific growth."[36] He endeavours to confine his treatment rigorously to the development of the science in the lines of these fundamental definitions. He is always stringently precise in his statement of theoretical conclusions and constantly has it in mind to pause for a careful adjustment of fact and theory. He closes each chapter of his "Political Economy" with a series of propositions which sum up the arguments of the chapter and seem meant to carry the sanction of a "Q. E. D."

Seeking thus to square every topic by a few standard theories and definitions, his effort is, of course, to simplify the science as much as possible. He consequently discards altogether, because discarding on principle, the usual great divisions of treatment. "How utterly misleading," he says, "seems the old description of Political Economy as 'the science of the Production, Distribution, and Consumption of Wealth.' A worse description of a good sci-

33 *Elements*, ed. of 1868, p. 1   34 *Pol. Ec.*, pp. 171-2
35 *Pol. Econ.*, p. 116   36 Id., p. 115.

ence could scarcely be put together in words. To say nothing more than has been already said about the irreducible word 'wealth,' this description . . . implies that 'production' is one thing, 'distribution' another, and 'consumption' still another! Professor Walker at the opening of his 'Wages Question' makes each of these distinct from the others, and then makes 'exchange' distinct from all three of them. This is not analysis but concision."[37]

Confident of his premises, Professor Perry's confidence in his conclusion is of the boldest. In 1877 he published, as a briefer handbook than his "Elements," an "Introduction to Political Economy" in the preface to which he declares it to be his aim "so to lay the foundations of Political Economy in their whole circuit that they will never need to be disturbed afterwards by persons resorting to" his book "for their early instruction, however long and however far those persons may pursue their studies in this science." When Mr. Cliffe Leslie ventures to ridicule this purpose to do impossible things, Professor Perry exclaims, "as if such foundations *could* not be laid, or at least had not yet been laid for the science. Mr. Leslie's words are of importance in this connection only in indicating clearly the dissatisfaction, or rather despair, of the second school as such." He supposes Mr. Leslie to belong to the "Commodities School" of Adam Smith, that is, and so not yet to have attained to liberty and certitude of definition.

Running all through the lines of Professor Perry's definitions, however, there is a strong substance of practical remark, of keen observation, of broad acquaintance with pertinent historical fact, which often seems a little incongruous because, though sometimes throwing doubt upon the value, it is never suffered to cast a shadow upon the serenity, of his theorizing. Although he introduces historical facts merely to establish propositions or to clinch illustrations, seldom for anything like induction; he uses them well—with quite the same force of elucidation that is derived from the "Feigned Cases" which constitute his principal illustrative tools. Time and again his clear processes of thought and vigourous commonsense lead him unconsciously away from his generalizations. He employs induction, as if to the manner born, in ascertaining the *per centum* of wages to the value of products; he abandons the wages-fund theory as if he had never liked and befriended it; and he acknowledges the infinite diversity of wages within each employment as if his theories had no instinctive kindness for the opposite view. Though clearly his methods are es-

[37] *Pol. Econ.* p. 169. For Prof. Walker's views see his *Pol. Econ.* p. 199, and this work post p.

sentially the same as those of the English classical school, he is distinctly independent in his thought. He adopts the premises of the English writers for the most part, and commonly reaches their conclusions; but his arguments are often cast in different lines from theirs, and if these new lines of view lead to doctrines unknown to his masters in the science, he is pleased, rather than startled or regretful.

Still, his chief labours are conscientiously within the field of orthodox doctrine, and his favourite rule of combat is, Deduction vs. Deduction. His freedom of thought is that of the latitudinarian, not that of the dissenter. He honestly seeks the truth, but he seeks it by means of the old standards of faith.

His doctrine of Value he takes from Bastiat. He regards value as something based upon *estimation*, upon *desire*, and he therefore rejects all suggestions of a fixed or determinable *measure* of value. Neither Ricardo's opinion, that it is the quantity of labour necessary to produce an article, nor that of Malthus, that it is the quantity of labour a thing can command, nor Mill's, that it is the cost of production, nor Carey's, that it is the cost of reproduction, seems to him tenable. These criteria may serve as indexes of the probable value of "many saleable things," but not of all. Exchangeability is the test, and *desire*, personal estimation of worth, the standard of value.

As to the growth of population, Professor Perry is comfortably optimistic; and as to the classical theory of Rent, he is skeptical. He admits,—nay, he defends—the law of diminishing returns, but he does not allow that law to serve as a basis for his beliefs about the rent of land. He looks upon leased land as differing no whit in principle from loaned money. Land is one of the "commodities" of the "All Sales School": to lend it to the cultivator is to render him a service, and rent is what he pays for that service. "The rent of leased lands is the measure of the service which the owner of the land thereby renders to the actual cultivator of it." "Land is a commodity made such by human efforts, and its sale, its produce, and its rent, come under the ordinary laws of value." "As lands are capital, so rents are profits."[38]

Professor Perry cites Mr. Gladstone's Irish Land Act of 1881 as in strict accordance with these principles, in those provisions which give to the tenant partial ownership in the land which he tills. Land is borrowed capital: the borrower is entitled to the increase which his skill and industry win from it: the lender should not have increased rents from the land which the bor-

[38] *Pol. Econ.*, pp. 288, 298, 299.

rower has improved; the improvements should be altogether the property of the borrower and should give him a certain hold, of partial ownership, upon the land, the original capital.[39]

Professor Perry is conscious, however, that "Ricardo's wrong doctrine of rent is too famous and too firmly embedded in many men's minds" to be passed by without formal refutation. It is in his view an "ingenious and plausible doctrine," though "as full of fallacies as an egg is full of meat." He believes that it was a direct offspring of the corn laws,[40] which, as he put it, "crowded cultivation down upon unfit soils by means of prices artificially made dear." It assumes, amongst other false things, "that mere cost of production determines the value of produce, while we have learned that the *desires* of purchasers have quite as much to do with value as the *efforts* of producers." "Worst of all, this law assumes, that there are 'original and indestructible powers of the soil,' and that 'rent is that portion of the produce of the earth which is paid to the landlord for the use' of these powers, and that the varying grades of soil become such and continue such without modification and reversal on the part of men; whereas, the truth is . . . that there are no such 'powers,' and that rent is *not* consequently paid for their 'use'." It is not diversity of soils, nor the law of diminishing return, that causes rent, since these continue as before when rent ceases to be paid; but it *is* the price of produce, under demand and supply, that causes rent. If this price be high, as under the corn laws, then rents tend to be high; if low, as under free trade in food, then rents tend to be low. . . . Of course, whatever makes lands more desirable for cultivation, such as greater proximity to markets, higher degrees of fertility, a better state of improvements, will influence both the price and the rent of those lands; while the variations of demand and supply as determining the *price of produce* are the main things to watch in order to find out about the value of lands and their rent."[41]

Francis Amasa Walker, now President of the Massachusetts Institute of Technology, was born in the year 1840. His father was Prof. Amasa Walker, the distinguished author of the "Science of Wealth." The son was bred to the law; but, the civil war broke out before he had fairly entered upon practice and he took service in the Union army, in which he did gallant service as an officer, being brevetted Brigadier General at the close of the war in 1865.

[39] *Pol. Econ.*, p. 289.
[40] See Bowen's view, p.
[41] *Pol. Econ.*, pp. 291-293, *passim*

After the war he entered the civil service of the federal government as Chief of the Bureau of Statistics, served for a short time as Indian Commissioner, and in 1870 was appointed Superintendent of the Census. In 1872 he became Professor of Political Economy in the Sheffield School of Science of Yale College. His principal works are, a "Statistical Atlas of the United States" (1874), "The Wages Question" (1876), "Money" (1878), "Money, Trade, and Industry" (1883), "Political Economy" (1883), and "Land and Its Rent" (1883).

Professor Walker's "Political Economy" is a compact manual, prepared for use as a text-book and having a text-book's conspicuous mechanical structure of brief chapters and prominent topical head-lines. It is, however, a thoroughly philosophical summary of the opinions advanced and maintained by Professor Walker in his several separate treatises on particular branches of the science, and may consequently be taken as the standard for his views.

Professor Walker stands, in his treatment of economic questions, quite apart both from those English writers who have made a psychology of political economy and from those writers of our own rearing who have grafted upon that psychological stock some strong branches of American commonsense and practical conclusion. He is essentially modern—essentially of to-day. He is never under bondage to preconceived theories of his own nor to the long-reverenced theories of his predecessors in the science. He is willing, however, to take all sound and good things, whether of doctrine or of fact, that the deductive school-men have to give, and he does not countenance the contempt nowadays offering to come into vogue in this country for the methods and standards of the classical English treatises. That contempt is not, in his opinion, "justified by a large view of the progress of Political Economy in the past, or by a consideration of the history of the other social sciences. Political Economy should begin with the Ricardian method. A few simple assumptions being made, the processes of the production, exchange, and distribution of wealth should be traced out and be brought together into a complete system, which may be called pure Political Economy, or arbitrary Political Economy, or *a priori* Political Economy, or by the name of its greatest teacher, Ricardian Political Economy. Such a scheme should constitute the skeleton of all economical reasoning; but upon this ghostly framework should be imposed the flesh and blood of an actual, vital Political Economy, which takes account of men and societies as they are, with all their sympathies, apathies, and antipathies; with every organ developed, as in life; every nerve of emotion or of sensibility in full play.

"On this subject what could be more pregnant with meaning than the aphorism of Bacon, 'those who have treated of the sciences have been either empirics or dogmatical.

" 'The former, like ants, only heap up and use their store; the latter, like spiders, spin out their own web.

" 'The bee, as a mean between both, extracts matter from the flowers of the garden and the field; but works and fashions it by its own efforts.

" 'The true labour of philosophy resembles hers: for it neither relies entirely or principally on the powers of the mind, nor yet lays up in the memory the matter afforded by the experiments of natural history and mechanics, in its raw state, but changes and works it in the understanding.' "[42]

Lavelaye has defined political economy as a branch of legislation, as 'the science which determines what are the laws which men ought to adopt in order that they may, with the smallest amount of effort or exertion, procure for themselves objects useful in the satisfaction of their wants, in order that they may distribute them in accordance with justice and consume them in conformity with reason.' Professor would regard this as a definition of the *art* of political economy. "It cannot be too strongly insisted on," he urges, "that the economist, as such, has nothing to do with the questions, what men had better do; how nations should be governed; or what regulations should be made for their mutual intercourse. His business simply is to trace economical effects to their causes, leaving it to the philosopher of every-day life, to the moralist or the statesman, to teach how men and nations should act in view of the economical principles so established. The political economist, for example, has no more call to preach free-trade as the policy of nations, than the physiologist to advocate monogamy as a legal institution."[43] There can, therefore, according to this view, properly be no such thing as a *national* political economy. The *art* may be national; the *science* must be universal. The art is akin to politics; the science must heed only economical, never political, reasons.

In insisting upon the usual divisions of treatment in handling his subject, Professor Walker advances opinions which serve to indicate still more clearly his position in the history of the development of the science. "Among those writers who have defined

42 *Pol. Econ.*, pp. 17-18.
43 *Pol. Econ.*, p. 21.

political economy as a Science of Exchanges," says he, evidently thinking principally of Prof. Perry,[44] "distribution is not recognized as a separate department of inquiry, involving principles peculiar to itself. Those writers find that the subjects of exchange are, broadly speaking, two, namely, services and commodities, or, labor and the products of past labor. To carry forward this distinction is not consistent with the simplicity of the science which these writers have in contemplation. The difficulty is soon solved. By analysis they discover that commodities are, after all, nothing but services which have taken-on a material form, and thereafter they speak only of services; make value to be the 'relation of mutual purchase, established between two services by their exchange,' and thereby secure to political economy 'one grand characteristic of the great sciences, viz., simplicity.'

"I venture to say," continues Prof. Walker, "that this forced simplicity, secured by compelling into a single form things having much that is not in common; this false peace, which disregards irreconcilable differences; this hasty generalization, by which services and commodities are made to be one and the same thing, has had the effect to render political economy signally barren through the very period when social philosophy has been most prolific, and, secondly, and by consequence, to forfit nearly all popular respect for, and interest in, the so-called science of exchanges.

" 'During the present century,' says the Duke of Argyle, in his Reign of Law, 'two great discoveries have been made in the science of government: the one is the immense advantage of abolishing restrictions upon trade; the other is the absolute necessity of imposing restrictions upon labor.' I do not quote this passage here for the purpose of raising the question of Ten-hour laws or factory inspection, but only to call attention to the clear, strong antithesis in which this eminent philosophical statesman places services and commodities. His statement does not exaggerate the general and still growing consent of social philosophers and legislators, that the rendering of services differs so widely from the exchange of commodities that the two must stand in very different relations to legislation. More and more fully has this distinction come to be recognized. If political economy denies the validity of the distinction, so much the worse for political economy in the eyes of social philosophers and statesmen alike. Surely the simplicity of the science may be secured at too high a cost!

"Equally against the pressure of enormous vested interests, and

[44] See *ante*, p.

against the protests of professional political economists, the legislation of almost every enlightened country has progressed by steady steps, through the last sixty, forty, and especially during the last twenty years, in the direction of discriminating vitally between commodities and services, allowing continually greater and greater freedom of contract in respect to the former, and bringing the contracts which involve the latter more and more completely under the authority and supervision of the State. And yet there is complaint that statesmen and the mass of the people entertain such slight regard for political economy, whose professors in the interest of the purity and simplicity of their science, discard from the premises of their reasoning all the 'sympathies, apathies, and antipathies' of mankind, and insist upon treating a Manchester spinner, with a wife and six children, ignorant, fearful, and poor, in debt to his landlord and his grocer, as possessing the same mobility economically, and under the same subjection to impulses of pecuniary interest, as a bale of Manchester cottons on the wharf, free to go to India or to Iceland, as the difference of a penny in the price may determine."[45]

These passages are worthy of quotation in full because they illustrate, as perhaps no other single discussion in his works could be made to do, Professor Walker's attitude towards theorizing after it has quit its proper function as skeleton and has taken to masquerading as the real body of the science. They contain really all that need be said directly concerning his position in the history of the science.

Professor Walker's discussion of Rent serves as an admirable illustration of his method of putting living flesh upon the inanimate bones of Ricardian theory. He believes that the Ricardian doctrine of rent is "as absolutely true in theory as that things equal to the same thing are equal to each other." "Rent is the surplus of the crop above the cost of cultivation on the least productive lands contributing to the supply of the market."[46] This law is true, however, only "hypothetically, that is, upon the conditions assumed, viz., that the owners and occupiers of land, each for himself, fully understand their own pecuniary interests, and will unflinchingly and unfailingly seek and find their best market."[47]

Immediately leaving the mere hypothesis in order to make a wide examination of actual facts, he discusses at considerable

[45] *Pol. Econ.*, pp. 199-200.
[46] *Pol. Econ.*, p. 214.
[47] Id., p. 216.

length the existing practical conditions of land-holding in America, England, Ireland, and Europe, and concludes "that *practically* there may be three classes of cases in respect to rent.

First—Where, under the influence of an active competition for the product of industry, with all the claimants substantially on an equality in respect to intelligence, alertness and freedom of mind, and with no laws or habits or sentiments opposing the complete exaction of all which anything that is the subject of bargain and sale may be worth, rents, as in the United States, conform nearly to the Ricardian formula. *Second*—Where, among a population presenting wide differences of wealth and intelligence, and perhaps, also, of rank and political power, sentiments of personal kindliness and mutual regard between landlord and tenant, and a strong, authoritative opinion throughout the community respecting the obligations imposed by the ownership of property, especially of landed property, serve, as in England, and in many countries of the continent of Europe, to reduce, in greater or less degree, the pressure of the land-owning upon the tenant class; making the landlord slow to seek occasions for raising rent to its full economical maximum; reluctant in forcing matters with the tenant to an extremity, and altogether unwilling, whether from his own individual interests, or out of respect to public opinion, to proceed, in any event, in the case of a decent, well-meaning tenant, to distraint and eviction; by which it comes about that rents vary widely from the Ricardian formula, always on the side of the tenantry. *Third*—Where, with a tenantry ignorant, degraded by long neglect or abuse, improvident, perhaps reckless in respect to family increase, and by consequence unable to offer effective resistence to an acquisitive, aggressive treatment of the question of rents, little in the way of sentiments of personal kindness on the part of landlords, and nothing in the way of an authoritative public opinion in favor of moderation in exercising the rights of property, enters to restrain the impulses which tend to advance rents up to the theoretical maximum, or even, as we have seen in the case of Ireland, above that point, with the result of ultimate injury to the economical interests of both parties, and of the entire community."[48]

In his separate treatise on "Land and Its Rent," published in 1883, Professor Walker, professing himself in this field "a Ricardian of the Ricardians," undertakes to confute the objections made to the doctrine of Ricardo by Bastiat, H. C. Carey, and Leroy-Beaulieu, and to meet the attacks made upon landed prop-

[48] *Pol. Econ.*, pp. 224-5

erty of John Steuart Mill and Henry George. Nowhere is his writing more pungent than in this little duodecimo volume of two hundred and twenty pages. It is not possible to reproduce here the points of the discussion. It will suffice to quote Prof. Walker's conclusions as to the holding of landed property. He believes "that the ownership of land, in the main, by the cultivating class, promotes frugality and a wiser application of the existing body of wealth,"[49] and that, whilst, "in a country like our own, with vast unoccupied tracts still available for settlement, with a population active, alert, agressive, both industrially and socially, and with no vicious traditions, no old abuses, perverting the natural operation of economic forces to ends injurious to the general interest, it is only needful that the State should keep off its hand, and allow the soil to be parted as the unhelped and unhindered course of sale and bequest may determine. . . . Wherever there is a peasantry unfitted for competition, upon purely commercial principles, with a powerful and wealthy class, under a painful pressure of population, there the regulation of the holding of land becomes a proper matter of State concern."[50]

Professor Walker has established a most suggestive analogy between the law of rent and the law of *profits*. He does not claim for himself complete originality of theory as regards this important contribution to the science. Archbishop Whately had spoken of rents and profits as belonging to the same *genus*, and Professor Walker accords Professor Alfred Marshal a share in the development of the completed analogy. As there is at the foundation of the theory of rent a no-rent class of lands, so there is at the foundation of the theory of profits a theoretical no-profits stage of production, and an actual no-profits class of entrepreneurs. "All profits are drawn from the body of wealth which is created by the exceptional abilities, or opportunities, of those employers who receive profits, measured from the level of those employers who receive no profits, just as all rent is drawn from the body of wealth which is created by the exceptional fertility (or facilities for transportation of products) of the rent lands, measured from the level of the no-rent lands."[51] In the one case the determining cause is the fertility or position of the land, in the other, the brain-fertility or opportunity of the entrepreneur.

Professor Walker therefore insists that *jealousy* should be directed against the no-profits, not against the *large*-profits, en-

49 *Land and Its Rent*, p. 210.
50 *Land and Its Rent*, pp. 219-20
51 *Pol. Econ.*, p. 253

trepreneur. "Profits are measured upwards from the level of the no-profits class of employers; and any cause which brings incompetent persons into the conduct of business, or keeps them there, against the natural tendency of trade to throw them out, increases the profits of the successful entrepreneur, by enhancing the cost of production and consequently the price of that portion of the supply which is produced at the greatest disadvantage. This enhancement of price is at the expense of all who consume the goods so produced; the laboring class equally with the others, in theory; probably in fact more than any other, on account of their limited ability to look out for their own interests in retail trade."[52] Anything that protects against the results of incompetency or decreases the efficiency of labor helps "to swell the proportion of incompetent employers of labor," and so to raise profits and prices.

The whole of Professor Walker's discussion of the employing class in industrial communities is indicative of a keen practical insight, and consequently, fruitful of much practical suggestion. "Unfortunately," he says, "the entrepreneur function has not been adequately treated, if, indeed, it has been in the smallest degree recognized. English and American economists, in general, have chosen to regard the capitalist as the employer of labor, that is as employing labor merely because of the possession of capital, and to the extent only to which he possesses capital." But the entrepreneur must not merely furnish food, tools, and materials; he must have "technical skill, commercial knowledge, and powers of administration." So important and difficult are the "duties of the entrepreneur, so rare are the abilities they demand for their satisfactory and successful performance, that he who can discharge these will generally find the capital required. If he be the man to conduct business, food, tools, and material will not, under our modern system of credit, long be wanting to him. On the other hand, without these higher qualifications, the mere possessor of capital will emply labor at the risk, almost the certainty, of total or partial loss. The employer, the entrepreneur, thus rises to be the master of the situation. It is no longer true that a man becomes the employer of labor, because he is a capitalist. Men command capital because they have the qualifications to employ labor. To a man so endowed, capital and labor alike resort, for the opportunity to perform their several functions and to entitle themselves to shares of the product of industry."[53]

[52] *Pol. Econ,* pp. 256-7
[53] *Pol. Econ.,* pp. 245, 246.

Professor Walker was one of the first economic writers to prick the bubble of the old wages-fund theory; and he succeeding in bursting it as effectually as any other of its now numerous opponents. That "wages are, in any philosophical view of the subject, paid out of the product of present industry, and hence production furnishes the true measure of wages," he declared in 1874 in an address at Amherst College; he defended the same thesis in an article in the *North American Review* for January 1875; and in his work entitled "The Wages Question," published in 1876, he so completed the refutation of the old theory as to entitle himself to speak of it as dead beyond all signs of life. "It would brutal," he exclaims, in 1883, "to inflict further blows upon a body so exanimate as the theory of the wages-fund."[54]

He defines wages as "the product of industry *minus* the three parts already determined in their nature and amount," viz., rent, interest on capital, and profits. Where perfectly free competition obtains, the laborer is "the residual claimant" of the product of labor; but practically there are generally in operation many causes which hinder the laborer from taking advantage of any situation which offers him opportunity for self-advancement. "To him that hath shall be given, and from him that hath not shall be taken away even the little that he seemeth to have" Professor Walker considers "an economic as well as a social law," operating to upset, in great part, in actual experience, the ideal 'harmonies' which Bastiat dreamed of as existing between capital and labor.

"The Wages Question" is valuable principally as reviewing the wide literature of the subject. We make take as a summary of Professor Walker's views in this field the following passage from his "Political Economy": "1st. Rejecting decisively the doctrine of the wages fund, . . . I hold, with Prof. Stanley Jevons, that wages equal the whole product, *minus* rent, interest and profits. 2nd. In reaching the origin and limit of profits, the remuneration of the employer, as distinguished from interest, the remuneration of the capitalist, I closely affiliate profits with rent. . . . 3rd. In determining how much in the shape of rent, interest and profit shall be taken out of the product before it is turned over to the laboring class to have and enjoy, I hold that the only security which the laboring class can have that no more will be taken than is required by the mercantile principles governing those shares, respectively, is to be found in full and free competition, each man seeking and finding his own best market, unhindered by any cause, whether objective or subjective in its origin. . . . 4th.

[54] *Pol. Econ.*, p. 384.

In the failure of competition, I hold that economical injury, more or less serious, may be wrought upon the laboring class. (a) By the lowering of the standard of the employers of labor, allowing persons to remain in charge of production who would be driven out by a stronger competition, and thus increasing the aggregate amount of profits, just as the driving of cultivation down to inferior soils increases the aggregate amount of rents. (b) By the bringing down of the industrial quality of the laboring class, through a reduction of wages which in time tells prejudicially upon their health, habits, and spirit, making them thereafter industrial agents of a lower, perhaps of a lower and still lower, order. 5th. In opposition to the orthodox doctrine that all such economical injuries are in their nature temporary and tend to disappear, I hold that, so far as purely economical forces are concerned, they tend to perpetuate themselves and to grow from bad to worse . . . ; that, again, so far as purely economical forces are concerned, in all industrial communities, the rich tend to become richer and the poor poorer; and that only social and moral forces, like charity, education, religion, political ambition, entering from the outside, or physical forces, like the discovery of new principles of chemical or mechanical action or of new resources in nature, can restore the economical equilibrium if once destroyed by the weakness of the laboring class. 6th. That among laboring populations whose freedom of movement has become greatly impaired, either by force of law or by their own poverty, ignorance, and inertia, restrictions and regulations from the outside, or combinations among the laborers themselves, although these do in form violate the principle of competition, may yet, in so far correspond to the infirmities of such populations as to have the effect to promote, it may be greatly to promote, the actual efficiency with which the laboring class seek their own interests, in the distribution of the product of industry."[55]

Professor Walker's power of analysis nowhere appears to better advantage than in his discussion of the causes and phenomena of financial, or commercial, crises. Speaking of the words "overproduction" and "under-consumption," which play so prominent a part in such discussions, he says, "Like all condensed phrases each of the large words signifies more than one thing; in a certain sense, each phrase embodies a great deal of arrant nonsense; taken otherwise, each embodies a vital truth; and finally, so far as either means anything at all, that meaning is exactly identical with what is expressed by the other." "Overproduction and under-

[55] *Pol. Econ.*, pp. 284-286.

consumption mean the same thing, that is under-production. This is of course a mere jingle of words, until the phrases are qualified as they should be. Over-production, as alleged by those who would explain hard times, is *partial over-production*, production, that is, which has gone on in certain lines, generally under speculative impulses, until it has exceeded the normal, or even, possibly, a highly stimulated demand. This excess of supply in certain lines yields an accumulation of vast stocks of unsaleable goods, which is *partial under-consumption*, these stocks melting slowly away through a period extending over months, it may be, over years. Commonly, *under-production* is the result. The bodies of labor and capital which have been called into the over-done branches of industry, cannot readily, if at all, be transferred to other branches; they remain where they are; half-employed, waiting for the renewal of the demand. In the dreary interval, producing little, they have little with which to purchase the products of others, who are consequently compelled to restrict their production proportionally." "Over-production, general over-production, is impossible, and, were it to occur, were the creation of wealth to outrun men's capacity to consume, no one would be injured thereby. But under-production is an inestimable evil. It means less wealth produced, and consequently fewer of the comforts and necessaries of life, on the average, to each member of the community."[56]

On the subject of Money Professor Walker has published two special works of which the one, consisting of lectures delivered before the Johns Hopkins University in Baltimore, may be called scientific, and the other, a briefer treatment consisting of lectures delivered in the Lowell Institute of Boston, popular. In the former, "Money" (1878), a history of doctrines is given, and the literature of the subject is reviewed at considerable length; in the latter, "Money, Trade, and Industry" (1883), many questions concerning the relations of money to trade and industry are discussed which were not touched upon in the earlier work, and much space is devoted to the consideration of the question of mono-metallism vs. bi-metallism and of the perplexities surrounding the subject of "fiat-money."

Professor Walker's principal contributions in this field of the science are contributions of clearness. He rejects the word 'currency', as having absolutely nothing in its favor "except that it forms its plural rather more agreeably than does *money*," and he extends the word money so as to include bank-notes. Indeed he

[56] *Pol. Econ.*, pp. 323, 325, 326.

uses the word in its broadest popular sense. Money is anything that serves as a medium of exchange, anything that "does money's work." He would call it, not "the measure of value," but "the common denominator of values," not "the standard of value," but "the standard of deferred payments." Following the lead of his father, he maintains "that paper money, nominally or really convertible into coin, is liable to be issued to excess under speculative impulses from trade"; and he supplies the needed proviso to Ricardo's propositions concerning the circulation of debased coins and inconvertible paper. "That Mr. Ricardo failed himself to qualify his proposition 'that, however debased a coinage may become, it will preserve its mint value,' has caused much misapprehension of his views and much needless controversy. . . . If debasement of the coin be carried so far and be carried on so long that a popular reluctance to receive the money pieces be generated, of a strength sufficient to cause men to modify or limit their production in order to avoid exchanges, or to cause them to encounter the inconvenience of barter rather than handle the distrusted coin, then depreciation may result: that is, the supply of money will become excessive through the blow inflicted upon the demand for money."[57]

In short supplemental chapters to his "Political Economy" Professor Walker has discussed many practical questions connected with commerce, labor, and finance which he recognizes as belonging within the domain of what he would call the *art* of political economy, inasmuch as they are more or less governed by considerations of State policy. To many of these questions, especially to that of bi-metallism, he has given a treatment much broader and more philosophical, and therefore more truly practical, than they had received from any other American writer.

[57] *Pol. Econ.* p. 156

WWhw MS. (WC, NjP).

To Ellen Louise Axson

My own darling,   Balto., May 26, 1885

If I were in your place, I should avoid saying to my lover anything that he would naturally find it very hard to believe. I should not say, for instance, such things as this: "I am fast gaining courage to *write* my deepest thought—whether I can *speak* it yet or not, I do not know." Do you expect me to believe, Miss, that you can love your husband and not tell him so to the last syllable? Think a moment, you dear shy little woman—my evasive little pupil—: the next time you see me I will be more to you than I have ever been before—I will be something more than your lover (for we wont count the few hours *before* the ceremony!); and do you think that there will be anything in my eyes then, or anything in the way I hold you to my heart then, that will check the words you want to speak, that will forbid you telling me what it means to you to be my bride? Do you think that there will be nothing in what I say to you then, with my eyes and with my lips, that will *compel* you to answer? Ah, sweetheart, I have a sort of sweet prevision of how it will be then. I seem to *know* what will come to pass. Maybe my darling's *words will* falter a little at first; but it will not take her many hours to find out how much more perfect the intimacy between us has grown than ever it was before; and *then*—why, precious, think how mortified I should be if it did not turn out so! You are the only pupil I ever have had or shall have in this delightful study of love-making; and if, after marriage (which we may call your graduation, the close of your preparatory training, in the art), you should show no ardor in putting my instruction into delighting practice, how overwhelmingly I should be convicted of failure! But I have no fears: I know my little mistress's heart, and I know that such hearts—if there *be* any more such in the world—cannot live and be undemonstrative, when they see that the happiness of the one they love depends upon their being demonstrative.

I think, my precious one, that there is a secret connected with this matter which you have not discovered. I was too little in advance of my pupil to be a good teacher. The words of love I have spoken to her have been said too much in spite of my own embarrassment (!), with too hot a flush and too violent a heartbeat to leave room for any art in drawing her out! But, sweetheart, it's worth while,—isn't it?—for our hearts' sakes to tell each other everything. After we are married you will freely exchange heart-secrets—wont you?—with the one who loves you perfectly, with

Your own Woodrow.

ALS (WP, DLC).

Two Letters from Ellen Louise Axson

My darling Woodrow   [New York, May 26, 1885]

How I have been wishing for you this afternoon, dear! I wonder if you have been having as good a time as I. I have been up to the Metropolitan to see the Watts collection once again; as I had not seen them at all since I began to paint—I knew it would be the best lesson I could have at present. That I would know better what to look for now, would see things that I missed before,—in short would *understand*, to some extent, the charm which I *felt* before. So I have spent a long, still, happy afternoon with them, letting them *soak* in. It was one of the pay days for all save students, so the place was almost empty and very peaceful and I have enjoyed it intensely. What noble pictures they are! I never had any other to impress me so much. I am sorry to think I have seen my last of them—though I think now that I can always carry them about with me. This afternoon, especially, has made them mine.

But it was for the sake of nature rather than art that I most wished for you. I never saw anything more beautiful than the park now. I never knew what green-sward was before. I understand now why Ruskin thinks the *green grass* the most beautiful thing in nature; I could never quite appreciate his ravings on that point because as I said I never saw grass in the South. But I don't believe there *is* anything so calculated to make the heart of man rejoice as that wonderful sunlit flower-bespangled sward.

> "Dimpled close with hill and hollow
> Dappled very close with shade.
> Summer snow of apple blossoms
> Running down from glade to glade."

I[t] was not apple blossoms however but dogwood and lilac—great masses of it everywhere. I walked from the Museum to an entrance lower down and all the way I wished for you—ah, I can't say *how* much! But we *will* be together soon!—and among scenes even fairer than this, because there *all* is of God's making and therefore on a larger, nobler scale.

I can't tell you how 'delightful' I think the Arden Park plan, darling. I am so very, very glad that we are going back to the beautiful place which is already so linked with our destinies. If I thought it, the first time I saw it, the sweetest place I had ever seen what will it seem to me the *second* time! It will tempt me to forget that "Heaven upon earth's an empty boast." Do you remember those lines of Wordsworth's—favourites of mine, they are. I was thinking of them, this afternoon, being "in that sweet mood when happy thoughts bring sad thoughts to the mind."[1] I shall give them to you

> "Pain entered through a ghastly breach
> Nor while sin lasts must effort cease
> Heaven upon earth's an empty boast

But for the bowers of Eden lost
Mercy has placed within our reach
A portion of God's peace."[2]

And, thank God, that is a peace which the *world* can neither
["]give nor take away." I believe,—indeed I know, that I have a
very "happy disposition"; but it would take a happier disposition
than anyone ever had, not to feel sometimes oppressed by ["]the
heavy and the weary weight of all this unintelligible world,"[3]
—and *especially* when one first takes up one's abode in a great
city—sees its wretchedness without having been hardened to it
from infancy. There is so much that seems to tear one's very heart-
strings;—and it seems to me that the pitiful sights of one sort
and another have indefinitely multiplied since I came to this
rather shabby avenue. Sometimes when it seems easiest to bear
one's own troubles it is well-nigh impossible to bear all the troubles of all the people in the world—as if we were called upon to
bear them!—but there it is!—we naturally cast *our* burden upon
the Lord but sometimes it seems harder to do the same with the
accumulation of burdens. And then there is the question of what
it means to leave all in God's hand; it certainly doesn't mean that
we can entirely "wash *our* hands" of it all; we may try but we
will be no more successful than Pilate. Ruskin says of some evils
that if they were properly mourned by us they would happen no
more forever. But this is a long and unintentional digression.

I certainly shall feel no suggestion of grief, my darling, that
the time has come for you [to] leave Balto. You greatly need
change of scene and occupation, if I am not mistaken; and to go
to the dear home circle in Columbia will be the best and most
restful of changes. No, I won't say that either! why shouldn't I
humour your fancy that there will be *one* change still better for
you? In things of this sort, you know, whatever we *believe* to be
true *is* true! So to make it doubly true we will *both* believe that it
will be well for *you too* to have me always by your side bound to
you by every sweet bond of love—pledged before the world to be
forever, as I am already   Your own Eileen.

As if all my letters were not sufficiently attractive in appearance,
this has received an additional attraction in the shape of all these
blots. Pray excuse them, the letter got bespattered with water
after I finished.

1 From "Lines Written in Early Spring."
2 From Wordsworth's "After-Thought," in *Memorials of a Tour on the Continent, 1820.*
3 From Wordsworth's "Lines Composed a Few Miles Above Tintern Abbey."

8[1]

My darling Woodrow,   New York,   May 27/85.

I shall be obliged to put you off with a very short note this morning for I have an engagement at nine and it is almost time to be off. I was rushing about so yesterday that when the day was over,—when I came home from prayer-meeting I was so tired I could'nt walk straight! And then I was *obliged* to write some other letters, so I was forced to postpone yours.

I had a perfectly delightful time yesterday at Mrs. Hamilton's. I lunched with them, you know. Every time I see Mrs. H. I fall more desperately in love with her than before;—she is "too sweet for anything." It is, altogether, an ideally happy home. She is a Phila lady, so that I shall see her hereafter,—isnt that nice? Her father is Judge Porter of that city—*the* Judge Porter!

No, sweet-heart, you *need* have no fears about my putting your instruction "into practice"! I can't live and be undemonstrative to *any* of those I love,—unless *they* are *very* undemonstrative. I don't overwhelm Uncle Randolph with caresses for instance. But I am too glad that you didn't "turn out" that way yourself—too fond of *being* petted—not to make the most of my sweet privileges in that direction. I love you, love you, darling, and I *must* tell it and show it as well as feel it. My heart is too full of it to keep it to myself. I am entirely and heartily   Your own   Eileen.

ALS (WP, DLC).
[1] Wilson wrote the "8" above Ellen's "7."

Two Letters to Ellen Louise Axson

My own darling,   Balto., May 28, 1885

This long letter of Tuesday night, full of the mood with which your "long, still, happy afternoon" with Watts and amidst the beauties of the Park had filled you, and admitting me so sweetly where I so dearly love to be admitted, to my darling's quiet, musing thoughts about the things which surround her and constitute part of her life, is *delightful*—but, precious, *must* you *always* continue to throw doubts upon my love—or is this passage with which your letter closes only an evidence that you have yielded to the temptation to pretend doubts which you do not really feel, in order to "draw me out" in vindication of my right to be believed? 'Why shouldn't you humour my fancy that there will be *one* change still better for me' than joining "the dear home circle in Columbia"? Is to believe that merely 'humouring a fancy' of mine? Then "it follows as the night the day" that there is no truth

in my love for you—that it also is a 'fancy,' which you are humouring by consenting to marry me! Suppose, for the sake of argument, that I really do love you more than any one else in the world
—more than I love father, mother, sisters, brother—more, infinitely more, than each or all—then will I not be infinitely happier
with you "always by my side, bound to me by every sweet bond
of love,—pledged before the world to be forever my own Eileen,"
than it is possible for me to be with every one else whom I love
in the world gathered in one single circle of sweetest home life
about me? If you believe in the love, you must believe in the
'fancy'! Either both are true, or both are lies.

Of course I know what my darling means. I *know* that she cannot doubt my love for an instant—and I know that this is only her
playful way of warning me anew of what she imagines will be
my disappointment when I discover her fancied inability to satisfy
me and my love. I am not misunderstanding you, sweetheart,—
I only want to *beg* you, with all the power that our love can give
to the prayer, never to *say* such things any more! There is a real
tragedy in them for me: they cut me to the heart. All that is true
and good in me has entered into my love for you; and all my
trust—as it were all the trust of a life-time gathered up into a single faith, supreme and unassailable—is given to you in return for
your precious love for me. To have the slightest shadow of doubt
cast—even cast half in fun—upon any part of this relationship
between us hurts me inexpressibly—seems a hint that my whole
life is false, hopes, purposes, and all. For our love's sake, my darling,—as you love me and value my happiness, don't, don't even
seem to doubt the genuineness and immeasurableness of my love
for you! All my life has entered into that love; my affections, my
thoughts, my hopes, my purposes are absolutely inseparable from
you! I have found out now what it meant that I was once reserved,
sensitive, morbid, almost cold. It meant that I had never begun
to live; that my nature waited for some one to awaken its one
absorbing passion, the one great love of which it was capable;
that when you came and called out that love—like one born to
discover and claim it—*I found myself*. That love contained all my
future. It is a great, a tragic thing—a thing of calm reason, expecting nothing of happiness which cannot come out of everyday
life such as all the race knows, dreaming no impossible romances,
expecting toil and disappointment and weariness; but, all the
same commanding my entire life, conditioning its happiness,
dominating its aims, making all the world, for me, turn about the
beloved form of the woman I love—about you, my queen, my dar-

ling, my all. Sweetheart, I believe in your love as I believe in my own: take this test, if you would find out what this letter means: If I should say, in reply to this sweet prediction of yours about the delight you will have in returning to Arden Park, 'I am so glad, my darling, that you are so soon to be with the dear home circle in Savannah. I know that you will be happy there; I know that you need such a change more than any other and that it will make you happier than any other could—No, I wont say that either! why shouldn't I humour your fancy that you will be still happier when I come to you? In things of this sort, you know, whatever we *believe* to be true *is* true! so to make it doubly true we will *both* believe that it will be well for *you too* to have me always by your side,'—would not such speeches hurt my darling to the quick? If I were again and again to say such things—as if returning to thoughts from which I could not escape—again and again to say 'Maybe you will be happy with me, as you think you will, and maybe you will not; maybe your love will suffice to keep you blind, and maybe it will not[']—as if repeating a thought constantly upermost in my mind—what would you think? Oh, darling, *my* darling, *please* believe in me! Let *any* one *else*—let all the world besides—think that I am loving you out of a fancy, one day to fade away and leave me desolate; but believe in me altogether yourself! You know my heart: it is no more capable of deceiving itself than it is of deceiving you. Of course, if you *have* doubts about our future, I would not for all the world have you withhold the least part of them from me; but if you believe in my love, believe also in that love's beliefs—for the two are inseparable!

Do you want a pleasant theme for your thoughts during your voyage, sweetheart? Then think such things as these—and I pledge you my life that you will be thinking the truth—think: 'I am going home where I shall meet my love; I am going to make preparations for him, for his reception; and all the time that I work, all the time that I rest, in every walk that I take, in every line that I read, I can know that all his heart is with me, all his heart is waiting on these preparations; my sewing is bringing his happiness; when I am through I can watch for him with the glad consciousness that I am ready to give myself to him to be his forever and that the gift will secure him the greatest happiness that he is capable of experiencing,—greater happiness,—*far* greater,—than any one else in all the world could give him. I am his joy and his life, and in giving myself to him I shall be giving him life and joy unspeakable. I am going to be his; my sewing shall be prologue to the sweet love-play of a life-time with him: a life-time in which I shall *see* it his constant delight to be my lover, if only I love him in return with all my heart, with unstinted faith and loyalty.' Ah, precious, think of me all the voyage through as absolutely dependent upon you for my happiness, and you will not then have thought half the truth of my love for you and my joy in the prospect of living with and for you!

You have not yet sent me the *ring*, my pet:—don't forget!

And, my little lady, don't forget, that I shall be desperately anxious till I know that the sea-journey is over, and that I shall want a telegram so soon as ever Palmer, or some one, can run down to the telegraph office after you get in.

I will write to-morrow to New York, of course, and I will write to Savannah every day after that, except Tuesday, the 2nd. I expect to travel all through Tuesday—leaving here on Monday night at ten (10) o'clock, and reaching Columbia between five and six in the afternoon on Tuesday.

May God bless my precious one and keep her from all danger! *I love you*, darling, and oh, how I long for the time to come when you will receive me—will come to me—as

Your own   Woodrow.

My own darling,   Balto., May 29, 1885

What message shall I send you to carry with you on your voyage? I should like to send one that would last you all the journey through, one that you would never get tired reading and re-reading. I wonder what message my sweetheart would find sweetest and most satisfying. Does she want to hear again that I love her? She *knows* that already—she knows that my love for her is as broad and deep as the great ocean that will bear her—and as *restless* until it be satisfied with her presence. It is without discoverable depths, and when my precious little voyager shall have set out for her life's journey on *its* bosom she may sail never so far without finding its bounds. It *has* no bounds for *her*!

How I hope that my darling will be spared sea-sickness! For I know how she delights in the water, and what a glorious treat the sea will be to her, if only she be her natural self to enjoy it. It seems only yesterday—and yet it seems a long time ago too—that I saw my little lady stand on the deck of the little steamer at Smithville drinking in with her glorious eyes all the breezy distances of the harbour, and of the ocean beyond, her pretty figure braced against the force of the eager wind that played boisterously amidst the folds of her gown and tried to snatch her hat from her; her whole face and attitude softened and transformed by the intense love of nature in her gaze! Ah, how I loved that sweet figure and that love of nature in those precious eyes—how I loved my darling as I watched her then! And how I value that pretty memory's picture, because it enables me to imagine the same lovely little lady standing on the deck of the great steamer which shall carry her home. What would I not give to see her *there*! But *you* need not wish that I was along, sweetheart; for I should almost certainly be sick, and so spoil your pleasure by exciting your anxiety and sympathy. You couldn't both enjoy the sea and think of the wretched individual below in his stateroom all by himself. So think, instead—if you want to think of me at all during your voyage—think of an individual who is packing his goods and chattels in the gleeful humour of a boy just about to leave all his school-tasks behind him and be off for a long summer of birds-nesting and hunting and fishing—only *this* boy, of whom you are invited to think, is possessed of a sense of joy much deeper than any that ever prospect of birds-nesting or fishing or hunting inspired. For the first time in his life, he is *enjoying* his packing. It *means* so much this time. He is leaving behind him something much more hateful than school-tasks. He is about to be emancipated from all the tedious drudgery of living for himself, all the dreariness of loneliness, all the pains of heart-silence. And the things that he is leaving behind, hateful as they are, are not half so hateful as the things before him are delightful and satisfying! I don't know how to describe those things. The sum of them all is *that I am going to my darling*. As I pack, I construct dreams for myself such as I was presuming enough to construct for you in yesterday's letter. It doesn't seem to me a bit pathetic—all the proprieties to the contrary notwithstanding—that this filling of my trunks and box is one of the last rites of my bachelorhood. I am so unconventional and blind as to *chuckle* over my realization of the fact! The truth is that I haven't been a real, 'sure-enough' bachelor for a long time. I abandoned the mental attitude of a bachelor some twenty months ago; and since then my thoughts have lived so constantly with you that I have not had time to be my old single self. And now I am getting ready to go and join my thoughts. They have been caressing my little sweetheart long enough; I am going to dismiss them from that function and turn them to finding out how I can *best* love and serve my precious one. They have hitherto been my deputies; henceforth they shall be my eyes, to see my darling's pleasure, that I may *do* it.

I have been doing something else in the way of preparation besides packing: I have been making farewell calls on numerous friends and acquaintances. And it has been a somewhat embarrassing business, because it is *hard* to feign *regret* at going away when going away means such things as it now means to me. I *am very* sorry to say good-bye to some of these delightful people—under ordinary circumstances it might depress me very much to feel that it was likely to be a *long* good-bye; but you spoil all the pathos of it, you little witch you. Thoughts of you fill my heart with laughter, with a sweet mirthful joy that you are waiting to receive me with unfeigned love and delight, that I am going to find in your sweet eyes all the dreams of my life reflected. Ah, precious, *my* sweet darling!—once more I pray God to keep you safe through your journey, and bring us to that sweet union for which we have so long been hoping and praying and living. *I* am coming to Savannah soon, sweetheart, and then how proud, how grateful, how joyful I shall be to tell all the world that with all my heart I am forever   Your own   Woodrow.

ALS (WP, DLC).

From Ellen Louise Axson

My darling Woodrow,   New York May 29/85
    For the first time this winter, I have missed a day altogether in my correspondence, and I am *so* worried lest you should be anxious again as you were before;—but it was a chapter of accidents, or rather *hindrances* which seemed utterly unavoidable and insurmountable. Annette had one of her nervous headaches last night; the light in such cases drives her perfectly *wild*, so that I was obliged to put it out, *very* early—even groping my own way about for a while. Then as I was not able to pack last night I had to get up at day-break to do it as I had an important engagement at nine. I thought I would at least write at lunch-time, but I was obliged to go on an errand or two which kept me *so* much longer than I expected that I did not get back until I knew it was too late for even the afternoon mails. And now, by way of conclusion, Annette has turned over the only ink-stand and left but one single drop of ink in it, with which I am struggling, desperately writing a syllable at a time[.] It would take till midnight to write a letter at this rate, and of course I am already tired, so I must give it up though my heart pleads with my judgment for time to answer that precious letter of this morning (Excuse pencil, please, I am *forced* to it)
    I am all ready to start now at a moments notice almost, trunks

packed and arrangements complete. I think I will get off without any trouble or perplexity. I bade farewell to the League today with many regrets,—though *they* were rather for the *Leaguers*. But I have had a happy winter there and I shall always love the dear old school. This was "criticism day" so I went over to get my last lesson this morning and Mr. Wier's parting words. He gave us a delightful little talk. He is decidedly the most *lovable* of all the teachers.

I did not tell you what a charming time we had yesterday afternoon when we went to the Lenox Library and home across the Park again. We saw two such superb Turners,—or rather two Turner's *one* of which was superb—and two *exquisite* ones by Sir Joshua; among the greatest treats in pictures that I have had this winter. Then they have very fine black letter books &c.—the first printed book, the first printed in English, &c. &c. The old librarian told us all about them. By-the-way, he was the most delightfully absurd old soul I ever saw,—a clever and very aimiable man in his dotage, I imagine. He is "devoted to young ladies" and was assiduous in his attentions, ending by asking us for our photographs! He called me "Miss Angelica" all the afternoon! I didn't tell you that he turned out to be "S. Austin Allibone," author of the ["]Biographical Dictionary", &c. &c., you know.

No, darling, I did not mean anything at all by the words you quote; but since you don't like that sort of trifling I will never do so any more! And that is a good deal to promise, since by so doing I "draw you out" in this delightful fashion. But I certainly need not *goad* you into to [*sic*] writing so, since yours are *always* the sweetest of sweet letters. Sweet-heart I *do* believe in your love as fully, as trustingly as woman ever did. Do *you* not *know* that I do? I could not love you just in the way that I do if I did not have perfect faith in *your* love. I do not believe that there is often an engagement, especially so long a one as ours, which has been so unshadowed by doubt of each others love, or by jealousy, or misunderstanding. Never for one moment has my perfect faith in your love and loyalty been disturbed. How could it be otherwise with the woman whom *you* love? My faith in *you* is so boundless that I must also have faith in your love, which is a part of you; for you are always so true "to thine own self"—"thou canst not then be false to any man." My doubts, love, were all about *myself*, but they too I have cast behind me. For weel or woe your heart is mine, so you tell me—so I believe, and believing it I could not be happy—(and you know how happy I am) if I did not also believe that the perfectness of *my love* has power to make it for your good. With God's help I will be a true wife to you my love. May you too have a prosperous journey, dear; and so good-bye for a little season. With all love and faith

Your own   Eileen.

ALS (WC, NjP).

From the Hopkins House of Commons

Dear Sir   [Baltimore] May 30–1885

We the Hopkins House of Commons take great pleasure in presenting you with the accompanying bronzes as a small token of our appreciation of your efforts in our behalf, of your kind encouragement and advice and of our esteem and regard for yourself. We further express our regret at your departure from the university and our congratulations on your approaching marriage. Hoping that this union may be as fortunate to you as your connection with the Hopkins House of Commons has been advantageous to us,

We remain

Very sincerely yours

The Hopkins House of Commons

Signed
 Theo. Hough.
 Chas E. Coates Jr.
 Allan C. Woods.
 A. A. Doub.
 Henry O. Thompson.
 Wm. C. Ferguson
Committee

ALS (WP, DLC).

Three Letters to Ellen Louise Axson

My own darling,   Balto., May 30, 1885

I have received no letter from you to-day, and of course I am being made desperately anxious by the fact, in spite of the most resolute efforts to summon philosophy to my aid. I suppose that the rush of preparation towards the last as the time for sailing draws near has robbed my precious of all chances to write. At any rate, I try to believe that her silence is caused by nothing else.

I am *very* busy myself to-day, visiting and packing, and, as it is now *late* in the day, I am completely tired out—much too tired to write such a letter as I should wish to send to greet my darling on her home-coming.

I had to give over the plan of going out to spend to-morrow with Webster. It could have crowded me too much in my preparations for leaving on Monday, as it turned out. If I had hurried more in order to make the visit possible, I should have been too worn out to enjoy the trip at all.

How glad I shall be when I hear that you are safely at home, my darling. You must give the dear ones there ever so much love from me. Tell them please to *try* not to think too hard things of me for taking you away from them. I shall try to make you as happy as even they could, and I will guard your welfare—will guard *you*—as the most sacred of all treasures. Does little Carry Belle [Axson] remember me at all? I imagine that little Ellen [Axson] *does*, because she seemed to me a thoughtful, observant little woman who would not forget easily or quickly. Maybe they will both remember me as I don't want to be remembered after I shall have taken cousin Ellie away from them! It seems strange now, sweetheart, to call you 'Ellie.' You have become in my thoughts so entirely my own *Eileen* that that sweet name seems the only one that you *ever* had. How shall we manage to keep it separately ours? I would not for anything have anyone else use that name, and yet I cannot keep it private—I cannot remember always to call you 'Ellie' when other people are around.

Remember, my precious one, not to work too hard during these three weeks to come. It will hurt me so to find my darling looking tired, with dark lines under her eyes. When the cool of the evening comes, take one of the cousins and go out for one of the walks we used to take together; wont you, pet?—and, as you walk try to think a little bit now and then about the eager individual in the next State who is thinking always of you, who loves you more than any words can tell, and is altogether

Your own   Woodrow.

My own darling,   Balto., May 31, 1885

I have been strangely excited all morning thinking of my treasure away out on the great, all-powerful ocean, thinking of the steamer that is carrying my destiny. My life, with all its hopes and purposes and possibilities, is bound up in the little lady who is that steamer's passenger to-day! Oh, if she could but know how much I love her! Maybe a sweeter light than ever would come into her eyes if she could. I wish that her happiness could be proportioned always to the power and gladness of my love—then I could be sure that she would always be as happy as I long to make her. My lovely little sweetheart! you are all the world to me!

You did not tell me till just the other day, precious, that you are fond of being *petted*. You had several times said, in Rome and in Wilmington last summer, that you liked me to kiss and caress you: but you said that only at my earnest and persistent solicitation, and I had a sort of lingering uneasiness lest you had said it out of indulgence, for fear of hurting my feelings. But if you now voluntarily base your promise of letting your love for me come out in whatever expression it will—if you call your right to pet *me*—a "sweet privilege"—on the express ground that you are too fond of being petted yourself to neglect such 'instructions' as mine, I have clear title to feel the delight with which I read that sweet statement. You didn't think—did you, sweetheart,—that *that* would be the part of your letter of which my heart would take special hold. Ah, my little queen, you don't know what a precious privilege it is in my eyes to be free to use *every* language of love to you. If you love to be petted, you are going to marry some one who dearly loves to pet you. His past conduct must have already satisfied you on that point! If I give you a prescription, Miss, whose end is to secure your perfect freedom in showing your love after—after I next come to see you—will you observe it? It is this: Begin now to think of me as near to you already as I will be after the 24th—and of my coming as the coming of the one who is closer than closest kin to you! Am I too bold, sweetheart? I don't mean to be bold. I only want my love to love me openly when I come—not publicly, Miss—as your reproving look says—but openly —openly to *my*—delighted—eyes. Ah, how I love to think of that time!

The ring came this morning, dear, safe and sound, with that sweet letter of Friday night.

Give my warmest love to all at 143[1]—and keep for yourself as much love as you can dream of in a score of day-dreams about such love as you want from   Your own   Woodrow.

[1] That is, to all the Axsons at 143 Broad Street, Savannah.

My own darling,   Balto., June 1st., '85
The 'last things' of preparation for leaving to-night have, of course, proved so many and so hurrying that I have time, here in the midst of them, for only a line or two. But you know what is in my heart this first day of *June* and don't need to be told what

things I am thinking of my darling. I am a profoundly happy man to-day—and all for the love my precious one has given me and the love for her with which my heart is full. You are my heart's queen and blessing, sweetheart.

I leave to-night at 9 o'clock, and shall reach Columbia about 5:15 on Tuesday afternoon. My address there will be 'care Dr. Geo. Howe,' you know, my pet.

Good-bye till Wednesday. I love you, *love* you, *love* you as

Your own   Woodrow.

ALS (WP, DLC).

Two Letters from Ellen Louise Axson

My darling Woodrow,   [At sea] June 1, 1885

I intended to have written you every day on the steamer; but here it is the last night and I am making my first attempt. Providence did not permit it in fact! I was not equal to anything yesterday but lying very quietly on deck using nothing but my eyes. In that position I was comfortable and happy, so that while I succumbed to the situation, I did not do it so completely as to destroy my enjoyment of the voyage. I have enjoyed it intensely, and to-day I am "all right" so there is nothing to even mar my pleasure,—unless one reckons a blistered face! The weather has been perfectly delightful yesterday and today;—we started in a rainstorm and had a heavy fog the first night—so I understand. I went to bed at seven and slept twelve hours, so I can't speak from personal knowledge.

We have only about twenty-one passengers on board, but three ladies beside myself—and one of them is a *child*! There are a lot of young men, three or four of whom make themselves rather "too numerous,"—though they are very nice. One of them is the freight agent, a brother of our superior judge, Pratt Adams. I know the family very well. Another is a New Yorker, a partner of Louis Tiffiny the decorator; and he is quite interesting because he knows personally nearly all the artists in New York and lives in that artistic atmosphere. But sooth to tell, there were reasons why my own thoughts were infinitely pleasanter company than the most entertaining of chance acquaintances. I have had nothing better to ask of the world, in these two sweet days than to be let alone to dream my dreams,—to think the thoughts which my own heart as well as your sweet letter dictate to me. Darling, the feeling that this voyage is bearing me to *you*, is so strong that it quite overshadows the fact that it is taking me first to the dear ones in Sav. You have been with me, indeed so constantly through it all and my heart has been, because of it, so filled with an unspeakable joy and peace, that I think this voyage will seem to me all my life long like a beautiful dream;—the sweet *stillness* after the noise and bustle of N. Y. adding to the dreamlike effect. But there is little of stillness about me now and the light is dreadful besides, so no more 'till tomorrow, dearest. We get in tonight at eleven they think. I want to mail this on my way to the house. Please excuse pencil and *every thing*. I love, *love, love* you sweetheart. Do you think you know how much I love you? With all my heart   Your own Eileen.

My darling Woodrow,   Savannah June 2/85

I am sure that I will take the prize *this time* for absolute stupidity and absence of mind! I was so anxious for you to get a letter as soon as possible that I sent it to be mailed at half past eleven last night; having before calmly slipped it into one of your *Baltimore* envelopes; so it is now taking it's way northward and will probably cross you somewhere on the road! I seemed to lose my reckoning altogether,—didn't realize that this was Tuesday,— for as if that were not enough I sent off a telegram this morning in great haste also to *Baltimore*! and am now about to send another to meet you in Columbia. Don't you think I must have been dazed. It must be because Sunday on shipboard was so unlike any other Sunday I ever spent that I did not know it had passed. Now I *must* catch the next train to make up for lost time, and so can write but a line now;—would have had time for a decent letter— but dear old Janie (Porter) has just been in making a long visit, and it is nearly twelve o'clock. I find all quite well except dear Grandmother who is very feeble. She has been quite sick for several days, but is better now.

I am feeling splendidly; enjoyed my trip *exceedingly*,—as I told you last night! Am perfectly charmed with sea travel. Yesterday and the day before were two of the most perfect days I ever spent —away from you. I found one of your sweet letters awaiting me, and another has just arrived. But I must not *begin* to answer them now or this will surely miss the mail. I *must* wait 'till tonight. There came also a sweet letter from Mrs. Green[1] and a wedding present!—already!—a pair of silver sugar tongs. I don't know how she happened to take time so by the forelock.

Give a heart-full of love to all the dear family circle in Colum-

bia, and keep for yourself just as much as you want, or as your
heart can hold from   Your own   Eileen.

ALS (WP, DLC).
    [1] Enclosed in ELA to WW, June 4, 1885.

From Albert Shaw

Dear Wilson: *The Minneapolis Daily Tribune.*June 3. 1885.
    I want to know just exactly what you think of the man A. Stick-
ney and his books. Have you seen "Democratic Government"? I
suppose I must make a bit of review of it for the *Dial*. It has been
sent me for that purpose. What do people think of him? But especially what do *you think* of him? I don't like him. Who is he?
When is your partnership Hist. Am. Pol. Econ. going to be published? So Levermore has a place! He sent me a postal. Who
will get fellowships? Will you remark to Dr. Ely that I am to have
an article (a short one) in July *Dial* on "Recent Books in Political
& Social Science" & that his "Recent Am. Socialism" is to be first
on the list. Sumner's new vol. of Essays, and Stickney's "Dem.
Govt" will be included. Ask him if he knows of anything pretty
new that ought to be rung into the list. But really I am commanding you too extensively. What I want you to do is to give me an
off-hand opinion of Stickney on a postal card by return mail. I
think of you often these days and rejoice much in your success
and approaching happiness. . . .
                        Yours as ever   Albert Shaw.

ALS (WP, DLC) with WWhw notation on env.: "Rec'd and Ans. June 9/85."

From Ellen Louise Axson

My darling Woodrow,   Savannah, June 3/84 [1885]
    I am sorry to be obliged to send you such a succession of
meagre letters, as I have been writing of late; of course, I know
you appreciate the necessity but that doesn't make me any less
sorry for it. It is now after eleven and I suppose I ought to curtail
my letter again as I was up 'till twelve last night. But of course,
I did not *really* see Uncle Randolph and Grandfather until tonight, and there was so much to talk over that it has grown late
before I was aware. Grandmother and the little folks, and myself
have been comparing notes all day. Tomorrow things will settle
into their old groove, and then I will write you a *letter* again. My

little pets are as sweet as ever,—bless their hearts!—I am *so* glad
to see them!—and Randolph is as great a rogue as ever. They all
remember you perfectly and take a deep interest in you.

Yes, sweet-heart, I shall remember not to work too hard. I mean
to be real conscientious about it. I have already had the hardest
work done in N.Y. and I mean to get a semptress to help me with
the rest. For your sake, I shan't be "penny wise and pound foolish," as girls are so apt to be in such cases;—'tis better to be bankrupt in pocket than in health!

And when I take the walks which you recommend I *will* "*try*"
to think a little about the young gentleman in the next state,—
perhaps I may succeed if he jogs my memory frequently.

And does that young gentleman expect me to believe him when
he tells me that he has only lately become convinced that I am
fond of petting?—oh fie! How wonderfully patient, uncomplain-
ing, self-denying, you must have thought me to submit with such
good grace to what I did not like;—and what an adept at concealing my true sentiments!

> "Hiding with many a light disguise
> The secret of self-sacrifice!"

But all that is "too thin" sir, I don't believe you[r] "uneasiness"
was very great. I have always congratulated myself upon being
small so that people—especially you—would have more excuse for
petting me. It would be a real misfortune to be a great big woman
—very dignified—whom no one ever thought of caressing, and yet
to have a nature which longs for that sweet love-language. Yes
dearest it is a sweet and precious privilege or right which love
grants us when it gives us "perfect freedom" in the use of that
language. It is a right so dear to me that I will even promise to
obey your latest instructions, my lord, if I may thereby gain larger
liberty in that direction; I *will* begin already to think of your coming as the coming of the one who is "closer than closest kin" to
me! For is it not true, sweet-heart[,] you are more—infinitely more
—than all the world beside to   Your own   Eileen.

ALS (WP, DLC). Postmarked Savannah, June 3, 1885.

Two Letters to Ellen Louise Axson

My own darling,   Columbia, June 3/85
     I arrived all right yesterday afternoon, 'on schedule time,' read
your uncle's telegram, and was happy—tho.' not so happy as I am

to-day, because now I am rested and it is Wednesday, just *three weeks* from the day of days!

I am so anxious to hear how my sweet pet stood the voyage. Of course you will tell me all about it in the letter I am so eagerly expecting.

I found the dear one's here quite well. Father is in Clarksville, on his way back from the General Assembly, but he will be here, we expect, before the end of the week. I can't tell you, sweetheart, how delightful it is for me to be at home, amongst those I love, once more. I wish with all my heart that you were free, as I am, to *enjoy* the company of the home-folks and did not have to busy, and tire, yourself so with your sewing. But then, if you were, I would not be waiting, would I? I should be claiming you, and not leaving you to enjoy your freedom at all, selfish chap that I am! Which would you prefer, my little queen, to be free to enjoy *your* dear ones, or to have me come and take you? Ah, my darling, how unspeakably I long for you! It is sweet, very, very sweet, to be with my loved ones in this wonderfully happy home; but some-thing—*every*thing is lacking without you! If you wanted proof of my love, you could find an amazing weight of it in my heart now, could you but look in and see. I feel all the time that there is some-one infinitely nearer to me than even these precious ones whom I love so much. In the midst of the most perfect home love and delight my heart cries out for you. And, as if to make the mat-ter worse, sister has put me at once into the tasteful room meant for you—for us—when you come. It *looks* as if it were meant for you; it seems to be waiting for you; it looks incomplete somehow without you—and so my loneliness without you is aggravated by this subtle sort of reminder of the time when my precious little mistress will be here to keep in countenance these pretty sur-roundings which were evidently not intended for an unapprecia-tive bachelor. Do you think I am very imaginative, Miss? Not a bit of it. But you are queen of all my thoughts and everything around me falls to talking to my heart of you—and of course things arranged for you talk of nothing else.

All the dear ones here send you their best and warmest love, darling; and *I* send you—ah, my pet, how can I tell you what I send!—love and loyalty and faith beyond all words! How can I wait the three weeks!

Love to all at 143 and kisses to the little ones. I will give you *your* kisses when I see you. With all my heart,
Your own Woodrow.

ALS (WP, DLC).

My own darling,   Columbia, June 4/85

I received your little note of the 2nd just after I had sent my letter off yesterday, and I was *so* glad to see my precious little sweetheart's handwriting again. It seemed such a long time since I had heard from her! You dear, absent-minded little woman, you! You *must* have been excited to "lose your reckoning" so far and send both the telegram and the letter to Baltimore: though I thought more than once, as I came southward, that I ought to have reminded you that I should probably have left Balto. before your steamer got in. The fact of the matter was that I took it for granted that you would get in about the middle of the day, and would have time to 'wire' me before I got off.

I am *so* glad, my pet, that you enjoyed the ocean trip. If you enjoyed it at all, I can imagine *how much* you enjoyed it: my picture of my little queen standing upon the deck, with all the glory of the scene in her sweet eyes, was realized. I shall expect very eagerly the return of your first letter from its wanderings. It makes me *very* happy, my darling, to hear of anything that you have enjoyed—of anything that has made *you* glad:—and that you are "feeling splendidly" in consequence of your trip is delightful, sweetheart. Take good care of yourself, precious, and try to be feeling splendidly on the 24th.

I must tell you, while I think of it, of a gratifying surprise I had before leaving Balto. "The Hopkins House of Commons" sent me a pair of very handsome, tasteful bronze figures for the mantel-piece (two cavaliers just 'drawing' on one another) in token of their esteem and of their appreciation of my efforts in their behalf. They hoped that my approaching marriage would bring me as much happiness as my connection with them had brought them advantage.

And now for something else I must not forget: How would you have me dress for the wedding, sweetheart? Maybe, if you are to be in white, it would be most appropriate for me to wear my dress suit. I can wear either that or a dark suit with 'cutaway' coat—a dressy walking suit. I can wear either with equal convenience, so you may freely express your preference; and I want to dress as you would have me. So you will give me full instructions, if you please, dearest, and I will follow them to the letter.

I am glad that your dear Grandmother is better. Give her my warmest love, pet. I hope that she will be quite strong again by the time I get there.

All the dear ones here send lots of love to my little queen; but I don't think that any of them—well as they know me, and much as they love you—have yet guessed how much love I have in all my thoughts for you—how *consciously* and entirely I am

Your own   Woodrow.

ALS (WC, NjP).

From Ellen Louise Axson

My darling Woodrow,   Savannah June 4/85.

We have had such a house full of guests today that it has been harder even than yesterday to find time to write; I begin to despair,—think I will try to get up and write before breakfast. Mr. and Mrs. [Thomas] Clay and the baby have been in spending the day;—from Richmond you know, or rather from Tivoli at present, —their summer retreat on the salts. Mr. Clay wants to know if you and I can't come out to see them,—I told him how much interested you were in Richmond. He says Tivoli is a pretty place too. I wish you could meet them, but I told him it would not be practicable; for Tivoli is sixteen miles from the station. But you might see Richmond itself, though they are absent. How would you like to come down in time to spend a day there?—going down on the morning train & coming back in the afternoon. Mr. Clay himself is there, of course, everyday. It is safe in the day time but almost death to sleep there.

I suppose you received telegram number two! Uncle Randolph has been having a great deal of fun at my expense over the "telegram business";—says he is going to send you one today to say that I overslept myself this morning! He told me with much glee that he had given me away to you in the one he sent yesterday; had told you about my sending one to Balt. I told him it was a failure after all, for I had already written you of it!—but he said his would reach you *first*, anyhow!

By-the-way, I did not tell you of our other invitation from Mrs. Green; I think I will enclose you her letter; it is so characteristic —and such a sweet letter besides.

Am *very* sorry your visit to Mr. Webster was crowded out,— was hoping that would in a small degree atone for the loss of the Princeton frolic;—and I cannot help regretting that you missed it dear. Perhaps I regret it the more because of the sort of feeling I have that somehow or other it is *my* fault! But after all it makes me much more happy about you than I have been for some time to think that you are away from Baltimore and *at home*!, and in such a sweet—such a perfect home. I am sure it will do you good in every way.

If we do not make for ourselves a *true home*, darling, it will not be because we have not had the model before our eyes among our own dear ones. May our Father in Heaven, the Hearer and answerer of prayer, help us to build wisely and well and upon the sure foundation of love for Him and service in His cause. May we build for Heaven as well as earth. Since life seems so short sometimes for all we wish to do, it is a great thing—is it not?—to begin something which we need not leave incomplete in any event, but may carry on to perfection in the *other* life. Give my truest love to all the dear family and keep for yourself, my darling, as much as your heart can hold from   Your own   Eileen.

ALS (WP, DLC). Enc.: Aminta E. Green to ELA, May 29, 1885, ALS (WP, DLC).

From James W. Bones

Dear Woodrow   Rome Ga June 5/85
I enclose check for $100. which you will please credit on the note. Should you be leaving Baltimore shortly let me know where I will address you or your mother. Before long I will pay balance on note. All are quite well with us
                    Your affec uncle   James W Bones
ALS (WP, DLC).

To Ellen Louise Axson

My own darling,   Columbia, June 5th/85
The hours for the mails here as [are] such that I must write in the morning and send, or take, my letter to the office at just the hour at which yours arrives, in order to be *sure* that it will get off at the right time. It's just as well that I have to wait twenty-four hours to answer your sweet little epistles, for, much as they delight me on first perusal, it requires many readings and a day's quiet thought about their contents to enable me to take in their sweetness in all its fulness. Instead of wearing off, my darling, the freshness of my delight in your love seems constantly to increase. The precious womanly love and faith that breathes in all these wonderful letters of my lovely little sweetheart's bring me *new* joy every day. As I open my heart to your love in reading your letters an inexpressible *peace* fills my mind and glorifies my thoughts. My heart must all my life long be young and strong with this precious little woman's love as its portion!
Such wonderful things are happening in my heart nowadays, sweetheart. You know how some beautiful scenes amongst the

grander sorts of mountains and valleys make one catch one's breath with a strange, overpowering *excitement*? Well, that strange exaltation in the presence of the greatest things of nature furnishes an imperfect analogy to the sensation daily growing stronger and stronger in my heart as my realization of the nearness of our marriage becomes more vivid. And my darling assists so sweetly in making that realization more and more vivid. These delightful, playfully earnest assurances of her fondness for petting—and especially for my petting—and this precious promise to expect my coming 'as the coming of one who is closer than closest kin to her,' tell me so plainly that I am loved as I love that I feel fully warranted in letting my imagination delight itself with anticipations of that sweet *near* time when these thoughts and these promises shall be translated into acts—and I'd be a very strange chap if such anticipations did *not* exalt my spirits with an exaltation such as they never knew before. The fact is, little lady, that I do love you sure enough; and if ever any woman had full love's-justification for confiding *all* her heart's secrets—for opening all her nature's sacred places—to a man, you have that justification. I don't claim any other right than *love's* right to know my darling—but I think that that's right enough, if I can offer you, what I can and do offer you, a love without limit and without question.

Thank you, precious, for you[r] promises to take good care not to overwork yourself, and to guard your health. I know that you will keep them—and, if you *do* succeed in thinking, during your walks, of the young gentleman in the next state, please, Miss, think of him with as much love as you conscientiously can, loving him as you would be loved by　　Your own　Woodrow.

ALS (WC, NjP).

From Ellen Louise Axson

My darling Woodrow,　　　　　　　Savannah, June 5/85
    Your sweet letter from Columbia reached me safely yesterday morning. Am so glad to receive news of your safe arrival,—your happy home-coming;—and to know that you are perfectly free to enjoy your home and dear ones. The political economy business I suppose is altogether finished? off yours [sic] hands for good and all? How glad I am that your father is soon to return and you will have him all to yourself for two or three weeks, for I know how intensely you enjoy his company. I hope he too will be "free." You see, sir, if I had not kept you all waiting on me for two or

three weeks, you would have missed all that, so you have me to thank for it!—and I hope you feel properly grateful to me! Which would you prefer, to be free to enjoy your dear ones or to come and claim me? You can't scold me this time, sir, for idle words, for foolish questions! since they are not my words at all! Ah dearest, if you only knew how constantly, my heart turns to you, —at all times, under all circumstances! Nothing has power to make me forget for one moment. I did not suppose before I loved that one *could* think so well of two things at once. But it seems to me that every day makes me feel more strongly how incomplete is my life without you, and the sweet love by which I am surrounded here does not avail to diminish the feeling one whit. They are all very dear to me; I have given them a strong and tender love,— but to you I have given *myself*, my whole life, all it's faith, hope, love—everything. Why should I not wish to be in the place where I *belong*, and that is at my darling's side. Do you wish me still to answer your question, dear? to tell you "which I would prefer," you or all the world beside? Or do you think you can imagine the welcome your little sweet-heart will give you when this little time of waiting is past? Give my warmest love to all the dear family. All here send love to you,—and there is waiting for you besides more than can be sent from   Your own   Eileen.

ALS (WP, DLC).

To Ellen Louise Axson

My own darling,   Columbia, June 6/85
    The letter you wrote on the steamer returned to me from Baltimore yesterday, and I am so glad that it did, for you never wrote a sweeter letter than that one, my little bewitcher. All its sentences seem to come so straight from *my* Eileen—seem to tell me so plainly that you *are* mine—and nothing else in the world can ever make me so happy as the evidences which you yourself furnish that your heart, with all its hopes and purposes, is entirely mine—entirely and forever. I love you, my precious!
    I don't think, darling, that I can accept Mr. Clay's kind invitation to spend a day at Richmond—unless you mean that you will go with me! Just at that time I shall not be in a frame of mind to enjoy such a trip away from you. I need not tell you what I shall be delightedly thinking about, to the exclusion of everything else —I need only say that I should not see much at Richmond except with my eyes only. For if you, Miss, think that it would be possible to enjoy a day so spent just at that juncture in my private affairs,

you very much overrate my philosophical powers. I appreciate the invitation most highly; but I can't go on any expeditions of the kind without you. Besides, I could hardly arrange to get to Savannah in time, for I am especially anxious to go down *with my family party*.

Here's a good story, little lady: Mr. Craig—as I may have told you before—is a young Irishman who came to board with sister Annie when she kept boarders and has, by special sufferance, staid on ever since. Yesterday, while I was out, sister A. got your picture from my room to show to him, and while he was looking at it little George came up and, with a child's curiosity, asked, "Who is that, mamma?" Sister showed him the picture. "Oh," said Georgie, "it's *Aunt Ellie*." It seems that the boys had had a conference as to what they should call you when you came—and of course it's never too early to begin a good habit. Mr. C. was highly amused, as you may imagine.

Dear father arrived last night, tired out, but in excellent health and spirits. It's no small undertaking to go to Houston, Texas, by way of Tennessee and return by the same way! He did secure a house in Clarksville, after all, and they wont have to board, as they had expected to do. I am frightened at the idea of dear mother's having to fix up another house for house-keeping; but, that done, the arrangement will be best in the long run.

Yes, sweetheart, we will start out upon the making of our own home with perfect models from which to copy; but we wont need to copy. Love has made these sweet home[s], and love will make ours, model or no model, with God's blessing upon it. I have nothing but sweet confidence concerning the sort of home my precious little wife's love will make for   Her own   Woodrow.

Warmest love to all—and unbounded love to you from all here.

ALS (WC, NjP).

Two Letters from Ellen Louise Axson

My darling Woodrow,   Savannah June 6/85.

Company again until late last night, and no chance to write!— and in consequence I must send another hurried letter this morning.

The gift from the "House of Commons" was indeed *very* gratifying; I am so pleased to hear of it. And what a nice selection they made of a present! I am anxious to see them;—what *did* you do with them, by-the-way?

Well, as I have so short a time to write I must come at once
to business! You consult a dreadful ignoramus, dear, when you
ask my advice as to what you ought to wear. I hadn't the vaguest
idea on the subject, so I told Aunt E. and Uncle R. just now that
you had asked me if I wanted you to wear a dress suit or not and
begged them to tell me what to say! Uncle R. is one who is apt
to know about all such things, being rather "particular" himself.
He said he would not think of *getting* a dress suit for the occasion.
I said I understood you had both, the dress suit and a "cut-a-way."
Then he said he would wear the former by all means; that it ought
to be either that or a *"frock"*!—a "Prince *Albert*" I believe he said,
(I am getting as much out of my depth as you were a few weeks
ago) and that the dress suit was, he believed, considered more
'the thing' at present. But,—by way of conclusion,—I have no preference, dear, in the matter and you must do whatever you choose.

Alas, alas for our nice little scheme for having it all 'strictly
private'! It is seriously threatened. We have had such a run of
company that there has been no time to consult until today; but
we have just been having a long discussion. Uncle R. asked if it
was to be in the church or house;—"Oh," I said, "the *house* by *all*
means!" And then I saw at once, to my surprise, that they were
dubious about it,—that they would have preferred the other. But
they said—"Well, it was my wedding and I must have it to suit
myself." Then they wished to know whom I would invite, and I
said only half a dozen or so of my intimate friends,—and *such* a
time as we had then over that! We couldn't invite *this* person
without *that* one, and then the others feelings would be hurt! So
at last I said, "Well, I won't invite a *solitary soul* and then no-one
will be offended." "No," they said, "you can't escape that way.
It is utterly out of the question not to ask the Porters,—seven to
begin with[,] Col Olmstead, and Mr. Baker too will have good
cause to be hurt if your father's daughter doesn't ask them; then
their wives must come too! Then the Gilberts will be mortally
offended if they are left out,—the Lawton's and Greens will think
it 'very strange' &c. &c.!" "In fact," said Grandmother, "Dr. Axson's granddaughter can't marry *clandestinly*, and she might
as well give up the idea!" and a minister's family must be so
careful too, about making invidious distinctions. Uncle R. said
the trouble was simply want of room, especially now that we have
but one parlour. If it were in the church, and it was understood
that it was a general invitation—no cards,—we need invite no one
to the house and no one's feelings would be hurt. I said it was so

much more of an ordeal in church, and I hated the display;—they answered that they did not think there was anything like "display" involved in a simple marriage in church. Of course there were some objections to every plan. But, they concluded, I must not do anything which I *shrank* from, I must consult you, learn your views and decide as we thought best. So there is the whole case laid before you; what do you think? I *do* shrink from the church, to tell the truth;—that sort of thing isn't 'my style'; but I see that it would be much less trouble to them, and so I am very undecided.

Have just had on my wedding dress and veil for the first time; have had it for a week and havn't had the curiosity to put it on before. It is *lovely*,—very simple but just as 'artistic' (!) as can be —a plain long skirt, with no fussiness about it, looped up on one side to show a lace short skirt.

But I must close. I have been interrupted twice by visitors since I began to write this and I fear it is too late already for the mail but I hope not, for in that case I don't know when it *will* reach you, as there are no mails tomorrow.

This is Stockton's eighteenth birthday,—and also Little Auntie's[1] wedding-day—the first Ellen Axson, you know,—nineteen years ago today, it was. *Our* wedding-day will be on Palmer's[2] birthday. Goodbye until tonight, dearest. Remember that I love you, my darling, more than life—that your love *is* the life of

Your own   Eileen

[1] Ellen Axson Walker.
[2] Ellen's cousin, Benjamin Palmer Axson.

My darling Woodrow,   Savannah June 6/85.

I have been to church tonight, and it is now growing late, but I must write a brief note in answer to the one this morning;— though I dare say the one I write tomorrow night will catch up with it.

I have had little opportunity today for doing anything but entertain visitors. My last were Daisy King and her husband [Clarence], Rose's sister, you know. She leaves for Sewanee next Thursday to my regret though I ought to be glad, for she has promised to do her best to send Rose down to me. She made me promise to "dress up" for her some morning so that she could "tell Rose all about it" in case she didn't come! By the way, I must tell you about my namesake,—little Daisy's pet kitten, which she has named, and always calls, "Miss Ellie,"—"because it is *so white*, and so is Miss Ellie"! You know I wear nothing but white dresses in summer and it seems to have made an impression on her.

This is a wonderfully sweet letter, my darling, which you have given me for my Sunday meditations, one that deserves what it will get, "many readings and a day's quiet thought to take in all it's sweetness." It will make tomorrow a *good day* for me, filling it full of a wonderful peace,—an inexpressible joy. Ah, darling, you do not know—I can not tell you how dear to me is this priceless treasure of your love; surely no one else is so rich as I! You call me 'queen,' but the crown which you have given me is one which queens might envy—which I am sure they *would* envy if they knew all. How it has dignified, enobled, *glorified* my life!— what new *meaning* it has given to life,—to womanhood! It has made it seem an inexpressibly sweet and blessed thing to *be* a woman. And I remember the time when—would you believe it,—I thought it rather a sad fate;—was inclined to be somewhat melancholy over it at times! But the clock is striking eleven,—reminding me of my good resolutions, so I will close abruptly. Believe me sweetheart always and altogether   Your own   Eileen

ALS (WP, DLC).

Two Letters to Ellen Louise Axson

My own darling,   Columbia, June 7th/85

Yes, I know that I owe it to you that I am left 'free' for these two or three weeks to enjoy the society of the dear ones here, and I believe that I *am* "properly grateful"—properly grateful for *such* a favour: which same, Miss, is equivalent to saying that I am not grateful at all! And *that*, sweetheart, is my answer to the question "which I would prefer." You are a dear little mischief to turn my own question against me; but I am glad to have a chance to answer it at your invitation—I only wish that I could answer it as sweetly as you did, my delighting little darling! I think I *can*, with the aid of that answer, "imagine the welcome my little sweetheart will give me when this little time of waiting is past." My imagination has been busy with nothing else these last few months, and it was only to *assist* it a little bit that I asked that question. That question was full of faith—I should not have dared to ask it, if it had not been—but I knew that my heart, full as it is with the love you have poured into it, could not answer it as well as *you* could, little lady. And now it seems to me that it must have been a happy inspiration, of love's own sending, that prompted me to ask it. It's all nonsense—isn't it, sweetheart?—to say that two persons must be the opposites of each other if the love and attraction between them are to be perfect. Their love for each other must be of the same kind, at any rate—and that cannot be unless they are kindred spirits. Doesn't it delight *you* to find that our love-tastes are so much alike? It fills me with a peaceful joy which cannot be described when I realize, from your sweet messages, that you are thinking of me and longing for me with the same thoughts and the same yearnings that possess me all the days through. Oh, my darling, I love you with all my heart! I would rather be with you than have the love of every one else in the world who seems to me lovable. The thought of living with you is the sweetest, most satisfying, most inspiring I ever had. There is a queer mixture of soberness and romance in my anticipations of our future. They are sober because they don't consist of 'castles in the air,' but of pictures of real, practical, even commonplace conditions such as surround all other people's lives; and yet they are romantic because they are penetrated with an ardour, an inspeakable eagerness and transforming tenderness of love which encircle my darling with the sweetest conditions of life conceivable. Yes, precious, I can imagine the welcome your lovely eyes and sweet lips will give me when I come: I expect to find my little love-pupil ready for her graduating (!) ceremony. Do you think that you can imagine what I shall say and do and feel then —what welcome will be claimed by   Your own   Woodrow.

My own darling,   Columbia, June 8/85
I must write only a little note to you this morning because I have not yet written to all my near kinsfolk to tell them of our wedding day, and I must devote this morning to the performance of that postponed duty.

I am a little heart-sick to-day, precious, because no letter has come from you for the last forty-eight hours. I am absolutely dependent on your sweet letters nowadays. Every day I seem to need you more than I ever did before, and when no letter comes it so emphasizes our separation that nothing seems to go right with me. I hope that you are well, darling,—that this trying hot weather is not telling on your strength. If loving thoughts could take care of you, sweetheart, it would be hard for harm to come near you, for there is never a moment of the day when my thoughts are not round about you. It will not be possible for me to *think* of you more after we are married, it seems to me, though there will be then a thousand other delightful possibilities of which we can now only *dream*. Oh, my little queen, my heart has been so long ready for our marriage that the waiting already seems interminable. I can hardly realize that it will be over *week after next*. I *love* you, Eileen, my lovely sweetheart; I love you passionately, loyally, with all my heart. It is life and happiness to me to be

Your own   Woodrow.

All here send warmest love—though dear father says he is *jealous* of you. Give my love to *all* at 143—minus visitors, unless Mrs. [William] Duncan be amongst them.   Lovingly   W.

ALS (WC, NjP).

To Thomas Woodrow

Dear uncle Thomas   Columbia June 8, 1885

I would give a great deal to be able to believe it possible that you and dear aunt Helen and Hattie would come on to Savannah —to be present at my marriage. I have already begged Jimmie to do the same. The wedding is to take place in Savannah on the 24th of this month—and the event would seem to me doubly happy if I could have all present who are dear to me. Do you think there is any chance of your coming. After the wedding we are to spend a week here (with sister Annie) before going into the N.C. mountains where we shall spend the rest of the summer probably.

Father and Mother and Josie are here—the house-keeping in Wilmington having been broken up in April. They will go on about the first of July to the neighborhood of New York in order that father may be able to do some necessary reading in the libraries of the city—preparatory to his courses in Tennesee.

All join me in warmest love to you and aunt Helen and Hattie and the dear little ones.

Your affectionate nephew   T. Woodrow Wilson

TCL (RSB Coll., DLC).

To Albert Shaw

Dear Shaw,   Columbia, S. C., June 8/85

Your letter of the 3rd., forwarded from Balto., found me here this morning. I got away from the Univ. just as soon as possible, leaving there about a week ago,—too soon to know any Commencement news.

I hardly know what to say about Albert Stickney. I have not

read his "Democratic Government" yet, but I did read "A True Republic" in 1879 when it first came out. My impressions about it are now of course somewhat indistinct,[1] but I remember that it seemed to me the production of a mind of great logical, perhaps one might say of considerable philosophical, power, but utterly without the *practical* instinct of the statesman. It exhibited a somewhat minute *knowledge* of practical conditions, but a strange neglect of those conditions when it came to drawing conclusions. The book had a carefully preserved air of practicality—and Stickney *is* a man of the world—but its scheme was as impracticable as it was logical. It regarded government as an affair of passionless business, rather than, as it really is, an affair of rules of action compounded of every human passion. His thoughts were good to revolve in one's mind, but they could be made to fit nowhere into a scientific comparative, historical treatment of the past, and possible future, growth of political institutions. But you don't want a disquisition.

Of Stickney himself I know only that he is prominent for ability and public spirit among the younger generation (the men in their forties, say) of the New York bar—a strikingly handsome fellow cured of apparently incurable woman-hating by a beautiful girl —dashing, cultivated, thoughtful—full of affairs and of acquired mental stores, a Mugwump.

I was very much obliged for your full letter about the Ill. senatorship contest. It was just what I wanted.

I concluded all but the bibliographical part of my writing for Ely before I got away from Balto.—and *that* can be done at a sitting now. But Ely himself and Dewey will probably not be ready for the press before written [winter].

My address till June 30 is care Dr. Geo. Howe; after that it will be Arden Park Hotel, Arden P. O., Buncombe Co., N. C. In haste,
        As ever,   Yours affectionately,   Woodrow Wilson

TCL (in possession of Virginia Shaw English).
[1] Wilson expressed his reaction to Stickney's *A True Republic* in, *inter alia*, the marginal notes in Vol. 1, pp. 546-48; in "Congressional Government," printed in Vol. 1, pp. 548-74; and in "Government by Debate," printed in Vol. 2, pp. 159-275.

To Charles Andrew Talcott

Dear Charlie,   Columbia, June 9th/85
    Your letter of May 22 reached me in Baltimore, just as I was beginning to enter the rush of work just preceding the end of the term, and I did not find time to answer it before leaving. As you

will guess from my whereabouts, it will not be possible for me to be in Princeton on the 15th. I need not say that I am sorry: I am more than sorry: I am bitterly disappointed that I cannot be with the gang, on this occasion to which I have so long been looking forward. But when I tell you the reason, you will, I am sure, forgive me for not being so sorry as I might be under other circumstances. The fact is, my dear fellow, that I am to be married, in Savannah, Ga., on the 24th of this month, and I had, of course, preparations to make for the event which made it necessary for me to come South as soon as possible.

'These presents,' therefore, old follow, are intended to extend to you a cordial and affectionate invitation to be present in Savannah on the 24th to see me set out on a new and better stage of my career. It would delight me, Charlie, if you could come. The ceremony is to be a private one—a family affair—but I feel as if some of the old gang—and notably one Charles Talcott—were almost as near to me as my own family, and if one or all of them could be present to give me a (moral) send-off, I should feel as if an additional element of happiness had entered into the occasion.

The Cow and his family enjoyed (?) very much your allusion to the refrigerator cars on the P.R.R.[1] The beef will undoubtedly be delivered all right. Give my warmest love to all the boys—and tell them I would give up anything but my wedding to be with them.

After my marriage, I (we) shall go up into the mountains of N. C. My address will be Arden Park Hotel, Arden P. O., Buncombe Co., N. C. Try to write to me there—my address here (Columbia, S. C.) is care of Dr. Geo. Howe.

As ever,   Yours affectionately,   Woodrow Wilson

ALS (photostat, RSB Coll., DLC).
[1] A reference to an unpublished portion of C. A. Talcott to WW, May 22, 1885.

To Ellen Louise Axson

My own darling,   Columbia, June 9/85

Your letter of Saturday reached me this morning. I wish that I had known before that there were no mails from Sav. on Sunday—it would have spared me a miserably unhappy day. Yesterday was the second day without any letter from you and I was tormented all through it with every distressing anxiety that a man's heart can suffer. I knew that it was through no *fault* of my darling's—it was because I did *not* know the cause that I was so wretched.

It is evident, my precious, that the choice left to us between a public and a private ceremony is no choice at all, as it is left in the conversation reported in your letter. If I were to tell you that action A alone was agreeable to my tastes, action B being incompatible with both my happiness and my just pride, but that of course you were quite free to do either as you pleased, since it was altogether your own affair, you would naturally regard your choice in the matter as somewhat restricted. And this case, it seems to me, is, as it stands, quite similar. It will be quite out of the question for you to have a private—a "clandestine"!—wedding, but you can have one if you wish. It is impossible to make any 'choice' on *that* basis. It is much better to begin all over again, and ask your uncle and grandmother to consider the whole thing from a different standpoint entirely. As the case presents itself to me— and has presented itself from the first—the primary and most imperative consideration is one, not of personal choice, but of *propriety*. I had taken it for granted that a public ceremony was out of the question in view of the fact that it is so short a time since your blessed father died—and I have already given that as a reason, to my most confidential friends, for the privacy of the ceremony. And I must say that, even when I have thought of the possibility of a *church* wedding, I have never dreamed of a "general invitation" to the public. That would, in my eyes, make the whole affair—*vulgar*, if you will pardon the word—I can think of no softer synonym. Surely, under *any* circumstances, we ought, out of respect for the sacred transaction and for our own dignity, to choose our company. Something stronger than my tastes revolt from the idea of exposing ourselves on such an occasion to the idle curiosity of a whole community.

Of course I understand the delicacy of choosing whom to invite —and recognize the (almost) impossibility of excluding such friends as the Olmsteads (would *Mrs.* O. come to see you sacrificed to *me*?), though I cannot understand how they could take *offence* at being left out from a strictly family affair. But, believing as I do that in any case a choice should be made in inviting, the alternative between church and house seems to me, as far as invitations are concerned, only a choice between a broad and a narrow selection of friends, according to accommodations. If the church be thought admissible, the selection will be necessary, according to my view of the matter, quite as much as if the house were decided upon—only it will be much easier.

I *wish*, my darling, that I could *help* you in this matter. I am painfully aware that this candid statement of my views, which I have felt bound to make, is no *aid* to you. If you find—or have found—that your uncle and grandmother are inclined to insist on the public arrangement, *of course* we must yield promptly and as cheerfully as we may, tho' I confess that a "general invitation" would cause me the keenest chagrin. It is idle to say that the choice lies with us. It must be a decision of common agreement—based upon proprieties and conven[i]ences such as we are all ready to recognize. I would give the world, if the worry—the distress—of the discussion were cast upon *me*, instead of upon my precious one, whom my heart so yearns to *aid* with its love and service: but be sure, darling, that I shall acquiesce, without *any* reservation, in whatever decision your family council comes to.

Oh, my little queen, you don't know what a leap of interest my heart gave at this sentence about your wedding costume. If I could only see you in it for a minute *now*! I did not know before, sweetheart, that your [you] were going to wear a *veil*. *Of course*, if that's the case, I must wear a dress suit. It would never do for one of us to be in full dress and the other not. You will observe, Miss, that in the matter of *my* suit, I asked *your* preference; and you cooly say that "uncle R." says so and so, but that you "have no preference in the matter." You dear, un-commanding little woman! Are you always going to decline to use your authority? I was consulting you, not as an authority on etiquette, but as my loving little mistress: I want to do what you wish.

I am afraid, my pet, that this continuous run of company, worrying you, as it must be doing, by making your work piece-meal, done at snatched intervals, and fatiguing as it must be under any circumstances, will wear upon my little sweetheart very sadly. She *cannot* be careful of herself when other people command all her time and strength. Never mind, week after next I shall constitute it *my* business to take care of her—to see that all the conditions are supplied for cultivating the roses in her cheeks and chasing all shadows away from beneath her eyes. My lovely sweetheart, I do so long to give my life to you—to prove by every service of love how absolutely and joyfully I am

Your own   Woodrow.

All send warmest love to you, precious. May-be you would like to know that the views I have expressed are fully endorsed by dear father and mother.   Lovingly,   W.

ALS (WC, NjP).

From Ellen Louise Axson

My darling Woodrow,   Savannah June 9/85

I was cheated out of writing Sunday night, after all, for just as I had written your name, out went the *light* and I had to grope my way to bed! Something is wrong with the gas in this room. These are bad times for letter-writing, dear. I am *very* sorry to give you such short rations; but let us hope you don't need them as much as when you were alone in Balti—at any rate you don't need them to assure you of my safty since I am no longer alone in N. Y. I really have *no* opportunity to see the family except at night; and as I don't know when I will see them again, I feel that I *must* embrace that opportunity; and then it is very important, I know, for me to get to sleep in good time, with hard work and the great heat combining to "pull one down." And of course there is no quiet time in the day to write. I really ought to stop now, for here is the semptress with half a dozen things to "try on." It is very inconvenient to be such a little "thin slip of a girl"!—to think you have bought things "ready-made," and then have to make them all over, though they are the smallest size! Think of patterns for a girl fifteen, being too large for me!

Miss Nora Lawton called yesterday; and was giving me a glowing account of you which she had received from Mrs. Bird, who she says "raves" over you. Miss Nora herself raves over your sister. I did not know before that Mrs. Howe died at her [Nora's] grandmother's.

I think it was very sweet as well as amusing in the little boys to adopt me so promptly. I feel a decided accession of dignity at the thought of being an 'Aunt'! How *rich* I shall suddenly become with so many charming new relations! Be sure always to give my dearest love to them all. All here send love to you, and they *mean* it too, with all their heart,—though Grandmother did say something the other day to the effect that she wished you would leave for parts unknown! But that was a terrible fib; for I am sure she don't want *me* to leave for parts, in very truth, unknown;—"that undiscovered country from whose bourne no traveller returns"! But I *must* not write longer. I love you, sweetheart, more than tongue can tell. I long for your dear presence always,—with a perfect longing; I am sure that you cannot imagine a gladder welcome than you will receive, my love. Your little pupil *is* ready for her graduating ceremony.

With all my heart   Your own   Eileen.

ALS (WP, DLC).

From Marion Wilson Kennedy

My dearest Woodrow: Little Rock, June 10th/85.

Your letter which came today, has almost *"broken my* heart"!
I *can't bear* to think of your being married, and I not even with
you long enough to see the ceremony. I know how wrong such
feelings are, however, and as my going is, from a financial point
of view, entirely and utterly out of the question, I am truly glad
I will have time to grow accustomed to the thought of this trial
before Ross comes home from Batesville.

Please, *all* of you,—yes, *even you*—, write me a full description
of everything connected with the trip to Savannah, *the wedding*,
and the trip back again. What would I not give to see it all, my
dear, *dear* brother! . . .

Give warmest love to dear Father and Mother, Annie and
George—to Josie and your dear self—

         Lovingly your sister,   Marion.

ALS (WP, DLC).

To Martha Carey Thomas

My dear Miss Thomas,   Columbia, S. C., June 10/85

I came away from Baltimore so much sooner and so much more
hastily than I expected that I did not have an opportunity to leave
with you my address—or, rather, my addresses—for the summer.
Until the first of July my address will be Columbia, South Carolina, care Dr. George Howe; after that date it will be Arden Park
Hotel, Arden P. O., Buncombe Co., North Carolina.

I suppose that the entrance examination papers will be sent to
me immediately after the examinations?—or will they be kept,
to be looked over with those of the autumn?

I trust that some new candidate for the fellowship in history
will present herself during the summer; though, so far, I have
not been able to hear so much as a rumor of one.

With sincere regard, Very truly Yours,   Woodrow Wilson

ALS (President's Files, PBm).

To Robert Bridges

Dear Bobby,   Columbia, S. C., June 10/85

You [Your] circular to the gang,[1] forwarded from Balto., reached
me yesterday. It is only too true that 'Wilson cannot come.' Miss

Axson gave me your kind message about staying with you until the 15th, and of course I was strongly tempted to accept the invitation; but it was simply out of the question, Bobby; I had to come South immediately. Try to think of me a bit on the 15th, old fellow, and remember that I shall think of you a big bit and with the keenest affection.

I don't know [William B.] Lee's address, Bobby; wont you give the enclosed note to him at the reunion—or mail it to him, if it will reach him sooner that way? I shall be very much obliged.

As ever,   Yours most affectionately,   Woodrow Wilson

ALS (WC, NjP).
  1 Robert Bridges to "Dear Fellows," June 5, 1885, handwritten form letter signed by Bridges (WP, DLC). Wilson was referring to the sentence: "Wilson is to be married on June 24 and cannot come."

Two Letters from Ellen Louise Axson

My darling Woodrow,   Sav. June 10/85

I have been prevented from writing until so late in the day that your letter of yesterday has arrived and I will answer it forthwith. The question under discussion was about decided, dear, before your letter came; and it of course settles it. It will be at *home*. Though Uncle R. *did* say at the table, just now, that I had better not tell you that it was *altogether* settled, since there were several things to be arranged before it could be so considered. They decided on the house chiefly because it would be much better for Grandmother, who continues very feeble,—she is in bed again today. I was so anxious to have it the way that would give less trouble, that I retired from the discussion altogether and begged them to decide.

I have done them great injustice, in giving you the impression that they meant to invite the *general public*; when I spoke of a "general invitation" I, of course, meant that it would be general among the friends of the family only. I said that if we had it at church we would need *invitations*, which would be more trouble than anything else; and they said that was unnecessary because those we wished to see would be sure to know it,—we could if necessary give them verbal invitations,—while at the same time it would be understood in the church that there were *no* special invitations, and therefore no one would feel slighted. In other words, all my friends would be welcome, and they were able to decide for themselves whether they *were* my friends or not. Perhaps a few persons who havn't the right of friendship intrude

themselves at a church wedding, but I shouldn't think many people would have so little sense.

When I said I was "surprised" to find that they preferred the
church, I of course referred to the fact of which you speak; for
I knew that on general principles they liked the church best. But
as I told you, they seemed to regard that in a different light from
myself; they did not think there was necessarily any more *gaity*
or *display* in a church wedding than in one at home; the one
could be as "quiet" as the other. As for Grandfather, who decidedly preferred the church, I think he has an idea that the
church is the place for a marriage, in the same way that it is the
place for a *baptism*! It is a good old *English* idea, so you ought
not to be too severe upon it. He may explain in the course of the
ceremony as he did while baptising Mrs. Clay's baby, the other
day, that this wasn't the proper place, but that as it was a special
case he thought they would [be] excusable this once in suspending
the rule. But pray don't think that anybody had any idea of exposing us to "the idle curiosity of a whole community"! I believe
that those who have so little delicacy as to go [to] a marriage
where they have no right, would go, cards or no cards. However
we need discuss that side of the case no more since it is practically
settled;—and I am more relieved than I can say that the reasons
in favour of the house did finally outweigh the others.

By the way, the Charleston train leaves a little after nine o'clock
and Aunt Ella says about *seven* P. M. would be the right hour.
Is it the Charlston train you are going to take? You know, you
havn't yet told me the details of your plans, or rather your sister's. When do [you] think you will get here?

I am *so* sorry dear that you were made anxious by the failure
of my letter to reach you. I was *afraid* it would be detained, but
I had no idea it would disturb you so now that I am at home. You
must try not be worried by any irregularities in my correspondence during the next two weeks. I will do the *very best* I can, dear,
but there is so much to do and such endless interruptions from
visitors that it is hard to "calculate" accurately in the matter of
times and seasons. I am writing at breakneck speed now so please
excuse *everything*;—havn't time to look it over even. I love you
darling with my heart of hearts. I am forever

                                        Your own   Eileen.

No, I didn't know myself that I was going to wear a veil and I was
a little dubious about it, being very much afraid of looking too
much "dressed up." But it was given to me, and I suppose I must

wear it;—not that I object *seriously* for it is "too lovely for anything"—and immensely *becoming*!

My darling Woodrow,   Sav June 10/85
   Uncle Randolph, who is a terrible tease in his quiet, dry way
has gotten a joke on me now which I am afraid will last him the
rest of my life! It is affording him such satisfaction that I wonder he has not already *"telegraphed"*! it to you. It has been pouring rain all the afternoon in a terrific manner, sky and earth
seeming all one sheet of water. "Ellie," said Uncle R. at tea, ["]sup-
pose the 24th is like this!" "Yes," I said absent-mindedly, watching
the storm, "it poured something like this the *last time*!" Imagine
the sensation! It will be necessary to explain that what I meant to
say was that it poured the last twenty-fourth of June when Janie
Porter married! The stormy weather is quite a relief to me though,
because it keeps visitors away. Though I did have a nice long visit
from Daisy King in the morning; she leaves tomorrow. She was
telling an amusing as well as astonishing story of plots and
counter-plots involving Mr. Gailor and—me! That absurd Mrs.
[Frank M.] Gailor! I told you a good deal about her,—did I not?—
what a terror she is, and how she makes things pleasant for her
son. It seems she took it into her head that "Tom" was, as Daisy
expresses it, "head over ears in love" with me; and she was dreadfully jealous of me, and was doing everything she could to keep
him away from me,—staying to talk to me herself, sending over
for him because she was sick, taking him off to make visits &c.
&c. While he on his side was anything but passive, but was expressing his opinion to them and to her too, it seems, in no very
measured terms. Indeed they seem to have had "all sorts of times"
about poor unsuspecting me. And I thought Mrs. Gailor was so
uncommonly nice to me, taking so much pains to talk to me, &c.,
and she was always as *sweet* as could be! Isn't it outrageous that
there should be all that domestic disturbance over a girl who was
so entirely out of the question. I should feel some compunctions if
it were anyone but that spoiled Mr. Gailor. But it *was* rather too
bad in the Anderson's to let it go on; Mr. [Jack] McRae was determined to tell him I was engaged and they were enjoying it so
that they wouldn't let him. He said he would tell him after I left
but Daisy says he[,] Mr. G.[,] was so "dreadfully depressed" for
some time after he came back from Cowan, where he went with
me, you know, that they thought I must have told him and that
it would be *unkind* (!) [—] they were grown suddenly considerate
[—] to say anything then. Don't you think the poor man has a

sweet life before him? He says it is as impossible for him to marry as if [he] had taken the vows of a monk, his mother falls into such a fury whenever the thing is suggested. She told the Anderson's that the woman, whoever she was, who married Tom should rue the day; she would see to *that*. I dare say she would kill her. But it is a shame to spend my time, when I have so little of it, in this manner!

No I don't think the work is wearing upon me very much, dear; —the hot weather, it is true *is* rather trying after the Northern climate. You don't say how it is using you,—though I suppose it is by no means so warm in Columbia. I hope you are fast getting "built up" now that "the proper conditions are supplied." I am sure darling that "week after next" there will be wanting no condition necessary to render it *well with* me in *every* respect. Whatever befall us, it can never be otherwise with me while your love encircles me. I am glad to find that in still another respect our love is of the same kind, for in my thoughts of the future there is that same "mixture of soberness and romance." I am sure that I have looked life straight in the face, that I don't imagine this to be an ideal world; but you know the most everyday scene is sometimes transfigured, as it were, into wonderful beauty by some rare sunlight effect; and so I expect this world of ours to be glorified by a light beyond even that of the sun,—"the light that never was on sea or land"—the light of love. Thank God for that light! for it's office is not merely to lend beauty to the world but to make our path plain before us;—and it is no will-o-the-wisp leading us astray, but a light beyond all others clear and pure and steady.

Yes, there *is* a spice of romance in my dream of the future, for I expect my lover to remain my lover, not through the morning hours only but all the day long; and I am afraid the majority of middle-aged people would smile pityingly at such an expectation. If I thought all the colour would wash out of our life as out of so many of those middle-aged folks I should pray to die in the next year or so. But it is pleasant to think that it is of no consequence to us what such people think; our treasure is in our *own* keeping, not at the world's mercy. What were those lines you sent me once?

> "Love, that what time it's own hands guard its head
> The whole world's scorn or rage shall not strike dead
> Love, which if once it's own hands dig its grave
> The whole world's pity and sorrow shall not save"—[1]

or words to that effect! I have left myself barely room enough to say "good-night." I love you darling—I am forever and altogether

Your own   Eileen

ALS (WP, DLC).

¹ From Swinburne's "Tristram of Lyonesse." See ELA to WW, April 15, 1884, n. 1, Vol. 3.

Two Letters to Ellen Louise Axson

My own darling,   Columbia, June 10, '85

Amongst the many things which I have noticed about you with a growing delight none has seemed to me fuller of sweet promises of happiness to me than this which is the burden of this delicious little note which reached me yesterday—the one you wrote on Saturday night:—my little queen finds my letters "wonderfully sweet" in proportion to the extent to which I indulge my love thoughts of her in writing them! My darling, if you want a sure, quick, easy receipt for making me happy, you have found it: you have but to *be* happy in my love, and to *show* me that you are! For that is just a part of that other, greatest secret which I have so often delighted to tell you, that your love for me constitutes the sum of my happiness. Your pleasure in being loved by me is just the sweetest of all manifestations that you love me; and when that pleasure appears in your words or in your glances or in your caresses—in *any* of the thousand sweet ways which you have of showing it—my happiness seems altogether too big for my heart. Why, sweetheart, I am *living*, these days, on the hope—the blessed *confidence*—of seeing that pleasure eloquent in all that you say and do two weeks from to-day. I may see you a *little* while by yourself—mayn't I—before the ceremony? I want to hear from your own sweet lips of your readiness for that act which is to crown our lives with a happiness such as we are now only *waiting* for. I don't know, Eileen, my precious one, *how* I am going to manage to behave myself that day! Maybe the excitement will make me unusually quiet—as excitement generally does—but I never before experienced excitement so mixed with overpowering delight as the excitement of that day will be: and so there's no telling how I shall be affected. I know some things about that day, though. I have dreamed more than once of a little damsel in a plain white skirt looped up on one side to show a lace short skirt —in a veil which will seem ashamed to hide the lovely face under it—who will seem to me to embody in her single self all the sweetness and loveliness of womanhood; and I have felt more than once already the thrill of joy that will make my heart beat as it never beat before with the consciousness that that precious little woman is *mine*—mine forever by the sure title of love! Oh, my darling, how wonderfully my love for you persists in growing—what a wonderful—hitherto un-dreamed of—heart-preparation I am undergoing for our marriage! I cannot tell you of it now, but I can, I am sure, then.

All here send warmest love to you, darling. Give my love to all at 143; and keep for your peerless little self all the love that your heart has imagined from   Your own   Woodrow.

My own darling,   Columbia, June 11, 1885
    I need not say that I am sorry that "these are bad times for letter-writing" with you; for, if possible, I need your letters *more* now than when I was alone in Balto. As the period of our separation grows shorter my longing for words of love from you grows more intense—somehow I *miss* you more than ever. It must be because I am consciously growing into oneness with my darling during these days which are so evidently days of mere waiting for our marriage. But all this is just one form of saying that I *love you*: and my love for you means, before all things else, a passionate desire to promote your welfare and happiness. It is, *of course*, perfectly natural and right that you should want to devote your evenings to enjoying the company of the dear ones whom you love, and whom you may not see soon again;—I would not have it otherwise. And it *is absolutely* necessary that you should "get to sleep in good time," in order that the heat and the hard work, which are making me so anxious, may *not* pull you down. It is, therefore, my *request*, Eileen—I *beg*—that you will sacrifice neither your rest nor your opportunity of seeing the family to my need for letters. A single page—a little note—each day, to let me know that you are not making yourself sick—but are taking *my* walks like a sweet girl—and that you love me with a love that longs for the 24th, shall suffice me. It need not cost you fifteen minutes a day —and surely you can find that much time of freedom in each twenty-four hours—that much time to talk to your lover. I am in earnest, sweetheart. I want to *insist* on this arrangement, if it is *at all* necessary to make it. I cannot bear to think that anything done *for me* is in any way a burden on my precious one—in any way interferes with either her duties or her health. And at this time especially I want to spare you all unnecessary exertion.

    Do you know, pet, that every mention you make of yourself— of your own dear little person—in your letters causes a special thrill of love to pulse through my heart? It is so sweet to have my little queen talk to me so freely and naturally about the work of preparation which her needle is doing. I love beyond all precedents of love my precious little, slender "slip of a girl"! I believe I should be capable of feeling a sort of respectful regard for the very patterns used in her sewing!

And my little "pupil" knows *herself* that she is 'ready for her graduating ceremony'? Oh, my peerless little sweetheart, you cannot say such things to me too often! You know you have not been saying them very long—and the time will never come when they will cease to awaken to its full gladness all the love of

Your own   Woodrow.

Love to all, darling; and as much as you could want from all the dear ones here for your sweet self.

ALS (WC, NjP).

From Ellen Louise Axson

My darling Woodrow,   Sav June 12/85

"Company company"—all day yesterday!—except when I was out,—not a minute to write!—not even at night for there was company then too. In the afternoon I went to prayer meeting and afterwards to one of our little mission festivals held in the basement of the lecture-room. Found all "my girls" there hard at work serving tables, and they had quite a jubilee over me. I was amused to see them begin just where they left off,—quarrelling about who should sit next me,—that was my chief trouble with them before. Mrs. Stoddard came here the first of the week to see if I would take the class as the girls were clamouring for me. But I was obliged to decline with thanks!

I have been amusing myself at the dentist's this morning, and so was prevented from writing early;—so your sweet letter written yesterday is now to be answered. I certainly will write you some time in each twenty-four hours, dear;—what I mean is that I can't take my own time for it, and so my letters are liable to be belated and miss the mail; especially as they are not so frequent as in New York. Did you not receive two letters on Tuesday? It is very hard *not* to write long letters every day for it seems to me I never had so much to say to you, darling,—so much that can't wait even one fortnight. Ah love, I *am* glad the time [is] so short! As long as separation is necessary one bears it quietly because one *must*; but when the end draws near,—when the necessity for repressing this longing to see you is past,—I wonder how I *ever* bore to be parted, the heart rebels so against it. To be sure you may see me, darling, before the ceremony—and hear from my lips of my readiness for that act which will make me *all yours*,—yours forever "by the sure title of love." Or rather for the act which will mark me,—set me apart—to the world as yours, for surely I cannot make the gift of myself more entire than it is already. It is wonderful what sweetness can be culled from just that thought that I am not my own,—I belong to another. Ah love, I give myself to you as joyfully as I do it completely. If I only *could* tell you how happy I am in your love I am sure, my darling your heart would be satisfied. It is "wonderful" how *my* love for *you* "persists in growing," but even more wonderful is the way in which my delight in *your* love for *me* has grown,—simply because there was more *room* for growth, you know! Now that I have come into a fuller knowledge of my own marvellous good fortune, I see, what I was not then conscious of, that my first faith as well [as] joy in your love left something to be desired.

> "For looking on myself I seemed not one
> For such man's love!—more like an out of tune
> Worn viol, a good singer would be wroth
> To spoil his song with, and which, snatched in haste,
> Is laid down at the first ill-sounding note.
> I did not wrong myself so—but I placed a wrond [wrong]
>   on *thee*."[1]

After all I cannot wonder that it should seem at first rather incredible that you should *really love me*!—it was not unnatural that I should be more distinctly *conscious* of *my* love for *you* than of yours for me. But *now* I feel through every fibre of my being that I *am* loved even as I love; and what words can tell the deep—the strange delight which comes to me with that consciousness. May *some* way be given me in our life together to repay you in some measure for the happiness which your love has *already* brought to   Your own   Eileen.

ALS (WP, DLC).
[1] From Elizabeth Barrett Browning, "Sonnets from the Portuguese," No. XXXII.

To Ellen Louise Axson

My own darling,   Columbia, June 12/85
    As if to test the sincerity of what I wrote yesterday, the mails have brought me no letter from you during the past forty-eight hours. I know that my precious one is safe, and she has promised me that she will carefully guard her health, so that the only

anxiety her silence causes me is that work and company together are robbing her of all *chance* of rest or recreation. Of course when I do not hear from her my loneliness fairly haunts me; but my love would not be worth a farthing if I were not anxiously insistent that she should not take a moment from either her rest or her duties for writing to me—and I can say with perfect truth that I feel not the slightest inclination to *complain* when she does not write. I doubt if the dear ones about me here, lovingly as they watch over me, notice any abatement in my cheerfulness when the mails fail me. The only thing is—well, sweetheart, you can imagine what it is—I am made more painfully *conscious* of our separation. Please, dear, don't try to write letters: notes will carry the words of love that my heart cannot do without. You need not fear that I will retaliate(!). I shall know that there has been no loss of the loving *desire* to write on my darling's part; and I will not cut *my* letters short. Although I too am busy about numerous little things, I have time always to write as usual; and my heart compels me to comfort it with this makeshift communication with my little queen. Letter-writing is at least better than silence. Silence would be unendurable; and yet silence is with my heart much more eloquent than speech. The thoughts which fill my mind about my Eileen—the ardent, longing, intensely loving thoughts which make these days like a time of sweet, solemn preparation for my life with her—sing songs of love, whisper hopes of happiness, command purposes of pure devotion such as I can never translate into *words*, but which, maybe, my darling can guess some of these days—can read by signs sweeter than words, *surer* than words, and more satisfying. My heart *needs* so much love, sweetheart, that its own necessities are, as it were, a sort of standard measure for its bounties. It would be only half a heart if it could not give love as perfect as that which its very life requires that it should receive: and its unbounded trust in your love has opened all its stores. Is not this an easy rule to observe, my pet: you have only to love me without reserve in order to win from me love as perfect and undivided as ever woman won. And oh, my little queen, I feel so rich, so strong, so complete, so ennobled, so blessed in the possession of your love. One whit's abatement in that love, one moment's pause in its growth, would kill me. I am nothing, if my heart be broken: and it would break if I could not have your love as absolutely as you have that of

Your own   Woodrow.

ALS (WC, NjP).

From Thomas A. Morris

Dear Sir   Arden, N. C. June 12th 1885

Rest assured we will try & give you pleasant & agreeable accommodations altho both the rooms you mention are engaged & were when we recd yr. first letter. Our intention now is to give you one large room in one of our new cottages or if I can have the partition taken down between the two rooms facing front over the ball room [I know] that you will like that. Both these situations have the best view and I believe that is what you wish. We are glad to hear from all your family again as we have only the pleasantest remembrances of them. With kind regards to all I am   Yours Respt.   Thos. A. Morris (per S.)

HwL (WP, DLC).

From Ellen Louise Axson

My darling Woodrow,   Savannah June 13/85

I was with Grandmother, who has been quite sick for two days, all last evening, so that it was impossible to write. This morning I have an engagement with the dentist at *half past eight*! You see therefore I must *really* write but a line this time, as I am afraid to wait until my return, tomorrow being Sunday. Will try and make up for this tomorrow.

I love you sweet-heart more than tongue can tell, I am consciously thinking of you *all the time*

As ever   Your own Eileen

ALS (WP, DLC).

From Thomas Kimber Worthington

My dear Woodrow   Baltimore, June 13th 1885.

Your welcome letter is just at hand and the contents noted with great joy on my part. I had no idea the happy event was so near. I hasten to give you my blessing, my dear Fellow, and wish that all peace and good may be with you and your dearest friend. I hope you dont think I am taking a liberty in wishing you well so earnestly but I care for you so much that I feel as if I had a right to do so.

If I had the pleasure of knowing Miss Axson (I hope I shall before long be introduced to Mrs Wilson) I should take another liberty and congratulate her.

However it would be needless to tell her about you as it goes without saying that she appreciates you.

As to your very kind invitation to be present at the wedding I must decline with many regrets. . . .

As I am up for a paper before the new State tax-commission in the fall, you see I have my hands more than full.[1] Indeed for another reason I could hardly leave Baltimore at present. I will impart it to you. The above can hardly interest you—about law and taxation, I mean—but in your present frame of mind a little love story will be more apropos.

In short my engagement with Miss Thomas will probably soon be a fixed thing. How it all came about, or is coming about, I havent time to tell you now. Suffice it to say that it is a great secret so dont you go writing to her about it like dear old Dave Dewey nearly did. I see my paper is more than out so must close with heart-felt wishes for the good and happiness of you and yours with sincerest affection.   Yours   T. K. Worthington

P.S. omitted. ALS (WP, DLC) with WWhw notation on env.: "Ans. June 19/85."
[1] He was a member of the Baltimore law firm of Carey and Carey.

Two Letters to Ellen Louise Axson

My own darling,   Columbia, June 13, '85
The mails here are enough to keep one who has anything to expect of them in a cronic bad humour. Yesterday at the usual hour I received the letter which you mailed on the 11th, and some hours later, in the afternoon, there came back to me *from Charlotte*, whither it had wandered, the letter which you had mailed on the *10th!* The latter contained your announcement of the family decision that the ceremony should be at home. I was profoundly relieved to hear that—and sincerely gratified: especially because the decision had been arrived at before my letter on the subject reached you. For I was conscious of having given my opinions in the matter in my usual absolute, plain-spoken fashion, and I was afraid afterwards that their so strong statement would seem to contradict my subsequent expression of my willingness to abide by whatever arrangement your family council might think best, and my readiness to accept it with cheerfulness. I had not the slightest wish to exercise any control in the matter. I wanted, as you did, to leave the decision altogether to those who were to have the trouble (?) of making the arrangements—only I did not know *how* to exercise that sweet *grace* of

submission which I so much admire—and love—in *your* part of the discussion. My lovely unselfish little sweetheart! How I wish I were like you, instead of being, as I am, fond of nothing so much as my own opinion and my own way! Will you teach me, precious? It *ought* to be easy for me to imitate what I love and admire with all my heart!

As to the "general invitation" to the church, my pet, of course it makes all the difference in the world, as to the taste and motive of the thing, for whom the invitation is intended—and it was, I confess, very stupid of me to imagine for a moment that you meant that the general public were to be *invited*; but, unless the common plan of requiring cards of invitation to be presented at the door for admission were adopted, the result would be the same in any case. The idle and curious—the general public—would come, invitation or no invitation. They would practically be invited.

I have not told you our plans, darling, because they were not definitely determined upon as to train and hour &c. Our party will leave here, Providence permitting, at 6.15 A.M. on Tuesday, the 23rd, and reach Savannah at 3.30 P.M. on the same day. We are to close the house and go in a body; and I want you to find out for us, my pet, at what hotel it will be most convenient for us to stop, if you please. "Uncle Randolph" will know. Could we get pleasant accommodations at the hotel (?) opposite the church? That would be *very* convenient. It don't make very much difference about the style, since we are to stay so short a time, but of course, on the ladies' account, we should like a comfortable house. No, dear, we will not return by way of Charleston, but by way of Augusta. The Charleston connections are very awkward; and the trains leave, according to the guide, at the same hour, 8:45 P.M. —maybe that is "a little after nine" by your town time. We shall leave for Augusta, therefore, at 8:45 P.M., expecting to reach Columbia at 1:32 on Thursday. That arrangement will involve some delay in Augusta, but not so much, nor at so unseasonable an hour, as the delay we should experience in Charleston, were we to return that way.

And so you 'expect your lover to remain your lover, not through the morning hours only, but all the day long'? Upon what do you base that fond expectation, Miss? Do you rely upon my promise always to be to you what I am now, and something more; or have you gone to the heart of my secret and found that you have power to keep me your lover by the mere edict of your love? That *is* the secret, sweetheart, whether you have found it out or not. I have not played the lover through any wooer's policy—through any craft of conquest, but simply and wholly because you were born my queen. I can never deny your sovereignty so long as you love me. I am your lover *by nature*, darling! For I was *made* to love you. How do I know it? I can't tell: no analysis of mine has ever plucked out the mystery of the matter. But a chap of my make knows when he is conquered—knows clearly what he loves; and *I* know that my Eileen combines in her single, peerless little self just that sort of womanly loveliness which must all my life through awaken the deepest tenderness and most passionate devotion of my love. I know that I *am* her lover; and, once her lover, I can never be anything but her lover. The single *reigning* power of my life—aside from my love for our God—is my love for her; and the only *condition* of that love is her love for me. With her love, life is full of strength and beauty for me; without it—I could not live, sweetheart.

And I, little lady, expect my sweetheart to be my sweetheart always, not only while her hair retains its sunlight, but also after it has grown tardily white with living for her lover, as his shall have grown with living for her. I expect it because I believe in her love with all the faith that can honour love like hers. No, indeed, we need not care what shallow-hearts may think at middle age of dreams like ours. I have seen such a dream realized in my own home. I know that love *can* retain *all* its youth and gladness; and I am sure that we shall only *begin* to be lovers on our wedding day. May God help me to serve you as truly as I love you, my darling. I am in every thought and purpose

Your own   Woodrow.

Warmest love to all precious; and from all here to my sweet one.

I was *so* much distressed to hear of your grandmother's sickness. I sincerely hope that she is much better ere this.

My own darling,   Columbia, June 14/85

That wonderful letter that you wrote on Friday reached me this morning and has filled my heart with a still, peaceful delight which I would give the world to be able to interpret to you, because it contains the whole story of my love for you. I love you as *my sweet treasure*, and this letter breathes all through the truth of the wholeness and gladness of the gift you have made to me. You are right, sweetheart, our marriage ceremony will mean no new thing for us, so far as the union of our hearts is concerned.

I have been married to you a long time in heart, my precious one; I *could* not be more entirely yours than I have been these many months gone by; and one of the odd (?) features of my impatience at our separation has been a sort of sub-conscious dissatisfaction at being compelled to live a bachelor's life when *really*, in the *essential* fact, I was no bachelor at all. That I should go and claim you and live with and for you seemed so *necessary* a result of my always conscious and always growing love for you, that I felt almost agrieved that circumstances were holding us unfeelingly apart.

But, sweetheart, this letter of yours makes me almost suspect that you are not so busy as you pretend to be. If you are so constantly employed with your sewing as you say, a visit from me would be only a serious interruption: and, knowing that, I have, of course, no idea of going to Savannah before the 23rd. And yet you seem to be deliberately tempting me to go! The little lady who tells me that she delights in nothing so much as in being altogether mine must have unbounded confidence in my power of self-control to think that I can hear her say such things and still stay away from her—so far away that I can only *dream* longingly of holding her in my arms and telling her in kisses uncounted how I value such speeches. My precious, my peerless little darling! You will not have to wait for a *future* chance 'to repay me in some measure for the happiness which my love has already brought to my own Eileen'! You *have* repaid me, you *are* repaying me, with this priceless love of *yours*, and these unspeakably sweet expressions of it! When you tell me next week (it *is next week* now, sweet one!) with your own lips how ready you are for your 'graduating ceremony,' I shall be repaid a thousand-fold for every heart treasure which I have so joyously laid at your feet. Darling, do you think that I *need* to be repaid with anything but *your love*? That love is the crown of my life, and nothing could crown me *more* than that *perfect* crown. You are to tell all the world that you are mine!—*that* is the fact which seems to me the sweetest and most significant in all the world—that it is which makes me so surpassingly glad to be

Your own   Woodrow.

ALS (WC, NjP).

From Harold Godwin

Dear Tommy: Princeton N. J. June 14–'85

Your letter came to me a few days since in the middle of a row which engaged all my time. Now I am at my leisure for a day and take the first chance I have, before my breakfast to tell you how glad I am that you are so soon to be married and how sorry that I cannot well be with you. I say this on general principles for it is of course not possible to do anything like making a journey to the South when married life is still freshly upon you. . . .

I have not seen the boys here yet, and fear I cannot be at the dinner. They all bear you in very affectionate remembrance. I shall leave it to Bobby to tell you how often you are spoken of and with how much regret that you cant be with them. I wish you a bon voyage for your start on the 24th and if I could get at your umbrella would play the trick on you which they did on me in England. They filled it nearly with rice and ten days later I used it for the first time. I could not help thinking of them as I found a shower of rice falling on me in a crowded street in Chester. If I could make you remember me on some such occasion be sure I would.   Ever Aff'y Harold Godwin

ALS (WP, DLC).

From Ellen Louise Axson

My darling Woodrow,   Sav. June 14 1885.

And so my letters were delayed again, and you were kept waiting again for forty-eight hours. I am *so* sorry. I will try not to let it happen again;—but would you really rather have a "line" such as I sent yesterday at the *right* time, than a *letter* at the wrong? Don't worry about the "work and company" dear; it is all right for the one counteracts the other; the company prevents my working too hard and furnishes "rest and *recreation*"! I had some real recreation yesterday afternoon; a *delightful* drive with Miss Nora Lawton to Bonaventure, the Scheutzen &c.¹ I have seldom had a pleasanter, and I have never seen the "low-country" looking so lovely. After the heavy rains everything was beautifully fresh and green, and we had a perfect afternoon and a glorious sunset.

By the way, I made an interesting discovery. Did I tell you about Mr. Pringle Mitchell my "compagnon en voyage"? I found him *very* "companionable" in more than one sense for he was always on hand, and he was quite entertaining as he knows intimately almost every artist in N. Y., being a partner of Louis Tiffany, the artist and house decorator. They are the firm who make those exquisite stained glass windows, you know. He was only here a day or two—went back on the next steamer—but he called before he left; and he chanced to tell me that his sister was a school mate and intimate friend of Miss Nora's, that she had visited at their house in New Haven. So I asked Miss Nora about them and to my surprise found that he is a son of *Donald Mitchell* —"Ike Marvell." She says they have a *lovely* home in New Haven, the most unique and picturesque of houses made of cobble-stones and covered with vines. It contains eighteen rooms,—one for *each child*! It was rather amusing to discover that the man who wrote "Reveries of a Bachelor" has twelve children—ten daughters. It is odd that the young gentleman did not tell me his parentage,—he *did* tell me all about his mother; how she was a Miss Pringle of Charleston;—it is a very old family, Grandfather says. And he also told me everything else imaginable about himself, about his life and surroundings, his hopes and fears[,] aspirations and disappointments! It is curious how confidential young men always become with me upon the shortest notice! I scarcely ever know one for a week before they begin to unbosom themselves in that way. My Southern friend on the steamer was just like Mr. Mitchell only more so! for he told me all about his misfortunes in *love*, and his religious troubles, how he had been very wild but how earnestly he had tried to change, becoming a member of the church &c., but how hard it was to be consistent living on the sea, cut off from church privileges, and all good influences, &c. &c.

And to think, sweet-heart that *next week* we begin our life journey together! How strange and wonderful—yes and how *sweet* it seems! Next week! How very, very near that makes it! That was my first thought as I opened my eyes this morning and it made my heart throb more quickly than it has ever done before in thinking of it,—but not at all with fear. "Perfect love casteth out fear"; —truly, my love, I too am undergoing a wonderful, hitherto undreamed of heart preparation for our marriage. I am so glad, my darling, that I can give you such a welcome as your love for me deserves—*demands*, for it is the greatness of your love which has prepared for you your welcome. *Mine* would be but half a heart if it could not give love as perfect as that it receives. I would not,— *could* not be so poor of nature as to dole out love or even the confession of my love in return for the unstinted portion which is filling my heart to overflowing with joy. By every proof possible my heart tells me that I am ready for our marriage, that my love and trust are unbounded,—that I am *absolutely*

Your own   Eileen.

ALS (WC, NjP).

1 Bonaventure is identified at ELA to WW, Feb. 11, 1884, n. 4, Vol. 3. "The Scheutzen" was Scheutzen Park, a suburban pleasure resort one-half mile from Bonaventure.

From James E. Rhoads

Dear Friend,   Philadelphia, 6 mo. 15, 1885.

Thine of the 10th came duly. I feared lest imperfect health had led to thy leaving Baltimore. Enclosed please find a form of application for the fellowship in History from Mary E Whipple. If after examining it thou thinks it best to ask her to write a thesis state whether thou wishes her to comply with any requirements as to subject &c. The application has not impressed the Dean or myself very favorably. But we ought to judge of it dispassionately, and in the light of duty towards the applicant as well as to the College.   Very truly thy friend,   James E Rhoads

ALS (WP, DLC).

From Houghton, Mifflin & Company

Dear Sir: Boston, June 15, 1885.

We have your favor of the 10th inst., & agree with you you that it would be well to add an Index to your "Congressional Government." We shall be glad to receive the copy for it at your earliest convenience, & will promptly put it in type & add it to the next edition of the work.

                    Yours very truly,   Houghton, Mifflin & Co.
                                            F. J. G.

ALS (WP, DLC).

From Jessie Bones Brower

My dear Cousin Woodrow,   Chicago Ill. 15 June 1885.

I was delighted to get your letter of the [blank], for do you know I actually began to be afraid that you would be married without letting me know of it before hand. I received the catalogue of the school in which you are to teach this next term, & would have acknowledged its receipt had I known your address. We were completely in the dark as to both your & Auntie's address.

Nothing would give me more pleasure my dear Cousin than to be present at your wedding, but of course it is out of the question as I have no one with whom to leave the children. This marriage is what I have dreamed of for many a year—ever since I was old enough to think of such things, & surely no match-maker ever had her plans turn out more beautifully, than did mine. And I can wish you no greater happiness my dear Cousin, than that your married life shall be as happy a one as has been mine. I say this now that I have been married almost 3½ years, which surely is some sort of a test. I think it takes a couple of years to rub off & polish up the differences in disposition between two people, & then comes the best love of all—the love that has been tested which is fuller & more complete than that of the honey-moon.

Now what could be nicer than for you to take a trip through the great lakes starting of course from Chicago? Just how much we would like to have you it is unnecessary for me to tell you, & you could afterwards join your Mother & Father in New York. I hope you will really take this place into serious consideration, for we have both quite set our hearts on it. . . .

Abe joins me in love to you all, & also in wishing you every happiness that a wife such as Ellie Lou ought to bring you.

Lovingly your Cousin,   Jessie B. Brower.

P.S. omitted. ALS (WP, DLC) with WWhw notation on env.: "Ans. Dec. 20/85."

To Ellen Louise Axson

My own darling,   Columbia, June 15th/85
Can you tell me, I wonder, why I am so *possessed* with the jubilant idea that this is the last week of our separation? One of the middle-aged persons, to whose opinions about life you sometimes refer, with no great deference, would, if he could but read my thoughts, conclude that I looked upon the end of our separation as the *beginning* of all that is worth living for, like most fond youthful dreamers; and if he were cynical, as we suppose him, he would write me down as one to be pitied, and would not stop to read me any further. But, if he could and would read my *heart* and my character, decypher the nature of my love for you and the real reasons of my dependence upon your love—the reasons which have their roots in the deepest soil of my soul—maybe he would not pity but would envy me. I have a heart which can be *filled* with love and there is but one woman in the world who can fill it—the peerless little woman whom I have won—and, once filled, it can never slacken in its joy so long as she is entirely its own. Its real, lasting, joy *is* to *begin* with the ceremony of the 24th—or rather with the sweet private ceremony which is to precede it— when it shall be put into possession of its own. It is of *that* that it is thinking now all the days through, and the joy of it all is that this present delight of certain expectation is to issue in a delight infinitely greater, the delight of that wifely love, and companionship, and sympathy which will be more to me than riches or power. Sweetheart, you can work wonders with your love if you

will! When once you find out how much I have needed you, you
will see what a part your love can play, and must play, in my fortunes. You have but to love me perfectly to strengthen me perfectly on the side on which I most need strengthening. It will, at
first, be as strange as it will be sweet—wont it, darling?—that our
separation is ended *for good and all*—that we can be together just
as much as we choose! And how much do you think that will be,
little lady? Do you think that you will want to go away from me
to spend Christmas—that you will ever think with complacence
of going back again for a little while to letter-writing? Imagine
my asking such questions if I were not as sure of your answer
as I am of my love for you! I can't abandon my old trick of tempting my darling to earnest confessions of the strength and wholeness of her love. Language never revealed its sweetness to me
until *she* cast it into forms of love! Her words are like kisses to
my heart. There's a single fact which sums up for me the beauty
and glory of my life: and that fact is, that my Eileen loves me
with all her heart and *needs* me as   Her own   Woodrow.

Special love to the dear grandmother, my pet; I do hope she is
much better.

ALS (WC, NjP).

From Henry Randall Waite

Dear Sir: Boston, Mass., June 15 1885
    In the announcement of the general plans of the Institute of
Civics already placed in your hands reference was made to The
Citizen, a publication to be issued under its auspices. It is the
intention of the corporation to commence the issue of this pe-
riodical as soon as the *necessary material can be secured.* Arrangements have been made by which the house of D. Lothrop
& Co. will publish it, the editorial columns to be under the absolute control of a committee of the Institute. It is the expectation
of this committee and of the publishers that within a reasonable
period authors will be compensated for articles furnished, but
in the initiation of the movement the committee have promised
to secure the contributed articles necessary without cost to the
publishers, a promise which they feel confident that they can
fulfil, in view of the expressed willingness of many friends of the
Institute to thus aid in the successful establishment of The Citizen. I am well aware that in asking you to thus contribute I am
making a request which you will be warranted in complying with
only because of the real merit and high promise of the work which

you will thus aid; as to this I trust you are already satisfied. Will you not therefore promise me for the first number an article in relation to Senatorial Courtesy—so called.[1]

I do not ask for a long article, but desire rather one equivalent to from a column and a half to four columns of a paper about the size of The Nation. I would not confine you to the subject indicated, but would be glad to receive matter relating to another subject if it can be furnished more conveniently. Please inform me on the enclosed postal at what date the committee may expect copy from you.

With the assurance that the aid sought will be of great value and highly appreciated, I have the honor to be,

Cordially Yours   H. R. Waite, President.

TLS (WP, DLC). Encs.: printed letter announcing forthcoming issue of *The Citizen*; certificate of membership for WW in the American Institute of Civics.
[1] Wilson responded with "Courtesy of the Senate," printed at Nov. 15, 1885, Vol. 5.

From Barnard E. Bee

Dear Sir,   Savannah, Ga. June 16 1885
Marriage licenses are obtained from the office of the Ordinary in the Court House. Mr. Russell the Clerk says he will be in his office at 9 A.M. on the 24th Inst.[1]

Yr Truly   Barnard E. Bee
Clerk S[uperior]. C[ourt]. C[hatham]. C[ounty].

ALS (WP, DLC).
[1] See the photographic section.

From Ellen Louise Axson

My darling Woodrow,   Sav. June 16, 1885
I have been asking Uncle R. about the hotels; he says the "Pavilion," opposite the church, is a private boarding house now and a very poor one. Possibly they *may* take "transients" occasionally. The "Screven" and the "Pulaski" are about the only ones, and there is very little choice between them. The Screven is one block nearer. Uncle R. says you can't make a mistake, they are both so bad. It suggests Bill Arp's remark that he is always sorry when there are two hotels in a town because whichever he choses he always wishes he had gone to the other! Uncle R. says you had better postpone the affair a year and then there will be a good hotel! He is a hard case; last night there was a ring at the bell

and it proved to be a coloured girl asking if Grandfather would marry her! The groom was waiting on the sidewalk while the bride made arrangements,—asked Grandfather how much he charged &c. She wanted it to be next Thursday night; whereupon Uncle R. called out to tell that it couldn't be done until "Wed. night week"!

We are expecting Stockton and Eddie today but I don't know at what hour; so I am a little excited. Stockton would not wait for his commencement, after all,—said he would have so little time to see me that he much preferred leaving as soon as the examinations were over. I was somewhat disturbed about it for I fear after he *has* seen me he will regret the commencement; but he would come. And of course I cannot but be glad for I am so anxious to see him; especially to know more fully how he is.

Grandmother is very much better now,—quite herself again.

Please excuse this hasty note, love; I have an engagement at nine and am scribbling "for dear life." It is very hard to write a short note when there is so much I want to say. I must try not to *begin* pouring out the love which so fills my heart, because then I will surely be late. But I am *very* glad that nothing need stop my *thinking* of you.

Believe me sweet-heart, with all love and faith,

Your own   Eileen.

ALS (WC, NjP).

To Ellen Louise Axson

My own darling,   Columbia, June 16/85

With all my resolute philosophy in the matter, I find Monday go *very* slowly and heavily without a letter from you. This morning has been *so* long in coming, and it is still so tedious a time to wait before the Savannah mail will be in! *Next* Monday it will be different: my last letter will have come and the next morning will be almost at hand to take me to my darling! Wont that be glorious, sweetheart?

Meanwhile, in imitation of truly philosophical conduct of which I have 'heard tell,' I am reading a little German every day and am struggling with the construction of an index to "Congressional Government." That work's lack of an index has been animadverted upon in various quarters, and I have asked the publishers to let me add one to the next edition, should another edition be called for.[1] It's no joke, is the making of an index, I find;

—especially in this case is it full of drudgery, for I am moderately
tired of the contents of the book to begin with. My interest in its
subject is perennial; but my interest in this particular treatment
of that subject has reached a decided wane!

Alas, for the short life of human friendships—at least of those
which are rooted in nothing deeper than mere good-fellowship!
Here is Miss Katie Mayrant arrived in town—visiting relatives just
across the street yonder from this same Howe residence—and I am
actually very much bored to think that I am bound to call on her.
It is only too evident now that our one-time intimacy, with its
romps and its energetic correspondence, was accidental—an accident of boarding-house association. She is a jolly girl, mischievous, affectionate, and interesting on close acquaintance; but she
is not deep, and does not *wear* well. I shall doubtless enjoy talking to her again when once I get over there; but I am not irresistibly inclined to rush over without delay.

I have been thinking, sweetheart, that, since we are to leave
at 8:45 on the 24th, seven o'clock would be rather late for the
wedding:—don't you think so? The ceremony and the congratulations, &c., which must follow it, will occupy at least half an hour,
I should say, and we *all* of us will have to make a complete change
of dress afterwards before giving our baggage to the express-men
to be carried to the train. Don't you think that we had better, if
possible, leave an ample margin for delays—for everything but a
certainty of being hurried and a chance of being left? But of
course you and "Aunt Ella" have thought of all these things, and
I need not suggest.

Warmest love to all at 143, dearest; is the dear grandmother
better?

All here send unbounded love to my darling. I love you, precious, unspeakably. I am with all love and faith and joy

Your own   Woodrow.

ALS (WC, NjP).
  [1] It was incorporated in what Houghton Mifflin called the "third edition,"
printed later in 1885.

From Ellen Louise Axson

My darling Woodrow,   Sav. June 17/85

If you were here you would be very glad for me and with me
today for I have my boys back! They came yesterday afternoon;
—are both looking *well* too in spite of all my anxiety about them.
Stockton is if anything less thin than he was last summer;—
though quite thin enough! But alas! how few pleasures come un-

mixed! I ended the evening, after all with a cry,—over poor little Ed;—because I found him stammering worse than ever. The doctors always said we were not to worry about that because with care it could *certainly* be conquered, since it was nothing more than a habit. He didn't stammer at all for two or three years after he learned to talk, and he always does it by fits and starts. But he is nine years old now and it isn't conquered yet; and I begin to feel utterly discouraged about it.

I was at the dentist this morning from quarter before *seven* to eleven! Do you think any further explanation is necessary for this tardy letter? But I have been for the last time now I am happy to say.

Today's letter has already reached me but I have not had an opportunity to speak to Aunt Ella yet about the time. You know 8:45 means 9.22 by our city time, so that we would have two hours and a quarter. Do you think that would be enough? Be perfectly free, dear, in giving your opinion and your mother's on these points. It *would* be *very* uncomfortable to be hurried;—ask your mother what hour she would choose.

Am *so* sorry to give you a hasty line again today but there is no help for it. I have company the whole of *every* afternoon, and I *must* work now. I think I will send you this sweet letter just received from Rose to make up! I want you to know my dear friend's heart. I don't know how Daisy managed to get the impression that there was any such "possibility." She *was* urging it—thought we "ought to come" when so near as Asheville; but I turned it off with a laugh and thought no more of it. Am sorry she has put the idea in Rose's head, to give her another disappointment.

But I *must* say "good-bye" darling for a few hours only for it is already afternoon, and I *will* write tonight. How sweet it is to think how soon we will be emancipated from this bondage to pen and ink! No indeed I *can't* "think with complacence of going back to letter-writing." In fact I can't think of it *at all*. I can't *imagine* myself following Réne's[1] example; can you? If you don't need me too much for me to think of leaving you upon slight occasion, I shall consider life a failure. "There is a single fact which sums up for me all the beauty and glory of my life": it is that you love me with all your heart and *need* me as   Your own   Eileen.

ALS (WC, NjP). Enc.: Rosalie Anderson to ELA, June 13, 1885, ALS (WP, DLC).
[1] Réné Fairbanks Beckwith.

To Ellen Louise Axson

My own darling,   Columbia, June 17, 1885

If your heart throbbed so quickly when you opened your sweet eyes *last* Sunday, what will it do when you wake *next* Sunday—and what will it say to you when you open your eyes *next Wednesday* morning? Ah, you matchless, delightful, loving little woman: how can I tell you my boundless joy in these sweet confessions! Each word that goes to make them up is more precious to me than aught else that I possess—and shall be until I possess the little lady who wrote them!—until one week from to-day—that sweet day from which all things in my life hereafter shall date, looking back to it as all things in my past life, consciously or unconsciously, have looked forward to it.

I received an exceedingly kind invitation yesterday—as, perhaps, you knew I should?—from Mrs. Gen. Lawton to be her guest during my stay in Savannah. Of course I had to decline. I could not and would not leave my family party at such a time. But I appreciated the attention very highly; and I shall, of course, call on Mrs. Lawton as soon as I get to Savannah, to take that much advantage of her desire to meet me.

I have just returned from making a call on Miss Katie Mayrant. I find that she expects to be here until the first of July: so that you will doubtless meet her! You will, I am sure, be amused at the odd, nervous girl. She is just now odder and more nervous than ever, for she has recently been unwell, in consequence of the strain of nursing a cousin whom she recently lost.

I am *so* glad, sweetheart, to hear that you had such a delightful drive with Miss Lawton, and to find that you derive recreation and rest, rather than additional fatigue, from the much entertaining of visitors. As for myself, I am feeling *ever* so much better than I did when I reached here. I was not *sick* then, but I was nervous and altogether 'run down,' so that there was very much room for improvement. And a good deal of that room has been taken up. You must not expect to find me anything but my usual thin self when I come next week; but you *may* expect, dearest, to see me looking well. And maybe the frame of mind and of spirits in which I shall be then will not detract from my appearance. Joy—supreme joy—does not usually make one *pale*, does it, my sweet one? If you were painting a face which covered a heart full of a delight such as it had never felt before, you would put some lustre into the eyes—wouldn't you?—and some lines of softness and health into the other features. All the best things of my

face will surely come out to view when once more I hold my darling close to my heart—and folks who can't see me then, can see
the light left by such moments—can see what a wonder and joy
it is to me to be   Your own   Woodrow.

ALS (WC, NjP).

From Ellen Louise Axson

My darling Woodrow,   Savannah June 17/85
    I have been driving with Miss Nora again this afternoon, and
she told me they had received "a nice letter" from you today and
they were *so* sorry you could not stay with them. I told them that
I appreciated their invitation as much as I was sure you did. It
was very sweet in them, was it not? They are all *so* lovely to *me*.
I never had kinder, more thoughtful and attentive friends. I am
so sorry that you won't meet Miss Nora. She leaves for Athens in
a few days to be bridesmaid for Miss Thomas, who also marries
on the twenty-fourth. I shall owe that young lady quite a grudge
for taking her off and for keeping Ed Brown, who is to be one of
her groomsmen.
    So Miss Katie Mayrant has appeared on the scene just at this
juncture!—how interesting! You must be sure, sir, to tell me all
about your affecting interview with her.
    And you are at work upon "Congressional Government" again;
—am glad you told me. I have been wondering what you were doing with yourself. Do you think you are getting decidedly stronger,
dear, since leaving Balt.? Have you had any headaches?—do you
feel less of that lassitude, &c.? I hope that when you combine rest
with the fine mountain air you will become as sound and strong
as one of the mountaineers themselves.
    I wonder if you know, sweet-heart, with what feelings I read
such letters as this before me—the one of the 15th—how my heart
lingers over the words which tell me that yours "can never slacken
in its joy so long as" one little woman is "entirely its own." Then,
love, how sure you are to find some sweetness in life, whatever
befall. If it is in the power of love to bless—no—I will not put it so,
for surely no one has greater reason to *know* that power;—*because*
it is in the power of love to bless, you *shall* be blessed. You shall
never want for wifely love and faith and sympathy, my darling,
or for anything that love can give. I have given you my *all*, sweetheart;—*my* all is so far below your deserts—below what I could
wish you to have that I cannot afford to hold back anything. I
know that I can make our accounts even in *one* respect. I can

give you love and devotion equal to your own, and it is my joy—my *life* to do it. Your little wife's heart will in very truth be yours altogether, irrevocably—yours in it's every throb, for I do indeed *live* for you. I love you, love you, dear, with a love that is stronger than death;—and I love you too "to the level of every day's most quiet need in sunshine and in shade." With all my heart

Your own   Eileen.

ALS (WC, NjP).

To Ellen Louise Axson

My own darling,   Columbia, June 18/85

What do you think of the fact that I am to have time for but three more letters to you, besides this one, before I shall go to you 'in proper person,' instead of in these poor representative epistles, with their incomplete messages and unsatisfying love missions? It seems to me, not only an unspeakably sweet, joyful fact, but also an almost solemn thought. It makes me long as I have never longed before to fill my letters with *perfect* messages of love. I would have those messages reflect in some sort the exalted feelings—the feelings of deep responsibility, of infinite tenderness, of all-controlling love, of awed joy, of passionate devotion and sweet hope—with which I approach the time which shall give to me my peerless little darling, to be my cherished wife, my beloved companion, my all in all. These feelings lift me altogether out of my former self, precious. They give to all my purposes and ambitions a bright side of love which quite transforms them, making them seem easier of accomplishment and surer of issue than they could ever have been without that seal of yours upon them. Ah, my sweet one, what a wonderful thing it is to be loved by you—to have won the heart of a little woman who knows how to bestow perfect love and vouchsafe perfect faith, and confess perfect joy in loving and trusting perfectly! Such love as yours could have brought happiness to any man with a heart, my darling; but surely it could have blessed very few as it has blessed me. Surely no man ever felt a more intense, eager longing for love, or had a more sensitive appreciation of its power to bless, than I feel and have! I *know* that you are the only woman in the world who could have matched my love *in kind.* Had you possessed no other charm or power but simply the nature to love as you have loved, and promise always to love, me, you would have been the one woman in the world to complete my life in marriage! I love you for a thousand lovely traits and sweet gifts for sympathy, but you have *won* me, you *reign absolute* in my heart, because of your capacity for loving—for loving with a woman's love and faith. It is my knowledge of that fact which has made me so ready to laugh at your fears about the future. I am sure that I am *not* mistaken in any essential part of my estimate of your power to give me fullest intellectual sympathy; but, even if I were mistaken as to your intellectual and many of your moral qualities, it would make not a peppercorn's difference in view of my certain knowledge of the depth and perfection of your love. You can satisfy my heart—and I would give a world of other things to secure that inestimable gift—*your* love, my Eileen's trust and devotion. It is *that* which I am coming to claim, and with it all the the [*sic*] other sweet things which are summed up in your priceless gift of yourself to   Your own Woodrow.

ALS (WC, NjP).

From Ellen Louise Axson

My darling Woodrow,   Savannah June 18/85

These boys—and the rest—and a necessary note or so have kept me until now it is half past eleven. But I *must* write a little, late as it is, for Minnie Hoyt comes in the morning at seven, and I am sure there will be no quiet for letters until after the mails. Isn't it delightful that Minnie can come down? Though we have been urging it, I only learned today by telegram that we might expect her.

By the way, tell Josie that he has made some friends here already. My little cousin Leila and her chums seem quite fascinated by his picture. I heard Leila making the most elaborate plans the other night, for the time when Stockton and "the new boy" were here;—how they were to be introduced to "Maggie" and "Daisy" and the whole lawn tennis club &c. &c. I listened with much amusement wondering when she meant to accomplish all that; but she suddenly bethought her to ask if Josie was to be here only "a few days," and was deeply disappointed to learn the facts of the case. It *is* a great pity that he can't meet all these "perfectly lovely girls."

My little cousin has just "done herself proud," and all the rest of us too, by taking the second honour. She graduates on Friday a week from today. She is a bright girl as well as a *very* lovely one, has the sweetest of dispositions.

Yes I knew the Lawtons were going to ask you; Miss Nora came Tuesday, to take me over the grand new Telfair Academy of fine arts, and she told me her mother had written you.

Miss Nora was here today, by the way, and she says she is going to Asheville this summer and means to drive out to Arden Park to see us and the place. She insists that I must put on my wedding gown for *her*, since she can't be at the marriage, so she is coming tomorrow to make me "dress up."

I am so happy, darling, at this good report as to your health. Such words from you are a *real* comfort because I can trust you so entirely, I know you would not say you were better if you were not.

There, the clock strikes twelve. This is naughty but nice; this sitting up to write you. However I can afford to laugh at these difficulties in conducting our correspondence because they are so soon to end. Though I am afraid I would not laugh if your letters were irregular in coming; for I am more entirely dependant on them *now*—and their words of love than ever I was before. What *should* I do if they were not forthcoming?—perhaps "back out" altogether! Ah darling, can I ever tell you how precious is your love to me—with what deep joy I *rest* in the fact that you love me, or what perfect joy I find in loving you. I *do* love you dear one, deeply, tenderly passionately. I can give you all the love you need, all your heart craves from   Your own   Eileen.

ALS (WC, NjP).

Two Letters to Ellen Louise Axson

My own darling,   Columbia, June 19, 1885

I *am so* glad that you have 'your boys' with you again. Your happiness comes home to my heart, my pet, as if it were my own —I believe it delights me *more* than my own! Maybe the best way of putting the truth of the matter is, that your happiness is the unselfish part of my own, and therefore the sweetest part. I can well understand your gladness at having Stockton and dear little Eddie with you once more. I wish you could *keep* them both. I don't yet understand how you can be willing to give up so much for *me*! I am delighted to hear that Stockton is looking so well. Tell him that I am anxious to hear that he has forgiven me for letting our correspondence die after having myself started it. A thousand things, my health among the rest, seemed to render it impossible for me to write one-half the letters I wanted to write.

I am as much distressed as you can be, dear, to learn that dear little Eddie's trouble is no nearer its cure than ever; but I see no reason to abate hope in the matter. He is scarcely old enough yet to set himself systematically to overcome the habit—and it is only him*self* that can cure him. When he is old enough to take himself in hand, there need be no insuperable difficulty in his way—especially since it is *only* a habit, and not an invariable one at that. Give him many kisses from me—and give Stockton too my warmest love.

Yes, indeed, my darling, this *is* a *very* sweet letter from Miss Rose. I have enjoyed reading it as much as you could wish me to. I too am sincerely sorry that her sister has prepared another disappointment for her. Give her my love when you write—and "Mac." my sincerest regards. We will manage to make up the 'quartette' for which she wishes *some* of these days.

No, my peerless little sweetheart—no indeed!—I *can't* imagine your "following Réné's example"! If I could, I should pray to die as soon as possible—I should wish to die *now*, before ever we could be married! Mrs. Beckwith may be a beautiful, a 'lovely' *creature*—I don't like to say *animal*—but she can scarcely be a lovable person—can scarcely have a woman's heart capable of love such as a man could live upon and not starve. There must surely be some explanation of her coldness hidden somewhere in her husband's character. If not, I hope I shall never hear of her again. Such examples of sham love give my heart a dull aching pain wh. is almost as real as if I myself were personally concerned. The only cure I can find is in turning to thoughts of *your* love— that wonderful, perfect love which is my supreme delight—that love which satisfies even my sensitive heart, which exalts my life and glorifies the love which I give in return—which blesses and delights and commands   Your own   Woodrow.

Columbia, June 20/85

Yes, my darling, I am getting decidedly stronger than I was before leaving Balto. My old headaches come now for only a few minutes at a time, because of some momentary worry, and the lassitude I feel occasionally is the result of *loafing*, I think, rather than of weakness. I have been, to some extent, following father's advice, that I should seek complete physical rest by leading, so far as possible, a mere animal life, with as much sleep and lounging and as little study in it as I could bring myself to stand. Consequently, I am said to have a little more flesh on my bones than I had three weeks ago. The only thing I need now is a *heart* completely at rest, sweetheart, and that will come with the possession of my precious little wife,—will be the inestimable dower which I shall get with you! You know the old saying, 'laugh and grow fat.' My heart cannot be filled with the joy of careless laughter until it shall be in complete possession of its sweet companion; but when she comes to make its contentment full, I shall have permission from every part of my nature to indulge in that whole-souled laughter which makes fat! What unspeakable delight will be mine then! How next to impossible it will be to grow thin! Nothing ever makes me ill so soon as a heart-want, and nothing ever cures me of all ailments so surely as the satisfaction of my heart-needs. The fact of the matter is, that I have been *pining* for you this long time past, my precious one—not in the sickly-sentimental sense, but in the sense in which every heart must pine which is forbidden all but a partial, maimed exercise of its strongest instincts—which loves in separation from the object of its love.

I received a very sweet, warm-hearted letter from Jessie yesterday in which she rejoices over our marriage, but promises me that the joy of our 'honeymoon' will not compare for fulness and completeness with the sweetness of the love we shall feel for each other two or three years from now. We have already accepted that belief, as supported by abundant testimony and by the analogy of our own past experience—haven't we, sweetheart? But we shall not enjoy the first gladness of being together any the less intensely because we expect to grow happier and happier in each other's love; shall we? I can imagine how I shall prize my little wife in the years to come—how my pride and delight in her will increase—; but all that will take care of itself. The thought which is near me, filling my heart with joyful excitement and eagerness is of the pride and delight which I shall take in my *bride*—my peerless sweetheart newly made my wife—my sweet love-treasure —my graduated 'pupil,' whom I shall strive to honour and cherish as her love and all her sweet womanly qualities deserve, that she too may be happy, in the possession of

Her own   Woodrow.

P. S. As for the time for the ceremony, my pet, dear mother says she can offer no advice. She is quite content, as I am, to leave you and your aunt to calculate how much time should be allowed for the ceremony and its accompanying circumstances, and how much for my party's getting back to the hotel and changing our clothes, in order to avoid the confusion and worry of hurry. Two hours would not contain time enough for *supper* in addition to the other things; but we might take that *before* the wedding. Arrange just as you think best, dear—and you will be sure to satisfy

Yours lovingly, W.

ALS (WC, NjP).

From Ellen Louise Axson

Savannah, June 20/85

And can it really be possible, my darling, that this is my *last* letter to you! I did not realize the fact until just now when I began to count up, and perceived that a letter written tonight or tomorrow would reach Columbia after you leave on Tuesday. How strange it seems to think that we will have no more need of letters!—how strangely *sweet*! And yet the letters have been *so* dear to me, and will always be my carefully guarded treasure, even when I have you too. They have made so large a part of my life for so long that I daresay I will still be listening and watching for the postman many a time when I am even at your side. You say well, dear, these are solemn thoughts as well as sweet ones,— thoughts which give me always the desire to fall on my knees and pray the Father to prepare me for whatever he is preparing for me;—to give us His blessing in all things, to choose all our changes for us,—and to teach me how to be all that I *wish* to be to you, all that your wife *should* be. And I am sure, love, that He *will* bless us, because we are *His*—because in spite of all our failures we *do* desire above all else to be under His guidance in everything,—to live and serve Him well and truly. Therefore, my darling, by my love for Him I pledge you true wifely love, and fealty and service, all the days of my life. I would that I could tell you in this last letter something more than I have ever told before of what *love* means for me. But there are few places in my heart which I have not opened to you, dearest;—I have shown you my heart of hearts, —I know because your own words tell me that you have read it and read it aright[.] You know as well as you *can* know, before the years have brought their proof how absolutely I am yours,—you know the depth and tenderness and fervour of my love,—this *"all-controlling* love"; you know how absolutely I *believe* in you,—with what unquestioning confidence. And I believe that you *trust me* as my love deserves, that you will *rest* in my love ever as I in yours; it is that which makes my joy in your love so great. Darling, my *faith* in you is a part of my *love* for you;—the one no less than the other has become the ruling *passion* as well as the controlling principle of my life. Thank God that the man I love is one who will *permit* me to obey *His* marriage law. I am to promise next week to *reverence* you! How many of the young men I have known do you suppose it would be *possible* to reverence! But you will be in very truth my head—my *king*, not only because *I* will it but because *God* wills it, because He made you so to be.

Sweet-heart, you never wrote a letter which brought with it sweeter joy than this of yesterday, which tells me that you *can* and *do* love me for "love's sake" alone, simply for its power to bless apart from all else. Did I not once,—many times perhaps,—pray you for such love,

> "do not say
> I love her for her smile, her look, her way
> Of speaking gently,—for a trick of thought
> That falls in well with mine, and certes brought
> A sense of pleasant ease on such a day
> For these things in themselves, Beloved, may
> Be changed or change for thee, and love so wrought
> May be unwrought so.
> But love me for loves sake, that evermore
> Thou mayest love on through love's eternity."[1]

When I feel that you give me such love as that, my heart is flooded with a deep peace—a perfect joy in loving and and [*sic*] being loved, such as no other thought can give. That *is true love*, the *only* true love I sometimes think. The other is but a stronger sort of *liking*! Yes I admit that I am *very glad* to be *liked* by you, looked at with *love's eyes* and *so* admired! But it would make me very *unhappy* to think that I held your heart by no stronger bond than that. I want to *depend* on something else, though all your words of praise are very sweet to me. It would be like trying to work out our own salvation. How little peace or joy we would find in life if that task had been set us. We are sons of Heaven by *free gift*;—and yet love of the Giver urges us to greater effort to please him,—to be what He would have us than any hope of gain.

Alas, I *must* close,—you don't know how much against my will, but if I don't, you will have no letter Sunday[.] I have been interrupted *three* times by callers since I began to write! I am afraid there is something else I ought to tell you which I don't remember;—but I hope not; at any rate there will be time after you come to see. Your father and Grandfather will of course arrange about their respective parts in the ceremony.

And now good-bye, my dear one, till Tuesday. I love you, darling as much as you would have me love you. Make out your check for *any* amount and I can fill it. Perhaps you have not yet sounded all the depths of my heart. Yet to the very bottom it *is all yours,–* and I am for life–and death   Your own   Eileen.

ALS (WC, NjP).
¹ From Elizabeth Barrett Browning, "Sonnets from the Portuguese," No. XIV.

From Hiram Woods, Jr.

My Dear Tommy,   [Baltimore] Sunday, 6/21/85
    It is 11.20 P.M. and rather too warm for comfort, but I want you to receive one more letter from me before you leave the state of *so-called* "single-blessedness"; hence I shall write you a few lines to-night.
    About the Princeton trip, I hardly know how to tell you. It was simply a delightful pleasure from beginning to end. Mitchell, Webster & I went up from Balto. Saturday morning.¹ At Philadelphia Bob Henderson joined us. At the Junction we met Prentiss, Riker & Billy Isham. When we reached Princeton we found that Bob Bridges had made admirable arrangements for our comfort. We had two large rooms in a house on Railroad Ave. The rooms communicated with one another. Mitchell, Henderson & I were in one, while the other end was held up by Webster, Bob B., Talcott (whom we found at Princeton) and Lee who did not get in till Sunday evening. It is needless to tell you all who were there, Al Dennis, Ridge, "Fee," "Katie," Jack Farr, "Pomp," Larkin & others were on hand. It didn't take long for us to forget the 6 years since we graduated. We were '79 again, and the old love soon had full sway in every heart. None of the fellows seemed particularly changed. There wasn't a discordant element there.
    On Sunday afternoon Talcott, Dan, Mitch, Bob, the Hen & I hired a carriage & went to Lawrenceville. We had a delightful ride. While we were at supper after reaching Princeton again, the "Heathen" put in appearance. The dear old boy was overwhelmed with his welcome. He is rejoicing in his engagement.
    On Monday A.M. we had a '79 game of base-ball, aided by Bickam '82. Bridges played. Talcott played every position, & played each with the same (lack of) skill. After a hard struggle of 4 innings, Comstock's nine had 25 runs, & Bridges' 9. I was L. F. on "Dutchie's" nine.
    During Monday afternoon each train brought in 79 fellows. By night we had 41 men in town. Then we took the town, we sang, cheered & made ourselves so generally *"observable,"* that an '85 man is said to have asked the question whether "this commence-

ment was '79's or '85's"[.] We sat down to supper at 10 P.M. Got up at 1.30. Everything was a success. The supper was excellent, and the attendance satisfactory. The speeches were capital. Possibly Chang Lee & Bob B. made the best of the evening. During supper the glee-club came around, and '82, '83 '85 & '77 also gave us a cheer. After the supper we all walked around the Triangle, and then every fellow either *went* or was *put over* the cannon. Day was breaking when, at 3.50, we got to bed. While plenty of wine was drunk, there was a noticeable absence of anything like drunkenness. On Tuesday the fellows began leaving. Mitch & I came down to Balto. in the afternoon, leaving (so-far as I know) only Ridge, Fee, Ned Webster & Talcott in Princeton. I would like to write something about our gang individually, but must postpone that till another time. Our reunion to me was the brightest spot in my life for a long time. In coming away, the uppermost thought with me was "Thank God for such friends as those we made at college." I believe, Tommy, college friendships are the most genuine & unselfish we ever make.

Many were the expressions of regret that you were not with us, and many a hearty wish was uttered that your future life may be full of success & happiness.

Now, old boy, a few words about what must be nearest your heart. Pardon me for trying to distract you by talking about even '79. It is unnecessary for me to tell you how glad I am that you are so soon to be married. I verily believe it will do you more good & do you good in more ways than 5 years of tuition under Adams. And then you'll have a heap better company, won't you? You and I found out at college what help there is in companionship. During those loved days we were the closest companions for eachother. Since then we have both been blest by having given us the love of a true, lovely woman.

In making your sweet-heart your wife you are anticipating me, I hope, only a little.[2] Will you kindly give to your Bride my best love, first as one who is a fast friend of yours, and secondly as one of the "gang." She will on Wednesday become a member of that charmed circle. All the family & Miss Hall "et al" unite with me in best possible wishes and congratulations to you & Miss Axson.

I fear you will have some difficulty in reading this. I am writing on a very unstable stand, because it is nearer the window than the table is. Let me hear from you soon as possible. I will write again shortly.   As Ever Your Friend,   Hiram Woods, Jr.

ALS (WP, DLC) with WWhw notation on env.: "Ans. Aug. '85."
[1] The members of the Class of 1879 mentioned in this letter were (in the or-

der of their first mention) Charles W. Mitchell, J. Edwin Webster, Robert R. Henderson, George L. Prentiss, Adrian Riker, William B. Isham, Robert Bridges, Charles A. Talcott, William B. Lee, Alfred L. Dennis, Jacob Ridgway Wright, Charles W. McFee, Louis C. Vanuxem, John Farr, Robert H. McCarter, Francis Larkin, and George Carlton Comstock. "Bickam '82" was Abraham S. Bickham.

2 Woods was engaged to Laura Hall of Baltimore.

To Ellen Louise Axson

My own darling,   Columbia, June 21, 1885

It sccms altogether too good to be true that our bondage to pen and ink is at last at an end! Hereafter we can speak face to face whenever we please—this letter will reach you on Monday, and on Tuesday I shall go in person to my darling, to *carry* the words of love of which my heart is so full, and to give her—oh, so gladly! —*myself* as a final lovegift—to consecrate to her my life, that it may be spent in making perfect the fulfilment of all the sweet promises in which our love for each other is so rich! Ah, my sweetheart, I wish that I could show you *some* of the gladness with which these thoughts fill me! But it is literally unspeakable. It is not translatable into anything but high spirits and a tumultuous throbbing at the heart such as maybe you can guess something about.

I wish that I could put into this letter, my precious, some words of love that would make you treasure it more than you have ever treasured any of my other letters. I feel as if this last love-*message* were in some sort sacred. My deepest, strongest desire in marrying you, darling, is to make you happy, and I would put into this letter some word of love which would seem to your heart a sort of sweet preface to the book of love which we are about to open together, to read new secrets of sympathy and companionship. I would have you catch a glimpse of my purpose for the future and of the joy which that future contains *for me*, of the gratitude I feel for your priceless gift of love, and of the infinite love and tenderness which is the gift of my whole heart to you. And think, my sweet one, with what unmixed delight we can look back upon our love for each other in the past. What a sweet preparation we have had for our wedding day! How *precious* the experience of these months of our engagement has been! It has brought us to a point where to marry is the only logical, natural, consistent thing we *could* do—hasn't it, darling? To wait longer *now* would be only to torture ourselves. I shall feel on Wednesday, sweetheart, that I am getting infinitely more than I deserve in getting you—I should have to be a vastly better man than I am to deserve such a little wife—but I shall not feel that the bargain is uneven so far as *love* is concerned, and I shall not be able to look back over the last two years without seeing that, whether I deserve it or not, this supreme good fortune was all along meant to be mine—through the marvellous goodness of God, who gave me a nature which needed above all things just such love and companionship as you alone could give me—you alone of all the sweet and lovable women in the world—and then brought you to me to satisfy that need: and not only to satisfy that need, but also to make me a better man through the gracious influences of your lovely womanly traits. Ah, little lady, I know whom I have loved! It cannot be *chance* that brought us together. Surely a man and woman who love each other as we love must have been born for each other. It may be, as Miss Rose says, that I do not *yet* know how great a treasure I have won in you; but I have a very confident idea that if Miss Rose could have known one or two of my greatest heart secrets she would have been slower to venture that opinion. She might change her mind if I could tell her how I discovered you—how I fell in love with you—how it all came about through a revelation which forced me, in spite of a great store of incredulity, to believe in the truth and possibility of dreams which I had all my life long been dreaming and disbelieving, that

> "Somewhere in the world must be
> She that I had prayed to see,
> She that love assigned to me";—

if I could make her see, as I see, that I have found "in thee, my sweet, Visions true and life complete,"—and that, in finding you, I found, not only the woman to whom I could give perfect love, but also the woman whom I had been loving, in my imagination, for I knew not how many years! How sweet it is to go back in thought to that time of this wonderful discovery, so hard to realize at the moment it was made. It seems a sort of seal and sanction of the future, that you should have come to me, as you did, as a verification and justification of all my longings in the past. And *this week*, sweetheart,—*next Wednesday*—I shall claim you! Oh, my peerless little darling, my joy is too great for anything but sweet tears!

But I *must* turn aside from the thought of these delights for just a moment—you will want to know the details of my plans. We expect to reach Savannah between three and four o'clock on Tuesday. So soon as I can make myself presentable after getting in, I will come to you. Then, if there be time, I shall call on the Lawton's (I don't want to make any calls on Wednesday, if I can help it), and in the evening the Wilson and Howe delegation want to come to pay their respects to you and yours. All this is *provided*, of course, that such arrangements suit your convenience.

Good-bye, then, sweetheart, till Tuesday. God willing, I shall come to claim a part of your welcome then—and, if you will promise not to tell anybody, I will tell you a secret: the next time that I hold you to my heart will be the happiest moment of all my life, and the delicious prelude to still happier hours when you will be constantly at my side to tell me of the love which is more than life to me! Darling, once more I pledge you all my love and honour. I *love* you, precious one. With all my heart, in all my thoughts and hopes and purposes I am   Your own   Woodrow.

Love to Miss Minnie. I am *so* glad she is with you!

ALS (WC, NjP).

A News Item

[June 25, 1885]

Miss Ellie Lou Axson, daughter of the late Rev. Edward Axson, of this city, and Mr. Wilson, son of Rev. J. R. Wilson, of Wilmington, N. C., were married last evening at the residence of Rev. Dr. I. S. K. Axson, pastor of the Independent Presbyterian church. The ceremony was performed by the groom's father and the bride's grandfather. The nuptials were celebrated quietly, only the immediate friends and relatives of the contracting parties being present.

Printed in the *Savannah Morning News*, June 25, 1885.

ADDENDA

Two Letters to Albert Shaw

My dear Doctor,   Wilmington, N. C. June 30th/84

Your letter[1] came while I was away from home on a flying visit to Georgia. I was *mighty* glad to see it when I got back. It was like yourself, whole-souled and straightforward; and I sincerely hope—seeing how much good it did me—that it's the first of a long series of epistles from the same hand.

The Arkansas business has been settled for me. The trustees of the "Industrial University," after declaring individually that they would reorganize the faculty, decided collectively that they would not: and so, there being no vacancy created, I did not reach even the stage of candidacy. I shall, therefore, do high and lofty tumbling for another year under the canvas of "the Greatest Educational Show on Earth." I am now face to face with the question, several times discussed with you, whether or not I shall apply for a degree. What say you now?

I wish I could give you exact information on the points about which you make inquiry, regarding the government of the University of Virginia. But I can't. I can give you only impressions: for I never looked into the matter and caught only such information as was current. It is altogether a State institution—unless I am very much mistaken only one of its chairs, that of agriculture, has an independent, private endowment—and the "Board of Visitors" is chosen by the Legislature, the Alumni, as such, having no representative upon it. I am quite sure that these are the facts —from what I observed of the actual government while I was there, and from what I heard during the time of "Readjuster"[2] ascendency, when it was feared that the Readjuster Board would replace the faculty by partisans of their own.

I was delighted to hear what you had to say about Shinn's skill in making his way in New York; for, though I had had a delightful letter from him, characteristically full of *confidences*, no man can give an outside view of himself—no matter how good may be the other "outside" work he is doing—and it was gratifying to know that he is *evidently* on the road to success. For the matter of that, however, I never doubted but that he was quite seaworthy enough to be launched anywhere.

Be sure to let me know when "Icaria"[3] comes out. What with moving about and not seeing many papers, I am apt to miss an ordinary advertizement in this quarter of the globe just at this stage of my existence: and I want to secure *that* volume as soon as may be. You've beat the crowd of us: the first to be out with "a book." Well, for my part, I am more than ready to say "hurrah!" with a will. I only hope that I may be as fortunate when my labourious product is finished! I am stalking along now through a "high and mighty" discussion of the Senate into wh. I am trying to admit as little nonsense as possible. My chief defence is an air of omnipotence. At any rate, I'm enjoying the masquerade!

Noting your fear of the effect of a Ph.D. beyond the Mississippi,[4] I have addressed the envelope simply "Mr." Am I discreet?

Write whenever you can to

Your sincere friend,   Woodrow Wilson

[1] Albert Shaw to WW, June 17, 1884, printed in part in Vol. 3, p. 214.

[2] See WW to R. Bridges, May 24, 1881, n. 1, Vol. 2, p. 71.

[3] Shaw's monograph, *Icaria: A Chapter in the History of Communism* (New York, 1884).

[4] Here Wilson refers to the following portion of Shaw's letter: "I don't feel a bit bigger now that I have the 'P.H. degree' as Shinn always calls it, and I think I shall drop it into the Mississippi when I cross. I'm much afraid it will injure my prospects in the far west. The people will think I'm an 'Independent kicker' in politics and an 'agnostic' in religion if I go swaggering around as a 'Ph.D.' " Shaw was about to begin work as an editorial writer for the *Minneapolis Daily Tribune*.

My dear Shaw,   Balto., Md., Nov. 28/84

Things have culminated today in a way that puts me in shape for answering your delightful letter that came a week ago.[1] "Icaria" came just now, and this morning I received a decisive communication from the publishers in Boston, with reference to my own essays.

I appreciate very highly indeed, my dear fellow, this gift of your book. I need not tell you that I shall value it very much beyond its market price, because I have already told you more than once my opinion as to your treatment of this particular "chapter in the history of Communism." I should esteem the book exceedingly valuable had it not come from you: as your gift, as well as your workmanship, I shall esteem it *precious*.

You have no doubt found out already, through the epistle which it moved Wright to compose, what a sensation your letter made here at No. 8.[2] It was like a fresh breeze from the prairies—and was all the more grateful to me because I had almost given up hope of such a breeze from that quarter. I say "such a breeze" because nobody but Shaw could set the like a-going.

I wish, my dear fellow, that I could reckon up the number of times and estimate the fervency with which I have wished for you this "semester." Of course there's Dewey and Levermore—my peers every way—at the board as of yore; but the new men are *so* uninteresting, and you were the only man who seemed to have thorough sympathy with my way of looking at things—the only man, consequently, who was able to get at me to stimulate and teach me. We "old men" are ranged on one side of the table, the newcomers on the other: I would give all that other side and most of our side for one Albert Shaw!

No, we haven't gotten back to the old school exercises of last year yet: but I fear we shall very soon. "Quizzes" are promised us for the near future—so soon as lecture material shall begin to give out. I think our side of the table will work, nay *intrigue*, to stave off the evil day as long as possible.

I finished my essays during the summer—adding three, on the Senate, the Executive, and some necessary Conclusions, to those you saw—and as soon as I got back here I sent the lot off to Houghton, Mifflin, & Co. Ever since that act I have been waiting in fear and trembling for their answer. To-day the suspense ended. They will "take pleasure in publishing the book at their own risk, and paying me the usual royalty of 10 per cent on the retail price of all copies sold"! The announcement completely took my breath away! My most daring hopes had not gone so far as an acceptance on any basis so eminently satisfactory as that. They "estimate that it will make a volume of about 350 pages similar to the volumes in their American Statesman Series." They expect to put the mss into the printers hands at once: so that I expect to have the pleasure of sending you a copy about the middle of the winter.

My special work this year is, of course, on Ely's history of American Political Economy. I have just finished going through delicious old A. L. Perry. What a treat to go through so complacent a treatise, where never a doubt obscures even the broadest generalization and where absolute finality of doctrine reassures you on every page! For a decided change of diet, I am going next to Walker. A little "horse sense" from him will do my etherialized spirit good. The earth will seem real again.

We had the examination on Colonial history, sure enough—and a very square examination it was. Adams gave us five broad topics from which to choose one on which to compose an essay during the two hours allowed us. That's the way to do, I think, with advanced students. Certainly it gave each man a chance to do his best.

Of course I have numerous private study, essay schemes of my own that I should like to get a chance to work up; but I fear they must seethe for a while, and wait till after the Ph. D. for a chance to bring forth fruit. That's a beautiful mixture of metaphors! but you won't mind, or give it away!

I am delighted to know of your success in the editorial line. I cannot say more than that my gratification at your having secured such a position overcrows my indignation at your having used that position to aid in the attempt to defeat the noble army of mugwumps and give the country to Blaine.

There are lots of fellows—as well as some other Fellows—who would, I know, want to send love to you if they were at hand; but since I'm here in my little den alone you will have to content yourself with the love of

Your sincere friend,   Woodrow Wilson

TCL (in possession of Virginia Shaw English).
1 Albert Shaw to WW, Nov. 16, 1884, Vol. 3, pp. 444-45.
2 Mary Jane Ashton's boardinghouse at 8 McCulloh St., Baltimore.

INDEX

NOTE ON THE INDEX

THE reader is referred to the Note on the Index to Volume I for a statement of general principles and practices for this series, including the treatment of Wilson's Marginal Notes. The alphabetically arranged analytical table of contents eliminates duplication in both contents and index, of references to certain documents, like letters. Letters are listed in the contents alphabetically by name, and chronologically for each name by page. The subject matter of all letters is, of course, indexed. The Editorial Notes and Wilson's writings are listed in the contents chronologically by page. In addition, the subject matter of both categories is indexed. The index covers all references to books and articles mentioned in text or notes. Footnotes are indexed. Page references to footnotes which place a comma between the page number and "n" cite both text and footnote, thus: "624,n3." On the other hand, absence of the comma indicates reference to the footnote only, thus: "55n2," the page number denoting where the footnote appears. The letter "n" without a following digit signifies an unnumbered descriptive-location note.

An asterisk before an index reference designates identification or other particular information. Re-identification and repetitive annotation have been minimized to encourage use of these starred references. Where the identification appears in an earlier volume, it is indicated thus: "*1:212,n3." Thus a page reference standing without a preceding volume number is invariably a reference to the present volume. The index will usually supply the fullest known forms of names of persons of more than casual interest, and, for the Wilson and Axson families, relationships as far down as cousins. Persons referred to in the text by nicknames or shortened forms of names can be identified by reference to entries for these forms of the names.

A sampling of the opinions and comments of Wilson and Ellen Axson covers their more personal views, while broad, general headings in the main body of the index cover impersonal subjects. Occasionally opinions expressed by a correspondent are indexed where these appear to supplement or to reflect views expressed by Wilson or by Ellen Axson in documents which are missing.

INDEX